Office X *for* Macintosh

THE MISSING MANUAL

*The book that
should have been
in the box*

Office X *for* Macintosh

THE MISSING MANUAL

Nan Barber, Tonya Engst, and David Reynolds

POGUE PRESS™
O'REILLY®

Beijing • Cambridge • Farnham • Köln • Paris • Sebastopol • Taipei • Tokyo

Office X for Macintosh: The Missing Manual

by Nan Barber, Tonya Engst, and David Reynolds

Published by Pogue Press/O'Reilly & Associates, Inc., 101 Morris Street, Sebastopol, CA 95472.

July 2002:	First Edition.
July 2002:	Second Printing.
September 2003:	Third Printing.
December 2003:	Forth Printing.

ISBN: 0-596-00332-3

Table of Contents

Part Two: Entourage

Part Three: Excel

Part Four: PowerPoint

Part Five: Microsoft Office as a Whole

Part Six: Appendixes

The Missing Credits

About the Authors

Nan Barber hails from Providence and holds a degree in Japanese from Brown, although she does most of her writing and editing in English these days. Her articles have appeared in publications such as *Macworld* and *TheSpook.com*. Nan is the principal Missing Manual copy editor, having edited most of the books in the series. She is managing editor for *Salamander*, a magazine for poetry, fiction, and memoirs, and lives with her husband near Boston. Email: *nanbarber@mac.com*.

Tonya Engst is best known for her work on TidBITS, a free email and Web publication covering the Macintosh Internet community, which she co-founded in 1990. Since then, Tonya has written several books about Microsoft Word, and numerous articles for magazines like *Macworld* and *NetProfessional*. Tonya works from her home office in Ithaca, New York. Her husband, Adam, works just across the hall while her son, Tristan, hangs out down the street at day care. You can reach her at *tonya@tidbits.com* or by visiting *www.tidbits.com/tonya*.

David Reynolds has been a Mac guy for over fifteen years, serving time as a Macintosh floor sales representative, a Mac consultant, an Apple Student Representative, and most recently as editor-in-chief of *MacAddict* magazine. Oh, and he co-wrote both *AppleWorks 6: The Missing Manual* and *Office 2001 for Macintosh: The Missing Manual*. If you'd like to reach David about this book—or anything else—send email to *dreynolds@mac.com*.

About the Creative Team

David Pogue is the weekly computer columnist for the *New York Times* and the creator of the Missing Manual series. He's the author or co-author of 30 books, including thirteen in this series and six in the "For Dummies" line (including *Macs, Magic, Opera, Classical Music,* and *The Flat-Screen iMac*). In his other life, David is a former Broadway show conductor, a magician, and a pianist. Family photos await at *www.davidpogue.com*.

John Cacciatore (copy editor) works out of his home office in Woburn, Mass., where he is ardently engaged in the English major's freelance trinity: writing, editing, and proofing. A collaborator on the past several Missing Manual volumes, John now understands the inner workings of the Mac and Windows more intimately than he ever dreamed possible. Email: *j_cacciatore@yahoo.com*.

Rose Cassano (cover illustration) has been an independent designer and illustrator for 20 years. Assignments have ranged from the nonprofit sector to corporate clientele. She lives in beautiful Southern Oregon, grateful for the miracles of modern technology that make living and working there a reality. Email: *cassano@cdsnet.net*. Web: *www.rosecassano.com*.

Dennis Cohen (technical reviewer) has served as the technical reviewer for many bestselling Mac books, including several editions of *Macworld Mac Secrets* and most Missing Manual titles. He's the co-author of *AppleWorks 6 for Dummies, Macworld AppleWorks 6 Bible, Macworld Microsoft Office 2001 Bible,* and *Macworld Mac OS X Bible.* Email: *drcohen@mac.com*.

Phil Simpson (book design and layout) has been involved with computer graphics since 1977, when he worked with one of the first graphics-generating computers, which were an offspring of flight-simulation technology. He now works out of his office in Stamford, Connecticut, where he has had his graphic design business since 1982. He is experienced in many facets of graphic design, including corporate identity, publication design, and corporate and medical communications. Email: *pmsimpson@earthlink.net*.

Acknowledgments

My thanks go to David Pogue for giving me the chance to become a published author—twice! I owe a great debt of gratitude to Ted and Kathy Spargo, the world's greatest parents. For helping me get my facts straight, I'd also like to thank Karen Sung, Microsoft's Erik Ryan, and Wolfgang Bauer (especially for that thing about the German Spelling Rules). Finally, thanks to Ben for letting me use his computer.

—*Nan Barber*

My contribution to this book would not have been possible without the folks who hang out with my son, Tristan, when I am busy. Thanks to Chris and Elaine for sleepovers, to Chris for covering sick days, and to Renee who runs an awesome day care. Thanks also to Adam for encouragement and technical support. A final thanks goes to David Pogue and my fellow authors for being fun to work with.

—*Tonya Engst*

I'd like to thank my wife Susan for her enthusiasm, support, and general good nature while I wrote this; my son, Jacob, for serving as the inspiration for a lot of the stuff that matters; my parents, without whom there'd be quite a paradox; my mother-in-law Judy for her encouragement and interest; my co-authors for working so hard to create a great book; and David Pogue for another shot at computer geek glory.

—*David Reynolds*

The Missing Manual series is a joint venture between Pogue Press (the dream team introduced on these pages) and O'Reilly & Associates (a dream publishing partner). I'm indebted, as always, to Tim O'Reilly, Mark Brokering, Cathy Record, and the rest of the gang.

I'm also grateful to proofreaders Jennifer Barber, Chuck Brandstater, Stephanie English, and Danny Marcus; to Erik Ryan and Kevin Browne of the Microsoft Macintosh Business Unit; the cheerful and gifted indexing team of Johnna and Tom Dinse; and to David Rogelberg for believing in the idea. And above all, thanks to Jennifer, Kelly, and Tia, who make these books—and everything else—possible.

—David Pogue

The Missing Manual Series

Missing Manual books are designed to be superbly written guides to computer products that don't come with printed manuals (which is just about all of them). Each book features a handcrafted index, cross-references to specific page numbers (not just "see Chapter 14"), and an ironclad promise never to use an apostrophe in the possessive word *its*. Current and upcoming titles include:

- *iPhoto 2: The Missing Manual* by David Pogue, Joseph Schorr, & Derrick Story

- *iMovie 3 & iDVD: The Missing Manual* by David Pogue

- *iPod: The Missing Manual* by J. D. Biersdorfer (covering iTunes, MusicMatch, and the iTunes Music Store)

- *Switching to the Mac: The Missing Manual* by David Pogue

- *Mac OS X Hints: Jaguar Edition* by Rob Griffiths

- *Mac OS X: The Missing Manual, Second Edition* by David Pogue

- *Mac OS X: The Missing Manual, Panther 10.3 Edition* by David Pogue

- *FileMaker Pro: The Missing Manual* by Geoff Coffey

- *Dreamweaver MX: The Missing Manual* by David Sawyer McFarland

- *AppleWorks 6: The Missing Manual* by Jim Elferdink & David Reynolds

- *Windows XP Home Edition: The Missing Manual* by David Pogue

- *Windows XP Pro: The Missing Manual* by David Pogue, Craig Zacker, & L. J. Zacker

Introduction

A New Day at the Office

To say that Microsoft Office is the world's most frequently-used software application is the understatement of the century. In most Mac- or Windows-based corporations, anyone *not* using Office is considered a weirdo.

So when Apple announced Mac OS X, Microsoft began rewriting the four big, attractive, sophisticated computer programs that make up Microsoft Office for the Macintosh: Word (a word processor), Excel (a spreadsheet application), PowerPoint (a slide-show program), and Entourage (a calendar/email/address book program). These Office programs were some of the first major ones to appear in *Carbonized* form (that is, adapted for Mac OS X), making it possible for millions of Mac users to start spending most of their time in Mac OS X.

Microsoft Scores a X

So why is Office considered a Mac OS X program? Here are some of the ways that Carbonization makes itself known in Office X:

- Office X *looks* like the rest of Mac OS X. Scroll bars and other controls appear in that soothing, shimmering blue color. The Formatting Palette (page 109) "genies" its way out of the Standard toolbar when you click its button. Furthermore, when you've minimized an Office document to the Dock, choosing it from the Window menu genies it back out again.

- As in most Mac OS X programs, Office's Open dialog boxes and Save dialog boxes (now called *sheets)* have a new column view, similar to Mac OS X Finder windows (see Figure I-1). They also offer options that let you convert documents in other formats from other programs.

• In one of Office X's most highly touted features, its drawing and picture editing tools take advantage of Apple's new Quartz graphics technology. If your copy of Office is up to date (page 12), your everyday word processing text shows up with softened, smooth, *antialiased* edges.

Note: Although you can apply Mac OS X-style transparency effects to images in Word and PowerPoint, as well as to charts in Excel, the transparency doesn't always show up in printouts (page 509).

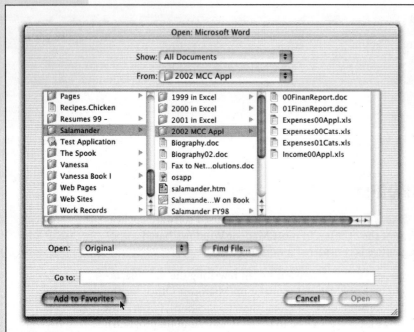

Figure I-1:
Burrowing down through folders is easier than ever in Office X, thanks to the horizontal scroll bar in the Open dialog box. Another timesaver is the From pop-up menu, which contains a list of the most-used and recently-used folders. The Add to Favorites button places documents in the Favorites menu, also shown here—another standard Mac OS X feature that can pay off when you're working in Office X.

More Integrated Than Ever

Word, Excel, and PowerPoint started out as individual, disparate programs. Starting with Office 2001, Microsoft began to design the programs of the suite as a cohesive whole. Word, Excel, and PowerPoint started to look and work more alike, and even share each other's components. For example:

• In your Entourage email, you can now use Word features like AutoCorrect and AutoFormat for bulleted lists and other fancy formatting.

• The names and addresses entered in Entourage become AutoText entries in Word, so that you can type just a few letters of a person's name to paste in the full address when typing up a letter. In fact, the Contact toolbar lets you select, find, update, and use contacts in any Office program, without even launching Entourage.

- Any text, picture, or table that you select can be dragged-and-dropped from any Office application into any other—or even to the desktop. If you've ever needed to put clip art in a spreadsheet, here's your chance.

- Office X has an abundance of drawing tools and picture editing tools (red-eye removal, cropping, and so on) in Word, Excel, and PowerPoint.

- The Office Clipboard is another one of those "why didn't they think of it before?" features. Finally, you can copy or cut items to a multiple-capacity clipboard and then paste them—one by one or all at once—into any Office document.

- By clicking a new flag icon on Word, Entourage, Excel, and PowerPoint toolbars, you can set up onscreen reminders that get added to the Entourage calendar. When the time comes, a dialog box appears on the screen to remind you when to follow up on a specific document or project.

UP TO SPEED

Having it Your Way

In the beginning, not many people bought Office X for Macintosh. Sales were far below Microsoft's expectations. Soon enough, a war of words heated up between Apple and Microsoft.

Apple claimed that the reason for the slow sales was that Microsoft had priced Office much too high ($500). Microsoft claimed that the reason was slow adoption of Mac OS X—and that was Apple's fault.

Following a period of public-relations tension, both sides backed down. Apple began assisting with the dissemination of Office X (by including a "test drive" version on every Mac), and Microsoft began to experiment with lower prices.

Starting in August, 2003 Microsoft reduced the price of Office X across the board and started offering, for the first time, standard and pro versions. Here are your options:

Standard Edition. The basic suite of four programs discussed in this book: Word, Excel, Power Point, and Entourage, plus perks like Windows Media Player and Microsoft Graph. (This book covers these freebies, as well, in Chapter 18.) The whole lot goes for $400. If you own a copy of Office 2001 or Office 98, you can save even more money;

an upgrade sets you back only $240. (Prices are even lower if you shop online.)

Professional Edition. The same as Standard, with one major addition: Virtual PC for Mac, a Windows PC emulator developed by a company called Connectix, which Microsoft purchased in 2003. (Presumably, Microsoft named it "professional" under the assumption that professionals are more likely to need to use Windows programs on their Macs.)

Professional Edition costs $500 (Virtual PC by itself costs $250). There's just one hitch: Virtual PC doesn't include the Windows operating system itself. You have to buy your own copy of Windows before you can run actual Windows programs.

Note: If you're thinking of buying the Professional Edition so you can play Windows-based games on your Mac, think twice. Not only do you have to buy Windows, which will run you a couple hundred more dollars, but your games will run a lot slower than on an actual Windows PC.

Student Edition. Same as Standard, but only costs $149 if you're a teacher, student, or the parent of a student.

- A single spelling checker looks over your Word essays, Excel spreadsheets, Power-Point slide shows, and even Entourage email.

- You can now scan or import digital camera images directly into any of the programs.

- The new Project Gallery lets you start a new Word, Excel, Entourage, or PowerPoint document from within any of the *other* programs.

Rather than marketing the programs individually, Microsoft pushes the Office suite for the same reason that there's one Missing Manual that covers all four programs: If you use only one of the Office programs without the others, you miss out on a lot of timesaving shortcuts.

What's New in Office X

When you get right down to it, Office X has only one big new feature: Mac OS X compatibility.

That's not to say that it offers *no* improvements over its predecessor, Office 2001. On the contrary, a handful of small new goodies awaits you.

New Features: Word

- **Multiselection.** We've lived so long without being able to select nonconsecutive chunks of text, that it can be hard to remember to use it. Keep pinching yourself, and press ⌘ as you select as many additional bits of text as you like. Then you can cut, copy, or format them all at once.

- **Clear formatting.** This addition to the Edit and Style menus changes any selected text to your Normal style.

New Features: Excel

- **Transparent charts.** Mac OS X's Quartz transparency really shows its true colors in Excel. As shown on page 507, 3-D charts become much easier to decipher when you can see through the layers.

- **Do-it-yourself keyboard shortcuts.** Excel fans can now assign any keyboard shortcuts they like to the program's commands, just as Word fans have been able to do for years.

- **ODBC queries.** If you know that ODBC stands for Open Database Connectivity, then run, don't walk, to *www.mactopia.com* to download Service Release 1. This update restores Excel X's ability to query ODBC databases, as described in the box on page 537. (If you work only with FileMaker Pro databases—or no databases—then never mind.)

- **Importing from FileMaker Pro.** Although Excel 2001 could import databases from FileMaker Pro into Excel worksheets, Excel X does it more easily and successfully than ever.

New Features: PowerPoint

- **Transparency.** You can now dress up your PowerPoint presentations with see-through graphics, thanks to Mac OS X's Quartz graphics technology.

- **Save as Package.** This new command (page 592) automatically saves all of the movies and large sound files from your presentation into a single folder. You no longer need to worry about copying them to a laptop or CD along with the rest of your presentations.

- **Improved PowerPoint movies.** Ever since PowerPoint 2001, you've been able to save your presentation as a QuickTime movie. Movies in PowerPoint X can now display all transitions and features in the original presentation, and look better, too. For instance, the fade in/fade out effects are enhanced by transparency.

New Features: Entourage

Although the primary offering in Entourage X is a much-improved design, you also benefit from smaller touches like these:

- **Improved calendar and other views.** Entourage X's views are easier to customize and switch between than ever. You can also view your tasks and calendar at the same time.

- **Office notifications.** Entourage's Flag for Follow-Up feature has been upgraded to Office Notifications (page 397), which is compatible with Microsoft's .NET Alerts in MSN Messenger.

New Features: Office as a Whole

- **Antialiasing.** If you have Mac OS X version 10.1.5 or later and Office X (with Service Release 1 installed), all text in your documents appears with smoothed edges (or *antialiased* edges, as the geeks would say). This effect makes large type look smoother and more professional, but can make smaller type look fuzzy. Fortunately, you can turn this feature off if you like; it's a checkbox called "Enable Quartz text smoothing" in the General panel of each program's Preferences dialog box.

- **Compatibility.** Office X can open and work with documents from Office 98 and 2001 for Mac; Office 97, 2000, and XP for Windows; and AppleWorks 6.

- **New Project Gallery options.** As described on page 15, the Project Gallery offers a wider variety of templates and wizards, as well as the new Based on Recent feature.

- **Help easier to search.** Office's Help system now uses a full-text search engine, as opposed to a question-based formula. The benefit to you is that Help is more likely to find the topic you're seeking.

- **Customizable toolbar buttons.** For real customization mavens, you can now create your own button icons (in Photoshop, for example) and use them on any of Office's toolbars.

- **Output as PDF.** Because Acrobat technology is integrated into Mac OS X, you can convert your Word or Excel documents, PowerPoint presentations, or even Entourage "documents" (such as an email message or calendar month) into PDF files for emailing or printing.

What Was New in Office 2001

Not everyone is a Bill Gates drone, dutifully spending another few hundred dollars for every Office upgrade that Microsoft dishes up. It's entirely possible, in fact, that you're coming from Office 98 or even an earlier version, having sprung for the upgrade to Office X only because you had to survive in Mac OS X.

Here's a recap of the new features that debuted in Office 2001, on which Office X is closely based; some of them may be new to you.

Best of the New Features: Word

- **Automatic typo corrections.** When Word is absolutely, positively sure what word you intended (as when you type *baeutiful* or *teh* or *gramar),* it corrects the typo instantly and silently, without any action on your part.

- **Definitions.** There's now a *definitions* dictionary available in all four programs, so that you can look up the meanings of words you encounter (or are thinking of using in your writing). You can check the meaning of a word, in fact, just by Control-clicking it in a Word document.

- **Live Word Count.** Instead of choosing from a menu to get a word count, you can just glance at the continuously updated word count at the bottom of the screen.

- **Click and Type.** In Word's Page Layout or Online Layout views, you can double-click anywhere in the document window and just start typing. (You don't have to press Return over and over again, or Tab over and over, to move the insertion point first.)

Best of the New Features: Excel

- **List Manager.** Excel's List Manager (see page 464) facilitates the process of using worksheets as database-like *lists.* The List Wizard and List Manager help automate tasks such as sorting and summarizing list data.

- **Formula Calculator.** This onscreen calculator is the easiest way yet to build and design formulas for the cells in your spreadsheet. It shows you placeholders for the various formula chunks you need to fill in.

- **AutoComplete.** As you begin typing into a cell, Excel offers you a pop-up list of guesses as to what you might be in the process of typing. It creates its guesses by studying the *other* entries you've typed so far in the same column.

- **Tiny tweaks.** Most of Excel 2001's new features were smaller blessings, all of which are welcome. It introduced the euro currency, a Font menu that displays your font names in their actual typefaces, four-digit year displays; and so on.

Best of the New Features: PowerPoint

- **Three-pane view.** You no longer need to spend your time flipping among three different views to get a feel for your slide show. The primary, three-pane Normal view shows your outline, notes, and the image of the current slide simultaneously.

- **Multiple masters.** A single presentation can incorporate multiple master slides, and it's easy to apply a certain master to many slides at once.

- **PowerPoint QuickTime.** You can save a PowerPoint presentation as a QuickTime movie that works just like a PowerPoint show. Just click to advance the slide on any Mac or Windows machine. What's amazing is that you, or a colleague, can then open that QuickTime movie in PowerPoint to make changes. The Quick-Time movie retains all of its PowerPoint characteristics behind the scenes.

Best of the New Features: Entourage

Best new features in Entourage? Entourage *was* a new feature in Office 2001. This calendar/email/address book/to-do list program is based on the powerful email smarts of Microsoft's Outlook Express for the Macintosh. Nevertheless, the time-saving benefits you gain with the addition of a calendar may surprise you.

Best of the New Features: Office as a Whole

- **Adios, Max.** Few features of Office 98 infuriated as many Mac fans as the dancing Help assistant called Max. Even if you closed his window, he still wasted another few seconds with an annoying wave—and still reappeared from time to time.

  Starting in Office 2001, the Help→Turn Assistant Off command deletes Max and his window, instantly and permanently.

Tip: The off switches for all of Word's other "helpful" features (automatically underlined Web addresses, automatically bulleted lists, automatically curlified quotes, and so on) are in one place: Tools→AutoCorrect. Page 96 offers complete instructions for toning down Word's infamous intrusiveness.

- **Project Gallery.** This first command on the File menu presents a master catalog of canned templates. From within any of the four Office programs, you can double-click to open any document or template in any Office program—even a to-do list task or a Web page. You can customize the Project Gallery by adding Word or PowerPoint templates you've created yourself.

- **The Formatting Palette.** This compact palette (see Chapter 3) packs a multitude of text-, paragraph-, image-, drawing-, slide-, and document-formatting features in a tiny amount of space. Because the Formatting Palette shrinks and grows depending on what's selected on the screen, screen clutter is greatly reduced.

- **Instant Web pages.** The Save as Web Page command, Web Page Preview, and other Web tools make it possible to design and create a Web page—complete with graphics, tables, links, and forms—without ever leaving Word, Excel, Entourage, or PowerPoint.

- **Windows suffixes.** One of Microsoft's greatest achievements (and the greatest joys for its customers) is that documents created in Word, Excel, or PowerPoint for the Macintosh are 100 percent compatible with the Windows versions. You and your Windows-using colleagues never have to convert or export your files. A Word file is a Word file regardless of the computer it's on, making cross-platform collaboration simple. (Specifically, documents created in Office 2001, 98, and X for the Mac, and Office 97, 2000, and XP for Windows, are all identical in format.)

There's only one fly in the ointment: Windows requires every document to have a three-letter suffix on the file name, such as *Letter to Mom.doc*. If you forget that step on the Macintosh, your Windows colleague may have trouble opening the file. Fortunately, a checkbox in Office's Save As box automatically adds the three-letter Windows file extension.

The Very Basics

You'll find very little jargon or nerd terminology in this book. You will, however, encounter a few terms and concepts that you'll see frequently in your Macintosh life. They include:

- **Clicking.** This book offers three kinds of instructions that require you to use the mouse or trackpad attached to your Mac. To *click* means to point the arrow cursor at something onscreen and then—without moving the cursor at all—to press and release the clicker button on the mouse (or laptop trackpad). To *double-click,* of course, means to click twice in rapid succession, again without moving the cursor at all. And to *drag* means to move the cursor while keeping the button continuously pressed.

When you're told to ⌘-*click* something, you click while pressing the ⌘ key (next to the Space bar). Such related procedures as *Shift-clicking, Option-clicking,* and *Control-clicking* work the same way—just click while pressing the corresponding key in the lower corner of your keyboard.

- **Menus.** The menus are the words in the lightly striped bar at the top of your screen. The menu titles are slightly different in each of the Office programs. You can either click one of these words to open a pull-down menu of commands (and then click again on a command), or click and *hold* the button as you drag down the menu to the desired command (and release the button to activate the command). Either method works fine.

- **Keyboard shortcuts.** Every time you take your hand off the keyboard to move the mouse, you lose time and potentially disrupt your creative flow. That's why many experienced Mac fans use keystroke combinations instead of menu commands wherever possible. ⌘-B, for example, is a universal keyboard shortcut for boldface type throughout Office X (as well as in most other Mac programs). ⌘-P opens the Print dialog box, ⌘-S saves whatever document you're currently working in, and ⌘-M minimizes the current window to the Dock.

When you see a shortcut like ⌘-W (which closes the current window), it's telling you to hold down the ⌘ key, and, while it's down, type the letter W, and then release both keys.

- **Pop-up buttons.** The tiny arrows beside many of Office X's buttons are easy to overlook—but don't. Each one reveals a pop-up menu of useful commands (see Figure I-2). For instance, the arrow button next to the Undo button on the Standard toolbar lets you choose any number of actions to undo. Meanwhile, the arrow next to the New button in Entourage lets you specify what *kind* of item you want to create anew—an appointment for the calendar, an address book entry, and so on.

- **Choice is good.** Microsoft wouldn't be Microsoft if it didn't offer you several ways to trigger a particular command. Sure enough, everything you could ever wish to do in Office X is accessible by a menu command *or* by clicking a toolbar button *or* by pressing a key combination. Some people prefer the speed of keyboard shortcuts; others like the satisfaction of a visual command array available in menus or toolbars.

Figure I-2:
The tiny arrows on Office X toolbars are a fascinating hybrid interface element called, in this book, pop-up button. Whenever you see the tiny black triangle pointing down from a toolbar icon (like the one next to the New button shown here), that's your cue to click the triangle and hold the cursor down for a pop-up list of options.

One thing is for sure, however: You're not expected to memorize all of these features. In fact, Microsoft's own studies indicate that most people don't even *know* about 80 percent of its programs' features, let alone use them all. And that's OK. Great novels, Pulitzer Prize–winning articles, and successful business ventures have all been launched by people who never get past Open and Save.

On the other hand, as you skim this book, be aware that the way you've been doing things in Word or Excel since 1998 may no longer be the fastest or easiest. Every new keystroke or toolbar you add to your repertoire may afford you more free time to teach ancient Greek to 3-year-olds or start your own hang gliding club.

As for the programmers in Redmond, let them obsess about how many different ways they can think of to do the same thing. You are under no obligation to try them all.

About This Book

Office X comes in an attractive box adorned with plastic bubbles that somehow call lava lamps to mind. What you won't find inside, however, is a printed manual. To learn this vast set of software programs, you're expected to rely on help screens (see Appendix B).

Such computerized help comes with built-in problems, however. Although Office Help is detailed and concise, you need to know what you're looking for before you can find it. There are no tutorials, annotated illustrations, or jokes. You can't mark your place (you lose your trail in the Help program every time you close an Office program), you can't underline or make marginal notes, and, even with a laptop, reading in bed or by firelight just isn't the same.

The purpose of this book, then, is to serve as the manual that should have accompanied Office X. Although you may still turn to online help for the answer to a quick question, this book provides step-by-step instructions for all major (and most minor) Office features, including those that have always lurked in Office but you've never quite understood. This printed guide should provide an overview of the ways this comprehensive software package can make you act like a one-person, all-purpose office.

About the Outline

This book is divided into five parts, each containing several chapters.

- Parts 1 through 4, **Word, Entourage, Excel,** and **PowerPoint,** cover in detail each of the primary Office programs. Each part begins with an introductory chapter that covers the basics. Additional chapters delve into the more advanced and less-frequently used features.

- Part 5, **Office as a Whole,** shows how the programs work together for even more productivity and creativity. For example, it covers the supplementary programs (WordArt, Graph, and so on), changing the menus and keystrokes (one of the strongest and most useful Office features), and more.

At the end of the book, Appendix A explains the Office online help system, and Appendix B offers guidance in installing, updating, and troubleshooting the software.

Tip: A third, free appendix awaits you on the "Missing CD-ROM" page at *www.missingmanuals.com* in electronic form: Appendix C, "Office X: Menu by Menu." It describes the function of each menu command in each of the four major programs, with cross-references to the book in your hands (where these features are discussed more completely).

OFFICE X FOR MACINTOSH: THE MISSING MANUAL

About→These→Arrows

Throughout this book, and throughout the Missing Manual series, you'll find sentences like this one: "Open the System folder→Libraries→Fonts folder." That's shorthand for a much longer instruction that directs you to open three nested folders in sequence. That instruction might read: "On your hard drive, you'll find a folder called System. Open that. Inside the System folder window is a folder called Libraries. Open that. Inside *that* folder is yet another one called Fonts. Double-click to open it, too."

Similarly, this kind of arrow shorthand helps to simplify the business of choosing commands in menus, as shown in Figure I-3.

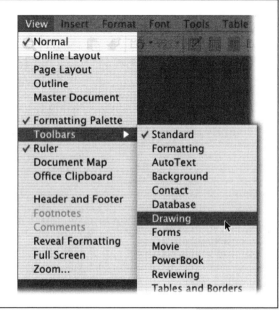

Figure I-3:
When you read "Choose View→Toolbars→Drawing" in a Missing Manual, that means: "Click the View menu to open it; click Toolbars in that menu; choose Drawing in the resulting submenu." (If you read "Choose Edit→ Preferences→Mail tab," that means you should click the tab called Mail in the dialog box that appears.)

About MissingManuals.com

At the *missingmanuals.com* Web site, you'll find news, articles, and updates to the books in this series.

But if you click the name of this book and then the Errata link, you'll find a unique resource: a list of corrections and updates that have been made in successive printings of this book. You can mark important corrections right into your own copy of the book, if you like.

In fact, the same Errata page offers an invitation for you to submit such corrections and updates yourself. In an effort to keep the book as up-to-date and accurate as possible, each time we print more copies of this book, we'll make any confirmed corrections you've suggested. Thanks in advance for reporting any glitches you find!

In the meantime, we'd love to hear your own suggestions for new books in the Missing Manual line. There's a place for that on the Web site, too, as well as a place to sign up for free email notification of new titles in the series.

Office Up to Date

Writing complex software is never easy—and few companies write more complex software than Microsoft. It's no wonder then, that the original version of Microsoft Office X had a few bugs—all right, 1,500 of them. It's also no wonder that few companies issue more "Service Releases" and updates than Microsoft—with the possible exception of Apple.

Bottom line: You'll do yourself a big favor by making sure that you have the most updated versions of both Office X and Mac OS X. As of August 2003, the latest Office X update is 10.1.4. To get it, go to *www.microsoft.com/mac* and look under "Quick Downloads" at the right of the page. The 10.1.4 download page instructs you to download the 10.1.2 update first, if you haven't already.

By the time you've downloaded and installed both of these updates, you'll be the proud owner of every update and fix that Microsoft has ever made to Office X, including the first and most important update, Service Release 1. Among other things, you'll find that Word crashes a lot less often.

(Incidentally, the download page lets you choose between a .hqx and a .bin version of the installer file. Install the .bin compression; the .hqx version is for older Mac systems, like OS 8—and if you had Mac OS 8, you wouldn't be using Office X!)

As far as your Mac goes, you can use Mac OS X version 10.1, 10.2, or (when it's available) 10.3. Visit Apple.com or use Software Update to make sure you have the most recent update of whatever version you have, though (10.2.6, for example). These little double-decimal updates are free.

Note, though, that like most programs, Office X runs much faster and more smoothly in Mac OS X 10.2. If you value your time, seriously consider taking the Jaguar plunge. (If you're upgrading to 10.3, "Panther," be sure to check for additional Office updates while you're at it.)

There's no downside to installing the Service Release and the subsequent Office updates. In fact, this book assumes that you've already done so. Using Office X without SR1 is just asking for frustration.

Part One: Word

1

Basic Word Processing

I t happens millions of times a day. Someone sits down at a computer, opens
Microsoft Word, and starts typing. When he wants to start a new paragraph, he
hits Return a couple of times and keeps going. When he's done, he clicks the
Print button and *voila!*—a page of text that's perfectly fine for handing out at a
meeting or posting on a bulletin board.

Of course, if that were the extent of your Office X ambitions, you wouldn't be reading a book about it. As you'll discover later in this book, Word X offers a staggering
array of advanced features that were once found only in page layout programs and
graphics software (not to mention space shuttles).

These first three chapters (all 140 pages of them), however, cover the basics: how to
start a document, type into and format the document, print it, and, finally, save it
all. These may sound like standard Mac techniques, no different from TextEdit or
SimpleText and not worth rehashing. But as you'll soon discover, Microsoft has its
own, greatly enhanced idea of the Macintosh Way.

New, Open, and the Project Gallery

The first thing you see when you initially launch Word is the Project Gallery (see
Figure 1-1), where you indicate what kind of document you wish to create.

If your reply is, "Well, *duh*—a word processing document!" then you must still be
under the impression that Word is a word processor, which it stopped being some
time in 1752.

The Project Gallery

The Project Gallery is proof. The icons in this window represent the kinds of documents Office X (not just Word) can create for you. (Use the scroll bar to see all of them.) They're canned *templates* for mailing labels, résumés, budgets, brochures, fax cover letters, and dozens of others—even Excel, PowerPoint, and Entourage documents like spreadsheets and blank email messages. The idea is that you can use Word as the launching point for your entire Office X experience, without having to know ahead of time which of the four Office applications is most appropriate for creating the document you want.

Tip: If you'd rather not visit the Project Gallery every time you launch Word, simply turn off "Show Project Gallery at startup." You can also choose Word→Preferences, click the General button (in the list at left) and turn "Show Project Gallery at startup" on or off.

When the Project Gallery opens, the Word Document icon is highlighted as shown in Figure 1-1. If you click OK (or press Return or Enter) now, a new blank Word document opens, just as if you'd chosen File→New Blank Document (or pressed ⌘-N).

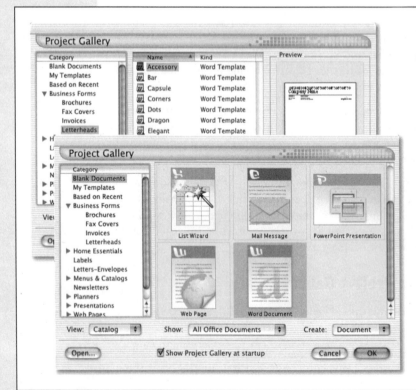

Figure 1-1:
The Project Gallery opens automatically when you first launch Word. When you wish to open another new document, just open the Project Gallery again by choosing File→Project Gallery or pressing Shift-⌘-P.

Back left: The List view (use the lower-left pop-up menu) offers a better overview than the Catalog view and saves you some scrolling.

Right: The Catalog view.

Opening any kind of document in the Project Gallery works the same way: Click the list items in the Category list on the left (see Figure 1-1) until you see the desired template or document type on the right. Then double-click the document icon to open it.

For instance, say you're writing a letter. Click the flippy triangle next to the Business Forms category (Figure 1-1). (You may have to keep clicking to find the type of document you're seeking. Résumés, for example, are filed under Home Essentials, maybe because Microsoft pictures you unemployed and lying around the house.)

Then click Letterheads; an assortment of colorful stationery templates appears in the window. (Catalog view is the best way to get an overview of what's available). Double-click a template; a new document opens, all formatted and ready for you to input your own address and other information.

Made for X

The following two items in the Category list (new to Office X) offer greater flexibility in creating new documents:

- **Based on Recent.** Clicking this category displays a list of the last nine documents you've worked on. But when you double-click one of these document icons, you get a *copy* of the document—not the original. You can make changes to it and save it as a whole new document.

  For instance, if you're writing a letter of complaint to the phone company, you can base it on the complaint letter you sent to the cable company last week. Since most of your choicest phrasings will probably remain the same, there's no need to start the letter from scratch. (The Open Copy option in the standard Open file dialog box serves the same purpose, but it's nice to have it in the Project Gallery.)

- **Writing Toolbox.** At last: multipage templates!

  In previous versions of Office, each template was only one page long. Now, however, you're offered a category containing two kinds of multipage documents: Journals, such as a Baby Book; and Reports, such as a Book Report. Each page is different. For instance, the Term Paper template contains a ready-made table of contents and example footnotes, which you replace with your own information.

Tweaking the Gallery

To customize the Project Gallery, use the following three pop-up menus found at the bottom of the dialog box:

- **View.** This pop-up menu lets you choose to view the Project Gallery either in icon view or as a list view (both are shown in Figure 1-1). In list view, the panel of large document icons is replaced by a list of smaller icons. At the right, a preview panel opens where you can see a more detailed view of what you're about to open.

- **Show.** This pop-up menu is like a filter. If you want to view *only* templates for Word documents, choose All Word Documents from here. You won't see Excel templates, PowerPoint templates, and so on.

  On the other hand, the setting called All Office Documents has its advantages. From this one panel, you can open up any kind of Office document or template without having to visit your Dock, for example, to click the appropriate program icon.

- **Create.** Choose Document or Template. If you choose Template, Word peels off a copy of the document you've selected and turns it into a *template* document, as described on page 202. It is now ready to save into your Templates folder for future use. (Yes, you're creating a template *from* a template; you're forgiven for any confusion.)

Tip: The Project Gallery lists simply reflect whichever files are in the Microsoft Office X→Templates folder on your hard drive. If you'd like to add to, trim down, rename, or reorganize the options in the Project Gallery, just return to the Finder, open the Applications→Microsoft Office X→Templates folder, and go to town. For example, you might add your corporate logo letterhead, after first saving it as a template (see page 202).

Ditching the Project Gallery

To dismiss the Project Gallery, click Cancel or press the Esc key (or ⌘-.). Word automatically opens a new blank document. If you'd rather open an existing document, use one of the methods described below. Word, a prince among Mac applications, always closes its default blank document whenever you open one of your own.

Creating a New Document

There are at least four ways to create a new document from scratch. They are as follows:

- Choose File→Project Gallery and click the Word Document icon, as described earlier.

POWER USERS' CLINIC

Keystrokes of the Very Busy

Within the Project Gallery, you can jump from the category list at left to the templates in the right or middle panel by pressing Tab. Once you've highlighted one of these lists, pressing the up and down arrow keys moves you up or down the lists. When the templates are in icon view, you can press all four of the arrow keys to highlight successive icons. (Sorry, Mac OS purists: You can't jump to a particu-

lar template by typing the first letters of its name.)

When you've highlighted a category (in the left-side list) marked by a "flippy triangle," press ⌘-right arrow to expand it, or ⌘-left arrow to collapse it again. And when you've finally highlighted the template you want, pressing Return or Enter, of course, opens it.

- Choose File→New Blank Document.

- Press ⌘-N.

- Click the New Blank Document button (the very first icon) on the Standard toolbar that appears just beneath your menu bar.

However you do it, the result is a fresh, empty document.

Tip: In fact, this new document is not really empty at all. Behind the scenes, it's already loaded up with such settings as a default font, margin settings, keystroke assignments, macros, style sheets, and so on. It inherits these starter settings from a special document called the Normal template.

You can read much more about Templates on page 202. For now, though, it's enough to know that you can modify the Normal template so that each new document you open automatically contains your own favorite settings.

Opening Documents with the Open Command

If you're entering the world of Word for the purposes of editing an existing document, just double-click the document in the Finder (or click it in the Dock, if that's where you stashed it). If you're already in Word, though, simply choose the fastest of the following options:

- Click the Open button in the Project Gallery.

- Choose File→Open.

- Press ⌘-O.

- Click the second (arrow-from-folder) icon on the Standard toolbar.

No matter which method you use, the standard Open File box appears (Figure 1-2). Actually, it may not look so standard to you, since it's Apple's new OS X Open dialog box. It features several advantages over the pre-Mac OS X Open box: It has a column view, just like the OS X Finder, and a From menu to make it easier to access the document you seek. (See *Mac OS X: The Missing Manual* for a complete list of Save and Open dialog box features, or the Introduction to this book for a quick summary.) Once you've located the document you want in this dialog box, double-click to open it.

Tip: When you choose File→Open, Word shows you the contents of the folder you last opened. But if you keep all your Word files in one folder, you might rather see *that* list of files when you use the Open command.

To make it so, choose Word→Preferences. Click the File Locations button (in the list at left), then Documents, then Modify; navigate to and highlight the folder you use most often, and then click Choose. From now on, choosing File→Open automatically takes you to the folder you selected.

In addition, Microsoft has added the following special features of its own to the Open dialog box:

- **Show.** Use this pop-up menu (at the top of the Open dialog box) to choose which kinds of documents you want to see listed on your hard drive. The setting "All Readable Documents" lets the Open dialog box display any possible document on your Mac that you can open in Word—not just Microsoft Office documents, but text files, JPEG graphics, HTML Web-page documents, and so on. If you know that the document you're seeking is of a certain type, you might save time by telling Word to show you *only* those choices.

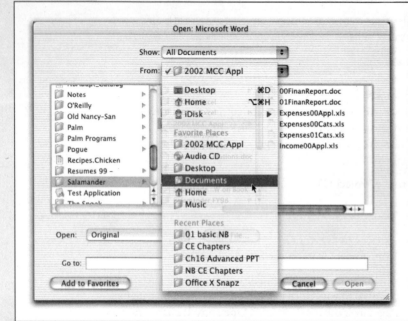

Figure 1-2:
The fastest way to use Mac OS X's new Open dialog box is to take advantage of the From pop-up menu. It lists the folders you've been using recently as well as the folders you've made Favorites in the Finder; it also contains a quick way to hop to the Desktop or your Home folder. Because Word X can open so many different document formats, leave the Show pop-up menu set to All Documents unless your hard drive is really congested. If the document you're looking for is plain text, for example, set it to Text Files to make your document easier to spot.

Tip: Don't miss the "Recover text from any file" option listed in this pop-up menu; it's a spectacular tool. It lets you extract recognizable text from *any file* and place it into a new window. It was intended to rescue usable prose from a corrupted Word document, of course, but it means what it says: *any file.*

- **Open.** This pop-up menu lets you choose one of the three different ways Word can open the same document. **Original** opens the document itself; **Copy** opens a copy, leaving the original untouched; and **Read-Only** opens the document but doesn't let you make changes to it.

Most of the time, you'll open the original and get to work. But opening a *copy* is a convenient way of leaving an electronic paper trail of your work. No matter how many changes you make or how badly you mess up a document, you still have an unsullied copy saved on your Mac. To save changes you've made to a Read-Only document, you must first save it under a different title.

GEM IN THE ROUGH

In Search of Files

The Open dialog box offers a streamlined means of traveling directly to the document you want to open—assuming you remember where you stored it. If you don't, the Find File button in the Open dialog box may be the quickest way of retrieving it.

Clicking Find File opens the Search dialog box, shown here at top. To find a file, type the portion of the file name you remember into the "File name" box. Choose a file type (Word document, text file, and so on) and folder location, if you know them.

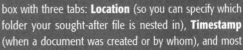

Word searches and displays a list of all files that have those characters in their titles. The Commands pop-up button lets you open, print, or even delete a file, right from within this dialog box. Its Sorting command lets you specify how you want the found-files list sorted—by name, date, size, and so on. (If you want to hang onto these results but add to them with a second search, turn on "Rebuild file list" first.)

The Saved Searches feature is useful when you're frequently rounding up documents that have something in common. For instance, you may want to find all the Word files you've saved today, or all the documents that your assistant created. When you've found a document or documents and think that you may need to repeat the procedure later, click Save Search As and name the search. Thereafter, just select that search from the "Saved searches" menu to do it again.

Sometimes you can remember just about everything about a document *except* its name. For those occasions, click Advanced Search. You get a dialog

box with three tabs: **Location** (so you can specify which folder your sought-after file is nested in), **Timestamp** (when a document was created or by whom), and most interesting of all, **Summary**. This most powerful tab doesn't require that you know where the desired file is located or what it's called. You can search for it via the information found in the file properties, such as Author or Keywords (see page 226), or any *words*—or even partial words—contained in the body of the document.

For the Summary feature to work well, use a word that's likely to be found in the document you're looking for, but not many others. For instance, searching for "people" is likely to find too many documents for you to weed through. A more specific term, such as "employees" or "benefactors," is more likely to round up the exact file you're seeking.

If you're really grasping at straws, enter whatever part of the word you remember—say you recall the document mentions a person whose last name begins with "Ber." Type *Ber* in the "Containing text" box and turn on "Use pattern matching." Choose "Beginning of word" from the Special menu. The Special menu also presents options that let you search for documents that do *not* contain a certain word, but instead contain a mathematical expression, and so on.

Finally, click OK to begin the search.

To cancel any search while it's under way, press Esc or ⌘-.. Click Clear in the Search dialog box if you change your mind about your search criteria and want to start over.

- **Find File.** This button opens Office's search function. While not as powerful as the Mac's own Sherlock, it has charms of its own—such as being available *within* the Open dialog box. It lets you search by name, file type, and location, and also provides advanced search functions such as searching by author or by keywords contained in the file. (Don't miss the Advanced button in this dialog box, which offers you the option to search for words *inside* your Word files, even if you can't remember what they were called. See "In Search of Files" on page 21.)

- **Go to.** If you know the folder you want to look in, you can type its *path* right into the "Go to" box. That is, you can type a folder path (such as *~/pictures*, or just *~/pi* and a press of the Tab key) right into the blank. (This is Mac OS X shorthand; the *~* denotes your Home folder, and the / means "the following folder is inside the previous one.")

  Add to Favorites. The Add to Favorites button adds a highlighted folder to your Go→Favorites submenu in the Finder, so you can jump directly to it the next time you need it. (Technically, Word places an alias of the folder in your Home→Library→Favorites folder. And as with any Favorite, you can delete it from the menu by dragging the alias out of the Favorites folder.)

Returning to Favorite Documents

Like most people, you probably work with the same documents and templates over and over again. In addition to giving you a chance to add folders to the Finder's Go→Favorites menu and the Based on Recent category in the Project Gallery, Word offers two shortcuts to retrieving files you've used recently or that you intend to use frequently.

The Recent Files list

First, there's the list of recently opened Word documents at the bottom of the File menu. Just choose a file name to open the corresponding document, wherever it may be on your machine. (Unless it's no longer *on* your machine, of course, in which case you get only a cheerful error message.)

FREQUENTLY ASKED QUESTION

Purging the Recent List

I'm not so sure I want my spouse seeing which files I've been working on recently. Is there any way to delete the document names listed in the File menu?

You bet. Open any Word document. Choose Word→ Preferences→General tab. Turn off "Recently used file list" and press Return. The list of names at the bottom of the File menu disappears, and Word stops remembering them. (You've also just wiped out the Recent Documents list in the Project Gallery.)

To cover your tracks even more completely, choose Word→Preferences→General tab again. Now turn on "Recently used file list" again. Word again starts listing files that you or your spouse open—but that last embarrassing batch remains gone.

Of course, you can avoid the whole issue by not naming your documents things like *ILuvWorf*.

Tip: You control how many documents are listed here by choosing Word→Preferences→General. Set the "Recently used file list" number to 0 if you don't want Word to track your files at all, or 9 for maximum tracking.

The Work menu

Word's Work menu is one of the program's best, but most overlooked, features. It's simply a list of the documents you use most often. Store your book outlines there, templates for your invoices, or the different drafts of your thesis. Figure 1-3 illustrates how to install new documents to the list.

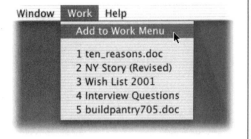

Figure 1-3:
To add to the Work menu, open the document (save it, if you haven't done so). Choose Work→Add to Work Menu. Now click the Work menu again; there's the name of your document, ready for opening just by choosing its name.

You can remove a document from the Work menu just as you'd remove any Word command: by pressing Option-⌘-hyphen. The cursor turns into a thick, black – sign. Use it to choose the name of the document you wish to banish from the Work menu. After your selection, it goes away for good (the menu listing, not your actual document).

The Work menu predates the Go→Favorites command in the Finder; it may seem redundant in Mac OS X. However, Go→Favorites saves you a step by letting you launch Word *and* open a document with one mouse click. On the other hand, once you're *in* Word, you may find that the Work menu is faster and prevents your Go menu from getting overloaded.

Word Processing Basics

Once a document is onscreen, your administrative efforts are complete, and the creative phase can begin. Odds are good that you've word processed before; nevertheless, Chapter 2 covers the nuts and bolts of editing in detail.

As a reminder, here are the very, very basics of word processing:

- **Don't hit Return at the end of a line.** Word automatically wraps the text to the next line when you reach the edge of the window.

- **Don't type hyphens to break end-of-line words, either.** To divide words at the end of lines, use Word's hyphenation feature, as described on page 153.

- **Press Return at the end of a *paragraph.*** To create a blank line between paragraphs, don't press Return twice; that can cause awkward problems, such as an extra space at the top of a page. Instead, change the paragraph's *style* to leave more space after each paragraph, as described on page 122. Using this more advanced and graceful method also lets you edit, add, and subtract paragraphs at will. As you do so, the spacing between the paragraphs remains consistent.

- **For similar reasons, don't press Tab to indent the first line of a paragraph.** If, instead, you set a *first line indent* using the Formatting Palette, as described on page 109, Word automatically creates the indents each time you start a paragraph. Indents created this way remain consistent as you edit the document. In addition, the amount of indentation you choose is not dependent upon the positions of your tab stops.

- **Don't press Return at the end of a page.** Word automatically wraps the text to the next page. If you want your next thought to start at the top of a new page, choose Insert→Break→Section Break (Next Page) instead. Now, no matter how much you edit before or after the section break, your new section will always start at the top of a new page.

POWER USERS' CLINIC

Document Protection

Word makes it easy to open documents; almost *too* easy, if you're trying to keep certain documents private or unmodified. Never fear: Word offers three levels of document-protection features designed to keep spies and busybodies out of your files.

- **Suggest Read-Only.** When someone tries to open a document protected in this manner, a dialog box politely suggests that he use the Read-only option. That person can make changes, but can only save the file under a new name. The original, read-only file remains intact.

    To save a file this way, choose File→Save As; click Options. Turn on "Read-only recommended," and press Return. Click Save or press Return to complete the process.

- **Password Required for Editing.** This trick makes Word ask for a password at the moment the document is opened, using a dialog box like the one shown here. Readers to whom you give

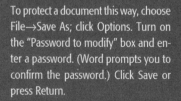

the password can edit the document and save the changes just as you can; for everyone else, the document opens as read-only, as described above.

To protect a document this way, choose File→Save As; click Options. Turn on the "Password to modify" box and enter a password. (Word prompts you to confirm the password.) Click Save or press Return.

- **Full Password Protection.** This highest level of document protection requires readers to enter a password before they can even open the document. In the Save As dialog box, click Options and then turn on the "Password to open" box and assign a password as described above.

If you use one of the password methods, write the password down and keep it somewhere safe. If you lose the password, nobody—not you, not the Recover Text from Any File feature, not even Microsoft—can open the protected document.

- **Press the Space bar only once—not twice—after punctuation such as periods, colons, and semicolons.** Double-spacing after punctuation is a holdover from the days of the typewriter, when you had to manually add extra space after punctuation for an attractive, readable result. On a Mac, Word automatically places the correct amount of space after each period or other punctuation mark. Adding an extra space is superfluous and clutters your file with extra characters.

- **Save early, save often.** Choose File→Save (or press ⌘-S) after every paragraph or sentence.

Note: Word 2001 veterans will be happy to hear that the "Disk is full" bug no longer exists in Word X. Now you can save a document as many times as you want, without worrying that Word will be unable to save changes because of an erroneous out-of-space message.

A Window into Word

The tools you use most often—those for navigating your document and for basic formatting—are clustered around the main text window, which is shown in Figure 1-4.

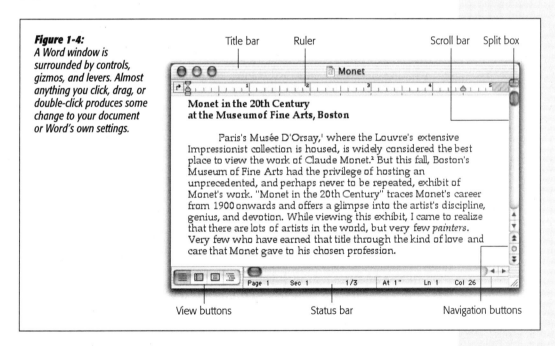

Figure 1-4:
A Word window is surrounded by controls, gizmos, and levers. Almost anything you click, drag, or double-click produces some change to your document or Word's own settings.

Title Bar

Word X's title bar does all the usual Mac things—sends the window to the Dock when double-clicked, moves it when dragged, etc.—but it has a few unheralded powers, too. It also performs like a Mac OS X *folder* window in two key respects:

• To find out what folder your document is nested in, ⌘-click the document's title. As shown in Figure 1-5, a pop-up menu appears, identifying your document *icon's* location on the hard drive. Click any folder or drive on the list to open it into a new window.

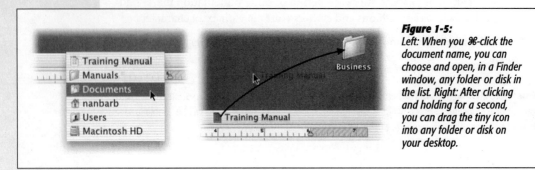

Figure 1-5:
Left: When you ⌘-click the document name, you can choose and open, in a Finder window, any folder or disk in the list. Right: After clicking and holding for a second, you can drag the tiny icon into any folder or disk on your desktop.

• See the tiny Word icon next to the document's name in the title bar? That's your *document proxy icon,* which works just like the *folder* proxy icon in every Finder window title bar. As shown at right in Figure 1-5, you can drag that icon just as you would any icon in the Finder. You might do so to move the current document to a different folder, to copy it to a different disk, or even to drag it directly to the Trash. In true Mac OS X fashion, you see a translucent ghost of the icon as you move it. (You have to hold the cursor down on this icon for about one second, making it turn dark, before you can drag it in this way. If you drag it too quickly, Word thinks you're simply trying to move the window on the screen.)

Tip: The document proxy icon appears faded out (disabled) whenever you've edited your document without saving the changes. (And you can't drag it to move, copy, or trash your document when you haven't saved changes.) Only when you choose File→Save (⌘-S) does the icon spring to life, ready for dragging.

The Ruler

The ruler across the top of the page displays the current settings for margins, tabs, and indents. See page 121 for details on how to use and change these settings.

Scroll Bar and Navigator Buttons

Figure 1-4 depicts the *Navigator buttons*—double arrows flanking a little round button at the lower right of the Word window. When you first open a document, these Navigator buttons act as page up/page down buttons. But once you've used the Find and Replace command (see page 75), or in some other way changed the *browse object,* the double arrows act differently.

For instance, after you've used Find and Replace, clicking the Navigator buttons takes you from each occurrence of the word you're trying to find to the next. For more detail on the Browse Object feature and Navigator buttons, see page 73.

Split Box

Figure 1-4 also shows the small blue *Split box* at the upper-right of the window. When you point to it, the cursor changes to a double-pointing arrow. Dragging that arrow divides the window into two panes, each with its own, independent, vertical scroll bar. (Choosing Window→Split, or pressing Option-⌘-S, accomplishes the same thing.)

This is a great arrangement when you're working at the end of a long document and need to refer back to material earlier in the document. You can use the upper window to scroll through the entire document, while in the lower window, you can go right back to where you were typing without losing your place.

Tip: It's often faster to simply *double-click* the split box. Doing so gives you two evenly split panes of the window; to adjust their relative proportions, just drag the *resize bar* (the gray dividing line between the panes) up or down.

Double-click this dividing line a second time to restore the window to its single-pane status. (The *bottom* half of the window disappears, even if it contained the insertion point—a potentially alarming behavior.)

Drag the light gray bar between the two panes up or down to adjust their relative sizes. Like the scroll bars, the page up, page down, and arrow keys work as usual *within* each pane, meaning you can't use them to travel from one pane to the next. To switch *between* panes, you can use the mouse, or just press F6, which acts as a toggle key to the other pane and back again.

To restore a split window back to a single one, drag the resize bar all the way to the top of the window, double-click the resize bar, or press Option-⌘-S again.

Window Menu

You can't split a window into more than two panes—nor create *vertical* panes—using the Split box as described above. However, you can get these effects using the Window menu (see Figure 1-6).

Choosing Window→New Window creates a clone of your document window, which you can scroll, position, or zoom independently; each can be in a different Word *view,* too (one in Outline view, one in Normal, and so on). The new windows are different peepholes into the same document; remember, you haven't created a new document. Therefore, any change you make in one window appears in both windows simultaneously. When you use File→Save, you save *all* the windows.

There's almost no limit to the number of windows you can create in this way. You can place two windows side by side and work on the first and last pages of your document at the same time, or you can create five windows, each scrolled to a different region of your manuscript. The title bar identifies the windows as "Introduction:1," "Introduction:2," and so on.

To reconstitute your document, just close the extra windows.

Status Bar

The light gray bar running across the bottom of the window (see Figure 1-4) is called the *status bar*. Divided into segments by etched vertical lines, the status bar presents a variety of statistics about your current location within the document.

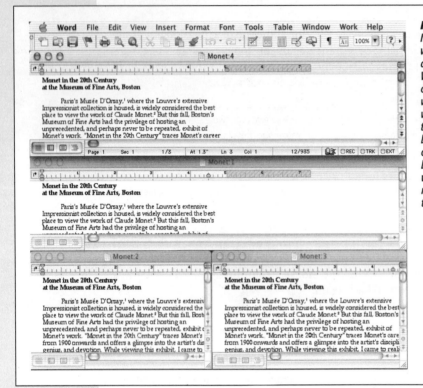

Figure 1-6:
If your screen is cluttered with documents and duplicate windows, the Window→Arrange All command turns each window into a screen-wide strip and stacks them from top to bottom. It's not a very convenient arrangement, but at least you can see what you've got. You can now resize and arrange them as you wish.

- **Page 10, Sec 2.** At the far left is the number of the page that contains the insertion point (not necessarily the page you're looking at), followed by the section number. If you haven't divided your document into *sections* (see page 137), which is likely, then the section readout always says Sec 1.

- **10/41.** The third set of numbers looks like a fraction; it shows the page number containing the insertion point (again) followed by the total pages. For instance, if you're at the end of a three-page letter, this readout says 3/3.

Tip: Double-click anywhere in the first two segments of the status bar to open the Go To tab of the Find and Replace dialog box, described on page 72. The idea, of course, is to provide you with a quick way to jump to a different page of your document without scrolling.

- **At 3.5".** The status bar's second segment provides information about your insertion point's location on the current page. The first number (1" in Figure 1-4, for example) is the distance, in inches, from the top of the page to the insertion point. It tells you where you're "at" along the length of your page, which could conceivably be useful if, for example, you need to determine column inches for a newspaper.

- **Ln 1.** The second number identifies the current *line* of your document, counting down from the top of the *printed page* (not the window) to the insertion point. It's useful when the number of lines is important, such as when placing a personal ad, or if you're a lawyer.

- **Col 15.** This peculiar statistic reveals the number of characters you've typed from the left margin.

- **34/1423.** The next divided segment of the status bar shows two numbers divided by a slash; the second number shows the total number of words in your document (journalists, kneel!), and the first indicates which word contains your insertion point, as counted from the first word of the document.

  If these numbers are blank, it's probably because your word count feature is turned off. To turn it on, choose Word→Preferences; in the Preferences dialog box, click the View button. Turn on Live Word Count (under "Window") and click OK. Now, when you start typing, the word count number is revised after every few words that you type; hence the name "Live Word Count."

Tip: Double-click the word-count segment to summon the Word Count dialog box, which provides the number of pages, paragraphs, lines, and other countable items, as well as the word count. (It's the same box that appears when you choose Tools→Word Count.)

Tip 2: If you highlight some text in your document, the number before the slash tells you how many words are in the selected passage.

- **The little book.** This is the spelling and grammar–checking status indicator, whose icon you can see change. As you type, a little pencil moves across the pages, indicating that Word is checking for spelling and grammar errors. Most of the time, when you're at rest, a red X appears on the book icon, meaning that somewhere in your document, Word has found an error. (That is, an error according to Word's sense of grammar.) When you've just completed a grammar check and made no new errors, the icon shows a checkmark instead of an X.

  To review Word's spelling and grammar flags starting from the beginning of the document, double-click the book icon. At each error, a pop-up menu offers alternative spelling and punctuation choices and commands that lead you to relevant spelling and grammar dialog boxes (see page 73).

Note: If you don't see the little book icon, it may be because you've turned off "as you type" spelling and grammar checking (Word→Preferences→Spelling & Grammar panel).

- **REC.** This button shows the status of the macro recorder (see page 270). It's almost always off (hollow). Clicking it on opens the Record New Macro dialog box, in readiness to create a new macro. See Chapter 6 for a full explanation of macros and how to record them. When the button is on (green), you're recording a macro.

- **TRK** corresponds to the Track Changes command (see page 183). When TRK is turned on, your own edits show up in a different color, so that your collaborators can see exactly which changes you've made.

Tip: Clicking the TRK indicator turns on revision tracking (or, if it's on, turns it off). That's a *huge* timesaver if you're used to turning on tracking in the usual way (Tools→Track Changes→Highlight Changes; turn on "Track changes while editing"; click OK).

- Clicking the **EXT** button turns your cursor into a high-powered text-selection tool. Normally, when the EXT is off (hollow), clicking in your text just places the insertion point there. You have to drag the mouse to select anything. But when you click EXT, the button turns green and you enter Extend Selection mode. Your insertion point, wherever it is at that moment, marks the beginning of a new selection. Clicking the mouse, pressing the arrow keys, or even pressing the Page up and Page down keys highlights text and keeps it highlighted until you turn EXT off again.

  Extend Selection mode is useful for selecting large amounts of text with a minimum of mouse work. (The Cut, Copy, and Paste commands work as normal in extend-selection mode.)

Tip: You can duplicate the mouseless-selection convenience of Extend mode without having to remember to click EXT again when you're done. Just hold down the Shift key to select text using the arrow keys and page up/down keys.

- **OVR** stands for *overtype* mode, another slightly peculiar editing mode. In overtype mode, when you click within existing text, what you type *replaces* what was typed there before. This is the opposite of the normal mode, where what you type is inserted *between* existing letters. Click OVR to turn overtype mode on (green) and off (hollow).

  (By the way, there's nothing worse than entering overtype mode by *accident*. Suddenly your typing eats away at whatever perfectly good prose was already there. Keep your cursor well clear of this status-bar doohickey.)

- **The stack of papers.** If you've created multiple *versions* of the current document (a feature described on page 189), you'll see an icon that looks like an overlapping stack of documents. Double-clicking it calls up the Versions dialog box, in which you create and manage your various versions of a file.

Tip: You may need to enlarge the document window to see all of the status bar icons. Just drag the resize box at the lower-right corner of the window.

- **Tiny floppy disk.** This fleeting icon appears only when Word is automatically saving your document during idle moments, thanks to its background-saving feature (page 40).

- **Printer icon.** A printer-shaped icon indicates your background printing status, which appears only when you're printing. You can watch the progress of your printout by examining the Dock icon of Print Center, Mac OS X's printing software.

Tip: If you don't find any of these status indicators particularly helpful—and you'd rather dedicate the screen space to your writing—just hide them. Choose Word→Preferences, click the View tab, and turn off the "Status bar" checkbox near the bottom of the dialog box. Then click OK.

Standard Toolbar

Word X can slip in and out of many guises—a picture or movie editor, a database manager, or a Web browser, to name just a few. Each primary function comes complete with its own *toolbar* filled with icons relevant to that task.

If all these icons were available all the time, your screen would be filled with toolbars. As a result, you'd have to do all your typing in a leftover space the size of a Triscuit. (Thousands of Word 6 veterans are nodding in agreement as they read this and remember.) Fortunately, Word X is very considerate of your screen real estate. You can open, close, resize, reshape, or relocate toolbars at will, like so:

- To open a toolbar, choose View→Toolbars and choose a toolbar from the submenu. Alternatively, carefully Control-click one of the etched dividing lines on any open toolbar and choose from the resulting list. Believe it or not, you can also see the toolbar list by Control-clicking any blank space on the Formatting Palette (page 109).

  Word comes with 24 toolbars, including the Standard toolbar; you can also design new toolbars of your own (see Chapter 17). There's no limit to the number you can have open at once. To close a toolbar, click the tiny close button in the upper-left corner, just like any other Mac window, or choose its name a second time from the View→Toolbars command.

- Each toolbar has a place where it likes to appear. The Drawing toolbar, for example, always opens vertically at the far left of the screen. However, you can move toolbars anywhere you like. To move a toolbar around on the screen, drag the textured bar at the top (or left side), just as though it's a shrunken version of a standard Mac title bar. As you drag a toolbar near one of the screen edges, or near another toolbar, it jumps neatly into place.

- To resize a toolbar, drag the tiny, striped, lower-right corner. Most toolbars can be changed from a long, narrow bar (either horizontal or vertical), into a squarish palette.

- If you forget a particular toolbar's function, position the cursor over the textured bar and wait for the yellow identifying *tooltip* balloon to pop up. Similarly, to find out the name of a *button*, just point to it without clicking and wait one second; a yellow tooltip, complete with a beautiful, 3-D Mac OS X shadow, appears.

The Standard toolbar is the only one that opens by default when you create a new Word document; it has icons for printing, saving, and other tasks that you perform frequently. Each button on it instantly does something that would normally take two or more mouse clicks: opening a new blank document, opening an existing file, saving the document, and so on.

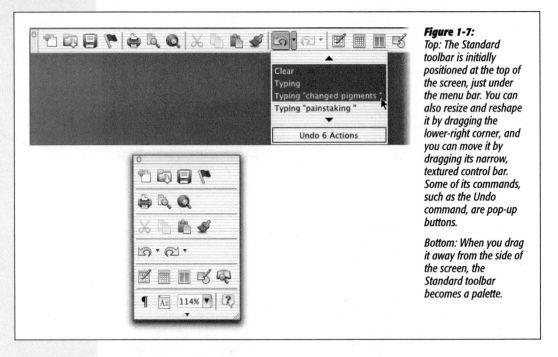

Figure 1-7:
Top: The Standard toolbar is initially positioned at the top of the screen, just under the menu bar. You can also resize and reshape it by dragging the lower-right corner, and you can move it by dragging its narrow, textured control bar. Some of its commands, such as the Undo command, are pop-up buttons.

Bottom: When you drag it away from the side of the screen, the Standard toolbar becomes a palette.

From left to right, the buttons on the Standard toolbar are:

- **New Blank Document, Open, Save.** These buttons correspond to the equivalent commands in the File menu.

- **Flag for Follow Up.** This button opens the Flag for Follow Up dialog box (also available at Tools→Flag for Follow Up), where you set a date and time. Word automatically creates a reminder on your Entourage calendar. When the appointed moment arrives, a reminder dialog box opens to remind you that it's time to quit procrastinating and finish up your work; see page 338 for a full description of this feature.

- **Print.** This button isn't the same thing as the File→Print command; it's a much more streamlined function. It prints the current document—all pages, one copy. For more control over what Word prints (number of copies, which pages), use the File→Print command (⌘-P), which opens the Print dialog box described on page 43.

- **Print Preview.** This button is another avenue into the printing process. It opens up the document in a window that offers a full view of the page, and a toolbar with various print commands. See page 49 for more on using the Print Preview feature. (*Keyboard shortcut:* ⌘-F2 or Option-⌘-I.)

- **Web Page Preview.** This button—a globe signifying the World Wide Web with a magnifying glass for *preview*—shows you what your document would look like if translated into a Web page. Like its menu equivalent (File→Web Page Preview), the button launches your Web browser and displays the document in a new browser window. (For those people unaccustomed to using their word processors for churning out Web pages, there's much more on this topic in Chapter 7.)

- **Cut, Copy, Paste.** These buttons correspond to the Big Three of the Edit menu. Cutting, copying, and pasting are described on page 63.

- **Format Painter.** Just as you can pour color onto a selected area in a painting program, you can also "pour" a set of formatting choices onto an entire paragraph. See page 126 for details.

POWER USERS' CLINIC

Secrets of the Re-branching "Undo" Tree

Having a multiple-level Undo is great; there's no debating that a program *with* one is much better than a program without one.

But the multi-Undo can also be frustrating in one occasional circumstance. Imagine something like this: You decide that you really wanted paragraph 13 the way you originally wrote it. Trouble is, you've since rewritten it *and* made hundreds of other changes to the manuscript. How can you recapture the glory of paragraph 13 the way it was two hours ago?

Unfortunately, you can't use a thousand Undos to re-create it. Remember, you've done a lot of great work in the meantime, in other paragraphs, that you want to keep. If you were to Undo all the way back to paragraph 13, just for the purpose of restoring it, you'll also lose all the other paragraphs you've written or edited in the meantime.

The sneaky solution is this: Undo all the way back to the point where paragraph 13 was originally by pressing ⌘-Z over and over again—all the while coolly watching all your great editing work disappear. When you finally see paragraph 13 return to its original version, highlight the paragraph and copy it (⌘-C).

Now *redo* all the changes, using ⌘-Y repeatedly until Word beeps, indicating that you've restored the document to its latest condition.

Finally, highlight paragraph 13 (which is back to its unsatisfactory version) and paste over it (⌘-V), replacing it with the good, earlier version. Fortunately, all those Redo's don't affect what you copied to the clipboard.

- **Undo.** Clicking this curved arrow undoes your last bit of typing, pasting, and so on. The tiny triangle next to it, however, is where the power of Undo is truly unleashed.

  Clicking on the Undo triangle pulls down a list that displays, in reverse order, the last several steps you took in Word—from major style changes to single deletions. You can retrace your steps pages and pages into the past. As you drag down this pop-up menu, the button at the bottom of the list (see Figure 1-7) tells you how many things you're about to undo. Letting go of the mouse button triggers Undo. If you change your mind, be sure to move the cursor off the Undo list until the button says Cancel before letting go. (*Keyboard shortcut:* ⌘-Z or F1, either of which only undoes one action at a time.)

- **Redo.** This button and triangle let you *redo* whatever you've just undone. If you just undid your last ten moves, for example, the Redo list can be dragged as far as "Redo 10 Actions." As with the Undo list, you can scroll up and down in this list to redo as much or as little as you like. (*Keyboard shortcut:* ⌘-Y or Option-Return, either of which only redoes one action at a time.)

- **Tables and Borders.** Clicking this button turns the cursor into a pencil, ready to draw a *table* anywhere in your document, and opens a palette of all the tools necessary to work with a table. See page 165 for full detail on using tables.

- **Insert Table.** Another quick way to create a table is to click this button, whose pop-up menu is a small expanse of white squares. Drag over the squares to select the table size you want: 2 x 2 (two rows by two columns), 3 x 3, and so on.

Tip: Don't feel cramped by the 4 x 5 maximum shape of the pop-up menu itself. If you drag beyond the boundaries of the proposed 4 x 5 grid, the pop-up menu itself expands until it's enormous.

When you release the mouse button, a table of the size you selected appears in your document at the insertion point. See page 165 for more on the Table tool.

- **Columns.** This button's pop-up menu lets you create columns; drag down and across to choose the number of columns you want. (You can drag beyond the borders of the pop-up menu if four columns across aren't enough, you crazed designer, you.) When you release the mouse button, you find yourself in Page Layout view, with your entire document divided equally into the number of columns you chose. For details on using columns, see page 150.

- **Drawing.** This button opens the Drawing palette, just as though you'd chosen View→Toolbars→Drawing. See Chapter 18 for full detail on using the Drawing feature.

- **Dictionary.** This tiny picture of a dictionary opens Word X's definitions-dictionary feature (Tools→Dictionary). Click on one of the words in the scrolling list in the left pane to read a brief definition on the right. Word's Dictionary is an abridgement of the Encarta World English Dictionary (*wwwencarta.msn.com*).

The definitions may not be comprehensive enough for card-carrying word nerds, but it's great for those times when you want to look up a word but just don't want to leave your chair.

- **Show/Hide ¶.** Clicking this button exposes paragraph markers (¶) and other nonprinting characters. This display is useful when, for example, you're copying a paragraph and want to make sure you're copying *all* the formatting. (Word

---

Look It Up

Like a pocket dictionary, Word's built-in Encarta Dictionary is handy, easy to use, and out of the way until you need it. Because it's electronic, it also has some unexpected features.

To look up a word in a document, highlight the word, and then choose Tools→Dictionary, or click the Dictionary icon on the Standard toolbar. (If no word is highlighted, you can still click to open the dictionary.) Or just Control-click the word right in your document, and choose Define from the contextual menu.

Now all of the tens of thousands of words in the dictionary are listed in the left pane of the dictionary window, as shown here. When you click a word in the left pane, the definition appears in the right pane. Here are some other ways to use the dictionary:

- If you began this process with a highlighted word, the dictionary opens to that word, or to the most similar dictionary entry. When you open the dictionary as you're typing, it opens to the word (or word fragment) you've most recently typed.

- To go directly to a word, start typing it in the small box at the upper left. The word list scrolls to match the word in progress, and the right pane automatically jumps to the current definition. Stop typing when the word you want appears.

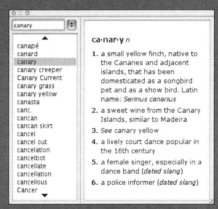

- Both left and right panes have arrows for scrolling at top and bottom. If you're unsure how a word is spelled, just scroll through the word list until you find it.

- The striped lower-right corner resizes the dictionary window, so that you can see more words in the left-hand list, and see the entire definition on the right, without scrolling.

- The pop-up menu next to the word box lists words you've recently looked up. You add to the list whenever you double-click a word in the word list in the left pane. (When you quit Word, this list is erased. You begin again the next time you start Word.)

- You can copy the text of the definition to paste in a Word document, email message, and so on. Just drag to select the text in the definition window and then press ⌘-C (or Control-click the definition and choose Copy Article or Copy Selection from the contextual menu).

- As in any dictionary, sometimes a definition isn't very helpful because it in turn includes a word that you don't know. Word understands. To view the definition for any word *within* a definition, Control-click it and choose Define.

---

stores formatting for each paragraph in the invisible ¶ mark that follows it.) Click it again to render the characters invisible once again. (*Keyboard shortcut:* ⌘-8.)

- **Formatting Palette.** This button displays or hides the Formatting Palette (see page 109). It's the same as choosing View→Formatting Palette, but quicker.

- **Zoom.** There are two ways to zoom (enlarge or shrink your document's representation on the screen) from the toolbar. First, you can enter a number in the box and press Return. (100% is roughly life-size; 125% is a more comfortable size on high-resolution monitors.)

Second, you can select a magnification from the pop-up menu. **Page Width** magnifies or reduces your view so that it fills the document window, no matter how wide or narrow you've made it. Even if you make the window bigger or smaller, Word automatically makes the text in it larger or smaller so that it always neatly fills the window, with nothing chopped off and no extra space.

In Page Layout View, you get a **Whole Page** command in this pop-up menu, too. It does the same thing as Page Width, but in both dimensions; in other words, Word scales the picture of your document so that the entire page fits within the window. Similarly, the **Two Pages** command forces two side-by-side pages to fit inside your window—a terrific option if you're the proud owner of one of Apple's gigantic flat-panel screens. (Make your window as wide as possible before choosing this option; otherwise, the font may become too small to read.) These and more zoom options are also available by choosing View→Zoom.

Note: Zooming never changes the actual printed size of your document. It only makes the type larger or smaller onscreen, as though you're moving closer to the page or farther from it.

- **Office Assistant.** This classic Help symbol—the question mark in the speech balloon—turns Max, the Office Assistant, on and off. (See page 689 if Max turns *you* off.) Whether you use Max or the Help system index, this button is the way to fire it up.

Note: Not all of the buttons on the toolbar have keyboard shortcuts. In fact, two of them don't even have menu equivalents: Format Painter and Show/Hide ¶. (Of course, you can always *add* these commands to your menus, as described in Chapter 17.)

Clicking the tiny triangle at the right end of the Standard toolbar reveals some extra buttons, plus commands that allow you to customize the toolbar (see Chapter 17). The extra buttons, accessible only by clicking the triangle, inexplicably remain hidden no matter how you resize the Standard toolbar. That's unfortunate, because some of them are just as useful as the buttons that are continually visible.

- **Spelling and Grammar.** Like choosing Tools→Spelling and Grammar, this button initiates a spelling and grammar check starting from wherever you are in the document. See page 73 for more detail.

- **Hyperlink.** This button (the globe with a chain link on it) opens the Insert Hyperlink dialog box, also accessible by choosing Insert→Hyperlink. This feature lets you create underlined links either to Web sites, other files on your Mac, or even other places in the same document (see Chapter 7).

- **Web Toolbar.** Clicking this little icon summons the Web toolbar—like choosing View→Toolbars→Web, but faster. The Web toolbar (see page 277) comes in handy if you've added any hyperlinks to your document.

- **Office Clipboard.** This button displays the contents of the Office Clipboard, not to be confused with the Clipboard that Word uses to hold material that you've cut or copied. See the tip on page 64 more on the Office Clipboard.

- **Document Map.** This button turns Document Map view (View→Document Map) on and off, as described on page 218.

- **Insert Excel Spreadsheet.** This button lets you create an Excel worksheet right in your Word document. (Since you're merely embedding the spreadsheet there, you must open Excel in order to edit it.) When you choose this command, Excel launches and opens a worksheet where you can enter your spreadsheet data. (This is a handy way to send income tax information in a letter to an accountant, for example.)

  When you're done inputting numbers, close the worksheet; the resulting table appears in your Word document. To edit the spreadsheet later, double-click the table to launch Excel. See page 659 for full detail on embedded worksheets. (To insert other kinds of Excel items into Word, choose Insert→Object.)

- **Close.** Like the File→Close command, this button closes the current document and gives you a chance to save it. (It's probably not worth asking who at Microsoft thought that it might be simpler to use this difficult-to-reach button to close a window, instead of simply clicking the close button at the upper-left corner of every Word window or pressing ⌘-W.)

- The next two buttons, **Envelopes** and **Labels,** open their respective dialog boxes, which can also be found on the Tools menu. As described on page 53, these features make creating, aligning, and printing envelopes and labels more painless than ever before.

- The final extra button, the universal magnifying glass icon for **Find,** is yet another way to open the Find and Replace dialog box, described on page 75. (*Keyboard shortcut:* ⌘-F.)

Formatting Palette
For details on this final, very important Word interface component, see page 109.

The Views

Word can display your document in any of five different views. Each offers different features for editing, reading, and scrolling through your work. Some people spend their entire lives in only one of these views, while power users may switch regularly back and forth between them.

In any case, using the Word X views feature doesn't change your actual document in any way; regardless of what view you're using, the document *prints* exactly the same way (the exception: Outline view). Views are mostly for your benefit while still preparing the document onscreen.

Here are the five Word views, as they appear in the View menu.

Tip: You can also switch views by clicking one of the four icons at the lower-left corner of your document window, to the left of the scroll bar.

Normal View

Normal view presents the Standard toolbar, the Ruler, and all the window accessories described in the previous section (see Figure 1-4). In Normal view, your entire document scrolls by in a never-ending window, with only a faint dotted line to indicate where one page ends and the next begins. Normal view is where you can focus on *writing* your document; many page-layout elements, including headers and footers, drawing objects, and multiple columns, don't appear at all in Normal view. As a result, Normal view offers the fewest distractions and the fastest scrolling.

Online Layout View

This view shows what your document will look like if you convert it to a Web page, as described in Chapter 7. (And if you'd never in a million years dream of using Microsoft Word as a Web-design program, then this is only the first of many discussions you can safely skip in this book.)

For example, in Online Layout view, you don't see any page breaks, even if a particular page requires 47 consecutive feet of scrolling; as far as Word is concerned, that's what the Web is like. The Ruler goes away, too, because Web pages don't actually offer true indents or tabs. (Your existing tabs and margins still work, but you can't make changes to them in Online Layout view.) Any backgrounds, drawings, and images you've added to your document are visible, and look as they would when your document is viewed in a Web browser.

Note: The little row of view buttons disappears when you're in Online Layout view. It's not your fault. You can switch out of this view only by using the View menu.

Page Layout View

This view offers a second ruler along the *left* side of the page—a vertical ruler. (The parts of the ruler that are your page margins are blocked out with diagonal gray stripes.) In Page Layout view, you can see—and manipulate—everything. You can adjust margins by dragging them as described in Figure 1-8. You can edit headers and footers by double-clicking where the cursor changes (see page 95). You can create drawing objects by clicking the Drawing button on the Standard toolbar (see Chapter 18 for more detail on drawings), and move them around by dragging. To see more of your page at once while in Page Layout view, change the Zoom box setting in the Standard toolbar.

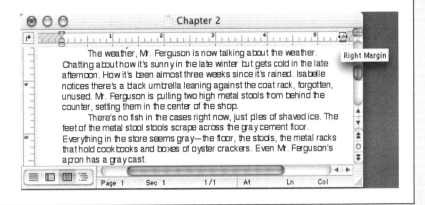

Figure 1-8:
When pointing to the ruler located at the margin boundary, the cursor turns into a double-sided arrow. You can now drag the arrow to reset the margin.

WORKAROUND WORKSHOP

Who is that computer and why is it staring at me?

Meet Max, the Microsoft Office for Mac mascot. This little animated, QuickTime-generated character acts as doorman to the Word Help system. Plus, when you're not using him for his day job, he entertains you with various antics as you type. (*Attempts* to entertain you, anyway.)

You either love him or you hate him. If Max gets on your nerves, you can dismiss him like any other window by clicking his close box. (Ever the friendly one, Max makes sure to wave goodbye before he leaves.)

Clicking inside Max's window does the same thing as choosing Help→Microsoft Word Help: It gives Max a speech balloon that helpfully asks, "What would you like to do?" Whatever you type

appears in the balloon and, when you click Search, triggers a search of the Word Help system. (See Chapter 18 for more on the Word help program.)

Clicking the Search button on the standard toolbar, however, calls up Max and his type-your-question balloon again, even if you've shut him down with the close box.

If you'd rather *never* see him, even when you click the Search button, here's the permanent solution: Choose Help→Use the Office Assistant to remove the checkmark and turn Max off until you turn him on again. Now when you choose Help→ Search Word Help, Word takes you directly to the Microsoft Office Help window, with a Max-free search function.

Outline View

In Outline view, Word automatically formats your paragraphs into outline form, saving you from remembering whether your next point should be labeled I., a., i., or whatever. Outline view lets you move your topics and supporting facts up and down, in and out of the hierarchy, using the mouse or keyboard—and remembers everything on the fly. Chapter 6 contains a full tutorial on using Word's outliner.

Master View

Master view is Outline view writ large. Where Outline view treats each *paragraph* as a movable, draggable entity, Master view allows you to manipulate entire *documents* within a giant, overarching master file. If you write a novel as a master document, for example, each *chapter* could be considered a subdocument. Each chapter would have its own custom-tailored headers and footers, but the book would have a consistent look because all chapters would use the same master template. (Not to mention how much easier it is to change the character's name throughout the entire novel when all the chapters are contained in a single file.)

See Chapter 6 for the full story on working with master documents.

Every Conceivable Variation on Saving

The first thing to do with a completed file—or even a file just underway—is, of course, to save it onto the hard drive, preserving it in case of an unforeseen system crash or accidental surge-suppressor power-switch toe-press. If you're still not in the habit of pressing ⌘-S every few sentences, paragraphs, or minutes, Word's AutoRecovery feature may save your hide.

Tip: If you have more than one Word document open at a time, hold down the Shift key as you choose File→Save. The Save command becomes Save All, which saves the changes to all open documents one by one. When you hold down Shift, you'll also notice that Close becomes Close All.

AutoRecovery

At preset intervals, Word saves the current document into a separate AutoRecover file. If your Mac freezes, crashes, or blacks out in a power failure, the AutoRecover file opens automatically (once *you've* recovered, that is). If you're satisfied that the "Recovered" file is the most recent and the one you want to keep, save it under a new name and continue working. (The file under the old name is the file as it was when you last conducted a real Save.)

Although AutoRecovery functions in the background as you work, it produces a momentary and detectable slowdown. In other words, you want Word to save often, but not *too* often. To set the AutoRecover interval, choose Word→Preferences and click the Save button. Under "Save options," turn on the "Save AutoRecover" box and enter a preferred number of minutes in the adjoining box.

Save As Options

The first time you save a document, or anytime you choose File→Save As, you open the Save dialog box (see Figure 1-9).

Note: If you're new to Mac OS X, this may be your first experience with a *sheet*—a new type of dialog box that scrolls down from, and is attached to, the title bar of a window. See page 2 for more on the Save and Open sheets.

Figure 1-9:
Word can convert your document into many formats. If you save it as a "Microsoft Word document" (the proposed choice), then any recent version of Microsoft Word—specifically Word 98 or 2001 (on the Mac), or Word 97/2000/XP (Windows)—can open it without any conversion or translation. To share with earlier versions of Word, choose their names from the pop-up menu.

The first thing to do is choose a disk or folder for storing your newly created document (see Figure 1-9). Next, click in the Save As box (or press Tab so that it's highlighted) and then name your document. (You certainly can do better than *Document1*.) Use the Format pop-up menu below to save your document into a different word processing file format, if you like (Figure 1-9).

Tip: If you frequently save documents in a different format, you can change the default setting so that you don't have to choose the preferred format every time the Save As box appears. Click the Options button in the Save dialog box, which is a shortcut to the Word→Preferences→Save panel (that is, click the Save button on the left side of the dialog box). There you'll find a pop-up menu called "Save Word files as," which lets you specify the format you prefer.

If you're sharing files over the Internet, or if you're unsure what software a document will be opened with, you may wish to try the Text or RTF options (page 64) on this pop-up menu.

One more thought: On your Office X CD, in the Value Pack→Shared Applications→Text Converters folder, you'll find a freely distributable program called Word 97-X Converter Installer. Feel free to give it to people who use Word 5.1, since they can use it to open Word 98/2001/X documents.

Finally, you'll generally want to leave the "Append file extension" checkbox turned on. It tacks a three-letter extension (*.doc* for standard Word files, *.dot* for templates, and so on) onto your file names—an essential feature that (a) lets Windows PCs identify the file, and (b) makes Mac OS X itself much happier.

Tip: You can hide these suffixes, if you like, either globally in Mac OS X (choose Finder→Preferences) or on a file-by-file basis (highlight the file, choose File→Show Info, and choose Name & Extension from the pop-up menu). The appropriate extension-hiding controls appear before you.

Fast Saves

In the olden days of Word, two conflicting urges generally raged inside you when working on long documents: the instinct to use the Save command often, and the instinct *not* to, since every save took longer and longer as the document grew.

Microsoft's solution was the *fast save* feature. In a fast save, Word doesn't bother saving the entire document. Instead, it saves just the changes you've made since your last save, by tacking that information onto the *end* of the document file. That's why a fast-saved document takes up more disk space than one saved the regular way—and why a fast save is quicker than a standard one.

Tip: Not only does the fast-save feature create larger files, it also poses a hypothetical security risk. Because material you've deleted is still, technically speaking, contained in a fast-saved document, a savvy villain could use a program like CanOpener (or even Word's own "open any file" option) to see every word you'd ever typed into the file.

You can solve both problems at once by using the File→Save As command as the last step before you're ready to submit a document. Doing so creates a new, non-fast-saved document that's both compact (in terms of disk space) and purged of all obsolete text.

Microsoft Gets Slick with Saving

In general, renaming or moving the Finder icon of a document that's *open and active* is a no-no. But in Word, you can be rather cavalier. With a Word document open on the screen, try switching back to the Finder and renaming its icon. When you return to the Word document and next use the Save command, the Word document instantly takes on the new name you gave it in the Finder!

Now try switching to the Finder and moving the icon into a different folder. When you return to Word, Microsoft's magic is on display yet again—if you ⌘-click the title of your Word window, you'll see that the program somehow knows about the icon's new location without missing a beat.

Another gem in the rough: When you close a document without first saving changes, Word displays the usual "Do you want to save the changes?" dialog box. Your choices—Don't Save, Cancel, and Save—can all be triggered from the keyboard. Just press D, C, or S, respectively.

You can turn this feature on and off like this:

1. Choose Edit→Preferences→Save panel.

2. Turn the "Allow fast saves" box on or off. Click OK.

Fast-saving doesn't work for documents shared over a network. Furthermore, you should always perform a full save when saving a document for the last time, as described in the tip on the previous page.

Backing Up

No discussion of saving would be complete without a word about backing up your work. Saving preserves your document in its current condition; backing up creates an additional, *extra* copy of the same file. For an extra measure of security, you can place this extra copy on a floppy disk, Zip disk, or even your electronic iDisk (see *Mac OS X: The Missing Manual*) in case something goes wrong with the copy on your Mac's hard drive.

Word can create backup copies automatically. Here's the process:

3. Choose File→Save As and click Options.

    You can also access this tab of Save options by choosing Word→Preferences→Save panel.

4. Turn on the "Always create backup copy" box and click OK. Click Save.

    Word saves both the current document and an identical backup copy in the same folder; the duplicate has "Backup of" in front of its file name.

From now on, Word will automatically update the backup whenever you save the original document, providing a useful "last saved" version.

Note: When you turn on "Always create backup copy," the "Allow fast saves" box is automatically turned off (see above). Backups can only be created during full saves, not fast saves.

Printing

Even in our era of email, you can't use a Mac for very long without printing something. As with so much else in Word, printing can be as simple or as complicated as you care to make it.

The Print Button

It doesn't get any simpler than this. Click the printer icon on the Standard toolbar to print one copy of your document. No dialog box, no page ranges, no options.

File→Print

This method is still simple, but more specific. Choose File→Print (or press ⌘-P) to open the Print dialog box, where you can tell Word how many copies of which pages of your document to print (and—new in Mac OS X—which printer you want to use, if you have several).

The Print dialog box has been restructured in Mac OS X. Instead of a series of dialog boxes for page range, layout, and so on, the box is now comprised of a series of *panels* that you expose by choosing from the pop-up menu in the middle of the box. This remodeling was much more than cosmetic, however, as you can now do things from the Print window (such as add a border or create an Adobe Acrobat [PDF] document), which used to require opening a separate dialog box—or a separate program!

The features in the Print box vary depending upon which printer you chose above, but here are a few of the classics.

Copies and Pages

This is the default pop-up menu choice when the Print dialog box opens. Often, these are the only settings you need.

- **Copies.** Enter the number of copies you need. Hit Return to print, or Tab to move on to more settings.

- **Collated.** Turning on this box prints out each copy of your document in page order. For instance, if you print multiple copies of a three-page letter with collating turned off, you'll get two copies of page one, two page twos, and so on. With collating turned *on,* you'll get page one, page two, page three, followed by another complete set of pages one, two, and three, and so on.

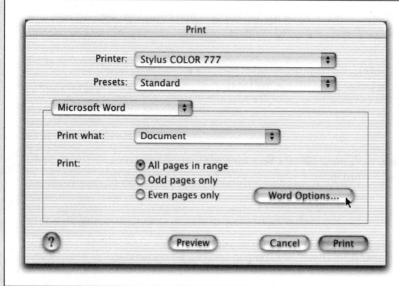

Figure 1-10:
In Office X, the ability to choose odd or even pages is hidden behind the easily overlooked Microsoft Word pop-up menu choice.

To print double-sided pages, print the odd pages first, then turn them over, reinsert them into the printer, and then print the even sides. (Experiment with just a couple of pages first until you figure out how to get them right side up on both sides.)

- **Pages.** The All button is initially selected, but you can also hit Tab and enter page numbers for a page range. For more control over which pages to print, read on.

Tip: If you don't see "Print odd/even pages only" or other common printing options, choose Microsoft Word from the pop-up menu, as described in Figure 1-10.

- **Range.** Clicking this button activates a text box where you can be more specific about which pages you want Word to print. Actually, you can be very, *very* specific. To print an individual page, type its number in this box (*12,* for example). Separate additional single pages by commas. (Typing *12, 20,* for example, prints one copy each of page 12 and page 20.) You can add ranges to your print batch as well, by using hyphens, like this: *12, 20, 25-30, 100-102.* This selection would print page 12, page 20, pages 25 through 30, and 100 through 102.

Layout

This menu choice offers a shortcut to a feature formerly available only in the Page Setup dialog box: the ability to print more than one Word page on each sheet of paper—a great paper-saving tool for printing rough drafts.

The Layout panel also contains a new Office X surprise: the Border menu. You can choose one of four simple page border options (single hairline, double hairline, and so on). The beauty and power of this menu is that you can apply the border to only one print job, or only one *page,* without actually changing your document in the Borders and Shading dialog box. (When you choose a border type from the menu, the preview box at the left presents an idea of what the border will look like.)

Output Options

This sheet contains the key to one of Mac OS X's best features: its ability to turn your Word document into a PDF (Acrobat) file.

Because all Macs and PCs can view Adobe Acrobat documents, you can attach a PDF file to an email and know that your recipient, no matter what kind of computer he has, will be able to open and read it, with all your fonts and layout intact. That makes PDF an ideal format for résumés, flyers or brochures, booklets, and other documents that need to look good for their intended audiences.

To "print" your Word document as an Acrobat file, turn on Save as File and choose PDF from the Format pop-up menu. (Even as of Office X version 10.1.5, the PostScript option here is dimmed and unavailable.)

Print Settings

The options in this panel depend on the kind of printer you've selected. This is where you can choose from a list of paper types (plain, glossy, and so on), and whether you want to use black and white or color. Choosing the print option that matches the type of paper you're using effectively changes settings in the printer (amount of ink released, printing speed, and so on) to achieve the best results on that paper. If you're using photo paper to print out digital photographs, for example, it's especially important to specify that here.

It's also where you can adjust print *quality,* high for good looks, low to save ink when printing out rough drafts or file copies.

Advanced Settings

This panel, too, appears only for certain printers. It may provide finer control over quality, such as letting you specify the exact dpi (number of dots per inch) that the printer uses. For a professional-looking invitation or newsletter, for example, use at least 300 dpi.

Microsoft Word

This panel lets you restrict your printout to odd or even pages, as described in Figure 1-10. It also offers the **Print what** pop-up menu, which is usually set to Document. However, this menu lets you print out some fascinating behind-the-scenes Word information sheets. They include:

- **Document Properties** provides a page of statistics for the pathologically curious. In addition to the usual number of pages, the title, and the author, you can see how many editing changes you made, and how many minutes you've spent on the document.

- If you're using Word's reviewing feature (see page 183), choose **Comments** to print out just the comments that you've attached to the document. When you print out a document with comments, you don't get to see the comments; this way, the comments appear on separate pages.

- If you do a lot of work with **Styles** (if you're charged with keeping them consistent in all your company documents, for example, or if you're just a total control freak), this choice lets you print a list of all styles the current document uses, complete with a full description of each. (Much more on Styles in Chapter 3.)

- Similarly, if you've created a lot of **AutoText entries** in your copy of Word X and you're getting confused, this option prints out a list of them. You can get the same information by choosing Tools→AutoCorrect→AutoText tab and scrolling through the list.

  If you're one of those power users who uses more than one *global template* (see page 209), this command is the way to create a separate AutoText cheat sheet for each template. It's also a quick way to print a list of all your address-book contacts, since they're considered AutoText entries; that way, you can review the list and decide which ones you want to add or delete.

- **Key Assignments** produces a handy cheat sheet to remind you of the keyboard-shortcut keystrokes you've created, as described at the end of Chapter 17.

This panel also contains the **Word Options** button, which opens the Print tab of the Preferences dialog box. Click the button and then click Print, which, misleadingly, does not immediately print, but opens the Preferences window.

Summary

This command calls up a box showing all current print settings: number of copies, page range, layout options, and so on. It's a quick way to review all your choices with one stroke of the pop-up menu. You can't print this information, and probably won't need to. Use the Custom option (described below) to save your favorite settings.

Saving Custom Settings

You've gone through every choice on the pop-up menu and gotten everything just the way you want it. For instance, you know you'll always print two copies, always want them collated, and almost always want to print with black ink (saving the more expensive color ink for photographs). To save this combination of settings for repeated use, choose "Save Custom Setting" from the pop-up menu *after* you've set all the other panels to your liking.

From then on, all you have to do is press ⌘-P and choose Custom from the Presets menu in the Print dialog box. Then press Return to print, or you can go on to adjust any of the settings if you need to deviate from your usual custom set (print three copies instead of your usual two, for example).

Preview, Cancel

The last items in the Print dialog box are the Preview button, your gateway to the magnificent built-in Mac OS X print-preview function, and Cancel, which you can click if you change your mind about printing. (Pressing Esc also dismisses the Print dialog box.)

Tip: If you click Preview, Mac OS X converts your Word file into a temporary PDF file, which it displays in the Preview program. Don't miss the Display menu, which lets you zoom in, zoom out, and navigate your document—and above all, don't miss the File→Save As PDF command. It lets you turn this temporary PDF document into a real, live one that you can send along to other people.

Yes, you can also turn your Word files into PDF documents using the Print dialog box as described above—but this way, you're allowed to review it before committing.

File→Page Setup

Some of the settings that appear when you choose Page Setup are a function of your printer's software, not of Word; as in the Print dialog box, choose your printer from the pop-up menu at top. Generally, however, you'll find options like these:

• **Paper Size.** Make sure the page size here matches what you've got in your printer. You can choose envelopes as well as paper, but if you use Word's envelope feature (see page 52), this setting is taken care of automatically.

• **Orientation.** You can change the direction that Word prints the "page" on the paper (upright vs. "landscape" mode).

• **Scaling.** Most of the time, you print at 100%, but in some cases this might not be your best option. For instance, if your document is just two lines too long to fit on one page, try printing at 90%. (You'll know if you've adjusted the document correctly by checking the File→Print Preview before committing the document to paper.)

For more advanced settings, choose Microsoft Word from the Settings menu, as shown in Figure 1-11. The settings here are what you need if you have a truly unusual page size or if Word is having trouble communicating with your printer.

Turn on "Use custom page size" and enter the dimensions of your paper. Remember that width is the measurement of the edge that you feed into the printer, which may not be the smallest measurement.

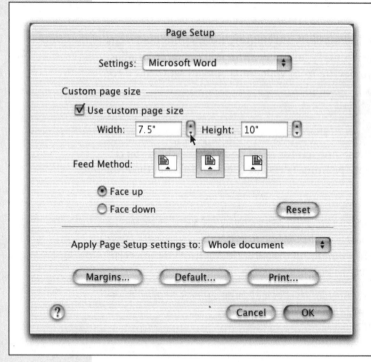

Figure 1-11:
Don't worry about the Feed Method unless you're printing on very nonstandard-sized paper. After you've entered the page measurements for width and height, you need to instruct Word how the paper is going into the printer (all the way to the left of the tray, for example), and which side of the page (Face up or Face down) your printer prints on.

After setting up your page, you can click the Print button to go directly to the Print dialog box. Clicking OK (or pressing Return) saves your page settings without starting the printing process. Click Reset to return all settings to their original configuration.

If you need to adjust the document's margins before printing, clicking the Margins button is a quick way to open the Format→Document→Margins tab, as described on page 135. Finally, if you find yourself frequently changing from the default settings to your own configuration (2 Up, 99% reduction, and so on), click the Default button to make that your *new* default page setup. Word will ask if you want to change the default settings for all new documents based on the Normal template (in other words, all new, blank Word documents that you open).

Note: Clicking Default in the Page Setup dialog box changes the defaults only for the settings *in the Page Setup dialog box.* If you took a side trip to the Margins dialog box, those settings won't be affected. To change the default margins, click Default in the Format→Document→Margins tab itself.

Finally, as in the case of margins (page 135), the Page Setup dialog box gives you a chance to apply these settings to the entire document, or just "This point forward" (as the "Apply Page Setup settings to" pop-up menu puts it). This feature may come in handy if you have letters and envelopes together in the same document, for example.

Print Preview

Word's Print Preview feature was created in the old days, before Apple added a system-wide Preview function to Mac OS X itself. Now you have a choice of both.

Like the Mac OS X version, the built-in Word view lets you see an onscreen representation of how your document will look on paper—a great way to avoid wasting paper on printouts that get chopped at the margin or contain straggling one-line hangovers on the last page. To see for yourself, choose File→Print Preview or click the Print Preview button on the Standard toolbar. (*Keyboard shortcut:* ⌘-F2.)

A special preview window opens, displaying a full view of one page of your document. You can't edit anything in this view, since you're just looking.

Because most windows are smaller than 8.5" x 11", the image is probably reduced. You can see the percentage of reduction in the Print Preview toolbar, as shown in Figure 1-12. (Unlike most toolbars, you can't choose this one from the View menu; you must open the Print Preview window to see it.)

Figure 1-12:
When you're ready to print, click the printer icon on this toolbar to access the Print dialog box (see page 43). You can dismiss the Print Preview window by clicking the close box, pressing Esc, or clicking back in any other document window.

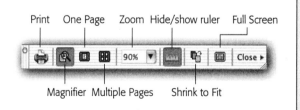

For a closer look at a certain word or a particular portion of your document, click the magnifying glass icon (Figure 1-12), and then click the page. The cursor changes into a magnifying glass and, with each click, toggles between the original view and the enlarged one. You can also change the view size by typing a percentage in the

Zoom box (also shown in Figure 1-12). Remember, 100% is not necessarily life-size; it's the size that allows you to see one full printed sheet at a time.

If your document is going to be bound with facing pages, you can see how the two-page spread will look by clicking (and holding the cursor down on) the Multiple Pages pop-up button. Drag to highlight two or more panes, and then click; Word simultaneously displays that number of pages.

The most powerful button on the Print Preview toolbar is the Shrink to Fit button. When the last page of a document contains just a few lines, you may want to avoid wasting that whole extra piece of paper. Or suppose you've been given a five-page limit, and you're just a couple of paragraphs too long. If you have neither the time nor the inclination to edit down your document, you can click the Shrink to Fit button. Word adjusts the type sizes, across the entire document, just enough to eliminate that last fraction of a page.

Note: If you don't like the effect of Shrink to Fit, you can choose Edit→Undo Shrink to Fit, press F1, or press ⌘-Z. But once you save and close the file, you can't get back the original font sizes with the Undo command. You must restore the font sizes manually.

Pointing to the other buttons on the Print Preview toolbar, without clicking, prompts their identifying tooltip labels. These other buttons include:

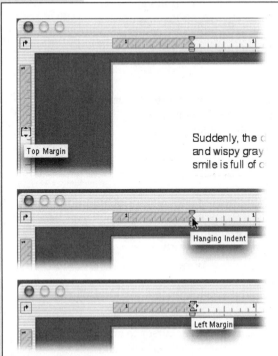

Figure 1-13:
Top: It's easy to adjust the top margin; just drag the intersection of the white and gray–striped regions on the rulers (you can see the special cursor shape at left).

Middle: Finding the spot to drag is extremely important, especially when adjusting the left margin; this tooltip indicates you're about to drag on the wrong spot. The indentation markers on the ruler don't do anything to the overall page margins.

Bottom: When you've found the correct location, your cursor changes shape, as shown here, and a tooltip appears.

- **View Ruler.** Click to make both horizontal and vertical rulers appear. As shown in Figure 1-13, you can use these rulers to adjust the margins of your document quickly and easily.

- **Full screen.** Because of the reduced view, Microsoft offers you this one-click way to maximize the available screen space. Clicking here collapses your tool palettes, enlarges the window to the edges of your monitor, and hides Word's usual assortment of status bars around the window edges.

- **Close button.** Click to return to whatever view you were using before opening the print preview.

Print Preferences

Believe it or not, Word X offers yet another swath of printing settings—none of which even appear in the usual Print and Page Setup dialog boxes.

Specifically, the controls that govern the printing of fields, hyperlinks, drawings, and other advanced features are tucked away in the Word→Preferences dialog box, as shown in Figure 1-14.

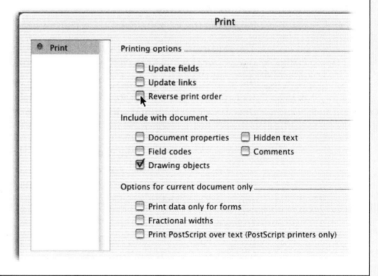

Figure 1-14:
The three checkboxes under "Options for current document only" need to be turned on each time you use them. You can also access this dialog box by clicking the Word Options button in the Microsoft Word panel of the Print dialog box.

- When **Update fields** is turned on, Word checks all the *fields* in your document (page 228) and verifies they contain the most recent information. The date is updated, for example, and captions are renumbered.

- Turning on **Update links** tells Word to check all hyperlinks (page 293) in the document and fix any whose destination document *on your hard drive* has moved. (Word can't update *Web* links this way, alas. You have to update Web links manually, as explained on page 299.)

- **Reverse print order** tells Word to print starting with the last page first. If your printer puts out sheets right side up, with each new sheet on top of the previous one, this option will save you from shuffling the pages into their proper order.

- Turning on **Document properties** prints the information from the General, Summary, and Statistics tabs of the File→Properties dialog box onto a separate sheet at the end of the document.

- When **Field codes** is turned on, Word prints the field codes (see page 228) instead of the *results* of those codes. For instance, a Date field would print as { DATE \@ "M/d/yy" * MERGEFORMAT } instead of 10/31/02.

- Turning on **Drawing objects** prints all images, including drawings, paintings, Clip Art, and WordArt. Turning it off suppresses images and prints text only.

- When **Hidden text** is turned on, any hidden text (page 116) in your document prints, along with all the other text.

- Turning on **Comments** prints the contents of the Comments pane (see page 179) on a separate page at the end of your document.

- **Print data only for forms** suppresses the main text of the form document and prints only information that has been entered into form fields, as described on page 300.

- The precision that the Mac can use to place characters *on the screen* is limited to the screen's resolution of 1/72 of an inch. But with **Fractional widths** turned on, the printer possesses much greater precision and flexibility to place each character in its typographically correct position on the page. For the best-looking printouts, turn on Fractional widths just before printing.

  Note, however, that when Fractional widths is turned on, Word's approximation of the printed appearance can result in overlapping, awkward-looking spacing on the screen. (Interestingly, when you switch to Page Layout view, Word *automatically* turns on Fractional widths, because Page Layout view is intended to show you how the page will look when printed.)

  If you're not connected to a PostScript printer and have not used any PRINT fields in your document, the **Print PostScript over text** box is grayed out. If you have—you desktop publishing professional, you—turning on this box prints watermarks and other PostScript–generated figures *on top of* the text.

Printing Envelopes and Labels

There's a big temptation to just hand-letter your envelope, but Word makes it so easy that there's no need to settle for anything less than a professional-looking, printed envelope. Moreover, the Labels command is equipped for printing business cards, Rolodex cards, and other odd-shaped items. These are tools worth learning.

Tip: You can also print a whole mass of labels or envelopes at once, based on addresses in your Office Address Book; see page 401.

Printing envelopes

Before starting, inspect your printer and the envelope you're going to use. Practice fitting the envelope into the feed slot. Check the printer's manual to see if you need to flip any levers to accommodate envelopes.

Now it's time for the Word part of envelope printing, as follows:

1. **Choose Tools→Envelopes.**

    The Envelope dialog box opens, as shown in Figure 1-15.

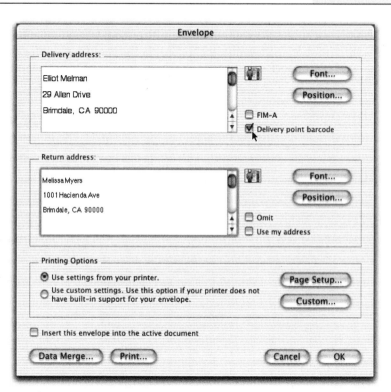

Figure 1-15:
When you check the "Delivery point barcode" box, Word will print the barcode used by the U.S. Postal Service's machinery. You may actually speed your letter's delivery as a result. Check the FIM-A box as well if you're printing a reply envelope.

2. **Fill in the Delivery address and Return address boxes.**

    To change the return address, turn off the "Use my address" box. (Word automatically fills in your name and address as you entered them in the Word→Preferences→User Information panel.)

    Alternatively, click the little person icon located next to the address box to select a name and address from the Office Address Book.

    Click the Font button to choose any of Word's fonts, type styles, and font sizes, as described on page 111.

3. **Click one of the Position buttons; use the arrow buttons in the Address Position dialog box to adjust the addresses on the envelope, if you wish.**

The Preview pane displays the results of your repositioning actions. Click OK when done.

4. **Click Page Setup or Custom in the Printing Options pane.**

If your printer has an envelope slot, and you're using a standard envelope size (as opposed to an oddly shaped greeting card envelope, for example), you're in luck. Click Page Setup and choose the envelope size in the Print dialog box (#10 is a standard business envelope). Click OK to print.

Click Custom if your printer doesn't have an envelope feed or doesn't accommodate your size envelope. In the Custom Page Options dialog box (Figure 1-16), choose the "Envelope size" menu, and then click the preview window that most closely resembles how you plan to insert that envelope into your printer's feed. Click OK when done.

You're almost ready to print. When you do, Word will create a new document to hold the envelope text. To store the envelope in the same document that you've been working in, check "Insert this envelope into the active document."

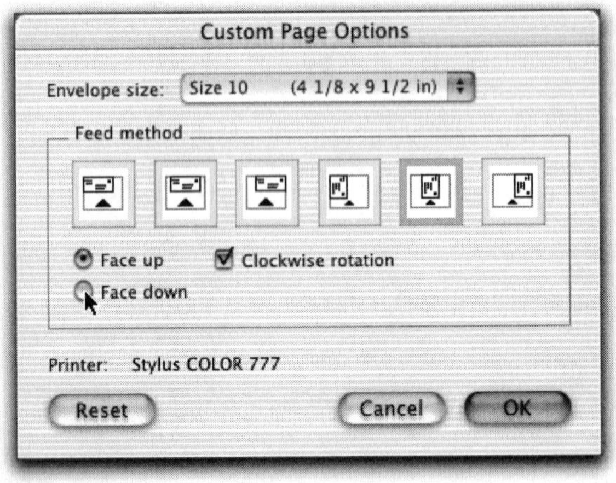

Figure 1-16:
When you turn the "Clockwise rotation" box on and off, and click the "Face up" and "Face down" radio buttons, the small preview windows show you the differences in how you'll be feeding the envelope into your printer.

5. **If you'd like to use the envelope you've just set up in a *data merge* (see page 254), click Data Merge to open the Data Merge Manager and use the envelope with a list of addresses.**

Otherwise, click Print or OK to print the envelope with the current address.

Printing labels

As mentioned above, Word's label function can print more than plain white address labels. You can make name tags, Rolodex or index cards, postcards, floppy disk labels, and so on.

Tip: When buying blank labels or cards for printing, make sure that they're going to work with your printer. Often, the labels or cards will come on a convenient 8.5" x 11" sheet that fits nicely into your printer's feed. You can then detach the individual labels after printing.

Figure 1-17:
When typing in the Address window, click Font to use any of Word's fonts or text formatting. Check the "Use my address" box to have Word insert your name and address from the Edit→ Preferences→User information tab (which is also reflected in the Entourage Address Book entry you created for yourself). Click the contact icon to choose a name and address from the Entourage address book.

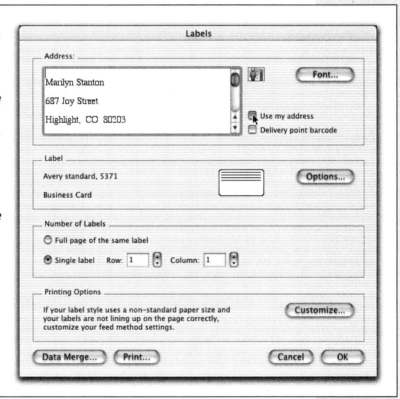

To print labels in Word, proceed as follows:

1. **Choose Tools→Labels.**

   The Labels dialog box opens, as shown in Figure 1-17.

2. **Type an address—or other label information—into the Address window.**

   (See Figure 1-17 for full detail.)

3. **Click Options in the Label pane to tell Word what kind of label or card you're using, as shown in Figure 1-18.**

The choices may seem overwhelming, but Word can help. Once you've chosen a manufacturer and item number, click Details to see a preview (with measurements) of the label itself.

If you have an odd-sized or unidentified label, click New Label. Word opens a dialog box in which you can enter your custom dimensions. (You'll need a ruler to measure the label itself in this case; however, Word has enough built-in labels that you'll rarely need to get this creative.) Click OK.

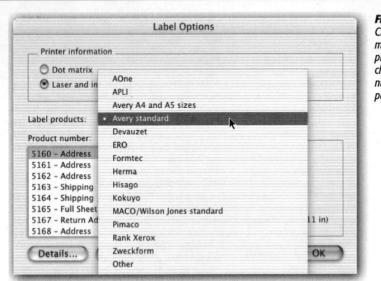

Figure 1-18:
Choose the name of the manufacturer from the "Label products" menu before choosing from the "Product number" list. Look on the label package for this information.

If your odd-sized labels come on odd-sized sheets (something other than 8.5" x 11"), click Customize in the Printing Options pane. Here you set the page size and feeding method, as described earlier and illustrated in Figure 1-19.

4. **If you're printing only one label, click the "Single label" radio button and choose a row and column to tell Word where to print the label.**

This way, if you have a sheet with some blank labels left over, you can have Word print on one of those remaining labels. No waste!

If you're printing more than one label, on the other hand, click Data Merge and use the Data Merge Manager (see page 254) to give Word a list of addresses to use.

5. **Click Print or OK when done.**

To avoid wasting labels, print on a blank piece of paper first. Hold the printed sheet over a label sheet (preferably against a window or light) to see if the labels are going to line up. If they don't align correctly, choose Tools→Labels, click Options, and click Details to adjust the print area and spacing of each label.

Sending It Electronically

These days, it's rare that a document is sent into the world on paper or disk. Instead, it's usually transmitted electronically. Word's File→Send To command offers two ways of transmitting your work electronically: via email and as a PowerPoint presentation.

- **File→Send To→Mail Recipient (as Attachment).** This long-winded command launches Entourage and opens a new email message. The document you were just working on in Word is automatically attached to the message, and your address book is open—ready and waiting for you to choose a recipient from your list of contacts. (See Chapter 8 for more on Entourage.) Congratulations—you've just saved several tedious steps.

- **File→Send To→Microsoft PowerPoint.** You can import a Word outline into PowerPoint for conversion into a slide show, but why go to all the trouble? When your Word document is ready to become part of your big show, choose this command. PowerPoint opens with your Word document now displayed as a PowerPoint presentation. See Chapter 15 for full details on working with your document in PowerPoint.

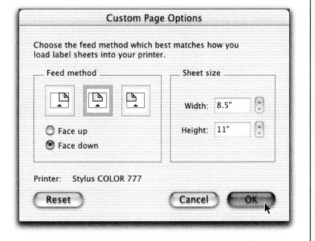

Figure 1-19:
Practice on a blank sheet of paper to determine whether your printer feeds face up or face down, and which corner the labels start to print from. Then use the buttons in this dialog box to match Word with what your printer is doing. If you're using one of the standard label types, you probably won't have to bother with these settings.

Editing in Word

D espite all the innovations in Office X, some things haven't changed, including the basics of editing your text. Adding, deleting, or moving text around works essentially the same way as it did in Word 1.0, which fit on a single floppy disk and had to be started up with a hand crank.

Most of the editing and formatting techniques in Word and the other Office programs require a two-step procedure: select, then do. That is, first select the thing (word, paragraph, sentence) that you intend to act upon; then use keystrokes or menu commands to tell the Mac *what* to do to it.

The Many Ways to Select Text

Dragging with the mouse is the way we all first learned to select text. In this time-honored method, you click at the start of where you want to select text, and while holding down the mouse button, drag until the text in question is highlighted.

For the first 17 years of Microsoft Word's life, you could only select one chunk of text at a time. But in Word X, you can select bits of text far apart from each other simultaneously and then cut, copy, and paste them all at once. (More on this later.) At last, you can grab a single sentence from the first paragraph of a document and a couple sentences from the second—and scrap everything else. Progress!

Assuming you mastered dragging a long time ago, here are some more streamlined ways to select text. (Some of these moves are second nature to power users.)

- **Shift-arrow.** If you undershoot or overshoot the mark when dragging manually, don't start over; remember the Shift–arrow key trick. After you release the mouse button, don't click again or do anything else. Hold down the Shift key and then press the arrow keys to expand or shrink the size of the selection—one character or line at a time. Add the Option key to expand or shrink the selection one *word* at a time.

- **Dragging with the mouse and Option key.** When dragging with the mouse, you'll notice that Word highlights text in one-word chunks, under the assumption that you'll very rarely want to edit only the first syllable of a word. Even if you begin dragging in the center of a word, the program instantly highlights all the way from the beginning to the end of that word, including the space after it. Usually, this behavior is what you want, and lets you drag somewhat sloppily.

Tip: If you dislike the way Word automatically selects in one-word increments, you can turn it off by choosing Word→Preferences and clicking the Edit tab. The checkbox called "When selecting, automatically select entire word" is the on/off switch for this feature.

Every now and then, however, you *do* want to edit only the first syllable of a word—perhaps to correct a typo. In those situations, Word's tendency to highlight the entire word can induce madness. On those occasions, press the Option key as you drag. Word responds by respecting the precise movements of your mouse.

Tip: Option-dragging *vertically* is a sneaky trick that lets you highlight only a tall, skinny block—a useful way to shave off the garbage characters at the beginnings of the lines of text you've pasted in from an email message, for example.

- **Clicking with the mouse.** Using the mouse and *not* dragging can save you time. Double-click a word to select that one word as a whole. Triple-click to select an entire paragraph.

  With one paragraph selected in this way, hold down Shift and click the mouse elsewhere, even pages away, to select more text in one-paragraph increments.

- **Using the Shift key and the mouse.** By using the Shift key, you can enjoy all the convenience of using the mouse without the wrist-wearying effort of holding down the mouse button. Just click at where you want to start selecting, hold down the Shift key, then click the mouse a second time where you want the selection to end (even if you had to scroll the document between clicks). Word highlights everything between the two clicks. If you overshoot the mark, you can back up in one-word increments by holding down Shift and clicking back into the selection. (Unfortunately, you can't change the *beginning* of the selection using this method.)

- **Using Shift with other keys.** If you do a lot of word processing, you may find it faster to keep your hands at the keyboard as much as possible, without stopping to grasp the mouse. In fact, it's possible to select text without using the mouse at all. Just use the arrow keys to get to where you want to begin selecting. Hold down the Shift key and use the arrow keys to adjust the size of the selection—line by line for the up and down arrow keys, and one character at a time for the right and left arrow keys.

If you hold down Option and Shift, the right and left arrow keys select in one-*word* increments, and the up and down arrow keys select in one-*paragraph* increments. (Your original selection is preserved, however, even if it was only part of a paragraph.)

You can use the Shift key with the Home, End, and Page Up/ Page Down keys as well. **Shift-Home** or **Shift-End** selects from the insertion point to the beginning or end of the line.

Shift-Page Up/Page Down selects one "screenful" (about half a page, depending on your monitor size) up or one down from the insertion point.

- **Using ⌘ with the mouse.** Here's a great command to memorize: ⌘-click anywhere within a sentence to select exactly that sentence, neatly and quickly, period and all. ⌘-click again to select a different sentence. To add complete sentences to the selection, Shift-click inside other sentences.

- **Using the selection strip.** To the left of your text, just inside the left window edge, is an extremely thin margin—an empty white space about an eighth of an inch wide. It's an invisible but extremely useful tool called the selection strip.

When your cursor ventures into this area, the arrow pointer points to the *right* instead of left as usual. Now you can click once to highlight a single line of text; twice to select a paragraph; or three times to select the whole document.

Tip: ⌘-clicking in the selection strip also highlights the entire document. As for the peculiar highlighting that appears when you Option-⌘-click in the selection strip: You tell *us* what Word's doing.

You can also drag vertically through the selection strip to highlight a vertical chunk of text—one of this strip's most frequent uses. (As always, you can click there once, then Shift-click elsewhere in your document to highlight all lines of text between the two clicks.)

- **Using Extend mode.** Turning on the EXT button in the Status bar (see page 25) or pressing F8 activates Extend mode, the most powerful (if disorienting) way to select text. Position the insertion point where you want to begin selecting, activate Extend mode, then use the arrow and page up or down keys to select text automatically. You know you're in Extend mode when the EXT button in the Status bar is on. To cancel Extend mode, click the button (or press ⌘-. to turn it off).

Exactly as when you're *not* in Extend mode, pressing the Option key with the arrows forces Word to select in one-word (right and left arrow) or one-paragraph (up and down arrow) increments.

Note: Previous versions of Word let you use the numeric keypad as cursor keys. By pressing Shift-Clear, you brought out the pad's second personality as a navigation keyboard, where the keys surrounding the 5 key acted as cursor keys, the 0 key acted as Insert, and so on. But Microsoft evidently fielded one too many desperate tech-support call from customers who'd entered this mode accidentally, and couldn't figure out why they could no longer type numbers with the numeric keypad. In Word 2001 and Word X, the number keypad does just one thing: types numbers.

Multi-selection

To use Word X's new multiple-selection feature, highlight a piece of text using any of the methods described above that involve the mouse. Then press ⌘ as you use the mouse to select more text. Bingo: You've highlighted two separate chunks of text.

For instance, drag to select part of a sentence. Then scroll down a couple of pages and, while pressing ⌘, triple-click to select another entire paragraph. Finally, you

Cut to the Spike

Before Word X's multiple-selection mode, the only way to paste nonconsecutive bits of text was a little-known and idiosyncratic feature called the Spike. As we all know by now, Microsoft only adds features, never removes them, so the Spike is still with us even though it's redundant in Word X. For old time's sake, here's the drill:

Select the first thing you want to collect in the Spike. (It can be text, a drawing or painting image, or even a table.) Press ⌘-F3. You've just cut the selection to the Spike, much the way you might cut it to the Clipboard. Now collect the rest of the things you want to paste; they can even be in different Word documents. As you cut text and picture selections, the Spike quietly gathers them up until you're ready to paste.

When you're done collecting, scroll to the spot in the document where you want the collected material to appear. Click there and then press Shift-⌘–F3. The entire contents of the Spike empty, in one fell swoop, into their new location.

A few more points about the oddly refreshing Spike:

- There is no menu command for the Spike. You must use the ⌘-F3 key combinations.

- You can't copy text to the Spike, only cut.

- You can paste the Spike's contents without emptying it. Instead of pressing Shift-⌘- F3, choose Insert→AutoText→AutoText and then click Spike in the list of entries; click Insert.

- Choosing Spike in the AutoText list, as described above, is also the way to see what's currently saved in the Spike. You can view the contents of the Spike in the Preview pane of the AutoText dialog box. Just click Cancel (or press Esc) instead of Insert when you're done.

- Because the Spike is part of the AutoText feature, you can also paste the Spike by typing the first four letters of the word "spike" and pressing Return.

- If you accidentally empty the Spike, immediately press F1 or choose Edit→Undo AutoComplete. The Spike is restored, and you can now paste it repeatedly.

Truth is, the Spike could still be useful even in the era of the multi-selection Word, since multi-selection doesn't work between different Word documents. The Spike is still your best option if you want to grab some text out of several open documents, then close them all and unload your selections in a new document.

can ⌘-double-click a single word to add it to the batch selection. (The only mouse method that doesn't work is using the selection strip. Because you're already pressing ⌘, clicking in the selection strip will select everything in the document!)

Note: Keyboard-selection methods that involve the Shift key don't work with multi-selection. When you've selected text using the Shift key and then press ⌘, Word doesn't recognize your subsequent mouse clicks as being additional multi-selections.

Also note that multi-selections must be in the same document (you can't select text simultaneously in different windows).

When you're done selecting bits of text here and there, you can operate on them en masse. For example:

- You can make them all bold or italic with one fell swoop.

- When you cut, copy, or paste (as described in the next section), the command acts upon all your multi-selections at once.

- You can drag any *one* of the highlighted portions to a new area, confident that the other chunks will come along for the ride. All of the selected areas will wind up consolidated in their new location.

Tip: This feature has special ramifications for the Find command described on page 75. The Find dialog box contains a new "Highlight all items found" checkbox. It makes the *software* perform your work for you, simultaneously highlighting every occurrence of a certain word or phrase within the entire file.

Moving Text Around

Three commands—Cut, Copy, and Paste—appear in every word processing program known to humankind, Word included. But Office X has more powerful ways of manipulating text once you've selected it.

Copy (or Cut) and Paste

To copy text, highlight it as described above. Then choose Edit→Copy (or click the corresponding Standard toolbar button), click the mouse or use the arrow keys to transport the insertion point to your new location, and choose Edit→Paste. A copy of the original text appears in the new locale. To move text instead of copying it, use Edit→*Cut* and Edit→Paste; the selected text moves from one place to another, leaving no trace behind.

Alternatively, after selecting the text, you can also Control-click the selection (or click the right mouse button if you have one), and choose Copy or Cut from the contextual menu. Similarly, when you arrive at the place where you want to paste, you can Control-click, then select Paste.

If this procedure sounds like a lot of work, you're right—especially if you're trying to choose these menu commands using a laptop trackpad. Cut/Copy and Paste is the sequence you'll probably use extremely often. By learning the keystroke equivalents, the time you save avoiding the mouse really adds up. For example:

Function	**Command**	**Keystrokes**
Copy	Edit→Copy	⌘-C or F3
Cut	Edit→Cut	⌘-X or F2
Paste	Edit→Paste	⌘-V or F4

___

Tip: The Office Clipboard, which debuted in Office 2001, remembers the last series of items you've cut or copied from any Office program. To see it, choose View→Office Clipboard. The Office Clipboard opens, showing every item you've cut or copied since you first launched an Office program for the day (memory permitting). The little letter in the lower-right corner of each window shows which program it came from.

To paste something from this window, drag it directly into your document, or click it and then use the Paste command. Paste Special

___

The Edit→Paste Special command gives you the opportunity to alter text *as* you paste it, so you can determine how it'll look and act once it reaches its final destination. Here are the options in the dialog box that appears when you choose Edit→Paste Special:

- **Microsoft Word Document Object.** This command nests one self-sufficient Word document inside another, which Microsoft calls an *embedded object.* See page 659 for more detail.

- **Formatted Text (RTF).** RTF stands for Rich Text Format, a file format that Microsoft devised to simplify the transfer of formatted text documents between incompatible programs. An RTF file is a lot like a text file, except that most common formatting specifications—bold, italic, font selections, line breaks, style sheets, and so on—survive the conversion to RTF and back again. Every modern word processor, for Mac or Windows, can open and export RTF documents.

  RTF is a big deal in Windows; on the Mac, you'll rarely need it for transferring text between programs, thanks to the Styled Text feature offered by most Mac programs (see below).

- **Unformatted Text.** Paste this way when you want to paste the text without any formatting (font, bold or italic, Word style, and so on). Text pasted as unformatted picks up the current font, style, and formatting at the insertion point wherever you paste it. (Unformatted text does carry its own paragraph breaks.)

- **Picture.** When pasting text *as a picture,* from that moment on, Word treats it just like a picture (and switches you into Page Layout view). Text pasted in this way plays with your head a little bit, since you don't get an insertion point for editing when you click inside the text. Instead, the Picture toolbar appears (see page 650); you can use any of its tools (color adjustment, brightness, contrast, and so on) to change the look of the text. (The Watermark toolbar icon is especially handy in this instance. It's harder to guess, on the other hand, what the Fix Red Eye button does to pasted text.)

What you can never do again is *edit* the text—check spelling, delete words, and so on. But once you have text just the way you want it, Paste Special→As Picture is a great way to create a poster, letterhead, watermark, or any document that you *don't* want anyone to edit later.

- **Styled Text.** This option preserves all font and paragraph styles in the pasted text. This Macintosh-only feature explains why you can copy some text from, say, a Web page or email: when you paste it into Word, the font sizes, boldface, and other formatting arrives intact.

  Most modern Mac programs, including word processors and page-layout programs, automatically copy styled text to the Clipboard whenever you copy.

- **HTML Format.** Use this option when you're creating a Web page (see Chapter 7) and pasting in text from another type of document. Word adds HTML formatting commands to the text you're moving.

Tip: If you've used older Macintosh programs, you may be wondering where the Publish and Subscribe features are in Word. What should you do when you want your new logo automatically updated in every document where it currently exists?

You can do this in Word, but not with Apple's Publish and Subscribe feature. Microsoft has officially discontinued the Publish and Subscribe commands in its software. (Come to think of it, so has Apple; these commands are missing from the latest version of AppleWorks, too.) You can achieve almost the same effect, however, using Microsoft's Object Linking and Embedding (OLE) technology, which is described fully in Chapter 18.

Paste as Hyperlink

This command is at the heart of a truly wild Word feature, one that lets a Word document become a living table of contents—a launcher—for the chapters in your book project, pages on the World Wide Web, people in your email address book, or even applications on your hard drive.

Text that's pasted as a hyperlink remembers where it came from, wherever that may be. Here are the kinds of hyperlinks possible in Word:

- **Within the same document.** Select some text, choose Edit→Copy, then use Edit→Paste as Hyperlink. Text that you've pasted as a hyperlink becomes a blue, underlined link to its point of origin.

  For example, using Paste as Hyperlink, you can paste text from the last chapter of your book into the introduction. From then on, you can click the link to jump directly to the last chapter. You can also use this command to construct a "live" table of contents, as shown in Figure 2-1.

When you position the cursor over a hyperlink without clicking, a yellow tooltip balloon identifies the name and location of the file it's connected to.

- **Between two different Word documents.** You can use the same technique to create a link between two different Word documents, even if they're on different disks. When you click the hyperlink, Word opens the document to the page you've linked to.

Note: If you click a link to a file on a removable disk (such as a Zip or floppy) that isn't currently in the drive, an error message appears.

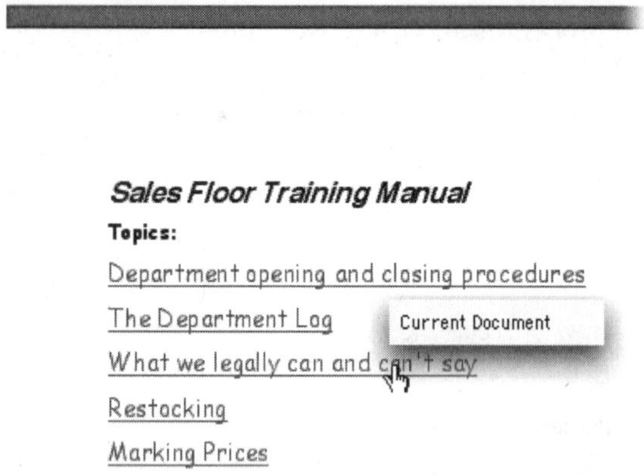

Sales Floor Training Manual

Topics:

Department opening and closing procedures

The Department Log   Current Document

What we legally can and can't say

Restocking

Marking Prices

Figure 2-1:
To create this linked table of contents, the headings from each section of the training manual were copied (Edit→Copy) and pasted as hyperlinks (Edit→Paste as Hyperlink). When you move the cursor over one of these links, it turns into a pointing hand. When you click it, you jump to that heading in the document.

FREQUENTLY ASKED QUESTION

Linking Word to the Web

When I copy a link from a Web site to paste into a Word document, the Paste as Hyperlink command is grayed out. I want to create a tutorial in Word that new employees can read on their computers. I want to link it to Web sites that the employees can refer to for more information. How can I do this if the command is grayed out?

Don't make things harder for yourself! You can create a link to the Web in any Word document simply by *dragging* the link from Internet Explorer into your document. (If you want the actual URL—beginning with *http://www*— to appear in your Word document, drag the actual *address* out of the browser's Address bar. If you want the plain-

English name of the Web page to appear instead, drag the tiny @ icon in the Address bar instead.)

When you click the resulting link in Word, your browser opens and takes you to the Web page specified by the link. (If you're not already online, the Mac may or may not dial up the Internet in the process, depending on your settings in the PPP tab of the Network panel of System Preferences.)

Note: Dragging from the Address bar doesn't work properly with either OmniWeb 4.1 or Netscape 6.2.1 for OS X, and not at all in Web browsers written for Mac OS 9 running in the Classic mode.

Editing a link can be tricky, since you can't exactly click it to plant the insertion point or drag to highlight some text. If you try, you'll simply trigger the link itself. The secret is to Control-click the link and choose Hyperlink→Edit Hyperlink from the contextual menu. A dialog box appears that lets you easily edit the link's text.

Note: When you put links of any kind into a Word document, the Web toolbar appears automatically. If it covers up any existing toolbars, just drag it out of the way using the handle at its left side. To dismiss it entirely, choose its name from the View→Toolbars submenu (or click its tiny close button).

Drag-and-drop

Drag-and-drop is the easiest way to move text from one place to another, especially if both the starting and ending locations are on the screen simultaneously. Because it lets you grab chunks of text and drag them directly around the paragraph or sentence before you, drag-and-drop is an extremely direct and satisfying way to rearrange your prose. As a bonus, drag-and-drop doesn't involve the Clipboard; whatever you've most recently copied or cut to the Clipboard remains there, ready for pasting, no matter how many times you drag-and-drop in the meantime.

After highlighting some text, position the cursor anywhere within the highlighted area. Press the mouse button and drag carefully. A dotted outline of the original text block moves as you drag, along with a nonblinking insertion point at your arrow-cursor tip. Move the mouse until the insertion point is where you want the relocated text to *start*. When you release the mouse button, the text jumps immediately into its new location. (If it didn't wind up exactly where you intended, choose Edit→Undo move, or press ⌘-Z or F1, to return everything to the way it was.)

Note: Within a Word document, drag-and-drop acts like a *Cut* and Paste operation—your text *moves* from one place to another. When you drag while pressing the Option key, however, or whenever you drag-and-drop between Office programs (see below), drag-and-drop acts like *Copy* and Paste—the original text remains where it was. (Drag-and-drop also acts like Copy and Paste when you drag between different open Word documents.)

Drag-and-drop between programs

In addition to working within Word, drag-and-drop also lets you drag text or graphic elements *between* Office programs. Position the two windows side by side (see Figure 2-2). Select your text or graphic, and then drag the highlighted block toward the destination window. Watch what happens before you let go of the mouse button:

- If you're dragging to an Excel spreadsheet, a dotted outline appears around the destination cell.

- If you're dragging to an Entourage email message, a gray line appears around the message, subject, or address text boxes. Text can be dropped into any of these locations.

- If you're dragging into a PowerPoint presentation, you can drop into a slide, notes area, or list. A colored outline indicates where the dragged material will appear when you let go of the mouse.

When your desired destination is appropriately highlighted, let go of the mouse button; your text appears in its new home.

Tip: Don't feel limited to dragging and dropping within Microsoft programs. Almost every modern Macintosh program can accept drag-and-drops. For example, you can drag from Word into AppleWorks (for Mac OS X or Classic), an America Online email, SimpleText, TextEdit, Stickies, and of course any Office 2001 programs running in Classic. Conversely, Office X programs can also accept drag-and-drops from other drag-and-drop-savvy applications. (When you drag into America Online for Mac OS X, the text appears as an uneditable picture instead of text. Still, your recipient will be able to read it.)

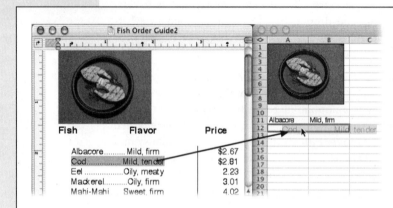

Figure 2-2:
Text being dragged from a Word file into an Excel spreadsheet. (The destination cell expands to accept the full text.) Pictures dragged from Word sit on top of a spreadsheet, without following cell boundaries.

Dragging and dropping to the desktop

When you drag-and-drop a chunk of selected text outside the boundaries of your document and onto the desktop, Word creates a *clipping file* (see Figure 2-3). Clipping files are pieces of text-in-waiting that you can later drag-and-drop.

As a bonus, when you drag-and-drop to the desktop, Word copies the text to the clipping file; it does not *cut* it. You can edit or even delete the original text, and still store an intact copy in the form of a clipping file on your desktop or the Dock.

Later, when you drag a clipping file back into a document, Word pastes a copy of the clipping text; the clipping file remains on the desktop, where you can use it again and again. In effect, you can use your desktop like a giant pasteboard to store boilerplate paragraphs that you use frequently. In fact, dragging the clippings to the Dock keeps them handy, but still out of the way.

Note: In Mac OS X, the Finder names every clipping "Picture Clipping," even if it contains text. Be sure to rename your clippings quickly and carefully so that you can remember what's in them.

You can also create clipping files from Word pictures or drawing objects. Just select the object and drag it to the desktop. (Word names it a *picture clipping*, as shown in Figure 2-3.)

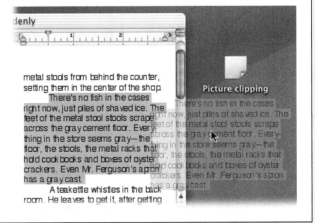

Figure 2-3:
You can rename a clipping file as you would any Finder icon: For example, click its name once, then twitch the mouse to make the "renaming rectangle" appear.

Cut Out to Be Smart

Have you noticed that when you cut and paste in Word, your pasted text is always perfectly spaced? In other words, when you paste a word with a space after it in front of a period, the extra space magically disappears and the period comes right smack after the word, where it belongs. And when you paste one word after another, a space appears between the two words, even if you forgot to put one there yourself. (Don't try *that* in TextEdit.)

That's Word's Smart Cut and Paste feature. You turn it on and off by the checkbox on the Word→Preferences→Edit panel—but turning it off is probably a bad idea. The golden rule of computing: Whenever your software offers to take over boring, microscopic, annoying work for you, let it.

Navigating Your Documents

Word X offers a multitude of ways to navigate your document, some of which aren't as immediately obvious as the scroll bar.

Tip: Using the scroll bar has its own reward; as you drag the "elevator" scroll-box handle up and down, a pop-out tooltip balloon identifies the major headings in your document as you scroll by. By scanning this readout, you'll know exactly where you'll be when you stop scrolling.

What the Keys Do

It's by far one of the most frequently asked questions among new (and unself-conscious veteran) Mac users: What on earth are all of those extra keys for on the standard Mac keyboard?

In many cases, the answer is "nothing." In most Mac programs, such keys as the Fkeys on the top row and the Num Lock key don't do anything at all. In Office, however, there's scarcely a single key that doesn't have a function. For example:

- **Esc.** Short for "Escape," this key provides a quick way of dismissing a dialog box without having to click the Close or Cancel button. It also closes a menu that you've pulled down, once you've decided not to use it. Esc acts the same as the ⌘-. key combination that Mac fans know and love.

- **Home.** This key moves the insertion point to the beginning of the line it's currently in. (You were expecting it to take your insertion point to the top of the document, weren't you? It's a trick; to do that, press ⌘-Home.)

- **End.** The End key, if you have one, takes you to the end of the current line. The ⌘-End combination takes you to the very end of the document.

POWER USERS' CLINIC

The Fkeys

On some Macs, they're tiny; on others, they're full-sized. On some Macs, you have twelve of them; on others, fifteen. They're the function keys (or Fkeys) stretched along the topmost row of your keyboard.

Once you're familiar with the many benefits of the Fkeys, you may become addicted. The following is how the function keys come defined in a new copy of Word X—but remember that it's easy enough to change their functions (see Chapter 17).

F1 means Undo (the same as ⌘-Z). (There's no predefined Fkey for Redo, although ⌘-Y or Edit→Redo are on hand if you change your mind *again*.)

F2, F3, and **F4** correspond to the Cut, Copy, and Paste commands described earlier in this chapter (⌘-X, ⌘-C, and ⌘-V).

You're entitled to wonder, by the way, why you might use the Fkeys for simple functions like copying and pasting when you're already in the habit of using the ⌘-key combinations?

The answer is on your keyboard: Many Mac laptops have only one ⌘ key—on the left side. If you have one of these, you'll probably find the single Fkey to be more convenient than a two-key combination.

F5 (Go To Same, also ⌘-G) calls up the Go To tab of the Find and Replace dialog box (see page 72).

F6 (Other Pane) moves the insertion point to the other pane of a split window. You can use Shift-F6 to go back to the original pane, but why? Hitting F6 a second time performs the same function.

F7 (Proofing, also Option-⌘-L or Tools→Spelling and Grammar) takes you to the first instance of a misspelling or instance of questionable grammar (as defined by Microsoft), and calls up the Spelling and Grammar dialog box.

F8 (Extend Selection) puts you in Extended selection mode, as described on page 30.

F9 (Update Fields) is useful only if you've added *fields* to your document, as described on page 228.

F10, all by itself, doesn't do anything. It's the key that time (or Microsoft) forgot. Open your Tools→Customize command and assign your favorite function to it (see page 633).

F11 (Next Field) works only when your document has fields (page 228).

F12 (Save As) opens the Save As dialog box. Note there is no Fkey shortcut for the Save function. (F10, anyone?)

- **Ins.** The Ins key (short for Insert), if you have one, is a very quick shortcut to the Paste command—even quicker than ⌘-V, and more intuitive than F4.

- **Delete.** The Delete key acts as a backspace key. It backs over and erases the last character you typed. In Word X, in fact, ⌘-Delete comes set to delete the entire *word* before the cursor, which is often far more useful than deleting just one character—especially when you're in the middle of a writing frenzy.

- **Forward Delete.** This key deletes the character to the *right* of the insertion point— not a function to which most Mac fans are accustomed, but an extremely useful one once you know it. For example, when trying to correct a typo, you sometimes place the insertion point on the wrong side of the letter you want, especially when you're working with italics. In such cases, one tap on this key does just the trick. (Many Mac keyboards lack this key; if you have a numeric keypad, you can use the Clear key instead, as described next.)

- **Clear.** This key acts as a forward delete key, too. On desktop keyboards, it shares a space with the Num Lock key.

- **Help.** Pushing the Help button opens the Word Help window or Max the Mac Plus's "what's your question?" window (depending on whether or not you have Max activated, as described on page 686). If the dog ate your Help key, ⌘-/ does the same thing.

- **Page up and Page down.** These keys move you up and down in the document, one screen at a time. (If you actually do want to jump from the top of one page to the top of the next, use the Navigator buttons instead, as described on page 73.)

Tip: Remember that you can combine some of these keystrokes–Home, End, Page up, Page down–with the Shift key to *select* text instead of simply scrolling.

Keystrokes: The Missing Manual

Microsoft apparently employs seething crowds of programmers who do nothing but dream up keyboard shortcuts for every conceivable Word function. With the Shift, Option, and ⌘ keys in various combinations, for example, the top-row function keys described in this chapter have second, third, fourth, and fifth functions— far more keyboard shortcuts than any human being could possibly remember (or fit in a 700-page book).

To see the master list of shortcut keys, choose Help→Word Help Contents; open the flippy triangle for the heading "Using Shortcut Keys." Then click either "About using shortcut keys" (for an overview) or "Shortcut keys" (to see the actual list).

To print out a list of all Word shortcut keys for future reference, choose Tools→ Macro→Macros. Choose "Word commands" from the "Macros in" pop-up menu, click ListCommands in the macro list, then click Run. In the dialog box that appears, click "Current menu and keyboard settings," then click OK. When the dialog box goes away and the shortcut key list appears, press ⌘-P or click the Print button in the Standard toolbar.

The list is several pages long and contains commands you may never use. But when you find yourself using the same menu commands over and over, it's worth taking a look to see if a keyboard shortcut exists.

The Go To Command

The scroll bar and arrow keys can get you pretty close to where you want to go in a long document, but now you can get there with much greater precision by telling Word. Double-clicking the Status bar (see page 25), pressing ⌘-G (or F5), or choosing Edit→Go To opens the Go To tab of the Find and Replace dialog box, as shown in Figure 2-4.

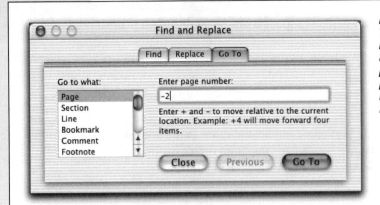

Figure 2-4:
Typing -2 in the "Enter page number" box will scroll the document back exactly two pages. It also moves the insertion point back. Choose your unit of measure (pages in this example) in the "Go to what" box.

The Go To tab looks simple, but there's quite a lot you can do with it:

- **Enter a page number.** If you know what page you want to access, just enter the number in the "Enter page number" box and hit Return (or click Go To if you're a mouser).

- **Jump a certain number of pages forward or back,** as described in Figure 2-4.

- **Step through your document** page by page. Just keep pressing Return (or Enter) without doing anything else in between—after entering 1, for example, in the "Enter page number" box. (Microsoft calls this "browsing.") (Of course, a less dialog box–intensive method of jumping from one page to the next is to use the Navigator buttons described below.)

- **Choose a specific item type to go to** in the "Go to what" box at the left. It can be as much as a section (see page 137) or as little as a line. You can check all your comments (see page 179) or footnotes at once by hitting Return repeatedly after selecting your unit of choice. (Jumping from one Heading, Graphic, Table, Comment, or Footnote to the next can be particularly useful in complex documents.)

The Navigator Buttons

All these nifty browsing features are also available by mouse, at the lower-right corner of every Word window, as shown in Figure 2-5. In the same illustration, you'll see that the double-headed arrows are called Navigator buttons. By choosing an item in the "Go to what" box (see Figure 2-4), you can click the Navigator buttons to move forward and backward from one to the next.

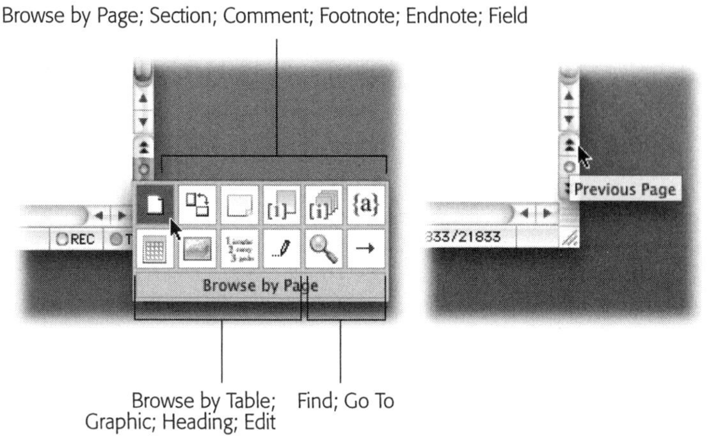

Figure 2-5:
The icons on the Select Browse Object palette (left) match the item types in the "Go to what" box in Figure 2-4. Once you've selected an item, you can click the Navigator buttons (right) to step directly to the next or previous one of the chosen item—Browse by Page in this example. This palette also contains shortcuts to the Find and Go To dialog boxes.

Browse by Page; Section; Comment; Footnote; Endnote; Field

Previous Page

Browse by Page

Browse by Table;   Find; Go To
Graphic; Heading; Edit

As shown at the left in Figure 2-5, click the tiny round Select Browse Object button to choose *how* you want the Navigator buttons to take you through your document. Just click one of the icons (described below) in the pane that pops up.

Changing the browse object affects all open documents. If you've been browsing a big document by *sections*, and then switch back to a shorter one that you want to review by *page*, you need to change the browse object again.

Tip: You can check the current setting by positioning the cursor over one of the double-arrow buttons without clicking. A little pop-up label says "next page," "previous page, " or whatever.

- **Browse by Page.** This is the default setting when you open a new document. With each click of a double arrow, you jump to the top of the next (or previous) page. (By contrast, the Page up/down keys scroll one *screen* at a time, even if that means you're jumping only half a page.)

- **Browse by Section.** When this setting is selected, the Navigator buttons take you from the top of one *section* to the next. Needless to say, this is most helpful if you've actually used section breaks in a document (see page 137).

- **Browse by Comment.** Word's Reviewing features (see Chapter 5) let you attach comments to a document, so that you can provide typed feedback to the author.

Either way, this setting lets you skip from one such comment to the next, bypassing the remainder of the text. (It's a very good idea to use Browse by Comment before you send a document out into the world.)

- **Browse by Footnote, Browse by Endnote.** Similar to Browse by Comment, these settings take you directly from one note to the next. (See page 197 for more on footnotes and endnotes.)

Tip: If you're viewing the notes in a split screen, the bottom screen (the one with the notes in it) has its own Navigator buttons, which are *always* set to the browse object of that pane's contents—be it footnotes, endnotes, or comments.

- **Browse by Field.** When you've used the Data Merge feature (page 254) or otherwise placed *fields* in your document (page 228), you can use the Navigator buttons to skip from one field to the next. This browse feature is really quite useful, since fields can look exactly like ordinary text and be easily missed. When browsing with this feature, Word helpfully highlights fields as it finds them.

- **Browse by Table.** This feature makes the Navigator buttons jump directly from one *table* to the next.

- **Browse by Graphic.** Choosing this browse object does nothing unless your document contains pictures, drawings, paintings, or scanned photographs. If it does, then the Navigator buttons move you from one graphic to another, skipping everything in between.

- **Browse by Heading.** This command is actually a two-in-one browse object. If you're working in Outline view (see page 40), the Navigator buttons move the insertion point item by item, hitting each entry in your outline.

GEM IN THE ROUGH

Back to Where You Once Belonged

The Go Back command is unique to Microsoft Word, and it's fantastically useful. No matter where you are in a document, this command scrolls directly back to the last place you clicked (usually the last place you edited text)—even if it was in another open document.

You'll find this command useful in a number of circumstances: after splitting and unsplitting the window, and then finding yourself deposited in the wrong part of a document; when you've just opened up a document that you were editing yesterday and want to return to the spot where you stopped; when reconsidering an edit after scrolling to a new location; and so on.

Better yet, Word doesn't just remember the last place you clicked; it remembers the last *three* places. Each time you use the Go Back command, your insertion point jumps among these four places—the last three edits and your current position—even if that means bringing different document windows forward.

You can trigger the Go Back command by pressing Option-⌘-Z, or Shift-F5, or using the Navigator buttons described above. If you fall in love with this feature, as you might, consider changing the keystroke to something easier to remember, such as ⌘-G or F10. (See Chapter 17 for instructions on changing a keystroke.)

This browsing method also works if your document's *styles* (see page 141) include any Heading styles. Use these preformatted font styles to set off chapter titles, captions, or subtopics. When you browse by heading, your insertion point skips from one heading to the next, bypassing all the mere mortal body text in between.

- **Browse by Edit.** Unlike the other browse objects, this one possesses a limited short-term memory. Word only remembers the last three places you clicked in your document. See the sidebar on the previous page for details.

Tip: Even though you've selected a browse object, you're not stuck with using the mouse to click the Navigator buttons. The keyboard shortcut ⌘-Page up or Page down takes you from one item to the next.

Finding and Replacing

When editing a document, sometimes you know exactly what you want to revise, but just don't know where it is. For instance, you want to go back and read the paragraph you wrote about *mansions*, but you don't remember what page it's on. Or suppose you've found out that you misspelled Sarah's name all the way through an article. Now you have to replace *every* occurrence of Sara with Sarah—but how do you make sure that you've got them all?

That's where Find and Replace comes in.

Find

If you just want to find a certain word (or even part of a word), choose Edit→Find (or press ⌘-F). The Find and Replace dialog box opens, as shown in Figure 2-6. Type the word you're looking for, and then click Find Next (or press Return or ⌘-F).

Tip: If you turn on "Highlight all items found in Main Document," the Find Next button changes to say Find All. Now Word will select all occurrences of the search term simultaneously. At that point, you can bold them all, italicize them all, cut them all, or perform other kinds of neat global maneuvers.

Now Word searches for your search term, starting from the position of the insertion point. If it finds what you're seeking, it scrolls to and highlights each occurrence of that word or phrase in your document. (If it doesn't find any occurrences, an error message tells you so.)

If Word finds an occurrence, but it's not the one you had in mind, you can keep clicking Find or hitting Return to find successive occurrences. When Word reaches the end of your document, it starts searching again from the beginning. When it finally wraps around so far that it finishes searching the whole file, another dialog box lets you know.

The Find box remains on the screen throughout the process, but don't let that stop you; you can pause and edit your document at any time. Just click in your document window, sending the Find box to the background. To resume your search, click the Find dialog box to bring it forward, then click Find Next.

Tip: The keystroke Shift-F4 (or Shift-⌘-Y) means "find the next occurrence of whatever I just searched for." The advantage is that it works even after you've closed the Find box altogether—and even if you performed your search hours ago (provided you haven't closed the document).

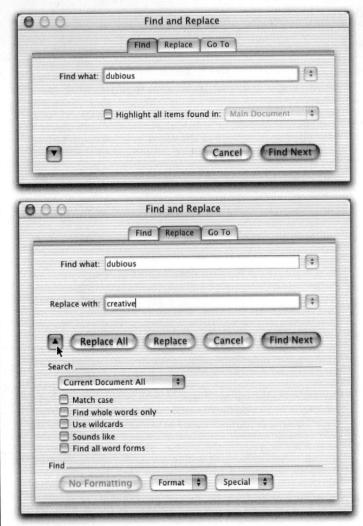

Figure 2-6:
Top: The Find dialog box.

Bottom: The expanded Replace box. The Format and Special menus at the bottom of this dialog box let you search for a font, typestyle, paragraph break, and so on. If you'd like to find all your italics and change them to boldface, or find all the dashes and delete them, this is the way to do it.

Replace

Although you can do edits and replacements in conjunction with the Find command as explained above, Word has a more streamlined process for making the same replacement over and over. Choosing Edit→Replace (Shift-⌘-H) opens the Replace tab of the Find and Replace dialog box.

Note: In previous versions of Word, the Replace keystroke was just ⌘-H. Of course, Apple has now claimed ⌘-H as its universal Hide command in Mac OS X, so Microsoft was forced to change the Replace keystroke to Shift-⌘-H.

It takes the Word veteran some time to unlearn ⌘-H for Replace. However, a few dozen shocks of seeing all your open Word windows disappear (and having to bring them back by clicking the W icon in the Dock) should train you to use the new protocol.

Once again, start by typing the word or phrase you want to replace in the "Find what" box. This time, however, you press Tab or ⌘-I to jump into the "Replace with" box; now type the new, improved replacement text.

When you click Find Next or press Return, Word searches the document and stops at the first match. Now there's a decision to make. After examining the highlighted phrase in context, click one of these buttons:

- **Replace.** This button means, "Replace this search term with my replacement text, then find the next occurrence of the search term."

Caution: If you simply press Find Next or Return, Word doesn't make the replacement. You must click the Replace button (or press ⌘-R) each time.

FREQUENTLY ASKED QUESTION

Converting Quotes from Curly to Straight, or Vice Versa

I've been told to convert all of Word's automatic, typographically correct "curly quotes" into Internet-friendly "straight quotes" before posting my work on a Web page or sending it by email. How do I do that?

As you've noted, Word converts your quotes automatically as you type, curling open and close quotes (and single quotes) as appropriate. To turn this feature off, choose Tools→AutoCorrect, click the AutoFormat As You Type tab, and turn off "Straight quotes with curly quotes."

You can also leave this feature turned on, while making the *occasional* curly quote straight—such as when you want a " mark to designate inches. The solution is simple: Just after typing the quote mark, press ⌘-Z or F1. Word straightens it instantly.

But to perform global surgery on an entire document, turning all curly quotes into straight ones, for example, choose Tools→AutoCorrect, click the AutoFormat As You Type tab, and turn off "Straight quotes with smart quotes." Click OK.

Now choose Edit→Replace. In both the "Find what" and "Replace with" boxes, type ' or ", and then click Find Next or Replace All. Word straightens all single or double quotes, as appropriate. (To curlify all straight quotes, repeat the procedure with the "Straight quotes with smart quotes" checkbox turned on.)

- **Replace All.** If you don't need this occurrence-by-occurrence interview, and you're sure you want to replace every occurrence of the search term in the entire document, click Replace All (or press ⌘-A).

Be very careful, however: in most cases, it's safer to check each case to make sure the replacement is appropriate. For instance, if you're replacing "rite" with "right," Word will change even "criteria" to "crightria," giving quite an unexpected surprise to your editor, professor, or boss. Use Replace All only when there's little chance for that kind of confusion; even so, you should proofread carefully afterward.

- **Find Next.** Suppose that, as you're searching for every occurrence of "Sara" to replace it with "Sarah," Word finds and highlights the first four letters of the word Saratoga. Clearly, you don't want Word to change this occurrence. In that case, just click Find Next (or press Return) to leave this occurrence alone and jump to the next one.

Advanced Find

Clicking the Expand button (the blue button with the down arrow on it) at the bottom of the Find or Replace tab makes the dialog box sprout an additional, secret panel. (Pressing ⌘-M does the same thing.) It offers the following precision controls for narrowing your search even further:

- The **Search** pop-up menu tells Word where to search. **Current Document All** starts the Find function from the very beginning of the document. **Current Document Down** and **Document Up** search forward and backward from the insertion point, and **All Open Documents** searches from the beginning of each document in the order that you opened them, moving automatically from one to the next.

- Turn on **Match case** when you want to find or change words only when they're capitalized a certain way; for instance, when you want to find the name Mike but skip over words like "mike."

- **Find whole words only** (⌘-Y) is a very powerful safety option. It tells Word to only look for the search term if it's separated from surrounding text by a space or punctuation mark—if it's a whole word unto itself, in other words. If you're searching for the word "men," for instance, checking this box prevents Find from stopping on (or, worse, replacing) "menu" and "document."

- Checking **Use wildcards** (⌘-U) lets you use special characters to *stand in* for actual letters, in cases where you're unsure of the right letter or want to look for more than one spelling at a time. For example, **?** stands in for any one letter or character. Entering *f?r* in the "Find what" box finds occurrences of "far," "for," "ferry," and so on. You can use * to represent any string of one or more letters (or other characters). Thus, entering *c*r* would find words like "car," "carrier," and "rancor."

When you'd settle for finding any one of several *specified* characters, put them in brackets. For instance, use *f[au]nny* to find all occurrences of both "fanny" and "funny" in your document.

Finally, an exclamation point indicates that you want to find any character *except* the one in the brackets. For example, *[!f]unk* finds "hunk," and "spunk," but not "funk."

Tip: There are quite a few more wildcard characters in Word, which you can use—independently or in combination—to send Word on incredibly complex, convoluted searches. For a list of all wildcards, enter *wildcards* in the Office Assistant's or Word Help window's Search box, and choose "Type wild cards for items you want to find."

- **Sounds like (⌘-S).** Turn on this box and enter a phonetic spelling for the word or words you're hunting for. Entering "thare" finds every occurrence of "there," "their," and "they're." This option really comes in handy when you can't remember the spelling of a name; enter "lee" to find Mr. Leigh or Ms. Li, for example.

- **Find all word forms.** This rather intelligent option finds all those irregularly spelled English nouns and verbs. For instance, if you're trying to find all the places where your article mentions running, type *run* and turn on this box. Word finds "ran," "runs" and "running"—but not "runner."

Finding by Format

Word is sometimes described as the Feature List that Ate Cleveland. Dozens or hundreds of features lie untapped by the vast majority of its owners.

But here's a buried feature that's well worth noticing: It's the Format pop-up button at the bottom of the Find dialog box, which lets you search for text according to its *formatting* (alone, or in combination with words typed in the "Find what" box). By opening this Format menu (or pressing ⌘-O), you'll see that Word lets you search for:

- **Font.** Finds occurrences of, say, Times or Palatino, as well as font *characteristics* like bold, italic, blue, 12-point, double-underline, shadow, and so on—in any combination.

- **Paragraph.** Locates paragraphs according to their indentation, line spacing, leading, outline level, page breaks, and so on.

- **Tabs.** Searches for tab stops by position and type.

- **Language.** Searches for text you've designated as being in a certain language (by highlighting the text and then choosing Tools→Language).

- **Frame.** Locates any *frame* (page 162), according to any of its attributes.

- **Style.** Lets you search for, or replace, any of your document's styles (see page 141).

• **Highlight.** Finds text you or a colleague has highlighted using the Highlighter tool on the Reviewing toolbar (page 180).

Tip: *Once you've popped open the menu with ⌘-O, you can "walk" down its commands with the arrow keys. Press Enter when you've snagged the one you want.*

This powerful feature is instrumental in dozens of situations. Sometimes it's useful when you just want to *find* something, like this:

• Type *the* in the "Find what" box. Choose Format→Style and choose one of the heading styles you've used in your document. (See page 141 for more on styles.) Word finds the word "the" only when it occurs in a heading.

• Click inside the empty "Find what" box; choose Format→Font. In the resulting dialog box, click Italic, and then click OK. Word will now find every italicized word in the document, one by one.

The uses of this feature become even more amazing when you use the Replace function at the same time:

• Suppose that, in keeping with your newspaper's style guide, you decide to put Microsoft's company name in bold type, everywhere it occurs. Type *Microsoft Corporation* in the "Find what" box. Click in the "Replace with" box, choose Format→Font, choose Bold in the Font Style box, and click OK. Now, when you click Replace All, Word changes all occurrences of the phrase "Microsoft Corporation" to boldface.

Tip: *You don't have to type Microsoft Corporation again into the "Replace with" box; if this box is empty, since you specified a format, Word assumes that you don't intend to change the text itself.*

• You want to create a quick table-of-contents document. You decide that the easiest way is to remove all the words in your document that *aren't bold,* leaving behind only what appears in bold type (your headings, that is).

Leave both the Find and Replace boxes empty. Click in the "Find what" box, choose Format→Font, click NotBold, and click OK. By leaving the "Replace with" box empty, you're telling Word to *delete* every occurrence of the specified "Find what" item (in this case, text that's not bold). When you click Replace All, Word vaporizes all the body text of your document, leaving behind only the boldface type.

• Click in the "Find what" box and choose Format→Tabs. Word displays a dialog box similar to the one where you set tabs (see page 127). Type *.5* in the "Tab stop position" box and click OK. Click in the "Replace with" box, choose Format→Tabs, and type *1* in the "Tab stop position box." Use the radio buttons in the "Find Tabs" dialog box to tell Word what kind of tab you're searching for. Word will not find tabs if the alignment doesn't match.

Finally, click OK. Word finds all the paragraphs with half-inch tabs and changes them to one-inch tabs.

- Someone has turned in an article to you that contains headings. But rather than using the Heading 1 *style* (see page 141), the author used simple boldface formatting for the headings. As a result, you can't use Word's Outline view to see just the headings.

   The solution is simple: Click in the empty "Find what" box. Choose Format→Font, choose Bold in the "Font style" box, and click OK. Now click in the empty "Replace with" box; choose Format→Style, select the Heading 1 style, and click OK. Now, when you click Replace All, Word changes all bolded paragraphs to Heading 1 style.

Your formatting selections are displayed just below the "Find what" box. Click No Formatting to erase them (in readiness for a different search, for example).

Note: If you've set up an elaborate string of formatting characteristics (Palatino, Heading 1 style, 12 point), there's no way to delete only one of them; you must click No Formatting to delete all of them and build the list again.

Finding Invisible Characters

The Special menu at the bottom of the Find and Replace dialog box lets you incorporate non-alphanumeric "characters" into your search. It also lets you search for document features that have nothing to do with words, such as column breaks, paragraph breaks, and hyphens.

When you choose one of these items from the Special menu, Word places its character code in the "Find what" box. You can use more than one of these choices and use them with wildcards, as described above.

Tip: Once again, you can manipulate this list with the keyboard. Press ⌘-E to open the Special pop-up menu, and then use the arrow keys to highlight the commands on it.

The Special menu really demonstrates its power in Find and Replace operations. Some examples:

- Suppose your document is filled with typographically correct dashes, which may turn into gibberish if posted on a Web page or emailed. To convert them into double hyphens, click in the "Find what" box and choose Special→Em Dash (for a long dash, like this —) or En Dash (for a shorter dash, like this –). Click in the "Replace with" box and type two hyphens (--). When you click Replace All, Word replaces dashes with hyphens.

Tip: To replace both kinds of dashes in one pass, choose one after the other in the Special menu. Now place brackets around them in the "Find what" box.

- To eliminate all comment marks (see page 179), you must first take an unexpected step: On the Formatting Palette, open the Document flippy triangle and click the ¶ button, so that Word displays symbols for such normally invisible symbols as spaces, tabs, and (here's the point) comment marks. Make sure revision tracking (page 183) is turned off.

   In the Find and Replace dialog box, click in the "Find what" box and choose Special→Comment Mark. Leave the "Replace with" box empty. When you click Replace All, Word will delete all comments (and yellow comment marks) from your file.

- To take out column breaks and let the text reflow, click in the "Find what" box and choose Special→Column Break. Click in the "Replace with" box and choose Special→Paragraph Mark to ensure that the paragraphs in the newly joined columns don't run into each other.

- A Word document may look fine if there's just one press of the Return key after each paragraph; the style in question may have built-in "blank lines" between paragraphs. But if you try to paste the document's text into an email message, you'll lose the blank lines between paragraphs.

   The solution is to replace every paragraph mark with *two* paragraph marks before copying the document into your email program. Click in the "Find what" box and choose Special→Paragraph Mark; then click in the "Replace with" box and choose Special→Paragraph Mark *twice*. Word replaces every paragraph mark (which Word represents with the code ^{p}) with two consecutive paragraph breaks ($^p^p$).

- To reduce typing, insert abbreviation codes into a Word document, then replace them with much longer passages of boilerplate text. Before searching, copy the replacement text to the clipboard, type the abbreviation code into the "Find what" box, click in the "Replace with" box, and choose Special→Clipboard Contents. Finally, click Replace All.

Tip: You'll see the Special→Clipboard Contents command only when you've clicked in the "Replace with" box. In other words, you can't search for something you've copied to the clipboard. That's unfortunate, since almost everyone, sooner or later, comes across a Word document filled with some strange symbol—little white squares, Symbol-font squiggles, or some other mysterious character. It would be nice if you could copy one instance to the clipboard, so that you could replace all instances with, say, nothing.

In such situations, you can usually get away with *pasting* the copied mystery symbol directly into the "Find what" box.

To undo selections you've made from the Special menu in the Find and Replace dialog box, select and delete the characters that Word placed in the "Find what" or "Replace with" boxes.

Spelling and Grammar

Whatever your document—term paper, résumé, or letter to the milkman—typos can hinder its effectiveness and sully your credibility. When you let mistakes remain in your document, your reader may doubt that you put any time or care into it at all. Word helps you achieve the perfect result by pointing out possible errors, leaving the final call up to you.

Tip: A spelling-related feature (new since Word 2001) may have been benefiting you without you even noticing. When you incur a typo that even a Sominex-drugged reader would notice, such as *wodnerful* or *thier,* Word makes the correction automatically, instantly, and quietly. (Press ⌘-Z or F1 immediately afterward if you actually intended the misspelled version.) Technically, Word is using its spelling dictionaries as fodder for its AutoCorrect feature, as described on page 98.

As a bonus, the spelling checker in Word X is smart enough to recognize run-together words (such as *intothe* and *giveme*) and propose the split-apart versions as corrected spellings.

There are two basic modes to Word's spelling and grammar features:

Check Spelling as You Type

Word's factory setting is to check spelling and grammar continuously, immediately flagging any error it detects as soon as you finish typing it. Each spelling error gets a red, squiggly underline; each grammatical error gets a green one. These squiggly underlines (which also show up in the other Office programs) are among the most noticeable hallmarks of Office documents, as shown in Figure 2-7.

If you can spot the problem right away—an obvious spelling error, for example—simply edit it. The squiggly underline disappears as soon as your insertion point leaves the vicinity. It's often more fun, however, to Control-click each error (see Figure 2-7), which opens a contextual menu to help you handle the correction process. Here are the commands you'll find in this contextual menu:

- **Help** opens the Word Help system, as described in Appendix B.

- The next segment of the contextual menu contains **spelling suggestions** from Word's dictionary. It says "(no spelling suggestions)" if Word has none.

  If one of these suggestions is the word you were trying to spell, click it. Word instantly replaces the error in your document, thus evaporating the squiggly line.

- Choosing **Ignore All** from the contextual menu tells Word to butt out—that this word is spelled exactly the way you want it. Once you've chosen this command, the underlines disappear from *all* occurrences of that term *in this document.* (If you use the same spelling in a new document, however, Word will flag it as an error again. To teach Word the word forever, add it to the custom dictionary, as described next.)

• As you've probably figured out by now, Word underlines a word not necessarily because it's spelled incorrectly, but because it's not on Word's list of correctly spelled words. Occasionally, you have to "teach" Word a new word. The **Add** command does exactly that.

Word maintains word lists called custom dictionaries. When Word checks a word's spelling as you type it, the Add command on the contextual menu instantly adds that word to the current custom dictionary. You can also edit a custom dictionary directly, as described on page 91.

Note: Adding words to the custom dictionary may trigger an error message saying, "custom dictionary is full." If you get this alert, install the Office X Service Release 1 (page 12), which fixes this bug.

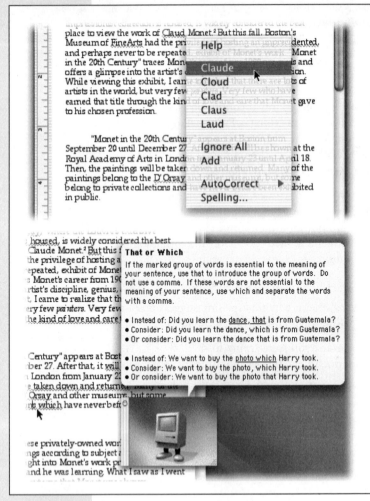

Figure 2-7:
Top: When Word is set to check spelling and grammar as you type, errors are underlined as you go.

Middle: Control-clicking each error opens a contextual menu that contains suggested spellings and commonly used Spelling and Grammar commands.

Bottom: Choosing "About this sentence" prompts the Office Assistant to explain the grammatical issue (bottom). Press Option-F7 to move on to the next error.

- The **AutoCorrect** pop-up menu provides access to matching choices from Word's AutoCorrect list (see page 96). Often, but not always, these choices are the same as the alternate spellings from the custom dictionary.

- **Spelling** opens the Spelling dialog box; it's the equivalent of the Tools→Spelling and Grammar command, in that it initiates a spelling and grammar check starting from your current place in the document. While it doesn't offer any more correctly spelled alternatives than the contextual menu, it is a convenience if, having discovered one typo, you decide to complete a full-fledged spell check.

Checking Spelling and Grammar All at Once

If it annoys you when Word flags incorrect or unusual spellings as you type, there's something you can do about it. Turn that feature off, as described in Figure 2-9, and check spelling on demand—once at the very end, for instance. If that's the way you like it, choose Tools→Spelling and Grammar (or press F7, or Option-⌘-L) to open the Spelling and Grammar dialog box (Figure 2-8).

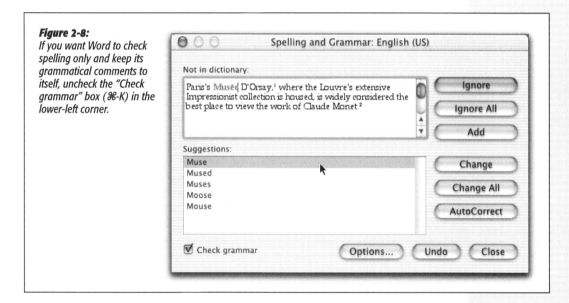

Figure 2-8:
If you want Word to check spelling only and keep its grammatical comments to itself, uncheck the "Check grammar" box (⌘-K) in the lower-left corner.

Word scans your document, starting at the insertion point, and displays errors one by one in the "Not in dictionary" box, as shown in Figure 2-8. As a courtesy, Word shows you the "error" in context, picturing the whole sentence in the text box with the specific spelling error shown in red. Your options are as follows:

- Click **Ignore** (⌘-I) to skip over the error without doing anything. If you don't want Word to flag this particular error again (in this document), click **Ignore All** (⌘-G).

- As described under "Check spelling as you type," clicking **Add** (⌘-A) adds the highlighted word to the custom dictionary. From here on out, in every document, Word will understand this spelling to be a correct one.

- In the lower, Suggestions list box, Word shows you some similarly spelled words from your main and custom dictionaries. Using the mouse or the up/down arrow keys, highlight one of them and click **Change** to accept that spelling just this once, or **Change All** (⌘-L) to swap all occurrences of the highlighted word—in this document—with the selected suggestion.

- If you agree that something is misspelled, but you don't see the correct spelling in the Suggestions list, you can make the correction directly in the top text area, using any of Word's editing tools. (This is a handy trick when Word discovers a typo like ";lkjijjjjjjj"—a sure sign that you'd fallen asleep on the keys. Just drag across the mess—right there in the dialog box—and press the Delete key to fix the error.)

  Then click Change or Change All, as described above, to apply your change to the document itself. You can also click **Undo Edit** (⌘-U) if you change your mind. (The Ignore button changes into Undo Edit as soon as you start typing in the window.)

- Whether you make a choice from the Suggestions window or make a change in the editing window, clicking the **AutoCorrect** (⌘-R) button tells Word to make the change from now on, using the AutoCorrect feature (see page 96). When you do so, Word enters your typo/correction pair to its AutoCorrect list, which you can view by choosing Tools→AutoCorrect and scrolling through the list. (See page 97 for more information on working with the AutoCorrect dialog box.)

- The **Undo** (⌘-U) button is a lifesaver for the indecisive. After you've made a correction, after you've clicked Change, even after you've created a new AutoCorrect pair, you can click Undo and take back your last change. Better still, the Undo command works even after you click Change, and Word has moved on to the next error. In that case, Word backtracks to the previous change and undoes it. In fact, you can keep on clicking Undo and reverse all the changes you've made since the beginning of your document.

  The Undo button is particularly valuable when you're spell-checking rapidly and realize that you've just accepted one of Word's suggestions a bit too hastily.

- The **Options** (⌘-O) button opens the Spelling and Grammar panel of the Preferences dialog box, shown in Figure 2-9.

- **Close** (Esc) calls a halt to the spelling and grammar check and dismisses the dialog box.

  When you're running a spelling and grammar check, the Office Assistant balloon often opens to explain the grammatical principle at work. Turn the Office Assistant off (see page 686) if you have no use for this reading material.

Word X's grammar checker is much smarter than it was in Word 2001. It's much less likely to underline perfectly correct sentences or make incorrect suggestions. (Remember when Word told you to change every occurrence of "that" to "which," and vice versa?)

Sometimes, however, you still need to rely on your own knowledge of grammar (and a healthy dose of common sense) in order to decide when to accept Word's suggested grammar changes—and when to click Ignore. A quick, online place to look for answers to your grammar questions is *www.grammarlady.com.* This Web site offers a free question-and-answer service, message boards, newsletter, and so on.

Figure 2-9:
The Word→Preferences→ Spelling and Grammar panel is command central for making Word's spelling and grammar features work for you. When you click "Check spelling as you type" or "Check grammar as you type," Word automatically unchecks the "hide" choices. You can still check "Hide spelling errors" or "Hide grammatical errors" to temporarily remove Word's squiggly underlines on a document-by-document basis.

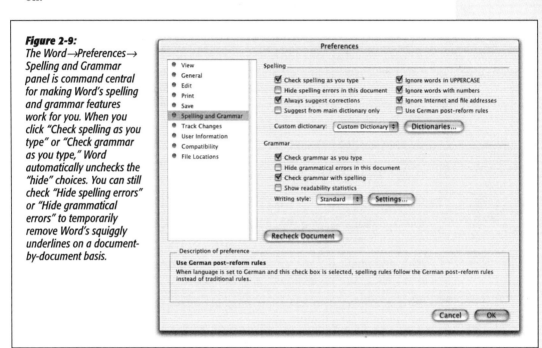

Spelling and Grammar Options

To tell Word how much (or little) help you need with your spelling and grammar, choose Word→Preferences; in the Preferences dialog box, click the Spelling and Grammar button. You'll find these options:

- **Check spelling as you type** turns on and off the red, wavy underlines that mark spelling errors in all Word documents.

- **Hide spelling errors in this document** turns off "Check spelling as you type" in the current document *only.*

- **Always suggest corrections** prompts Word to show you alternative spellings during spelling checks that use the Spelling dialog box. Without this option, Word will flag errors without proposing suggestions.

Note: Control-clicking a squiggly-underlined word produces spelling suggestions regardless of the "Always suggest corrections" setting.

- **Suggest from main dictionary only** instructs Word to use only the list of words that came installed with it, ignoring your custom dictionaries. (See page 91 for more detail on custom dictionaries.)

- Turn on **Ignore words in UPPERCASE** if you frequently use acronyms or stock symbols (such as WFMI or ADM). Otherwise, Word will interpret them as misspelled words.

- Turn on **Ignore words with numbers** if you'd like Word to leave words like 3Com and R2D2 alone.

- **Ignore Internet and file addresses** governs whether or not Word interprets URLs (*www.missingmanuals.com*) and file paths (Macintosh HD:Documents:Tests) as spelling errors. Because it's unlikely that most Web addresses are in Word's dictionaries, you'll usually want this option turned on.

- **Use German post-reform rules.** Turning on this box tells Word to use the new German spelling rules that were instituted in the 1990s—in Germany. (So if it works only on German-language Macs, why you can still see and turn it on on English-language Macs? As a conversation starter, we guess.)

- **Custom dictionary.** See page 90 for a full explanation of this feature.

- **Check grammar as you type** turns on and off the green, wavy underlines that mark what Word considers grammatical errors in all Word documents.

- **Hide grammatical errors in this document** turns off "Check grammar as you type" in the current document only.

- Turn off **Check grammar with spelling** to proceed through spelling checks without stopping for grammar issues.

- **Show readability statistics** will please educators and testers, but is probably of little value to anyone else. If you turn on this checkbox, Word applies a readability formula to the document. ("Check grammar with spelling" must be on as well.) The readability formula calculates an approximate grade level based on the number of syllables, words, and sentences in the document. These statistics are displayed in a box at the end of the spelling and grammar check.

Word uses one of two formulas to interpret the results. The *Flesch Reading Ease* score uses a scale of 0 to 100, with 100 being the easiest. A score of 60 or 70 indicates text that most adults could comfortably read and understand. The Flesch-Kincaid Grade Level Score, on the other hand, calculates grade level according to U.S. averages. A score of 8, for example, means that the document is on the eighth-grade reading level. If you're writing the minutes for your next MENSA meeting, this reading level may seem a little low; for a general audience, though, it's a good level to shoot for.

Either way, remember that this is a software program analyzing words written by a human being for specific audiences. By no means, for example, should you base somebody's entrance to a school on these scores—they're only crude approximations of approximations.

GEM IN THE ROUGH

Checking Foreign Language Text

The spelling checkers in ordinary, middle-class word processors choke on foreign terms. But not Word, King of the Feature List; it actually comes with different spelling dictionaries for dozens of languages. The program can actually check the English parts of your document against the English dictionary, the French portions against the French dictionary, and so on—all in a single pass.

This amazing intelligence works only if you've taken two preliminary steps. First, you must install the foreign-language dictionaries you intend to use (they're not part of the standard installation), using the technique described on page 681.

Second, you must *tell* Word what language each passage is in. To flag a certain word, passage, or document as Danish, for example, first highlight it. Then choose Tools→Language; in the resulting dialog box, select the language and click OK.

You've just applied what Microsoft calls language *formatting*—that is, you've flagged the highlighted text just as though you'd made it blue or bold. From now on, your spelling checks will switch, on the fly, to the corresponding spelling dictionary for each patch of foreign language text in your document.

Writing Styles

As it's probably occurred to you by now, grammar can be very subjective. Contractions, for example, aren't incorrect; they're just appropriate in some situations and not in others. In an academic or medical paper, long sentences and the passive voice are the norm; in a magazine article, they're taboo. On the other hand, other kinds of errors, such as writing the contraction "it's" when you mean the possessive "its," are something you *always* want to avoid. And when writing poetry or a play in dialect, the usual rules of grammar simply don't apply.

In other words, there are different writing styles for different kinds of documents. Word X not only recognizes that fact, it lets you choose which one you want to use in a given situation. Better still, it lets *you* decide which grammatical issues you want flagged.

To select a writing style from Word's preconfigured list, choose Word→ Preferences→Spelling and Grammar. In the resulting dialog box, choose a writing style from the pop-up menu near the bottom of the box under Grammar.

To customize writing styles to your own needs, thus becoming your own grammar czar or czarina, click Settings. The Grammar Settings dialog box opens, as shown in Figure 2-10. (If the Grammar settings are dimmed in the dialog box, it's because the Grammar module isn't installed. See Appendix A for installation instructions.)

The choices you make from the pop-up menus under Require apply to all writing styles. Each menu gives you a chance to customize points of style that are more a

---

matter of individual choice than grammar. By default, Word doesn't check for any of the three Require items listed here: whether you put a comma after the second-to-last item in a list (as in: *planes, trains, and automobiles*), whether punctuation goes inside or outside of quotation marks, or the number of spaces between sentences.

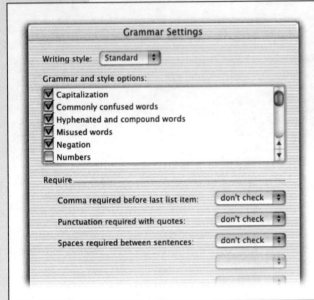

Figure 2-10:
You can modify existing writing styles (Standard, Casual, Formal, or Technical), or create your own combination of grammar standards (Custom), by checking and unchecking options in the list. Clicking Reset All returns the currently selected style to its original condition. (To restore all writing styles to their original settings, you must reset them one by one.)

If you learned how to write in England, you probably put periods and commas *after* the quotation marks at the end of a quote. In the United States, punctuation is expected to go *before* the quotes. Choose "inside" or "outside" from the second pop-up menu to have Word check if you're doing it consistently, one way or the other.

If sending your text to an editor or layout person for desktop publishing, you'll probably be asked to put just *one* space between sentences; you probably learned how to type with *two* spaces after every period. You can choose 1 or 2 from the bottom menu to instruct Word to check the spacing for you.

You can create your own unique style by choosing Custom from the pop-up menu at the top of the box and turning on any combination of options. When you click OK, the custom style applies to your document; you can't name the style or create more than one custom style at a time.

Custom Dictionaries and Preferred Spellings

As noted earlier, Word maintains a list of thousands of words that it "knows" how to spell. When it checks your spelling, Word simply compares the words in your document to the words in the list.

To teach Word the words that you're going to be using frequently, you have two options: you can add them to a *custom dictionary,* or, if you have large batches of words that you only use for specific situations, you can create multiple custom dictionaries. Then choose which dictionary you wish to apply to the document you're currently working on.

You can't add words directly to Word's *main* (built-in) dictionary, which is permanently "hard-wired"—specially encoded for speed. In fact, you aren't even allowed to see the main dictionary. However, when you add words to a custom dictionary, Word uses them seamlessly along with the main dictionary (as long as you haven't turned on the "Use main dictionary only" box in the Word→Preferences→Spelling and Grammar panel).

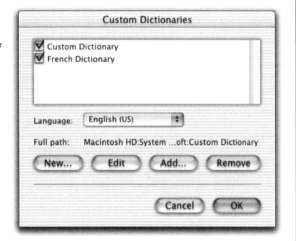

Figure 2-11:
The checked boxes show the custom dictionaries currently in effect. Uncheck one if you would like Word to stop using it in spell checks. For example, if you turn off French Dictionary, Word will interpret French words as spelling errors.

Editing the custom dictionary

To add words to a custom dictionary, choose Word→Preferences; click the Spelling and Grammar panel (Figure 2-9). Then click the Dictionaries button; in the Custom Dictionaries dialog box that opens (Figure 2-11), one custom dictionary, by default, is listed and checked, meaning that it's currently in use. Any words that you've ever added to Word's dictionary during a spelling check appear in this custom dictionary.

To look over the list of words, click Edit. (If a message appears to warn you that Word will now stop checking your spelling, click Continue.) Suddenly, all your added words appear listed in a new Word document, which you're now free to edit. You can add, delete, and edit words using any of Word's editing tools; just remember to use the Return key to ensure each word is on a separate line.

Creating a new custom dictionary

In some cases, you may want to create a new custom dictionary for specific projects. For instance, suppose that you're writing something in a foreign language or a paper filled with technical terms. If you add these foreign or technical terms to the same custom dictionary that you use for everyday correspondence, they'll show up in spelling checks and sometimes even create false errors.

To create a new custom dictionary, click New in the Custom Dictionaries dialog box (Figure 2-11). Type a name for the new dictionary, and then click Save. Word saves the new custom dictionary in your Home folder's Library→Preferences→Microsoft folder.

Now you can add words to the custom dictionary in one of two ways:

- To add new words occasionally, in the course of your everyday writing career, click the name of the new dictionary in the Custom Dictionaries dialog box. (Turn off any other dictionaries that may be listed in the box. Otherwise, Word will add newly learned terms to the default custom dictionary, for example, instead of your own foreign/technical one.) Then just go to work in your document. Whenever you check spelling, choose Add (see page 86) to place the unfamiliar term in your new custom dictionary.

- You can also add words all at once, by selecting the custom dictionary in the Custom Dictionaries dialog box and clicking Edit as described above. If there's a list of vocabulary words or technical terms in front of you, simply type or paste them into the text document that is the custom dictionary. Just make sure that each word is on a separate line before you click Save.

You can also copy and paste words from one custom dictionary into another. Thus, you can always copy the contents of the original custom dictionary into your specialized dictionary, so that you'll always have access to all your preferred spellings.

Tip: When editing custom dictionaries, you can access them easily by going directly to the Library→Preferences→Microsoft folder in your Home folder. You'll see icons marked with "ABC," which you can open in a program like TextEdit and edit away.

You can also rename these files. For example, if you've created new custom dictionaries, you may want to rename the default custom dictionary "original," "default," or "old."

Adding and removing custom dictionaries

After creating a new custom dictionary, you may decide to exclude it from certain documents. To do so, uncheck its box in the Custom Dictionaries dialog box as described in Figure 2-11.

If you select a dictionary and click Remove, it disappears from this list and no longer appears in the pop-up menu in the Preferences→Spelling and Grammar panel. This is the way to go if you never again want this custom dictionary as an option and don't want anyone else to see it in Preferences. However, a removed custom dictionary doesn't go away forever. It remains in the Library→Preferences→Microsoft folder (in your Home folder), or wherever you stored it on your Mac's hard drive. To return it to the Custom Dictionaries dialog box, click Add and choose it in the Add Dictionary dialog box.

Foreign language dictionaries

If your new dictionary is in a foreign language, there's an extra step. After creating the new custom dictionary, as described above, select the new foreign dictionary in the Custom Dictionaries dialog box. Then choose the appropriate language from the Language pop-up menu. Now Word will know to apply the correct spelling rules for that language.

Choosing custom dictionaries before spell-checking

From now on, before you check spelling, you can specify which custom dictionaries you want Word to consider as it pores over your document. To do so, choose Word→Preferences→Spelling and Grammar panel, and then choose a custom dictionary from the pop-up menu.

Exclude dictionaries

As noted earlier, you can't edit the built-in Word dictionary. The previous discussions guide you through *adding* words to Word's spelling wisdom—but how do you *delete* a word from the built-in dictionary? After all, as noted above, the main dictionary is a hermetically sealed, specially encoded, untouchable entity that you can't edit using any tool known to man.

The answer: by creating an *exclude dictionary.* This is a special kind of dictionary document format that stores the words that you want Word to flag as spelling errors. Whereas a custom dictionary "teaches" Word which words are spelled correctly, the exclude dictionary teaches Word what spellings are *wrong*, even though Word's main dictionary lists the spelling as correct.

For instance, say you prefer "focussed" to "focused." The second spelling, "focused," is the one that comes installed in Word. You should put the word "focused" into the exclude dictionary, so that Word will question that spelling during spell checks, giving you a chance to change it to "focussed."

To create an exclude dictionary, open a blank document. Type or paste in any standard spellings that you want Word to treat as errors. For instance, if you work for the Trefoil Theatre, you'll want to put "Theater" in the exclude dictionary. (The exclude dictionary is case-sensitive; if you want Word to flag both "focused" and "Focused," for instance, you'll have to type both versions into the dictionary.)

When your list of excluded spellings is complete, choose File→Save As. In the Save box, navigate to the System Folder→Preferences→Microsoft folder. Before saving, also do the following:

• Type a name for the exclude dictionary. "Exclude dictionary" is fine.

• Most importantly, you must choose a special format for this dictionary. In the Format pop-up menu, choose Speller Exclude Dictionary.

Click Save. You have to quit and relaunch Word for the exclude dictionary to take effect.

Five Ways to Type Less

At first glance, the Word window looks much like any computer screen. You type, and letters appear, just as in that classic Mac word processor, TextEdit. But there's actually much more to it than that. While you're typing, Word is constantly thinking, reacting, doing things to save you precious keystrokes.

As noted earlier, for example, Word corrects obvious spelling errors as you go along. But it also lets you create your own typing shortcuts, and even tries to anticipate your next formatting move, sometimes to the frustration of people who don't understand what the program's doing. The more you know what Word is thinking (it means well, it really does), the more you can let Word do the work, saving those precious brain cells for more important stuff—like writing.

Click and Type

Since the beginning of Word time, our screens have given us a continually blinking insertion point, located in the upper-left corner of the screen. That's where you typed, period. If you wanted to type in the middle of the page—for example, to create a title page of a report—you couldn't just click there and start typing. Instead, you had to take the ludicrously counterintuitive step of moving the insertion point over and down by tapping the Space bar, Tab key, or Return key until it was where you wanted it.

No more. The Click and Type feature lets you go directly to your desired spot on the page just by double-clicking. Here's how it works:

1. **Switch to Online view or Page Layout view.**

   These are the only views where Click and Type is available; choose from the View menu to change views.

2. **Move the cursor around on the blank page, letting it hover for a second at the point where you'd like to place some text.**

   In some cases, you'll see the cursor change to indicate that Word is about to provide some free formatting help. If your cursor is near the left or right margin, Word assumes that you want your text to be left- or right-aligned; you'll see tiny left- or right-justified lines appear next to the hovering insertion point (see Figure 2-12). When you hover in the middle of the page, the insertion-point icon changes to centered text. If your cursor is near the top or bottom of the page, the cursor changes shape again to illustrate that you're about to edit the document's *header* or *footer* (see page 193).

If Word guesses wrong about the alignment, you can always adjust the text alignment later using the Alignment and Spacing tools in the Formatting Palette (see page 121).

3. **Double-click.**

The insertion point turns into a standard blinking bar, and you're ready to begin typing. (If the insertion point doesn't end up quite where you wanted it, just double-click again.)

Note: Behind the scenes, Word actually fills the page with Tabs and Returns, exactly as you did manually in the old days; that's how it gets your insertion point to the spot where you double-clicked. Knowing that (or *seeing* that, by clicking the ¶ button on the Standard toolbar) makes troubleshooting or adjusting Click-and-Typed text much easier.

To turn Click and Type on and off, choose Word→Preferences→Edit panel. Check or uncheck the "Enable click and type" box.

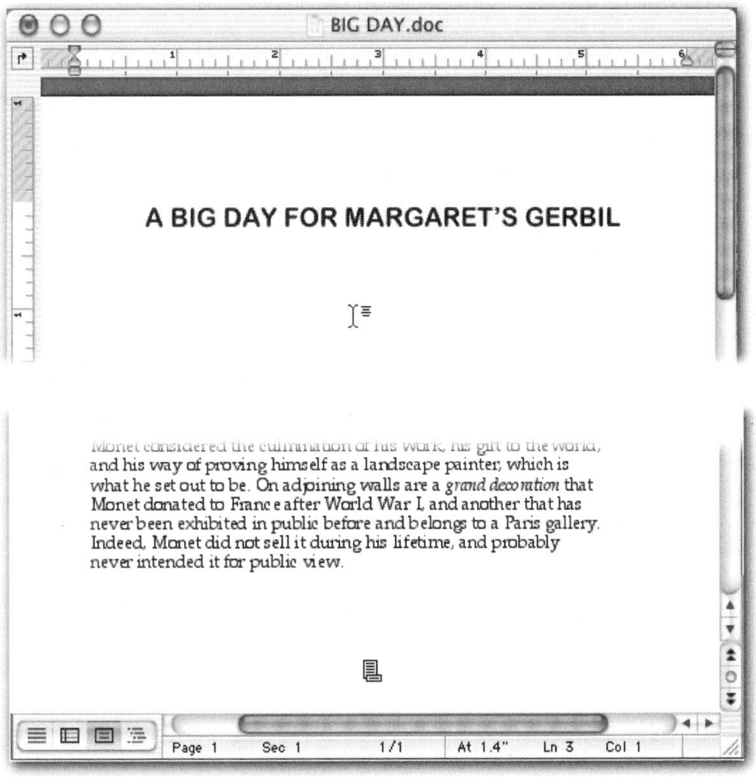

Figure 2-12:
Top: The Click and Type I-beam cursor is poised to click and type centered text.

Bottom: This special cursor appears to let you know that you're about to create a footer using Click and Type.

BIG DAY.doc

A BIG DAY FOR MARGARET'S GERBIL

Monet considered the culmination of his work, his gift to the world, and his way of proving himself as a landscape painter, which is what he set out to be. On adjoining walls are a *grand decoration* that Monet donated to France after World War I, and another that has never been exhibited in public before and belongs to a Paris gallery. Indeed, Monet did not sell it during his lifetime, and probably never intended it for public view.

Page 1   Sec 1   1/1   At 1.4"   Ln 3   Col 1

AutoCorrect

Word seems psychic at times. You type *teh,* and Word changes it to "the" before you even have a chance to hit Delete. You start to type the name of the month, and all of a sudden today's date pops up on the screen—and you didn't even know what day it was.

You're witnessing Word's AutoCorrect and AutoType features at work—two of the least understood and most useful tools in Word's arsenal. They can be frustrating if you don't understand them, and the writer's best friend if you do.

Think of AutoCorrect as Word's *substitution* feature. All it does is replace something you're typing (the typo) with a replacement that Word has memorized and stored (the correct spelling). The correction takes place as soon as you type a space after the incorrect word; no further action is required from you. And it happens so fast that you may not notice you've just been autocorrected unless you're watching for it.

Telling AutoCorrect to Shut Up

Sometimes Word is more diligent in correcting errors than you'd like. What if you're trying to type a letter to a Ms. Porvide, and Word changes it to Provide? Or maybe you work for a company called Intelligance, and you're tired of changing the "e" to an "a" every time Word helpfully "corrects" it.

You don't want to turn AutoCorrect off, because you want Word to catch all your *other* typos. And you could press ⌘-Z after Word makes each change, but that gets wearisome about the 35th time. Fortunately, there's a solution.

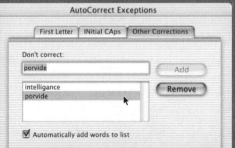

Click the Exceptions button on the AutoCorrect tab (see Figure 2-13). Then click the Other Corrections tab. Type your preferred spelling into the "Don't correct" text box and click Add. If you have many preferred spellings that you'll need to reeducate Word about, turn on the "Automatically add words to list" checkbox. Now, each time Word

makes an incorrect correction, click the Undo button on the Standard toolbar, choose Edit→Undo, or press ⌘-Z. *Intelligance* turns back into *Intelligance,* for example, and Word automatically adds your exceptional spelling to its AutoCorrect Exceptions list.

But you're not done yet, since the substitution pairs in the AutoCorrect dialog box (Figure 2-13) *override* the list in the Exceptions box. In other words, even though you've listed a preferred spelling as an exception, Word will still make the correction, and change *Porvide* to *Provide,* for example. The final step, then, is to *delete* the original AutoCorrect substitution pair. Choose Tools→AutoCorrect→AutoCorrect tab, scroll down until you find the offending correction pair, click to select it, and then click Delete. You may now Porvide to your heart's content.

Crucial Tip: If you retain one tip from this book's advice about Microsoft Word, remember this: *You can undo any automatic change Word makes,* under any circumstance, by pressing ⌘-Z or F1 just after Word makes it. That goes for automatic capitalization help, spelling help, formatting help, curly quote help, and anything else that seems to take place without your explicit command.

Word maintains a file of common misspellings and their corrections. That's why Word makes certain corrections and not others: not all possible error/correction combinations that you need come installed on the list. To see this list, choose Tools→AutoCorrect and click the AutoCorrect tab (Figure 2-13). (Here you'll also find the most important checkbox in the world of AutoCorrect: the master on/off switch, called "Replace text as you type.")

The first three checkboxes cover capitalization errors; they save you from the errant ways of your pinky fingers on the Shift keys. When the first two boxes are checked (see Figure 2-13), Word makes sure that you get a capital letter at the beginning of every sentence, whether you hold the Shift key down too long ("Correct TWo INitial CApitals") or not long enough ("Capitalize first letter of sentences").

Figure 2-13:
Feel free to add your own word combinations here, too. Put the "typo" in the Replace box, and the replacement version in the "With" box, then click Add. Think beyond typos, too—remember, you can make Word expand anything into anything. Make it replace int *with* Internet, *your initials with your full name, and so on.*

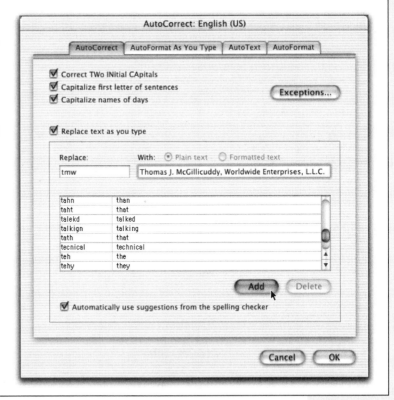

CHAPTER 2: EDITING IN WORD   **97**

Tip: Efficiency-addicted Word fans eventually stop capitalizing the first letters of sentences altogether. Word does it automatically, so why twist your pinkies unnecessarily?

If you turn on "Capitalize first letter of sentences," bear in mind that Word assumes every period is the end of a sentence. So why doesn't it auto-cap the first word after you type *U.N.* or *Jan.?* Because it's smart enough not to auto-cap after all-cap abbreviations (U.N.), and because it maintains a list of lowercase abbreviations that *shouldn't* be followed by capitals. (To see the list, choose Tools→AutoCorrect, then click Exceptions; you can add your own abbreviations to this list, too.)

If you turn on "Automatically use suggestions from the spelling checker," AutoCorrect will go above and beyond the list of substitution pairs in this dialog box. It will use Word's main dictionary as a guide to proper spelling and automatically change words that almost, but not quite, match ones in the dictionary. (When Word can't decide on a match, it simply squiggly-underlines the misspelled word in the document.)

AutoText: Abbreviation Expanders

AutoText is another Word feature that automatically changes what you've typed, once again delighting the expert and driving novices batty. In short, it's an abbreviation expander.

Figure 2-14 shows AutoText in action.

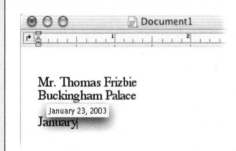

Figure 2-14:
You're typing along. Suddenly you see a floating yellow tooltip just above the insertion point. That's Word's AutoText feature in action. It's proposing a replacement for what you just typed—today's date, in this case. If you want to accept the suggestion, press Return or Enter; if not, just keep typing and pretend the tooltip never happened.

AutoText works by maintaining a preinstalled list of commonly typed terms and their replacements. You can also add your favorite terms to the list—the name of your company, your phone number, email address, and so on (see Figure 2-15). You can also add longer items—entire paragraphs, full addresses, lists, and even graphics, as described on page 101.

Setting up an AutoText entry

Word comes set up with dozens of ready-to-use AutoText entries; in fact, it's more powerful in Office X than in previous versions. It completes not only the names of days of the week and months of the year, but also today's date and names from your Entourage address book (see Chapter 10).

But the real joy of becoming an AutoText addict is creating your own abbreviations. You can use AutoText to save form letters or contracts that go on for pages and pages, and then dump them into your documents just by typing a few keys. If you're a lawyer, realtor, or medical professional who's not using AutoText to save time on boilerplate copy, you're missing out on a great timesaver.

To create a new entry, select a block of text (from a word or two to many paragraphs) and choose Insert→AutoText→New. (If the AutoText toolbar is visible—to make it so, choose View→Toolbars→AutoText—you can just click its New button.) Name your selection carefully; the name you choose is the abbreviation that will trigger the expansion. Choose something easy to remember, but not something that you might type unintentionally. Click OK.

Tip: If you've carefully formatted the copy that you want to use as AutoText—with different type styles and colors, for example—you can preserve that formatting no matter what the style of the document you eventually use it in. Click the Show/Hide button (a ¶ symbol) on the Standard toolbar or Formatting Palette. Now when you select the text, select the gray ¶ symbol at the very end along with it; the selection's formatting will come along into AutoText.

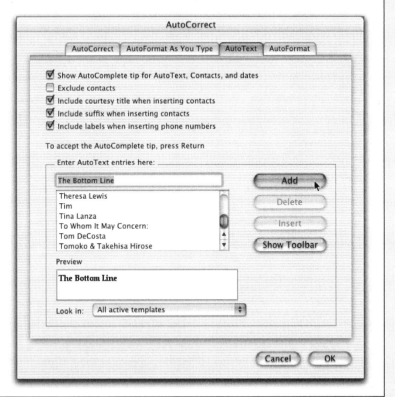

Figure 2-15:
This tab (Insert→AutoText→ AutoText tab, or Tools→ AutoCorrect→AutoText tab) is where you choose words, phrases, and fields to insert into your document without typing. You can also add your own items to the list by typing them into the "Enter AutoText entries here" box and clicking Insert. Select and click Delete to banish from your list any items you never use. You can also insert AutoText items into your document from this tab. Press the down arrow or Page down key to scroll down until your desired entry appears in the Preview box (you can also use the scroll bar). Hit Return to drop the entry into your document; it lands wherever your insertion point has been blinking.

Triggering AutoText entries

You can drop any item in the list into your document in one of two ways.

- **AutoComplete.** It doesn't get any less labor-intensive than this. When you type the first four letters of any word on the AutoText menu, AutoComplete, if turned on, shows you the full, expanded version in a pop-up tooltip (see Figure 2-14), hovering above the area where you're typing.

  To accept it, just hit Return; Word finishes the typing for you. If you don't want the choice that AutoComplete is offering, just keep typing (or hit Esc). If you inadvertently accept a completion that you didn't want, just press ⌘-Z to undo it. You can also choose Edit→Undo AutoComplete.

  There's little downside to leaving AutoComplete turned on; after all, you can ignore all of its tooltip suggestions, if you dislike the feature. But to turn off even these suggestions, you'll find the on/off switch by choosing Tools→AutoCorrect→ AutoText tab; it's the "Show AutoComplete tip for AutoText, Address Book Contacts and dates" box (see Figure 2-15).

- **Choosing from AutoText menu.** Choose Insert→AutoText. The current Auto-Text items are listed in the submenus that have arrows. (Any items you added yourself, as described in Figure 2-15, are under the Normal submenu.) Drag

---

POWER USERS' CLINIC

AutoText Toolbar

If you use AutoText frequently, or when you're first using Word X and adding lots of new entries, consider keeping the AutoText toolbar visible at all times. Choose View→ Toolbars→AutoText, or click Show Toolbar on the AutoText tab of the AutoCorrect dialog box (see Figure 2-15).

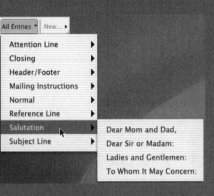

The first button on the toolbar, which looks like an A (representing text) and a mechanical cog-wheel (representing automation), calls up the AutoText tab, saving you several clicks.

All your AutoText entries are found under the All Entries menu, making them more easily accessible than the Insert→AutoText submenu.

The New button is usually grayed out. It's active only when you *select* a word, phrase, paragraph, or graphic. Clicking New brings up a dialog box where you can confirm, and name, your selection as a brand-new AutoText entry, never to be typed in full again. (The first four letters of the name entered here will trigger AutoComplete, so make sure to use the first four letters of what you want to type, or something equally easy to remember.)

---

through the submenus until you find the entry you want to avoid typing, and click it to drop it into your document. Your choice appears wherever you left your insertion point, and it inherits whatever text style and formatting is in place at that point.

AutoText graphics

Despite its name, AutoText can be used to automate more than just text. It can easily store frequently used graphics, as well. Create a drawing in Word (see Chapter 18), or paste a graphic from another program into a Word document—a logo that you've created in a drawing or painting program, your scanned signature, or a favorite photograph, for example. Click the graphic to select it, then choose Insert→AutoText→New (or click the New button on the AutoText tab or toolbar).

You can't insert an AutoComplete graphic by typing; to drop it into a document, you must choose its name from the Insert→AutoText submenu (or the AutoText toolbar).

AutoText fields

Some of the preinstalled AutoText entries are *fields*: placeholders that, when you print, Word fills in with the date, type, page number, and so on. Word lists them in the Header/Footer section of the AutoText submenu, because that's where you're most likely to use them.

For example, you can place a page number at the top of each page by putting a— *PAGE*—AutoText field in the header. To remind yourself (and everyone else) who wrote a particular document and when, place the "Author, Page #, Date" AutoText in the footer. (Word uses the name you entered when first setting up Office. To override that name, enter a different name in the Word→Preferences→User Information panel.)

POWER USERS' CLINIC

AutoText for Polyglots

If you have the English version of Office X, and you never type in any language other than English, this sidebar is not for you.

But suppose you're typing a letter to your lover in Paris, only to realize—*sacre bleu!*—that the entries listed in the AutoText tab of the AutoCorrect dialog box are in English, and will do you no good at all.

Not to worry. Instead of using the AutoText tab, use the submenus on the Insert→AutoText menu, or the All Entries menu on the AutoText toolbar. Those menus reflect the language *currently in effect at the insertion point,* while the list in the AutoCorrect box always reflects the language of the *version* of Word that you've purchased.

How does Word know which language you're typing in? You told it so by highlighting the foreign language text, choosing Tools→Language, and then selecting a language in the dialog box that appears next. So, before typing your letter to Jean-Marc, choose Tools→Language, select French in the list that appears and click OK. *Et voila!*—your choices on the AutoText submenus and AutoText tab are in French. (If you've already begun typing in French, be sure to select that text first. Otherwise, Word will think it's very poorly spelled English.)

Project Gallery Templates

A *template* is like Word stationery; it's a special kind of document with formatting and preferences options set the way you like them. A *wizard,* on the other hand, is Microsoft's term for a series of interview-style dialog boxes that request information from you and process your responses.

The templates in Office X's Project Gallery combine the two features, with the ultimate aim of, once again, saving you much of the grunt work of typing and formatting. Here's how you might use one of these template/wizard combos to create a business brochure:

1. **Choose File→Project Gallery.**

   The Project Gallery opens, as described on page 15. Except for Blank Documents and My Templates, all the categories in the list box at the left contain lists of built-in templates (see Figure 2-16).

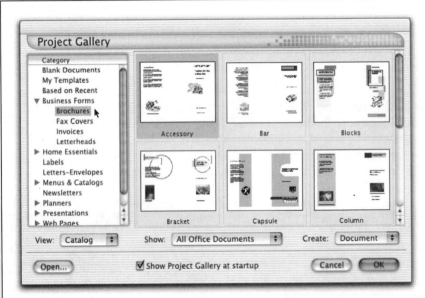

Figure 2-16:
Click the "flippy triangles" next to the categories to see a larger selection of templates. To see only the ones that work in Word, select "Word documents" from the Show pop-up menu at the bottom of the Project Gallery.

2. **Double-click Business Forms, then click Brochures.**

   Word displays a list of prefab brochure designs. (If you're not seeing the thumbnail images, make sure the View pop-up menu says Catalog.)

3. **Double-click the brochure design you want.**

   The template's wizard windows open. Some of the wizard fields may be already filled in, using information from the Word→Preferences→User Information tab or from the last template you used.

The Content tab collects information, such as your name and address, that will be inserted into corresponding fields in the template.

4. **Fill in the blanks; specify the tables or other elements you want in your finished brochure.**

As you make changes to the wizard, you can see them reflected in the new document window behind the wizard window. However, you can't click in or scroll the new document while the wizard remains open.

5. **Click the Layout tab to add a preformatted order form, price list, or one of the other professional brochure elements.**

In an advance over the Template Wizards in Office 2001, Word X anticipates some of the more complex features you're likely to include in a brochure. You can choose a table (such as an event schedule or price list) or form (such as an order form or sign-up form), as shown in Figure 2-17.

If you have the option of changing the color scheme, the wizard offers you a Theme & Color tab. (You do, in the case of the brochure.) If you like, click the tab and specify a different color scheme or graphic design theme.

6. **Click Save & Exit.**

The wizard closes. (If you click Cancel, the wizard closes, and everything that was in the template disappears, leaving a blank document.)

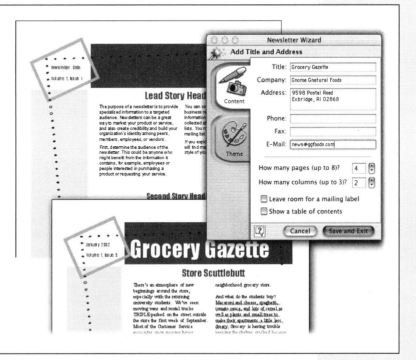

Figure 2-17:
Top left: A template is a canned Office document filled with "dummy" text. You could, if you wished, simply drag through it and replace it with new text of your own.

Top right: The Newsletter Wizard, on the other hand, presents a dialog box full of empty boxes (fields) to fill in, partially automating the process of replacing the template's text.

Bottom left: The template has turned into a meaningful document, with your own text substituted for what was previously in the template.

Finally, you arrive in your new document—a heavily formatted Word file, almost ready to print, but filled with dummy text and placeholder images. Although this dummy text isn't going to be around very long, it's worth a quick read. It contains advice and tips for your own writing (such as "This is a good place to briefly, but effectively, summarize your products or services").

If you've prepared your letter, newsletter or other text in another document, open that document and select the text. Choose Edit→Copy or press ⌘-C. Return to the template, select the prefab dummy text that you want to delete, and choose Edit→Paste or press ⌘-V. You may have to adjust the size of text boxes by clicking on them and dragging their handles.

AutoFormat

Has this happened to you?

- You type a numbered list, and suddenly the next number in sequence appears on its own.

- You type a Web address, and suddenly Word turns it into a blue, underlined, working hyperlink (that you can't edit, since clicking inside it opens your Web browser).

- You type an email smiley—which looks like :)—and Word, on its own, decides to replace your punctuation symbol with an actual graphic smiley face, like ☺.

- You start typing a letter, and Office Assistant Max offers to help. How did *he* know you're writing a letter—and how do you convince him that you're perfectly capable of formatting a letter on your own?

Tip: Remember: Just because Word steps in and formats something for you doesn't mean you're stuck with it. You don't even have to backspace over it; just press ⌘-Z or F1 (or choose Edit→Undo Automatic Change). Whatever it is that Word just did—making a smiley face, turning a URL into blue underlined text, numbering a list—is restored to the way you originally typed it.

All of these behaviors—considered helpful by Microsoft and unspeakably rude by many Word users—are triggered by a technology called AutoFormat. This tool doesn't have to be annoying. In fact, once you learn the workings behind AutoFormat, you can control and use it to your own advantage.

There are two ways to use AutoFormat: You can have Word autoformat words and paragraphs as you type them, or you can autoformat manually, in one pass, after the typing is complete.

Autoformatting as you type

To turn AutoFormat on and off, choose the Tools→AutoCorrect→AutoFormat As You Type tab. There they are: the master on/off switches for all of Word's meddlesome behavior (see Figure 2-18).

To turn AutoFormat off completely, uncheck *all* the boxes and click OK.

You should also turn AutoFormat off if your document is destined for plain text, or if you're going to paste and format it in a different program anyway. Also, be aware that curly quotes and bullets can turn into funny characters when pasted into an email. (They look fine in Entourage email, but your recipient's email program may not translate them properly. And borders don't work at all.) Later, you can turn the same plain text into a nicely formatted Word document by conducting a single AutoFormat pass, as described below.

There's a checkbox for each feature that Word can autoformat. Here's what each AutoFormat option does:

- **Headings.** If you type a short phrase and press Return, Word interprets it as a heading and applies a big, bold style (Heading 1) to it.

- **Borders.** Word draws a bold horizontal line across the page when you type three hyphens in a row (or three underlines) and press Return—a handy way to break up sections in a document, if that's indeed what you want.

  AutoFormat also creates a double line if you type three equal signs (===); a dotted line for asterisks (***); a wavy line for tildes (~~~); and a triple, picture frame-like line for number signs (###). (Press Return after the symbols.) Later, you can reformat the line or turn it into a full border by clicking in the paragraph and using the Borders and Shading tools on the Formatting Palette (page 130).

  The first time it makes the change, Word asks your permission. Click Yes. After that, Word will do it without asking.

- **Tables.** This feature lets you create Word tables (see page 165) by using typed characters instead of the Draw Table tool. Type a plus sign (+) to start the table, a row of hyphens (---) to set the width for the first cell, another + sign to end the cell, more hyphens, and so on. The line must begin and end with + signs. To

Figure 2-18:
There are two separate tabs in the AutoCorrect dialog box for the two different ways of using AutoFormat. This one, called AutoFormat As You Type; and the one on the far right, simply called AutoFormat.

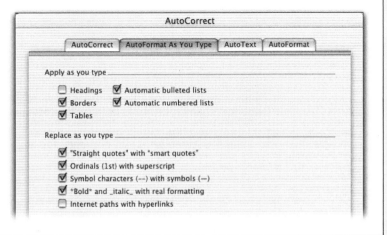

create the next line, click below this first row and start typing + signs and hyphens again. You can also switch to using Word's table tools to reformat or expand the table at any time.

Note: Because Word's table feature is so easy to use, it's hard to imagine why anyone would create a table using + signs and hyphens. The answer is that tables sent by email, as well as those posted on Web pages and newsgroups, *already* use this format. By pasting them into Word and performing an AutoFormat pass, you turn existing Internet tables into proper Word tables. Few people build a *fresh* table using this method.

- **Automatic bulleted lists.** When you type a common "bullet" character, such as *, -, >, or =>, and follow it with a space or a tab, then some text, and then press Return, Word changes the character to its proper bullet symbol (• or ➤, for example). It also switches to the ListBullet style in your document's template (page 202). When you type a return at the end of a line, Word continues with the next bullet. Press Return twice to end the list.

  You can also start a bulleted list by inserting a bullet of your choice. Choose Insert→Symbol (page 200) followed by *two* or more spaces and your first list item, then press Return. You can even use pictures as bullets; just choose Insert→Picture→Clip Art, and then click Web Bullets and Buttons in the Category pane. Now select a bullet by clicking it. (Keep them small; a graphic used as a bullet must be no more than one-and-a-half times the line height of your text.)

- **Automatic numbered lists.** When you type a number followed by a period (or a hyphen, close parenthesis, or close angle bracket [>]) and a space or tab, Word understands that you're starting a numbered list. After you press Return, Word automatically types the next number in the series and uses the ListNumber style (page 141) from your document's template. Pressing the Return key twice in a row instructs Word to end the list.

- **"Straight quotes" with "smart quotes."** When you type a quotation mark (Shift-apostrophe), Word replaces the double-apostrophe straight quotes with more attractive, typographically correct curly quotes.

  Most of the time, this is a useful option. If your document is going to be sent by email, however, turn this feature off. (See page 77 for details.)

- **Ordinals (1st) with superscript.** If you type "1st," Word instantly changes it to 1st.

- **Symbol characters (--) with symbols (—).** When you turn on this box, Word changes a single hyphen to an en dash–like this–and two hyphens to an em dash—like this. It's a handy feature, especially because the keystrokes for those dashes are so hard to remember (Option-hyphen and Shift-Option-hyphen, respectively.)

Tip: Grammatically speaking, an en dash is used to indicate a range or gap in a sequence ("The poetry reading went from 6:30 p.m.–11:00 p.m., and featured a reading from pages 23–142 of *Letters My Father Never Wrote Me*"). The em dash is the real dash, which indicates a pause for impact ("I can't stand readings–especially poetry").

- ***Bold* and _italic_ with real formatting.** When Word encounters words bounded by asterisks and underscores, it changes them to boldface and italics, respectively.

  You may already be familiar with the use of asterisks and underscores for emphasis on the Internet. For the same reason, you can use this feature during a final AutoFormat pass (see below) to reformat text you've copied from an email or chat room. (Few people use this feature *while typing;* it's easier to press ⌘-B for bold. Most people use it only when massaging text from the Internet.)

- **Internet paths with hyperlinks.** When this box is checked, Word changes URLs that you type (*www.msn.com,* for instance) into working hyperlinks. Hyperlinks are usually formatted in blue and underscored, unless you change these settings in the Format→Style dialog box (see page 300).

- **Format beginning of list item like the one before it.** This option combines automation with the freedom of doing your own formatting.

  For example, suppose you want to start each item in your list with a Roman numeral, followed by a space, followed by the first word in bold, followed by a period and the rest of the sentence in plain text. To begin, type the first item that way and press Return. Word asks if your intention is to start a numbered list. Click Yes and continue. Word starts a new list item every time you hit Return. Press Return twice to end the list.

  The key is to start the first item with a number or bullet to let Word know that you're starting a list. If you want the first word or words to appear in, for example, bold (like the first sentences in this bulleted list), you must follow it with a period, colon, hyphen, dash, or other punctuation mark.

- **Define styles based on your formatting.** Here's the most powerful option on the AutoFormat tab. It tells Word to update the document's styles (see page 141), based on the formatting done directly in the document. For example, if you change your first heading to 14-point Helvetica Bold, Word applies that font to *all* occurrences of that style; you've just redefined the style, in fact. This option *overrides* any formatting you've done in the Styles dialog box, so use it with caution.

Tip: AutoFormat "cues" can be memorized for other autoformat options, too (in addition to using asterisks for bold and underlines for italic). For instance, if you frequently make bulleted lists, try to get in the habit of typing an asterisk for a bullet, knowing that Word will automatically change it to •.

To see the list of Word's autoformatting cues, type *formatting automatically* into the Search box of Word's Help window or the Assistant's Help balloon. Click Search. In the resulting list of links, click "Results of formatting a document automatically." The resulting Help window contains a table correlating what you type with Word's automatic replacements. Peruse this table and memorize the characters to type for your favorite kinds of borders, bullets, and so on. You can now format complex documents without ever reaching for the mouse.

AutoFormatting in one pass

Even if you don't like Word making changes as you type, you can still benefit from AutoFormat—by running your finished document through what you might call its AutoFormat-O-Matic. For instance, you can take text that uses the Internet style for *bold* and _italic_ and have Word change them into proper **boldface** and *italics*. AutoFormat can also clean up a document by changing URLs into live hyperlinks or adding attractive bullets to lists, all at once.

First, choose Tools→AutoCorrect→AutoFormat As You Type and turn off all the boxes; now Word won't make any of these corrections *during* your typing.

When you're ready to AutoFormat, click the AutoFormat tab; the checkboxes here correspond, for the most part, to those described above. You're offered only a couple of new ones here. They are as follows:

- **Other Paragraphs.** Ordinarily, Word's AutoFormat feature applies a Heading style to whatever it recognizes as a heading, and a List style to anything it recognizes as a list. But if you turn on this option, Word also applies other styles when autoformatting. For example, Word can format plain text to your default Body Text font and paragraph style.

  Word does this by comparing the text in the document to the styles in your Normal template (see page 202) and automatically applying the closest matching style. If this box is checked and the document appears to be a letter, Word also applies letter features such as Inside Address.

- **Preserve Styles.** Turn on this box if you've already done some formatting of your own in the document *before* starting the AutoFormat pass. Word won't change the style of any text you've manually formatted.

When you click OK, you won't notice any changes in your document; all you've done is specify what will happen when Word *does* conduct its editorial pass through your document. To trigger that event, choose Format→AutoFormat. Choose a document type from the pop-up menu—General document, Letter, or Email—which tells Word what kind of document it's going to be autoformatting. For instance, if the document is a letter, Word knows to apply letter styles such as Inside Address and Closing. If you choose Email, Word eliminates formatting options that usually don't work in email, such as first-line indents. (Clicking Options returns you to the AutoFormat tab described above.)

If you choose "AutoFormat and review each change," Word opens a dialog box that shows each change Word is about to make; you can choose to accept or reject it. If you choose "AutoFormat now," Word goes through the document and prepares all autoformatting changes without pausing. Even so, you have a second chance to click Review Changes at the end, or to accept or reject all Word's changes outright. You can also click Style Gallery to apply one of Word's document templates (see page 202), with all its colors and fonts, to the finished document.

Formatting in Word

Formatting is the part of word processing that lets you loosen up and have a little fun. You can dress up your bland 12-point Times with any typeface you choose—bold or italic for emphasis, color for variety, borders around certain paragraphs, and so on.

It's important to understand that Word offers independent formatting controls for each of four entities: *characters* (individual letters and words), *paragraphs* (anything you've typed that's followed by a press of the Return key), *sections* (similar to chapters, as described on page 137), and the entire *document*. Attributes like bold and italic are *character* formatting; line spacing and centering are *paragraph* attributes; page numbering is done on a *section-by-section* basis; and margin settings are considered *document* settings. Understanding these distinctions will help you know where to look to achieve a certain desired effect.

The Formatting Palette

The Formatting Palette, which debuted in Office 2001 and received a complete overhaul for Office X, puts Word's most common formatting commands within easy reach. It opens when you first open a Word document. If it's been hidden, you can bring it back by choosing View→Formatting Palette or clicking the Formatting Palette button on the Standard toolbar; both methods alternately hide and show the palette.

The options on the Formatting Palette change depending on what you're doing. When you click a photo or drawing, for example, the palette changes to show the tools you need to work with graphics. Most of the time, however, the Formatting Palette displays the commands you most frequently need to work with fonts, paragraph formatting, and other elements of text.

Note: In Office 2001, you could navigate around the Formatting Palette using the Tab key. (By pressing Shift-⌘-F to highlight the Font menu, using the arrow keys to select a font, and then tabbing down to the Size menu, for example, you could keyboard your way through the entire Formatting Palette.) Unfortunately, Microsoft no longer provides this feature in Office X.

Some of the keystrokes still work, such as the Font trick mentioned above, and Shift-⌘-S to highlight the Style menu. And, of course, you can still use the keystrokes for Bold (⌘-B), Italic (⌘-I), and so on. The buttons on the Formatting Palette respond accordingly.

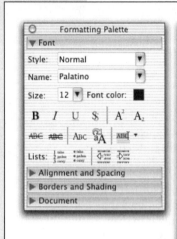

Figure 3-1:
In Word X, almost every conceivable formatting control resides in a single convenient window, a jam-packed command center called the Formatting Palette (shown here in two different states of expansion). Clicking the close button makes the Formatting Palette genie back into its toolbar button in true Mac OS X fashion.

Character Formatting

The Font panel of the Formatting Palette—the one that's open the first time you use the Formatting Palette—deals mostly with what your letters, numbers, and other characters look like.

Choosing Fonts

Installing Office X adds about 50 fonts to your Library→Fonts folder—an unannounced gift from Microsoft.

To change the font of text you've already typed, select the text first, using any of the methods described on page 59. If you choose a new font in the middle of a sentence or even the middle of a word, the new font will take effect with the next letter you type.

Now, open the Font menu to reveal your Mac's typeface names in their own typefaces (a Mac-only feature). This what-you-see-is-what-you-get (WYSIWYG) fonts feature has a few ramifications, such as:

- If you have a very long list of fonts, you don't have to scroll all the way down to, say, Zapf Chancery. Once the menu (or Formatting Palette pop-up list) is open, you can *type* the first letter or two of the target font. The menu shifts instantly to that alphabetical position in the font list.

Figure 3-2:
Top left: When you pick from the Font menu, you get to see what each font looks like.

Top right: If you use the Formatting Palette to choose a font, the fonts you've used most recently are conveniently grouped together at the top.

Bottom: The Font dialog box (Format→Font or ⌘-D). Not only are there more font style options here than in the Formatting Palette, you also receive a preview at the bottom of the box. If you like what you see, click OK.

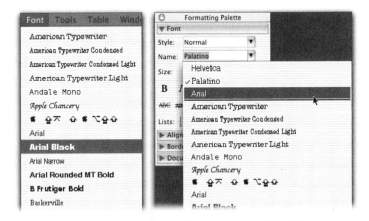

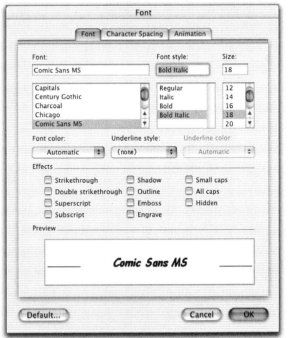

Note: You can still press the arrow keys to select a different font once the menu is open, but power users can no longer highlight a font's name in the menu by typing the first couple letters of its name. Microsoft promises to fix this bug—someday. (Service Release 1, discussed on page 12, does *not* fix this bug.)

- You can open the font list faster if you *don't* use the WYSIWYG fonts feature. Pressing Shift before opening the Font menu or Fonts list in the Formatting Palette allows you to see all the fonts listed in plain type.

  This is also the solution for the person trying to figure out the name of a font that shows up as symbols. (You can turn off the WYSIWYG feature for good by choosing Word→Preferences→General panel and turning off "WYSIWYG font and style menus," then clicking OK.)

Note: You may find that turning off WYSIWYG font menus turns off WYSIWYG only in the Formatting Palette and toolbar Font menus. The Font menu in the bar remains WYSIWYG until you quit and relaunch Word. Service Release 1, as described on page 12, fixes this glitch.

- Once you've turned off WYSIWYG font menus, you can still summon the WYSIWYG font when you *do* want it by pressing Shift before opening one of the Font menus.

Even the Formatting Palette doesn't offer every possible font manipulation tool; for that, you'll need the Font dialog box, as shown in Figure 3-2. To open it, choose Format→Font or press ⌘-D. In the following pages, you'll read about both the Formatting Palette and the more complete controls available in the Font dialog box.

Font Sizes

Font sizes are measured in points. A point is 1/72 of an inch in letter height, but you don't need to know that; what you *should* know is that most text is printed at 10- or 12-point sizes.

Some fonts (New York) look too large at 12 point. Other fonts (Times and Times New Roman) are almost uncomfortably small at 10 point. Print a test page to be sure, since the font size may look different on paper than on the screen, depending on your monitor's resolution. (If you have a high-resolution monitor, your tendency will be to make the font too large in order to achieve a comfortable size to read on the screen. Rather than increasing the font size, use the Zoom box (page 36) to make sure your font will print out in a proper size.)

To select a font size, choose one from the list in the Formatting Palette, type a size into the Size box in the Formatting Palette, or choose a point size in the Font dialog box (Format→Font or ⌘-D).

Tip: You can always bump selected text to a slightly higher or lower point size by pressing Shift-⌘-> (that is, period) or Shift-⌘-< (comma) for larger and smaller type, respectively. Each time you press the combination, the text grows or shrinks by the intervals listed in the Formatting Palette's Size box (from 12 to 14 to 16, for example).

Styles of Type

You can apply different type styles to your regular, unembellished font for emphasis or effect. Most font styles are available in the Formatting Palette with a single click; a few extra ones reside in the "Font style" box in the Font dialog box (see Figure 3-2). Those type styles, as they appear in the Font dialog box, are as follows:

• **Regular** denotes plain, unadulterated text. Not bolded, not underlined.

Tip: You can return to plain text at any time without even opening the Font dialog box. Just highlight the text you've been playing with in your document and choose Edit→Clear→Formats or Clear Formatting from the Style menu in the Formatting Palette (*Keyboard shortcut:* Shift-⌘-N).

The Clear Formatting command, however, takes you all the way back to the Normal *style* (see page 141), which generally means your 12-point body type. To strip font effects from selected text without changing its underlying style definition (such as 24-point Futura for a headline), press Control-Space bar instead.

• **Italic** is commonly used for foreign words and phrases. Also italicize the titles of books, movies, and magazines. *Shortcuts:* Click the capital I in the Formatting Palette, or press ⌘-I.

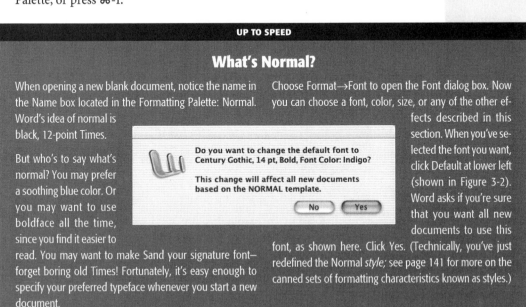

UP TO SPEED

What's Normal?

When opening a new blank document, notice the name in the Name box located in the Formatting Palette: Normal. Word's idea of normal is black, 12-point Times.

But who's to say what's normal? You may prefer a soothing blue color. Or you may want to use boldface all the time, since you find it easier to read. You may want to make Sand your signature font— forget boring old Times! Fortunately, it's easy enough to specify your preferred typeface whenever you start a new document.

Choose Format→Font to open the Font dialog box. Now you can choose a font, color, size, or any of the other effects described in this section. When you've selected the font you want, click Default at lower left (shown in Figure 3-2). Word asks if you're sure that you want all new documents to use this font, as shown here. Click Yes. (Technically, you've just redefined the Normal *style;* see page 141 for more on the canned sets of formatting characteristics known as styles.)

Do you want to change the default font to Century Gothic, 14 pt, Bold, Font Color: Indigo?

This change will affect all new documents based on the NORMAL template.

No   Yes

- **Bold** is the most common way of making a single word or phrase stand out from the surrounding landscape. Use bold for emphasis. *Shortcuts:* Click the capital B in the Formatting Palette, or press ⌘-B.

- **Bold Italic** is a beautiful effect for headings and headlines. Use either method described above to choose both bold and italic, one right after the other. You'll know you've got it when both the B and the I are highlighted in the Formatting Palette. In the Font dialog box, just choose Bold Italic.

- **Underline.** Clicking the underlined U in the Formatting Palette, or pressing ⌘-U (Shift-⌘-D for a double underline), draws a line under the text, as well as the spaces between words. In the Font dialog box, use the "Underline style" pop-up menu to choose from a number of fancy underscores, and to specify whether you want Word to underline the words only, not the spaces.

You can also choose a color for the underline itself in the Font dialog box; see the next section for more detail.

Typing in Color

Color is a great way to liven up your documents—an increasingly valuable option in a world where many documents are read onscreen.

Click the tiny "Font color" color swatch or pop-up menu in the Formatting Palette or the Format→Font dialog box to survey your selection of 40 colors, as shown in Figure 3-3. To choose a color, just click it.

Tip: When using Word to prepare a document for the Web, remember that colors look different on different computers. For example, someone viewing your page on a Windows machine or an older monitor may see your true colors very differently.

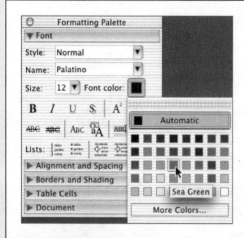

Figure 3-3:
Word has helpful (and occasionally creative) pop-up labels for all colors in the palette. To choose from a broader rainbow, click the More Colors button. Doing so opens the Apple Color Picker dialog box, which offers several different ways to specify any color under the sun, as described on page 651.

Special Text Effects

Bold and italic offer enough variety for most documents, but many more buttons await in the Formatting Palette, and still more choices in the Font dialog box. Some of them, such as Outline and Shadow, are clearly just for show (they usually look amateurish in printed documents); others, such as Subscript and All Caps, are invaluable tools.

Here are the options, in order, as they appear in the Font dialog box:

- **Strikethrough** and **Double strikethrough** indicate that something's crossed out, but you don't want to delete it outright. (Word's change-tracking feature adds strikethrough style to deleted text automatically; see page 185.) *Shortcuts:* Click the ~~ABC~~ or ABC buttons on the Formatting Palette.

- **Superscript** and **Subscript** shift characters slightly higher or lower (respectively) than the other text on its line and slightly decreases their size—perfect for chemical formulas and exponents. (You don't need these effects for footnotes; Word handles footnote formatting automatically, as described on page 197.)

  You can make letters or symbols super- or subscripted, too, not just numbers—very handy if you like taking things to the Nth degree. *Shortcuts:* Click the A^2 or A_s in the Formatting Palette, or press ⌘-= for Subscript or Shift-⌘-= for Superscript.

- **Shadow** and **Outline** reverse the color of the type, making the letter white and the outline black (or whatever text color you're using). Shadow creates a heavier outline that makes the words appear slightly raised. Both were popular when the Mac first appeared, but seem dated nowadays. *Shortcut:* For Shadow, click the shadowed capital S on the Formatting Palette; there's no shortcut for Outline.

- **Emboss** and **Engrave** make letters appear slightly raised or carved out, as if with a chisel. They work best on a colored background, such as on a Web page. On a white background, the words gain a subtle drop shadow. (These infrequently used effects are available only in the Font dialog box, not on the Formatting Palette.)

Small Caps, All Caps

Word offers several variations on the when-to-capitalize scheme you probably learned in English class. For example, you can apply either of these formats to text you've highlighted (or are about to type):

- **Small Caps** creates a formal look for headings and letterheads; all the letters are capped, but "lowercase" letters are shown in smaller capitals, Something Like This. *Shortcut:* Click the ABC button on the Formatting Palette.

- **All Caps** simply converts highlighted text to all capital letters. You can choose "All caps" in the Font dialog box, or click the a→A button in the Formatting Palette.

  Even though the visual result is the same, there's a big difference between using the All Caps style and simply typing some words with the Caps Lock key down.

Text you've formatted as All Caps is still, in Word's brain, actually mixed upper- and lowercase letters. It thinks you've applied the all-cap format just as a visual, the way you'd apply bold or blue or underlining. That is, by turning off the All Caps style, the text reverts to the capitalization you originally used when typing it—something you can't say about text you typed with the Caps Lock key.

You can therefore search for text in the All Caps style using the Find and Replace command, or define it as part of a *style* (see page 141).

Tip: To change the capitalization of words you've already typed—or to fix an email message that arrived IN ALL CAPITAL LETTERS—highlight the text and then choose Format→Change Case. By choosing from the list in the Change Case dialog box, you can make Word instantly "retype" the text as all lowercase (all small letters), all uppercase (all caps), Sentence case (where the first letter of every sentence is capitalized, as usual), or Title Case (where the first letter of every word is capped).

(Unfortunately, these options aren't terrifically smart; Sentence case still leaves names and the word *I* lowercase, and Title Case doesn't leave small words like *of* and *the* lowercase.)

The most interesting choice here is tOGGLE cASE, which reverses the existing capitalization, whatever it may be.

POWER USERS' CLINIC

Drop Caps

Have you ever wished you could duplicate those extra-large capitals that start the chapters of so many books (like this one)? Unfortunately, just enlarging the point size of the first letter doesn't work. True *drop caps,* as they're called, are not only large, but they drop *below* the other letters on the line; hence the name.

But Word X can do it. After typing the first paragraph of your chapter, choose Format→Drop Cap. Choose one of the drop-cap styles, then adjust the Options settings (font,

number of lines to drop down, and distance from text) until you've got the look you like. When you click OK, Word sends you into Page Layout view—if you weren't there already—where the drop cap appears as an independent graphic box that you can enlarge or drag as you would any graphic (see Chapter 18).

If you return to Normal view, you won't see the drop cap in its correct position; that's perfectly normal.

Hidden Text

Word's Hidden Text feature can remove your personal notes and reminders from plain sight in a document. You can make the hidden text reappear only when you want to; you can also choose whether or not you want it to show up when printed.

To turn certain text invisible, first select it. Choose Format→Font→Font tab. (There's no button for hidden text on the Formatting Palette.) Turn on the Hidden box and click OK; the text disappears until you choose to show it. (To turn hidden text back into normal text, show the hidden text as described next, select it, choose Format→Font→Fonts tab, and turn off the Hidden box.)

When you want Word to display the text you've designated as hidden, use either of these techniques:

- Choose Word→Preferences→View tab. Turn on "Hidden text" and click OK.

- Click the Show/Hide button (¶) on the Standard toolbar (or the Document section of the Formatting Palette).

Either way, hidden text appears with a dotted underline to distinguish it from the rest of the text.

Tip: Whether or not hidden text *prints* is up to you. To print hidden text along with the rest of the document, choose Word→Preferences, click the Print button, turn on the Include with Document→Hidden text box, and click OK.

Lists

If you're in the business world, or even the business of organizing your thoughts, you can't get far without using numbered or bulleted lists.

Bulleted lists are an attractive way of presenting little nuggets of information. Here, for example, is a bulleted list that illustrates how useful they can be:

- Each paragraph is indented from the left margin (like this one) and is preceded by a *bullet* (the round dot shown at left).

- You can always create a numbered list by typing a number at the beginning of each line, but it won't be nicely indented.

- You may know how to create a bullet (•) at the beginning of every line by using the keyboard shortcut Option-8. But again, that won't produce the clean left margin on your bulleted paragraphs.

- Furthermore, creating lists manually can get messy. For example, inserting an item between two existing ones in a numbered list requires some serious renumbering. And if you want your list indented, you'll have to fiddle with the indent controls quite a bit.

Word has partially automated the process. A quick way to start a numbered or bulleted list is to click one of the list icons on the Formatting Palette (next to where it says Lists). Word promptly indents the paragraph containing the insertion point and adds a bullet (or the number 1). Even the indenting is perfect: The second and following lines of a list item start under the first letter, not all the way back to the left margin. To start a new list item, just hit Return. When you're finished building the list, press Return once more and then click the same icon in the Formatting Palette a second time.

If you create a *numbered* list this way, Word does the numbering automatically as you go. Better yet, if you insert a new list item between two others, Word knows enough to renumber the entire list.

When you click one of the list icons in the Formatting Palette, a new palette segment labeled Bullets and Numbering appears directly below, complete with its own flippy triangle (see Figure 3-4).

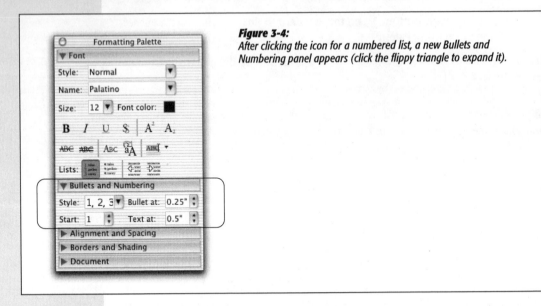

Figure 3-4:
After clicking the icon for a numbered list, a new Bullets and Numbering panel appears (click the flippy triangle to expand it).

Each of the four pop-up menus in the Bullets and Numbering panel controls a different aspect of how your list will look (the *entire* list, no matter which individual list line contains your insertion point).

- **Style** specifies the kind of numbering (Arabic numerals, roman numerals, and so on), or the size and shape of the bullet.
- **Start at** tells Word what number to start the list with.
- **Bullet at** tells Word, in inches, how far from the left margin to set the bullet.
- **Text at** tells Word, in inches, how far to indent the words from the left margin. It must always be a larger number than "Bullet at."

You can also adjust the indents by clicking the indent left and indent right icons on the Formatting Palette, which are right next to the list icons.

Extra Features in the Bullets and Numbering Dialog Box

The Formatting Palette is great for quickly designing a list, but the Bullets and Numbering dialog box offers even more options. Open it by choosing Format→Bullets and Numbering (see Figure 3-5).

Customizing a bulleted list

Bulleted lists as delivered by the Formatting Palette are fine, but there may come a day when simple black, round bullets just don't cut it for the radical new-age business plan you're writing up. In such cases, click the Bulleted tab in the Bullets and

Numbering dialog box. If one of the styles appeals to you, choose it by clicking; then click Customize to open the dialog box shown at bottom in Figure 3-5. Watch what happens in the Preview box as you make changes.

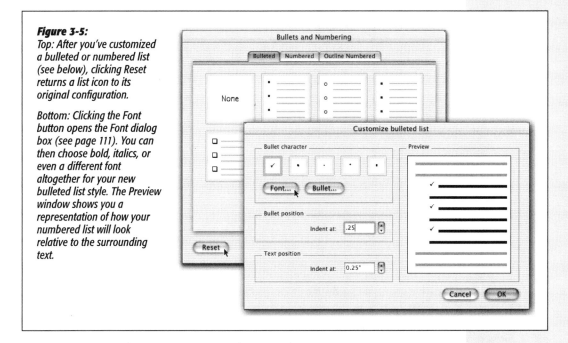

Figure 3-5:
Top: After you've customized a bulleted or numbered list (see below), clicking Reset returns a list icon to its original configuration.

Bottom: Clicking the Font button opens the Font dialog box (see page 111). You can then choose bold, italics, or even a different font altogether for your new bulleted list style. The Preview window shows you a representation of how your numbered list will look relative to the surrounding text.

- **Bullet character.** Choose an alternate bullet symbol, or click the Bullet button to open the Symbol dialog box (see page 200), where you can choose any character in any font to become your new bullet.

- **Bullet position.** The indentation point of the bullet is measured from the left margin.

- **Text position.** The text indentation is also measured from the left margin. It's usually indented farther than the bullet; note how, in Figure 3-5, the text position indent is a larger number than the bullet position one.

Click OK to return to the Bullets and Numbering dialog box. The bulleted list style now appears as one of the eight list icons (see Figure 3-5), easily accessible if you want to use the same style of bulleting later in the document. Click OK again to apply the new bulleted style to the current paragraph.

Customizing a numbered list

Like the Bulleted tab, the Numbered tab in the Bullets and Numbering dialog box presents a selection of eight preconfigured list styles (one of which is None). Click the one that suits your purposes, or at least comes the closest. Click Customize to open a dialog box much like the one at the bottom of Figure 3-5—but this one, of course, applies to numbers:

- **Number format.** You can't edit the number or numeral shown here; it's determined by your choices in the "Number style" and "Start at" tools. You can, however, type additional text into this window, such as the words *Figure, Item,* or *Commandment*—whichever word you want to appear before the number in each list item.

- **Number style.** This pop-up menu lets you choose Arabic or roman numerals, letters (*A, B, C,* and so on), or even words (*First, Second,* and so on).

- **Start at.** Usually, you'll start at 1, but you can also start at 0 or any other number by entering it in the box or choosing it with the arrows.

- **Number position.** Choosing Left, Right, or Centered from the pop-up menu aligns the number relative to the space between "Aligned at" and "Indent at."

- **Aligned at.** This is the distance from the left margin to the numbered item. For instance, if you choose Left from the number position menu and .5" for "Aligned at," the number itself will be placed half an inch from the left margin.

- **Text position.** This is the distance from the left margin to the text part of the numbered item. The larger you make this measurement, the farther from the number the text begins.

Click OK to return to the Bullets and Numbering dialog box; the custom numbered list style now appears as one of the eight list icons (see Figure 3-5). Click OK again to apply the new numbered style to the current paragraph.

GEM IN THE ROUGH

Picture Bullets

There are a host of bullets preinstalled in Word, both in the Bullets and Numbering dialog box and in the Symbol dialog box, as described on page 200. For added creativity, insert a *picture bullet,* as in the example shown here.

To do so, choose Format→ Bullets and Numbering→ Bulleted tab. Click Picture. Now you can choose any graphics file on your Mac; Word starts you off with a folder full of its own preinstalled picture bullets. Choose one of those to add the selected picture as a bullet to the current paragraph. Otherwise, navigate to your own picture file (something you've scanned, drawn, or downloaded

from a Web site, perhaps), select the file in the list box, and click Insert.

More often than not, the typical picture will be unreasonably large for a bullet. Click to select it and drag the resize handles (at its corners) to make it smaller. In fact, you can actually edit the picture right within Word; see Chapter 18 for full detail on Word's picture tools.

It may sound like a lot of work, but you only have to do it once. When you press Return to make another list item, Word automatically continues using the edited picture bullet.

- Run, don't walk, to the closest emergency exit.
- Breathe through your nose.
- Yell softly into your shirt.

Tip: If there's more than one numbered list in your document—if you're writing, say, a book about Office X that contains many numbered tutorials—you'll need a way to make the numbering start over at 1 for the second list. (Otherwise, Word will cheerfully keep your number sequence going all the way through a document.)

To tell Word to start over, click the first item in the *second* list and choose Format→Bullets and Numbering. Click the radio button for "Restart numbering," or press ⌘-R. ("Continue previous list" gives the list item the next number in the series, no matter how many pages have elapsed since the first part of the list.) Click OK.

Paragraph Formatting

The lower half of the Formatting Palette pertains mostly to settings that affect entire *paragraphs.* Just as the Formatting Palette's top section offers the most useful controls of the Format→Font dialog box, its second section offers a subset of the Format→Paragraph dialog box (Figure 3-6).

And just as character formatting applies *either* to highlighted text *or* to text you're about to type, paragraph formatting applies to only a selected paragraph (the one containing the blinking insertion point), several selected paragraphs, or the paragraph you're about to type (from the insertion point's location).

Figure 3-6:
Left: The Paragraph dialog box offers dozens of controls that apply to the selected paragraphs.

Right: The expanded Formatting Palette reveals the most useful controls. For example, the controls at the bottom of this panel are a quick way to change indents.

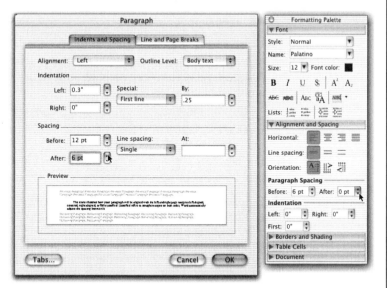

Alignment and Spacing

When you click the flippy triangle next to Alignment and Spacing, the Formatting Palette almost doubles in size (Figure 3-6, right). All the commands here pertain to how your text lies on the page.

Horizontal

These icons illustrate how your paragraph will be aligned with the left and right page margins: left aligned, centered, right aligned, or fully justified. (*Justified* refers to straight margins on both sides. Word automatically adjusts the spacing between letters and words to make the right margin come out even, exactly like a newspaper. Justification works best if you turn on hyphenation, too, as described on page 153.)

You may find yourself changing alignment frequently when writing something like a newsletter, in which it's common to go from a centered headline to a left-aligned article to a justified column of classified ads. Fortunately, alignment is fully equipped with keyboard shortcuts: ⌘-R right-aligns the current paragraph, ⌘-L is for left alignment, ⌘-E centers the current line or paragraph, and ⌘-J justifies the current paragraph.

Line spacing

Word's factory setting is for single-spaced lines, like the ones in this book. If you like more space between lines, or if you're required to use double-spacing for school-work or legal work, use these icons to change the spacing. The three line-spacing controls on the Formatting Palette correspond to single-spaced, one-and-a-half-spaced, and double-spaced text.

Choosing Format→Paragraph→Indents and Spacing tab (Option-⌘-M) generates even more spacing options. As shown in Figure 3-6, you can choose a setting from the pop-up menu under "Line spacing" and, to get even more specific, type an exact number in the At box.

- **At least.** Choose this setting to add graphics or vary font sizes within a paragraph. In the box, type a minimum number of points (12 is a good size for single spacing); Word will automatically adjust the spacing to accommodate any larger items in a line.

Tip: Here's a trick you can use in this or any Office X measurement text box: You don't have to be content with *points* as the units. After typing the number you want, type *cm, mm, in,* or *pi* for centimeters, millimeters, inches, or picas, respectively. The software makes the conversion automatically. (You can also change the proposed measurement value by choosing Word→Preferences→General panel and using the "Measurement units" pop-up menu.)

- **Exactly.** Choose this setting for projects where you've been asked to use a specific line spacing in points. Enter the number of points in the box. (If any letters or pictures are too high for the spacing you've specified, they'll simply be decapitated.)

- **Multiple.** Use this setting to refine the double-single-triple spacing system. For instance, choosing Multiple and entering *1* in the At box denotes single spacing. Typing *1.3* in the At box tells Word to increase single-spacing by 30 percent. Specifying *3* in the At box creates triple spacing.

Finally, you can change line spacing using the keyboard: ⌘-1 tells Word to single-space the current paragraph, ⌘-5 is for one-and-a-half space (1.5, that is), and ⌘-2 results in double-spacing.

Orientation

The Orientation icons on the Formatting Palette aren't actually paragraph-specific, like the other controls in their section. In fact, they work very differently depending on what you're editing:

- In a table cell, they rotate the text in the selected cell (see page 157).

- If you've divided your document into sections (page 137), you can use one of these icons to rotate *entire pages* within a document—to get a couple of horizontally oriented (landscape) pages in a document whose pages are otherwise oriented vertically (portrait). Here's the trick: Before using the Orientation controls, insert a "Section Break (Next Page)" break before and after the pages you want rotated (page 137).

- If your document has neither tables nor section breaks, these icons rotate your *entire window* by 90 or 180 degrees. They don't affect how the document is *printed*; for that purpose, use the Orientation icons in the File→Page Setup dialog box. Instead, this feature rotates the image of your document on the screen to make it easier for you to edit the *text* that you've rotated 90 degrees, such as the vertical label of a table cell.

POWER USERS' CLINIC

Windows, Orphans, and Paragraph Relationships

Ordinarily, when your text reaches the bottom of the page, Word chops a paragraph in half, if necessary, so that it continues on the top of the next page. The result isn't always especially good-looking, however; it may leave what publishers call a *widow* (the last line of a paragraph at the top of a new page) or an *orphan* (the first line of a paragraph all by itself at the bottom of a page). You can avoid these problems by highlighting a paragraph (or paragraphs), choosing Format→Paragraph→Line and Page Breaks tab, and turning on "Widow/Orphan control." This control instructs Word to allow no less than two lines at the top of any page before a paragraph break.

Similarly, to keep *any* paragraph or group of lines unbroken, just select any number of paragraphs or lines, choose Format→Paragraph→Line and Page Breaks tab, and turn on the "Keep lines together" box.

Another easily avoided typographical problem: a heading at the bottom of a page whose body text is split onto the next page. The solution: Select the heading, choose Format→Paragraph→Line and Page Breaks tab, and turn on "Keep with next." (It means, "Keep with next *paragraph.*")

Sure, these tools are useful when applied to individual paragraphs, but they're especially ideal for defining *styles* (see page 141). For example, you may as well turn on "Keep with next" for *all* of your heading styles; it's virtually always ugly when a heading appears on one page, while its body text appears on the next.

In other words, if you were hoping that these icons would let you rotate, say, a particular heading, thus mixing text direction on a single page, forget it; Word can't do it. Your best bet is to fill your page with a borderless table (page 171) that confines the rotated text to a cell of its own.

Paragraph Spacing

If you're in the habit of pressing Return twice to create space between paragraphs, it's time to consider the automatic alternative. The Paragraph Spacing tools on the Formatting Palette let you change the amount of space that appears, automatically, before and after the current or selected paragraph. (The same controls show up in the Format→Paragraph→Indents and Spacing tab, as shown in Figure 3-6.) When you click the arrows beside the Before and After boxes, the spacing increases and decreases in six-point increments; for finer control, you can enter any numbers into the boxes. (Four to eight points is a good place to start.)

Change the spacing in the Formatting Palette or Paragraph dialog box at the outset of your document, or press ⌘-A to select all existing paragraphs first. The advantage of doing it this way is that the extra space is added automatically, with no danger of accidentally deleting any of the extra line breaks. Furthermore, if you change your mind about the extra space, you can press ⌘-A and readjust paragraph spacing, without having to delete any extra line breaks.

POWER USERS' CLINIC

Formatting Revealed

In looking at a Word document, there are very few outward cues to tell you what's going on in terms of formatting—since you can't see the behind-the-scenes formatting parameters. However, when troubleshooting a formatting snafu, you might want to see exactly what Word is *thinking*.

You can. Choose View→Reveal Formatting. The cursor turns into a small word-balloon. If you click the balloon on any word or in any paragraph, it opens into a larger balloon listing all of its font and paragraph formatting specifics: font, type style, indents, spacing before and after, and so on. You can click as many places as you like. As soon as you start to type again, or if you click anywhere outside the margins, Reveal Formatting turns off and the balloon goes away.

Indentation

To the horror of academics and typesetters everywhere, most people indent the first line of each paragraph by hitting the Tab key. Trouble is, Word's default tab stops are set at half-inch intervals—much too wide for professional use.

It's a far better idea (from the purist's standpoint, anyway) to use Word's dedicated indenting feature, which lets you specify individual *paragraph* margins (and first-line indents) that are independent of the document margins (see page 135).

Tip: If you do indeed press Tab to begin a paragraph, Word tries to guide you toward the proper way. It automatically moves the first-line indent marker (see Figure 3-7) to the first tab stop on your ruler. Now you've got a quick way to correctly indent your paragraphs. Adjust the marker (making the indent *smaller*, for best results) and then type away. All subsequent paragraphs will have the same first-line indent.

If you'd prefer that Word abandon this behavior, choose Word→Preferences→Edit tab and turn off "Tabs and backspace set left indent." Now the Tab key and indents are totally disconnected.

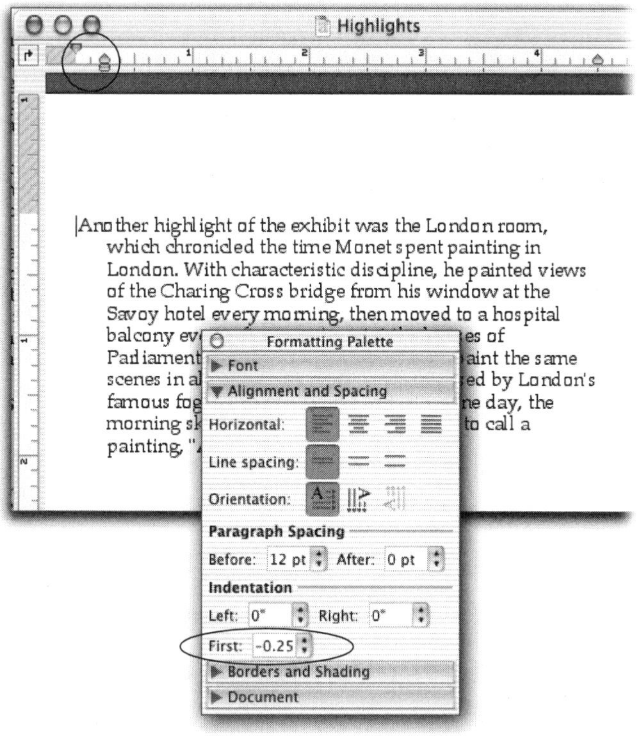

Figure 3-7:
Top: A paragraph with a hanging
indent *of a quarter-inch, and a* right
indent *of a half-inch, as shown on the
ruler.*

*Bottom: The Indentation settings on
the Formatting Palette for the
paragraph shown.*

*Note: To create a hanging indent, you
must type a negative number in the
First box.*

There are two ways to adjust indents for highlighted paragraphs: by dragging the indent markers on the ruler (Figure 3-7), or by setting numerical values (in the Formatting Palette or Format→Paragraph→Indents and Spacing tab). When you want to give a paragraph its own distinctive style, use one of these indents:

- **First line indent.** Drag the top left marker (the first-line indent handle) to where you'd like the first line of each paragraph to begin. One-quarter inch is a typical amount. To set an exact measurement, adjust the "First line" indent setting in the Formatting Palette (or Paragraph dialog box).

- **Hanging indent.** As illustrated in Figure 3-7, you create a *hanging indent* by dragging the lower, house-shaped marker. (The square left-indent marker moves along with it.) To set an exact measurement, type a negative number into the First box on the Formatting Palette (such as *-.25"*); or, in the Paragraph dialog box, click the Indents and Spacing tab and select Hanging from the Special pop-up menu.

- **Left and right indents.** Left and right indents are the internal left and right margins for a paragraph. Most people aren't aware of them, because they usually match the right and left margins of the *document*. But there are times when you want a paragraph to be narrower—either indented from the left margin or on both sides—such as when creating a *block quote*, for example (a longish quotation that you want separated from the rest of the text).

To adjust the paragraph margins for highlighted text, drag the left and right indent markers (identified in Figure 3-7) on the ruler, or change the Left and Right settings on the Formatting Palette. (The Indents and Spacing tab of the Paragraph dialog box offers the same options.) The distances you specify here are measurements from the document's right and left margins, not from the edges of the paper.

Tip: You can also drag the first-line indent or left-indent marker *left,* into the margin, to make a line or paragraph extend into the margin. This is called a *negative indent,* which gives the effect of a hanging indent without changing the left margin. However, if you have a narrow left margin and use negative indents, you may get an error message when you print the document. That's because the negative indent is too close to the left edge of the page.

GEM IN THE ROUGH

Format Painter

It could happen to anyone. You finally have a paragraph exactly the way you want it. In fact, you want to use these settings for all the paragraphs you've previously typed.

Instead of going back to change them one by one, now is the time to use the Format Painter. Select the text you worked so hard to perfect. (If it's just the font characteristics you want to copy, then select as little as a single letter; if paragraph formatting is involved, triple-click a paragraph to select the entire thing.)

Once you've selected the text, click the Format Painter—the paintbrush icon in the Standard toolbar. Now you can perform the following:

- Drag across the text that you want the new formatting applied to. As you let go of the mouse button, Word applies the formatting.

- To copy the new formatting to a large amount of text or to nonadjacent paragraphs, double-click the Format Painter; it's now locked on. (A tiny + symbol on the toolbar icon alerts you that it's locked.) From now on, every paragraph you click or blurb you select will get the new formatting—that is, until you click the paintbrush again or press ⌘-period.

Press Esc or ⌘-period to cancel the Format Painter; press ⌘-Z or F1 (repeatedly, if necessary) to back out of what you've just done.

There's even a keyboard shortcut to "pour" formatting from one block of text to another. Select the first text sample, press Shift-⌘-C, then select the text you want to format and press Shift-⌘-V. You've just copied and pasted both character and paragraph formatting.

Tabs

To tell the truth, the era of the Tab key is fading.

In the typewriter days, it was useful in two situations: when indenting a paragraph and when setting up a table. But in the Microsoft Age, newer, far more flexible tools have replaced the Tab function in both of those circumstances. The indentation controls described above are much better for paragraph indents, and the Table tool (page 165) is a far superior method of setting up tabular data.

Still, millions of people are more comfortable with the tab-stop concept than Word's newfangled tools. This section shows you how they work (and assumes that you remember how tab stops work on typewriters).

Default tabs

Every Word document has a ruler (choose View→Ruler if you don't see it), which starts out with an *invisible* tab stop every half inch across the page. These are the *default* tab stops; you can prove that they exist by pressing Tab over and over again, watching as the insertion point moves from one to the next, exactly as on a typewriter.

But the default tab stops aren't permanent; they start to disappear when:

- You choose Format→Tabs to open the Tabs dialog box (Figure 3-8) and change their default placement (in the "Default tab stops" box). You can do this by clicking the arrow buttons beside the box or by entering a new setting.

- You set new tab stops, as described next. When doing so, all of Word's default tab stops to the *left* of your hand-placed tabs disappear. For instance, when you set a new tab at .75" from the margin, the default tab stop at .5" goes away; when you

Figure 3-8:
You can change the spacing of the default tabs in the "Default tab stops" box (or by clicking the arrows next to it). You can also add a tab leader—that is, a dashed line, dotted line, or underline that automatically fills in the gap between the end of your previous typing and the tab stop.

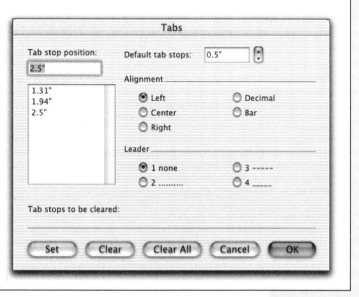

press Tab, the insertion point goes straight to .75". (All remaining default tab stops to the *right* of the new tab remain in place until you add more new tab stops.)

Setting tabs

The quickest way to set new tab stops is by using the ruler; just click anywhere in its tick marks to place a new tab stop. After tabs are set, you can reposition them by simply dragging them along the ruler. To delete one, drag it directly down *off* the ruler until it disappears into thin air.

To set tabs with more exactitude, choose Format→Tabs (or double-click any tab stop on your ruler) to open the dialog box shown in Figure 3-8. Any hand-placed tab stops are listed in the list at the left, according to their distances from the left margin.

To create a new tab, type its location in the "Tab stop position" box, choose an alignment (described next), and click Set (or press ⌘-S). To delete a tab, click it in the list and then click Clear (or press ⌘-E). To change a tab's position, clear the existing tab and type the new position in the "Tab stop position" box. To delete *all* tabs in the list, click Clear All (⌘-A). Press Return or click OK when you're ready to close the Tabs box.

Tab types

When clicking a tab stop in the dialog box list, you'll be shown its *type*. As illustrated in Figure 3-9, pressing the Tab key doesn't necessarily align your insertion point with the *left* side of your tab stop. The following types of tab alignments help you arrange text on the page:

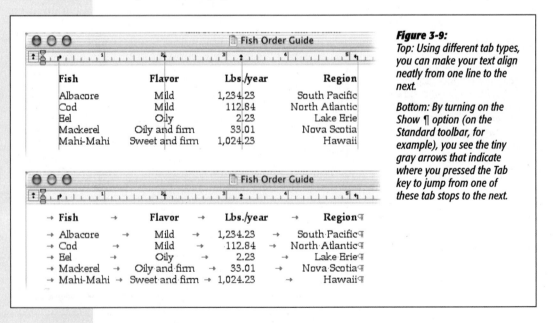

Figure 3-9:
Top: Using different tab types, you can make your text align neatly from one line to the next.

Bottom: By turning on the Show ¶ option (on the Standard toolbar, for example), you see the tiny gray arrows that indicate where you pressed the Tab key to jump from one of these tab stops to the next.

- **Left (⌘-L).** This is the kind of tab stop you're probably used to. When you press Tab and then start typing, your text flows rightward from its origin beneath your tab stop.

- **Centered (⌘-N).** The text is aligned with the tab stop at its centerline, creating a balanced effect that's ideal for things like invitations and brochures.

- **Right (⌘-R).** When you press Tab and then start typing, your text flows *left*ward from its origin beneath your tab stop. Several of these rows together create a neat right margin.

- **Bar (⌘-B).** This kind of tab stop isn't a tab stop at all; instead, it's a method of producing a *vertical line* down your page, directly beneath the tab stop. You don't even have to press Tab to get this vertical line; any paragraph that contains this tab type on the ruler continues the line down through the page. (Insert your own joke here about picking up the bar tab.)

- **Decimal (⌘-D).** This behaves exactly like a right tab stop—until you type a period (a decimal point, in other words), at which point your text flows to the right. In other words, this very useful tab type lets you neatly align a series of numbers (such as prices), so that the decimal points are aligned from row to row.

You don't have to use the Tabs dialog box to change tab-stop types, by the way. If you repeatedly click the *tab well* at the upper-left corner of the ruler (see Figure 3-9), Word displays the icon of each tab type until you stop. If you click the spot on the ruler where you want the tab, you'll plant that tab type. For example, to set a left tab at 1/4", click the tab button until the left-bending arrow appears, then click at 1/4" on the ruler.

Applying tabs to paragraphs and styles

When you set, clear, and move tabs, the changes apply to the paragraph that contains your insertion point. Often, however, you'll want to use the tab settings for many paragraphs—or an entire document. Here are the ways you can accomplish that:

- **Set the tabs before you start typing.** This is a common trick if, for example, you need to insert a little columnar table in the middle of a report. Every time you press Return to begin a new line, the same tab stops will be available.

- **Select all paragraphs.** If you've already done some (or a lot of) typing, select the paragraphs by dragging over them, or press ⌘-A to select the entire document. Set tabs as described above.

- **Make tab stops part of a style.** If you make your preferred tab stops part of a *style* (see page 141), you can apply them to any paragraph just by clicking that paragraph and choosing from the Style menu on the Formatting Palette. If you're *really* attached to certain tab stops, you can even make them part of your Normal style.

Tip: The Ruler *toolbar* contains buttons for tabs, as well as other controls for alignment and spacing. To open it, choose View→Toolbars→Ruler.

Borders and Shading

Black text on a white page is clear and easy to read, but it can get monotonous. When a little zest is required, try using borders, background shading, and fill patterns to emphasize various parts of your document. For instance, light gray background shading can highlight a useful list in the middle of your article. A plain border can set off a sidebar from the body of your text. And a fancy border can be part of an invitation.

Text and paragraph borders

To put a border around some text, first select the text in question; to put a border around an entire paragraph, just click anywhere in the paragraph. Click the flippy triangle next to Borders and Shading on the Formatting Palette to expand it, as shown in Figure 3-10. The controls are:

- **Type.** Clicking the square icon next to Type opens a palette of placement choices for your border: a square, a line above or below, and so on. Click the one you want. The light dotted line, No Border, automatically disables the remaining controls described here.

- **Style.** This pop-up menu shows a selection of solid, dashed, and multiple-line styles to apply to the border you've just specified.

- **Color.** Clicking the color square displays Word's standard palette of 40 colors. You can choose one, or click More Colors to use Office's color-picking tools, as described on page 651.

- **Weight.** This control denotes the thickness of the line in points (to 1/72 of an inch). The pop-up menu shows a variety of thicknesses ranging from 1/4 point to 6 points.

Extra features in the Borders and Shading dialog box

For more customization options than those available on the Formatting Palette, highlight the paragraphs you want to change and choose Format→Borders and Shading. The dialog box shown in Figure 3-10 opens. When you click the Borders tab (Figure 3-10), you see these options:

- **Setting.** Most of the time, you'll choose to put a *box* around your paragraphs, as represented by one of the lower icons on the left. The shadow and 3-D options create a very professional, modern look.

  If you choose Custom, Word doesn't assume anything—not even that you want a four-sided box. As the Custom button implies, you can use a different line style on each side of the box—solid top and bottom and dotted on the sides, for instance. Click the sides you wish to use from the buttons in the Preview panel, then design each one in the Style panel. Click the side button again to make changes.

- **Style.** Choose a line style, a width in points, and a color.

- **Horizontal Line.** Rather than a border, this tool adds a horizontal line *under* the paragraph in question. The line is actually a picture embedded into your document; that's why the lines you choose from are stored in a clip art folder. You also have the option of turning on "Link to File" to make the line a *linked object* instead of an embedded one. These lines are mostly intended for use on Web pages. (See page 659 for more detail on linked and embedded objects.)

- **Options.** Clicking Options opens a dialog box where you can choose how far away from the text you want to set your border. The default settings are 4 points on each side, 1 point top and bottom. If you have room, consider increasing the amount of space between the text and border for a clean, elegant look.

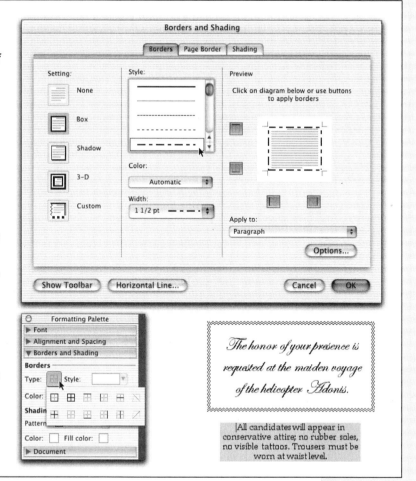

Figure 3-10:
Top: As you work, watch what happens in the Preview box at the right of the dialog box. The only way to see how the final result really looks, however, is to return to your document.

Bottom left: The Formatting Palette, expanded to show the border controls and the Type pop-up menu—the first step in applying a border.

Bottom right: Borders and shading vary from the ridiculous to the sublime. Here are two examples of borders used to different effect. Above, 3/4 point double wavy-line border, 12 points from text, no shading.

Bottom Left: 15% gray shading, 1 point from text, no border.

Note: If your text is in a *text box* (see page 155), don't add a border around it—you'll just end up with two borders. Text boxes come with *built-in* borders, which you can format using the line tools on the Drawing toolbar and the Colors and Lines tab of the Format→Text Box tab.

That said, you *can* put borders on parts of the text *inside* text boxes. (If you also want to hide the border surrounding the text box, click the border, then choose No Line from the Line Color palette on the Drawing toolbar.)

Once your border is complete, click OK. You can now use the tools in the Borders and Shading section of the Formatting Palette (or the Tables and Borders toolbar) to make further refinements.

Page borders

When it's time to create a title page, certificate, or phony diploma, nothing says "professionally published" like a handsome border around the edges of your page. To add one, choose Format→Borders and Shading→Page Border tab. (The Formatting Palette has no controls for adding a page border, but if you decide to add one at the last minute, you can add a quick and dirty border from the Print dialog box, as described on page 45.)

Most of the tools for designing a page border are the same as those for a paragraph border (described previously). But there are subtle differences: Page borders trace the page margins, regardless of the size or amount of text on the page, and the page border changes size automatically as you change the margins (page 135).

The Page Border tab contains a few extra features specific to page borders:

- **Art.** The Art pop-up menu offers dozens upon dozens of small clip-art border motifs in repeating patterns (little marquees, banners, and—for those "You've Been Potty-Trained!" certificates—ice cream cones).

- **Apply to.** This menu on the Page Border tab lets you put a border on the first page of your document or section only. (Can you say "title page"?)

- **Options.** The Options button opens a dialog box with settings that control how the border frames the page, including the Margin settings described in Figure 3-11.

  "Align paragraph borders and table edges with page border" does more than align them; it actually *connects* them if they're adjacent. Thus, the side borders of a paragraph will extend out to and meld with the side borders of the page.

  Turn on "Always display in front" unless you plan to place text boxes or images *over* the page border. (If you do so, you may want to give the border a lighter shading or lighter color.)

  The "Surround header" and "Surround footer" options determine whether the page border encompasses the header and footer (see page 193) along with the rest of the page.

Shading

When you decide to fill in a gray or colored background behind a paragraph or text box, the key words to remember are *light* and *subtle*. Patterns and shading can make text difficult to read, and the interference is often worse on the printed page than on the screen.

Figure 3-11:
The Margin settings control the distance of the text from the margin (or the paper edge, depending on what you choose from the "Measure from" menu). The border, however, still hugs the margins. In other words, when you increase the Margin settings in this dialog box, the text area will decrease as it moves farther in from the page margins. (Yes, some of the text may flow onto the next page as a result.)

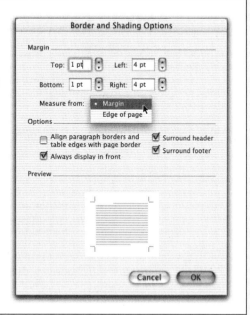

To put a fill or pattern behind text, you must first select the text (or click anywhere in a paragraph). Click the flippy triangle next to Borders and Shading on the Formatting Palette to expand it, as shown in Figure 3-12

Figure 3-12:
Left: The Formatting Palette reveals that even if you don't think you're using a pattern, you are. Text with no background or a plain, unshaded fill color has a clear pattern. The Fill color is a background that underlies both text and any pattern you apply.

Right: The Borders and Shading dialog box offers more options.

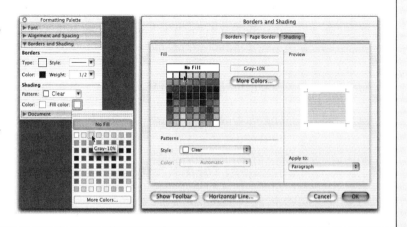

- **Pattern.** The Pattern pop-up menu offers a long list of choices, from Clear (no pattern), to a series of percentages of *halftone* shading (like newspaper photographs), to line patterns such as diagonal stripes. Most of the time, you're probably best off leaving this pop-up menu alone; use the "Fill color" control instead for a professional, even tint.

Tip: Choosing "Solid (100%)" from the Pattern pop-up menu will result in solid black behind your text. Ordinarily, your text would therefore disappear completely, but Word thoughtfully makes the text white, producing an effect called *reversed type,* like this.

- **Pattern color.** If you decide to choose a pattern, the "Pattern color" pop-up menu becomes active. The color you choose here becomes the "black" color of the pattern you chose from the Pattern pop-up menu.

- **Fill.** This is the color that appears behind text or under any pattern you've chosen. You can choose from 40 colors and 24 grayscale shades.

Note: There's a difference between choosing No Fill and White fill color. No Fill is transparent; when you layer a picture beneath text with no fill, you can see the picture. On the other hand, when you layer something beneath text with White fill, the fill blocks out whatever's below.

You can combine these options in fascinating and grisly ways. For example, any pattern you choose overlies the fill color of your paragraph, even if that's No Fill, in which case all you see beneath the pattern is the color of the paper. When you choose one of the percentage shadings from the Pattern pop-up menu, you're choosing a percentage of black or color to overlie the fill color.

Extra features in the Borders and Shading dialog box

A few extra features are available only in the Format→Borders and Shading dialog box. For example:

- You can control how far the fill extends beyond the text. For example, after choosing a fill color, choose Format→Borders and Shading→Borders tab. You'll notice that the None border setting is chosen. However, you can now click the Options button and adjust the "From text" settings, as described on page 161. The settings will apply to the boundary of the fill, as if it were an invisible border.

- Also in the Borders and Shading dialog box, the Horizontal Line button opens a "Choose a Picture" dialog box showing the decorative horizontal lines in Word's clip art gallery. Select one and click Insert to place the line across the text at the insertion point. (You can't make borders with these lines, just horizontals.)

Document Formatting

When you start with a blank document, Word provides a one-inch margin at the top and bottom of the page, and a stately one-and-a-quarter inch margin at each side.

Most people never change these settings; in its own, almost accidental way, Microsoft has dictated the standard margin formatting for the world's business correspondence. But if you learn how to work with margins—as well as paragraphs and indentation—you can give your document a distinctive look, not to mention fit much more text on a page.

Margins

You can adjust the margins of a Word document in either of two ways: by entering exact measurements (in the Formatting Palette or the Document dialog box), or by dragging the margins directly onto the ruler.

To use the numeric option, choose Format→Document→Margins tab, or click the triangle next to Document on the Formatting Palette. There you'll find individual boxes that let you specify, in inches, the size of the left, right, top, and bottom margins.

Figure 3-13:
Top: The house-shaped controls set indents (see page 124). The line where the color of the ruler changes indicates the margin limits.

Bottom: Drag the blue/white boundaries (circled) to adjust the margins.

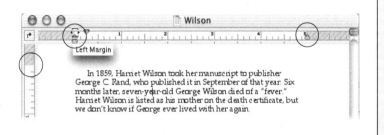

To set your margins by dragging, which produces immediate visible feedback, you must be in Page Layout view. (Choose View→Page Layout.)

- **Left, Right, Top, Bottom.** To set margins by dragging, point to the line where the ruler changes from white to striped, without clicking. (The striped area is *outside* the limits of the margin.) When the cursor changes to a box with double arrows, drag the margin line to any point on the ruler you wish (see Figure 3-13). Now you can change the margins on both the horizontal and vertical rulers.

Tip: You may find it extremely hard to adjust the left margin, since the trio of *indent* markers (Figure 3-7) lie directly on top of the blue/white boundary. Let the cursor hover until the Left Margin tooltip appears and the cursor shape changes as shown in Figure 3-13. You may even find it worthwhile to move the first-line indent handle out of the way while you adjust the margin.

- **Header and Footer.** Headers and footers (see page 193) appear *within* the normal margins. For instance, if you've set the bottom margin for 1", you can have the page number (footer) appear a half-inch from the edge of the paper—half an inch below the bottom of the text. To do so, set the Footer margin for 0.5", as shown in Figure 3-13.

Tip: When you've got your margins just the way you want them, you can make that setting the default for all new documents you open. Just choose Format→Document and click Default at the lower left of the Document dialog box.

Gutters and Mirrors

Word's *gutter* and *mirror* margin features make margins work when your document is destined to be bound like a book.

In an open book, the *gutter* is the term for the inner margins where the pages attach to the spine. Usually, the gutters have to be wider than the outer margins to allow room for the binding and the spine. (You may want to talk to your publisher—the fine people at Kinko's, for example—to learn about margin requirements.) Word can add this extra space automatically. For instance, if you set a gutter space of 0.25", Word will *add* a quarter-inch to the gutter margin on each page.

Another useful tool for book margins is the *mirror margin* feature, which is designed to let you set up margins that are uneven on each *page,* but reflected on each two-page *spread* (see Figure 3-14).

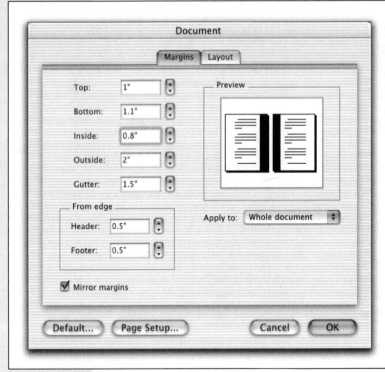

Figure 3-14:
A quick way to open this dialog box is to double-click on the ruler located along the top-left side of the page. The gutter is an extra area for binding; the mirror margins feature is handy when you want the outer and inner margins to be uneven.

Section Formatting

The Formatting Palette doesn't say anything about *section* formatting; in fact, most people have never even heard of it.

Still, section formatting is important in a few special circumstances, such as these:

- Sections allow you to divide a document into chapters, each with its own headers or footers.

- Sections let you change from, say, a one-column format for your opening paragraph to a three-column format for the body of the article. They also let you insert a landscape-orientation page or two into a paper that's primarily in portrait orientation.

- Sections give you flexibility in printing; you can print your title page on colored paper from a different paper tray on your printer, for example.

- You can set different margins for each section of your document; this might come in handy if your training manual contains multiple-choice quizzes for which you could really use narrower page margins.

The bottom line: A section is a set of pages in your document that can have its own independent settings for page numbering, lines, footnotes, and endnotes. It can also have its own layout features, such as page borders, margins, columns, alignment, text orientation, and even page size. Finally, it can have its own printer settings, such as orientation and paper source.

Inserting and Removing Section Breaks

To start a new section, choose Insert→Break, then choose one of the Section Break *types*—depending upon where you want the new section to begin (relative to the current page). For instance, to change the number of columns in the middle of a page, choose Section Break (Continuous); to start the next chapter on a new page, choose Section Break (Next Page). If you're self-publishing a novel, remember that new chapters usually begin on a right-hand page; choose Section Break (Odd Page).

You'll see the change reflected right away; in Normal view, a section break shows up as two finely dotted lines labeled "Section Break (Next Page)" or whatever kind you inserted (see Figure 3-15). In Page Layout view, you see only the *effect* of the page break; if you chose the "Next Page" type, your text abruptly stops in the middle of one page and picks up again on the next. But if you click the Show/Hide (¶) button on the Standard toolbar, the breaks appears as double dotted lines, just as in Normal view.

Choosing a section type may sound like a big commitment, but don't fret—you can always go back and change it. To do so, click anywhere in the section that you want to *change*—that is, just after the section break itself—and then choose Format→Document→Layout tab. Choose a new section type from the "Section start" menu. (This menu offers an additional section-break option: New column, which is useful solely if you're designing your document with multiple columns, as described on page 150. To make an existing column start at the top of the page, click it and choose "New column.")

To remove a section break, just click its double dotted line and press Delete.

Caution: Deleting a section break, or the last paragraph marker in a section (click ¶ to see it), also deletes its formatting. The section *before* the break will take on the formatting of the section *after* it. The sudden appearance of 24 pages of a two-column layout, for example, can be disconcerting if you're not prepared for it, to say the least.

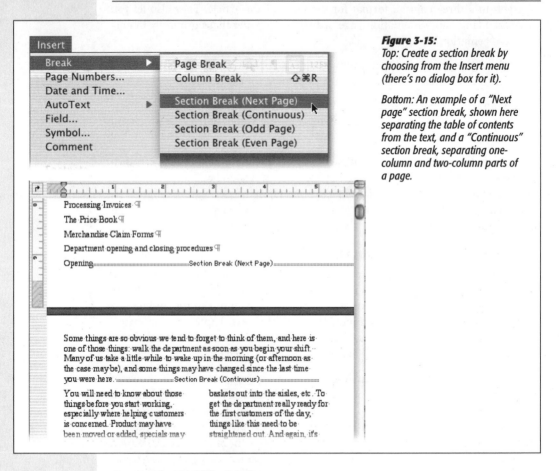

Figure 3-15:
Top: Create a section break by choosing from the Insert menu (there's no dialog box for it).

Bottom: An example of a "Next page" section break, shown here separating the table of contents from the text, and a "Continuous" section break, separating one-column and two-column parts of a page.

Formatting Within Sections

To change formatting or other settings within a section, such as page numbering or headers and footers, just click in the section and use the commands in Word's dialog boxes and toolbars. Settings like margins, alignment, columns, and page orientation, plus any feature involving numbering, such as page and line numbering, headers and footers, and so on, operate independently of the other sections in the document.

Page numbering across sections

When you use a header or footer and page numbers in your document, you can either number each section independently or number the document continuously from beginning to end. For example, suppose you've written a term paper with an introduction in its own section, which you want to number with Roman numerals. (You want regular Arabic numerals for the body of the paper.) Here's how you'd set things up:

1. **Click at the end of the introduction and choose Insert→Break→Section Break (Next Page).**

   The double dotted lines appear, if you're in Normal view (click the Show/Hide if you don't see them).

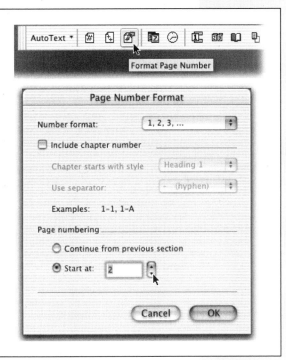

Figure 3-16:
Top: The Header and Footer toolbar.

Bottom: Clicking the "Continue from previous section" radio button carries over the page numbering from the section before. You can start a section at any page number you choose by clicking "Start at" and entering a number in the box.

2. **Click anywhere in the introduction (*above* the section break) and choose View→Header and Footer.**

   The header and footer areas of your page appear, as described on page 193. The Headers and Footers toolbar opens, too.

3. **Scroll down to the footer on one of the pages in the introduction.**

   The footer is labeled "Footer – Section 1."

4. On the Headers and Footers toolbar, click Insert Page Number (the # icon), then click the Format Page Number icon (shown in Figure 3-16).

   The Page Number Format dialog box opens, also as shown in Figure 3-16.

5. From the "Number format" pop-up menu, choose "i, ii, iii…"; click the "Start at" radio button. Click OK.

   The number *i* appears in the box, which is right where you want the numbering for the introduction to begin.

6. Click in one of the footers in the second section (*after* the section break). On the Headers and Footers toolbar, click the "Same as Previous" icon, so that it's no longer highlighted.

   This button is about halfway across the toolbar; use the tooltip balloons to find it (point to each icon without clicking).

7. Again on the toolbar, click Insert Page Number, then click Format Page Number.

   Again, the Page Number Format dialog box appears.

8. This time, choose the Arabic numerals (1, 2, 3, …) from the "Number format" pop-up menu. Click the "Start at" radio button; make sure *1* appears in the box. Click OK.

Now, no matter how you add material to, or remove material from, the introduction and the body of your paper, the introduction will be numbered starting on page i. The numbering of the main body, meanwhile, will start over with 1. Should you change your mind and decide to number your paper consecutively from the intro to the end, you won't have to remove the section break. Just click one of the footers *after* the section break and then click the "Same as Previous" button on the Headers and Footers toolbar.

Styles, Page Layout, and Tables

Once you've polished the *content* of your document, it's time to work on the packaging. Word can take you deep into the realm of page design and layout.

For example, an endless block of text running across the page is fine, but columns are sometimes easier to read—and they look more professional. Or perhaps you'd like to add some well-placed borders, but you've never been sure how to work with them.

This chapter builds upon the formatting concepts in Chapter 3 and describes how to add the finishing touches that give your document polish and flair.

Styles

Creating Word documents usually requires a small assortment of formatting styles, which you'll use over and over again throughout the document. In a short piece, reformatting your chapter titles (for example) is no big deal; just highlight each and then use the Formatting Palette to make it look the way you like.

But what about long documents? What if your document contains 49 chapter headings, plus 294 sidebar boxes, captions, long quotations, and other heavily formatted elements? In such documents—this book, for example—manually reformatting each heading, subhead, sidebar, and caption would drive you to distraction. Word's *styles* feature can alleviate the pain.

A style is a prepackaged collection of formatting attributes that you can apply and reapply with a click of the mouse. You can create as many styles as you need: chapter headings, sidebar styles, whatever. The result is a collection of custom-tailored styles for each of the repeating elements of your document. Figure 4-1 should clarify all of this.

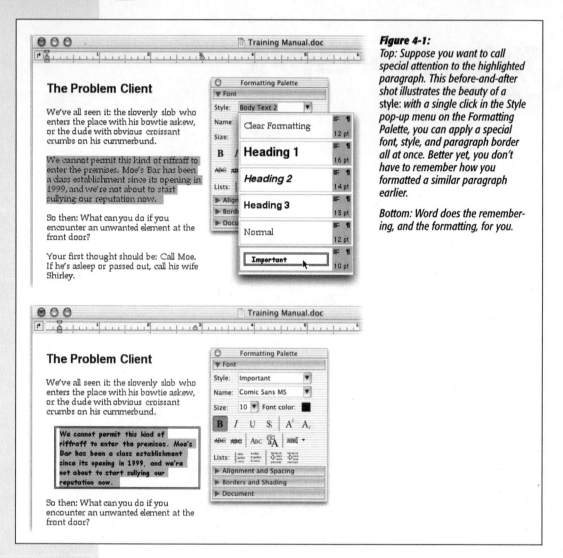

Figure 4-1:
Top: Suppose you want to call special attention to the highlighted paragraph. This before-and-after shot illustrates the beauty of a style: with a single click in the Style pop-up menu on the Formatting Palette, you can apply a special font, style, and paragraph border all at once. Better yet, you don't have to remember how you formatted a similar paragraph earlier.

Bottom: Word does the remembering, and the formatting, for you.

After creating your styles, just apply them as you need; they'll be consistent throughout the document. During the editing process, if you notice you accidentally styled, say, a *headline* using the *Subhead* style, you can fix the problem by simply reapplying the correct style.

You'll appreciate styles even more when it comes time to change the formatting of a particular style. If you change a style's description, Word offers to change *every occurrence* of that style in your document.

Styles aren't one of Microsoft's masterpieces when it comes to ease of understanding. But grasping how they work, where they're stored, and when they change helps to explain many of Word's idiosyncrasies, and pays off handsomely in the long run.

Where Styles Are Stored

Every document has a collection of ready-to-use, built-in styles, whether you're aware of it or not. (To be more precise, every document is based on a *template* that stores a canned set of styles, as described on page 141.) Word opens each new blank document with the *Normal* paragraph style preselected.

The styles available in your document are listed in several places: in the Font panel of the Formatting Palette, the Formatting toolbar, the Ruler toolbar, and the Format→Style dialog box (see Figure 4-2).

Tip: There are many more styles in the Style dialog box than in the Formatting Palette or the toolbar menus, which contain only a selection of the most useful styles. To see that comprehensive list of styles without opening the Style dialog box, just Shift-click one of those menus.

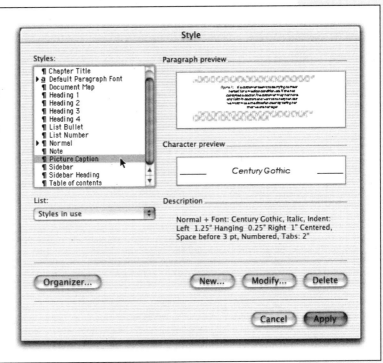

Figure 4-2:
Choose Format→Style to see the styles available in your document. Each document comes with a few heading styles, such as the Normal style and Heading 1, because the Normal template has these starter styles built right in. (See page 202 for more on templates.) Starting from a different template might produce a different set of starter styles.

Applying Styles

To apply a canned style to text you've already typed, highlight the text. For example, drag through some text, or click once inside a paragraph to select it. (You can also choose a style for a new paragraph *before* you begin typing it.)

Now choose a style from one of Word's style boxes, using one of the following methods (listed in ascending order of speed):

- Press Shift-⌘-S to highlight the Style list in the Formatting Palette. Use the up and down arrow keys to step through the styles in the list until the one you're seeking is highlighted. Press Return to apply the style.

Tip: You can save time by typing the name of the style and then pressing Return.

For this very reason, some people use very short style names when they format a style. For instance, if you name a style GX, you only have to press Shift-⌘-S, type *gx,* and Return to apply the style—never having touched the mouse. Better yet, give the style *two* names, separated by a comma—one in English for your own reference in using the Style menus, the other its "keystroke name." For example, your Sidebar style might be called *Sidebar, sb.*

- Click the arrow button next to the Style list in the Formatting Palette, then drag the mouse to highlight the desired style (see Figure 4-1). Click the style name to apply it.

- Choose Format→Style; double-click one of the style names in the Styles list box (see Figure 4-2)—or click the style name once, then click Apply.

GEM IN THE ROUGH

WYSIWYG Styles

As you may have noticed, the Formatting Palette's Style pop-up menu displays the names of the styles in their actual fonts, sizes, and colors; even paragraph borders show up around the relevant style names.

You can open the Style list faster if you *don't* use this WYSIWYG feature. To turn it off, choose Word→ Preferences→General panel, turn off "WYSIWYG font and style menus," then click OK; now all of the styles listed in the Formatting Palette appear in a demure Lucida Grande.

Of course, this also turns off the WYSIWYG *font* menus; you can't turn them off independently. (You can still summon a WYSIWYG font display on a case-by-case basis by pressing Shift before you open the menu, but that trick doesn't work for the Style menu.)

Finally, if turning off WYSIWYG font menus turns off WYSIWYG only in the Formatting Palette and toolbar Font menus, but not the Font menu in the bar, you need to install the Office X Service Release 1, as described on page 12.

Creating Styles by Example

There are two ways to create your own styles: You can use the Styles dialog box to build one from scratch, or you can "create by example"—that is, you can format the text in the document the way you want it, and then tell Word to memorize that formatting. The second method is usually easier.

For example, suppose you want to create a style for illustration captions. Start by typing out the caption, ending with Return to create a paragraph.

---

1. Select the paragraph (by clicking inside it, for example).

   Now use the formatting controls to make it look exactly like you want it:

2. Using the Formatting Palette or Format menu, choose the Century Gothic font, at 10-point size, italic, centered, indented on both sides.

   Chapter 3 offers details on using these controls.

3. Click in the Style box on the Formatting Palette (or press Shift-⌘-S) to highlight it. Type the new style name (*Picture Caption,* for example), and press Return.

   To apply this style more quickly in the future, consider assigning it two names separated by a comma—the second one can be an abbreviation (see the Tip above).

That's it; your style is ready for use.

Creating Styles in the Dialog Box

For more control over what Word associates with a style, use the Style dialog box shown in Figure 4-2. To use it, choose Format→Style and then click New (or press ⌘-N). The New Style dialog box opens, as shown in Figure 4-3.

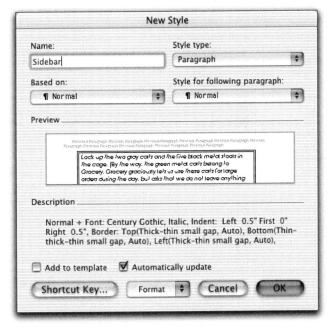

Figure 4-3:
As you develop your new style, the Description in the middle of the New Style dialog box will change to indicate a written definition of the style.

Use the various controls here to define this new style:

- **Name.** Give your style a name that reflects how you're planning to use it: Headline, Sidebar, and so on.

- **Based on.** Choose Normal or whatever existing style is closest to what you envision for the new style. Basing your new style on an existing one has two payoffs. First, it saves you time, since some of the formatting is already in place; second, when you modify the underlying style (such as Normal), all styles *based* upon it change as well, keeping your document design coordinated. For example, if you base a heading on the Normal style, and then change the Normal font to Palatino, the heading style's font changes to Palatino as well.

- **Style for following paragraph** is a big timesaver. Let's say the new style you're creating is a heading, and after each heading, you always return to typing in Normal style. Instead of manually changing the font back to Normal after each use of the Heading style, just choose Normal here. Now, whenever you press Return after using the heading style, the font automatically returns to Normal.

- If you chose *Paragraph* in the **Style type** menu at upper right, the style will include the current settings for indents, tabs, and other aspects of paragraph formatting (as described in Chapter 3). If you chose *Character* formatting, then Word memorizes only the font and other type characteristics of your new style. You can apply a character-formatting style in a paragraph independently of the paragraph style.

- Turning on **Add to template** stores your new style in the *template* on which your document is based (see page 202). All new documents based on this template will offer this style, too, ready to go. (To find out which template you're using, choose File→Properties→Summary tab. The name of the template is shown near the bottom of the dialog box.)

- Turn on **Automatically update** with caution. When this box is turned on, any formatting change you make to any *one* occurrence of text in this style will change the style's definition—and with it, *every* occurrence of the style in your document.

- **Shortcut Key** opens the Customize Keyboard dialog box (see page 633), where you can assign a keyboard shortcut to this style. For example, you can assign Control-⌘-Z to your favorite heading style and apply it with a quick tap of the left hand. If you frequently change styles as you type along, or if you have trouble using a mouse, this feature is a godsend.

Clicking the **Format** pop-up menu (or pressing ⌘-O) gains you access to the dialog boxes, where you actually format the style you're building:

- **Font** opens the Font dialog box, described on page 111.

- **Paragraph** opens the Paragraph dialog box, described on page 121.

- **Tabs** opens the Tabs dialog box, described on page 127.

- **Border** opens the Borders tab of the Borders and Shading dialog box (page 130).

- **Language** lets you associate a foreign language with your style, for the benefit of the spelling checker and other proofing tools.

- Placing a **Frame** around a paragraph gives it some of the qualities of text boxes. See "Workaround Workshop" on page 162 for more detail on the differences between text frames and text boxes.

- **Numbering** opens the Bullets and Numbering dialog box, which is described on page 215. The menu option's name, "Numbering," is only half accurate, since it's used for bulleted lists as well as numbered ones.

When you click OK after making changes in any of these formatting dialog boxes, you return to the New Style dialog box, where the Description information tells you which characteristics you've assigned to this style.

When you click OK again to return to your document, the newly created style's name appears along with all the others in the Formatting Palette; now it's ready to apply.

Changing, Deleting, or Copying Styles

There are several ways to change an existing style, listed here in order of speed:

- Select some text in your document and make the desired changes to it. Then choose the style's name in the Formatting Palette and press Return.

  The Modify Style dialog box opens, as shown in Figure 4-4; click OK to update the style, and with it every occurrence of text in that style. (Use the Reapply option if you've made a mess of a certain paragraph, and you want it restored to its virginal, true-to-its-style condition.)

- Choose Format→Style; click the style's name in the Styles box; click Modify (or press ⌘-M); and use the Format menu to make changes to the font, paragraph, and so on, just as if creating a new style (as described above).

Figure 4-4:
Turning on "Automatically update the style from now on" has the same effect as the "Automatically update" box in the Style dialog box (see page 146). It also means that you can change the style in the future without seeing this message again.

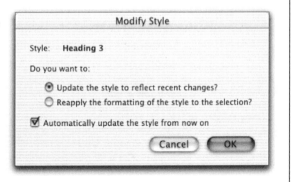

Deleting styles

To delete superfluous styles, choose Format→Style, then click the style in the Styles list box and click Delete.

Note: Word won't let you delete certain built-in styles (such as Normal, Heading 1, 2, and 3, and so on). If you click one of these styles, the Delete button is grayed out.

To delete many styles at once, choose Format→Style and click Organizer (or press ⌘-O). The Organizer opens, as shown on page 207. In the list box for the current document, ⌘-click the styles you want to delete, then click Delete. (If the list of styles you wish to delete are consecutive, click the first one, then Shift-click the last style name; click Delete.)

Transferring styles

Once you've cultivated a crop of magnificent styles, you may want to spread their sunshine to other documents. You can do so in the Organizer dialog box, described in the previous paragraph and on page 207, but that's a lot of trouble.

The sneaky, much faster way is to *copy* paragraphs formatted in the styles you want to transfer and then paste them into another document. Word automatically adds the pasted styles to the second document's list of styles. (If the document already contains a style of the same name, it ignores the new one you've pasted.)

Tip: If you're ever confused about which styles you've applied where, try this: Choose Word→Preferences→View panel. Set the "Style area width" to about one inch, then click OK. Now Word opens a new strip at the left side of your document window that identifies the style of every paragraph!

Page Layout

Word automatically flows text from line to line and page to page. However, an important part of document design is placing text right where you want it, breaking it up, and generally controlling the flow.

Inserting Breaks

A *break* is an invisible barrier that stops your text in its tracks, and then starts it again on a new line, column, or page.

Paragraph break

In Word, pressing Return (or Enter) creates a paragraph break; although you may not have been aware of the term, this is what you've been creating every time you end a paragraph. Unless you've chosen a different "following paragraph" style (see page 146), the new paragraph takes on the same formatting as the one above.

Line break

Pressing Shift-Return inserts a *line break*. It's similar to a paragraph break except that the text on the new line remains part of the original paragraph, and retains its style and paragraph formatting. No matter how you edit the surrounding text, the line break will remain where you inserted it—until you remove it, of course.

Page break

Choose Insert→Break→Page Break (or press Shift-*Enter)* to force a *hard* page break. No matter how much text you add above the break, the text *after* the break will always appear at the top of a new page.

Use a page break when, for example, your report has a separate title page. Inserting a hard page break at the end of the title page text forces the body of your paper to begin on page 2. You may also want to start a new page for each topic in a document, if you're writing a manual on chores for the kids, for example. In this case, you could start a new page for the cleaning instructions for each room in the house.

Tip: In Page Layout view, page breaks are generally invisible. The text just ends in the middle of a page and won't go any further, which can be disconcerting if you've forgotten about the page break you added.

To view the dotted lines that represent a page break, choose View→Normal, or click the Show/Hide ¶ button on the Standard toolbar or Formatting Palette.

Column break

To make text at a certain spot jump to the top of a new *column* (in multicolumn layouts like those described in the next section), choose Insert→Break→Column Break. Word ends the current column and, when you start typing again, begins at the top of the next column at the top of the page.

If you choose this option when you're not using multiple columns (see page 150), it behaves like a hard page break. (On the other hand, if you later switch to a two- or three-column format, the column break behaves like a normal column break. If you plan to make two different versions of your document—one with columns and one without—you may therefore want to use column breaks instead of page breaks.) *Keyboard shortcut:* Shift-⌘-Return.

Figure 4-5:
Click the ¶ (Show/Hide) on the Standard toolbar to see which breaks are where in your document. This is the sure-fire way to get rid of breaks you want removed. Now that you can see them, you can delete or backspace over them.

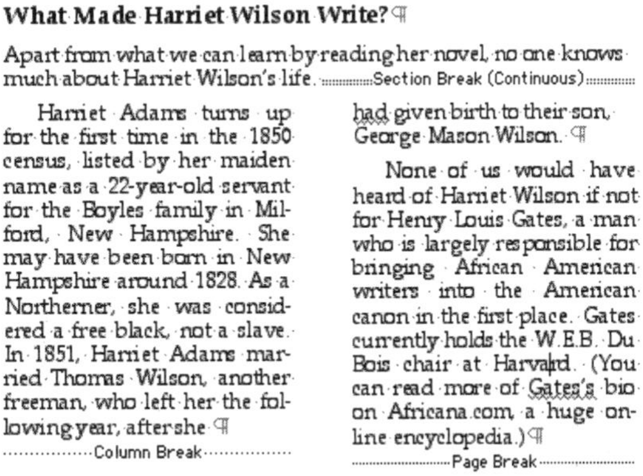

What Made Harriet Wilson Write? ¶

Apart from what we can learn by reading her novel, no one knows much about Harriet Wilson's life. ⠀⠀⠀⠀Section Break (Continuous)⠀⠀⠀⠀

Harriet Adams turns up for the first time in the 1850 census, listed by her maiden name as a 22-year-old servant for the Boyles family in Milford, New Hampshire. She may have been born in New Hampshire around 1828. As a Northerner, she was considered a free black, not a slave. In 1851, Harriet Adams married Thomas Wilson, another freeman, who left her the following year, after she ¶
⠀⠀⠀⠀Column Break⠀⠀⠀⠀

had given birth to their son, George Mason Wilson. ¶

None of us would have heard of Harriet Wilson if not for Henry Louis Gates, a man who is largely responsible for bringing African American writers into the American canon in the first place. Gates currently holds the W.E.B. Du Bois chair at Harvard. (You can read more of Gates's bio on Africana.com, a huge online encyclopedia.) ¶
⠀⠀⠀⠀Page Break⠀⠀⠀⠀

Section break

A *section* is like a chapter—a part of a document that can have formatting independent of the other parts. For instance, you can give each section different margins, page numbering, pagination, headers and footers, even paper size for printing. See page 137 for more detail on sections.

To begin a new section, insert a section break by choosing Insert→Break→Section Break. You can choose to begin the new section on a new page or in place (see page 152).

Caution: When deleting a break as shown in Figure 4-5, bear in mind that the usually invisible ¶ marker at the end of a paragraph "contains" the formatting for the paragraph that comes before it. If you join two paragraphs or sections together by backspacing until there's no break between them, they blend into one and take on the formatting of the *second* section or paragraph.

Working with Columns

If you're putting together, say, a newsletter or some classified ads, you can often make your publications look more professional by pouring it into multiple parallel *columns* (see pages 4-6). Newspapers and magazines, for example, use columns in their layouts because the shorter lines are easier to read.

Tip: You can see multiple columns only in Page Layout view (View→Page Layout). Only one column per page appears in Normal view, much to the confusion of anyone creating columns for the first time.

Adding columns using the Standard toolbar

The quickest way to create columns is via the Columns button on the Standard toolbar, as shown in Figure 4-6. If you want your entire document in columns, make sure nothing is selected; if you want columns for only part of the document, select that text.

Then click the Columns pop-up button on the Standard toolbar; drag downward and across to highlight the number of columns you'd like to use, as shown in Figure 4-6. If you need more than four columns, drag beyond their borders to expand the choices to five or six.

When you release the mouse, Word divides your text into columns of equal width. (If you highlighted only part of the document, Word automatically creates invisible *section breaks* above and below the selected portion; see page 137.)

Adding columns using the Columns dialog box

Although the Columns pop-up button on the toolbar is quick and easy, Word, as usual, offers far more control if you're willing to visit a dialog box. To use this option, select text or click in your document and proceed as follows:

1. **Choose Format→Columns.**

   When the Columns dialog box opens (see Figure 4-6), the number of columns is preset to One, meaning that your text takes up the entire width of the page.

2. **Choose one of the icons at the top of the dialog box, or enter a number in the "Number of columns" box.**

   The buttons labeled Two and Three create two or three columns of equal width. Left and Right mean, "Give me the number of columns I've specified in the 'Number of columns' box, but for some visual spice, make the first column half as wide, or twice as wide, respectively, as the other columns."

3. **Click the arrow buttons next to the Width box for each column or the spacing boxes.**

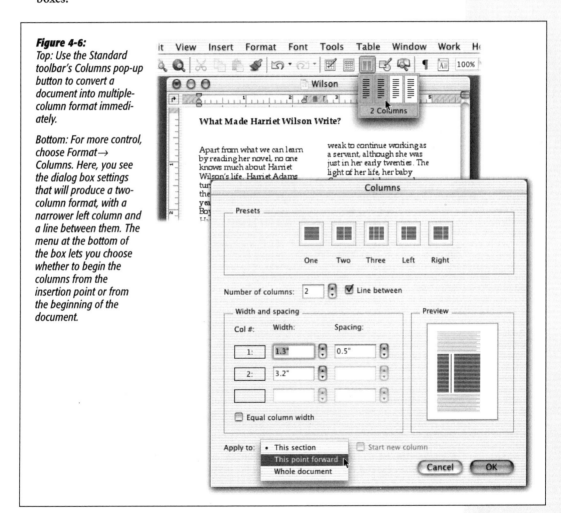

Figure 4-6:
Top: Use the Standard toolbar's Columns pop-up button to convert a document into multiple-column format immediately.

Bottom: For more control, choose Format→ Columns. Here, you see the dialog box settings that will produce a two-column format, with a narrower left column and a line between them. The menu at the bottom of the box lets you choose whether to begin the columns from the insertion point or from the beginning of the document.

Width boxes are available for the number of columns you've requested. The Preview box displays the results. To create columns of equal width at any point, check the "Equal column width" box.

4. **If you so desire, turn on "Line between" to draw a thin vertical line between columns. Click OK.**

You return to the document, where the fancy columns are now in place.

How columns look and flow

As you type down to the bottom of a column, the text automatically flows to the top of the next column. To end one column and move on to the next, choose Insert→Break→Column Break.

Columns start out left-aligned, with an uneven right margin. The general consensus, though, is that fully justified columns offer the tidiest, most professional look. To justify columns, select all the text in your columns (⌘-A if that's your entire document), and then click Alignment and Spacing→Justification on the Formatting Palette. (Consider turning on automatic hyphenation, too, for better word spacing, as described in the following section.)

Adjusting column widths

You can resize columns by dragging the column margin markers on the ruler, as shown in Figure 4-7.

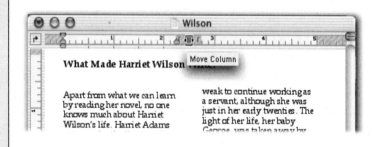

Figure 4-7:
The quickest way to adjust column widths is by eye. First choose View→Page Layout. Then place the cursor over the ruler near the column boundary that you'd like to adjust (at the top of the page). When the cursor turns into a double-arrow box, drag to move the column margin.

Using the Format→Columns dialog box to resize columns gives you better control over the measurements, and provides access to the "Equal column width" feature (see Figure 4-6). If you turn on this box, the columns remain the same width no matter what; if you resize one of them using the arrow buttons, the others automatically grow or shrink to match.

If you don't turn on "Equal column width," you can resize each column individually; the other columns grow or shrink to fill the page width. You can also adjust the spacing with the arrow buttons (or by entering numbers in the boxes). Keep an eye on the Preview pane to see the effects of your changes. The total width of the columns and spacing always equals the full text width on the page: the width between the left and right indents.

Tip: If you're experiencing trouble getting your column lengths to come out even at the bottom of the page, check the Paragraph Spacing (under Alignment and Spacing in the Formatting Palette). Leaving just a small amount of space before and after each paragraph makes it easier for Word to balance the columns.

Automatic Hyphenation

When you're using columns, hyphenation (a feature that automatically breaks longer words at the right margin) creates a straighter, more even right margin (see Figure 4-8). It also grants you more regular spacing within each line in *justified* text (text that's stretched to be flush with both margins).

Word's factory setting is programmed not to insert hyphens until you type them— or until you turn on the automatic hyphenation feature. To do so, choose Tools→Hyphenation, then turn on "Automatically hyphenate document." When you click OK, Word scrutinizes the document and hyphenates words where necessary, using its built-in dictionary as a guide to "legal" syllable breaks. Word will continue hyphenating automatically as you edit and add on to your document.

Figure 4-8:
Top left: By default, hyphenation is turned off, so that if a word is too long, Word moves it down to a new line. The result can be ugly gaps between words.

Bottom: Turning on "Automatically hyphenate document" can produce much better-looking spacing (top right).

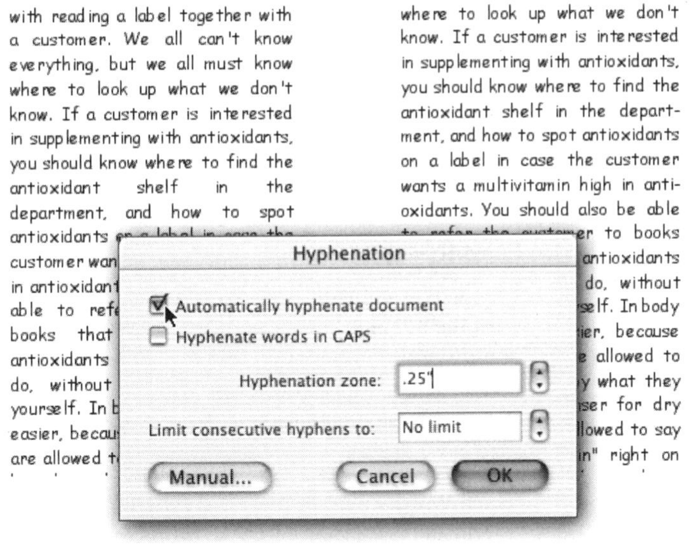

with reading a label together with a customer. We all can't know everything, but we all must know where to look up what we don't know. If a customer is interested in supplementing with antioxidants, you should know where to find the antioxidant shelf in the department, and how to spot antioxidants on a label in case the customer wan

where to look up what we don't know. If a customer is interested in supplementing with antioxidants, you should know where to find the antioxidant shelf in the department, and how to spot antioxidants on a label in case the customer wants a multivitamin high in antioxidants. You should also be able

Hyphenation

☑ Automatically hyphenate document
☐ Hyphenate words in CAPS

Hyphenation zone: `.25"`

Limit consecutive hyphens to: `No limit`

(Manual...)   (Cancel)   (**OK**)

Hyphenation Settings

Before clicking OK, be sure to review the following hyphenation settings:

- If you turn *off* "Hyphenate words in CAPS," Word leaves your acronyms whole; that's probably what you want it to do.

- The "Hyphenation zone" is the amount of space Word will allow at the end of a line before it resorts to using a hyphen. The larger you set this number, the fewer hyphens you'll end up with in your document. The smaller the number, the more even the right margin will be—and the more hyphens you'll have.

- Set "Limit consecutive hyphens" to 2 or 3. If you set it to more than that, all the hyphens at the end of consecutive lines will look like a little ladder climbing up the page (a big no-no in professional publishing).

Undoing hyphenation is easy: Just choose Tools→Hyphenation and turn off the "Automatically hyphenate document" box. Word returns your document to its pristine, prehyphenated condition.

Manual Hyphenation

The automatic hyphenation feature is an all-or-nothing deal; it applies to the entire document, or not at all. If you'd like more say in what Word hyphenates, use manual hyphenation. This method affords you the chance of saying Yea or Nay to each word that Word wants to break up.

To do so, choose Tools→Hyphenation and click Manual. Word goes through your document, stopping at each word it wants to hyphenate, just as in a spelling check. In the Manual Hyphenation dialog box that appears, you can click No (don't hyphenate), Yes (hyphenate at the blinking hyphen), or use the arrow keys to move to the point where you want Word to put the hyphen; *now* click Yes. Clicking Cancel both dismisses the dialog box and ends manual hyphenation.

If you expect to conduct major editing after hyphenating manually, then consider another hyphenation pass. Unlike automatic hyphenation, manual hyphenation doesn't add or remove hyphens automatically as your text reflows during editing. (You can also rehyphenate only *parts* of the document by selecting the text before performing a manual hyphenation.)

Hard Hyphens

For the true control freak, Word offers two ways to place hyphens right where you want them. These keyboard shortcuts are effective whether or not you use the manual or automatic hyphenation features. For example, if you feel your document has too many hyphens in a row, even after your manual hyphenation pass, you can still change a hyphenated word to have a nonbreaking hyphen.

- **Optional hyphen.** By clicking inside a word and then pressing ⌘-hyphen, you tell Word where to place a hyphen *if* the word needs to be hyphenated. As you edit the document, if the word moves away from the end of a line, the optional hyphen disappears, returning only if the word needs to be divided again.

- **Nonbreaking hyphen.** Click inside a word and then press Shift-⌘-hyphen. You've just told Word that you *do not* want to break this word up—ever.

To delete optional hyphens and the oxymoronic nonbreaking hyphens, click the Show/Hide (¶) button on the Standard toolbar or the Formatting Palette. The invisible hyphens become visible (they look like an L-shaped bar and an equal sign, respectively) and are ready for you to delete.

Note: If Hyphenation is grayed out on the Tools menu, you may be in Outline or Master Document view, where hyphenation is unavailable.

Text Boxes

Putting text in a box of its own, sitting there independently on the page, represents a quantum leap in text-flow management (see Figure 4-9). You can now format and color a text box independently from everything else on the page, as well as use drawing tools on it. In other words, text boxes let you think outside the box.

Note: A text box is fundamentally different from a paragraph with a *border* around it, although text boxes can (and often do) have borders. For one thing, you can't drag to resize a bordered paragraph, or flow text around it, as you can with a text box. On the other hand, if all you want is a border and none of the other fancy features, then creating a border around a plain old paragraph is the easiest way to do it.

Text boxes also emulate the way desktop publishing programs such as Quark XPress and PageMaker handle text. If you've never used professional desktop publishing software, consider this your first training ground.

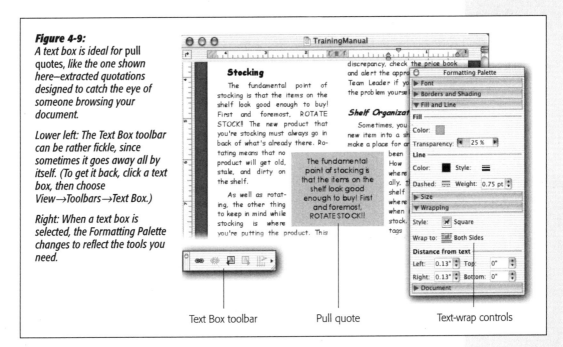

Figure 4-9:
A text box is ideal for pull quotes, like the one shown here—extracted quotations designed to catch the eye of someone browsing your document.

Lower left: The Text Box toolbar can be rather fickle, since sometimes it goes away all by itself. (To get it back, click a text box, then choose View→Toolbars→Text Box.)

Right: When a text box is selected, the Formatting Palette changes to reflect the tools you need.

Text Box toolbar   Pull quote   Text-wrap controls

Note: Text boxes *completely disappear* in Normal view. To work with text boxes, make sure you're using Page Layout view (View→Page Layout)—or be prepared for some surprises when you first see the printout.

Creating Text Boxes

To start a text box in your document, choose Insert→Text Box. (Another avenue: If the Drawing toolbar is open [page 644], click the Text Box button, which looks like a capital A with an I-bar next to it.)

Move the mouse to where you'd like the box to appear, and drag diagonally; Word shows you the rectangular outline of the box you're creating. The box is complete when you let go of the mouse; you can always resize or move it later. To place text inside your new text box, click inside it and type or paste.

Tip: To enclose existing text in a text box, first select the text, then choose Insert→Text Box or click the Text Box button. Your text appears in a small text box, which you can then resize.

The Text Box Toolbar

The diminutive Text Box toolbar appears when you first create a text box, as shown in Figure 4-9. Its buttons let you:

- **Link and unlink text boxes.** *Linking* text boxes sets up an automatic text flow from one to another, exactly as in PageMaker, QuarkXPress, or any newspaper on earth that makes you "Continue on page 13A." As you add text to the first text box, overflow text falls into the second one, even if it's many pages away. Most people never suspect that Word is even capable of this page-layout feature, perhaps because it's buried in this shy toolbar.

   To link two text boxes, click the first box, and then click the Create Text Box Link button (see Figure 4-9); the cursor turns into a pitcher, as if to pour text into the next box. Now click the second box. Excess text flows automatically from the first box into the second. (Press Esc or ⌘-. to back out of the process.)

Tip: There's nothing preventing you from repeating this process, linking three, four, or many text boxes together into a continuously linked chain. You may drive your readers crazy, but you can do it.

   To break a link between two boxes, click anywhere in the first of the two boxes and click the Break Forward Link button. The text from the second box now flows back into the first one, leaving the second box (and any subsequent boxes in the chain) empty.

- **Navigate from one text box to another.** The next two buttons on the Text Box toolbar (see Figure 4-9) come in handy if there are many text boxes distributed far and wide in your document. They step you forward and back through the text boxes, skipping over everything in between.

- **Change text direction.** Clicking this button rotates the text within the box (and all others linked to it), as shown in Figure 4-10.

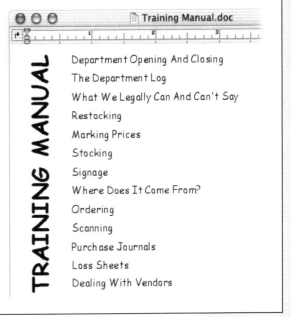

Figure 4-10:
Clicking "Change text direction" on the Text Box toolbar (or choosing Format→Text Direction) allows you to create eye-catching mastheads like this one. You can make text read top to bottom, bottom to top, or back to normal. (You can't turn text upside down.) Use this trick for creative layout effects for newsletter mastheads or letterheads.

TRAINING MANUAL

Department Opening And Closing
The Department Log
What We Legally Can And Can't Say
Restocking
Marking Prices
Stocking
Signage
Where Does It Come From?
Ordering
Scanning
Purchase Journals
Loss Sheets
Dealing With Vendors

Formatting Within Text Boxes

To use Word's formatting features on text within text boxes, just select the text first. The tools on the Standard toolbar and the Formatting Palette pertain to the text within a box, so long as the insertion point is in that box.

Tip: Choosing Edit→Select All or pressing ⌘-A, while the insertion point is in a text box, effectively selects all the text in that box *and* any boxes that are linked to it.

To adjust the margins within a text box, choose Format→Text Box. (This choice only appears when the insertion point is within a text box.) Click the Text Box tab, as shown in Figure 4-11. The settings you establish in these boxes control the distance between the borders of the text box and the text itself.

Changing the background color or border style

When a text box is selected, the Formatting Palette changes to offer specialized controls for formatting its line thickness, line color, and background ("Fill") color or pattern. In fact, because a Word text box is like a cross between a text block and a *drawing object* (see Chapter 18), many of the icons on the Drawing toolbar affect text boxes. For example, the Drawing toolbar offers 3-D and shadow effects, which look great on text boxes.

Tip: To use the drawing tools on a text box, make sure to select the box itself, not the text inside it. To do so, position the cursor on the box's outline until the cursor turns into a hand, and then click. (When you click *inside* the box, the tools on the Formatting Palette turn back to text tools.)

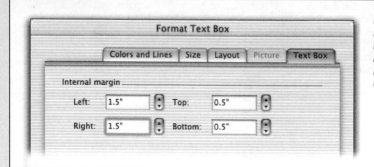

Figure 4-11:
Even if text boxes are linked, the internal margin settings (shown here in the Format Text Box dialog box) apply only to the text box containing the insertion point.

Sizing text boxes

If you can't see all the text in a box, you can either link it to another text box or just make this one bigger. Here's how: Select the box by clicking it, and then drag any of the tiny white resize handles at its corners. Or, for numerical precision, use the boxes on the Formatting Palette's Size section; the relevant portions of the Formatting Palette are shown in Figure 4-9.

Working with Linked Text Boxes

Microsoft's name for a group of linked text boxes is a *story*. There's no limit to the number of text boxes you can link together—just keep creating new ones and linking them (page 156) until there's room for all your text.

Copying linked text boxes

You can copy or cut an entire story (or part of one) for pasting into another document. To do so, select the text *box* (not the text) of the first box in the story and Shift-click any additional text boxes you want to copy. Once they're selected, you can now copy or cut and paste the chain of boxes using any of the copy/paste methods described in Chapter 2. Use this method if, for example, you want to copy a series of text boxes and then change the text inside of them; this will also save you the work of creating and sizing new text boxes.

Note: Word can't link text boxes across documents in order to keep the text flowing "live" from one to the next.

To cut or copy the *text only* from a story, click in any box in the chain and choose Edit→Select All (or press ⌘-A). Now when you use the cut or copy and paste commands, you'll be pasting just the text, not the boxes.

Deleting one text box in a chain

If you delete one box in a story, the text remains intact, flowing from beginning to end through the remaining text boxes in the chain. Select the box that you want to delete by holding the cursor over the box's boundary until it changes into a hand icon; click the box edge. Then choose Edit→Clear (or press Delete). If necessary, enlarge the remaining linked text boxes to show all the story text.

Grouping text boxes

You can *group* text boxes just as you would group any graphic objects (see page 646); the only trick is selecting them. As noted above, the trick is to click their *borders;* Shift-click to select the additional boxes that you want to group. Once they're selected, choose Group from the Draw pop-up button (the top button on the Drawing toolbar). (If you change your mind, the Ungroup and Regroup commands are on this same menu.)

POWER USERS' CLINIC

Character Spacing

When working with text flow, you're usually concerned with the big picture, such as where the text goes and whether a word is divided. But in times of page-layout stress, your control in Word can get much finer than that; you can actually adjust the letter spacing between individual letters—an especially useful control in text boxes.

Select the text that you'd like to work on. (You'll probably want to adjust the character spacing of only a single line or a few words at a time.) Then choose Format→Font→ Character Spacing tab.

As you use the Spacing (horizontal) and Position (vertical) settings, keep an eye on the Preview window, which displays all results. The Scale percentage controls the magnification of the Preview window, in case you need to look *really* closely.

- **Spacing.** Choose Expanded or Condensed from the pop-up menu, then click the arrows to choose the amount of space that Word puts between each character in your selected text. (One point is 1/72nd of an inch.)

- **Position.** Choose Raised or Lowered from the pop-up menu, then click the arrows to tell Word

how much higher or lower to position the selected text. Thus, if you're concerned with the amount of space between two lines, select one of the two lines and move it higher or lower until you get the desired results.

Note that *character spacing* isn't quite the same thing as what professional typesetters called *kerning.* Kerning refers to the space between certain specific pairs of letters, such as capital T and lowercase o. Especially in larger type sizes, the word "To" can look odd, for example, because there's too much space between the T and o. Kerning moves the o closer so that it's slightly *under,* rather than coming after, the top arm of the T.

In Word, kerning is a feature that you can set to kick in automatically according to your text's size. (Kerning is usually unnecessary in body text; it's more critical in headings and other large point size text.) If your headings are in 14-point type, for example, set the "Kerning for fonts" box to 14 points and above. That's all you have to do; Word makes sure that the kerning pairs are shifted automatically, based on information embedded in the font itself. (Word offers no manual kerning controls.)

When you drag a grouped text box, they all move together. When you drag the sizing handles, they all grow or shrink by the same amount. Likewise, when you use the color and fill commands, they act upon all boxes in the group.

Text Wrapping and Layering

Whether you're creating a Web site or printed document, one of the most enjoyable parts is putting in a few images—photos, clip art, or drawings. But too often, the text and graphics don't share the space as harmoniously as they should. Many people find topics like *text wrapping* too intimidating to bother learning.

Don't be one of them. Word's layout features are more intuitive than ever, especially for you, the wise and discriminating Mac user.

Wrapping text around things

The "things" around which you can wrap text can be clip art from Word's own collection (see "Adding Insertions" in the next section); drawings you've done in programs like Word, AppleWorks, or Illustrator; AutoShapes from the Drawing toolbar; or text boxes. (See Chapter 18 for a review of the various graphic objects you can place into a Word document.)

To get started, select the graphic or text box you want to wrap your text around. Ignore the text for now. Just worry about getting the picture where you want it on the page. Then consult the Wrapping section of the Formatting Palette (Figure 4-12), as it offers a pair of pop-up buttons that specify how you want the text to wrap.

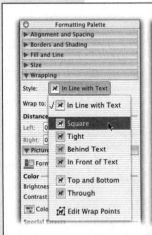
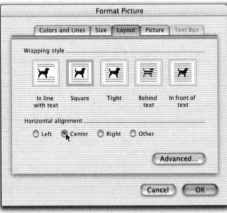

Figure 4-12:
The wrapping controls in the Format dialog box (right) mostly correspond with the Style and "Wrap to" pop-up controls in the Formatting Palette (left). Your text can leave a hole for the graphic (Square), hug its irregular sides (Tight), sit superimposed (Behind Text), be covered up by the graphic (In Front of Text), or treat it as just another typed character (In Line With Text).

Advanced text wrapping

As always in Word, the Formatting Palette is the quickest way to achieve a result (text wrapping, in this case), but more control awaits in a dialog box. Here's how to get there:

1. **Click to select the graphic or text box, then choose Format→whatever.**

   In other words, choose Format→Picture, Format→Object, Format→AutoShape, or Format→Text Box; the wording of the bottommost choice on the Format menu depends on the item you've selected. In any event, the appropriate Format dialog box now appears (Figure 4-12, left).

2. **Click the Layout tab. Choose one of the text-wrap styles by clicking its icon.**

   These wrapping controls correspond to those on the Formatting Palette. For example, choose Tight if you'd like the text to hug the outlines of an irregularly shaped object. Choose Behind Text to create a watermark, or choose Square for a neat, businesslike look.

3. **To keep the object right where you placed it on the page, click Other under "Horizontal Alignment."**

   The other buttons move the object to align with the left margin, center line, and right margin, respectively.

4. **Click Advanced.**

   A new dialog box appears (see Figure 4-13).

5. **Make the changes you want, as shown in Figure 4-13; click OK twice.**

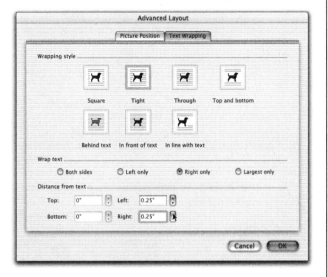

Figure 4-13:
Top: A Word clip art inserted into a document; left alignment, tight wrapping, one side only, 0.25" from text.

Bottom: The Advanced Layout tab contains additional options. For example, you can **Wrap text** *on one side only, instead of both sides. One of these may be a better choice if the text wrapping is down one side of a column. "Largest only" wraps text only on one side—the side that has the most room, even if that changes in the middle of the object. This is a good choice for irregularly shaped objects.* **Distance from text** *lets you choose how close you want the text against the object it wraps—in hundredths of an inch.*

Layering text with graphics

Most of the time, you'll want to wrap text *around* objects. But sometimes, for effect, you'll put text right *over* an object, or vice versa. To pull this off, use the "Behind text" or " In front of text" options shown in Figures 4-12 or 4-13.

If superimposing a graphic has made the text difficult to read, there are a couple of fixes. Either lighten the object beneath the text, or, if the text has a fill, change it to a clear or semitransparent fill.

- To lighten an object, select it. If it's a picture, click the Image Control button on the Formatting Palette and select Watermark. Another way to lighten a picture is to click Color Adjustment on the Formatting Palette and choose the Saturation radio button. Then use the Setting slider to lighten the image as much as you need.

- If the object is a drawing or AutoShape, you can use the Transparency slider on the Formatting Palette to make it easier to see through. (The slider has no effect on lines. For less-intrusive, thinner lines, use the Weight box on the Formatting Palette, or choose a lighter color in the Line Color box.) You can access the same controls by choosing Format from the Draw pop-up button on the Drawing toolbar.

WORKAROUND WORKSHOP

Text Boxes and Text Frames

Before Word 98, all text boxes were called text *frames*, and they had fewer features than they have now.

When you open a document from an earlier version of Word that contains frames, they remain intact. You can continue to work with the text frames by selecting them and using the Format→Frame dialog box.

To reiterate, frames are far more limited than today's text boxes. You can't link or group them, rotate the text inside them, or format them using the Borders and Shading dialog box or the Drawing toolbar, as described in this section (use the Formatting Palette instead).

If you'd like to convert old text frames *into* text boxes, there's only one way to do it, and it's a workaround. Create a new text box (see page 155), and then cut and paste the text from the frame. Finally, select and delete the orphaned text frame.

Or, to remove a text frame *without* putting its text into a text box, choose Format→Style. At the bottom of the Modify Style dialog box, choose Format→Frame, and then click

Remove Frame.

On the other hand, frames aren't dinosaurs altogether. Some Word features work in text frames but *not* in text boxes, including footnotes and endnotes (see page 197), comments (page 179), field codes for tables and indexes, and AUTONUM fields.

To create a text frame around a paragraph, choose Format→Style and click Modify. At the bottom of the Modify Style dialog box, choose Format→Frame; use the settings in the Frame dialog box to adjust the text wrapping and other attributes. You can resize and move text frames in your document just like text boxes, but you can also enter exact position settings here. To reopen the Frame dialog box at any time, click inside the frame and then choose Format→Frame.

Finally, there's an even quicker way to create a text frame: Create a text box as usual (page 155), and then, with the text box selected, choose Format→Text Box→Text Box tab. Click Convert to Frame.

Tip: You can even layer text with text—a great trick when using your company's name as a watermark on your letterhead, for example. To do so, make a text box containing the logo, apply a light color or light shade of gray to it in the Formatting Palette, and choose "Behind text" from the Style pop-up button in Formatting Palette's Wrapping section. Drag the logo into place.

Pictures and Drawings

Word comes with enough graphics features to make AppleWorks quake in its boots; in fact, "Microsoft Word and Picture X" might have been a better name for the program. More and more, the skilled use of pictures, drawings, and other embellishments is necessary in the creation of a comprehensive, readable document.

The Insert menu offers a long list of graphic objects that you can pop onto a Word page: clip art, scans from a digital camera or scanner, drawing objects called AutoShapes, and so on. Because this Insert menu is available in most of the Office programs, its graphic commands are described in Chapter 18.

Inline vs. Page Graphics

Using graphics in Word entails only a few special pieces of knowledge. First, you can specify how the existing word processor text interacts with each graphic—whether it wraps around or passes over or under the image. (That's the purpose of the Text Wrap commands described earlier in this chapter.)

Second, it's important to understand that you can paste a graphic in either of two ways:

- As an **inline** graphic, one that sits right in the text. If you delete or insert text in preceding sentences, the graphic moves backward or forward as though it's just another typed character.

- As a **page** graphic, one that's married to a particular spot on the *page*. If you add or delete text, nothing happens to the graphic; it sits right where you inserted or pasted it.

Note: *Page graphics don't appear* in Normal view, Outline view, or Master Document view. To see them, you must switch into Page Layout view, Online Layout view, or the print preview.

The distinction between inline and page graphics has been a source of confusion since Word 1. And Microsoft continues to fiddle with the design of the controls that let you specify which is which.

In Word X, the scheme is simple, as long as you understand the technical difference between the two kinds of graphics that Word handles.

- **Drawing objects** always begin life as *page graphics*, floating on the page with no relationship to your text. (Drawing objects are graphics that *you make yourself*,

---

right in Word, using the tools on the Drawing toolbar. They include AutoShapes, text boxes, arrows, rectangles, freehand lines, and so on.)

- **Pictures** always begin life as *inline graphics,* embedded right in a line of text. (*Pictures* are images you import from other sources; they include Word's own Clip Art gallery, scans and other digital photos, Photoshop files, and the like.)

Tip: See Chapter 18 for more detail on the distinction Word makes between drawing objects and pictures.

Converting Inline Graphics ↔ Page Graphics

Just because drawings start out floating on the page and pictures start out hooked into your text doesn't mean they have to stay that way. It's easy enough to convert an inline graphic into a page graphic or vice versa. Here's how:

1. **Double-click the graphic.**

   In order to double-click a *drawing,* you obviously need to *see* the drawing, which means you need to be in Page Layout or Online Layout View. You can double-click *pictures,* and thus access all formatting tools, in any view except Outline or Master Document.

   In any case, the appropriate Format dialog box appears.

2. **Click the Layout tab.**

   The dialog box shown in Figure 4-12 appears.

3. **To convert a page graphic to an inline graphic, click "In line with text"; to convert an inline graphic to a page graphic, click any of the remaining Text Wrap icons. Click OK.**

   Word automatically switches views, if necessary, so that it can display the graphic in its new environment. Thus, your former inline graphic is now floating on the page in Page Layout view, or your former page graphic is now just another typed character in Normal view.

Charts, Spreadsheets, and Equations

Word's Insert→Object command lets you embed a variety of data—charts, equations, graphics, and other Office documents—from other Office programs right into a Word document.

You'll find a complete description of this feature, which technically is called Object Linking and Embedding technology (abbreviated OLE and pronounced "oh-LAY"), in Chapter 18.

Tables

How do you use Word to create a résumé, agenda, program booklet, list, multiple-choice test, Web page, or other document where numbers, words, and phrases must be aligned across the page? In the bad old days, people did it by pressing the Tab key to line up columns. As Figure 4-14 illustrates, this method is a recipe for disaster. (Unfortunately, thousands of people *still* use this method—or, worse, they still try to line up columns by continuously pressing the Space bar.)

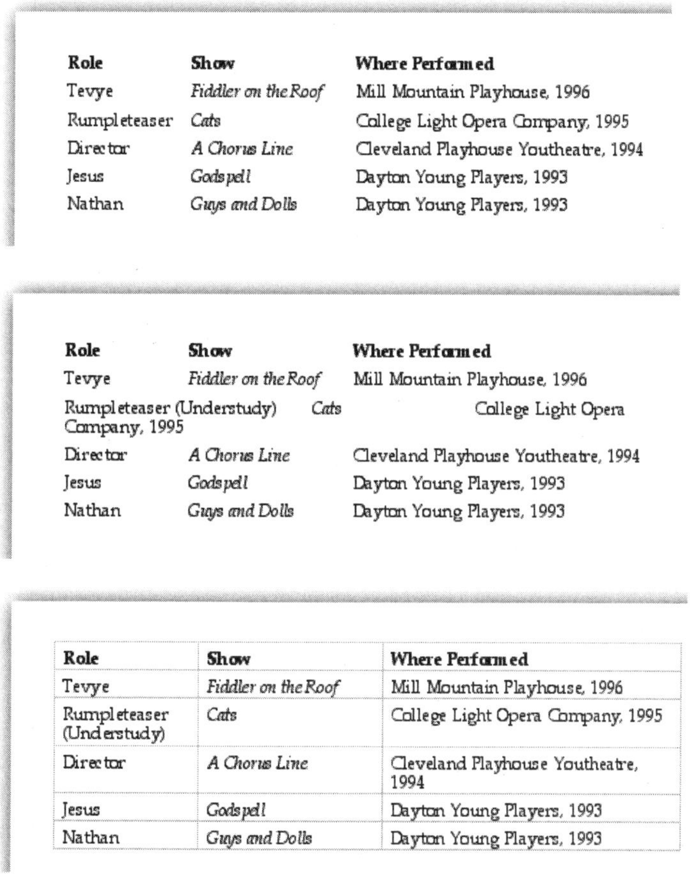

Figure 4-14:
Top: If you use tabs to set up a table, things may look good at first—as long as every line fits within its space and you never plan to insert any additional text.

Middle: Here's what's wrong with the tab approach. When you insert the word Understudy *into one of the columns, it pushes too far to the right, causing an ugly ripple effect that will take you a long time to straighten out.*

Bottom: If you use a table, you never have this kind of problem. Just type as much text as you like into a "cell," and that row of the table will simply expand to contain it. (The light gray gridlines don't print unless you want them to.)

Role	Show	Where Performed
Tevye	*Fiddler on the Roof*	Mill Mountain Playhouse, 1996
Rumpleteaser	*Cats*	College Light Opera Company, 1995
Director	*A Chorus Line*	Cleveland Playhouse Youtheatre, 1994
Jesus	*Godspell*	Dayton Young Players, 1993
Nathan	*Guys and Dolls*	Dayton Young Players, 1993

Role	Show	Where Performed
Tevye	*Fiddler on the Roof*	Mill Mountain Playhouse, 1996
Rumpleteaser (Understudy) *Cats*		College Light Opera Company, 1995
Director	*A Chorus Line*	Cleveland Playhouse Youtheatre, 1994
Jesus	*Godspell*	Dayton Young Players, 1993
Nathan	*Guys and Dolls*	Dayton Young Players, 1993

Role	Show	Where Performed
Tevye	*Fiddler on the Roof*	Mill Mountain Playhouse, 1996
Rumpleteaser (Understudy)	*Cats*	College Light Opera Company, 1995
Director	*A Chorus Line*	Cleveland Playhouse Youtheatre, 1994
Jesus	*Godspell*	Dayton Young Players, 1993
Nathan	*Guys and Dolls*	Dayton Young Players, 1993

Using Word's *table* feature is light-years easier and more flexible. As illustrated in Figure 4-14, each row of a table expands infinitely to contain whatever you put into it, while everything else on its row remains aligned. Tables also offer a few simple spreadsheet features.

Creating Tables

There are two ways to insert a table: You can let Word build the table to your specifications, or you can draw it more or less freehand.

Inserting a table

The quickest way to insert a table is to use the Insert Table pop-up button on the Standard toolbar (see Figure 4-15).

If the toolbar isn't visible, choose Table→Insert→Table. The Insert Table dialog box opens, also shown in Figure 4-15.

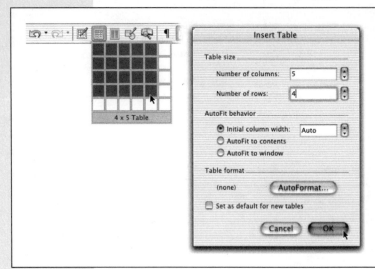

Figure 4-15:
Left: A quick way to make a small table is to drag from the Insert Table button on the Standard toolbar. As you drag through the resulting grid, you're specifying the grid size you want. (You can drag beyond the boundaries shown here, by the way, to specify a 9 x 9 table, for example; the pop-up grid grows as necessary.)

Right: If you frequently use the same kind of table, check the "Set as default for new tables" box to make your favorite settings the new defaults. They will appear in this dialog box each time you choose Table→Insert→Table.

After choosing the number of rows and columns you wish to start with (you can always add more later), click an AutoFit radio button to instruct Word how to size the columns across your table. If you know how wide in inches you'd like each column to be, click "Initial column width" and set a measurement in the size box. "AutoFit to contents" creates skinny columns that expand as you type into them, and "AutoFit to window" (the easiest way to go if you're not sure) spaces the selected number of columns evenly across the page. The table appears in your document at the insertion point when you click OK. Figure 4-16 depicts a small 6 x 4 table.

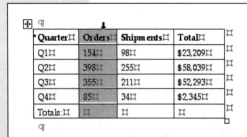

Figure 4-16:
The light gray markings shown here appear when you click the Show/Hide ¶ button on the Standard toolbar or Formatting Palette. To select an entire column, click near the top of it; the cursor turns into a tiny arrow. To resize a row or column, drag the horizontal or vertical lines when the cursor turns into a double arrow. The resize box at lower right keeps all rows and columns in proportion as it expands or shrinks the entire table.

Drawing a table

Word's Draw Table tool gives you free rein to form the table of your dreams—the trick is learning to control it.

To summon this toolbar, click the Tables and Borders button on the Standard toolbar, choose View→Toolbar→Tables and Borders, or choose Table→Draw Table. The Tables and Borders toolbar opens and the cursor turns into a pencil. (Press Esc whenever you want the normal cursor back.)

When you drag the pencil horizontally or vertically, it draws lines; when you drag diagonally, it draws boxes. Using these techniques, you can design even the most eccentric, asymmetrical table on earth.

The tidiest way to begin drawing a table is to drag diagonally to create the outer boundary (Figure 4-17, left), then drag horizontal and vertical lines to create the rows and columns. Drawing your own table is the best option when you want a variety of widths in your rows and columns, as shown in Figure 4-17, rather than evenly spaced ones.

To remove a cell or line you've just drawn, hold down the Shift key (or click the eraser tool on the Tables and Borders toolbar) and drag it across a line. The line promptly disappears.

Figure 4-17:
Left: Drag diagonally to create the outer border of your table.

Right: The Draw Table tool lets you create rows and columns of any size and shape just by drawing them.

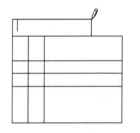

When you're done designing your table's framework, you can dismiss the Tables and Borders toolbar. On the other hand, if you leave it open, you'll have buttons for sorting and formatting your table, or drawing more tables, ready at hand. The insertion point is now blinking in your new table, all set to begin typing.

If you really make a mess of things, press ⌘-Z to undo what you've done, one step at a time. Alternatively, vaporize the entire table by clicking inside it and choosing Table→Delete→Table.

Typing into tables

To type into a table cell, click in that cell. You can use the up or down arrow keys to change rows; press Tab and Shift-Tab to jump forward or backward through the cells. (There's not much call for tabs within cells—after all, you've *already* aligned the text the way you like it. But if you need a tab character, press Option-Tab.)

Note: Pressing Return or Enter *doesn't* take you to the next cell; it puts a line break in the *current* cell instead. Get in the habit of pressing Tab to move on to the next cell.

You can also navigate like this:

To move to:	Press these keys:
First cell in the row	Control-Home
Last cell in the row	Control-End
Top cell in the column	Control-Page up
Bottom cell in the column	Control-Page down
Highlight whole table	Option-Clear

As you type, text wraps within the cell, forcing the row to grow taller as necessary. To widen the cell as you type, choose Table→AutoFit→AutoFit to Contents. (Even then, the cell will widen only until the table reaches the edge of the page—then the text will start to wrap down.)

Of course, this automatic wrapping is the principal charm of tables. But if you find yourself wishing Word would *not* wrap text in this way, select the cells in which you want wrapping turned off, and then choose Table→Table Properties→Cell tab. Click Options and uncheck the Wrap Text box. You can still enter as much text in a cell as you like, but the cell won't expand downward to show it—it will just disappear beyond the cell boundary.

Selecting cells

To cut, copy, or drag material from cells in a table, you must first select it, as with any other Word text. Because it's a table, however, you have the following options:

• Drag the mouse—down, across, or diagonally over the cells you'd like to select.

• Click at the top of a column—the cursor changes into a downward-pointing arrow—to select an entire column. Likewise, click at the left of a row—the cursor changes into a right-slanting arrow—to select an entire row.

• Click the thin, invisible *selection bar* at the left edge of a cell to highlight that cell. (Double-click the selection bar to highlight a whole row.)

• Click one cell, row, or column, and then Shift-click another to extend the selection by additional cells, rows, or columns.

• Option-click anywhere in a column to select the entire column.

• Triple-click the cursor at the beginning of any row to select the entire table.

• Use the Shift key in conjunction with any of the navigation keystrokes described above.

Sizing rows and columns

You can make a row taller or shorter, or a column wider or narrower, much the way you adjust Word's text boxes or margins. Point to any line or boundary of a table without clicking, then drag when the cursor turns into a double-sided arrow.

You can also rely on Word's own automatic table features to help you design the table. They include:

- **Balanced columns.** If a symmetrical, balanced look is what you crave, Word can automatically arrange the rows or columns across your table so that there's equal space between them. First select the rows and columns that you want to balance, then choose Table→AutoFit→Distribute Rows Evenly or Distribute Columns Evenly. (Corresponding buttons on the Tables and Borders toolbar and Formatting Palette can do all this with a single click.)

- **Automatic sizing.** Often, you want the columns to stretch and shrink depending on what you type into them. Or, you just don't know in advance what size you want or need the columns to be. In such cases, choose Table→AutoFit→AutoFit to Contents. As you work, the columns will stretch to just the width necessary to accommodate the contents. For maximum room, Table→AutoFit→AutoFit to Window stretches your columns—no matter how many of them there are—to fill the page from margin to margin.

  At any time, you can resize the table using the mouse; doing so overrides and cancels the previous AutoFit setting. When you have the column widths right where you want them, choose AutoFit→Fixed Column Width. The same menu choices are available on the Tables and Borders toolbar (click the little arrow next to the Insert Table button) as well as the bottom of the Formatting Palette.

- **Numeric precision.** To set row and column sizes using exact measurements, select the rows or columns in question and then choose Table→Table Properties. The resulting dialog box (see Figure 4-18) contains size boxes where you can enter exact measurements.

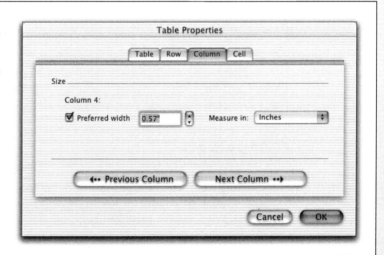

Figure 4-18:
When using the Table Properties dialog box, you can select a group of rows and columns and size them all at once, or you can use the Previous and Next buttons to work on each row or column one at a time.

For columns, you can also specify a percentage of the table width instead of a measurement in inches. For rows, you have the option of setting an exact measurement, or an "At least" measurement. When "At least" is chosen, the cells in that row will stretch downward to wrap text as you type—even if you've turned off "Wrap Text" on the Cell tab.

• **The whole table.** To resize the table as a whole, drag the lower-right corner. The rows and columns remain evenly spaced, or in whatever proportions you have chosen.

Adding rows and columns

If you run out of room and need more rows at the *bottom* of your table, it's easy to add more: Click the lower-right cell and press Tab. A new row appears, identical to the one above, ready for your typing.

To add a new row or column *anywhere* in your table, click in the table and then use the Table→Insert submenu. Choose one of the options from the menu that appears: "Insert Columns to the Left," for example. (These commands are also available in the Insert Table pop-up button on the Tables and Borders toolbar.)

Adding multiple rows or columns at either end of your table, or anywhere within it, is a two-step process. First, highlight the *same number* of rows or columns as the ones you want to insert; to add two rows, select two existing rows.

Next, choose Table→Insert, and one of the submenu options (Insert→Rows Below, for example). Word instantly creates the requested number of new, empty rows or columns.

Inserting individual cells works much the same way. Insert one cell at a time by choosing Table→Insert→Cells, or by using the Insert Table menu on the Tables and Borders toolbar. To insert multiple cells, select the equivalent number of *existing* cells at the desired location in your table before choosing from the menu.

Of course, you may find it more fun simply to click the Draw Table tool on the Tables and Borders toolbar and *draw* the extra columns and rows onto your table.

Note: If Word crashes when you're working with a very long table, or when you draw a table *within* a table cell, install the Office X Service Release 1, as described on page 12.

Deleting table parts

It's easy to dismantle a table in various ways:

• **Deleting cells.** Select one or more cells and choose Table→Delete→Cells. Word asks if you want to move the remaining cells up or leftward to fill the void; choose one and click OK (or press Return).

• **Deleting rows and columns.** Select them (as shown in Figure 4-16) and choose Table→Delete→Rows (or Columns). You may find it faster to click anywhere in the row or column and choose Table→Delete→Cells, then choose a radio button to delete the *entire* row or column. Click OK or hit Return to confirm the deletion.

- **Deleting the whole table.** Click anywhere in the table and choose Table→ Delete→Table.

Formatting Tables

When you click inside a table, the ever-responsive Formatting Palette sprouts a new set of formatting tools—a section called Table Cells. In conjunction with the existing Borders and Shading section, you now have all the formatting controls you need.

To use them, begin by highlighting the cells, rows, or columns that you want to work on. Then you're all set to format any of these table elements:

- **Table border or gridlines.** The Borders tools let you choose a line style (solid, dashed, and so on), color, and weight (thickness in points). Clicking the Type button triggers a menu where you can choose which sides of the table you want borders to appear on. For instance, you may want only vertical lines inside the table and no outside border. Or you may want a heavier top border on the top row of cells only. (The same border formatting tools appear on the top row of the Tables and Borders toolbar.)

Tip: You can also eliminate certain table lines entirely. Just click the eraser tool on the top row of the Tables and Borders toolbar, and drag along each line you want to disappear from the table. Doing so *merges* the table cells (page 174).

- **Background shading in cells.** Shading in a table is similar to a *fill* (see page 133), except that you don't use the Fill palette; you use the Shading palette in the Formatting Palette (or Tables and Borders toolbar). You can choose from 40 colors and 24 shades of gray, or choose More Colors to use Word's color pickers (see page 651).

FREQUENTLY ASKED QUESTION

The Thin Gray Lines

I like the concept of a table, but I don't want thick black lines in my résumé (or Web page). How do I get rid of them?

You're right: Unless you intervene, these lines will actually print out. One of the quickest ways to delete the borders and gridlines is to click inside the table and then choose Format→ Borders and Shading; in the resulting dialog box, click None, then click OK.

Even then, however, you may still see thin *gray* lines. These don't print; they're just on the screen to help you understand the "tableness" of your table. You can hide even these lines, if you like, by choosing Table→Gridlines so that the checkmark disappears.

At this point, you might want to consider clicking the Show/ Hide (¶) icon on the Standard toolbar. The end-of-row and end-of-cell marks become visible, defining the bounds of your table.

Autoformatting tables

With creative combinations of borders, lines, and shading, you can make a table look right for anything from Citibank annual reports to Sesame Street. When you're in a hurry, though, choose a Table AutoFormat for instant good looks.

Click anywhere in your table and choose Table→Table AutoFormat. There's a long list of potential formats in the list box at the left of the Table AutoFormat dialog box. Simply click on each for a preview. If you want to use *some* of the features in the format but not others (font, color, and so on), then just turn on the boxes for the ones you wish to use.

Tip: Turning on AutoFit is a good idea, since it ensures that the new format will exactly fit the existing information in your table, instead of vice versa.

Many of the formats have a different typeface or shading applied to the top (heading) row, first column, last column, and so on. The checkboxes in the "Apply special formats to" section control whether you take those features along with the rest of the format. For instance, if you're not using the last row of your table for totals, don't turn on the "Last row" box.

Table headings

For the purposes of Autoformatting, Word considers the first row of a table to be a heading. But what if your table is longer than a page? Wouldn't it be nice if Word could *repeat* the column titles at the top of each page? Well, it can, thanks to the Heading Rows Repeat feature.

Select the top row of your table (and any additional rows that you'll want to repeat). Then choose Table→Heading Rows Repeat; that's all there is to it. When your table flows onto a new page (page breaks you insert yourself don't count), the heading will appear at the top of each new page of your table.

Cell margins and spacing

To enhance the look of your text in a table, adjust the gap between the characters and the borderlines. You can also put a little space around the outside of each cell—an especially attractive effect on Web pages (see Chapter 7).

Just select one or more cells and choose Table→Table Properties→Cell tab. Click Options, and set measurements in the size boxes for the distance between the text and the top, bottom, left, and right edges of the cell. The "Same as the whole table" box changes the margins of the selected cell to match the default cell margins for the table. To set the default margins for all cells in the table at once, choose Table→Table Properties→Table tab; click Options and enter measurements in the "Default cell margins" boxes.

To add more spacing around the *outside* of cells, click anywhere in the table and choose Table→Table Properties→Table tab. Click the Options button and turn on "Allow spacing between cells"; enter a setting in the size box. When you click OK, that amount of white space will surround each cell, simulating the effect of thicker cell walls. Usually .1" or less looks good. More space than that creates a waffle-like effect, as illustrated in Figure 4-21.

Text formatting within cells

Like text anywhere in Word, you can change the direction and alignment of selected text in a table using the Format→Text Direction command—a great effect for row or column labels (Figure 4-21, right). In the resulting dialog box, choose the text orientation—horizontal, vertical, or bottom-to-top—and click OK.

Figure 4-19:
Left: You can create some unusual table looks using, for example, .15" spacing between cells.

Right: Rotated text.

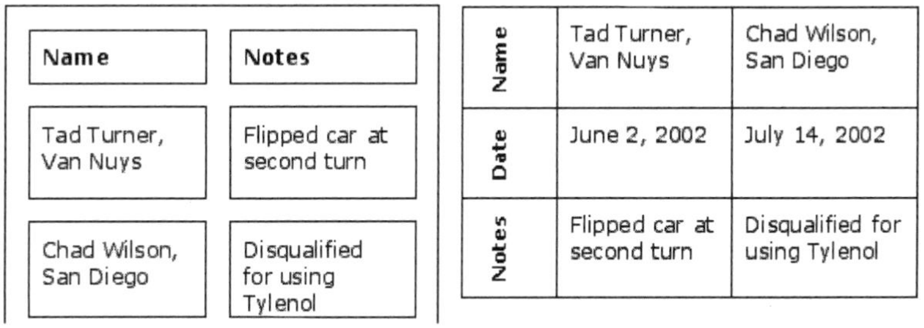

Name	Notes
Tad Turner, Van Nuys	Flipped car at second turn
Chad Wilson, San Diego	Disqualified for using Tylenol

Name	Tad Turner, Van Nuys	Chad Wilson, San Diego
Date	June 2, 2002	July 14, 2002
Notes	Flipped car at second turn	Disqualified for using Tylenol

You can also make the text in selected cells hug the left or right side of its cell, center it right in the middle, or make it stick to the "floor" or "ceiling" of a cell. After selecting the cells, click the arrow button next to the alignment button on the Tables and Borders toolbar and choose the alignment pattern you're seeking. Align Top Left, for example, aligns text to the top and left margins of the cell, so that the text starts in the upper-left corner.

Table layout on the page

When you created your table, you probably dragged it where you wanted it, or built it starting from the insertion point. To position it exactly where it looks best on the page and apply advanced features like text wrapping, use the tools in the Table→Table Properties→Table tab, shown in Figure 4-20.

Note: If you try to drag a table down in your document (to add text above the table, for example), the table may not break properly across pages. The workaround: Copy the table, open a new Word document, type the new text, then paste the table below it.

- **Size.** Use this box to set a width for the entire table. (It says "*Preferred* width" because it may change if you use the AutoFit feature, as described on page 169.)

- **Alignment.** Choose left, centered, or right alignment. "Indent from left" tells Word where to start aligning, measured from the edge of the page. (If your table already spans the page, margin to margin, you won't see any difference.)

- **Text Wrapping.** For large tables, you'll usually choose None. If you choose Around, the Positioning button becomes activated; clicking opens a dialog box where you can use advanced layout features like those described on page 160.

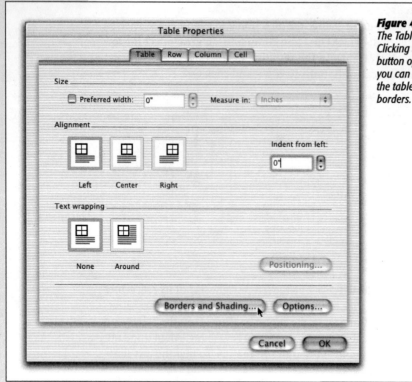

Figure 4-20:
The Table Properties dialog box. Clicking the Borders and Shading button opens a dialog box where you can choose lines and fills for the table, as well as page borders.

Nested tables

A *nested table* is a table-within-a-table, or, more specifically, a table within a *cell* of another table. This feature is especially valuable when you're using Word as a Web-design tool. For example, you can create a table with four large cells to divide your Web page into quarters, and put a smaller table in each one.

To create a nested table, click in the cell where you want the table to start, then click the Insert Table button on the Tables and Borders toolbar. Choose the number of rows and columns for your nested table. Now you can click in one of the nested cells and start typing. (Because the nested table must remain within one cell, either resize the cell to hold the nested table, or choose Table→AutoFit→ AutoFit to Contents to allow the holding cell to expand.)

Merging and splitting cells

Merging and splitting are nothing more than ways of subtracting or adding columns en masse. Merging cells (or rows or columns) turns two into one, and pours their contents together. Splitting cells (or rows or columns) divides them, forcing their contents into the cell above or to the left of the split.

Start by highlighting the cells, rows, or columns you want to merge. Then choose Table→Merge Cells, or click the Merge Cells button on the Tables and Borders toolbar; the selected cells instantly merge. Another way to proceed: Use the eraser tool to remove the line dividing two cells, columns, or rows; this way you can see directly how merging cells works.

Figure 4-21:
Top: A 2 x 2 table.

Middle: The same table after merging the top two cells.

Bottom: The table after splitting the top two cells in two. If the "Merge cells before split" box had been checked in the Split Cells dialog box, Farewell would immediately follow So Long in the upper-right cell.

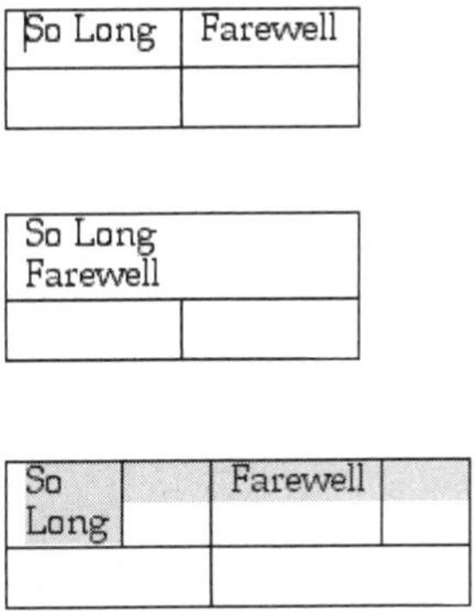

So Long	Farewell

So Long Farewell	

So Long		Farewell	

The quickest and most satisfying way to split cells is to draw new lines right smack across existing cells, using the Draw Table tool on the Tables and Borders toolbar.

If you need computer-aided precision, however, you can split cells, rows, or columns perfectly evenly by selecting them and then choosing Table→Split Cells (or click the Split Cells button on the Tables and Borders toolbar). In the Split Cells dialog box, choose the number of rows and columns you want *each* cell to be divided into. For example, the cells at the right in Figure 4-21 were split into two columns and one row; the one row that was selected stayed one row, and the two columns became a total of four.

Tip: You can also split a *table,* creating a blank line between its top and bottom portions—a great trick when you need to insert some regular text into the middle of it. Just click where you want the split and then choose Table→Split Table.

Converting text to a table

Sometimes you want to create a table from information that's already in Word, such as a table that a novice Word person (perhaps even a younger you) created by trying to line up text with the Tab key. At other times, you've got a table and want to extract its information *without* maintaining its tableness (before importing into a page-layout program, for example, because page-layout programs don't understand Word tables). Word is happy to be your obedient servant.

The key to turning highlighted text into a table is the Table→Convert→Convert Text to Table command. Presumably, the text is a list, a number of words separated by tabs, or some other vaguely table-like blob of text. In the Convert Text to Table dialog box, start with the "Separate text at" settings. Choose the most logical place to divide your selected text into cells. If that's not a paragraph, comma, or tab, then click Other and press the key that represents your choice—Space bar, Return, period, and so on.

Word automatically suggests the number of columns you'll need to hold all the text; you can also specify the number of rows and columns you want. You also have the chance to use the AutoFit and AutoFormat features now—or you can always save them for later. Click OK to begin the conversion process.

If the table doesn't look quite as you had hoped, examine it and learn how Word interpreted your choices in the Convert Text to Table dialog box. Then press ⌘-Z to undo the conversion and try again with different selections. Or just reformat your table using the tools described in this section.

Converting a table into text

Converting a table to text is easier still. Click the table and choose Table→Convert→ Convert Table to Text.

Your only decision is how to divide the contents of one cell from the next—you don't want them all to run together, of course. You have a choice of paragraph marks (each cell's contents will become a new Word paragraph), tabs, commas, or any other character you enter in the Other box by pressing its key. If you choose tabs, the result is what you've heard described as *tab delimited text;* that is, one tab separating each word or phrase that formerly occupied a cell on a single row, with a Return character at the end of each line.

Formulas in tables

Word is no Excel, but Microsoft is at least aware that you may want to do simple math from time to time. Fortunately, a table can carry out many of the most common spreadsheet tasks with the help of functions and operators. You can add up a column of numbers, for example, or have Word average them and display the results.

To add a column of figures, click in the bottom cell of the column (making sure that it's blank, of course) and click the AutoSum (Σ) button in the Tables and Borders toolbar (see Figure 4-22, left). Your answer appears immediately against a gray background (which doesn't print). This gray box indicates that you're dealing with an uneditable *field* (see page 228).

Note: This kind of field doesn't update automatically. If your table numbers change, you must repeat the click on the AutoSum button (or click the field and then press F9).

For more complex formulas, click the cell where you want to place the results of your calculations and choose Table→Formula. Word's guess at what formula you're looking for already appears in the Formula window. If that's not right, press Delete, type an equal sign to begin your formula, and build it with the following (see Figure 4-22):

- **Cell references.** Cells in Word tables are named the same way as in Excel spreadsheets, except that you can't see the row letters and column numbers. The columns are named A, B, C, and so on, from left to right; the rows are numbered 1, 2, 3, and so on, from top to bottom. The upper-leftmost cell is A1.

  To refer to the entire column above the formula cell, use the expression *(ABOVE)*; to refer to the entire row, use *(LEFT)*. For a *range* of cells (a block of them), use a colon to separate the top left and lower-right cells of the range, such as A1:B2 to name a four-cell range.

Figure 4-22:
Top: Clicking in the bottom cell and the clicking AutoSum adds up the numbers in each column.

Middle: The Tables and Borders toolbar shows the AutoSum button responsible for this magic.

Bottom: The Table→Formula command reveals that the AutoSum function does nothing more than insert the invisible formula =SUM(ABOVE) into the selected cell. You could have typed it in this dialog box yourself, if you had very little else to do. In this case, currency formatting was selected from the pop-up menu. You can also choose simpler formatting without the dollar sign and decimal point.

Quarter	Orders	Shipments	Total
Q1	154	98	$23,209
Q2	398	255	$58,039
Q3	355	211	$52,293
Q4	85	34	$2,345
Totals:	992	598	$135,886.00

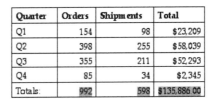

AutoSum

Formula

Formula:

=SUM(ABOVE)

Number format:

$#,##0.00;($#,##0.00)

Paste function: Paste bookmark:

Cancel   OK

- **Operators.** *Operators* are symbols like + for addition, – for subtraction, * for multiplication, / for division, and > for greater than. To view a complete list, type *Mathematical and relational operators* into the search box of Word's Help system. Using operators in combination, you can set up a table cell to add sales tax (* *1.06*) to a subtotal column, for example.

• **Functions.** Choose formulas from the "Paste function" list in the Table→Formula dialog box. These are the same as the Excel formulas described in Chapter 12.

• Click the arrow next to the **Number format** box to tell Word what you want the results to look like—AutoFormatted with a dollar sign, with commas, and so on.

Click OK to place the formula in the current cell; see Chapter 12 for much more on using formulas in Office X.

Sorting tables

If your table contains names, dates, or other listed items, you may want to arrange them in numerical or alphabetical order. To do so, click the table and choose Table→Sort.

In the "Sort by" box, Word helpfully suggests that you start with "Column 1," the first column on the left. All the columns in the current table are listed in a menu; click the arrows to choose one. For instance, to sort chronologically, choose the column that contains your dates. You can sort by Text (alphabetically), Number, or Date; just choose the one that matches your data.

You can choose second and third sort columns as well. For example, after the first column sorts by date, you may want to sort names alphabetically *within* each date. Use the "Then by" boxes to set up these second and third internal sorts.

Click OK to begin the sort. (Note that you can't sort columns—only rows.)

Comments, Change Tracking, and Versions

Most of the time, the point of your work in Office is to create documents you'll eventually send or show to *other people*. (The exception: Keeping a diary in Word. You know who you are.)

In the modern working world, more and more people find it valuable to be able to mark up and revise such distributed documents. Thanks to the features described in this chapter, you, the original author, can look over other people's edits, incorporate them if you agree, or delete them if you don't. Whether you're working with one partner or an entire team of co-workers, Word's collaboration features make it easy to track the various revisions and versions of the electronically transmitted documents that you'll inevitably create.

Comments

Often when reviewing someone else's document, you'll want to add comments without making them a part of the text itself. You'll have a query for the author, an idea, a suggestion, or a joke—the kind of thing that you'd write in the margin or on a sticky note if you were working on paper. Fortunately, the days of typing boldfaced or bracketed comments directly into the text are over.

Adding Comments

To add just a single comment in Word, select the text that you're commenting on and then choose Insert→Comment (or press Option-⌘-A). The Comments pane opens at the bottom of the document window, as shown in Figure 5-1, with an insertion point at the beginning of a newly numbered comment marked with your initials. The text you originally selected now appears marked with a yellow highlight. Type your comment; press F6 to return to the main (upper) pane of the document window (or just click there).

If you plan to make more than a few comments, however, you may find it more convenient to open the *Reviewing toolbar,* which lets you add a comment with a single click. After highlighting the text you'd like to praise, criticize, or deconstruct, proceed as follows:

1. **Choose View→Toolbars→Reviewing.**

   The Reviewing toolbar opens.

2. **Click the Insert Comment button on the Reviewing toolbar (see Figure 5-1).**

   Word splits your window, showing the Comments pane at the bottom.

3. **Type your comment; click back in the upper pane of the document window to return to it.**

   You can also press F6 to toggle between the two panes.

4. **When you're finished adding comments, close the Comments pane by clicking its close button or by pressing Shift-Control-C.**

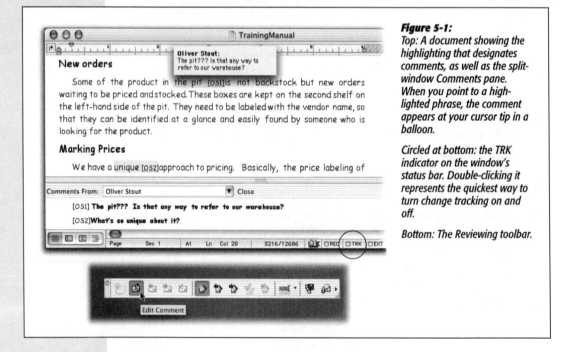

Figure 5-1:
Top: A document showing the highlighting that designates comments, as well as the split-window Comments pane. When you point to a highlighted phrase, the comment appears at your cursor tip in a balloon.

Circled at bottom: the TRK indicator on the window's status bar. Double-clicking it represents the quickest way to turn change tracking on and off.

Bottom: The Reviewing toolbar.

Reviewing Comments

When you open a document with comments, the Comments pane doesn't automatically open. Instead, you see only strips of yellow highlighting, indicating the places where comments have been lodged. Point to each, without clicking, to view the comment in a tooltip balloon like the one shown in the previous illustration.

Note: In long and complex documents, these comment balloons can take a long time to appear, and sometimes never appear. Clicking in the window and then pointing the cursor again sometimes helps, as does turning off "Check spelling as you type" and "Check grammar as you type" (in the Word→Preferences→Spelling tab). If you're unable to make these balloons appear, just open the Comments pane, as described next.

If you like, you can open (or close) the Comments pane, where all the document's comments are listed sequentially. To do that, click the Edit Comment button on the Reviewing toolbar, shown in Figure 5-1, or choose View→Comments. Or, you can just double-click the bracketed initials of the person who made the comment (the *comment mark*). Among other things, opening the Comments pane makes it easy to incorporate your editors' comments into the document itself, either by copying and pasting the text from the Comments pane or by drag-and-dropping it.

Tip: To delete a comment after reading it, Control-click its yellow highlighting and choose Delete Comment from the contextual menu.

Navigating Comments

The main document pane and the Comments pane have independent vertical scroll bars. You can move around in each one using any of Word's usual navigation tools (see page 69). You can also use the Previous Comment and Next Comment buttons on the Reviewing toolbar (Figure 5-1), or the Object Browser described on page 73, to hop from one comment in the document to the next. (The main document window scrolls automatically to keep up.)

If the Comments pane isn't visible, choose View→Comments, or double-click a comment mark, such as *[NB3]*. Now you can edit comments—yours or anyone else's— or click Delete Comment (on the Reviewing toolbar) to do away with a comment completely.

Change Tracking

When it's time to mark up a document for revision, many people who otherwise use their Mac for everything still turn to paper, pencil, and highlighter. After all, marking up a printout lets you see both the original and your handwritten edits at a glance. And when you collaborate with others on a paper or project, you can use different colored ink to differentiate the various editors.

The problem with the paper method is that you eventually have to retype the document, incorporating all the handwritten comments, into Word.

To avoid all that hassle, edit onscreen in Word instead. Word has tools that let you highlight with different colors and see at a glance who made what changes. Even better than paper, Word can automate the process of comparing and merging edited documents.

Getting Ready for Change Tracking

In order for Word's change tracking tools to work properly, you have to tell Word how you want your name to appear (when it's used to "sign" comments and changes) and how to display the changes.

Identify yourself

Especially if you're working with others, Word needs to know who you are so that your name can be attached to your version and your changes. To ensure that Word knows you correctly, choose Word→Preferences→User Information panel. If your name isn't already there, fill in the Author box, as shown in Figure 5-2. Word will use the name or initials in the author box to identify and label any changes and comments you add to the document. Click OK when you're finished.

Note: The User Information tab and your own address book "card" in Entourage are linked; that is, when you change User Information, you also change your Entourage "this is me" card, and vice versa. (You tell Entourage which set of contact information is yours by opening the card with your info and choosing Contact→This Is Me.)

By the way, none of this has anything to do with the Author name that appears in the File→Properties→Summary tab, which Word pretty much ignores.

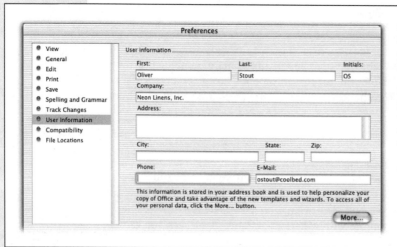

Figure 5-2:
Every time you annotate a document—whether it's yours or somebody else's—Word "signs" the comment, insertion, or deletion with your own name. And how does it know your name? Because your name and initials appear here, in the Word→Preferences→User Information panel.

Setting Word to track changes: Method 1

Suppose you receive a document from a colleague who's asked you to help clean up the prose. If you just dive right in, editing away, she'll have no way of spotting the changes you made. When you intend to review a document, whether it's your own draft or a Word document given to you by someone else, you must ask Word to track your changes *before* making them.

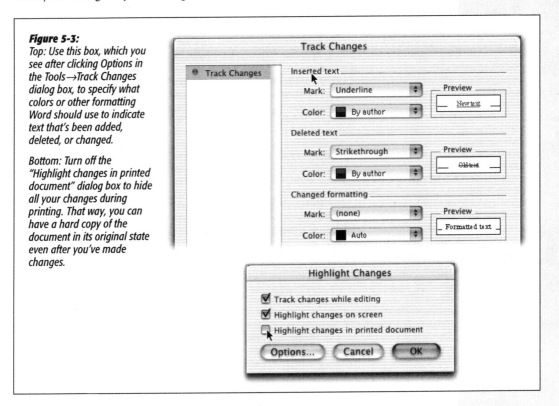

Figure 5-3:
Top: Use this box, which you see after clicking Options in the Tools→Track Changes dialog box, to specify what colors or other formatting Word should use to indicate text that's been added, deleted, or changed.

Bottom: Turn off the "Highlight changes in printed document" dialog box to hide all your changes during printing. That way, you can have a hard copy of the document in its original state even after you've made changes.

By far the easiest way to activate change tracking is to turn on the tiny TRK button at the bottom edge of your document window (Figure 5-1). (The button turns green when you click it.) From now on, Word will record any changes you make, as described in the next section.

Note: If your changes don't appear in a different color after you've turned on change tracking in the Status bar, then you need to turn on change *highlighting*, as described next.

Setting Word to track changes: Method 2

If you prefer the long way, however, you can turn on change tracking and gain some additional options, as follows:

1. Choose Tools→Track Changes→Highlight Changes.

The Highlight Changes dialog box opens, as shown in Figure 5-3.

2. Turn on "Track changes while editing."

You also have the option to turn "Highlight changes on screen" on or off. If it's *off*, you won't see any special markings as you edit the document; the usual coloring and strikethrough annotations won't appear. You'll feel as though you're editing a Word file *without* change tracking turned on. (The only difference: Every now and then, Word will abruptly refuse to let you backspace any farther than you have. That's because your insertion point has collided with a deleted word—which you can't see because it's currently invisible.)

Behind the scenes, though, Word will indeed record every change you make. At any time, you or a collaborator can choose Tools→Track Changes→Highlight Changes and turn "Highlight changes on screen" *on* again to make them show up.

Now proceed as described in "Making Changes," below.

Making Changes

After turning on change tracking as described above, now you can edit the Word document as usual. You can use any of the tools described in Chapter 2, including inserting text, formatting it, and deleting large blocks of text or even entire pages. Word keeps track of it all, as shown in Figure 5-4.

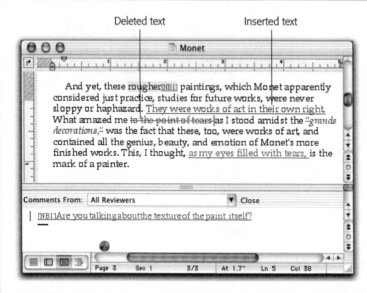

Figure 5-4:
If your work comes back to you appearing heavily marked up by your editors, don't feel too depressed. Remember that every proposed replacement text results in two colorful blotches on the screen—one passage with a line through it, the other appearing as an insertion.

Changing tracking options

The Track Changes dialog box in Figure 5-3 and the sample document in Figure 5-4 show Word's default settings, regarding the following onscreen changes:

- Word places a thin vertical line in the margin where *any* kind of change has been made.

- Text you've inserted is underlined; it's color-coded by author, too. Text typed by the first person to review the document appears in red; the second author in blue, the third in pink, and so on, for up to eight authors. Then Word starts over again with red.

- Deleted text displays strikethrough style, ~~like this~~, *and* is color-coded by author.

- Formatting changes (to boldface or italic, for instance) don't leave any visual trace except for the thin margin line. (You can change this setting, however, as described next. In Figure 5-4, for example, this setting was adjusted so that reformatted text would appear in a different color.)

Here is how to work with these options:

1. **Choose Tools→Track Changes→Highlight Changes. Click Options.**

   The Track Changes dialog box opens (see Figure 5-3).

2. **For each kind of change, use the pop-up menu to indicate a highlighting style.**

   For instance, you could choose "none" for "Deleted text" so that it will disappear instead of being struck through; choose bold instead of underlining for "Inserted text" for a less cluttered look. The pop-up menus offer different marks for each context.

3. **If you don't want to use Word's "By author" color system, as described above, choose different colors for "Inserted text" and "Deleted text."**

   Unless everyone in your work group can agree on a different color scheme, it's probably best to stick with Word's color choices. Having different editors in the same document can get confusing, and Word does a great job of keeping track of the colors.

   Choose different colors for reformatted text ("Changed formatting") and the marginal lines ("Outside border") only if you want to make these items more obvious.

4. **Click OK.**

Reviewing Changes One by One

When a Word document comes back to you after having been edited using the tracking feature, it's very easy for you to review the changes one by one, accepting or rejecting each proposed revision, until you wind up with a normal, clean-looking document. (For documents with multiple authors or editors, see "Merging Tracked Changes" below before proceeding.)

To get started, open the document or merged document.

Reviewing changes: Light edits

If there's only light editing, the easiest way to approve or reject each change is simply to Control-click the changed text; from the contextual menu, choose Accept Change or Reject Change. When you accept a change, Word removes the color and marking and turns the change into normal text. When you *reject* a change, Word removes the marked or colored text and restores the original.

Reviewing changes: Heavier edits

If there are many changes likely to be approved, you may as well pull out the heavy artillery—the Reviewing toolbar:

1. **Choose View→Toolbars→Reviewing.**

   The Reviewing toolbar appears.

2. **Click at the beginning of the document; click the Next Change icon on the Reviewing toolbar.**

   Word scrolls to the first change and highlights it. Look over the suggestion; decide whether, in your estimation, it's an improvement or not.

3. **Click the Accept Change icon (with the checkmark) or the Reject Change icon (with the x) on the Reviewing toolbar.**

   Again, when you accept a change, Word turns the change into normal text. When you reject one, Word restores the original.

   If you change your mind after accepting or rejecting a change, press ⌘-Z to undo it.

4. **Click the Next Change icon and continue the process.**

   If change tracking is turned on, any new editing you do will be highlighted on the screen with your author color. To eliminate this during your last pass, click the Track Changes button on the Reviewing toolbar to turn it off, or turn off the TRK indicator at the bottom of the document.

   After you've reached the end of the document, but missed reviewing some changes along the way, Word asks if you want to return to the beginning.

5. **Click OK.**

Accepting or Rejecting All Changes

If you trust your editors completely, you can accept or reject *all* changes in a document, all at once. You don't even have to look at them first (although you should, unless you're sure your editors are *much* smarter than you are). Word also makes it possible to view the document as a whole, with or without all changes.

1. **Choose Tools→Track Changes→Accept or Reject changes.**

   The dialog box shown in Figure 5-5 opens.

2. **Choose a way to view the document.**

   The dialog box now onscreen is small for a reason: It's designed to be moved aside, so that you can survey the document before making the radical move of accepting or rejecting all of the edits that have been made to it.

   To help you with this pursuit, you're offered three radio buttons. They let you see the document with all changes highlighted (as shown in Figure 5-4); as if all changes were accepted ("Changes without highlighting"), or in its original state before any changes were made. These humble-looking radio buttons are one of the most powerful aspects of the change-tracking feature.

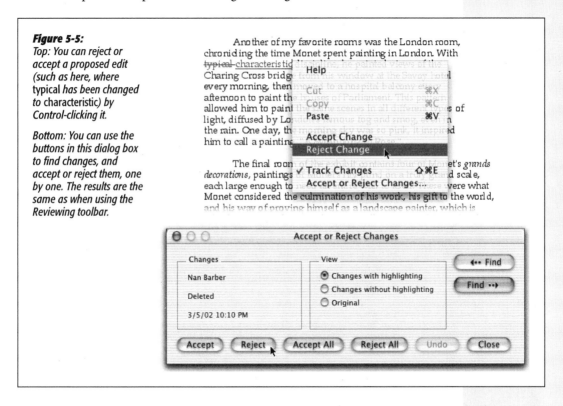

Figure 5-5:
Top: You can reject or accept a proposed edit (such as here, where typical *has been changed to* characteristic*) by Control-clicking it.*

Bottom: You can use the buttons in this dialog box to find changes, and accept or reject them, one by one. The results are the same as when using the Reviewing toolbar.

3. **To go ahead and make all proposed changes, click Accept All. To return the document to its original condition, click Reject All.**

   Word asks if you're sure before proceeding. Even after accepting all or rejecting all, you can change your mind by clicking Undo.

4. **Click Close.**

Merging Tracked Changes

One of the most common scenarios for using change tracking is to email or otherwise transfer the same original document out to several reviewers, each of whom peppers it with edits and comments. If they all came back on paper, it would be quite a challenge to sort through and incorporate all the good ideas.

In Word, it's easy to merge the edited documents together, one by one. To do so, open the original file—or any one of the edited documents—and proceed as follows:

1. **Choose Tools→Merge Documents.**

   Word opens the Choose a File dialog box, where you'll choose the first file to merge into the currently open document. If you're unsure where the document is saved, but have some idea of the file name or certain words found in it, click Find File to have Word search for it.

2. **When you find the file, double-click it.**

   Word begins the merging process. When it's over, the original document contains both its own tracked changes *and* those merged in from the second document. The changes from different authors appear in different colors.

3. **If you have more files to incorporate, repeat Steps 1 and 2.**

   When all the documents are merged, place your insertion point at the beginning of the document and review the changes as described on the preceding pages.

UP TO SPEED

Preparing to Send a Reviewed Document

If someone *else* will be merging the reviewed documents, there are a few things you can do to make his job easier when you send your edited copy:

Make changes visible. Choose Tools→Track Changes→ Highlight Changes, or click Highlight Changes in the Reviewing toolbar, before you send your document off. That way, the recipient can see immediately that it's been edited.

Change the name. Add your initials to the file's name in the Finder, for example, so that it won't be confused with the original during the merging process.

Send the most recent version. As you edit the document, you can freeze it in time by using Word's *versioning* feature (described later in this chapter). When you're ready to return your final edits, choose File→Versions and open the version that you want to submit. Choose File→Save As and save it as a separate document under a new file name before you send it off. Using this method, you still have a record of all versions you created, but your recipient only gets the one you intended to send out. (What's more, using the Save As command produces a much smaller file.)

Comparing Documents

The merging process described earlier in this chapter works well if *all* documents have been edited using Word's change-tracking feature. But often enough, you wind up with two drafts of a document, one of which has been edited (by you or somebody else). Word's Compare Documents feature can help you see where edits have been made—a feature that has saved the bacon of more than one lawyer in back-and-forth contract negotiations.

To use it, round up both the edited version and your original or master copy and proceed as follows:

1. **Open the changed copy of the document. Choose Tools→Track Changes→ Compare Documents.**

   Word opens the Choose a File dialog box. Here's where you select the *original* document—the one you want to compare the edited version to. The original could be the one that's never been edited, or one that's been edited with change tracking or even merged. Just make sure that you've reviewed it and accepted or rejected all tracked changes before you begin the comparing process.

2. **When you locate the original version of the document, double-click it.**

   Word compares the two documents. Their differences are depicted as tracked changes in the first document you opened. In other words, text that's in the edited version but *not* in your original appears in color and underlined; text that somebody deleted from the edited version appears with strikethrough lettering.

If there were already tracked changes in either of the documents, Word ignores them and gives priority to the actual, unmarked text. If either of the documents has untracked changes, Word asks before proceeding with the comparing process. Usually, you'll want to click OK and go ahead. The unmarked changes may be edits you made to the document while you were writing it, before you started the reviewing process.

Versioning

The File→Versions command performs a kind of temporary Save, by creating a snapshot of your document at a moment in time—without actually creating a new document. All versions of a document are stored in the same file on your hard drive with the same file name; even though it may contain eleven different drafts, you still see only a single icon in the Finder.

Saving versions, in other words, creates listings in the Versions dialog box, not separate document files. Thus, you can save as many versions as you like without losing them or creating a mass of documents on your hard drive.

Saving a Version

Suppose you open your first draft of a document. You're about to do some heavy editing, but you're not sure you're going to like your own new direction. By saving the current draft as a version, you'll always be able to return to the document the way it used to be.

To save a version of the document you're working in, proceed as follows:

1. **Choose File→Versions.**

   The Versions dialog box opens, as shown in Figure 5-6.

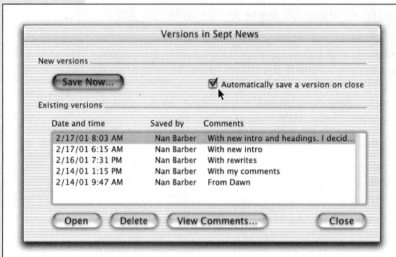

Figure 5-6:
You can see the first few words of your comments in the Versions dialog box. Double-click one of the drafts listed to return to that previous version. Or, to see the full comments you wrote for each version, click View Comments.

2. **Click Save Now.**

   The Save Version dialog box opens. Type some comments that will help you remember what the version is all about (such as *Halloween XXV: Romantic comedy approach*) then click OK.

You have just saved a version.

GEM IN THE ROUGH

Automatically Saving a Version

You don't have to remember to save a version every time you cultivate a new draft of your document; Word can do so automatically.

Just choose File→Versions, and then turn on "Automatically save a version on close" in the Versions dialog box (Figure 5-6). Click OK. From now on, Word saves a new version every time you close the file—a logical time to do so, preserving each session's editing efforts as a separate draft. (You don't have the opportunity to name each automatic draft; Word calls each one "Automatic version," although it does date-stamp each one in the Versions dialog box.)

You can now forget all about the Versioning feature. To save, choose File→Save (⌘-S) as usual. When you open a document that has versions, Word always shows you the latest draft.

Opening a Version

To return to a particular version, first open the document. Then choose File→Versions. Double-click the name of a version in the list. To help you keep track of what's going on, Word opens the selected draft in a separate window. Both the latest document and your selected earlier version are now visible, with their windows tiled one above the other. (The date and time stamp in the window name helps you identify the earlier version.)

Spinning Off a Version

The beauty of saving lots of versions is that you can open any one of them and save it as a separate document at any time. To do so, open a version as described above. Click the version's window and choose File→Save or Save As (or F12). A standard Save sheet opens in the version's window, where you can choose a name and location for the new document.

Deleting a Version

If you have too many confusing versions in the Versions dialog box, you can delete some of them. To delete a version, select it and click Delete. Word asks if you're sure (you can't undo this deletion). Continue selecting and deleting as many versions as you wish.

Click OK to exit the Versions dialog box.

Advanced
Word Processing

A Word document, like a book, is only as good as the sum of its parts. Chapters, a table of contents, an index, footnotes, and cross-references all work together to help orient your audience in the material. No matter how important the information or how brilliant the fiction, if the words are presented as pages and pages of plain text, your reader will get lost and maybe even give up. You need to break it up into parts, and the parts need to work together. It's all about the packaging.

This chapter takes you deep into the woods of Word's power-user features, well off the beaten path trod by millions of everyday, casual users. The material you'll find here is at your disposal when you need to write a dissertation, full-length book, or another complex, structured document.

Headers and Footers

A header or footer is a special strip that can show the page number—as well as your book title, chapter title, name, date, and other information—at the top or the bottom of every printed page in your document (or one section of it).

Creating Headers and Footers

Word treats the header and footer as a special box at the top or bottom of the page. To view these special text areas, choose View→Header and Footer; dotted lines appear around the header and footer areas of your document, and the Header and Footer toolbar appears, as shown in Figure 6-1. The rest of your document, meanwhile, fades to gray. (If you find even that faded representation of your body text distracting, hide it by clicking the Show/Hide Document Text icon on the Header and Footer toolbar.)

Tip: If you're working in Page Layout view, you don't have to bother with the View→Header and Footer command. Just move the cursor to the top or bottom of the page; when the cursor turns into this shape 🖹, double-click. The header/footer dotted lines appear.

Fill your header or footer by typing inside it and clicking icons in the Header and Footer toolbar. For your convenience, Word places a centered tab stop in the middle of the typing area, and a right-aligned tab stop at the right. You can choose View→ Ruler and adjust these tab stops, of course (see page 128), but they're especially handy when you want to produce a header like the one shown in Figure 6-1.

1. **Make sure the cursor is at the left margin. Type the chapter title.**

   After typing *Chapter 1: The Beginning,* you can highlight and format it; for example, italicize it by pressing ⌘-I.

2. **Press Tab.**

   The cursor jumps to the center-aligned tab in the middle of the header or footer.

3. **Insert the date.**

   Click the Insert Date icon on the toolbar, as shown in Figure 6-1. (Word inserts the date as a *field,* which is continuously updated; whenever you print or send this document, the date will be current.)

4. **Press Tab.**

   Now your cursor is aligned at the right margin.

5. **Type *Page,* and a space; insert the page number by clicking the Insert Page Number icon on the toolbar (Figure 6-1); type *of;* insert the total number of pages by clicking the Insert Number of Pages icon.**

   (If you need help identifying an icon on this toolbar, point to it without clicking. As usual in Office X, a yellow tooltip balloon appears to identify it.)

   Word inserts placeholder fields (indicated by a nonprinting, gray background) into your header or footer, so that it says *Page 3 of 15,* for example. When you print or scroll through your document, you'll see that each page is correctly labeled in this way. (Of course, most people don't use the "Page X of Y" notation; if you want just the page number to appear, simply click the Insert Page Number icon and be done with it.)

Tip: If, at this point, you want more control over page numbering, click the Format Page Number button on the Header and Footer toolbar, as shown in Figure 6-1. In the dialog box that appears, you can specify how you'd like the page numbers to appear (*a, b, c,* or in Roman numerals, or with chapter numbers included). You can also indicate that you'd like them to begin with some number other than 1, which is ideal when your document is the *continuation* of a document you've already printed.

6. Double-click the dimmed body portion of your document (or click the Close button on the toolbar) to exit the header/footer editing area.

Tip: Headers and footers don't appear or print when you save your Word files as Web pages. But leave them in—they will appear and print if you return to using the same file as a Word document.

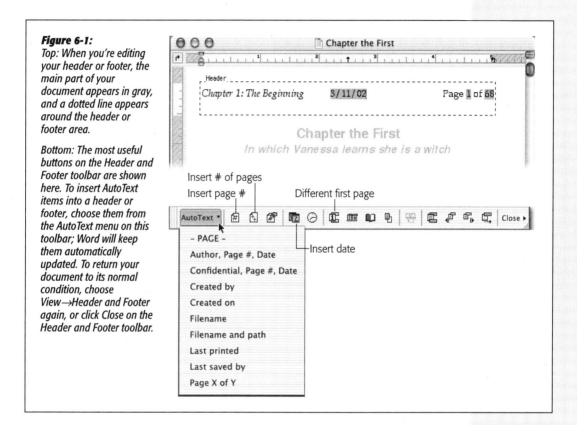

Figure 6-1:
Top: When you're editing your header or footer, the main part of your document appears in gray, and a dotted line appears around the header or footer area.

Bottom: The most useful buttons on the Header and Footer toolbar are shown here. To insert AutoText items into a header or footer, choose them from the AutoText menu on this toolbar; Word will keep them automatically updated. To return your document to its normal condition, choose View→Header and Footer again, or click Close on the Header and Footer toolbar.

Positioning headers and footers

By default, headers and footers extend from the left margin to the right margin. To make them wider than the text and extend them into the margins, give the header or footer a *hanging* or *negative indent* (see page 125).

To move a header or footer higher or lower on the page, click in it and choose Format→Document→Margins tab; adjust the numbers in the "From edge" boxes. (Higher numbers move the header or footer text closer to the middle of the page.) Alternatively, you can adjust it visually by clicking in the header or footer and then dragging its margin up or down in the vertical ruler at the left side of the page. This adjusts the distance between the header or footer and the body of the text.

Title pages

If your term paper has a title page (featuring the name of the paper centered on an otherwise blank page), it would look a little silly if the paper's title also appeared at the bottom.

Fortunately, you can give your first page a different header or footer—or none. To do so, go to the first page of your document. Choose Format→Document→Layout tab, click "Different first page," and click OK. (Alternatively, click the Different First Page button on the Header and Footer toolbar.)

Tip: The "first page" setting applies only to the *section* that contains your cursor (see page 137). In other words, you can control the header/footer's appearance independently for each section in your document.

Now you can edit and format the unique header and footer for your first page, or just leave them blank. (You can also apply this technique to the first page of each *section* of your document; see page 137 for more detail on sections.) If you haven't formatted the header and footer for the rest of the document, click the Show Next button on the Header and Footer toolbar; Word takes you to the second page, where you create the headers and footers for the rest of the pages.

UP TO SPEED

Page Numbers: The Other Method

Page numbers are the most popular use of headers and footers. That's why Word provides buttons for adding and formatting them right on the Header and Footer toolbar (see Figure 6-1).

But there's an even easier way to number your pages in Word: Just choose Insert→Page Numbers. The Page Numbers dialog box opens, as shown here. Watch the Preview window change as you set up the controls found here, such as Alignment (which includes Inside or Outside, for use when you're setting up bound-book pages); "Show number on first page" (turn it off if your document has a title page); and the Format button,

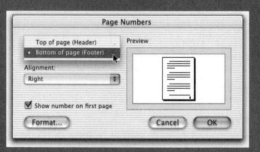

which opens a dialog box where you can specify what kind of numbering you want (1, 2, 3; i, ii, iii; a, b, c; and so on).

When you turn on "Include chapter number," Word includes the chapter number along with the page number—in a "Chapter 1, Page 1" scheme. In the "Chapter starts with style" menu, choose the heading *style* that you used for the chapter number (you have to use one of Word's built-in headings—or a style based upon one of them—to make this numbering feature work). Then, choose a separator (a hyphen, dash, or whatever).

Bound-book pages

If your document is going to be bound like a book, you'll probably want different headers and footers on odd and even pages, exactly like those on these book pages (book name on left-side pages, chapter name on right-side pages).

To create these mirror-image headers and footers, choose Format→Document→ Layout tab, click "Different odd and even," and click OK. (Alternatively, click the Different Odd and Even Pages icon on the Header and Footer toolbar.) Then edit the headers and footers for the odd and even pages in your document; when you edit *any single* odd or even page, Word applies the changes to *all* of them.

Different headers (and footers) for different sections

If you've divided your document into *sections* (see page 137), you can have different headers and footers for each section—a very common technique when you want to break your document into chapters.

By default, all headers and footers in a document are the same, even when you insert section breaks, so the trick is to *sever* the connection between the header and footer in consecutive sections. For instance, if you want a different header in each of your document's three sections, go to a page in the *second* section and choose View→Header and Footer. Click in the header and click the Same as Previous icon on the Header and Footer toolbar. (This button breaks or rejoins the header/footer connection between each section and the one before it. You can use it to restore the header and footer connections if you change your mind, and once again make them uniform throughout the document.)

Repeat the process for the third section, and so on.

Footnotes and Endnotes

Footnotes, as any research scholar can tell you, are explanations or citations located at the bottom of each page, referred to by a small superscript number or symbol in the main text. (See Figure 6-3 for an example.) *Endnotes* are similar, except that they're listed together in a clump at the end of the document, instead of on each page. Word can handle each kind of annotation gracefully. Here's how to insert a footnote or endnote into your document:

1. **Click at the exact point in your document where you want the superscript note number to appear; choose Insert→Footnote.**

   The Footnote and Endnote dialog box appears, proposing a footnote. (Press the keystroke ⌘-E, or click Endnote, for an endnote instead.)

   If left to its own devices, Word will number your footnotes sequentially (1, 2, 3…). If you'd rather use a symbol (such as an asterisk), click "Custom mark" and type the desired symbol, or click the Symbol button and choose one from the various palettes.

2. **If you want nonstandard numbering, click Options.**

If you're some kind of radical, you may prefer Roman numerals, letters, symbols, or something else. In the resulting dialog box (see Figure 6-2), you can also choose where to place footnotes and endnotes: at the bottom of the page or immediately after the text, for instance. Click OK to close the box.

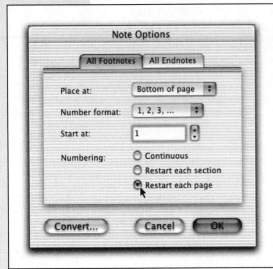

Figure 6-2:
The radio buttons on the All Footnotes and All Endnotes tabs let you choose where to start and restart the numbering. For instance, if you choose "Restart each page," the first footnote on each page will be marked "1."

3. **Click OK to close the Footnote and Endnote dialog box.**

Word opens up a pane at the bottom of the document window where you can type the actual text of the note. (To toggle between displaying and hiding the note pane in Normal view, choose View→Footnotes; in Page Layout view, no such shenanigans are necessary—the notes simply appear at the bottom of the page. You can edit them directly.)

Word usually draws a horizontal line, a third of the way across the page, above your footnotes. If you'd like to edit this line to say, for example, *NOTES:*, choose Footnote Separator or Endnote Separator from the Footnotes pop-up menu (in the bar at the top of the note pane). Now edit the text (or line) that you find there. You could even make the line a different color, for example, or delete it entirely by clicking it and pressing Delete.

4. **Type your footnote.**

A footnote is often a *citation*—a reference to a specific book or article that provided your information. One standard format for citations is called MLA (Modern Language Association) style, and it looks like this:

Watanna, Onoto, *A Japanese Nightingale* (New York, Harper & Brothers, 1901) 41.

The definitive guide to correct MLA-style footnotes is the *MLA Handbook for Writers of Research Papers* (for high school and undergraduate students) or the *MLA Style Manual and Guide to Scholarly Publishing* (for graduate students, scholars, and professional writers); for more information visit *www.mla.org*.

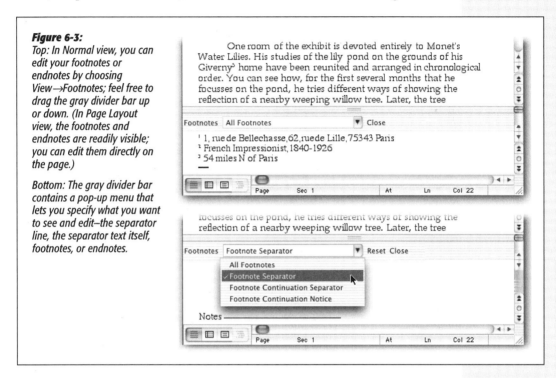

Figure 6-3:
Top: In Normal view, you can edit your footnotes or endnotes by choosing View→Footnotes; feel free to drag the gray divider bar up or down. (In Page Layout view, the footnotes and endnotes are readily visible; you can edit them directly on the page.)

Bottom: The gray divider bar contains a pop-up menu that lets you specify what you want to see and edit–the separator line, the separator text itself, footnotes, or endnotes.

5. **Repeat from step 1 to add more footnotes, or click Close to move the Footnotes pane out of your way.**

   Each footnote is marked in your text by a small number or symbol, as specified by you. At any time, you can jump back and forth between the footnote symbol (in the main window) and the Footnotes pane by pressing F6.

Tip: You can combine footnotes and endnotes in a single document. For example, footnotes might contain explanations and elaborations of text, while endnotes might contain citations.

Deleting Footnotes and Endnotes

To remove a footnote or endnote, select the superscript number or symbol in your text (not in the Footnote pane) and press the Delete key. The number and the entire note disappear, and Word renumbers the remaining notes, if necessary. (Deleting the note number in the footnote or endnote itself, or in the Footnote pane, works no such magic. All you do is delete the little superscript number before the note. The rest of the note, and the number in your text, stay right where they are.)

Tip: You can convert footnotes to endnotes, or vice versa—a blessing for the indecisive. In Normal view, choose View→Footnotes, choose All Footnotes or All Endnotes from the pop-up menu in the gray divider bar, select the notes you want to convert, and Control-click the selection. Choose Convert to Endnotes or Convert to Footnotes from the contextual menu.

UP TO SPEED

Inserting Symbols

You can use hundreds of different symbols in Word. The following terms, for example, all depend upon symbols for correctness and clarity: 98.6°, Oscar™,¿Que pasa?, and so on. Larger symbols called *dingbats* let you do cool things like put a ☎ next to your phone number. High-tech dingbats, like those in Microsoft's Webdings font, come in handy on Web pages, such as 🖃 to indicate an email link.

To enter the wonderful world of symbols, choose Insert→Symbol. The Symbol dialog box appears, offering a palette of symbols in the Symbol font. Drag your cursor—now a magnifying glass—across them for a closer look.

If you don't see the symbol you're looking for, choose another symbol font from the Font menu. If you want a standard typographical symbol, such as © or ®, choose "Normal font" from this pop-up menu (or just click the Characters tab, where you'll find a cheat sheet of such common symbols and the keystrokes that produce them).

When you've finally highlighted the doohickey you're seeking, click Insert (or press Return) to place it into your document at the insertion point.

If there's a symbol you wind up using frequently—you're a Valentine's Day consultant, for example, and you use the ♥ symbol about 20 times a day—you can set it up for easier access in either of two ways.

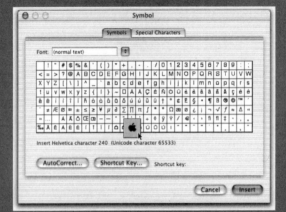

First, you can assign a keyboard shortcut to it. To do so, click the ♥ in the Symbol dialog box (in the Zapf Dingbats font, for example), and then click Shortcut Key. In the resulting dialog box, press the keys you want to trigger this symbol (Control-H, for example). If you chose a key combination that's already assigned to another Word function—which is fairly likely—you'll just get an alert sound. Keep trying until you stumble onto an unassigned combination. (The keystroke will become part of the Normal template [see page 202], and so it'll work in all documents based upon it.)

But you may find it easier to use a word or letter combination to insert a symbol. For instance, if you want ⌘ to appear every time you type *Apple*, or your favorite dingbat (say ✌) to appear when you type a code like *xq*, click the symbol and then click AutoCorrect. The AutoCorrect dialog box opens, showing your chosen symbol in the Replace With box. Type the word or code you want to trigger the appearance of the symbol (four letters or longer) and then press Return twice.

If you use Option keystrokes to type symbols (such as letters with foreign accents), you may find that they don't work properly, especially if the Formatting Palette is open. You may have to press Option twice, for example. If this kind of problem rears its head in your copy, upgrade to Office X Service Release 1, described on page 12.

Controlling Footnote Flow

If your footnotes are too long to fit on their "home" page, they flow into the footnote section of the next page. (Endnotes flow to the *top* of the following page.) As a courtesy to your reader, you may want to add something to the separator line—"Continued on next page," for example. Word, being equally thoughtful, lets you do exactly that.

Open the note pane as shown in Figure 6-3 and choose Footnote (or Endnote) Continuation Notice from the Footnotes menu. Type your thoughtful text, ("See next page," or what have you), and click Close.

Tip: Word positions endnotes immediately after the document or section's text, according to your specification. To put them on a separate page for printing, click in front of the first endnote and choose Insert→Break→Page Break. If you have numerous endnotes, you may want them to start on a new page so they're easier to check against your paper.

Line Numbers

If you're a lawyer, Bible scholar, or aspiring Hollywood scriptwriter, you're already familiar with *line numbering:* tiny numbers in the left margin every five or ten lines (see Figure 6-4). But even in everyday business, they're occasionally useful; you could email a press release to your boss and ask, "Let me know if I come on too strong in lines 5–8," for instance.

Line numbers show up only in Page Layout view (choose View→Page Layout). To add them to your document, select the text whose lines you want numbered. If it's a single section, for example, click anywhere in that section; if it's the whole document, choose Edit→Select All or press ⌘-A. If you're at the start of a new document and want to start numbering immediately, read on.

Tip: By choosing Format→Paragraph→Line and Page Breaks tab and turning on "Suppress line numbers," you make Word skip over the selected paragraphs in its numbering. Keep this checkbox in mind when defining a style, too, since you can use it to ensure that your captions are *never* numbered, for example.

Choose Format→Document→Layout tab. If you've selected text as described above, choose "Selected text" from the "Apply to" menu at the right; click Line Numbers. Turn on "Add line numbering" and set the following:

- **Start at** tells Word what line to start counting with. Select 2, for instance, if you want Word *not* to include the heading at the top of the page.

- **From text** is the distance from the left margin of the text. **Auto** is a good start unless a certain distance has been specified.

- **Count by** tells Word: "Show numbers only on every ___th line." The most common settings are 5, 10, and 20.

- **Numbering,** when it's *continuous,* begins at the first line and goes all the way to the end of the document. You can also tell Word to start over on each page, or after each section break.

To delete line numbers, just select the text again, choose Format→Document→ Layout tab, and turn off "Add line numbering."

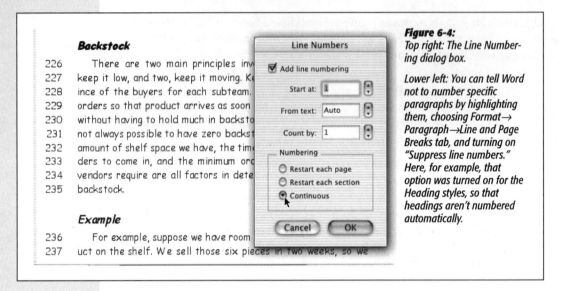

Backstock

226   There are two main principles inv
227   keep it low, and two, keep it moving. Ke
228   ince of the buyers for each subteam.
229   orders so that product arrives as soon
230   without having to hold much in backsto
231   not always possible to have zero backst
232   amount of shelf space we have, the tim
233   ders to come in, and the minimum ord
234   vendors require are all factors in dete
235   backstock.

Example

236   For example, suppose we have room
237   uct on the shelf. We sell those six pieces in two weeks, so we

Line Numbers

☑ Add line numbering

Start at: 1
From text: Auto
Count by: 1

Numbering
○ Restart each page
○ Restart each section
◉ Continuous

Cancel   OK

Figure 6-4:
Top right: The Line Number-ing dialog box.

Lower left: You can tell Word not to number specific paragraphs by highlighting them, choosing Format→ Paragraph→Line and Page Breaks tab, and turning on "Suppress line numbers." Here, for example, that option was turned on for the Heading styles, so that headings aren't numbered automatically.

Templates

This chapter may cover the most advanced features of Microsoft Word, but nothing you've read so far can touch the exasperating complexity of *templates,* the system of special files that Word uses to store your keystrokes, AutoText entries, styles, and dozens of other preference settings. There are two kinds of templates—global and document. Because you can simultaneously load more than one template, some-times they interact in complex ways, including making all of your text switch to radically different formatting.

When using Word as a basic word processor, you can safely ignore templates. Mil-lions of people use Word every day, in fact, unaware that lurking behind the scenes of every single document is one critical global template called Normal. Every setting they change, every keystroke they redefine, every style they apply—everything gets stored in this template file. Most people, in other words, never need step into the piranha-infested Template River.

Learning about templates, however, can pay off for the ambitious and technically undauntable. For example:

- If you collaborate with other people, you can send them a template you've cre-ated that contains an officially sanctioned set of styles, so that all your docu-ments will have a consistent look.

- Similarly, your boss or network administrator may give *you* a template file, filled with styles, so that your corporate correspondence will resemble everyone else's.

- Or maybe you plan to use your laptop, and want to ensure that all of the custom keystrokes, AutoText entries, and styles that you've carefully worked up on your desktop Mac are in place on the laptop.

The following pages take you through this insanely challenging topic with as few migraines as possible.

Document Templates

In any normal program, a template is simply a stationery pad, a locked icon in the Finder that, when opened, automatically generates a blank, untitled copy of the original. If you frequently (or even occasionally) need to create documents that incorporate certain standard elements, such as the top of your letterhead or boilerplate text on a contract, document templates can save you a lot of time.

Word offers something like this kind of template, too. You see dozens of these templates, called document templates, whenever you choose File→Project Gallery. These are regular Word documents—brochures, labels, newsletters, and so on—that have been saved in a special, self-duplicating format. You can read more about the Project Gallery at the beginning of Chapter 1.

Creating a document template

It's very easy to create your own document template: Just prepare a Word document. Then dress it up with graphics, font selections, dummy text, tables, forms, whatever you like. It's very important to understand that you can also customize this document with Word's more advanced features, such as:

- Styles

- AutoText entries

- Macros

- Margins and tab settings

- Customized menus and toolbars

- Page layout (columns, for example)

- Headers and footers

Then choose File→Save As. You can, if you wish, choose Document Template from the Format pop-up menu, but it's not technically necessary; *any* Word document— even a normal one, which you save into the Applications→Microsoft Office X→Templates folder—behaves like a template in the Project Gallery. The primary advantage of choosing Format→Document Template is that Word jumps to that folder (or, rather, the Applications→Microsoft Office X→Templates→My Templates folder) automatically.

Name the file and then click Save.

Using a document template

From now on, whenever you'd like to peel off a copy of that template, choose File→Project Gallery, click My Templates (or whatever folder you selected inside the Templates folder), and double-click the name of the corresponding template. It's just like opening a regular Word document, except that instead of appearing as a blank, stripped-down document, it comes complete with a number of predefined elements. The keystrokes you defined in the template, the styles you set up, the AutoText entries, dummy text, and so on will all be ready to use. All you need to do is save the new, untitled document and name it.

If you send a copy of this document template to another person or another machine, all of these preference settings will similarly be ready to use any time they open it. (If a Windows person might be the recipient, remember to add *.dot* to the end of the file's name; otherwise, Word for Windows won't recognize it.)

However, the settings, keystrokes, macros, toolbars, and so on, will not be available in any other Word document—only new ones "peeled off" from the document template. You or your colleague may wind up longing for a method of making these customizations available universally, to any Word document, including existing ones. That's perfectly possible—and it's the purpose of *global* templates.

Global Templates

Every Word document, even a new blank one that you've just opened, is based on a template; that's why you see a list of styles available in the Formatting Palette of even a brand new file. Behind the scenes, every Word document is based, at the minimum, upon a template called Normal.

Normal is what Word calls a *global* template, meaning that it's available to all documents, all the time (unless you intentionally *unload* it, as described on page 211). Exactly as with document templates, a global template determines which styles, macros, toolbars, page layout elements, AutoText entries, and other features are available when you use the document—but you don't have to go through the Project Gallery to open one, as you would with a document template.

Note: There's no technical difference between a document template and a global template–the same template file can serve as either one. The only difference is how you *load* it. If you use the Project Gallery, the template affects only a single document; if you use the Templates and Add-Ins command, as described on page 210, the template affects all documents.

Modifying a Template

No matter how hard you try to create a template the way you want it, the time comes when you have to go back and change it. You want to make your heading sizes smaller, or you have a new logo, and so on.

In a nutshell, you make such changes by opening the template file (choose File→Open, navigate to the Applications→Microsoft Office X→Templates folder, and open the template you want to modify). Make whatever changes you want to the document—adjust the styles, margins, zoom level, default font, whatever—and then choose File→Save. From now on, all new documents you spin off from that template will reflect your changes.

Tip: When you modify a template, the changes don't automatically ripple through all *existing* documents you peeled off of it before the change. You can open each of those older files, however, and force them to update their styles, macros, keystrokes, and so on, to reflect the changed template. To do so, choose Tools→Templates and Add-ins. Turn on "Automatically update document styles." Click OK.

Attaching a Document Template

It happens sometimes that 20 minutes into working on a new document, you realize that there's a template that would be just perfect for it. Fortunately, Word lets you *attach* a new template to a document, even if it began life as the offspring of a different document template. For instance, you begin a letter and decide that the Normal template looks a little too plain. You can look through the Project Gallery, find a letter template whose styles appeal to you, and attach it.

Here's how to attach a new document template:

1. **Choose Tools→Templates and Add-ins.**

   The Templates and Add-ins dialog box appears.

2. **Click Attach. In the Choose a File box, navigate to, and open, the template you'd like to attach, as shown in Figure 6-5.**

   The file name of the newly attached template appears in the "Document template" box of the Templates and Add-ins dialog box (see Figure 6-5).

3. **Click "Automatically update document styles"; click OK.**

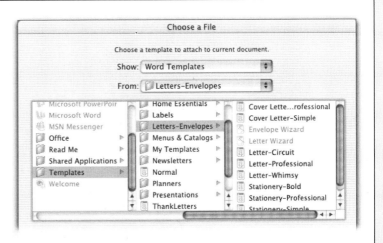

Figure 6-5:
The templates that come with Office X are stored in the Applications→Microsoft Office X→Templates folder, but you can use this dialog box to navigate to a template anywhere on your Mac. Remember that any document, template or not, in your Templates folder (or a folder in your Templates folder) is automatically treated as a template, and shows up in your Project Gallery.

Choose a File

Choose a template to attach to current document.

Show: Word Templates

From: Letters-Envelopes

The Normal *style* in your document (which, confusingly, is unrelated to the Normal *template*), along with other built-in styles (Heading 1, Heading 2, and so on), change to match those in the template you just attached. Moreover, your document now uses any macros, AutoText entries, custom toolbars, shortcut keys, and custom menus that were stored in the attached template. (If you want to use the macros and customizations without changing styles, do *not* click "Automatically update document styles" in step 3.)

Note: Boilerplate text and graphics from the newly attached template don't suddenly appear in your document. Styles from the template don't appear either, unless the current document has styles whose names match. If you still want the new template's styles imported into your document, you must copy them into your document using the Organizer (see page 207), or use the Format→Style dialog box.

Word only allows one document template to be attached at a time. When you attach a new one, the old one goes away. This is one of the ways that document templates are different from global templates, which you can gang up simultaneously.

POWER USERS' CLINIC

Different Definitions of Normal

Before Mac OS X, Word only had one Normal template, and it was always in the same place—the Templates folder. But because Mac OS X is a multiple-user system, Word X respects the notion that each person who uses your Mac can sign in with his own name and password to find his own unique environment, with his own Home folder, desktop, and other settings. So why shouldn't he have his own Normal template, with his own favorite font, margins, and so on?

If you currently don't bother with the Login screen (which appears at startup, offering a list of account holders), then Word maintains a single Normal template just as it always has. Any customizations you make to the Normal template potentially mess everything up for the next person to use the Mac, forcing people to spend a lot of time changing fonts and other settings back the way they like them.

The solution, of course, is to set up individual *user accounts* for the various people who log in to your Mac (see Chapter 11 of *Mac OS X: The Missing Manual*). The next step is to change everyone's Normal template privileges to read-only.

To do so, select the Applications→Microsoft Office X→Templates folder in the Finder. Choose File→Show Info. Choose Privileges from the pop-up menu, choose "Read only" from the Everyone pop-up menu, and then close the Show Info box.

From now on, Word will automatically save a different Normal template for each person who logs into the Mac (in each person's Home→Library→Preferences→Microsoft folder).

If you're working along and Word prompts you to choose a place to save the Normal template, here's what's going on: Someone changed your Template folder privileges to read-only, but you don't have an Administrator account (again, see Chapter 11 of *Mac OS X: The Missing Manual*). Word doesn't let nonadministrators change the Normal template.

The best thing to do is tell Word where to save your Normal template (in your Preferences folder, for example). From now on, Word will automatically use *this* Normal template for you, so you'll never have to worry about it again.

The Organizer

Any style, AutoText entry, custom toolbar, or macro that you create and save to a document becomes part of a template (either the Normal template or a document template). Because of a little-known but very timesaving Word feature called the Organizer, you never have to create one of those custom items more than once. The Organizer, the great-great-grandchild of Apple's 1984 Font/DA Mover program, lets you transfer these items from file to file (see Figure 6-6).

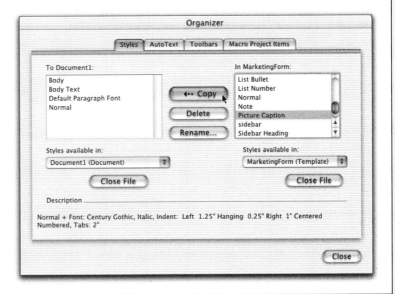

Figure 6-6:
When you click an item in either list box, the direction of the arrows on the Copy button changes accordingly. You can Shift-click to select a number of consecutive list items, or ⌘-click to select (or deselect) nonconsecutive items in the list.

To use the Organizer, proceed like this:

1. **Choose Tools→Templates and Add-ins; click Organizer.**

   You can also get to the Organizer by choosing Format→Styles and clicking Organizer, by choosing Tools→Macros and then clicking Organizer, and probably by tunneling underneath your kitchen floor. In any case, the Organizer dialog box opens, as shown in Figure 6-6.

2. **Inspect the file names above the two list boxes.**

   The left box always represents the current document or document template if there is one; the right box represents the current global template. However, it doesn't matter which is which. You can move a style, AutoText entry, toolbar, or macro from any document or template to any other, in either direction.

3. **Set up the two lists so that the files you want to copy to and from are visible.**

   If you don't see the document or template that has what you want, click Close File below one of the boxes. When the button changes to Open File, click it again.

The Choose a File dialog box opens; use it to navigate to, and open, the template or document that has the features you want.

Tip: To save frustration, note that the Show pop-up menu at the bottom of the Choose a File dialog box always defaults to *Word Templates.* In other words, if you're looking for a standard Word file that contains styles you like, you won't see it in the Choose a File dialog box until you choose Show→All Word Documents.

If you began this exercise with the destination document (target document) open on the screen, it should already be listed on the left side of the Organizer. If not, however, it's easy enough to click its Close File/Open File button so that the correct destination file is also listed.

4. **Click the appropriate tab at the top of the Organizer dialog box, depending on the kinds of items you want to copy.**

For example, suppose you created some terrific AutoText entries while working on a different Mac, and now you want to use them on your home-based Mac. So, you cleverly emailed yourself the file, sending those AutoText entries along for the ride.

Now you've opened the Organizer; on the left side, you've opened the document that contains the AutoText entries. On the right side, you've opened the Normal template, so that Word will autocomplete those entries all the time on *your* Mac. Click the AutoText tab to see all the AutoText entries contained in the files on both sides.

5. **When you find an item you want to copy from one document or template to another, click it and then click Copy.**

See Figure 6-6 for advice on selecting more than one entry. In any case, after you click Copy (or press ⌘-C), the selected items now appear in both lists. (If there's already an item of the same name in the target file, Word asks you to confirm that you want to replace it.) You can copy in both directions, as much as you like.

Tip: You can also use the Organizer to *rename* template items, such as styles and macros. Just click one and then click Rename. Enter the new name in the small dialog box that appears and click OK.

If you ever want to *delete* items—AutoText entries that pop up too often, or macros that you no longer need, for example—the Organizer is the place to do that, too. Select the item in one of the list boxes and click Delete.

---

6. **Click Close.**

Word asks if you want to save the changes you made to your documents; click OK. You return to your document, where the changes you made in the Organizer are now in effect.

Normal and Global Templates

Every Word document is based on a global template. As noted earlier, 99 percent of all Word documents are based on the Normal global template, usually unbeknownst to their authors. In fact, the very first time you launch Word and click the icon for a blank document, you're using the Normal template.

The Normal template

Because Word documents are based on the Normal global template, the very first one you ever created (and probably most of them since that time) came set up to use certain default settings—the Normal font style (Times, 12 point), three heading styles, one-inch page margins, and so on. Whenever you create new styles (as described on page 141), they wind up being saved as part of the Normal template, so that they'll appear in the Formatting Palette Style list of any other Word document you open.

But what if you want to change the default page margins, or change the Normal font to something a little less, well, normal?

The easiest way is simply to choose File→Open, navigate to the Applications→Microsoft Office X→Templates folder, and double-click the Normal template. Make whatever changes you want—to the Normal font style (choose Format→Style); to the paragraph containing the blinking insertion point, which all subsequent paragraphs will inherit (Format→Paragraph); to the document margins (Format→Document); and so on. Save and close the document. Your modified Normal template will now determine the specs of any subsequent documents you create.

Tip: The default setting that most of the world's Word users want to change is the *font;* experienced Word veterans don't care if they ever see Times 12 again. For this reason, Microsoft provides a shortcut to modifying the default font in the Normal template—a method that protects the novice from even having to know about templates.

It's the Default button. Choose Format→Font, choose a typeface, and then click Default; click Yes to confirm. Any new documents you create using the File→New command automatically reflect your changes.

This useful Default button also appears when you're modifying your margins (Format→Document), page setup (File→Page Setup), proofing language (Tools→Language)—all of which represent the most popular default formatting changes. In this way, you can change the Normal template on the fly, without opening it.

Loading a template as global

Suppose someone has sent you a Word template containing macros, AutoText entries, custom toolbars, shortcut keys and custom menus that you'd like to use frequently. Instead of re-creating them, you can turn that person's document into a *global* template, and use those settings at will. To do so, open the document and proceed as follows:

1. **Choose File→Save As. Navigate to the Microsoft Office X→Templates→My Templates folder. Click Save.**

   Word saves the document as a template.

Tip: To save time, don't bother choosing "Document Template" from the Format pop-up menu. Whenever you save a document—even a regular Word file—into the My Templates folder (or any other folder in the Templates folder), Word understands that you want to use it as a template.

---

2. **Open a new blank document. Choose Tools→Templates and Add-ins.**

   The Templates and Add-ins dialog box opens, as shown in Figure 6-7.

3. **Click Add. Navigate to the My Templates folder; open the template you just saved.**

   The template now appears in the list box as checked, (see Figure 6-7).

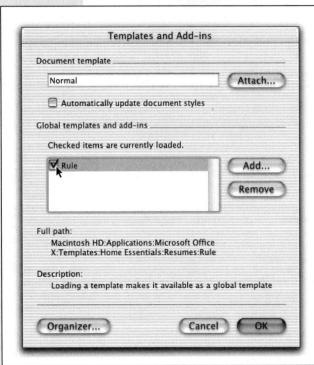

Figure 6-7:
You can make the custom items in any Word template available in every Word document by loading the template as a global template.

4. **Click OK.**

   Loading a new global template has a similar effect to attaching a new document template (macros, AutoText, custom menus, and shortcut keys are transferred to your document), but because it's a *global* template, these items are available in all documents—until you either unload the template or quit Word, that is.

Note: You don't get a global template's *styles* when you attach it in this way. You can transfer them into your document using the Organizer, as described on page 207, or attach the same template as a document template.

Unloading a global template

Having several global templates open uses up memory, therefore slowing your Mac down. To unload a global template you no longer need, choose Tools→Templates and Add-ins and uncheck it in the list, or click Remove.

POWER USERS' CLINIC

Using a Template as a Startup Item

Word automatically unloads any global templates you load (other than the Normal template) when you quit Word. When you open Word again, the Normal template is, by default, the only global template loaded.

If you want to make the AutoText entries, macros, and other attributes of another global template available all the time, you can pursue one of these two avenues:

- Copy them into the Normal template using the Organizer, as described on page 207.

- Turn the additional global template into a *startup item.*

To do the latter, navigate to the template on your Mac's hard drive; it's probably in the Microsoft Office X→Templates folder. Click the template's document icon to select it and choose File→Duplicate. Drag the copied file to the Microsoft Office X→Office→Startup→Word folder.

From now on, this startup template is automatically loaded to every Word document you open. In other words, this global template is *not* automatically unloaded when you quit Word.

The Outliner

Your teachers were right: The more time you spend on the outline, the less work you'll have to do when it comes time to writing your actual paper, story, article, or book. Word's outline maker is an underused tool that can revolutionize the way you work and even think. It frees you from the drudgery of keeping track of all the letters and numbers in an outline, while encouraging you to categorize and prioritize your ideas.

Building an Outline

To outline your document from the beginning, open a blank document and choose View→Outline, or click the fourth tiny icon at the lower-left corner of your document window. (You can also apply Outline view to an existing document, which is described later in this section.)

Whenever you switch to Outline view, the Outline toolbar appears (see Figure 6-8). When you first start typing, your words are formatted as Heading 1—the highest level in the outline hierarchy. (Outline headings correspond to Word's built-in heading styles.)

Now you're ready to build your outline. Press Return after each heading. Along the way, you can create the subheadings using either the mouse or the keyboard, as described next.

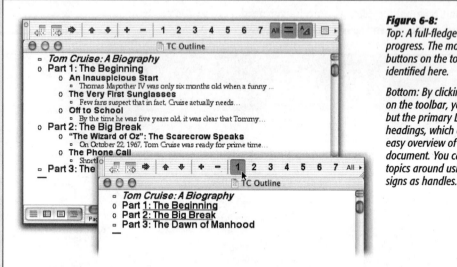

Figure 6-8:
Top: A full-fledged outline in progress. The most important buttons on the toolbar are identified here.

Bottom: By clicking the big 1 on the toolbar, you hide all but the primary Level 1 headings, which offers an easy overview of your document. You can drag topics around using the + signs as handles.

- **Promoting and demoting.** Moving topics out toward the margin (toward Heading 1, making them more important) or inward (less important) is called *promoting* or *demoting* them.

  To promote or demote a heading, click within it and then press Tab (to demote) or Shift-Tab (to promote). Keep pressing until you reach the desired level. (You can also press Tab or Shift-Tab *before* typing a heading.)

  Or, if you're a mouse-driven kind of person, click the Promote and Demote buttons at the left of the Outline toolbar (see Figure 6-8). *Keyboard Shortcuts:* Shift-Control-left arrow to promote; Shift-Control-right arrow to demote. You can also drag with the mouse, as shown in Figure 6-9.

Tip: You can promote or demote an entire batch of headings at once. Drag through an outline to select certain headings, or neatly select a heading and all of its subheadings by clicking the + symbol. (To eliminate subtopics from the selection, first click the + sign, then Shift-click where you want the selection to *end.*)

- **Inserting body text.** You wouldn't impress many people if everything you wrote were a headline; fortunately, you can flesh out your headings with regular body text by clicking the double-arrow icon on the Outline toolbar. (It stands for "Demote to Body Text.") Use this style, denoted by a tiny white square in Figure 6-9, for the actual, longer-than-one-line paragraphs and thoughts that constitute the main body of your writing. *Keyboard shortcut:* Shift-⌘-N.

- **Rearranging headings.** To move topics up and down on the page without promoting or demoting them, just drag them by the + and – handles (see Figure 6-9). Alternatively, you can select the topic or topics and click the Move Up and Move Down arrows on the Outline toolbar. *Keyboard shortcuts:* Control-Shift-up or -down arrow.

- **Breaking up headings.** You'll probably come across instances, especially when outlining an existing piece of writing (see below), where you need to separate one sentence from the previous one in order to make it a new topic. Just click before the first letter of the sentence and then press Return to put it on a new line.

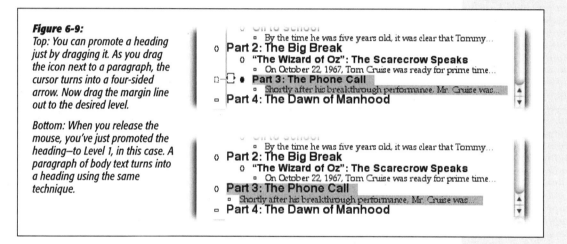

Figure 6-9:
Top: You can promote a heading just by dragging it. As you drag the icon next to a paragraph, the cursor turns into a four-sided arrow. Now drag the margin line out to the desired level.

Bottom: When you release the mouse, you've just promoted the heading—to Level 1, in this case. A paragraph of body text turns into a heading using the same technique.

Collapsing and expanding an outline

The whole point of creating an outline is to organize the topics you're presenting, to ensure all the major points are there and to arrange them in a logical order. Therefore, it's helpful to see just your main points at a glance, unencumbered by the minor details. Here are some ways you can control how much or how little of your outline you see:

- **To show only Level 1 headings:** To get a quick "big picture" view of your outline, click the large numeral 1 on the Outline toolbar, or press Shift-Control-1; now Word shows *only* your Level 1 headings, the real main points of your document. Everything else is temporarily hidden.

  Similarly, clicking 2 (or pressing Shift-Control-2) shows heading Levels 1 *and* 2, so you can check how your subtopics are looking, and so on. (Figure 6-8 illustrates this trick in action.)

- **To collapse only one section of an outline:** Double-click the puffy + sign next to it. All subtopics of that heading disappear, leaving just a gray bar behind as evidence that something's been hidden. To expand it again, double-click the + again. (Double-clicking a minus sign doesn't do anything, since there's nothing to collapse.) This trick is helpful when you're closely examining a small portion of a long outline and just want to move some minor details temporarily out of your way.

- **To view first lines only:** Click the Show First Line Only button on the Outline toolbar, or press Shift-Control-L, to make Word hide everything but the first line of every paragraph—whether it's a heading or body text. (This button is shown performing its magic in Figure 6-7, which is why every body paragraph there ends with an ellipsis, like this …)

- **To hide all body text:** You can collapse all the material that you've relegated to body text so that only headings are visible by clicking the All button on the Outline toolbar (or pressing Shift-Control-A).

- **To expand everything:** In an outline where you've collapsed at least one heading somewhere, the All button takes on a different role. Clicking it now expands any headings or body text that have been collapsed. Click All or press Shift-Control-A to get everything out in the open and return to work. (If you click All again at this point, it will hide all body text and return to its role as body-text toggle.)

Tip: If the heavy boldface type and dark fonts make your outline hard to read, click the Show Formatting button on the toolbar. It displays all headings in plain, unformatted type.

Outlining an Existing Document

Say you've been typing away on your latest essay or annual report, and you're stuck. You've run out of ideas, and the ones you did have no longer look so clear now that you see them onscreen. It's still not too late to apply the organizational power of an outline. Just choose View→Outline; Word displays your document in outline format, using your own line breaks, indents, and headings as a guide. Now you can use the navigational tools described above to reprioritize and clarify your thoughts.

Numbering an Outline

If what you remember about outlining came from high school English class, you may be wondering about the I's and a's and funny little iii's that you were taught to use as outline numbers. Not only can Word number your headings and subheadings automatically, but it can also automatically renumber the outline as you move topics around.

To add numbering to an outline, choose Format→Bullets and Numbering→Outline Numbered tab. Then proceed as shown in Figure 6-10.

Now continue working as usual with your outline. Even if you drag topics around or insert new ones, Word automatically updates the numbering.

Renumbering a numbered outline

You can't edit a numbered outline in your document; when you click the numbers or letters, nothing happens.

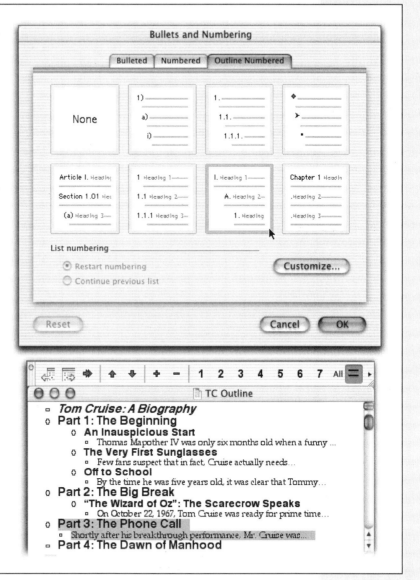

Figure 6-10:
Top: When this dialog box appears, choose one of the seven outline styles; the ones on the bottom row add numbering and apply heading styles to the text on each level. There's also an option for automatically adding the "Article" and "Section" labels used in legal documents (Article 1, Article 2...), and another for using Outline format for chapter headings. If one of the illustrated numbering styles fits your needs, click it and then click OK. If not, see "Customizing an Outline" in the next section. Click OK when you're set.

Bottom: The resulting outline is numbered automatically, according to the style you've selected.

But what if you're starting a new section with a completely different outline in it, and want the numbers to start all over again? Click in the heading whose number you wish to change. Then choose Format→Bullets and Numbering→Outline Numbering tab, and click Customize. To change the number of the current heading, you must first change the number in the "Start at" box, as shown in Figure 6-11. Any numbered headings following this one will be numbered in a continuing order.

Customizing an Outline

The seven built-in numbering formats cover most purposes, especially if you're creating the outline for your own benefit. But if you've been asked to turn in a document in outline format, or if you're using Word to create a legal document, you can achieve a more consistent result by customizing the outline's AutoFormatting yourself.

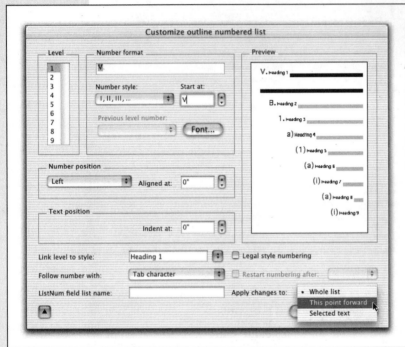

Figure 6-11:
The "Apply changes to" menu lets you make only part of a document into an outline. If it's grayed out, try selecting some text before opening the Bullets and Numbering dialog box and the Customize box. (Click the blue expand arrow to view these choices.)

Using the Custom Outline dialog box

To set up an unusual numbering style for your outline, choose Format→Bullets and Numbering→Outline Numbered tab, and click Customize.

When the Custom Outline dialog box first opens, as shown in Figure 6-11, the settings you see pertain to the numbering style you've chosen in the Bullets and Numbering dialog box, and to the current heading level at the insertion point.

In the Level box at the left, choose the outline level you want to tailor. For instance, you may accept Word's built-in typeface for chapter titles, but want your secondary headings to look different. In that case, leave Level 1 alone and click the 2 in the Level box. The Preview box presents an example of the current numbering; it changes as you make changes in the Custom Outline dialog box.

- The **Number Format** panel shows the numbering style—letter, Roman numeral, and so on—for the current level.

- Word generally begins counting headings with the number 1. But if you want to print out an outline that's supposed to be a continuation of another document, you may want its numbering to start with, say, 17. That's the number you type into the **Start at** box.

- When you want to display level numbers together, choose from the **Previous level number** menu. Ordinarily, the title might be numbered 1, and the three subheadings a, b, and c. But if you want the subheads numbered 1a, 1b, and 1c instead, choose Level 1 from this menu. This numbering tactic is useful when your outline has long paragraphs, since it'll keep you from getting lost in the levels.

- The **Font** button lets you choose a font and typeface for the outline *number* only. (To change the font for the heading *text*, use "Link level to style" as described below.)

- The **Number position** panel is where you can choose left, centered, or right alignment, relative to the distance between the text (see below) and the left margin. The **Aligned at** box is where you set the left indent. Watch what happens in the Preview box as you click the arrows.

- The **Text position** box sets the distance of the text from the left margin. It operates independently of the number position.

Advanced outline customization

If you click the blue arrow button, the dialog box expands, sprouting a handy fold-out panel that offers even more intimidating-looking options.

- In the **Link level to style** menu, you can choose to apply any of the styles in the current document template (see page 202) to the level that you're formatting.

- The **Follow number with** menu lets you insert a tab, a space, or nothing at all between the number and the text. (You do it here because you can't directly format outline numbers in your document, not even in Outline view.)

- The **ListNum field list name** box lets you insert a *second* number into an outline numbered item.

- Use the **Legal style numbering** box to apply legal style (no letters, no capital Roman numerals) to any numbering style. This box grays out the "Number style" menu and gives Legal style numbering complete control.

- When you choose a new level in the Level box, the **Restart numbering after** box is turned on by default. That's because each subtopic is numbered from the beginning, under the main topic that contains it (1a, 1b; 2a, 2b)—you wouldn't want your headings labeled 1a, 1b, 2c, 2d. Thus, under subheading (a), sub-subhead numbers start again with i, ii, iii, and so on, as shown in Figure 6-11.

Click OK to close the Customize box and apply your selections from the Bullets and Numbering dialog box. If you plan to always use the outline in Outline view, you're done; otherwise, consider switching into Normal or Page Layout view for further refinement. You'll discover that the nice, even indenting of your various headings in Outline view may not exist in Normal or Page Layout view. As a result, you may have to adjust the indentation of your various heading styles to make the indenting levels correspond in the other views.

The Document Map

The Document Map doesn't actually look like a map; it looks more like a portable table of contents that's open beside you as you read. It's identical to the left-side table of contents list you might find in an Adobe Acrobat (PDF) document, if you've ever used one of those. No flipping pages—not even much scrolling (see Figure 6-12).

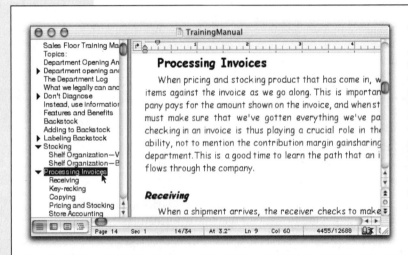

Figure 6-12:
When you click a heading in the Document Map in the left pane, you automatically jump to that point in your document in the right pane. There's no quicker way to get from one place to another in a long document. Plus, when you click the mouse somewhere in your document, that topic is highlighted in the Document Map.

What's in the Document Map

In essence, the Document Map is a navigating pane revealing just the headings in a document. A heading, in this case, can be any text in one of Word's built-in heading styles, a style you've *based on* one of the built-in heading styles, or text to which you've applied an *outline level*.

Viewing and Navigating the Document Map

To see the Document Map, choose View→Document Map. A narrow panel with its own vertical scroll bar opens down the left side of your document window.

The Document Map doesn't have a horizontal scroll bar at the bottom; if you can't read the full text across the Document Map pane, drag the narrow gray bar—the resize bar—to widen its pane. Actually, you can read the full text of any topic in the Document Map without resizing anything. Just point the cursor at any line in the Document Map, and a yellow, tooltip-like label appears, revealing the full heading text.

The flippy triangles in the Document Map work just like those in a pre–Mac OS X Finder window: Click one to reveal or conceal all its subtopics. If you're a fan of contextual menus, you can also Control-click a heading in the Document Map and choose Expand or Collapse.

Because the items shown in the Document Map have levels, like headings and outline topics, you can collapse or expand the entire "outline" so that, for example, only the Level 1 and Level 2 headings show up, exactly as you can in Outline view. To do so, Control-click in the Document Map pane and choose a heading level from the contextual menu. If you choose Show Heading 4, for instance, the Document Map will display only Levels 1 through 4, hiding everything else.

To dismiss the Document Map, choose View→Document Map again, or just double-click the resize bar.

Customizing the Document Map

By default, the Document Map shows up as black Helvetica text with blue highlights. (Microsoft isn't exactly known for its aesthetic prowess.)

To jazz up the Document Map font (or just make it less ugly), choose Format→Style and choose Document Map in the Styles list box. Click Modify to bring up the Modify Style box.

Now choose Font from the Format menu. Whatever font, color, size, case, or text effect you specify now will apply to all text in the Document Map.

Tip: At this point, you can even change the highlight color, which appears when you click a heading in the Map. Click OK; then, from the Format pop-up menu, choose Borders. Click the Shading tab in the resulting dialog box. Choose a new fill color as described on page 651.

Click OK, OK, and Close when you're satisfied. (Clicking Apply will change the current paragraph in your main document to the Document Map style; that's probably not what you want to do.) If you have a change of heart at this point, press ⌘-Z to restore the Document Map to its original, bland condition.

Master Documents

In the beginning, there was Word 5.1. It had fonts, sizes, styles, tables, and graphics.

But the people weren't satisfied. They wanted to bind together many different chapter documents into a single, unified book. They wanted to knit together files written by multiple authors who had edited their respective sections simultaneously on the network. They wanted to print, spell-check, or search-and-replace across dozens of different Word files at once; or generate tables of contents, indexes, and cross-references for all component Word files at once.

On the sixth day, Microsoft created the Master Document.

A Master Document looks much like an outline. However, each heading in the Master Document can refer to a section or an entirely different *Word file*. As in the Document Map, you click these headings in Master Document view to travel directly from one part of the document to another.

In essence, a Master Document is like a binder holding all the individual Word files that comprise it (which Microsoft calls *subdocuments*). Each subdocument can be formatted independently, moved or removed, split up, or combined with another subdocument—all while remaining safely under the umbrella of the Master Document. The Master Document concept is slightly alien, difficult to understand, and sometimes a bit flaky; but if you're putting a book together, Master Documents may be the only way to go.

Creating a New Master Document

To start building a Master Document, open a new document and choose View→ Master Document. The Master Document toolbar appears, and your document is set up for outlining (see Figure 6-13).

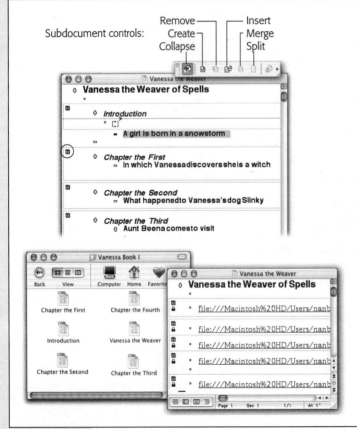

Figure 6-13:
Top: The Master Document toolbar and a Master Document, showing three subdocuments. A subdocument icon, like the one circled, represents each document. In Master Document view, you can drag text from one subdocument to another. Here the heading "A girl is born in a snowstorm" is being dragged from the Master Document outline into the subdocument "Introduction."

Middle: Behind the scenes, each master document is comprised of individual Word documents on your hard drive.

Bottom: If you click the Collapse Subdocuments icon on the toolbar, the nature of your subdocuments becomes all too real—you see only hyperlinks to their locations on your hard drive, spelled out as file paths.

Subdocument controls:
Remove
Create
Collapse
Insert
Merge
Split

Vanessa the Weaver

Vanessa the Weaver of Spells

Introduction

A girl is born in a snowstorm

Chapter the First
In which Vanessa discovers she is a witch

Chapter the Second
What happened to Vanessa's dog Slinky

Chapter the Third
Aunt Beena comes to visit

Vanessa Book I

Back · View · Computer · Home · Favorite

Chapter the First
Chapter the Fourth
Introduction
Vanessa the Weaver
Chapter the Second
Chapter the Third

Vanessa the Weaver

Vanessa the Weaver of Spells

file:///Macintosh%20HD/Users/nanb
file:///Macintosh%20HD/Users/nanb
file:///Macintosh%20HD/Users/nanb
file:///Macintosh%20HD/Users/nanb
file:///Macintosh%20HD/Users/nanb

Page 1   Sec 1   1/1   At 1"

Setting up your über-document is exactly like creating an outline (see page 211), in that you use all the same techniques. Each heading, however, will eventually become the name of a separate file on your hard drive. Because a Master Document will wind up as a herd of individual files, you'd be wise to save it on your hard drive in a folder of its own; the subdocuments will wind up there, too.

Spinning off a document

Once you decide to spin off a particular heading as a subdocument, click it and then click the Create Subdocument button on the Master Document toolbar (see Figure 6-13). (You can also highlight several headings at once before clicking the Create Subdocument button. Just make sure the first heading is at the level you'll want represented as subdocuments.)

A light gray box that defines the boundaries of the document appears onscreen; you can type or paste into it. Behind the scenes, you've just created a new, linked file icon in your Master Document's folder (Figure 6-13, middle). You or your network comrades can edit these individual files independently; whenever you open up the Master document, you'll see the changes reflected.

Note: Subdocument files are stored in the same folder as the Master Document and behave like perfectly normal Word files. But don't drag their icons to another folder, rename them by clicking the icon's name, and so on. If you do, the Master Document won't be able to find them. Instead, move and rename subdocuments using the techniques described later in this section.

The safest way to copy a Master Document and all its subdocuments to another location is to select them all and move them all at once (or just move the folder that contains them).

Incorporating a document

You can turn an existing Word document on your hard drive into a new subdocument, too. Just click the Insert Subdocument icon on the Master Document toolbar to open its dialog box. When you navigate to and select a file and click Open, the contents of the document appear in your Master Document as a subdocument, just like all the others.

Tip: You may find that your outline headings have lost their sense of identity—this is where building a Master Document gets iffy—but you can usually regain your composure by adding a new heading inside the gray boundaries of the imported document.

Viewing Master Documents

Master Documents look and act vastly different in each of Word's views. If you can remember to switch into the correct view, you've won more than half of the Master Document battle.

- **In Normal view**, subdocuments become *sections* (see page 137), with a section break separating each. Use Normal view to type and edit your document. Be careful not to remove the section breaks. Removing them will inadvertently combine the Word documents that make up your Master.

If, in Normal view, your document looks like a series of hyperlinks, with no other text, you have two choices: Click on a hyperlink to open that subdocument in a new window, or choose View→Master Document and click the Expand Subdocuments button. Now when you return to Normal view, the text in your Master Document will flow continuously, with a section break between subdocuments.

- **Online and Page Layout views** function just as they normally do. Your document appears to be a seamless whole, with no visible breaks between subdocuments.

- **Outline view** turns the Master Document into one big outline; here too, if you see hyperlinks instead of text, expand the subdocuments as described above. This view is useful for organizing your document at any stage of the process because it's so easy to drag-and-drop. In Outline view, subdocuments are represented by continuous section breaks.

Working with Master Documents

In Master Document view, not only can you see all your subdocuments, you can also open them, arrange and organize them, and control access to them.

Opening and expanding subdocuments

When you click the Collapse Subdocuments button (first on the Master Document toolbar), something very odd happens: Each subdocument is listed as a blue, underlined hyperlink, with only its heading visible (Figure 6-13, bottom). The rest is collapsed, exactly as in an outline. The text of the hyperlinks may look unfamiliar to you, since they are the *folder path* and *file name* of the subdocument. Clicking a link opens the subdocument in its own window.

You also see a padlock icon next to each heading. It's a bug; that document is not, in fact, locked in any way. If you double-click it (to open the file into its own window) or expand it, you'll find that it's easily editable.

Tip: You *can* lock a subdocument so that it's protected from errant mouse clicks in Master Document view; just click in the heading and click the padlock icon on the toolbar. Even so, double-clicking that heading opens it into its own window, which is easily editable. In other words, the Lock function doesn't offer what you'd call government-level security.

But when you open a subdocument into its own window, the padlock in the Master Document indicates that you (or anyone else) cannot edit the same document in Master Document view. The lock feature is really effective only when sharing a Master Document over a network, where it prevents two people from editing the same document at the same time.

Once you've collapsed your subdocuments, you can drag their little document icons up or down to rearrange them (or press Delete to remove them).

When you then click the Expand Subdocuments button on the Master Document toolbar (the very first icon again), the subdocuments open within the Master Document window. A light gray box outlines the contents of the subdocument in outline form.

Moving and renaming subdocuments

Don't rename or move a subdocument in the Finder; if you do, the Master Document will no longer be able to find it. If you really want to rename or move one of these documents, do so from within the Master Document, like this:

1. **Open the subdocument using any of the methods described above, and choose File→Save As.**

2. **Type a new name for the subdocument and, if desired, choose a new location for it. Click Save or press Return.**

With these two steps, you've updated the Master Document's *link* to the subdocument. The next time you open the subdocument from within the Master Document, the one with the new name and location will open. (The subdocument with the old name and location is still there, sitting on your hard drive as an independent Word document. You can delete it, unless you have some further use for it.)

Splitting and combining subdocuments

Suppose you want to chop a long chapter into two shorter ones. Or perhaps two people who were collaborating on a report have had a big fight, requiring you to solve the problem by giving them individual assignments. Fortunately, the process of dividing a subdocument in two, which Word calls *splitting,* is comparatively painless.

To do so, expand the subdocuments in Master Document view. Click where you want your split-off document to begin, and then click the Split Subdocument button on the Master Document toolbar.

At other times, you may want your subdocuments to meld together. For instance, you may want to combine two short chapters into one longer one, without restarting the pagination. You could cut and paste text from one subdocument into another, but there's a more elegant way, which Word calls *merging.*

To perform this task, move the subdocuments that you intend to merge so that they're next to each other in your outline. Highlight them, then click the Merge Subdocument button on the Master Document toolbar.

The new, merged subdocument carries the name of the *first* subdocument that you combined. The original, unmerged versions of the second (and other) subdocument files remain in their original folder locations on your hard drive, but they're no longer connected to the Master Document. If you're not going to reuse the files, delete them to save disk space.

"Removing" a subdocument

The Remove Subdocument button on the Master Document toolbar doesn't actually delete it (for that, see below). Instead, this function brings the document's contents into the Master Document itself, so that it's no longer linked to an external file on your hard drive. For example, you might use it when, for formatting reasons, you want your introduction to be part of the Master Document, instead of giving it a subdocument of its own.

To do so, expand the subdocuments. Click the subdocument icon, then click Remove Subdocument on the Master Document toolbar. The contents of that subdocument now appear in the body of the Master Document. (You may delete the old subdocument file, which is now orphaned on your hard drive—unless you want to keep it as a backup.)

Deleting Subdocuments

Deleting a subdocument from a Master Document is easy: With the subdocument expanded and unlocked (see page 222), click the subdocument icon to select it and then press Delete. (When you delete a subdocument, you only remove it from the Master Document; you don't actually delete its file. The original subdocument file is still in the same folder where you left it, and where it will stay until you Trash it.)

Master Documents and Formatting

Like all Word documents, every Master Document is based on a template (see page 202). Not surprisingly, all subdocuments have the same template as the Master Document.

What is surprising, and potentially confusing, is the fact that a subdocument can have its *own* template, independent of the Master Document—and yet it can still take on the Master Document template when you want it to.

In Master Document view, all subdocuments share the same Master Document template—its styles, headers, footers, and so on. When you print *from this view,* all subdocuments print in the styles of the master template, resulting in a very consistent look. But when you open a subdocument *in its own window,* the subdocument's own independent template applies—with its own type styles, headers, footers, and so on. All the template parts listed on page 203 can operate independently in the Master Document and its subdocuments.

Master Document Security

Master documents were designed for sharing. The fact that two different people can simultaneously work on subdocuments of the same Master Document makes collaboration easy. When the individual subdocuments are done, you can review and print the finished product in Master Document view, ensuring that the formatting is consistent throughout. An added challenge, however, is keeping people from messing with subdocuments that they shouldn't, whether or not they're doing it maliciously.

Locking and unlocking subdocuments

The simplest (and most easily foiled) way of keeping someone from tampering with a subdocument is to lock it, as described on page 222. When a subdocument is locked, you can open and read it, but you can't edit or change it.

Fortunately, anytime someone is working on a subdocument, it gets locked automatically when viewed by anyone else on the network. It remains locked until its editor finishes and closes it.

Assigning passwords

Locking a subdocument by using the Lock Subdocuments button is a good way to prevent others from making accidental changes to a subdocument, but it doesn't actually lock out those who know about the Lock Document button. For true security, Master Documents and subdocuments must be password-protected just like any other. As always, you can password-protect either the Master Document or (if you've opened one into its own window) a subdocument; either way, the instructions on page 24 apply.

Sharing a Master Document on a Network

One of the most popular uses for Master Documents is file sharing. For instance, members of a public relations department can each work on a separate section of their company's annual report. The report is a Master Document, and each section is a subdocument.

Here are some tips for successful Master Document file sharing:

- Choose one person to be team leader. That person will format the Master Document, hold the passwords, and oversee the final proofreading and distribution of the completed document.

- To prevent accidental or mischievous tampering with the subdocuments, assign a password to each one, as described on page 24. Make sure the team leader keeps a record of them in a safe place.

- Make sure all Macs involved are networked and set up for file sharing. If any team members are not familiar with file sharing, a consultation with the network administrator is in order. To learn more about setting up file sharing, including the Owner and Group designations described below, choose Help→Mac Help in the Finder and search for *file sharing,* or consult *Mac OS X: The Missing Manual.*

AutoSummarize

Imagine this scenario: Five minutes to get to the professor's office, and you suddenly remember that she wanted you to include an abstract (a summary) at the beginning of your thesis. Or this one: You proudly plunk your report on your boss's desk and he says, "I'm not reading all this. Give me the 15-minute version." Word's AutoSummarize feature comes to the rescue in situations just like these.

Unfortunately, Word doesn't actually read your document and then write a well-crafted summary. (Maybe in Word 2021.) What Word does is scan the document for frequently used words, then string what it believes to be the key sentences together into a summary. ("Key sentences" are those that include those most common words.)

In other words, you're best off setting fairly low expectations for this feature. Think of AutoSummarize as a glitzy feature for demos at trade shows, or perhaps as something that helps you come up with a *rough* summary; you can (and should) edit the summary later.

Creating an AutoSummary

Open the document you wish to summarize; choose Tools→AutoSummarize. Word immediately gets to work, compiling a list of key words in your document and flagging the sentences that contain them. Since it may take some time, especially in a long document, kick back and watch some TV. If nothing's on, you can press ⌘-. to cancel the process.

When Word's behind-the-scenes work is done, it presents you with a dialog box like the one in Figure 6-14.

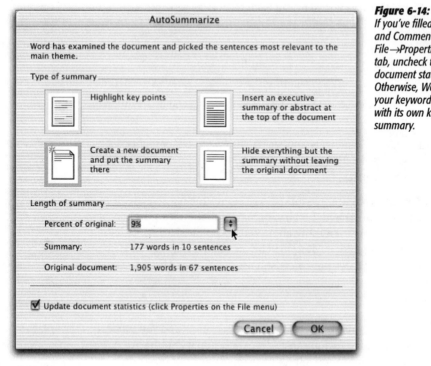

Figure 6-14:
If you've filled in the Keywords and Comments boxes on the File→Properties→Summary tab, uncheck the "Update document statistics" box here. Otherwise, Word will replace your keywords and comments with its own keywords and summary.

Type of summary

The icons under the "Type of summary" heading let you choose how you want Word to display the summary it has generated:

- Click **Highlight key points** if you'd like to scroll through your document and see which sentences Word flagged as being key points for inclusion in the summary. This is an effective way to see how Word has interpreted your document.

  When you click OK, your document appears with yellow highlighting on certain sentences. You also get a tiny toolbar containing a button for toggling between your original document and the highlighted version, as well as a slider for adjusting the length of summary percentage (see below). Click Close on this toolbar to return your document to its original condition.

- **Insert an executive summary** copies the sentences Word has chosen as representative and displays them at the *beginning* of the document. If the summary is either too long or too sketchy, press ⌘-Z to undo the AutoSummary. Now see "Length of summary" on page 228.

- **Create a new document** opens a blank Word document and puts the summary there (instead of at the top of the document).

- **Hide everything** is the choice for those who can't commit. When you click OK, it shows you the summary, hiding the balance of the document without actually closing it. A small toolbar also opens, in which you can adjust the length of the summary (see below), and toggle between the summary and the full document.

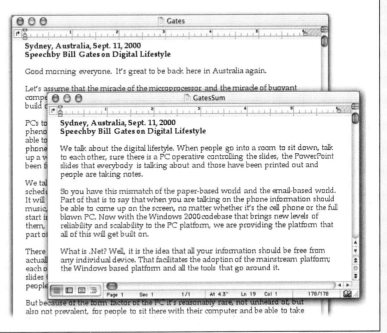

Figure 6-15:
Back: Bill Gates rambled on for quite some time in a 2000 speech to a Sydney, Australia, audience.

Front: The ten-sentence summary of the speech really tells you everything you need to know.

• Under **Length of summary** at the bottom of the dialog box, Word shows you the length of the summary relative to the full document. The default is 25 percent, which means that the summary is exactly one-quarter the length of the document as a whole. When you change the percentage and then click OK, the AutoSummarize dialog box goes away, and Word re-creates the summary according to your whims.

Working with Fields

The concept of *temporary placeholders* is one of mankind's greatest inventions. When you change a tire, the jack acts as a stand-in for the tire, supporting the car until the new tire is in place. When technicians set up the lighting for a particular Hollywood movie scene, a low-paid extra stands there patiently as a model, so the highly paid star doesn't have to stand there for hours while the technicians fiddle with shadows. When a magazine designer doesn't yet have the photo that will go on page 3, he'll simply place a box there in the correct size and label it FPO (for position only), with the intention of replacing it with the finished photograph when it's ready.

In Word, *fields* are temporary placeholders that stand in for information that may change or may come from another location on your hard drive—the current date, a page number, a place you've bookmarked, the name of a Word file, and so on. Fields, in fact, are the basis of some of Word's most powerful features. They let you:

• Create form letters and address labels, and merge them with your contact information (see page 254).

• Create indexes (page 247) and tables of contents (page 242).

• Create invoices that calculate their own totals (page 176).

• Create cross-references (page 239) and captions (page 235).

Inserting Fields

You can't *type* a field into a document. You must ask Word to create it in one of the following ways:

• Choose a command that creates a field. These are usually found on the Insert menu, such as Insert→Date and Time.

• Choose Insert→Field and choose one of the available field types from the Field dialog box (see Figure 6-16).

• Press ⌘-F9 and type the field *code,* if you know it. (The field code is a short piece of code, enclosed in braces {like this}, that tells Word what kind of information will go there.)

You may never have to create a field manually. Most of the time, fields are built right into a Word feature or another command. For instance, when you choose Insert→Date and Time, Cross-reference, Bookmark, Footnote, or Caption (all of which are described in the following sections of this chapter), Word uses a field to define the location and content of these features. When you choose any of the items on the Insert→AutoText→Header/Footer submenu, Word uses fields to insert these pieces of document information.

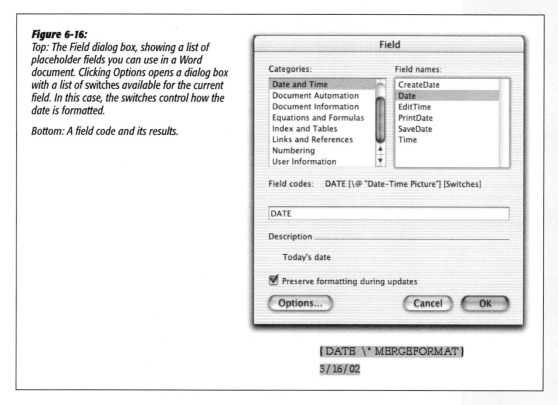

Figure 6-16:
Top: The Field dialog box, showing a list of placeholder fields you can use in a Word document. Clicking Options opens a dialog box with a list of switches *available for the current field. In this case, the switches control how the date is formatted.*

Bottom: A field code and its results.

However, there are hundreds more fields at your disposal in Word, and inserting them is as easy as choosing them from a list in the Field dialog box.

Building fields in the Field dialog box

To place a field where the insertion point is located, choose Insert→Field to open the Field dialog box as shown in Figure 6-16. Because there are so many fields in Word, the program displays them in category groups. When you click a category in the left box, the list of fields in that category appears in the right box.

When you click a field name on the right side, the field code appears in the "Field code" box below (DATE in the Figure 6-16 example). A more complete description appears in the Description panel near the bottom of the dialog box. You can learn a lot about fields just by clicking and reading the descriptions.

Modifying Fields with Switches

The Field dialog box has an Options button that lets you specify in more detail how you want a field to look and act. When you click it, the Field Options dialog box displays any applicable *switches* (software options), as shown in Figure 6-17. Like the Field dialog box, the Field Options dialog box has a Description panel below the "Field code" box; as you click each option, its description appears. You can read more about switches in the following tutorial.

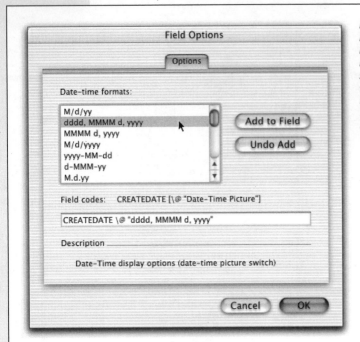

Figure 6-17:
Depending on the field you're modifying, the Field Options dialog box may show one Options tab, as shown here, or two Switches tabs. A switch is an instruction that modifies the field results. In this case, Date-Time switches tell Word how to display the current date and time.

As you build a field by adding switches or other options, you see the field code grow in the "Field code" box at the bottom of the Field dialog box. (Field veterans can type directly into this box, using the syntax shown above the box as a guide.)

Tip: If you know a thing or two about field codes, you can also edit them directly in the document. Just click in the field code (press Shift-F9 to display the field code instead of the results) and edit away.

When you've selected any options or switches, click OK (or press Return) to dismiss the Field and Field Options dialog boxes. Word returns you to your document with the newly placed field highlighted in dusky gray. The highlighting alerts you to the fact that you're looking at a field rather than normal Word text. (The highlighting doesn't show up when you print.)

Tip: If highlighted fields are just too obvious for you, then take the gray away. Choose Word→ Preferences→View tab. Choose When Selected or Never from the "Field shading" menu. Caution: If you choose Never, it will be much harder to tell where fields are. And since you can't edit field text as ordinary Word text, confusion may ensue.

What a Field Does

A field is a bit of computer code that, in one way or another, processes information. For instance, a Caption field remembers what number a caption is supposed to be, and displays that information (see page 235). The field code contains all the computerish instructions that tell Word how to figure out the Caption number and then format it. In another example, a Merge Field code (see page 254) tells Word what piece of information to grab from a database. Finally, a Date field retrieves the date from your Mac's Date & Time Control Panel and places it in your document.

For example, suppose you're creating a fax cover sheet you plan on using every day. Since you keep forgetting to date your faxes, you want to create a document with a Date field in it. This way, when you fax your daily dispatch, it's automatically dated. Here's the process:

1. **Open a blank Word document and begin typing your fax cover sheet. Click wherever you want to place the date. Choose Insert→Field.**

   The Field dialog box opens, as shown in Figure 6-16.

2. **Click "Date and Time" in the Categories box (left) and "Date" in the Field Names box.**

   You actually have two options here. *CreateDate* inserts today's date, which is what you'll always see. *Date* updates automatically; it inserts the current date each time the document is printed. In this case, you obviously want the current date each time.

3. **Click Options. Choose your favorite Month/Day/Year combination from the list box, as shown in Figure 6-17.**

   The date codes are not exactly in common English, but there is a logic to them. In general, a single letter in one of these codes (M) stands for a number (*1* for January, and so on), and a repeated letter (MMMM) stands for a full version (*January* spelled out).

4. **Click Add to Field, then click OK twice.**

   The date appears in your document. When you click it, it appears highlighted in gray to indicate that it's a field, not a typed-in date.

5. **Save your document.**

   You could also save this document as a template. The Date field works either way.

Working with Fields in a Document

To change the text formatting for a field, select the entire field by dragging across it (either the field results or the field code, whichever is showing at the moment), and then use any of Word's formatting commands: press ⌘-I for italics, choose a font or font color from the Formatting Palette, and so on.

Tip: If you format fields this way, make sure that the "Preserve formatting during updates" box is turned on in the Field dialog box (see Figure 6-16). Otherwise, the field will revert to its original formatting whenever you *update* it (see below).

Displaying fields

When you look at a field in your document, you may see one of two things: the field code (which looks like intimidating gobbledygook) or the result of the field code. For example, when you insert the DATE field into a document, it might show up either as *{ CREATEDDATE\@"m/D/YY"*MERGEFORMAT }* (the field code) or simply *6/20/02* (the result).

If you're seeing one of these but you'd rather see the other, Control-click the field and choose Toggle Field Codes from the contextual menu (or click inside the field and then press Shift-F9).

Or, to switch *all* fields in your document from field codes to their results, press Option-F9.

Updating fields

Because fields are just placeholders, the information that eventually fills them will change from time to time. The date changes, for example, or you may change your user information (which affects AUTHOR fields).

Word doesn't automatically update fields *while a document is open.* In other words, if you change your Mac's date in System Preferences, the date fields in your open documents don't reflect the change. However, if you change your Mac's date and then *open* a document with date fields, Word does update them upon opening. To update fields in open documents, press ⌘-A (selecting an entire document automatically selects all the fields in it) and press F9. A quick way to update a single field is to Control-click it and choose Update Field from the contextual menu.

Tip: If you like, Word can update your fields automatically each time you print. The secret is to choose Word→Preferences→Print tab and turn on the "Update fields" box.

Locking, unlocking, and unlinking fields

There will be times, especially when you send someone else a copy of your document, when you really don't want anyone to change your carefully planned field codes. To protect a field from changes, click in it and press ⌘-F11. This *locks* the field, meaning that you can't update the field or edit its code. You can still format the field results, however. (To lock all fields in the document at once, press ⌘-A, then ⌘-F11.)

To unlock a field, thus enabling updating and editing again, select it and press Shift-⌘-F11.

If you *really* want closure on a field, you can freeze it in time forever with its current results. To do so, click in the field and press Shift-⌘-F9. Unlinked from its code, the field is now ordinary Word text; it's no longer a field, and will never be automatically updated.

Field printing options

Normally, you'll want to print your document with the field results; you want people to see a date, not { DATE MMMMd, yyyy * MERGEFORMAT }. However, it is possible to print out a copy that shows the field codes, so that a technical-type person can look them over, for instance. To do so, choose Word→Preferences→Print panel and turn on the "Field codes" box (under "Include with document").

Bookmarks

Bookmarks in Word are the digital equivalent of folding down the page or underlining a paragraph that you want to refer to later. You can use bookmarks in long documents as you write them, perhaps to mark places that need more work later. They're also useful in Word documents you get from others, to mark places that you have questions about or pages that you're going to use most often. And because you give each digital bookmark a *name,* it's easy to jump to specific spots in a long (or even short) document.

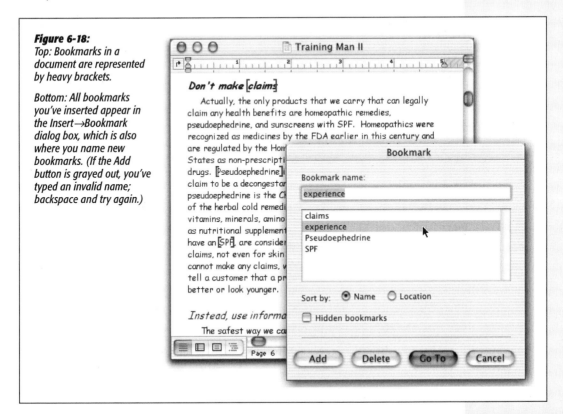

Figure 6-18:
Top: Bookmarks in a document are represented by heavy brackets.

Bottom: All bookmarks you've inserted appear in the Insert→Bookmark dialog box, which is also where you name new bookmarks. (If the Add button is grayed out, you've typed an invalid name; backspace and try again.)

Adding Bookmarks

Select the word, phrase or paragraph that you want to bookmark, or just click in the text at the appropriate spot. Choose Insert→Bookmark (or press Shift-⌘-F5), and assign your bookmark a name in the "Bookmark name" box (see Figure 6-18). When creating a name, adhere to these parameters: Be descriptive and specific; use underlines instead of spaces (Word, in its ornery way, doesn't permit spaces in bookmark names); use numbers, if you like, but not as the first character; and do not exceed 40 characters.

Click Add or press Return when you're done.

Deleting Bookmarks

To delete one or more bookmarks, press Shift-⌘-F5 or choose Insert→Bookmark, click the name of the bookmark you want to discard, and click Delete. Of course, your other option is to delete the text or graphic object (if any) that the bookmark is attached to. When the text or image goes away, the bookmark goes with it.

Navigating by Bookmark

After you've scattered bookmarks throughout your document, you're ready for the fun part: leapfrogging from one bookmark to another, skipping all the extraneous stuff in between. Your choices are to take Word's word for it that you're at a bookmark, or make all bookmarks visible on the Preferences→View panel, as described above.

Note: What you see when you leap to a bookmark depends on what you did when you created it. If you had highlighted text or graphics before choosing Insert→Bookmark, that text or object is selected when you jump to it. If you had only clicked in some text *without* highlighting anything, you get a blinking insertion point at the bookmark when you jump to it—that's all.

- **Use the Bookmarks dialog box.** To go directly to a bookmarked location, press Shift-⌘-F5 or choose Insert→Bookmark; the Bookmark dialog box lists all the bookmarks you've created. Double-click the name of a bookmark. The insertion point moves to the selected bookmark; the Bookmark dialog box remains open so that you can repeat the process. Press Return or click Close to dismiss it.

- **Use the Go To command.** Another way to travel to a particular bookmark is to press F5, ⌘-G, or choose Edit→Go To. Each of these actions opens the Go To tab of the Find and Replace dialog box (see page 72). In the "Go to what" list box at left, click Bookmark and choose a bookmark name from the menu at right. Click Previous and Next to jump around by bookmark.

- **Use the Navigator buttons.** Start by using the Go To procedure described above to jump to the first bookmark. Now you can close the Find box and use the Navigator Buttons (see page 26) to move forward and backward through your bookmarks, or press the keyboard shortcuts, Shift-page down and Shift-page up, instead.

Tip: When using the Bookmark dialog box, checking the Hidden Bookmarks box adds cross-references (see page 239) to the bookmark list. Now you can use the Bookmark dialog box and the Go To feature to browse your cross-references.

Viewing Bookmarks

Bookmarks are invisible; even the Show/Hide (¶) button on the Standard toolbar or Formatting Palette doesn't uncover them. If you really want to see where they lie on your document, choose Word→Preferences→View tab; turn on the Bookmarks checkbox. (To hide them again, just turn off the box.)

When visible, text bookmarks are surrounded by thick brackets; location bookmarks appear as big, fat I-bars.

Captions

Captions are labels that identify illustrations, tables, equations created by Microsoft Equation Editor, and other objects by number (see Figure 6-19).

Most people type in captions manually, but Word's captioning feature has huge advantages over the manual method: It can number, renumber, and even insert captions automatically. Letting Word handle the captions not only saves you time, but could potentially save you from repeating a caption number, for instance, or leaving out a caption entirely.

Inserting Captions

To caption an item—table, picture, text box, or some other object—first select it, then choose Insert→Caption. Instead of typing a caption, you *build* it using the Caption dialog box, as shown in Figure 6-19.

- **Caption, Label.** You can't directly edit the words in the Caption box (such as "Figure"), which is how the caption will appear in the document. Instead, this box reflects whatever you select from the Label pop-up menu. If none of the three labels provided (Figure, Equation, Table) strikes your fancy, click New Label and type your own—*Illustration* or *Chart,* for instance—and hit Return.

- **Position.** This pop-up menu lets you choose one of the two most popular places for the location of your caption: above or below the captioned item.

- **Numbering.** Word numbers your captions automatically; this feature, after all, is the whole point of this exercise. Use the Numbering dialog box, as shown in Figure 6-19, to choose a number format (Roman numerals or whatever).

  If you choose to include the chapter number in the captions (perhaps before the hyphen—"Figure 6-20," as in this book, for example), you need to tell Word how to *find* the chapter numbers. A couple of conditions apply: The chapters must all be within the same document, and you must use one of Word's built-in chapter-heading *styles* (see page 141) for the chapter headings.

For instance, suppose you've formatted all your chapter headings using the Heading 1 style. Furthermore, suppose you've autonumbered them as described on page 118: you chose Format→Bullets and Numbering→Outline Numbered tab and selected one of the numbering styles with Heading 1, Heading 2, and so on.

Now, when you turn on the "Include chapter number" box (Figure 6-19) and choose Heading 1 from the pop-up menu, your captions include the correct chapter number. (And your chapter headings are automatically numbered, to boot.)

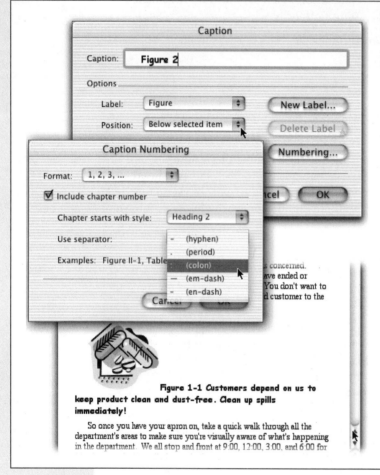

Figure 6-19:
Top: Labels you add using the New Label button appear on the pop-up menu with the three preinstalled labels.

Middle: If hyphens don't do anything for you, choose a different separator such as a period, colon, or dash. Because the chapter headings in this document use one of Word's built-in heading styles, figures are automatically numbered 1-1, 1-2, 1-3, and so on.

Bottom: A caption in place. Note that if you're planning to import your Word document into a desktop publishing program, you'll probably lose your captions. The text of the captions may appear, but the numbering will be lost.

When you finish creating the caption, click OK. The caption (numbered 1) appears in a separate paragraph above or below the selected object. As you insert more captions, Word will number them in order. (*Deleting* or rearranging captions is another matter, however, as described on the next page.)

Adding Text to Captions

If the caption for your bird picture reads "Figure 1," you can simply click after the 1 and type a description, such as *Blue-footed Booby*.

If you accidentally type over or delete the label or caption number, hit ⌘-Z (or choose Edit→Undo Typing) to restore order. If it's too late to Undo, then your only alternative is to delete and reinsert the caption. The document's captions may then need to be updated (see below).

Tip: A neat way to add supplementary text to captions is to click the caption and choose Insert→Caption; you can then type the extra text in the Caption window itself. This technique produces a caption that you can't edit in the document itself.

Deleting and Editing Captions

To delete a caption, select it and press Delete. To change a single caption—for example, to change Figure 1 to Table 1 and leave all the other Figure captions untouched—you must delete the caption and insert a new one as described above.

Word's captioning feature makes it exceptionally easy to change *all* captions of the same label at once. For example, if your document has a series of captions labeled Figure 1, Figure 2, and so on, you can easily change them to the more descriptive Photo 1.1, Photo 1.2, and so on. Just select any of the captions (be sure to select the *entire* caption) and choose Insert→Caption to open the Caption dialog box. Now you can choose a different label, create a new label, pick a different numbering system, and so on. Any changes you make will apply to *all* captions under the original Figure label.

Tip: Technically, captions are *fields,* which are described in full on page 228. So if you've used captions in your document, you may start to see strange-looking codes like { SEQ FIGURE *ROMAN } instead of the caption. Don't be alarmed—and don't delete them!

What you're seeing is Word's *field code*—its own, internal geek instructions for creating the caption. You need to tell Word to display the field *results*—the caption itself—instead. To do that, Control-click the field code and choose Toggle Field Codes from the contextual menu.

Or, to return *all* caption field codes to normal, press ⌘-A (or choose Edit→Select All), Control-click any single field code, and *then* choose Toggle Field Codes. (Be sure to press Control *before* clicking, otherwise you'll undo the Select All.)

Updating Captions

When it comes to automatic caption numbering, Word's fairly good at counting—but not infallible. When you delete a caption or drag one out of sequence, the others don't get renumbered automatically. If you want your figures numbered sequentially, you must *update* the captions after making such a change.

To update a single caption, select it by selecting all of its text; then press F9. (Alternatively, Control-click the caption and choose Update Field from the contextual menu.) Updating all captions in a document at once couldn't be easier: Just press ⌘-A (Select All), then F9.

AutoCaptioning

Inserting captions is easy enough, but you can make it downright effortless. Word's AutoCaptioning feature can automatically add a caption to any Clip Art, picture, or table whenever you add one to your document. Here's how it's done:

1. **Choose Insert→Caption; in the dialog box, click AutoCaption.**

   In the AutoCaption dialog box, you're presented with a list of checkboxes for the kinds of objects Word can automatically create captions for—a picture, a Microsoft Organization Chart, and so on.

Note: AutoShapes are *not* on the list. Captions for AutoShapes and other drawing objects must be inserted manually; fortunately, Word still numbers them correctly along with all those created automatically.

---

2. **Turn on the boxes—as many as you wish—for the kinds of graphics you want captioned.**

   You can have more than one kind of label in your document, and you can choose different object types for each one. For example, use "Table A" for tables and "Figure 1" for pictures and charts. To do so, turn on the "Microsoft Word Table" box and go on to step 3; choose "Table" for the labels. Then repeat the procedure, turning on the boxes for the items you want the "Figure" label applied to. You can have as many kinds of labels AutoCaptioned at once as you like, provided you can keep them all straight in your head!

3. **Using the pop-up menus, choose a label and a position for the captions.**

   When you check a box as described in step 2, you may notice that the Label menu changes. Word is suggesting a label for that type of object. You can override it by making a different choice from the Label menu.

   The label and position choices here work as described on page 235; as always, you can create new labels by clicking the New Label button.

4. **Choose a numbering style for the AutoCaptions.**

   If you're using more than one type of caption label, each can have a different numbering style.

5. **Click OK.**

Now insert the pictures or tables in your document. The captions will appear automatically.

Turning AutoCaptions Off

To turn AutoCaptioning off, choose Insert→Caption, click AutoCaption, and un-check the boxes for the captioned objects. All existing captions stay as they are, but no new ones will be added automatically.

Cross-References

In long, technical, or scholarly documents, you frequently find phrases like "see Chapter 12" or "see Figure 8 on page 313." These are *cross-references*—words that refer the reader to another place in the document. Of course, you can always type your own cross-references—but what a mess you'll have when you decide to cut a few pages from the first chapter, and all 1,424 of your cross-refs now point to the wrong page numbers!

Word stands ready to create smarter cross-references that update themselves no matter how you edit your document. What starts out saying "See page 24" will change automatically to say "See page 34" after you insert a ten-page introduction.

Remember these two principles as you start on the road to becoming a master cross-referencer:

- Word thinks of cross-references as pointing to *objects* in your document, not places.

  In other words, a cross-reference must be connected to a figure, bookmark, or a heading.

- Cross-references can only refer to something within the same document.

  If you're creating a document with multiple chapters, you must combine them into one Master Document (see page 219) before working with cross-references.

Inserting Cross-References

When creating a cross-reference, start by typing appropriate lead-in text into your document: *See, Turn to, As shown in,* or whatever you like. Then it's time to get Word involved.

Here, for example, is how you might build a cross-reference that reads, "See Figure 1 below" (see Figure 6-20).

1. Type *See Figure;* then choose Insert→Cross-reference.

   The Cross-reference dialog box appears.

2. Make a selection from the "Reference type" pop-up menu.

   The list contains only the things that Word can recognize as a cross-reference: a figure (anything with a *caption,* as described in the previous section); a Word table; any text that's formatted with one of Word's built-in headings or num-bered lists; an equation created with Microsoft Equation Editor; or a footnote, endnote, or bookmark.

Tip: If you don't use any of the above items in your document, but just want to refer to some text, you can always bookmark it (see page 233). For instance, if you want a cross-reference to read "See the discussion of komodo dragons on page 30," first go to page 30 and bookmark the paragraph where you talk about komodo dragons. Name the bookmark "komodo dragons." Now go to where you want the cross-reference positioned, choose Bookmark in the "Reference type" menu, and continue as described below.

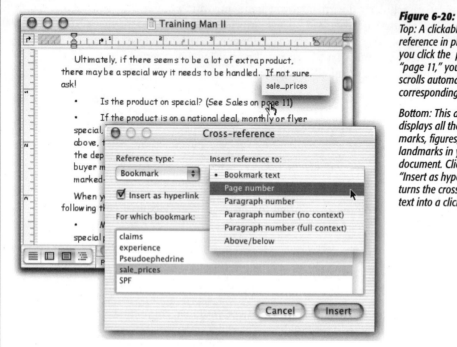

Figure 6-20:
Top: A clickable cross-reference in place. When you click the phrase "page 11," your document scrolls automatically to the corresponding paragraph.

Bottom: This dialog box displays all the bookmarks, figures, or other landmarks in your document. Clicking the "Insert as hyperlink" box turns the cross-reference text into a clickable link.

3. **Choose the specific item you're cross-referencing in the "For which" list box.**

   In Figure 6-20, "Bookmark" is the chosen reference type; the "For which" box lists all the numbered items in the document—an employee training manual in this case. If you had chosen "Numbered item," all the list items in your document would appear, and so on. From this list, choose the correct destination for this particular cross-reference.

4. **In the "Insert reference to" menu, specify what type of item you want the reference to point to.**

   You have a choice of the actual text (of the caption or paragraph), the number (of the page, list item, or outline paragraph), or simply "above" or "below."

   In other words, this is where you finally get to tell Word what you want the cross-reference to *say*. In Figure 6-20, the choice "Paragraph number" places the number "1" in the cross-reference after the typed word "See." If you were to go back and renumber the list in the training manual, the number in the cross-reference would change automatically.

If **above/below** is not one of the choices on the "Insert reference to" menu, turn on the "Include above/below box" to add "above" or "below" to the end of the cross-reference, as shown in Figure 6-20.

Thereafter, no matter where you move the referenced item—as long as it's within the same document—Word will change "above" to "below," or vice versa, as necessary.

5. Click Insert or press Return when you're done creating the cross-reference.

Modifying, Deleting, and Cross-References

To change a cross-reference (in case you've changed a figure or divided your document into two shorter ones), just select it, choose Insert→Cross-reference, and modify the settings. This lets you change a cross-reference to Figure 2 instead of Figure 1, for example.

To delete a cross-reference, select it and press Delete. (When selecting a cross-reference, drag over only the shaded part, as shown in Figure 6-20; do not include any additional text you've typed.)

Like captions, cross-references are a type of *field* (see page 228), and also like captions, cross-references can sometimes spontaneously combust. Similarly, you fix them as you would broken captions. For example, if you see some cryptic characters like { REF_Ref372221765\r\p } instead of the cross-reference you were expecting, Control-click the shaded part of the cross-reference and select Toggle Field Codes from the contextual menu.

Again like captions, Word sometimes misses a few—despite the fact that the program updates cross-references automatically when you move text in your document. Therefore, as part of the finishing touches on any document in which you've used cross-references, press ⌘-A and then press F9. You've just signaled Word to update all cross-references (and captions, for that matter).

Creating a Table of Contents

Word's Table of Contents (TOC) feature shines in its versatility. Once you've built a table of contents in Word, you can use it to navigate your document (just as you might with the Document Map); you can custom format it to get just the look you want; you can save yourself the task of updating page numbers if you add or delete text from your document (which can be a major pain); and you can use it as a Web site map (because in Online view, a Word Table of Contents is automatically hyperlinked).

TOC the Easiest Way: Using Built-in Headings

If you have a well-organized document, and you've used Word's outliner or one of its built-in heading styles (Heading 1, Heading 2, and so on) to introduce each new topic, Word's Table of Contents feature was made for you. Go directly to step 1 below.

If you wrote your document without headings, on the other hand, insert them before creating the table. (Use Word's built-in heading *styles,* as illustrated on page 143.) Be descriptive when you design the headings; instead of just "Chapter 10" or "Advanced Techniques," use "Chapter 10: Underwater Architecture" or "Advanced Card-Counting."

When you're ready to smack a table of contents on the first page of your masterwork, proceed as follows:

1. **Click where you want the TOC to begin.**

   To put the TOC on the first page, click at the very beginning of the document. (You can also insert it after a title page or introduction.)

2. **Choose Insert→Index and Tables→Table of Contents tab.**

   You should now be staring at the Index and Tables dialog box shown in Figure 6-21.

3. **Choose a style in the Formats box, as described in Figure 6-21.**

   If none of the format styles thrills you, choose "From template" and see "TOC the Harder Way: Using Other Styles" on page 244.

4. **Decide how many levels you want to show, using the "Show levels" control.**

   For example, you may want your table of contents to show only chapter titles; in that case, choose 1 in the "Show levels" box. If you've divided your document into many levels of detail, each with its own heading level, you may want to show only the first two or three levels to keep the table from getting too long. (The table of contents in this book, for example, shows chapter titles and the first-level subject headings.)

5. **Format the page numbers.**

Most printed tables of contents include page numbers, of course, but if you're preparing a document for the Web where page numbering is irrelevant, then turn off "Show page numbers."

If you elect to use page numbering, you can also indicate whether you want them to be right-aligned (as in the Preview window in Figure 6-21) and what style of Tab leader you want (the dots, spaces, or lines that connect each title with its page number). The Preview window in Figure 6-21 shows a dotted line, but the "Tab leader" menu offers several other choices.

6. **Click OK.**

Figure 6-21:
Top: The "From template" format uses the styles in the current document template and results in a consistent appearance with the rest of your document. (See page 141 for more on styles.) Click on each one and look in the Preview window; choose the one that makes the best impression.

Bottom: The Options dialog box lets you build your table of contents from styles you've used in your document other than Heading 1, Heading 2, and so on. Here, the Caption style is being added to the list so that captioned pictures will appear in the table of contents.

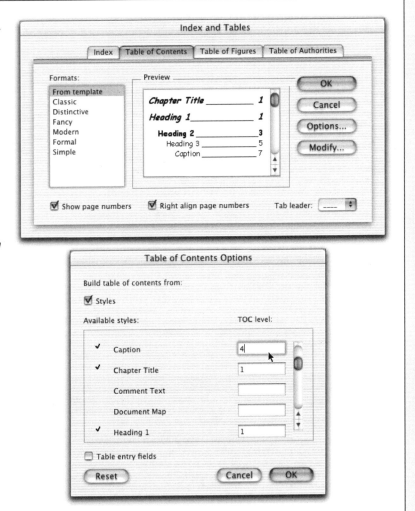

You now return to your document. If you switch into Page Layout view (View→Page Layout), you'll see the table of contents, complete with page numbers (see Figure 6-22).

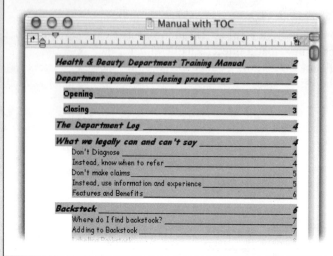

Figure 6-22:
A table of contents created from the headings in an actual Word document. The gray doesn't print; it simply informs you, the editor: "These are fields, and I, Microsoft Word, will be responsible for maintaining and updating them. Don't try editing anything here yourself."

TOC the Harder Way: Using Other Styles

Life is easiest if you use Word's built-in heading styles (Heading 1, Heading 2...) when preparing your manuscript—but that's not your only option. If your document is delineated by other styles, whether built-in or ones you've created, you can use those as the basis for your table of contents headings instead.

To do so, chose Insert→Index and Tables→Table of Contents tab. Follow steps 1 through 5 on page 242, and then click Options.

In the Table of Contents Options dialog box, you see a scrolling list of all styles in your document (see Figure 6-21). If you scroll down, you'll see that Heading 1, 2, and 3 have been assigned to corresponding TOC levels. This is your opportunity: Delete the numbers from these heading styles and type new TOC level numbers (1, 2, and so on) into the boxes next to your own styles, exactly as shown in Figure 6-21.

POWER USERS' CLINIC

Custom Formatting the Table of Contents

You can change the typographical look of your TOC headings just as you would any style (see page 141 for more on styles). Just choose Format→Styles, click the TOC1 style name, click Modify, and proceed as described on page 145.

Click OK to return to the Style dialog box. Click the next TOC heading level, click Modify again, and repeat until you've designed a table of contents to call your very own.

Tip: You can even type each level number next to more than one style. For instance, if you want your captions to be listed in the table of contents under each main topic, like your Level 3 headings, just type *3* in the box next to Caption (as shown in Figure 6-21).

In fact, you don't even have to use different levels. If you make *every* heading style Level 1, every item in your Table of Contents will have equal weight—no indents or typeface changes.

Click OK and return to the Preview box to check your work.

Updating or Deleting a Table of Contents

Like many Word features, TOCs rely on self-updating, noneditable blocks of gray-background text called *fields,* as described earlier in this chapter. As you may recall, Word updates the results of its field calculations only when you *open* the document. If, during an evening of sleepless self-doubt, you decide to rewrite the names of the different sections in your thesis, it may come as something of a shock to discover that your table of contents still shows the original section names. And if you cut out that 31-page digression into the mating habits of the Venezuelan beaver, you may be surprised to discover that the table of contents page numbers haven't been updated to reflect the new, shorter status of your paper.

The solution is simple: After editing your document and before printing or sending it, update the Table of Contents by *updating* its fields. To do so, click at the left side of the first line of the TOC, and then press F9.

Tip: The field-editing process *wipes out* any formatting or editing you've done to the text in your table of contents—which is an excellent argument for formatting your TOC using the dialog boxes as described on page 242 instead of formatting them by hand.

To dispense with a TOC, click at the very beginning of the first line of the Table of Contents. Press Shift-F9 to display the TOC field code against its gray background ({ TOC\o"1-3" }, for example). Select the entire field code, brackets and all, and press Delete. You've just vaporized all remnants of the Table of Contents.

Table of Figures and Table of Authorities

Creating a table of figures or table of authorities is very much like creating a table of contents. Word takes captions (for the Table of Figures) or citations (for the Table of Authorities) and compiles them into a table. You can custom design type styles just as in a TOC, and you can update and delete these tables exactly as described above. There are only a few differences.

Table of Figures

A table of figures is a list of captions, as opposed to headings. If you've inserted captions for pictures, tables, graphs, or equations in your document, Word can list them, along with their page numbers and tab leaders, just as in a table of contents. The steps for creating one are precisely the same as for creating a table of contents (page 242), except that you click the Table of Figures tab in step 2 instead of Table of Contents.

Table of Authorities

Lawyers, legal secretaries, and paralegals: This section is for you. In fact, nobody else is likely to know what a table of authorities *is*.

A table of authorities doesn't automatically use existing document styles like headings or captions. You have to mark each citation (case, statute, or document) that you want the TOA to use. To create a table of authorities in Word, follow these steps:

1. **In your document, select a citation.**

   For example, you might highlight "Title 37, Code of Federal Regulations, Section 1.56(a)."

2. **Choose Insert→Index and Tables→Table of Authorities tab; click Mark Citation.**

   The keyboard shortcut, for the nimble-fingered, is Shift-Option-⌘-I.

3. **Select the current citation type in the Category menu.**

   If you want to use a category that's not shown, click one of the numbers (8 through 16) in the menu. Click Category; then type the new category name in the "Replace with" box. Click Replace, and then click OK.

4. **Edit the text of the citation in the "Selected text" box.**

   Do this only if you want the citation to appear differently in the Table of Authorities. Add boldface or underscores, for example.

5. **Type an abbreviated version of the citation in the "Short citation" box.**

   In the next step, Word is going to search for the next occurrence or occurrences of this citation. If you used a specific abbreviation in your document, use that here as well—"Title 37," for instance.

6. **Click Mark or Mark All.**

   If you want to go through your document and find citations individually, click Mark and then click Next Citation. To let Word find, and automatically mark, all long and short versions of the current citation, click Mark All. Word marks citations with TA *field codes* (see page 228).

7. **After marking all your citations, click Close.**

   The Mark citation box goes away.

When you're done marking the citations, it's time to create the Table of Authorities itself.

1. **Click where you want the Table of Authorities to begin. Choose Insert→Index and Tables→Table of Authorities tab. Choose from the category menu.**

You can make a table of authorities for All citations, or create a separate one for each category. If you formatted citations in the "Selected text" box (step 3 above), be sure to turn on the "Keep original formatting" box.

2. **Choose a design in the Formats box and continue formatting your Table of Authorities.**

   See page 243 for more detail on formatting.

3. **Click OK.**

If you add a new citation after completing the Table of Authorities, it's easy to add it in. Just select the new citation, press Shift-Option-⌘-I and follow steps 3 through 7 in the first set of instructions above.

To update a Table of Authorities, click at the very beginning of the table and press F9. The same rules apply as described in "Updating or Deleting a Table of Contents," on page 245.

Indexing

Although Microsoft may hate to admit it, few people actually use Word to publish books. Most "real" books may be *written* in Word, but they're usually then poured into a proper page-layout program like PageMaker, QuarkXPress, or InDesign for the rest of the process.

That doesn't stop Microsoft from wishing its word processor were up to the challenge, though. As evidence, here's Microsoft's indexing feature, which can spew forth a professional-looking index for a document, complete with page numbers, subentries, and the works. (The operative word, however, is *can;* indexing involves considerable patience and tolerance on your part. As you'll soon find out, indexing often involves a descent into Word's sub-basement of field codes—a pseudo-programming language that's not intended for casual experimentation.)

Phase 1: Create Index Entries

As smart as Word X is, it can't read your document and ascertain what the important topics are; you must tell it which concepts you want indexed.

You do so by reading over each page of your document. Each time you come to an important point that you want included in the index, perform the following steps:

1. **Select the word or phrase that you want to index.**

   For instance, in a book about birds, you might want to create an index entry for *eggs.* So you'd highlight the word *eggs* in the manuscript.

2. **Press Shift-Option-⌘-X.**

   You could also choose Insert→Index and Tables→Index tab and then click Mark Entry in the dialog box—but life's too short.

Shift-Option-⌘-X is a keystroke well worth learning (or redefining to something easier—see page 633), since you'll be using it often. It opens the Mark Index Entry dialog box, shown in Figure 6-23.

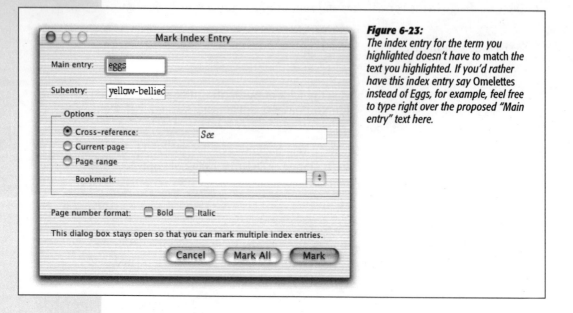

Figure 6-23:
The index entry for the term you highlighted doesn't have to match the text you highlighted. If you'd rather have this index entry say Omelettes instead of Eggs, for example, feel free to type right over the proposed "Main entry" text here.

3. **Choose Bold or Italic for the page number, if you like.**

   Use this feature to make the principal mention of the indexed term boldface or italic. This will make it stand out from the rest of the page numbers for the same term—to indicate a page where an illustration appears, for example (Eggs, 9, 11–13, 34, 51–52).

4. **Specify a subentry, if applicable.**

   For instance, if the material on the current page is mainly about yellow-bellied nuthatch eggs, you may want the index to show "yellow-bellied nuthatch" as a subentry under "eggs" (see Figure 6-23). Type *yellow-bellied nuthatch* in the Subentry box. Word assumes that you want this particular phrase indexed as a subentry under "eggs" (or whatever your main entry was in step 1).

5. **Click Mark to create an index entry for your selected word or phrase.**

   If you click Mark All instead, Word creates an index entry for *every* occurrence in the document of the word or phrase you selected in step 1. (The fact that it flags only the *first* occurrence in each paragraph is actually beneficial, since the entry may be repeated frequently in a paragraph. The purpose of the index is to direct the reader to the correct paragraph or page; to index each occurrence would create an overly long, cumbersome index.)

Note: Mark All is case-sensitive. In other words, Mark All will create entries for each occurrence of *eggs,* but not *Eggs.*

6. **Highlight the next entry in your document.**

   The dialog box remains open even after you click Mark or Mark All. However, to move on to the next entry, you have to select another word or phrase and then press Shift-Option-⌘-X again.

7. **Proceed through your entire document, marking each entry you want in the index by highlighting it and then pressing Shift-Option-⌘-X.**

   A *field code* (see page 228) appears in your document after each term you've indexed. Because these fields are formatted as *hidden text* (see page 116), Word automatically turns *on* the Show/Hide button on the Standard toolbar. That's why you see line breaks, paragraph breaks, and any other hidden text in addition to the index field codes.

8. **Click Close.**

   Now you're ready to build the index as described on page 252.

Cross-references

A cross-reference in an index looks like this: "Eggs, *See reproduction.*" It tells your reader: "*You* may be looking under Eggs, but actually I've listed all of these entries under Reproduction." (Of course, if you create a cross-reference for "reproduction," you have to actually create index entries for that topic!)

To create a cross-reference, follow the steps above; but before clicking Mark Entry in step 3, type the cross-referenced term into the "Cross-reference" box. The word "See"

POWER USERS' CLINIC

Indexing on a Deadline

If time doesn't allow reading—or even skimming—your entire document for the topics you'd like to index, there's a quicker way. By typing the topics you want to index directly into the Mark Index Entry dialog box, you can create a quick, emergency index without having to do any re-reading.

After all, if you wrote the document, you have a pretty good idea what the important points are.

Start by choosing Insert→Index and Tables→Index tab. Click Mark Entry to open the Mark Index Entry dialog box (see Figure 6-23).

Type the relevant word or phrase that you want to appear in the index in the "Main entry" box, then click Mark All; Word indexes all occurrences in your document of the word or phrase you typed. Type the next term you want indexed and click Mark All again; repeat this process until you've told Word about every important topic you can remember. Finally, click Close and proceed as described under "Building the Index" on page 252.

You can always redo or expand the index later, when time allows. Just select any word or phrase you want to add to the index, and proceed as described on page 247.

---

already appears in the "Cross-reference" box; you can type text after it (or over it). For instance, you can change it to "See also" or just "also."

Page range entries

Occasionally, the information related to your index entry spans several pages, like this: "Eggs, 9–19." Unfortunately, Word requires that you *bookmark* the range of pages before creating the index entry. To do so:

1. **Select the entire block of text that you want indexed, even if it's many pages long. Choose Insert→Bookmark; name the bookmark in the "Bookmark name" box, then click Add.**

   You can name the bookmark anything, because this name doesn't affect the index entry name. If this is the first mention of eggs in the document, for example, you could call it Eggs1. After you click Add, the Bookmark dialog box closes. (See page 233 for more on bookmarking.)

2. **Back in your document, click at the end of the selected bookmark text.**

   This tells Word where to mark the index entry field. (If you don't see the bookmark brackets around the text, turn on Bookmarks on the Word→Preferences→View panel.)

3. **Press Shift-Option-⌘-X.**

   The Mark Index Entry dialog box appears.

4. **Type the index entry, but then click "Page range." From the pop-up menu, choose the name of the bookmark you just created.**

   This menu contains all the bookmarks you've created so far in the document you're indexing.

5. **Click Mark and continue creating index entries, if you wish.**

When you later create the index, the range of pages you bookmarked will appear next to the index entry.

Phase 2: Editing Index Field Codes (Optional)

Like many Word features, Word's indexing feature relies on *fields* (invisible placeholders, as described on page 228). Because index entry fields are marked as hidden text (page 116), you can only see them when the Show/Hide (¶) button located on the Standard toolbar (or Formatting Palette) is on. At that point, the indexing codes show up, looking something like this: { XE "eggs" \r "eggs1" } .

In other words, if you'd like to see the field codes—so that you can delete them, edit them, or just see where they are—click ¶ on the Standard toolbar or the Document section of the Formatting Palette.

Once you've made your field codes visible, you can edit or delete them. To delete an index entry, select it by dragging over its field code (including the brackets), and then press Delete.

Unless you want to fool around with editing field codes, deleting an entry is also the easiest way to *edit* an entry; after deleting the faulty field codes, simply create a new replacement entry, as described on page 247.

If you're unafraid to edit field codes directly, however, here's how to edit the four kinds of index field codes:

- **Single page entry (eggs, 234).** The field code looks like { XE "eggs"\b }. If you misspelled the main entry, made an error in capitalization, or whatever, you can edit the word between the quotation marks. But be careful not to disturb any other part of the code, including the spaces. Also in this example, the *b* after the backslash indicates boldface; an *i* here stands for italic. To change a boldface page number to plain text, for example, delete both the letter *b* and the backslash.

- **Cross-reference entry (eggs, *See* reproduction).** The field code looks like { XE "eggs" \t "*See* reproduction" }. In addition to editing the main entry, you can also change the cross-reference (reproduction) or the additional text (*See*). Again, be careful not to disturb any other part of the code.

POWER USERS' CLINIC

AutoMarking Long Documents

If your document is very long, reviewing it to find each item to mark can be an exercise in tedium. Although the Mark All button helps, Word's AutoMark feature can accelerate the process even further. However, this feature is only worth using on very long documents—maybe 100 pages or more—because it entails an extra step that offers its own brand of tedium: creating a *concordance file.*

A concordance file is a Word document with a two-column table that you create yourself from a blank document. In the first (left) column, you type the text that you want Word to look for and mark in your document. In the right column, you type the index entry itself, which may not necessarily be the same term. (Using this technique, you can index, under *printing,* five pages of discussion about *dot-matrix printers, laser printers, fonts,* and *ink cartridges;* the actual word *printing* may never appear in the text.)

Another example: You could type *egg, eggs, Egg, laying, reproduction* in the left column (each in its own cell), and *eggs* directly across from each in the right cell (as shown here). (To create a subentry, use a colon, also depicted in the illustration.) At the end of this exercise, Word will find each word in the left column and index it under the term you've specified in the right column—all of the sample terms shown here, for example, will be indexed under "eggs."

After logging each important term in your document this way, save and close the concordance file. Then open the manuscript document. Click at the end of the document, and then choose Insert→Index and Tables→Index tab.

In the resulting dialog box, click AutoMark. Navigate to your concordance file and open it. Now Word automatically places index entry fields in the document; you can see them highlighted as you scroll through it. If you missed any major topics, just create another concordance file and repeat the process.

Now build your index as described on page 252.

egg	eggs
eggs	eggs
laying	eggs
reproduction	eggs
Egg	eggs
Eggs	eggs
robin's eggs	eggs:robin's
hen's eggs	eggs: chicken's
chicken's eggs	eggs:chicken's
Chicken's eggs	eggs:chicken's
Henhouse	eggs:chicken's
henhouse	eggs:chicken's

- **Page range entry (eggs, 234-236).** The field code looks like { XE "eggs" \r "Eggs1" }. This one's tricky to edit, because in order to change the range bookmark name (see "Page range entries" on page 250), you have to type in the *exact* name of the bookmark. However, you can change this into a single-page entry by deleting the bookmark name with its quotes, the backslash, and the *r*. And, of course, you can edit the main entry name.

- **Subentries (eggs, robin's, 21).** The field code looks like { XE "eggs:robin's" }. The main entry is before the colon, the subentry is after. You can edit either one, and also create additional layers of subentries just by adding another colon followed by another subentry, and so on.

Phase 3: Building the Index

Once you've marked index entries in the document you're indexing, you can generate the index itself, as follows:

1. **If the field codes in your document are showing, turn off Show/Hide by clicking ¶ on the Standard toolbar to hide them.**

   This step ensures that your document is paginated correctly. When field codes are showing, they take up room just like extra words and throw off the page numbers.

   Most of the time, you'll want to insert a page break or section break just before the index, so that the index will begin at the top of a new page. Then:

2. **Click in your document where you want the index to begin. Choose Insert→ Index and Tables→Index tab.**

   The Index and Tables dialog box opens, as shown in Figure 6-24.

   Choose a Type radio button to specify the layout of your subentries.

   If you click Indented, each subentry appears indented under the main entry. If you click Run-in, all entries in the index are flush left. (Watch the Preview window for an example of each.)

3. **Choose a Format from the Formats list.**

   If you choose "From template," Word uses the *styles* (page 141) in your current template. To see what the other canned index designs look like (Classic, Modern, and so on), click each and view the results in the Preview window.

4. **Choose a number of columns in the Columns box by clicking the arrows or entering a number.**

   You can choose one, two, three, or four columns per page. To save space, most indexes use a multiple-column format. If your document already *has* columns, choose Auto to make your index match the same number of columns.

5. **Turn on "Right align page numbers" to move the page number out to the right margin of the page or column.**

Turning this on affords you the option of using a *tab leader* (dots or dashes between the entry and its page number), as shown in Figure 6-24. Choose it from the small pop-up menu at the lower right.

6. **Click OK.**

Word creates an index, as shown in Figure 6-24. This will take a few minutes, especially if your document is long. You can stare at the watch icon or go get a snack.

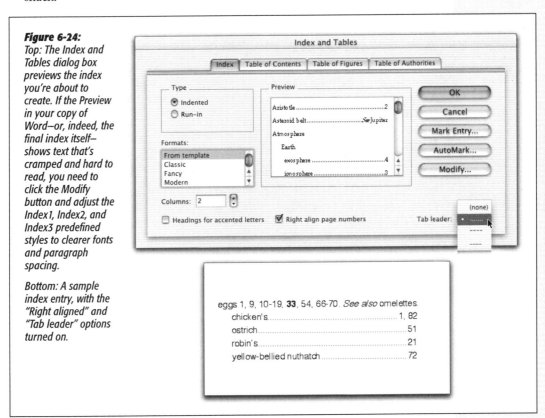

Figure 6-24:
Top: The Index and Tables dialog box previews the index you're about to create. If the Preview in your copy of Word—or, indeed, the final index itself—shows text that's cramped and hard to read, you need to click the Modify button and adjust the Index1, Index2, and Index3 predefined styles to clearer fonts and paragraph spacing.

Bottom: A sample index entry, with the "Right aligned" and "Tab leader" options turned on.

Phase 4: Cleaning Up the Index

Once Word has finished building the index, you can edit it as you would any text. You can also revisit it in any of these ways:

• **Reformat the index.** Click the index and choose Insert→Index and Tables; in the resulting dialog box, you can change any of the options on the Index tab, as described above. (Because you clicked the index first, any changes you make will apply to it, even though this dialog box normally creates a *new* index.)

• **Update the index (F9).** If, after sleepless nights of soul-searching, you decide to edit your document by inserting or deleting text, Word doesn't automatically update your index; all of its page numbering is now off. Similarly, if you decide to add, delete, or edit some index entries themselves, they won't be reflected in the index you've already generated.

The solution, either way, is to click in your index and press F9. Word updates the index; as when you created the index, this will take some time.

- **Deleting an index.** To remove an index from your document, click it and press Shift-F9 (it will be represented as a field code). Select and delete the entire field code to delete the index.

Tip: Deleting the index doesn't delete the index *entries* you've marked in your document. Usually, leaving them in place does no harm, since they're marked as hidden text and generally don't print or show up onscreen. But if you need a genuinely clean document, use the Replace command described on page 75. Using the Special pop-up menu, choose Field and replace it with nothing. Word will neatly extract them from your file.

Data Merges

If the term *data merge* is new to you, perhaps it's because "data merge" is a kinder, gentler euphemism for its result: *form letters*. A data merge grabs information from a database, and uses that information to automatically fill in the blanks of a Word file ("Dear <<name>>, As a fellow <<city>> resident, I thought you might be interested in contributing <<income>> to our fundraiser"). In the example above, a data merge can effectively churn out what seem to be personal, individually written letters. Merging data can also create labels, envelopes, or a catalog.

Having Office X on your Mac puts you at a definite advantage: You get to use all the document-beautifying features of Word (see Chapter 3) to write the placeholder letter, and you have your choice of programs to organize the data. You can use an existing Excel file, your Entourage Address Book, a FileMaker Pro database, or a Word table to supply the data that you want plugged into the generic letter.

The placeholders Word uses when you write the letter are *fields* (see page 228). And because fields can process information like computer code, Word data merge documents are very powerful. For example, you can set them up to prompt you for information before proceeding with the merge ("What amount to ask for?").

To make these interactive functions easier to use, Office X offers the Data Merge Manager. Just as the Formatting Palette consolidates dozens of different formatting features, so the Data Merge Manager also collects and automates the features you need for four of the most popular merges: form letters, labels, envelopes, and catalogs.

Preparing Data Sources

Before you begin your mail-merge experience, figure out what computer document will contain the *source data*—the names and addresses for your form letters and envelopes, for example, or the items and prices in your inventory database that you'd like to merge into an attractive catalog.

The most common data source is a database of names, addresses, and other personal information. Office X can grab data from Word tables, tab-delimited text files (such as ASCII), Excel files, the Entourage address book, or FileMaker Pro databases.

As you delve into merges, you'll need familiarity with two important pieces of database terminology: *records* and *fields*. A *field* is a single scrap of information: the phone number or the shoe size. (This *database* field isn't quite the same thing as the gray-text placeholder *Word* fields described earlier in this chapter—although the database kind of field will indeed be represented by a Word field in your form letter.) A *record* is the complete set of fields for one form letter, mailing label, or envelope—the name, address, phone number, and so on.

Tip: Whether you create a new database for your merge or use an existing one, make sure that each record is set up the same way. If you're using a database where the first and last names are in separate fields in some cases and together in others, you're going to have trouble getting the merge to work properly.

Figure 6-25:
The data-merge feature of Word isn't a shining example of simplicity. But the section structure of the Data Merge Manager palette, which looks a lot like the Formatting Palette, at least makes the steps sequential. The file name and main document type appear here–in this example, it's called MergeLetter (see it near the top?). So do the fields in the database you've selected (see them in the Merge Field section?).

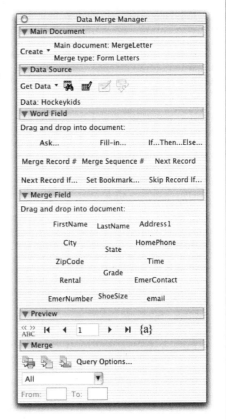

Creating a New Data Source

Let's say you have a bunch of application slips filled out by kids signing up for your hockey lessons, and you want to write each student a welcome letter. However, you don't have the database in electronic format yet.

The easiest way to start a data source file is to launch Word and choose Tools→Data Merge Manager. What you'll see is something like Figure 6-25.

The list of database fields you'll need depends on what you plan to say in the form letter. In the example in Figure 6-26, the coach realized she'd need date, first and last name, address, shoe size, school grade, the instructor name, and the entrance where the student's hockey class would gather for their first meeting. A few fields already in the database for other purposes—phone number, for example—won't be used in this letter; that's OK.

To create a data source for your project, proceed as follows:

1. **Open the *main document*.**

   "Main document" means the file that will contain the letter itself—the text that won't change from one printout to the next. Choose Tools→Data Merge Manager, if the palette shown in Figure 6-25 isn't already open.

2. **On the Data Merge Manager, choose Create→Form Letters.**

   As you can see from the pop-up button, Word comes ready to access information from your Office (Entourage) Address Book or a FileMaker database—or to create a new list of data from scratch. That's what you'll be doing in this example.

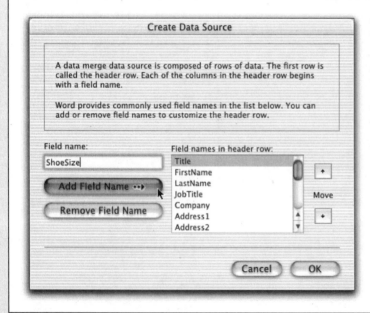

Figure 6-26:
Scroll through the "Field names in header row" box and click "Remove Field Name" for any you don't plan to use. To add fields you will need for your hockey letter (ShoeSize, for instance), type them in the "Field name" box and click Add Field Name. Note that Word does not permit spaces in the names of your fields.

3. On the Data Merge Manager's Data Source section, choose Get Data→New Data Source.

The Create Data Source dialog box appears, as shown in Figure 6-26. It has a list of suggested fields for form letters. Edit the list of fields, also as shown in Figure 6-26.

4. **Click OK. Name the database (*Hockey Kids,* for instance) and click Save.**

You've just created a Word document with a table that will hold all your data.

Now you're confronted with a Data Form window like the one shown in Figure 6-27. It's time to play fill-in-the-blanks; use this dialog box to type in the information for each kid in your class.

5. **Enter the first kid's name, address, and other bits of information, pressing Tab or Return to jump from blank to blank. Click Add New to save the first record and clear the form for the next set of data.**

Click Delete to "backspace" over the record you just entered; click Restore to bring it back. The counter at the bottom reminds you where you are; use the navigation buttons to move backward and forward through the records.

6. **When you're finished typing in the data, click OK.**

A list of the fields you've created appears on the Data Merge Manager (see Figure 6-25).

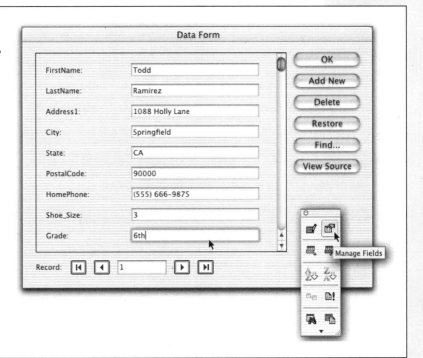

Figure 6-27:
The Find button lets you search the records you've entered. Of course, you can always click View Source and see all your data in table form. The data source is a Word document that you can see anytime by choosing File→Open. To reopen this entry form anytime, click Manage Fields on the Database toolbar.

To add more records to your data source at a later time, you have two alternatives. You can choose File→Open, open your Hockey Kids document, and add rows to the Word table you'll find there (see page 165 for full detail on working with tables). You can also choose Get Data→Open Data Source on the Data Merge Manager palette, and click the Edit Data Source button to pull up the Data Form shown in Figure 6-27. Once the data source is open, you can use the Database toolbar to sort and edit it. (If you don't see this toolbar, choose View→Toolbars→Database.)

You're ready to perform the merge; skip ahead to page 261.

Using an Existing Data Source

To merge an existing database into a form letter or envelopes, say in FileMaker Pro or Excel for Windows, you must first save the file. Then follow the steps below:

1. **Open your form letter (or create a new blank document).**

   If the Data Merge Manager palette isn't already open, choose Tools→Data Merge Manager.

2. **On the Data Merge Manager palette, choose Create→Form Letters (for this example).**

WORKAROUND WORKSHOP

Header Rows and Header Sources

To set up a data merge, you must insert fields from a database called the *data source* into the form letter or document. The data source usually takes the form of a table in which each column's name appears at the top (Name, Address, Phone, and so on). In fact, that's exactly what the steps described on page 256 do—they lead you through the construction of a correctly formatted Word table. (You could just as easily make your own Word table by hand, as long as the first row contains the field *names* and subsequent rows contain the records you want to merge.)

To know where to place what data, Word relies on the table's column names (like First, Last, and Phone), located in the *header row*. In other words, when Word comes to the FirstName field in the main document, it plugs in the next name from the FirstName column of the data source.

When creating a data source and main document from scratch, as described on page 256, your header row auto-matically matches the fields in your main document. If you're using an existing data source with a main document that already contains fields, you can change the top row or first record of the data source to match—usually.

But if you can't edit—or don't want to edit—the existing database, you can still make it match the fields in your main document by creating a *separate header source*.

To do so, choose Get Data→Header Source→New Header Source. Word opens a dialog box just like the Create Data Source box. The difference is, Word uses the field names you enter here as a substitute top row for your existing database. For instance, if the first names are stored in the second field of your database, make FirstName the second field in the separate header source, even if the field is called something else in the database. The header source must have the same number of fields as the database, even if you don't plan to use them all in your merge.

If you've already produced a main document with fields, then add to your existing database a first record (a header row) whose entry names match the fields in your main document (see "Header Rows and Header Sources" on page 258).

3. **On the Data Merge Manager, choose Get Data→Open Data Source.**

If the existing database is in FileMaker Pro or your Office Address Book in Entourage, choose the appropriate command from this pop-up button instead. (You need a copy of FileMaker on your Mac for that option to work.)

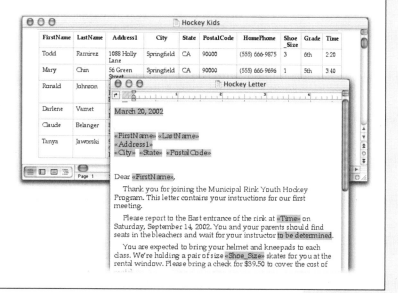

Figure 6-28:
This form letter and data source were created in Word. If you want to abandon the main document and start again, choose Create→ Restore to Normal Word Document on the Data Merge Manager. To add a field to a data source, select a column and click the Insert Columns icon on the Standard Toolbar.

POWER USERS' CLINIC

Delimiting Numerous Fields

A Word table used for a data source can contain a maximum of 63 columns or fields. If you need more than that—if you're creating a catalog, for instance—you must turn the document into a *tab-delimited text file* before using it as a data source.

A tab-delimited text file is a plain text document in which the information for each record (each person's mailing information, for example) appears on its own line, with a tab between each field (between Name and Address, for example).

You can create a tab-delimited text file in any database program, although the commands to do so vary slightly. In Excel, for instance, choose File→Save As; choose Text (tab delimited) from the Format pop-up menu. In AppleWorks, choose File→Save As and choose ASCII text from the File Type pop-up menu. And if you've built your data source as a Word table, turn the whole table into tab-delimited plain text using the instructions on page 175.

Before you use your tab-delimited file as a data source, inspect it in Word (choose File→Open to open it). Make sure that its very first row identifies the *names* of the columns (Name, Address, Phone, and so on).

---

4. Navigate to the file on your Mac and click Open.

You're ready to proceed. If you haven't written your form letter yet, go to the next section. When both your form letter and data source are ready, go to page 261.

Creating the Main Document

When you're ready to write the actual form letter, you have a choice—like thousands of Publishers' Clearinghouse Sweepstakes form letter writers before you. You can either use an existing Word file as the body of the letter, or start from scratch.

To showcase the power of fields in a data merge document, here are the steps used to create the letter shown in Figure 6-28. In the Data Merge Manager, make sure the flippy triangle next to Merge Field is pointing downward, so that you can see the fields available in your data source. (If you haven't selected or created a data source, see "Creating a new data source" on page 256 or "Using an existing data source" on page 258.)

1. Open a new Word document. Type the date, if you like, and then press Return two or three times.

   You're about to insert the first addressee's mailing address, as is customary in a standard business letter. But you don't want to have to *type* that information— that's *so* 1985. You want Word to fill it in for you, not just on this letter, but on every one of the 44 letters you're about to write and print.

2. Drag-and-drop merge fields from the Data Merge Manager palette to place the mailing address into the letter, as shown in Figure 6-29.

3. Type *Dear* and a space, and then drag-and-drop the FirstName field.

   Word represents the field (which, when you print, will be replaced by somebody's *actual* first name) using brackets. You should now see, in other words, *Dear <<FirstName>>*.

   If your data source contains a field for titles (such as Mr., Ms., or Dr.), you can insert it instead, and then drag the LastName field.

4. Continue writing the letter, drag-and-dropping merge fields as appropriate (see Figure 6-29).

5. Insert an Ask field to collect the instructor's name for the letter.

   Our hapless hockey coach *still* doesn't know who the instructor will be. In fact, she won't know until it's almost time for the letters to go out. Therefore, she'll fill in the instructor's name during the merge itself.

   This is where the *Fill-in field* comes in. On the Word Field section of the Data Merge Manager palette, drag "Fill-in" to the point in the letter where the instructor's name should go. A dialog box appears; type *What's the instructor name?* or something else that will help you (or whoever's filling in the forms) remember what was supposed to go there.

This dialog box also gives you a chance to specify a fallback entry—default text that will appear in the letter in case you don't get the instructor list on time ("name to be determined," for example). If you turn on the "Ask once" box, Word will ask you once for the missing information, then merge it into *all* the letters.

Tip: You may be tempted to use the Fill-in field with abandon, so that Word will ask you, in the process of printing out the form letters, to fill in personalized information for each record. But you can't *see* the records *during* the merge, so you won't have any way of knowing which information should be filled in for each person's letter.

The way to customize the Fill-in field is with a *query* (page 262). For instance, filter the student database by grade and then conduct a separate pass for each, so that you can type a different instructor name for each batch of letters.

Figure 6-29:
You build your form letter by dragging the fields from the Data Merge palette directly into the letter. This example is almost complete; the ShoeSize field is one of the last fields to add to the form letter. The cursor reveals a small box when you drag the fields. Note that Word automatically places a space between two merge fields on the same line.

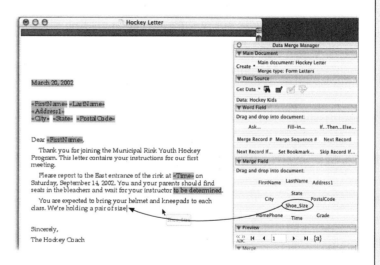

6. **Finish typing the letter and save the document as usual.**

   Word has inserted field codes for all the merge fields you've just drag-and-dropped. To see them, choose Preview→View Field Codes ({a}) on the Data Merge Manager.

Previewing, Formatting, Preparing to Merge

After you've prepared a main document and inserted merge fields, you can see how the document will look with the actual data.

On the Preview section of the Data Merge Manager palette, click the View Merged Data button (identified as step 4 in Figure 6-25). Word shows you the first finished form letter, complete with *Dear Garfinkle* (or whatever the FirstName is in the first record from your data source). Click the arrows in the box on the Preview panel of the Data Merge Manager to browse the other merged records.

In Preview mode, you can make formatting changes to the main document as well as to the merge fields. Just select text or fields in the usual way and use the Formatting Palette to add bold, italic, or other formatting. (When you reformat a field, the change applies to that *entire* field—for *all* documents in the merge.)

Once you've filled and prepared a data source, designed a main document, and outfitted it with merge fields, you're ready to merge. Check the Main Document and Data Source panels of your Data Merge Manager to ensure that the file names of your main and database documents appear correctly. Use the Preview feature as described above. Proofread your main document carefully, especially if you have numerous records in your database—you don't want a tiny mistake copied many times over!

When everything looks good, Word stands ready to merge your data and your form letter in any of three ways: sending it directly to the printer, merging into a new Word document, or merging into outgoing email messages.

Merging Straight to the Printer

If you've already previewed your merge, simply click the Print button (on the Standard toolbar) or Merge to Printer (an icon on the Data Merge Manager, shown in Figure 6-25). Specify the number of copies you need in the print dialog box and hit Return. Word prints the merged documents on your labels or paper.

Customizing merge printing

By default, the pop-up menu just below the Merge to Printer icon reads All, meaning that Word will print a merged document for *all* records in your chosen data source. The other choices are Current Record (to print just the record you're currently previewing in the document window) and Custom.

When you click Custom, you can use the From and To boxes below it to specify a range of records to merge. For example, if you have sticky laser labels that come 30 on a sheet, and you just want to print the first page of labels, enter *1* and *30*; Word will print only the first 30 records (that is, one page of labels). For the second page, enter *31* and *60*, and so on.

Query Options

If you want to print nonconsecutive records, use the Data Merge Manager's Query Options. This feature lets you *filter* your records before merging (choose only the records that meet certain criteria) or sort them.

With your main and data source documents chosen in the Data Merge Manager, click Query Options. The dialog box shown in Figure 6-30 appears. Let's say you want to send a special letter to clients in Denver, letting them know that you're going to be visiting their city next month. Your data source contains *all* your clients, even those in San Francisco, whom you obviously don't want to receive the same letter.

Since you're filtering by city, choose the City field on the Query Options→Filter tab and type *Denver* in the "Compare to" box. As you can see in Figure 6-30, there are lots of filtering options. You can even apply more than one.

For instance, you can filter out only the people who have a work phone number *and* who live in your state. You can filter out people who were born after a certain date *and* who are women. Click OK when you're done; now you can print the merged documents as described earlier.

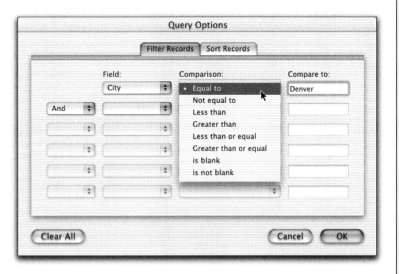

Figure 6-30:
Clicking the Sort Records tab lets you sort your data records as any Word table. (See page 165 for more detail on tables.) You can combine filtering and sorting. If the Office Address Book is your source, this dialog box looks a bit simpler, offering checkboxes that let you select only certain names and addresses for inclusion (or all names in certain categories).

Merging to a New Document

Instead of sending your form letters (or mailing labels) to a printer, it's often more useful to have Word generate a new Word document, looking exactly as though a tireless secretary had painstakingly typed up a copy of each form letter with the correct addresses inserted. This is the only way to go if, for example, you want to tweak the wording of each outgoing letter independently. You can always print the thing *after* looking it over and editing it.

Creating a new mass form-letter document is easy: After setting up your main document and data source, click the Merge to New Document icon on the Data Merge Manager palette. Word churns for a moment and then produces the document (with a page break automatically inserted after each copy of the letter).

Save the merge document to your hard drive. Edit, print, or duplicate it just as you would any Word document.

Merging to Email

You *know* it's the Internet age when your word processor comes with a feature that lets you send out form letters by email. Here's how this feature works:

1. **Create a form letter main document and a source document as described on the previous pages.**

   For best results, don't use complex formatting, since certain email users can only view email as plain text (see Chapter 8).

2. **Click the Merge to E-Mail icon on the Data Merge Manager palette.**

   If the button is dimmed, it could be that Entourage isn't selected as your default email program. Quit Word, choose →Control Panels→Internet, click the Email tab, and choose Microsoft Entourage from the pop-up menu at the bottom of the window. Start again from step 1.

   If all is well, however, the Mail Recipient dialog box opens, as shown in Figure 6-31.

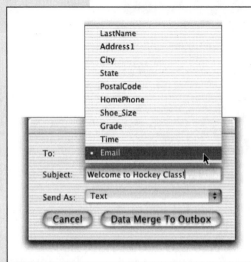

Figure 6-31:
If you choose to attach the letter as a file attachment, the name of your attachment will be the same as the file name of your main document. You may want to rename it for the benefit of your recipients, especially if you have a tendency to give documents unflattering names, like LettertoStupid.

3. **Using the To pop-up menu, choose the field that contains the email addresses. Complete the email message as you would any other.**

   For example, type a Subject line in the box.

4. **Using the bottom pop-up menu, specify whether to send the letter as text (in the body of the email) or as an attachment. Click Data Merge to Outbox.**

   The data merge proceeds as usual: Word asks you to type Fill-in fields, and so on. Entourage opens automatically, and you can watch the boldface digits next to its Outbox skyrocket as Word crams newly generated messages into it. There they wait until you click Send (or until a scheduled Send runs). There's no preview, but you can open any of the merged emails in the Outbox and look at them.

Labels and Envelopes

Two of the most common Word data merges are automated for you: address labels and envelopes. Either way, this is an extremely powerful feature that lets you combine the database flexibility of your Entourage Address Book with the formatting smarts of Word. Whether you're the local Scout-troop master or an avid Christmas-card meister, letting Word prepare your mass mailings beats addressing envelopes by hand any day.

Prepare for one of these data merges as follows:

- Prepare a data source, as described on page 254.

- Know the size of the labels or envelopes you're going to use. Have some on hand as you begin the process. (You can buy sheets of self-adhesive labels at Staples or any other office supply store; Avery is one of the best-known names. These labels come in every conceivable size and shape; the 30-per-page version is the most popular.)

- Set aside some time for trial and error.

Merging onto labels

Make sure that the labels you buy will fit into your printer and feed smoothly—buy inkjet or laser labels, for example, to match the kind of printer you have.

To create labels, open a new blank Word document and proceed as follows:

1. **Choose Tools→Data Merge Manager.**

   The Data Merge Manager palette appears.

2. **On the Data Merge Manager, choose Create→Labels.**

   The Label Options dialog box appears (see Figure 6-32, top). Unless you're that rare eccentric who uses a dot matrix (impact) printer, leave "laser and inkjet" selected.

3. **From the "Label products" pop-up menu, select the brand of labels you have.**

Word lists every kind of label you've ever heard of, and many that you haven't.

Tip: If you've bought some oddball, no-name label brand not listed in Word's list, click New Label. Word gives you a dialog box, complete with a preview window, for specifying your own label dimensions.

---

4. **Inspect your label package to find out what label model number you have; select the matching product in the "Product number" list box. Click OK.**

   The main document becomes an empty sheet of labels. It's time to start dragging field names from your source document.

5. **On the Data Merge Manager, use the Get Data pop-up button to select the database or file that contains your addresses.**

For example, to use your Entourage Address Book, choose Office Address Book from this menu. If your addresses are stored in an Excel spreadsheet or a tab-delimited text file, choose Open Data Source instead (then navigate to your database or data source file and open it).

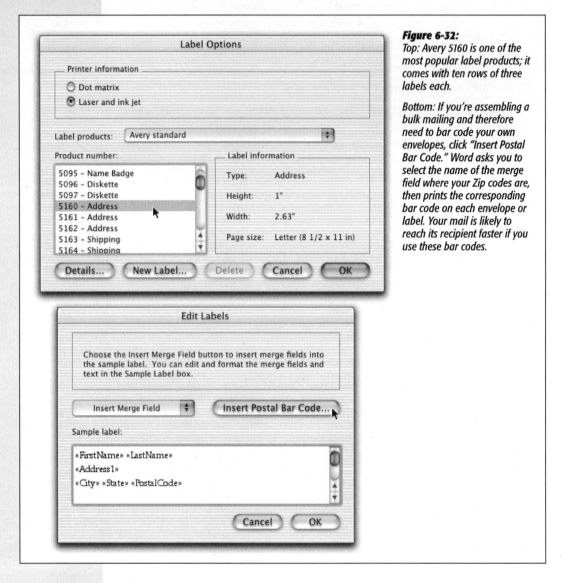

Figure 6-32:
Top: Avery 5160 is one of the most popular label products; it comes with ten rows of three labels each.

Bottom: If you're assembling a bulk mailing and therefore need to bar code your own envelopes, click "Insert Postal Bar Code." Word asks you to select the name of the merge field where your Zip codes are, then prints the corresponding bar code on each envelope or label. Your mail is likely to reach its recipient faster if you use these bar codes.

If you haven't set up your database yet, choose New Data Source and follow the steps on page 256.

6. **In the Edit Labels dialog box that appears, choose field names from the "Insert Merge Field" pop-up menu to build your address.**

As illustrated at the bottom of Figure 6-32, use the Space bar and Return key as you go. For example, choose First_Name, insert a space, choose Last_Name, then press Return to start a new line. Choose City, type a comma if you like, and then choose State; add two spaces before choosing Zip code.

7. **Click OK.**

You return to your main document window, where placeholders for your labels now appear. (Click the <<abc>> icon on the Data Merge Manager's Preview panel to preview the actual names and addresses as they'll be printed.)

Now you can format the text using, for example, the Formatting Palette; you can change the font or size, add bold, italic, or color, and so on. Just select the text or the field placeholders to format them.

8. **Click Merge→Merge to Printer and print out one page of labels on a blank piece of paper.**

This way, you can check to see if the labels are properly aligned without wasting an expensive sheet of labels. Hold the paper printout over a label sheet and line them up in front of a window or light.

9. **If your labels need realigning, choose Create→Labels on the Data Merge Manager and click Details.**

A dialog box pops up, displaying the dimensions and specifications of your currently chosen label model, along with boxes and arrows for adjusting them. You can move the label text up, down, and side-to-side in order to better fit on the labels.

10. **When everything's working properly, load the labels into your printer, and click Merge→Merge to Printer. Click Print.**

Take advantage of the Merge→Custom box (see page 262) if you have a long mailing list. Some printers tend to jam if you try to print too many pages of labels at once.

Editing labels

You can edit a label document by opening it, just like any main document. But because of the unique problems involved in changing a sheet of labels, Word provides a couple of special tools. To make changes to an existing label document, proceed as follows:

1. **Open the label document.**

Word opens the document and the Data Merge Manager. (If not, choose Tools→Data Merge Manager.)

2. **Click the Edit Labels for Data Merge button.**

It's the third icon in the Data Source section of the Data Merge Manager palette. The Edit Labels dialog box opens, as shown in Figure 6-32.

3. Make changes to the label format.

4. Add or remove merge fields or change text formatting, for example, by selecting the merge fields and using the Formatting Palette. Click OK and proceed with the merge.

Propagating labels

You can also edit labels right in the main document, which you may find easier than using the Edit Labels dialog box. The secret is in the Propagate Labels button on the Data Merge Manager (the rightmost icon in the Data Source section of the Data Merge Manager palette). Here's how to use this method of label editing:

1. **Open the label document; click the *first* label on the page.**

   Word opens the document and the Data Merge Manager. (If the Data Merge Manager is not open when you need it, choose Tools→Data Merge Manager.)

2. **Edit the label document.**

   For instance, you can drag merge fields from the Data Merge Manager, type additional text, and format the text or field placeholders (font, color, and so on). Remember, you're doing this only in the first label.

3. **Click the Propagate Label Document button on the Data Merge Manager.**

   Word changes all labels on the sheet so that they match the changes you just made in the first label.

   When you're done propagating, merge and print the labels as described on the previous pages.

Merging onto envelopes

Printing envelopes on computer printers has always been an iffy proposition; in essence, you're trying to ram two or three layers of paper through a machine designed to print only on sheets one-layer thick.

You'll have an easier time if your printer is envelope-friendly. If your printer has guides for feeding envelopes, so much the better. You may find that some brands of envelope fit your printer better than others.

When you're ready to begin, open a new blank document and follow these steps:

1. **Choose Tools→Data Merge Manager, then choose Create→Envelopes.**

   The Envelope dialog box opens, as shown in Figure 6-33. If you don't care for Helvetica, click Font to call up a Font dialog box. You can use any of Word's fonts and effects.

2. **Click Position. In the Address Position window, click the arrows to move the return and delivery addresses around on the envelope, if necessary.**

   If the return address is too close to the envelope edges, for example, or the delivery address is too low, now's your chance to fix it.

3. Click Page Setup.

Word opens your printer's usual Page Setup dialog box. Choose the envelope size from the pop-up menu and click OK. (If you don't see the correct size, click Cancel; under Printing Options, click the "Use custom settings" button, then click Custom. In the Custom Page Options dialog box, choose an envelope size and tell Word how you plan to feed it into the printer.)

Figure 6-33:
If your return address does not automatically appear in the Return Address window, type in the address you want to use in the "Return address" box. Check the "Use my address" box to pull up the name and address you entered when you set up Office X. Turning on Omit will print the envelopes with no return address at all.

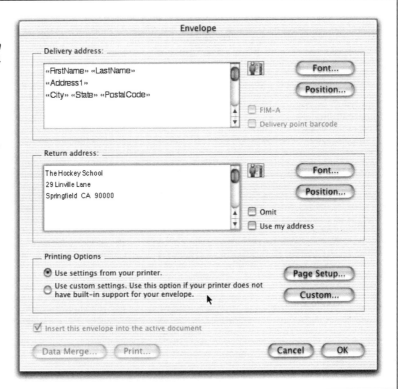

4. Click OK, then OK again to dismiss the Envelope dialog box.

Your chosen envelope format appears in the main document; it's time to "type in" the addresses you want to print.

5. If you want to print just one address from your Entourage Address Book, click the Address Book icon at the upper right of the Delivery Address window, and proceed as shown in Figure 6-34.

If you want to run an actual mass printing of envelopes, however, do this:

6. On the Data Merge Manager, choose Data Source→Get Data→Open Data Source; select and open your database.

Again, Excel spreadsheets, FileMaker databases, and tab-delimited text files are fair game. If you haven't set up your database yet, choose New Data Source and follow the steps on page 256.

7. **Drag field names from the Merge Field panel of the Data Merge Manager into the address box of the envelope in the main document.**

   Add spaces and line breaks in the usual way, as shown in Figure 6-32.

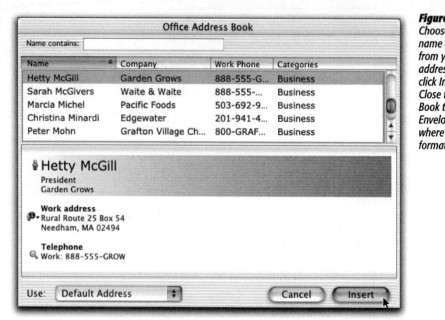

Figure 6-34:
Choose the desired name and address from your Entourage address book, then click Insert as shown. Close the Address Book to return to the Envelope dialog box, where you can format the envelope.

8. **Prepare your printer's feed for envelopes; click Merge→Merge to Printer. Click Print.**

   If the envelope gods are smiling, your printer now begins to print the envelopes perfectly. (If they're not, then you may discover that you'll have to rotate the envelopes in the paper slot, for example.) Depending on your printer model, you may have to print one envelope at a time—if so, choose Current Record from the drop-down menu at the bottom of the Data Merge Manager.

Working with Macros

A *macro* is like a script: a step-by-step series of commands that Word performs, rapid-fire, each time the macro is run. Although they definitely qualify as a power-user feature, you should consider this feature any time you find yourself facing a repetitive, tedious editing task. For example:

- Changing three different character names in one pass (which is required for each chapter of the novel you just finished).

- Drawing a table with the months of the year automatically listed down the first column and the names of all salespeople across the top. (All you have to do to complete the daily sales report is fill in the figures.)

- Saving the table document above as a Word document in your Sales folder and saving an additional copy as a Web page (which you can now upload to the company intranet).

Office's macros are actually tiny programs written in a programming language called Visual Basic. People with programming skills and a lot of time on their hands can make Visual Basic do astounding tricks; fortunately, you don't need to learn the language. You can generally get away with using Word's *macro recorder,* a "watch me" mode where Word writes the macro for you as you traverse the various steps once yourself. Once you've recorded the macro in this way, Word is ready to execute those actions automatically, like a software robot that's wired on caffeine.

Tip: A macro is saved into a document or a template. Thereafter, it works only when you've opened that same document (or a document based on that template).

To make a macro available in all Word documents, move it into the Normal template, as described under "The Organizer" on page 207. Fortunately, macros you create by recording are stored in the Normal template, so they're always available.

Creating a Macro

Even without knowing Visual Basic, you can create a macro for anything you know how to do in Word. Think of the macro recorder as a tape recorder that "listens" to what you do, and then replays it on command.

Note: The macro-recording feature in Word can't record mouse movements (other than menu selections and button clicks); so if your macro involves selecting text or moving the insertion point on the page, do it using keyboard shortcuts.

In this example, the company you work for has been sold, and you'd like to create a macro that goes through a document and replaces the old company name with the new one. Because you'll have to do this on dozens or hundreds of existing documents, you decide to store it as a macro that you can trigger at will.

1. **Open a document that needs your Find/Replace surgery. Choose Tools→
   Macro→Record New Macro.**

   Alternatively, click to turn on the REC button on the bottom edge of your document window. The Record Macro dialog box opens, as shown at bottom in Figure 6-35.

2. **Type a name for the new macro.**

If you find it a bit nerdy that you have to name the macro before you've even created it, just wait—Word's nerdiness is only warming up. For example, you're not allowed to use commas, periods, or even spaces in the name of your macro. In Figure 6-35, the macro has been named ReplaceCo.

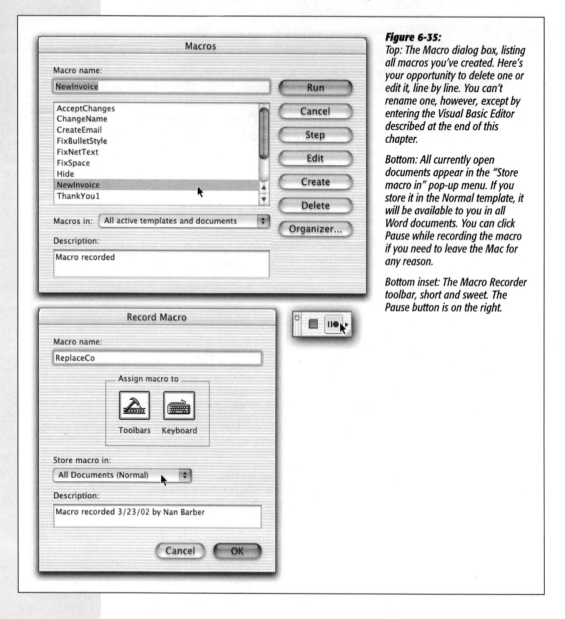

Figure 6-35:
Top: The Macro dialog box, listing all macros you've created. Here's your opportunity to delete one or edit it, line by line. You can't rename one, however, except by entering the Visual Basic Editor described at the end of this chapter.

Bottom: All currently open documents appear in the "Store macro in" pop-up menu. If you store it in the Normal template, it will be available to you in all Word documents. You can click Pause while recording the macro if you need to leave the Mac for any reason.

Bottom inset: The Macro Recorder toolbar, short and sweet. The Pause button is on the right.

___

Caution: If you assign a macro the same name as an existing macro, Word replaces the original one without so much as a by-your-leave. If you give your macro the same name as a preinstalled Word macro, for example, you'll lose the Word macro.

___

Type a description, too, so that later you'll remember what this macro was designed to do.

Again, before you've even created the macro, you must now tell Word how you intend to trigger this macro in the future. To do so, either press a key combination of your choice or click a button on a toolbar. (You can always change your mind, or choose both methods, later.)

3. **To create a button on one of your toolbars for this macro, click Toolbars.**

   The Customize dialog box appears, with a mutant version of your macro's name (such as Normal.NewMacros.ReplaceName) displayed on the right.

   Drag the macro's *name* from the Customize dialog box to the Standard toolbar or any open toolbar. (More on dragging to toolbars in Chapter 17.)

4. **If you want this macro to be available in only one document (as opposed to all Word documents), choose the name of the current document from the "Store macro in" pop-up menu.**

   Word assumes that the document you want to store the macro in is already open. If not, click Cancel, open the correct document, and start over.

5. **To assign a keyboard shortcut to the new macro, click Keyboard.**

   The Customize Keyboard dialog box opens, with the cursor blinking in the "Press new shortcut key" box. Press a key combination on your keyboard (Control-R, say) that will be easy for you to remember.

   The combination must include Control, ⌘, Control-⌘, or Shift-Control plus one or two other keys, such as letters and numbers. If the combination you press is already in use, you'll see the name of the conflicting command under "Currently assigned to"; see page 633 for more on changing Word keystrokes.

   Click Assign.

6. **Click OK to begin recording the macro.**

   You now return to your document. Everything appears to be as it was, except for the presence of a tiny, two-button toolbar (Figure 6-35). (On the right: a Pause button, which you can click before and after you do something that you don't want recorded.) You'll also notice that the arrow cursor becomes translucent when you pass it over text or over the edges of a window.

   This is your opportunity to actually perform the steps that you want Word to reproduce later. In this example, you'll record a search-and-replace operation, thusly:

7. Choose Edit→Replace. Type the old company name in the "Find what" box, press Tab, and then type the new name in the "Replace with" box (see page 77). Click Replace All.

Word makes the replacement everywhere in the document.

8. Close the Replace tile box, and then click the Stop button (the small blue square) on the Macro Recorder toolbar—or just double-click the REC indicator on your status bar.

That's it—you've just recorded a macro. If you'd like to test it on the document that's still open before you, choose Edit→Undo Replace All (to undo the effects of your manual search-and-replace), and then trigger the macro as described below.

Tip: The macro doesn't become immortalized in your Normal template until you quit Word. If your Mac has a tendency to crash or freeze every now and then, you'd be wise to quit Word shortly after recording any important macros. Otherwise, you'll launch Word after a freeze or crash only to find that the macro has disappeared.

Running a Macro

As with so much else in Office, there are several ways to run a macro that you (or other people) have recorded. Here's a list:

- Press the keystroke that you assigned to the macro when you created it.

- Choose the macro in the Tools→Macro→Macros dialog box (Figure 6-35, top) and then click Run.

- Click the toolbar button that you assigned to the macro when you created it.

- Set up a macro to run automatically. To do this, give the macro one of these special names: **AutoExec** (runs when Word first launches), **AutoExit** (when you quit Word), **AutoOpen** (when you open an existing document), **AutoNew** (when you start a new document—very useful), or **AutoClose** (close a document).

You can also add your macro to any of the Word menus, as described on page 630.

The Macro Organizer

As with styles, AutoText, and toolbars, you can copy macros between documents or templates using Word's Organizer (see page 207 for complete instructions). Only these two subtleties make macro copying different:

- In the steps on page 207, click the Macro Projects tab instead of the Templates tab.

- You can't copy individual macros—only macro bundles called *macro projects*. (All of the macros *you* create wind up in a single macro project called NewMacros.)

Learning about Visual Basic

When you record a macro, Word automatically translates it into the Visual Basic programming language. To see how it looks, click a macro in the Macros dialog box (choose Tools→Macro→Macros) and click Edit. A supplementary program called Visual Basic Editor opens, displaying all the code for that macro. If you know anything about programming, you can learn quite a bit about Visual Basic just by examining the code.

Note: If Word crashes when you're trying to use the Visual Basic window, install the Office X Service Release 1, as described on page 12.

Sometimes even the novice can make some sense of this code. For example, if you've recorded a macro that blows up your document window to 150 percent, you'll see a line of code that says *ActiveWindow.ActivePane.View.Zoom.Percentage = 150*. You don't have to be a rocket scientist to realize that you can edit the 150 if it turns out to be too much magnification. You could replace that number with *125* and then choose File→Close and Return to Microsoft Word, having successfully edited your macro. (The same trick works very well for modifying search-and-replace macros; it's very easy to change the phrases Word searches for and replaces with.)

Word also has help screens that describe the Visual Basic *objects* (commands) that you assemble to create a macro. Some commands are difficult or impossible to record in a macro. If you create lots of macros, or feel inclined to debug existing macros, the time may come when you need to delve into Visual Basic.

Word Meets Web

It may be that this Internet thing has gotten out of control. It seems as though every piece of self-respecting software, from databases to games, has been Internet-enabled. Where would you be if you couldn't convert, say, your recipe file into a Web page for all the world to see?

PowerPoint, Excel, and Entourage are capable of converting your slide shows, spreadsheets, and calendars into Web pages. But for traditional, everyday Web pages, Microsoft intends Word to be the Web workhorse.

Word as Web Browser

In truth, Word isn't much of a Web browser. It does have a Web toolbar (choose View→Toolbars→Web), complete with Back, Forward, Stop, Refresh, and Home buttons (see Figure 7-1). There's even a Favorites menu, which you may be delighted to discover comes populated with the bookmarks in your Internet Explorer Favorites menu.

Figure 7-1:
When you type a Web address in the box in the Web toolbar, Word launches Internet Explorer (or whichever browser is selected on the Web tab of your Internet control panel) and opens that Web page. You don't even have to type the "www" or ".com".

But this toolbar is actually just a remote control for Internet Explorer itself. Whenever you use one of its controls or type an address into its Address bar, your Web browser launches (if it isn't open already) and handles the actual task of displaying the Web page in question.

Opening Web Pages from the Web

That's not to say, however, that Word can't display Web pages in its own window, because it can. Just choose File→Open Web Page; a small dialog box appears, in which you can type the URL (Web address) of the Web page you want. When you click OK, Word connects to the Net and brings the specified page into its own window.

Unfortunately, Word is really only the strange preteen cousin of Internet Explorer; not only do Web pages take a long time to appear in Word windows, but they may also look peculiar, with a shuffled layout, enormous margins, unpredictable movie capabilities, and other anomalies. Still, this feature may be just the ticket when you want to grab some text out of a Web page article you just read. By bringing text into Word, you can copy, paste, reformat, and perform other editing tricks.

Tip: When you open in Word any kind of Web-related document—a Web page, a Web template from the Project Gallery, a Word document you've saved as a Web page, or any other HTML file—it automatically opens in *Online Layout* view. If you ever find that you can't see images, background colors, or other Web features in your document, you've probably somehow gotten into the wrong view. Choose View→Online Layout.

Opening Web Pages from Your Hard Drive

These days, documents that have been written using the HTML Web-design language are no longer confined to the Internet. Because they're relatively small, include formatting, and open with equal ease on Macs, Windows PCs, and every other kind of computer, HTML documents are now a common exchange format for Read Me files, software user manuals, and the like. (You know when you have one because its file name ends with *.htm* or *.html*.)

Word can open such documents directly: Just launch Word and choose File→Open, then navigate to the file on your Mac and click Open. The file opens into Word's Online Layout view. Hyperlinks work, but otherwise the file acts more like a Word document than a Web page. For example:

- Scrolling text (see page 286) doesn't scroll.

- Animated GIFs, such as Active Graphics (see page 282) work, but only in Online Layout view.

- Movies designed to play automatically (and anything else requiring a Web-browser plug-in) don't work.

- Text flow and the positioning of images on your page may be different in Word than in a browser. Using a table for layout alignment (see page 165) results in more consistency between Word and browser views.

Viewing HTML Code for a Web Page

When you open an HTML document, Word does its best to show you the images and text of that document just as though you're viewing it in a Web browser. In other words, you see the *results* of the HTML programming, not the HTML code itself.

If you're comfortable working in the HTML programming language, however, Word is only too happy to show you the underlying code:

1. **Open the Web page in Word. Choose View→HTML Source.**

   If that menu choice is grayed out, save the Web page document first. The Web page opens as a document full of HTML code. A tiny, one-button toolbar, ("Exit HTML Source") also opens.

2. **Edit the HTML in Word. Click Exit HTML Source when you're finished.**

   Word returns you to Online Layout view, where the changes you just made in HTML are reflected.

Creating a Web Page in Word

Most people who are serious about Web design use dedicated Web-design programs, such as Dreamweaver, GoLive, or the free Netscape Composer.

But Word can convert any of its own documents into a Web page, ready to "hang" on the Internet. Make no mistake: Professional Web designers may sneer at your efforts, since Word fills the resulting behind-the-scenes HTML code with acres of unnecessary computer instructions that can make a Web page take longer to load into visitors' browsers. Furthermore, they can also render your design layout imprecisely. But when you need to create only the occasional Web page, or when simplicity and a short learning curve are more important to you than impressing professional Web designers, Word can suffice.

Designing a Site Map

Before you start working on your Web page in Word, it's a good idea to have a plan of action. Take a blank piece of paper or Word document, draw a box for each page of your Web site, and label them to figure out how many Web pages your site will have, and how they'll be connected by navigational links. For instance, you might have a home page, an FAQ (frequently asked questions) page, a page of scanned photos, a long article on a page of its own, and a page with your contact information. Figure 7-2 shows an example sketch.

Basic Web-Page Layout

Once you've figured out which Web pages you'll need to create for your Web site, the next step is to create individual Word documents that represent those pages. You'll probably wind up taking advantage of Word's advanced graphics and design tools—especially tables and hyperlinks—much more in a document that will ultimately become a Web page than, say, a run-of-the-mill memo. But otherwise, editing and designing a Web-bound Word document is much the same as editing and designing any other Word file.

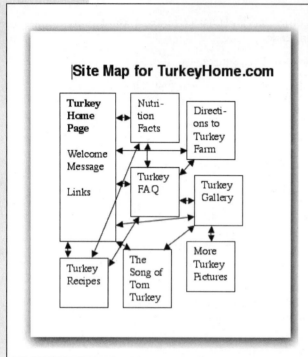

Figure 7-2:
You'll save yourself from temporary insanity if you begin your Web design with a site map. Draw arrows in all the directions that you're going to link the pages together, remembering that you'll want to link each page back to the home page, or at least to the page before it.

Tip: The following pages assume that you're interested in designing your Web pages essentially from scratch. The File→Project Gallery command, however, offers a Web Pages category filled with predesigned Web-page templates, such as a Frequently Asked Questions page, a Personal Web Page, and so on. If the Web page you have in mind is one of these basic types, by all means use the Project Gallery templates to save time. See page 15 for more on the templates.

Themes

As you contemplate your site's graphic design, think simple. Although Word's Web tools let you use a riot of background and font colors, nothing looks cleaner and more readable on the Web than black type on a plain, light background.

Still, Word comes with a long list of canned color schemes for Web pages (and other documents) called Themes. Each theme incorporates professionally selected choices for font, bullet graphics, horizontal lines, headings, background colors, and other elements (see Figure 7-3).

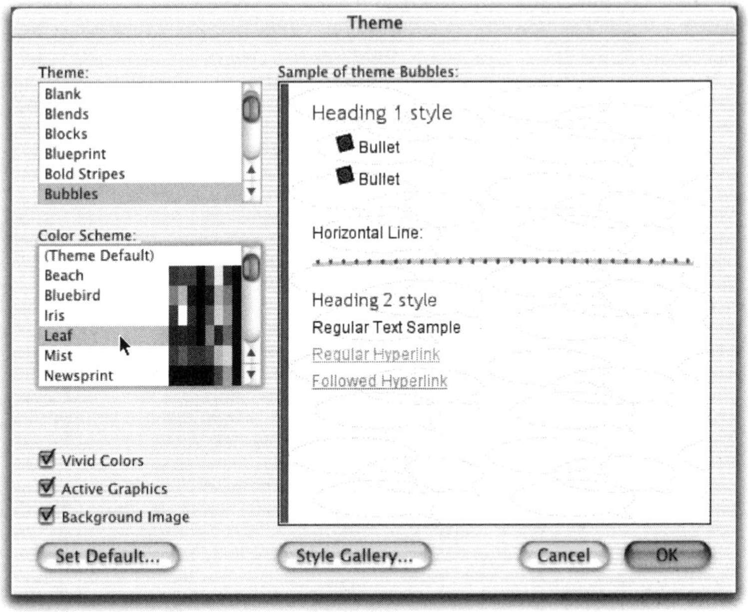

Figure 7-3:
In addition to the background color, each theme contains an optional picture, which you activate by turning on the Background Image box. Also make sure the Active Graphics box is turned on so you can see the effect of any animations you're going to use. (Uncheck the box to work on your Web page without distraction.)

To review your options, choose Format→Theme. The Theme dialog box opens. Click the various theme names for a preview of each. If you find one that appeals to you, click OK. Word applies the theme and returns you to your Word document, where you'll notice major differences only if you used Word's built-in heading styles, picture bullets, horizontal lines, and hyperlinks. (These are the elements a theme can affect.) If you've already saved the document as a Web page, or if you're in Online Layout View, you'll also get the full effect of the background pattern or color.

Here are more things you can do with Themes:

- Choose a different color scheme. Each theme has a default scheme, but you can substitute any of the eighteen other color groupings listed in the **Color Scheme** box. Keep an eye on the Sample box (see Figure 7-3) until you find the colors that grab you.

- Once you've chosen a theme, check the **Vivid Colors** box and watch what happens to the colors; the background in particular changes to a brighter color. On the other hand, if your Web page contains lots of text, bear in mind that a dark or bright background can make it hard to read.

- Turning on **Active Graphics** *animates* the bullets and borders on the screen. Animated graphics blink, alternate between two different colors, or otherwise scream for your reader's attention. For the full effect, choose File→Web Page Preview to view your document in your Web browser.

- The **Background Image** checkbox turns on the default background pattern for each theme. If you find it detracts from your text, or if you prefer a plain background, simply turn it off.

- Finally, after applying the theme and returning to your document, you can tailor it to your liking. Just use the Formatting Palette and Word's other tools to change the background color, border style, and so on.

Style Gallery

The Style Gallery button in the Theme dialog box (see Figure 7-4) opens a window where you get another look at the templates listed in the Project Gallery (see page 15).

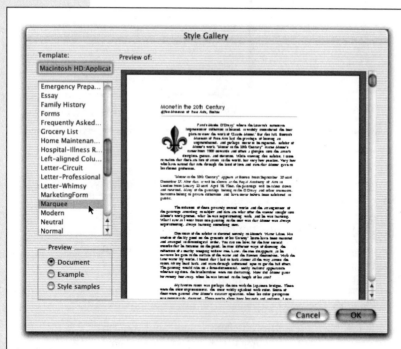

Figure 7-4:
The list at the left displays all of Word's preinstalled templates, as well as those you've created yourself and stored in the Microsoft Office X→Templates folder. If you've stored templates somewhere else, you can enter the path in the box at upper left.

As illustrated in Figure 7-4, the preview window (eventually) shows how your Web-page-in-progress will look in the selected template. (You might not notice much difference unless you've used styles—especially Word's built-in Heading styles—in the document.) It's a good thing, too, because not all the templates work very well with all pages. For instance, if your document has lots of text, the Comic Sans font and pastel-colored headings of the Corners theme may make your words hard to focus on.

If you find one you like, click OK. As always, you can adjust the formatting once you've returned to your document.

Backgrounds

Although a white or very light background is generally your best bet for legibility on Web pages, Word lets you choose anything, from graceful to hideous, as the backdrop for your page. It can be a solid color background, a pattern or gradient, or a picture. (If you don't specify a background color, your visitors' Web browsers will use a default color, which is usually white or light gray.)

To choose a background color for your Web page, choose Format→Background; in the Background color palette, click one of the color blocks to make it the background color. You can choose a different color by clicking More Colors and using one of Word's color pickers as described on page 651. If you choose No Fill, your background will be the default color of your reader's Web browser.

Note: When you're adding a background color to a Web page template that already contains a background *pattern,* the color overrides the pattern. To remove the color and restore the pattern, click No Fill on the Background color palette.

You can also click Fill Effects on the Background palette; you'll be offered a wide range of fancy backdrops, from burlap to shimmering gradients. (See page 652 for more on these options.) Most of them are much too busy for a Web page that you actually expect people to read. For the sake of humankind, please use background textures, patterns, pictures, and gradients sparingly—with only very light colors— or not at all.

When you choose a color, it appears instantly as the background of your Web page document. Word automatically switches into Online Layout view, if you weren't there already.

Font colors

You specify the color for the text of your Web page just as you would in any Word document—for example, using the Font Color button on the Formatting Palette.

When choosing a font color, the most important thing to remember is how it will show against your background. Remember, you want a lot of contrast between the background color and the font color. Black, blue, and red are good font color choices for light backgrounds.

White text on a black background sounds elegant, but it's not a good choice when working on a Web page in Word, since the black background shows up only in Online Layout view. When you switch to Normal view, you'll get white text on a white background—the new millennium version of invisible ink. You lose the ability to print your page from Normal view for the same reason. (Furthermore, black backgrounds—solid color backgrounds of any kind, really—gulp down color ink from your Web site visitors' printers like it's Gatorade.)

Also, be aware that some people, in an effort to make Web pages load faster, turn off graphics in their Web browser. (In Internet Explorer, for instance, you do this by choosing Explorer→Preferences, then clicking Web Browser→Web Content in the left pane and turning off "Show pictures.") Because background pictures and patterns are, in fact, graphics, readers who've turned graphics off won't see them. Instead, they'll simply see your text against their browser's default background color, which is usually white or light gray—yet another reason why black, red, and dark blue are safe font colors for Web pages.

POWER USERS' CLINIC

Automatic Color

When you open the Font Color section of the Formatting Palette, you'll notice that your first choice is Automatic Color. If you choose Automatic Color for text in a Web page, your reader will see it in whichever default color she's chosen for her Web browser. (In Internet Explorer, for example, you can specify your default text color by choosing Explorer→Preferences. Click Web Browser→Web Content in the left pane and click the Text color block. Choose a color using one of Office's color pickers as described on page 651.)

Choosing No Fill for your background color and Automatic Color for your font is the ultimate in consideration for your reader. It does, however, limit your creativity.

Other text effects

You can use any of Word's text formatting—such as different fonts, typefaces, and paragraph formatting—in documents you'll be saving as Web pages, but bear in mind that they may look different, or be lost completely, depending on your reader's browser. (See Chapter 3 for more detail on text formatting.)

Word also offers special effects for use on Web pages: animated text and scrolling text. Use them with caution—for two very good reasons. First, they may not be visible in all browsers or on all computers; in some cases, the affected text may be lost completely. Second, flashing and animated text, as noted earlier, strikes many Web citizens as extremely annoying.

- **Animated Text.** To use Word's animated text effects, first select the text in your document. Then choose Format→Font; in the Font dialog box, click the Animation tab, as shown in Figure 7-5. Click each of the listed Animations and watch what happens in the Preview box. If you find one you like, click it and then click OK.

Note: Beware of the Default button in the Font dialog box. If you click it, you'll apply the animation style to your Normal font, the one you see by default in every new Word document. Chances are you don't want Las Vegas Lights around everything you type in every Word document—or maybe you do. Either way, Word asks you before proceeding.

- **Scrolling Text.** Scrolling or marqueeing text is, unfortunately, a very popular text effect on Web pages. As shown in Figure 7-5, a single dialog box lets you determine all aspects of how the text looks and scrolls.

To open this box, highlight the text you want to scroll and then choose Insert→HTML Object→Scrolling Text. Choose a font, size, and typestyle in the lower panel of the dialog box, a different background color from the Background pop-up menu, and an animation style from the Behavior, Direction, and Loop pop-up menus.

Figure 7-5:
Top: The Las Vegas Lights and Sparkle Text animations feature multicolored speckles. Blinking Background alternates a black background with white or with the font color. You get the idea.

Bottom: The Font pop-up menu in the Insert→HTML Object→ Scrolling Text dialog box lets you apply scrolling to text in any Word font. Scrolling or "marqueeing" text rolls across the width of your Web page from one side to the other.

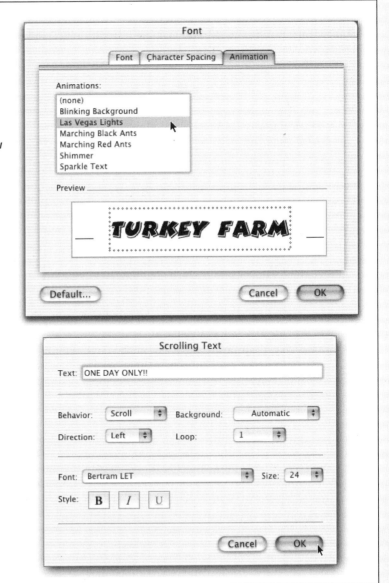

For example, *Scroll* makes the text roll across the screen just like the letters on the marquee of a Broadway theater. (Use the Direction pop-up menu to specify whether it starts from the left or the right.) It goes all the way across until it disappears, then reemerges at the opposite edge and starts over again. From the Loop menu, choose the number of times you want the scrolling action to take place: one through five times, or Infinite.

Slide scrolls the text to the opposite edge of the page, and then stops. *Alternate* means that the text bounces back and forth across the screen as though in a slow-motion game of Pong.

To edit your scrolling text, select the text and choose Insert→HTML Object→ Scrolling Text. Make any changes in the Scrolling Text dialog box.

Note: You won't see any text animation in Word; you have to save the result as a Web page and then open it in a Web browser.

Tables in Web page layout

These days, it's a very rare Web page whose design is nothing but a single river of text running down the middle of the page. Most professional Web pages, including those at *macworld.com, nytimes.com,* and *missingmanuals.com,* are composed of several parallel columns. Each can contain an independent flow of text, as well as such standard elements as a graphic or navigation bar.

To create this effect in Word, use a Word *table,* as described in Chapter 4. Aligning objects using the HTML language alone is notoriously difficult. But if you compose your Web page with a table, you can use its rows and columns to align the text and graphics on your page. If you hide the borders, as described in Figure 7-6, your visitors won't even be aware that they're viewing a table. (You can still view the gray gridline indications in Word, but they won't show when the finished Web page is viewed in a browser.)

Tip: To ensure that as many people as possible can read your text—including people using older or text-only browsers—consider also designing a simple, table-free, text-only version of your Web page and link it to the front page of your Web site.

A single cell of your table can be extremely tall, if necessary. If yours is like a typical Web page, in fact, the entire page may be composed of a single row of the table, whose cells stretch the full height of the page. That's perfectly OK, and it's a clever way to get two or three parallel columns with independent text flows. (See page 165 for information on creating Word tables.)

Tip: Consider using *nested* tables for the smaller objects in your Web page.

For example, create a table eight cells long by two cells wide to hold a list of links. Fill the table, then drag it into a large cell in your main table. The main table will help align the list relative to the rest of the page. (See the list of links in Figure 7-6, for example.)

Figure 7-6:
A simple Web page laid out in a Word table. The table gridlines ensure that the text blocks, bullets, and links line up properly with each other. To make the black lines disappear, choose Table→Table Properties; click the Borders and Shading button; click None, OK, and OK. You can also select the entire table and choose No Border on the Borders and Shading panel of the Formatting Palette.

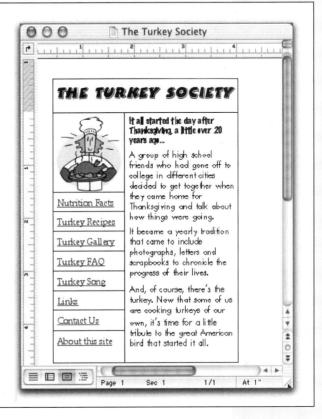

Graphics, Sounds, and Movies

Both Word's Clip Art Gallery and the Web itself are brimming with images that you can use to adorn your Web pages. You can also use any of Word's drawing tools, such as AutoShapes and WordArt (see page 640), in the Web pages you create. When you save the Web page, Word saves the graphic in the Web page's folder as a GIF file (see the sidebar box on page 288).

Downloading Graphics from the Web

When you see a picture you love on a Web site, you can download it and use it on your own Web site. (Of course, you'll do your best to avoid using a copyrighted image without permission.) Here are the easiest ways to download Web graphics:

- Click and *hold* the hand cursor on the image that you'd like to capture (or just Control-click it). From the contextual menu, choose Download Image to Disk (Internet Explorer), Save Image (Netscape), or Image→"Save image to" (OmniWeb). In the resulting dialog box, select the folder on your hard drive where you like to keep downloaded images. Click Save.

- Drag the image itself right out of the browser window and onto your desktop or the folder where you're keeping downloaded images. Let go of the mouse button when the outline of the image appears on the desktop or when the destination folder appears highlighted.

Text wrapping and graphics

Wrapping text around images on Web pages works the same way as in other Word documents, as described on page 160. If you're using a table to lay out your Web page, you can even use text wrapping within a table cell.

The instructions for wrapping text around a graphic image are exactly as described on page 160—with one difference. In HTML, you can place graphics over text, behind text, with text above and below it, or wrapped around either side of it. What you can't do, however, is wrap text around *both* sides of a centered graphic. Thus, in Online Layout view, that option is grayed out on the Wrapping section of the Formatting Palette. To activate the choices on the "Wrap to" menu, drag the graphic to either side of the table cell or page.

UP TO SPEED

Graphics Formats on the Web

Like Internet Explorer, Netscape and other modern Web browsers, Web pages created in Word use images in any of three formats: GIF, JPEG, and PNG. If you place any other kinds of images in your Web page, such as PICT or bitmap, Word converts and saves them in one of the three compatible formats listed above, based on the following criteria:

- Photographs are saved in *JPEG* format. (JPEG graphics use a compression system that is especially effective with photographs.)

- Clip art, drawing objects, and PICT files are saved as *GIF* files. (GIF images are limited to 256 colors, but download very quickly. In other words, they lend themselves to drawings and other simple images.)

- If you've chosen "Allow PNG as an output format" in Preferences (see below), Word saves all images in PNG—Portable Network Graphics format.

The newest of the major graphics compression formats, PNG represents an improvement over both JPEG and GIF. PNG works equally well for both simple images and photographs. If you save all your Web page images as PNG, your Web page will load faster, take less storage space on your Mac, and work on all modern Web browsers.

To do so, choose Word→Preferences→General panel and click Web Options. Click the Picture tab and turn on "Allow PNG as on output format." Because PNG is gradually replacing GIF as the most popular Web graphics format, the only reason not to use it is that certain older browsers won't recognize such images.

Bullets and Dividers

Bullets and lines are very effective ways of "punctuating" your Web page and keeping its layout organized. Large, uninterrupted blocks of text make for difficult reading on the Web, so using these small graphic elements to break up your text helps prevent eyestrain—for both you and your readers.

Web bullets and divider graphics work just like other Word Clip Art, including the way they're inserted.

1. **Choose Insert→Picture→ClipArt.**

   The Clip Gallery appears. (See page 637 for more on this feature.)

2. **In the Category list in the Clip Gallery, scroll down to and select Web Bullets & Buttons or Web Dividers.**

   Each of these categories has several pages; click the "Next" icon at the bottom of the preview pane to see the next page.

3. **Click the image you want, and then click Insert.**

   You return to your document, where the newly placed graphic appears.

Horizontal Lines

Another great way to break up the text on a Web page is to insert a horizontal line between sections. If you started your Web page with a Word Web Page template or chose a theme, then Word has a line in a coordinating color and pattern already picked out for you. To insert one, proceed as follows:

1. **Choose View→Toolbars→Tables and Borders.**

   The Tables and Borders toolbar opens.

2. **Click the arrow button next to the Borders button on the Tables and Borders toolbar. Choose Horizontal Line from the pop-up menu.**

   Word inserts the line for your theme at the document's insertion point.

You can also insert a horizontal line in any Web page by choosing Insert→ Picture→Horizontal Line. The Choose a Picture dialog box opens, showing you the contents of your Mac's Applications→Microsoft Office X→Clipart→Lines folder. Select a line (based on what you see in the preview window) and click Insert. Word places the line across your Web page document at the insertion point.

Tip: You can use even more lines by installing the Clip Art in the Value Pack, as described in Appendix A. Then, when you choose Insert→Picture→Horizontal Line, you can navigate in the Choose a Picture dialog box to the Microsoft Office X→Clipart→"Bullets and Lines 1" and "Bullets and Lines 2" folders and choose one of the many lines there. Click Insert to use the line in your Web page.

Movies

Web pages created in Word can store and play digital movies in any of several formats: QuickTime, QuickTime VR, MPEG, and some AVI files. (Word converts AVI to QuickTime when you save the Web page.) Any such movie that you have on your Mac, whether you downloaded it or made it yourself, can be used on a Web page you create in Word.

To use a movie from the Web in your Web page, you need to download it onto your Mac. If you just click a link to watch a movie, that doesn't necessarily download a copy for you. You have to Control-click the link and then, from the contextual menu, choose either Download Link to Disk (Internet Explorer), Save Link As (Netscape), or Save Link To (OmniWeb). Either way, you'll get a chance to name the file and choose a folder location for it on your Mac, such as the desktop or your Documents folder.

Then:

1. **Choose Insert→Movie.**

   You must be in a Word document, not an .htm document, and you should be in Page Layout or Online Layout view. The Open File dialog box appears. (If you use the Insert→Movie command in Normal view, Word automatically switches to Page Layout view.)

Note: If you can't find the Movie command on your Insert menu, see the sidebar on the facing page for a workaround.

---

2. **In the Insert Movie dialog box, navigate to the movie file on your hard drive and then double-click it.**

   The movie appears on your page, where you can drag to place it anywhere on your Web page, wrap text around it, and resize it just like any Word picture—all using the Picture toolbar or Formatting Palette.

Giving a movie a poster frame

The *poster frame* is the still picture that you see when the movie is not playing. To give your movie a poster frame, click to select it and proceed as follows:

1. **Click the Play button on the Movie toolbar (see Figure 7-7).**

   As the movie plays, watch until you see an image that would make a great poster frame. If you've made the movie controls visible, you can also use it (or press the arrow keys) to locate just the right frame.

2. **Click the Set Poster Frame button on the Movie toolbar.**

   Repeat the process until you get the perfect poster frame.

3. **Click the Format Picture button on the Movie toolbar to open the Format Picture dialog box.**

The poster frame is like any Word picture (see page 636). You can resize or crop the poster frame, apply a transparency to it, change its fill color, and so on, as described on page 650.

4. **Click OK.**

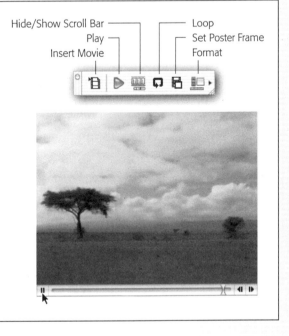

Figure 7-7:
The Movie toolba helps you find the "poster frame" that will represent the movie when it's not actually playing.

Start by clicking the Show Movie Scroll Bar icon to make the standard movie controls appear at the bottom of your movie frame (bottom). Play the movie, or step through it one frame at a time by pressing the arrow keys. When you spot a good still frame, click the Set Poster Frame icon on the toolbar. That's now the movie's stationary stand-in.

Hide/Show Scroll Bar
Play
Insert Movie
Loop
Set Poster Frame
Format

Removing a movie
Deleting a movie is easy: Click the icon or poster frame to select it and press the Delete key.

WORKAROUND WORKSHOP

The Crazy Movie Workaround

You can't put a movie on a Web page in Word when you're *in* a Web page. If you're working in a document that you've saved as a Web page, you can look on the Insert menu all you want; the command is just not there. Only in a standard Word document does the Insert→Movie command appear.

In Word 2001, you could see the Insert→Movie command in all documents and in all views, but you could only insert and view the movies in Page Layout view, Online Layout view, or a Web page document opened in Word.

In Word X, you must learn a whole different way of thinking. You'll have to design *most* of your Web page in a standard Word document, taking care to insert all your movies *before* saving the document as a Web page. You can play, reposition, format, and set a poster frame for movies after you've saved the document as a Web page, but you can no longer add new movies.

Tip: Your movie won't play on the Web unless each visitor to your page has installed the QuickTime plug-in. Not all Mac users have the most recent version, and Windows users may not have it at all. You can help them by giving them a link to the Web site where Apple gives downloads of a free version for both Windows and Mac. For example, you might add this text somewhere on your Web page: "You need the free QuickTime plug-in for Mac or Windows to view the movies on this Web page. Download it at www.apple.com/quicktime." (See page 293 for more on inserting hyperlinks.)

Background Sounds

If your movies, background pictures, and animated text aren't enough multimedia to send your visitors' 56 K modems falling to their knees sobbing, don't give up; Word also comes with a library of sounds that play as your reader views your Web page. You can use one of them, or any sound you've downloaded in the WAV, AIFF, or MIDI format:

1. **Choose Insert→HTML Object→Background Sound.**

   The Background Sound dialog box appears.

2. **Click Select; navigate to the sound file and double-click it.**

   The standard drag-and-drop installation of Office (see Appendix A) offers a handsome set of sound effects in the Microsoft Office X→Office→Sounds. If you use the Value Pack (also described in Appendix A) to install the Clip Art package, you get extra sets of sounds in the Microsoft Office X→ClipArt→Multimedia→ Sounds and ThemeSnd folders.

Tip: Unfortunately, the Value Pack sound files in the ClipArt folder don't have descriptive names. To preview them, you must open each in QuickTime Player, which comes on every Mac.

3. **Choose the number of times you'd like the sound to play from the Loop menu, and then click OK.**

GEM IN THE ROUGH

Web Page Preview

As you build your Web page, you'll need to preview your work-in-progress from time to time. Yes, choosing View→Online Layout shows what your document will look like in a Web page; but you won't be able to see your animated text and certain other browser-only features. Fortunately, the File→Web Page Preview command actually shows it in your Web browser, which provides a much more accurate preview.

The document name in the title bar may not match the file name that you gave the document when you saved it. That's because Word takes the Web-page name from the title box on the File→Properties→Summary tab. In other words, if you'd like to change the name that appears in the Web browser's title bar when opening your Word document as a Web page, simply choose File→Properties→Summary tab and change the title.

When your viewer opens the Web page, the background sound plays the number of times you chose to loop it.

To remove a sound, choose Insert→HTML Object→Background Sound. The name of the current background sound file is shown at the top of the dialog box. Click Clear to remove it from your Web page.

Hyperlinks

Hyperlinks—buttons, graphics, or text phrases that, when clicked, take you to a different document—are what Web sites are all about. In Word, you can make just about any kind of link you've ever dreamed of—links to Web pages, to other documents or pages you've created, to movies or sound files, or to a particular point in the same document or another document.

Tip: Hyperlinks are not just for creating Web pages. They work extremely well right on your own hard drive, where you can use them to create a living, clickable list of all the files—or even applications—that you open frequently. They also work as described here in Excel and PowerPoint.

The following examples show you how to create links to various locations on your hard drive or on the Web.

Linking to Another Place or Another Word Document

If your document is long, you may want links to help your reader navigate it. For instance, on a Web page (or even a senior thesis), you can place a link called "Back to top" at the bottom of your page, or a list of links at the top of the page that link to paragraphs further down. Either way, this can save your reader lots of scrolling.

Hyperlinks can also jump from one *document* to another. This simple feature is the key to two dramatic Word features:

- For everyday Mac work, you can set up links to other Word files on your hard drive.

- When you're building a Web page, you can set up links to other Web pages you've created. For instance, you may have a Web site about birds, with a main page and a separate page for each bird.

Remember that you'll have to upload all such Web documents to the Web along with the linking page; otherwise, the hyperlink won't work.

The easy way (copy and paste)
The routine goes like this:

1. Copy some text in the document or paragraph you want to jump *to*.

   A heading makes an especially handy target, but it can be anything at all, anywhere in the document.

2. **Switch to the document or paragraph where you want the link to appear; choose Edit→Paste as Hyperlink.**

   (If the command is dimmed, then you need to save the target document.)

   The copied material appears in your document; it should be blue, underlined, and ready to click. (You can change the text of the link itself as described later in this section.)

The beauty of this technique is that it can take you even to a particular *spot* in a different document—whether its ultimate destination is the Web or just your own Mac. For example, in a technical document, you could create links to specific entries in a glossary of terms. (This "jump to a certain spot" feature works only if the destination document isn't already open; if the target document *is* open when you click the link, you go to the *beginning* of it. Nobody ever accused Microsoft of consistency.)

Tip: If you create these types of links frequently, use the ultimate link-creation shortcut. Set up both documents so that you can see their windows simultaneously. Highlight the "jump to here" text in the target document, then Option-⌘-drag it *out of its window* and into the document where the link will appear. When you release the mouse, a contextual menu appears, offering commands like Move Here and Copy Here; click Create Hyperlink Here. You've just created a link to the text you highlighted.

The longer way (using bookmarks or headings)

You don't have to use the copy-and-paste routine. If you've used Word bookmarks (see page 233) or its built-in heading styles in the target document, you can use them as anchors—the targets—for your links, like this:

1. **Select the text ("Back to top," for example) or graphic that will be the hyperlink; choose Insert→Hyperlink.**

   The Insert Hyperlink dialog box opens, as shown in Figure 7-8. The text you selected in your Web page document appears in the Display box. If a graphic will serve as the link, then <<Selection in Document>> appears in the box.

Tip: Microsoft doesn't kid around about the Insert→Hyperlink command; it offers about 731 alternate methods of triggering it. For example, you can also Control-click the selected text or object and choose Hyperlink from the contextual menu, or click the Insert Hyperlink button on the Standard toolbar, or press ⌘-K.

---

2. **Click the Document tab, then click Locate.**

   The Select Place in Document dialog box appears.

3. **Choose the bookmark or heading, click OK, then click OK.**

   If you haven't successfully created any bookmarks or used one of Word's built-in heading styles, Top of the Document is the only available choice. If you do have headings and bookmarks in the document, click the flippy triangles to view the entire list.

After you click OK to close the Insert Hyperlink dialog box, the text you selected in step 2 turns into a blue, underlined hyperlink. To test it, just click the link; the document scrolls so that the heading or bookmark anchor jumps to the top of the screen.

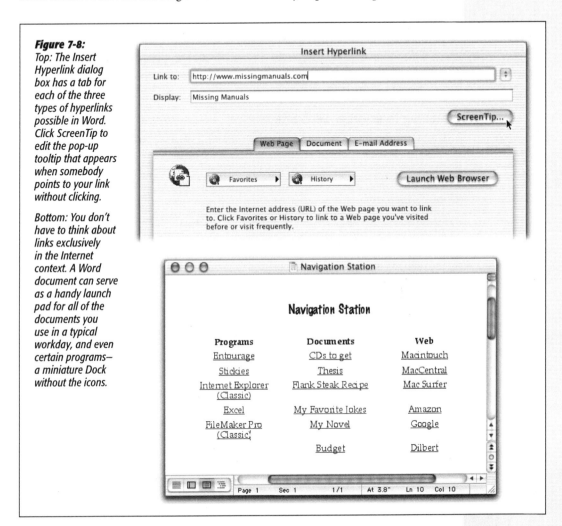

Figure 7-8:
Top: The Insert Hyperlink dialog box has a tab for each of the three types of hyperlinks possible in Word. Click ScreenTip to edit the pop-up tooltip that appears when somebody points to your link without clicking.

Bottom: You don't have to think about links exclusively in the Internet context. A Word document can serve as a handy launch pad for all of the documents you use in a typical workday, and even certain programs— a miniature Dock without the icons.

Linking to an Application or Mac File

If you spend most of the day in Word, consider making yourself a launching pad document like the one shown in Figure 7-8, which serves as your "home page" for the entire computer. It works like this:

1. **Highlight the text or the image that will be the link "button"; choose Insert→Hyperlink.**

   The Insert Hyperlink dialog box opens, as shown in Figure 7-9.

2. **Click the Document tab. Click Select.**

   Word opens the Choose a File dialog box.

3. **Navigate to the destination document or program on your Mac and select it; click OK.**

   You return to your document, where there now exists a living, working link to another file or program on your Mac.

Linking to Another Web Site

If you're designing a Web site, of course, the kind of link you're probably most interested in creating is one that jumps to *another* Web page. That's why Word provides so many different ways of creating a hyperlink to another page on the Web.

By typing a URL

As many an annoyed Mac fan can tell you, Word comes factory set to turn *any* Web address you type into a living hyperlink. When you're creating Web pages with Word is the one time you'll actually be grateful for this behavior. Just type the Web address into your Web page document, beginning with *www* and ending with *.com, .org,* or dot-whatever. Word automatically creates the hyperlink (unless you've turned off this feature, as described on page 107).

WORKAROUND WORKSHOP

A Link to the Past

In Word 2001, you could create a link to virtually any application on your Mac. In Word X, many Mac OS X application icons in the Choose a File dialog box are grayed out when you're creating hyperlinks. The reason: Most Mac OS X program icons are actually *packages*—thinly disguised folders—each of which contains both the program itself and its supplementary software and files. Microsoft Office X's own programs (and other Mac OS X programs that haven't been turned into packages) are all you see in this list.

You *can,* however, still link to Classic applications in Word X. Thus, if you're using hyperlinks to create a launcher as described on page 65, you're limited to three choices: documents, Classic applications, and Office X applications.

If you're sneaky, however, you can work around this obstacle. Link to a *document* in a Mac OS X application—even a blank one. Word X is perfectly happy to open a document, and therefore the program you're trying to launch opens automatically.

There is a drawback to this method: After doing some editing, you must remember to use Save As instead of Save for the first time, so that you don't commit your typing to the blank startup document.

By dragging a URL

You don't have to memorize and type a URL in order to place a hyperlink in your document. All you have to do is find it on the Web; then you can drag and drop the Web address into your Web page.

To see how this works, open your Web browser and visit the Web page that you'd like to link to. Switch back to Word; drag the icon next to the Address window from the browser into your document, as shown in Figure 7-8.

When you let go of the mouse button, Word creates a hyperlink *field*. (If you see the field code [see page 228] instead of the title of the Web page, select the entire field code and press Shift-F9.)

The text of the final hyperlink in your document will be the Web page's title (as seen in the title bar of your browser window), not the URL itself. If you want to see the underlying URL, point to the Web-page name without clicking to make the identifying yellow balloon appear.

If you'd like to use different text other than the Web page's real title for the hyperlink, edit the hyperlink as described on page 299. For example, if the Web page you're linking to is titled "Actor Bio 2," you might want to change it to the more descriptive "Brando: The Early Years."

Figure 7-9:
You can make a Web link in a Word document just by dragging the @ sign out of the address bar in Internet Explorer—in this example, to make a "home page" of links you like to visit frequently.

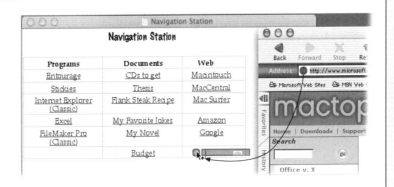

By using a Favorite or History

If you have Internet Explorer on your Mac, the Favorites list in the Insert Hyperlink dialog box displays your Internet Explorer Favorites, while the History list displays the Web sites you've most recently visited in *Internet Explorer*. This pop-up menu can be a real timesaver; here's how to go about it:

1. **Highlight the text or the image that will be the link "button"; choose Insert→Hyperlink.**

   The Insert Hyperlink dialog box opens, as shown in Figure 7-8.

2. Click the Web page tab.

Make sure the correct text for your hyperlink appears in the Display box; if not, change it.

3. From the Favorites or History pop-up list, choose the Web site you want to link to.

If the Web site you're looking for isn't in one of the lists, click Launch Web Browser to search the Web for it.

4. Click OK.

You've just added a link to the Web page you selected.

Note: Although there is an Anchor box on the Web Page tab in the Insert Hyperlink dialog box, it almost never works in Web sites. In order for this feature to work, the page must contain HTML anchor tags or Word bookmarks, as described in "To a specific location on another page."

Email Hyperlinks

An *email* hyperlink, also known as a *mailto* link, opens a new, preaddressed message in your default email program (or the program of whoever clicks the link). When you create a Web page, it's common practice to include an email hyperlink to yourself, so that your readers can contact you with questions, comments, or orders. To do so, just follow these steps:

1. Type and select the text ("Contact me") that will become the email hyperlink.

As with any other hyperlink, you can use a graphic, but you should also include some text to make clear what the link does.

2. Choose Insert→Hyperlink. In the Hyperlink dialog box, click the Email Address tab. Type the email address you want the link to mail to in the To box.

The Recent Addresses list contains a list of email addresses for which you've recently created hyperlinks (not necessarily ones you've actually used). To look up an address in your Entourage Address Book instead, click Launch Email Application. No matter what your default email program, Entourage launches. There's no further integration with Entourage, however, so you'll have to manually copy and paste the address you want out of its Address Book.

3. Press Tab; type a subject line, if you wish.

In other words, when your visitor clicks the "Contact me" link, his email program will automatically open. When it does, an outgoing blank email message will appear, preaddressed to you *and* with the Subject line already filled in. Including a subject line can help you keep track of emails that come from this particular Web page. However, not all Web browsers, or all email programs, work with the subject-line-in-an-email-hyperlink feature.

4. Click OK.

The email link is ready to click.

Note: If all you need is a simple Web or email hyperlink, just type it into Word. Word creates the hyperlink instantly (if, that is, you haven't turned off this feature in the Tools→AutoCorrect→AutoFormat As You Type dialog box). Later, should you want to change the link to read "Contact Me" or something more elegant-looking than your plain old email address, edit the link as described on page 299.

Likewise, for simple addresses like *www.apple.com*, just type the URL into your document. You can always go back and change the text later, as described next.

Selecting and Editing Hyperlinks

When you click a hyperlink in Word, Word follows the link, even if that means launching your Web browser or opening some program or document on your Mac. But if clicking triggers the link, how are you supposed to *edit* the hyperlink text?

The easiest way is to Control-click the link and choose Hyperlink→Edit Hyperlink from the contextual menu. The Edit Hyperlink dialog box opens; here you can change the URL, email address, display text, ScreenTip (see below), anchor, and so on.

Hyperlink ScreenTips

When you browse the Web with Internet Explorer 4 or later, you can point to a hyperlink without clicking to summon a small, yellow, identifying ScreenTip (like a tooltip). The information shown in the ScreenTip depends on what kind of hyperlink you've created.

By default, Word creates ScreenTips for each type of hyperlink automatically: the URL for a Web link, *mailto:myname@mac.com* (or whatever your address is) for an email link, or the full path and file name of the document on your Mac or other computer on your network.

You can change the ScreenTips to say whatever you like. For instance, say you have a picture of a house that links back to your home page. If your reader doesn't get it from the picture, the URL (which could be something like *http:/*

/www.geocities.com/~bobtheduck) may not be much help. You could change the ScreenTip so that when your reader passes the cursor over the house picture, "My Home Page" is the tip that pops up.

To write your own ScreenTip, Control-click the hyperlink and choose Hyperlink→Edit Hyperlink from the contextual menu. In the Hyperlink dialog box, click ScreenTip.

The Set Hyperlink ScreenTip dialog box (shown here) opens; here you can type up to 254 characters of text for your ScreenTip. That's enough room to write a fairly long sentence, if you wish.

Click OK when you finish editing the ScreenTip. Click OK to close the Edit Hyperlink dialog box after making any other changes you like.

If the dog ate your Control key, you can also highlight the link by carefully dragging across it, then pressing ⌘-K (or choosing Insert→Hyperlink) to open the Insert Hyperlink dialog box. In fact, if all you want to edit is the display text for a hyperlink, just drag carefully across it (or Control-click it and choose Hyperlink→Select Hyperlink) and then retype—no overnight dialog box stay required.

Similarly, you can edit graphic links without triggering them; once again, the trick is to select the link without activating it—by Control-clicking it. After editing the image using the Formatting Palette or the Drawing or Picture toolbars, press Esc or click elsewhere to deselect the object and avoid inadvertently making further changes.

Hyperlink colors

In Word, text hyperlinks appear in blue type until they're clicked, whereupon they change to purple. You can change these default colors, if you like; the trick is to change the Hyperlink *style*, just as you'd change any Word style (see page 147 for instructions).

If you're *that* kind of person, you can even change the color that clicked hyperlinks change *into* after being clicked. Just modify Word's built-in FollowedHyperlink style.

These new hyperlink colors will override default hyperlink colors when the page is opened in Internet Explorer and Netscape Communicator. If your colors don't work, it's because your visitor has changed his browser preferences to override the color choices that have been programmed into Web pages.

Removing Hyperlinks

To remove a hyperlink you no longer want, you have two options:

- Drag over the hyperlink text and press Delete. Both the hyperlink and the display text or object are deleted.

- To cancel out the link while leaving the display text or object in place, Control-click the link and choose Hyperlink→Edit Hyperlink on the contextual menu. Click Remove Link.

Web Forms

If you've ever searched a Web site, taken a poll, or made a purchase online, you've used a Web *form*. Web forms take the form of pop-up menus, checkboxes, and little text boxes. They're designed to collect information from the Web site visitor and save it on a server for processing.

You can build a Web form in Word, but you'll need the help of a Web programmer to write the necessary CGI scripts that make the form work. (CGI stands for *common gateway interface*, a software convention for transferring and processing data between Web pages and servers.)

To build a Web form, you must insert various *form controls* in your page—checkboxes, radio buttons, pop-up menus, buttons, and so on—which your visitors will use for submitting the information and resetting the form. You'll find them in the Insert→HTML Object submenu. With the help of a programmer, select settings and values from the resulting dialog box.

Saving Web Pages

If you started your Web page from a Web-page template or a blank Web page, as described at the beginning of this section, all you have to do to save it is press ⌘-S or choose File→Save or Save As. You can also save a standard Word document or template as a Web page, like this:

1. **Choose File→Save as Web Page.**

   The Save dialog box opens, as shown in Figure 7-10.

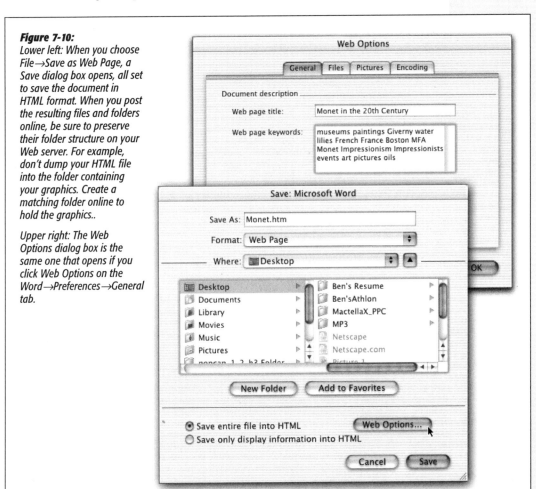

Figure 7-10:
Lower left: When you choose File→Save as Web Page, a Save dialog box opens, all set to save the document in HTML format. When you post the resulting files and folders online, be sure to preserve their folder structure on your Web server. For example, don't dump your HTML file into the folder containing your graphics. Create a matching folder online to hold the graphics..

Upper right: The Web Options dialog box is the same one that opens if you click Web Options on the Word→Preferences→General tab.

2. **Click one of the radio buttons depending on how you'd like to save the file.**

   The **Save entire file into HTML** option creates a dual-purpose document. It stores the information *both* for display on the Web *and* for returning to it as a Word document. Such word processor–only elements as headers and footers, comments, page numbers, and page breaks will reappear when you open it again in Word.

   Save only display information into HTML saves *only* the document attributes that work in a Web browser. Other information, such as page and section breaks, columns, and headers and footers will be lost. This option makes a smaller, more compact HTML file, which is a good thing if your Web service provider charges based upon how much server space you use.

Tip: If you choose this option, use Save As first to save a copy with all the normal Word elements intact; you may decide to use the document in Word again.

---

3. **Click Save.**

   Word takes longer than usual to save the document. When it's finished, you can switch to Online Layout view (if you weren't already there) to see the Web page as it will appear online.

Web Options

When you click Web Options in the Save dialog box (see Figure 7-10), you can specify special Web features that would normally require mucking around in HTML code.

- The Web page *title* you enter on the **General Tab** appears in the title bar in a Web browser. The Web page *keywords* are the terms that search engines like Google and Yahoo spot when searching. (In HTML, these words are known as *meta tags*.)

- "Update links on Save" in the **Files** tab comes already turned on. If you've changed or moved any of your Web page's supporting files, such as bullets, graphics, or background patterns, Word updates the links so the page will work when you reopen it. The "Save only display information into HTML" checkbox turns on the corresponding radio button in the Save dialog box (see above).

- Checking "Allow PNG" on the **Pictures** tab saves all the images in your Web page in Portable Network Graphics format, as described on page 288. The "Screen size" pop-up menu shows just about every screen size and resolution combination your Web page visitors are likely to have. 1024 x 768—standard on iBooks and iMacs, for example—is the smallest screen most people use today, and therefore a pretty safe bet.

   In the "Pixels per inch" box, 72 is the best setting for Mac monitors; your text will look gigantic on Windows PC screens. If you're creating a page that's going to be viewed primarily on Windows PCs, change this setting to 96; unfortunately, your text will look tiny when viewed by Mac monitors. (You're witnessing the unfortunate side effect of competing Mac/Windows standards. There's no simple solution, other than encouraging your Mac friends to use Internet Explorer 5.0 or later for its automatic text-enlargement feature.)

- The menu on the **Encoding** tab displays all the foreign languages and browser formats Word can use for saving your Web page. If your page contains text in a different alphabet system (such as Cyrillic or Japanese), choose it from this menu.

Tip: As you complete your Web page, consider testing it in different Web browsers. Text may wrap differently, colors and graphics may look different, and movies and marquees may not operate the same way, if at all, in different browsers.

If you have a copy of the America Online program, for example, open your page using its File→Open command. Try the same experiment in Netscape Navigator (available free at *www.netscape.com)*. You would do well to also check the increasingly popular browsers, OmniWeb *(www.omnigroup.com)* and Opera *(www.opera.com)*. You can even see what your site looks like when viewed on a Microsoft WebTV, just by downloading the free WebTV Viewer simulator (at *developer.msntv.net).*

Lost in the Translation

Despite all its Web-savvy trappings, Word, when you get right down to it, isn't actually an HTML editor. The Web pages it creates capture the spirit of the original Word document you prepared, but not the letter, since you lose quite a bit of its look in the conversion to a Web page. Among the casualties: text boxes; fancy text effects like embossed type, shadow, and strikethrough; drop caps; page numbering; margin settings and page borders; headers and footers; multiple columns; and styles. All of these Word features drop out when the document is converted to HTML. Fields (see

---

POWER USERS' CLINIC

HTML Text Styles

The HTML styles in the Format→Style dialog box let you transform a saved Web page into an attractive Word document. For example, suppose that someone at your company created an online training manual, but no one made a paper version. Or maybe you want to download an article from the Web and create a printed version (with permission, of course).

These Web pages are HTML documents, and the text in them is formatted using HTML codes. For instance, one HTML code creates a first-level heading, another denotes an address or citation, and another creates hyperlinks. These labels are listed in the Styles list box in the Format→Style dialog box; except for Hyperlink and Followed Hyperlink, their style names all begin with the letters *HTML*.

You can format and redefine these styles as you would any Word styles; when you do, Word will use them for HTML-formatted text whenever you open a Web page in Word. You may want to make all hyperlinks match your Normal style, for example. (Headings in HTML are automatically changed into your Word heading styles.)

To convert a Web site into a Word document, open the Web page in your browser. Choose File→Save or Save As; save the page onto your Mac in HTML format. Open the page in Word by choosing File→Open and navigating to the Web-page file. You will see the text in the document, but not the images (they don't get saved along with the rest of the page).

---

page 228) *sort* of carry through; the resulting Web page shows the field information (such as the date), but it's no longer self-updating. Tabs aren't reliable, either, since Word converts them into HTML tabs, which, in some Web browsers, turn into spaces. (Use tables wherever you're inclined to use tabs.) Footnotes, on the other hand, perform beautifully. The superscript numbers turn into hyperlinks that scroll to the notes at the bottom of the page.

Posting Your Web Site Online

Creating HTML documents is only the first step in establishing a Web presence. The final step is uploading them to a *Web file server*—a computer that's always on and connected to the Internet. You have several options:

- **Use your own Mac.** If you have a full-time connection (cable modem or DSL), you can use the built-in Web Sharing feature of Mac OS 9 or Mac OS X to make your Web site available to the Internet at large. Your Web address won't be very memorable (along the lines of *http://192.168.34.2*), the speed won't be great, and not very many people can visit your site at once, but the price ($0) is right. The Mac's online help and *Mac OS X: The Missing Manual* contain instructions.

- **Use your ISP.** Most Internet service providers (ISPs), as well as America Online, offer somewhere between 5 and 10 megs of free space to hold your Web pages as part of your monthly fee. Into that space, you can upload your Web pages directly, making them available for public browsing. Your ISP takes care of keeping its computer up, running, and connected to the Internet.

- **Use the Apple HomePage feature.** Apple offers every Mac user 20 MB of free Web space in the form of the Sites folder on your iDisk—a virtual hard drive. (Visit *www.apple.com/itools* for details.) Just put the HTML documents you've created— name your home page *index.html* for best results—and graphics into the Sites folder of your iDisk. (Don't bother using the iTools HomePage-building tools; Web pages you've designed using Word don't show up. But if you just drag them into your iDisk's Sites folder, they're instantly available to the Internet.)

UP TO SPEED

Naming and Nesting Folders

If you've had experience creating Web pages using a *real* HTML editing program, you know about the headache of creating sets of folders to organize all the pages and picture files that compose your Web site. If the various HTML documents (the individual Web pages) and their graphics (your picture bullets, background patterns, and so on) aren't on your hard drive and on the Internet in precisely matching folder hierarchies, you'll get dead links, missing graphics, and worse. You also need to save the graphics files (for picture bullets, background patterns, and so on) in folders.

When you save a Word document as a Web page, you create one document (whose name ends in *.htm*) containing the text, and an accompanying folder that contains all of the graphics, sounds, and movies. All you have to do is post them online in the same relative folders.

If you're making a large Web site with many pages, you may want to nest folders within one larger folder to help keep things organized.

Part Two: Entourage

2

Entourage Email and Newsgroups

For longtime Microsoft Office users, one program in the Office X application lineup is a relative newcomer: a program called Entourage. Entourage is closely based on Outlook Express, Microsoft's free email and newsgroup reader. But to those Internet features, Entourage adds a calendar and a to-do list. True to its name, entrusting your schedule and communications to this program is like having an entourage of lackeys at your command. And who couldn't use an entourage of lackeys?

At first, you might wonder what the point is of adding a calendar and task list to an email program. As it turns out, however, this arrangement offers numerous payoffs—cross-fertilizing features that let all of this information work together, both within Entourage and among the other Office programs.

The Big Picture

The Entourage main window is divided into three main areas: buttons for Entourage's main functions at top left, a list of "file folders" for your email at bottom left, and a big viewing area for your actual messages, calendars, tasks, and so on, on the right. Like changing stations on a car radio, you can switch among Entourage functions by clicking their buttons.

Entourage Functions

When you first launch Entourage (Figure 8-1) and complete the setup wizard (described in a moment), the Mail button at the upper left is already selected. But mail is only one of Entourage's functions. This chapter and those that follow cover all of them in depth, but here's a quick overview to let you know what you're in for. The six big icons at the upper-left corner of the Entourage screen correspond to the following features:

- **Mail.** This, of course, is the big Kahuna feature: email. This chapter covers the Mail feature in detail.

- **Address Book.** Your electronic "little black book"—home to not just the email addresses in your social entourage, but also phone numbers, home addresses, and so on. The Address Book also features predefined Address Book *Views* that let you find subsets of your data—every member of your family, for example. See Chapter 10 for complete details on the Address Book.

- **Calendar.** Plan your day, your week, your month…if you dare, plan your year! You can manage your schedule and track important events using the Entourage Calendar. Once again, a set of Views can quickly show you only work- or family-related events, recurring appointments, or whatever. See Chapter 9 for details.

- **Tasks.** Your to-do list. When you click this button, the right side of the screen shows the list of tasks you've set up for yourself. See Chapter 9 to read everything about Tasks.

- **Notes.** Memo-pad-like musings that you can attach to names in your address book, tasks in your to-do list, and so on. See Chapter 10 for details.

- **Custom Views.** The Custom Views button collects together all of Entourage's predefined views for its Mail, Notes, Calendar, Address Book, and Tasks functions, along with any views you've created yourself. More on Custom Views on page 425.

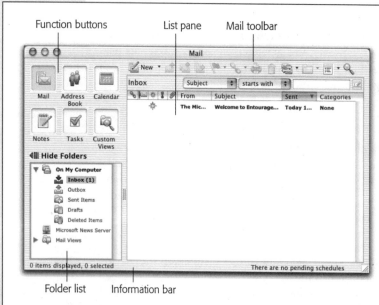

Figure 8-1:
In addition to the Folder list and an email-specific toolbar, Entourage has a List pane that lists all of the messages in a particular folder. There's also an information bar at the bottom of the screen that shows how many messages are in a given folder, how many are selected, and what schedules (if any) Entourage has on deck. Don't miss the Fonts tab in Entourage→ General Preferences, where you can specify the type size and style you prefer for reading your email and other Entourage components.

Tip: Entourage starts out showing each of its major functions one at a time in its main window. But what if you want to see your calendar and your email at the same time?

You can—by opening them into separate windows. To do that, Control-click any of the six major function buttons, and choose the Open in New Window command from the contextual menu. Now you can see two views simultaneously, such as your Calendar and Notes, two Mail windows, your Address Book and Tasks, and so on.

The Toolbar

Entourage has only one toolbar (see Figure 8-2), which changes to reflect your current activity. For example, if you've clicked an email folder, the toolbar's buttons all pertain to email functions; if you click the Calendar button, the toolbar gains calendar-appropriate commands. You'll encounter these commands in the context of the email, newsgroup, calendar, address book, notes, and task discussions in this and the following chapters.

POWER USERS' CLINIC

The Mighty Morphing Interface

You don't have to be content with the factory-installed design of the Entourage screen. You can control which Entourage panes are visible, how big they are, and which columns show up in list views.

Some people like to read email messages in separate windows, while others like to use the Preview pane, which displays the current message right in the main Mail window. To turn on Entourage's Preview pane, choose View→Preview Pane, or press ⌘-\. (You can turn it off again the same way.) Try Entourage both with and without the Preview pane.

You can also hide or show the toolbar or the Folder list using the View menu. For example, to hide the toolbar, choose View→Toolbars.

To change the size of a pane, drag its border, as shown here. You can drag any border that features two parallel lines in the center. (You don't have to drag right on those lines, though.)

Entourage also lets you decide what columns appear in Mail's List pane. If you don't care about seeing the Categories column for your email, for example, you can hide it, leaving more space for Subject and Date. To switch columns on or off, choose from the View→Columns submenu.

You can also *rearrange* the columns, which can be handy if you'd rather see the Subject column first instead of the Sender, for example. Just drag the column's header horizontally; release when the vertical dotted line is where you'll want the column to wind up. To make a column wider or narrower, drag the short black divider line between column names horizontally.

You can't resize the skinny icon columns on the far left, but you can move any of them except the first two.

Tip: Like most other windows in Mac OS X, the main Entourage window has a close button. Be wary of it: closing the main window disables nearly all Entourage's functions, and you may find it difficult to get them back again! Even the View→Go To submenu is disabled, and its key commands (⌘-1 through ⌘-6 for Entourage functions) are gone with it.

If this happens to you, the trick is to choose File→New→Open New Main Window (Shift-Option-⌘-N, if you have enough fingers). A new main Entourage window appears, and you're back in business. Alternatively, just switch to another Mac OS X application (like the Finder) and then back to Entourage: if a main window wasn't open, Entourage will create one for you when you switch back.

Figure 8-2:
Entourage's toolbar commands change to match the Entourage function you're using. This figure shows the fully expanded email toolbar, shown here broken in half so that it will fit this page. If the Entourage main window isn't wide enough to show everything, the program omits button names and shows only their icons, to make the toolbar fit.

Setting Up Entourage

When you first launch Entourage (or when you create a new *identity*, as described on page 420), the Entourage Setup Assistant presents itself. The Setup Assistant presents a long series of question-and-answer screens that give you the opportunity to set up your email accounts, import your address book information from whatever mail program you used to use, and so on.

Any email program requires a number of technical details that define your particular email account. If you have another email program that's been working fine (Outlook Express, Netscape Communicator, Eudora, or Claris Emailer, for example), Entourage can usually copy all the details from the older program (and from the settings in the Internet pane of your Mac's System Preferences program).

If you've never used your Mac for email before, however, or if you're using a Mac that doesn't have a functioning email program, you'll need to type these email settings into Entourage directly. Unless you're quite a technical person, your sole source of this information is the help line (or Getting Started booklet) of your *ISP* (Internet Service Provider), the company to whom you pay a monthly fee for Internet access. You need the account information your ISP gave you in order to receive or send email, so have this info on hand as you set about getting Entourage ready.

Note: Entourage can't check America Online mail.

Then let the Setup Assistant take you by the hand like this:

1. **By clicking Yes or No, indicate whether or not you want Entourage to be your** *default* **email program.**

   The very first thing you see the first time you run Entourage is a question: "Would you like Microsoft Entourage to be your default email program?" If you answer in the affirmative, the program makes the change in the Internet pane of System Preferences. From now on, Entourage will open whenever you click an email link (on a Web page or in a program's online help, for example).

Tip: If you later decide that you'd prefer a different email program—Apple's own Mail program, for example—open the Internet pane of your System Preferences (choose →System Preferences, then click the Internet icon). Click the Email panel, and then select a different email program in the pop-up menu at the top of the pane.

   After you've made your choice, the Setup Assistant asks for your name.

2. **Enter your first and last name.**

   Entourage will use this information in the From field of all outgoing mail. Most people, having nothing to hide, provide this information, but you can type anything you want (or nothing) here, depending on how courteous an Internet citizen you want to be (see the box on Email Netiquette on page 361). Click the right arrow button (or press Enter) to continue.

3. **Enter your home information.**

   Entourage asks you for your street address, city, state, Zip code, country, and telephone number. If you'll be using Entourage mostly from home, also turn on "This is my default address."

   You've just specified the address that Office X will use whenever it needs your home address; for example, this is the address Word proposes printing on envelopes as your return address. If you're nervous about the Microsoft Evil Empire collecting your data for its own nefarious purposes, you can leave these blanks empty.

Tip: The information you specify here is the same information you can access in Word by choosing Word→Preferences→User Information panel. It also creates a special entry in your Entourage Address Book, marked with a lowercase *i* icon, denoting it as your own information "card."

   As in any Office X dialog box, you can advance from one field (text box) to the next by pressing the Tab key. Once you've specified your home address (or decided not to do so), click the right arrow button or press Enter.

4. Enter your work address.

Entourage gives you the option of making *this* address Office's default address for you. Click the right arrow to continue.

5. Import your calendar, address book information, and email from your older programs, if you like.

As part of Entourage's campaign to serve as the only communication and organization program you'll ever need, the Setup Assistant now offers to import email and address book information from whatever email program, calendar program, or address book program you *used* to use, before the great day of Entourage's arrival.

This feature saves you astronomical amounts of time. Since all of your familiar data is instantly available, you can get comfortable with your new email/calendar/address book program in record time.

The assistant now offers five choices: to import nothing at all; or to import information from Entourage 2001, from an email program, from a calendar/address book program, or from *both* your email program and a calendar/address book program.

If you choose to import email, the Setup Assistant presents you with a list of email programs from which it can import information: Outlook Express 5, Eudora, Netscape Communicator 4.0 or higher, or Claris Emailer 2.0v3. You can also tell Entourage that your email program isn't listed, at which point it does its level best to import the information anyway. In addition to the email messages themselves, Entourage can sometimes import email filters (rules), email filing folders, and other bits of information that you've created in your former email program. (For some unfathomable reason, Microsoft Entourage is especially good at importing information from Microsoft Outlook Express.)

If you choose to import data from another PIM (personal information manager—that is, calendar/address book), you'll be presented with a choice of software whose information Entourage understands: Claris Organizer, Palm Desktop, Now Contact, and Now Up-To-Date. Select the program that currently contains your addresses and calendar, and then click the right arrow to continue. (The older program needs to be still installed on your Mac for this to work.)

Tip: Unfortunately, Entourage X can't import email and other information from Apple Mail, the email program that comes with Mac OS X. However, the Office X Value Pack has an AppleScript that can move personal mailboxes in Apple Mail to Entourage X.

To get the script, run the Value Pack Installer on your Office X CD-ROM or installation folder, and then select the "Import from Mail" script for installation. Once it's installed, you can run the script from your Microsoft Office X→Utilities folder.

Finally, you'll be presented with a list of individual items to import: your mail messages, addresses, account information, filters, signatures, calendar items, tasks, and notes. Once you've selected the items to import, click the right arrow to start the process, which can take a long time. (Better go grab a snack.)

When the importing is complete, click Finish. If you didn't previously indicate that you wanted Entourage to be your default email program, the Setup Assistant will ask you again. Tell this eager-beaver software Yes or No.

If you successfully imported your email account's settings, you're ready to start using Entourage. Skip to the next section.

UP TO SPEED

POP, IMAP, and Web-based Mail

When it comes to email, there are three flavors of accounts (not counting America Online mail, which is a mutant breed): *POP* (also known as Post Office Protocol or POP3), *IMAP* (also known as IMAP4), and *Web-based*. Although the lines between them are often blurry, each has its own distinct nature, with different strengths and weaknesses.

POP accounts are the most common kind. This type of account usually transfers your incoming mail to your hard drive before you read it, which works fine as long as you're only using one computer to access your email.

If you want to take your Entourage email world along with you on the road, you have to copy the Documents folder on your desktop Mac's hard drive—or, at the very least, the Documents→Microsoft User Data folder—into the corresponding location on your laptop's hard drive. Then, when you run Entourage on the laptop, you'll find your messages and attachments already in place.

(Another travelers' tip: Entourage can leave your POP mail on the server, so that you can read it while on the road, but still find it waiting on your home Mac when you return. See page 323.)

IMAP accounts don't enjoy as much popularity or support as POP accounts. (IMAP is most often found among educational institutions and corporations.) Unlike POP, where your mail is stored on your hard drive, IMAP keeps your mail on the remote server, downloading it only when you want to read or act on a message. Thus, you can ac-

cess the same mail regardless of the computer you use. IMAP servers remember which messages you've read and sent, too.

The downside to this approach, of course, is that you can't work with your email except when you're online, because all of your mail is on an Internet server, not on your hard drive.

Web-based servers are similar to IMAP servers, in that they store your mail on the Internet; you use a Web browser on any computer to read and send messages. (As a Microsoft service, Hotmail.com offers a twist on Web-based accounts: you can check your Hotmail email with Entourage instead of having to use a Web browser.)

Although Web-based accounts are convenient, they're also slower and more cumbersome to use. Most also put ads in your email, and you'll usually find it awkward to compose and manage messages using a Web browser. That's the price of a free email service.

POP and IMAP accounts offer by far the quickest service and greatest reliability. The only downside is that if you switch ISPs, you have to switch your email address as well. To prevent this problem, you can try a free service like *mail.com, pobox.com, bigfoot.com*), or Apple's *mac.com*, which give you a permanent email address. If your "real" email address changes, these services simply forward your mail to whatever new address you specify. That way, you'll never have to send out a change-of-email-address again.

If you didn't import settings from an existing email program, however, or if the importing didn't go smoothly, you may now have to type in the email settings for your account.

6. **Enter the name with which you'll want to "sign" your email and newsgroup messages.**

   You've now moved into the account setup portion of the Entourage Setup Assistant. The text box already contains the name that you entered in step 2, but you can put any name you like here—*Queen of the Universe,* if you like. (Again, though, read up on etiquette on page 361.)

7. **Tell Entourage your email address.**

   In this step, either you can set up an account for an existing email address, or you can sign up for a Hotmail account (a free account provided by Microsoft, as described in the box on the facing page).

   If you do, in fact, have an Internet account, it came with an email account as part of the package, so the first option is the one most people choose. Enter your email address in the text box. Click the right arrow to continue.

   If you'd prefer to set up a Hotmail account, click the Hotmail button and then the right arrow. On the next screen, you'll be given the option to open your Web browser and go online to the Hotmail sign-up page, where you can get a Hotmail ID and password.

   Once you have an account set up, you can return to Entourage and enter your ID and password to finish setting up your Hotmail account.

8. **Tell Entourage what kind of incoming mail server you'll be using, and type in your incoming and outgoing *mail server addresses.***

   As noted above, you need to consult the account information your ISP gave you when you signed up (or ask your network administrator, if you're on a corporate network) to figure out what settings to use on this screen.

   Click the right arrow button.

9. **Enter your account ID and Password.**

   In this step, you'll need to enter your *email account ID* (the portion of your email address that comes before the @ symbol) and the password for your account.

   Entourage is willing to store your password in the Mac OS *Keychain* (a handy Mac OS X feature that memorizes all of your email and file-sharing passwords for you). Turn off the "Save password" box only if you want to have to type your password every time Entourage checks your email.

   The buttons "Click Here for Advanced Receiving Options" and "Click Here for Advanced Sending Options" open dialog boxes where you specify security options and alternative ports for mail services. Your network administrator or ISP help desk will tell you if you need to use these options. (For example, you may have to turn on *authentication* in the sending options in order to send email if you travel or access the Internet using another ISP.)

Click the right arrow button to continue.

10. **Name your account.**

Entourage needs a name for your brand new account, such as *Earthlink Account* or *Hotmail account.*

A word about the other checkbox here: The Entourage toolbar contains a button called Send & Receive All. If you have more than one email account, a click on this single button can check *all* your email accounts. Turn off the "Include this account in my Send & Receive All schedule" option on this screen if you *don't* want this account to be checked automatically.

11. **Click Finish to wrap things up.**

Entourage now has all the basic information it needs to start work. If you haven't already selected Entourage as your default email program, it will ask you yet again whether you want Entourage as your default program: even though you've long-since made up your mind on this issue, again click Yes or No.

GEM IN THE ROUGH

Using Your Mac.com Address with Your ISP

If you're looking for an email address with a little Macintosh flair, or if the address your ISP has given you is hopelessly hard to remember, check out Apple's mac.com email service, part of the company's iTools Internet service.

Mac.com can forward mail from your mac.com address to your ISP, but you can also send and receive mail *directly* via your mac.com address. This can avoid confusion: your correspondents simply use your mac.com address, and your messages appear to come *from* your mac.com address rather than a hard-to-remember ISP address. No one needs to know about your ISP. In fact, as noted earlier, you can *change* ISPs and continue using your mac.com mail without anyone having to update their address books.

Here's how to do it: Choose Tools→Accounts. In the window that pops up, click the Mail tab. Double-click the mac.com account that you just created. In *that* window,

click the Account Settings tab and enter your mac.com email address in the "E-mail address" field. Enter your ISP's mail server address (its *SMTP server*) in the "Sending mail" section.

Now, mail sent using your mac.com address will appear to come from your mac.com account; that is, your recipients will see the mac.com address as your return address.

If you get an error when you try to send mail from your mac.com address, return to the account settings, click "Click here for advanced sending options," turn on "SMTP server requires authentication," and enter the account ID and password for your ISP email account.

(Apple's iTools site also offers instructions for sending and receiving mail via mac.com, which might help if you still have problems and your ISP can't help.)

Setting Up a Second Email Account

The Account Setup Assistant described above offers a relatively painless procedure for setting up your main email account. But if you have additional accounts to set up, you can return to the Setup Assistant like this:

Configuring IMAP Options

IMAP accounts offer lots of flexibility—but as usual in the software world, that means that they also offer lots of complexity. To find Entourage's staggering array of email options, choose Tools→Accounts; double-click the name of your IMAP account; and click the Options tab. Here you'll find special options, in addition to those described at the end of this chapter:

- **Download complete messages in Inbox.** Normally, when you connect to an IMAP account, Entourage grabs only the message's *headers*—its size, subject line, sender's name, and date. The body of the message stays on the server until you click the message's name in your message list, at which time Entourage retrieves the whole thing. If you turn on this box, however, Entourage downloads both the headers *and* the message contents to your Inbox, making them instantly available. This option, in other words, makes your IMAP account behave a lot like a POP account.

- **Root folder.** If you haven't heard from your IMAP account administrator that this is something you need to fill in, ignore it.

- **Live Sync.** These options let you choose how Entourage manages its connection to IMAP servers—for example, whether it tries for a connection as soon as Entourage is launched, how long it should stay connected, and whether it should connect to all of your mail folders or just the Inbox.

- **Check for unread messages in subscribed folders.** If you've subscribed to IMAP folders, turning on this option makes Entourage check them for new mail automatically. Turning it off means you'll have to look inside the folders yourself.

If you're an especially technical IMAP user, you can also tweak the Advanced tab in the Edit Account window. There, you'll be able to fine-tune two sets of preferences:

- **Special folders.** Ordinarily, an IMAP account stores your incoming, deleted, and filed messages on an Internet server. Messages you've sent or haven't yet sent (because they're in your Drafts folder), however, remain on your hard drive. If you turn on "Store special folders on IMAP server" and then turn on the corresponding folder checkboxes, Entourage stores the contents of the Sent Items and Drafts folders on the server, too, so that you'll have access to them from anywhere. (You'll need to specify a server's folder path for these items, should they be named anything but "Sent Items" and "Drafts.")

- **Delete options.** This feature has nothing to do with wiping out stock holdings. Instead, it has to do with how your IMAP Internet server processes a message that you delete: It can either delete it outright or move it to its own Deleted Items folder. You can also indicate here when deleted messages are actually deleted—when you quit Entourage, after messages reach a certain age, or when you close an IMAP folder.

1. With Entourage open, choose Tools→Accounts.

   This brings up the Accounts window, the central point for dealing with email, Usenet news, and directory services accounts in Entourage.

2. With the Mail tab selected, click the New button.

   Entourage's Account Setup Assistant reappears. Continue with step 6 of the previous instructions.

Note: If you have more than one email account set up in Entourage, one of these accounts is the *default account*. The default account is the one that's used to send and receive mail unless you specify otherwise. To specify the default account, choose Tools→Accounts and click the Mail tab in the resulting window. The current default account is shown in bold. Select the account that you want to make the default, click Make Default, and close the window.

Configuring Your Account Manually

If you've got all the necessary settings for a new account on a slip of paper in front of you, then the screen-by-screen assistant may seem unnecessarily slow. Here's how to create a new email account without any help from the Setup Assistant.

Choose Tools→Accounts to open the Accounts window. Then, with the Mail tab selected, click New. When the Account Setup Assistant appears, click Configure Account Manually. Entourage now asks what kind of account you want to set up: POP,

Figure 8-3:
Left: The Account Settings tab of the Edit Account window contains the same basic information as the Account Setup Assistant, but in a much more compact form.

Right: A click on the Options tab, however, reveals a slew of options that are not available through the Account Setup Assistant.

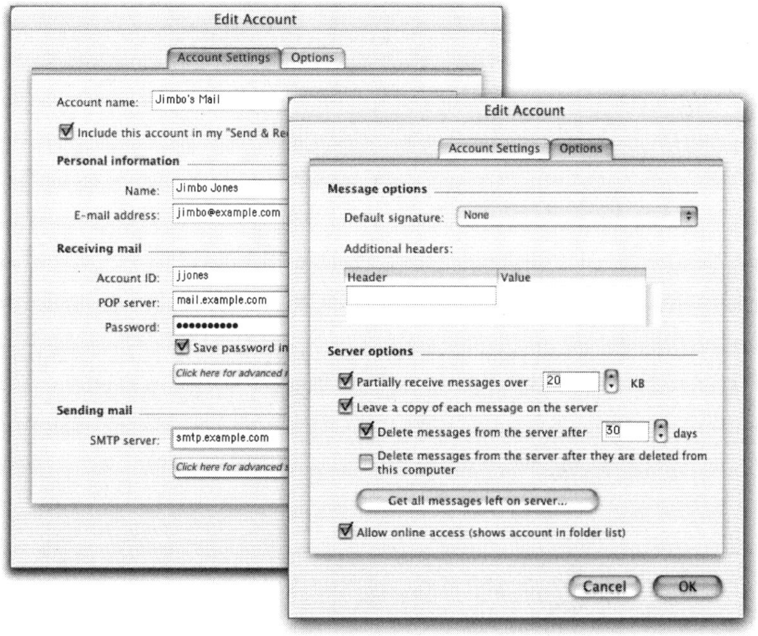

IMAP, or Hotmail. Choose the account flavor you want from the pop-up menu, and click OK. A window opens displaying two tabs in which you can enter all of your relevant information.

Note: Setting up an account manually has another payoff: it offers advanced control over how Entourage sends and receives mail. (Hotmail accounts aren't included.) These are options most people can and should ignore (unless your ISP requires them).

Under the Account Settings tab (see Figure 8-4), click "Click here for advanced receiving options." You get a window in which you can specify a secure connection, choose a different port for your POP or IMAP connections, or force Entourage to use a secure password.

If you click the Options tab, you can specify the default *signature* for this account (page 356), additional *headers* you want added (for geeks only), and whether or not you want to limit message sizes (page 325).

If you have an IMAP account, you're also offered some additional options, which are described on page 316.

Sending and Receiving Mail

All of this setup has been leading up to this: telling Entourage to check for incoming mail and send any outgoing mail. The basic process is easy, but several subtleties can make your email experience more satisfying.

Send and Receive All

When Entourage opens for the first time, you've got mail; the Inbox contains a message for you from Microsoft. It wasn't actually transmitted over the Internet, though— it's a starter message built into Entourage just to tease you. Fortunately, all your future mail will come via the Internet.

You get new mail and send mail you've written using the Send & Receive command. You can trigger it in any of several ways:

- Click the Send & Receive button in the toolbar.
- Choose Tools→Send & Receive→Send & Receive All.
- Press ⌘-K. (If you're used to ⌘-M from Office 2001, note this change. Microsoft had to avoid ⌘-M, which is the Minimize command in Mac OS X.)

Tip: You can also set up Entourage to check your email accounts automatically according to a schedule, as described on page 320.

Now Entourage contacts the mail servers listed in the account list, retrieving new messages and downloading any files attached to those messages. It also sends any outgoing messages and their attachments.

Tip: After it's done, Entourage tries to communicate its success or failure by playing a cheerful chime—one for "You've got mail," a different one for "You've got no mail," and so on. You can change these sounds, opt to have Entourage flash the menu bar instead, elect to have Entourage bring itself in front of your other open Mac programs when there's new mail, or even choose a completely different sound *set*. All of this fun awaits in the Entourage→General Preferences→Notification tab.

In the list on the right side of your screen, the names of new messages appear in bold type. Folders *containing* new messages show up in bold type, too (in the Folder list at the left side of the screen). The boldface number in parentheses after the word "Inbox" lets you know how many of its messages you haven't yet read.

Finally, after messages are downloaded, Entourage applies its filters—what it calls *Rules*—to all new messages, putting mail from mailing lists into specific folders, for example. More on rules on page 345.

The Progress window

While it's connecting to the Internet and transferring messages, Entourage displays brief details of its activity at the bottom of the main window. If you'd like more detail, open Entourage's Progress window, as shown in Figure 8-4, by choosing Window→Progress or pressing ⌘-7.

Figure 8-4:
Top: The Progress window first appears as a small window with a flippy triangle on the left side.

Bottom: When you click it, the window shows you all of the details when it makes a network connection: what server has been checked, the number of messages left to be downloaded, where they're coming from, and how much of each message has been downloaded.

Checking a specific email account

You don't have to check *all* of your email accounts whenever you want to get mail. Suppose, for example, that you want to send a message to *yourself*, from your work account to your home account. In that case, you'd want to send/receive mail only from your office account; if, later in the day, Entourage also downloaded messages from your home account, you'd wind up with the same message in your office Mac's copy of Entourage, defeating the whole purpose.

You can exclude an account (or several accounts) from the "Send & Receive All" routine easily enough. Open the Accounts window (Tools→Accounts), double-click the account's name, turn off "Include this account in my 'Send & Receive All' schedule," click OK, and close the Accounts window.

But suppose you *usually* want to check all accounts, but *occasionally* want to check only one of them. On such an occasion, choose that account's name from the Send & Receive pop-up button menu on the main Entourage window. (Alternatively, choose the account name from the Tools→Send & Receive submenu.)

Advanced Mail-Getting Features

Hundreds of thousands of people are perfectly content to use Entourage for email just as it comes out of the box. But if you're willing to slog through some technical options, you can unleash some extremely useful variations on the "Click a button to download mail" routine.

Automatic checking on a schedule

You don't have to press a button to check your email. You can set up Entourage to check your email according to a regular schedule. To be sure, this is an advanced feature, which may force you to think, just for a moment, like you're a computer. But there's no debating the convenience of checking Entourage in the morning to find that, for example, it has fetched all your new mail automatically during the night.

To create a schedule, choose Tools→Schedules to bring up the Schedules window (Figure 8-5, left). Click the New button in the window's toolbar, which brings up the Edit Schedule window with an untitled schedule (Figure 8-5, right). (If you want to edit an existing schedule, double-click it in the Schedules window.)

In this window, you can set three options: the schedule's name, when it happens, and what happens. To give the schedule a name, just type it in the Name field at the top of the window.

The *When* portion of this window lets you determine when a schedule runs, using a pop-up menu:

- **Manually.** Nothing will happen automatically. To run the schedule, you'll have to choose its name from the Tools→Run Schedule submenu.

- **At Startup.** Entourage will run the schedule whenever you launch the program.

- **On Quit.** Entourage will run the schedule when you *quit* the program.

- **Timed Schedule.** You can set specific times and days for schedules to execute. That is, you can set a schedule to run every Thursday and Sunday at 12:27 p.m., if you like.

- **Repeating Schedule.** Unlike with a timed schedule, you can set a schedule to run at regular intervals, such as every 30 minutes or every three days.

- **Recurring.** This option lets you use a recurring schedule to run in a recurring pattern over a defined period of time—such as monthly on the 21st day of each month for a period of three months, starting two months from today.

For Timed and Repeating schedules, you can set the particulars by clicking the button next to the pop-up menu, which opens a window in which you can set exact days, hours, and minutes for schedules to run.

By clicking the Add Occurrence button, you can add up to three "triggers" for this automated action. For example, you might set up a Timed Schedule, an At Startup action, and an On Quit event, so that, for example, your email gets checked once when Entourage is launched, then every hour, and once again when Entourage quits.

Tip: If you turn on "Only if connected," you can prevent Entourage from trying to connect to the Internet when the schedule is run (e.g. dialing furiously and seizing command of your Mac over and over again). Instead, Entourage will trot off to the Internet only if your Mac is already connected.

Now that you have specified *when* your schedules are to be run, you need to determine *what happens* when a schedule is run; Entourage can do much more on a timetable than check your mail. You do this in the Action section of the Edit Schedule window. The pop-up menu offers seven options:

- **Receive Mail.** Entourage will connect to a mail server and download any waiting mail. This is an ideal action to schedule at startup.

- **Receive News.** If you want to download the latest newsgroup postings, you can tell Entourage to download that information—another one that's useful in a startup schedule.

- **Send All.** This action sends all waiting mail—a useful one to schedule for when you quit Entourage. That way, you can make sure that all of your outgoing mail goes out before you walk away from your Mac.

- **Run AppleScript.** AppleScript scripts can be made to do just about anything—they're especially good for integrating functions of several programs, not just email. For instance, you could tell Entourage to run a script that backs up your Documents folder onto a different hard drive when you quit Entourage. (AppleScript is a programming language—an easy one to master, but still a programming language. *Mac OS X: The Missing Manual* offers beginning AppleScript tutorials, and getting-started information and links to online resources are also available at Apple's AppleScript Web site, *www.apple.com/applescript.*)

- **Delete Mail.** Entourage will delete mail from your Deleted Items folder, which might be something that you want to do whenever you quit the program.

- **Launch Alias.** This schedule item opens an alias to any document or program on your hard drive—powerful stuff if you want to launch, say, your Web browser whenever you launch Entourage.

- **Excel Auto Web Publish.** This item has to do with Excel's Save As Web Page feature, which lets you publish an Excel workbook as a Web page automatically.

So why is an Excel option showing up in an Entourage dialog box? When you set a workbook to publish on the Web on a recurring basis, Excel hands the task off to Entourage's scheduling feature, where it appears as a schedule. Once it's in Entourage, you can further customize *when* the automatic publishing of that workbook takes place. When Entourage executes an Auto Web Publish schedule, it opens the workbook in Excel and saves it as a Web page. (This option is not available unless you've already created an autopublishing workbook in Excel.)

Once you've selected one of these options, you can also select parameters for it. For example, if you choose Receive News, you can specify which subscribed newsgroups (see page 363) you want to read.

You can add dozens of actions to take place in a single schedule. To add an action, click the Add Action button. A new pop-up menu appears. (To delete one, too, click its "block" in the dialog box and then click the Remove Action button.)

Entourage comes with three prefab schedules that you can edit to meet your own evil ends: Empty Deleted Items Folder, which deletes all messages in the Deleted Items folder; Send & Receive All, which sends all outgoing mail and receives any waiting mail for all the accounts you've set up; and Send All, which sends all outgoing mail without checking for *incoming* mail. You can run these schedules, as well as any you've set up yourself, by choosing from the Tools→Run Schedule submenu.

Figure 8-5:
The Entourage Schedules window (top left) shows all of the schedules currently available in your copy of Entourage. By clicking the New button (or by editing an existing schedule), you get the Edit Schedule window (lower right). In it, you can tell Entourage what to do and when to do it.

This particular schedule runs whenever Entourage is launched, and it checks for new mail, runs an AppleScript script that archives all the email, and then grabs new news articles from the Microsoft news servers. It performs these actions only if you're connected to the Internet, and it leaves your Mac connected when it's finished running.

The hotel-room feature: online accounts

As noted earlier in this chapter, the world's most common email account types are POP (in which your messages are transferred from the Internet to your hard drive) and IMAP (in which your messages always remain on your mail server rather than your computer). The kind of account you have depends on your ISP.

But like many hip email programs, Entourage can let you use POP accounts almost as if they *were* IMAP accounts—that is, you can grab your messages without removing them from your Internet server. Better yet, the program can download only the *headers* of the messages, which takes but an instant, even over a slow (or expensive) connection. Once you have the headers, you can survey the subject lines or the names of the senders, and choose which messages you want to download in their entirety.

This feature is ideal for use when you're in a hotel room, dialing your Internet account over a slow modem connection, for two reasons. First, you're spared the tedium of downloading a bunch of messages and attachments you don't really need while on the road. Second, the mail stays on the server until you delete it manually; it'll still be there when you return home, when you can again download the messages, this time onto your main Mac.

Note: Most Internet service providers allow you to accumulate only five or ten megabytes' worth of mail. Beyond that limit, incoming messages get "bounced" back to their senders. In other words, you can't delay downloading your messages indefinitely, and attachments can easily consume a lot of your quota. Unfortunately, there's no way within Entourage to see how much space your mail is using on your ISP's server.

Microsoft calls this feature *online access*, by which it means that you will be accessing mail in this account only via the Internet, rather than downloading it to your hard drive. To set up your account this way, choose Tools→Accounts, which brings up the Accounts window. Double-click the account that you want to make available for online access.

In the resulting Edit Account window, click the Options tab and turn on "Allow online access," as shown in Figure 8-5. You wind up with a new icon in the Folder Items pane: the online representation of your account, bearing the same name.

Setting up an account for online access doesn't remove its mail or folders from your hard drive. It just sets up a different way of accessing the account, as represented by a new icon in the Folder List for that account. (Yes, this is confusing.)

Tip: When you set up an account for online access, it's usually a good idea to turn off Entourage's Preview pane (View→Preview Pane). You'll see why in a moment.

To make Entourage check the Internet for new messages sent to this account, click this icon in the Folder Items list—just one click. Entourage starts by downloading only the *header information* of the waiting messages: subject lines, sender names, date and time the message was sent, and so on. It doesn't download the messages themselves.

CHAPTER 8: ENTOURAGE EMAIL AND NEWSGROUPS

If you see a message whose subject line or sender looks promising, click it. If Entourage's Preview pane is showing, Entourage downloads the message and shows it there. If not, double-click the message to make Entourage download it and display it in the message window.

Either way, the message also remains on the Internet email server: that's the big difference between using the online access feature and using the Send & Receive command for that account.

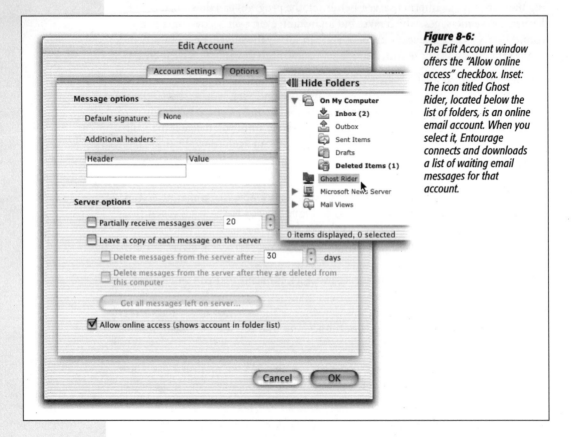

Figure 8-6:
The Edit Account window offers the "Allow online access" checkbox. Inset: The icon titled Ghost Rider, located below the list of folders, is an online email account. When you select it, Entourage connects and downloads a list of waiting email messages for that account.

To delete mail from an online account, select the messages that you want to delete, and then press the Delete key. (Now you see why it's a good idea to turn off the Preview pane—when you click a message to delete it, you simultaneously tell Entourage to *download* it if the Preview pane is on the screen.)

The message doesn't move, but a "deleted online message" icon appears in the message's Online Status column (see Figure 8-7). When you next connect to that account in online mode, Entourage deletes the message from the server, if you're still connected to the Internet.

On the other hand, if you change your mind and want to *keep* a message you've marked for deletion, click the deleted online message icon. From the pop-up menu, choose Leave Message on Server, so that the "deleted online message" icon disappears. The message will be there waiting for you when you check your email account in one of the "normal" ways.

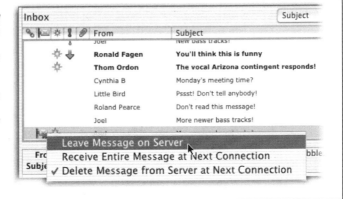

Figure 8-7:
Online messages that have been deleted still show up in the message list, bearing an icon that looks like an envelope with a red X. The next time you connect to an online account, any messages marked for deletion will be shown the door. If you change your mind, you can click the deleted online message icon to bring up a menu; select Leave Message on Server from the menu to leave the message there.

Restricting download sizes

For road warriors stuck with slow modem connections, you can tell Entourage to grab only the first portion of a message, so that you don't have to sit through an hour-long modem connection to download that "You Want It When?" cartoon that your friend thought was just *so* funny.

To do this, select Tools→Accounts and then open the account for which you want to limit the size of downloaded messages. Click the Options tab at the top of that window, and then turn on "Partially retrieve messages over ___ KB." You can set how much of a message that you want to grab (see Figure 8-6).

Note: It's crucial to remember to turn this option *off* once you get home, or you'll be wondering why Entourage keeps chopping off your messages and giving you half-downloaded, unopenable attachments.

Offline access

When you're in the plane or bus terminal, you probably don't have an Internet connection. In such situations, you may want to read and write replies to your email—but you may find it annoying that, every 15 minutes or so, Entourage tries vainly to get online, resulting in an avalanche of error messages.

To shut it up, choose Entourage→Work Offline. A checkmark appears next to the menu item. From now on, you can read and write replies to your email without interruption from Entourage. In fact, if you click Send & Receive, Entourage will ask you if you're sure you want to go online before attempting to make a connection. (Choose Entourage→Work Offline again to return to the normal "connect when ready" mode.)

Figure 8-8:
Top: Messages that Entourage has only partially retrieved show a half-completed picture of an envelope in the Online Status column (circled).

Bottom: If you decide that you want to download the whole message, click this icon; choose Receive Entire Message at Next Connection from the menu that pops up. The next time you hit Send & Receive, Entourage will download the complete message (or complete attachment) for you.

Reading a Message

Just seeing a list of new messages in Entourage is like getting wrapped presents; the best part is yet to come. There are two ways to read a message: using the preview pane, and opening the message into its own window.

To preview a message, first make sure the preview pane is showing. (If not, choose View→Preview Pane.) The right side of the Entourage main window splits in half. When you click a message's name in the list in the top portion, the body of the message appears in the preview pane below. Don't forget that you can adjust the relative sizes of the List and Preview panes by dragging the gray border between them.

To open a message into a window of its own, double-click its name in the List pane. An open message has its own toolbar, along with Previous Message and Next Message arrows in the left corner. These are pop-up menu buttons; they offer commands that let you move to another read or unread message, delete the current message, and so on.

Tip: Entourage tries to condense the lettering of messages in list views, if necessary, to show you their entire names. This tightened letter spacing isn't particularly attractive, but may make the difference between your being able to read the subject line of a message and seeing it chopped off.

You can, if you like, resize Entourage's columns to make more room for the text: just drag the border between the columns. You can also point to a particular bit of condensed text without clicking. A small, yellow pop-up balloon appears, revealing the entire, non-condensed message name.

Regardless of your viewing preference, any attached pictures, sounds, or movies *also* appear in the body of the message. You can even play those sounds and movies in the email message itself. (Entourage displays and plays any kind of file that Quick-Time can understand—JPEG, GIF, PICT, Photoshop files, and so on—and can also call on Mac OS X's graphics smarts to preview Acrobat PDF documents.)

Tip: If the text of a message is too small to read, click the Increase Font Size button on the message's toolbar at the far right of Entourage's Preview pane. If a message's text is too *big* (for a narrow window or a laptop screen, say), Option-click the Increase Font Size button to make Entourage decrease the size of the text.

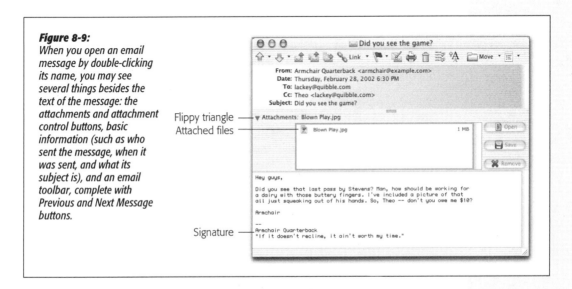

Figure 8-9:
When you open an email message by double-clicking its name, you may see several things besides the text of the message: the attachments and attachment control buttons, basic information (such as who sent the message, when it was sent, and what its subject is), and an email toolbar, complete with Previous and Next Message buttons.

Flippy triangle
Attached files

Signature

Once you've read a message, you can view the next one in the list either by pressing ⌘-] or by clicking its name in the List pane. (If you're using the preview mode, and haven't opened a message into its own window, you can also press the up or down arrow keys to move from one message to the next.)

POWER USERS' CLINIC

Where Are the Headers?

As a favor to you, and to make Internet email look less intimidating, Entourage normally hides the blobs of technical-looking text known as *Internet headers*. This information shows all the email servers a message has visited on its way to your Inbox, along with dates, times, and other data.

Sometimes this information can be enlightening or helpful in troubleshooting or reporting a problem to an ISP. To view the header information, open a message into its own window and then choose View→Internet Headers (Shift-⌘-H).

Tip: To mark a message that you've read as an *unread* message, so that its name remains bolded, choose Message→Mark as Unread (Shift-⌘-T), or Control-click the message's name and choose Mark as Unread from the contextual menu.

Here's another timesaver: You can *hide* all the messages you've already read. Just choose View→Unread Only (Shift-⌘-O). To bring the hidden messages back, choose View→Unread Only again.

Icons in the message list

After you've received some messages in Entourage, you'll notice that some of those messages have icons at the left side of their list-view lines. These badges or flags give you useful information about the messages:

- **Links.** A chain-link icon here (🔗) indicates that a message has been *linked* to another message, calendar event, task, note, or the like. (See page 339 for more on linking.)

- **Online Status.** An icon that looks like an emaciated folder (📁) indicates that a message has only been partially retrieved—a dead giveaway that you've turned on the "Partially download" option described on page 325. A folder with a red X through it (📁) indicates that the message has been deleted from the server in an *online account* (page 323). Finally, an icon with a red, downward-pointing arrow indicates that the message will be fully downloaded the next time that you connect (page 325).

- **Status.** The status column shows the status of particular messages. A blue star (✦) means that the message has been received but not yet read. A curved arrow facing left (↩) denotes a message that you've answered. A purple, angular arrow facing right (↗), on the other hand, indicates that you've *redirected* the message (see page 335). A green, curved arrow facing right (↪) denotes mail that you've forwarded to someone else.

Note: Unfortunately, Entourage displays these last three icons only after your replies, forwards, and redirects have actually been sent, rather than when you write the reply, or choose to forward or redirect a message. As a result, it can be difficult to determine whether or not you've processed a message if you don't happen to be connected to the Internet and checking mail every 30 seconds.

If you modify the subject or text of a message you've received (see page 333), the status column shows a pencil (✏️) to let you know. If a message is associated with a calendar event (or invites you to an event—see page 386), the message status icon offers a small calendar (📅). (Caution: the calendar status overrides things like the symbols for forwards and replies.)

- **Priority.** This column's icons indicate a message's priority: a red exclamation point (❗)for highest priority; an orange one for high priority; a dark blue downward arrow (⬇) for low priority; and a pale blue downward arrow for lowest priority. No icon means normal priority.

Note: You see a priority icon only when your correspondents used their email program's priority-labeling feature, or if you change the priority of a message once you've received it. After all, what Bob at the office thinks is wildly important may not even be a blip on your radar.

- **Attachments.** If a message has one or more files attached (see page 341), a paper-clip icon (🖈) appears in this column.

- **Thread.** If you're using Entourage's threaded view of email or newsgroup messages (see page 329), the first available message in a thread will display a flippy triangle (▶) at the far left of the message listing: click the triangle to expand or collapse the thread.

GEM IN THE ROUGH

Nice Threads

As email begins to take over your life, you may notice that one person sends a message, you reply, the other person replies to the reply, and so on. The two of you have just created a *thread.*

Entourage can group messages by thread, so that it's easy to follow an electronic conversation from beginning to end: choose View→Threaded to make Entourage sort the current message listing by subject with threads bunched to-gether. Click the flippy triangle next to the first message of a thread to expand or collapse the list of messages in that thread.

Threading is particularly useful for reading *newsgroups* (see page 363), since newsgroups are all about conversational exchange, but it's sometimes handy for everyday email exchanges, too.

How to Process a Message

Once you've read a message and savored the feeling of awe brought on by the miracle of instantaneous electronic communication, you can process the message in any of several ways.

Deleting messages

Sometimes it's junk mail, sometimes you're just done with it. Either way, it's a snap to delete a message that's before you on the screen: just press the Delete key. Alternatively, you can:

- Press the forward-delete key, if your keyboard has one.

- Click the Delete (trash can) button on the toolbar.

- Choose Edit→Delete Message.

- Press ⌘-Delete.

You can also delete a batch of messages at once by highlighting them and then using a delete button, menu command, or keystroke.

Tip: If you want to delete a message and move to the next in one easy step, press Option-⌘-]: that's the same as the key command for moving to the next message (⌘-]) plus the Option key. If you want to delete the current message and move to the *previous* message, press Option-⌘- [instead.

Either way, the message or messages don't actually disappear, just as moving a file icon to the Macintosh Trash doesn't actually delete it. Instead, these commands move the messages to the Deleted Items folder. If you like, you can click this icon to view a list of the messages you've deleted. You can even rescue messages by dragging them into any other mail folder (such as right back into the Inbox, as illustrated in Figure 8-9).

Entourage doesn't truly vaporize messages in the Deleted Items folder until you "empty the trash." You can empty it in any of several ways:

- Control-click the Deleted Items folder. Choose "Empty 'Deleted Items'" from the contextual menu.

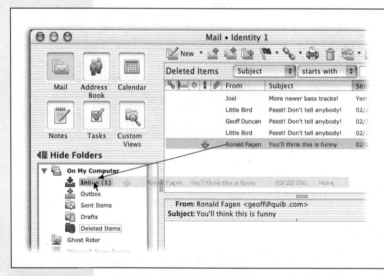

Figure 8-10:
By dragging an item out of the Deleted Items folder and into another folder, you can save it from certain doom. You can also delete messages by dragging them into the Deleted Items folder, for that matter.

Selecting Messages

When you want to process a group of messages simultaneously—to delete, move, or forward them, for example—you need to master the art of multiple message selection.

To select two or more messages that appear consecutively in your message list, click the first message, then Shift-click the last. This trick selects every message between the two that you clicked.

To select two or more messages that *aren't* adjacent in the list (that is, skipping a few messages between selected ones), ⌘-click the messages you want. Only the messages you click get selected—no filling in of messages in between.

After using either technique, you can also *deselect* messages you've managed to highlight—just ⌘-click them again.

- Click a message, or a folder, within the Deleted Items Folder list and then click the Delete icon on the toolbar (or press ⌘-Delete). You'll be asked to confirm its *permanent* deletion.

- Choose Tools→Run Schedule→Empty Deleted Items Folder.

- Set up a schedule to empty the folder automatically when you quit Entourage, for example, or to delete only messages that are older than, say, 60 days. See page 330 for instructions.

Replying to messages

To reply to a message, click the Reply button in the toolbar, choose Message→Reply, or press ⌘-R. Entourage creates a new, outgoing email message, preaddressed to the sender's return address.

To save you additional time, Entourage pastes the entire original message at the top of your reply, complete with the > brackets that serve as Internet quoting marks. (It's also a feature you can turn off; choose Entourage→Mail & News Preferences, click the Reply & Forward tab, and turn off "Include entire message in reply.") Entourage also tacks *Re:* ("regarding") onto the front of the subject line, a long-stand-

---

TROUBLESHOOTING MOMENT

Fixing the Entourage Database

Entourage keeps all of its messages in a single, gigantic database file on your hard drive. It's called Database, and it sits in the Documents→Microsoft User Data→Office X Identities→Main Identity folder in your Home folder (in the Finder, choose Go→Home).

As you add and delete hundreds of messages from this database over time, some digital sawdust gets left behind, resulting in peculiarities when addressing messages, or general Entourage sluggishness. You also wind up with *massive* Entourage files, which can consume hundreds of megabytes of disk space. That's a particular bummer if you like to copy your message database to your laptop when you go on a trip, or if you back up your data every day.

Fortunately, it's easy enough to *rebuild the database,* a procedure that cleanses, repairs, organizes, and purges your message files. You wind up with a much more compact and healthy database.

To rebuild the Entourage database, quit any other Office X applications you're running. Then hold down the Option key when launching Entourage. After the logo screen pops up, you'll be given two choices: Typical Rebuild or Advanced Rebuild. Most of the time, a typical rebuild does the trick, taking several minutes to repair and compact your database.

If you're still having problems, launch Entourage again with the Option key held down, and this time choose Advanced Rebuild. This should clear up any problems you may be having, but it also requires you to redownload folder lists and messages for your Hotmail or IMAP accounts, and replace any pictures of contacts in your Address Book.

In either case, you'll now find *two* sets of database files in your Microsoft User Data folder—one set bears the prefix "Old." You can throw the "Old" files away after the rebuild is finished, and you've confirmed that the new ones work fine.

If you're curious, the Entourage X database has a maximum size of 2 GB (or if you've installed Service Release 1, described on page 12, 4 GB).

ing convention of Internet email, and prefixes the quoted message with a one-line label indicating who originally wrote it, and when it was written.

Tip: If you only need to quote *part* of a message in your reply, select the text you want to quote, then hold down the Shift key as you choose Message→Reply (or simply press Shift-⌘-R). Entourage creates a reply that includes only the text you selected as the "quotation." See the box on page 361 to find out why keeping your quoted material brief is a thoughtful gesture for your correspondents.

Meanwhile, if you want to include text you've copied from some another source—a Word file, for example—as a quotation, click in your message where you'd like the text to appear, and choose Edit –> Paste Special→Paste As Quotation (or press Shift-⌘-V). Entourage inserts the text in the clipboard as it would any other quoted material in your email message.

Your cursor appears at the bottom of the message area, below any quoted text; you can begin typing your reply. You can also:

- Add recipients to the message by adding email addresses in any of the recipient fields (To, Cc, or Bcc).

- Remove one or more recipients (by clicking their names and then clicking the Remove button in the window that appears, or pressing the Delete key).

- Edit the Subject line or the original message.

- Use the Return key to create blank lines within the bracketed original message in order to place your own text within it. Using this method, you can splice your own comments into the paragraphs of the original message, replying point by point. The brackets preceding each line of the original message help your correspondent keep straight what's yours and what's not.

- Attach a file (see page 357).

Note: If the original message came with an attached file, Entourage doesn't fasten the attachment to the reply.

There are three kinds of replies, each represented by a different icon on the toolbar:

- A **standard reply** (click the Reply button) goes only to the sender of the message. If that sender is a mailing list (see the box on the facing page), then the message may be sent to the *entire* mailing list, which could get you in trouble. Check the To address to make sure you're sending a message to the right place!

- **Reply To Sender** creates a reply that goes to the person who wrote the original message (or posted the message to a newsgroup; see page 363). Use this option if you'd like to reply privately to a message posted to a mailing list or a newsgroup, avoiding sending the message to the entire mailing list or group. (If you use this command on a message that *didn't* come from a mailing list or a newsgroup, Entourage treats it as a standard reply.)

- The **Reply To All** button addresses a message to *all* recipients of the original message, including any Cc recipients. This is the button to use if you're participating in a group discussion; all six of you can carry on an email correspondence, always sending each response to the other five. (Reply To All doesn't send the reply to anyone who may have been in the secret Bcc field, as described on page 349.)

Tip: Entourage starts out placing the insertion point at the bottom of any quoted text in a reply. If you're the kind of person who likes to put your response *above* the quotation, choose Entourage→Mail & News Preferences, select the Reply & Forward tab, and turn on "Place insertion point before quoted text."

Editing messages

Entourage lets you edit a message somebody *else* wrote. For once in your life, you can edit down some long-winded person without hurting his feelings.

Just double-click a message to open it into a window, and then choose Message→Edit Message. (If it's HTML formatted, you'll be warned that the note is about to become a plain-text message.) Feel free to delete or rewrite the text. When you close the window, Entourage asks if you want your changes preserved. After you click Save, a notepad icon appears next to the message's name, a reminder of your meddling.

Reformatting messages

Some messages are forwarded and replied to about a million times. With each round, more brackets get added at the beginning of each line. Sooner or later, these messages become almost illegible (see Figure 8-10).

Fortunately, Entourage can usually clean up a message's text. It can, for example, make a message's text all uppercase or all lowercase, increase or decrease its quoting levels (those multiple brackets >>>), or even straighten out curly quotes (which often arrive at the other end of Internet email as gobbledygook).

UP TO SPEED

About Mailing Lists

During your email experiments, you're likely to come across something called a mailing list. Mailing lists come in two general forms: *discussion lists* in which members of the mailing list contribute to a group discussion via email, and *broadcast-only lists* that transmit messages to subscribers. For example, a group of Celtic music fans might have an email discussion list in which members write about anything they like, but a particular Celtic artist might have a broadcast list to announce concerts and albums to fans who've signed up for updates. By searching Yahoo (*www.yahoo.com*) or similar Web directories, you can turn

up mailing lists covering just about every conceivable topic.

Many Internet discussion lists are *unmoderated,* which means you can send a message to all members of the group by sending a message to a single address—the list's address. That's why you have to be careful when you just want to reply to *one person* in the discussion group; if you accidentally reply to the list address and not to a specific person, your message may be distributed to *everyone* on the mailing list—sometimes with embarrassing or disastrous consequences.

The most useful of these tools is Rewrap Paragraphs. When you have a badly wrapped message, the Edit→Auto Text Cleanup→Rewrap Paragraphs command does its best to remove all those funky line breaks so that the message is clean and legible once again.

Tip: When you use the Rewrap Paragraphs command on a message you've received, Entourage asks if you want your changes to the original made permanent. Sometimes that's just fine, but other times you may want to keep the original (bad) formatting around, just in case Rewrap Paragraphs messed up a chart or specially formatted text like pop-song lyrics.

No biggie: you can have *both* the original and the cleaned-up version. Just make a duplicate of the message (select the message, choose Edit→Duplicate Message), and then use Entourage's reformatting tools on the copy.

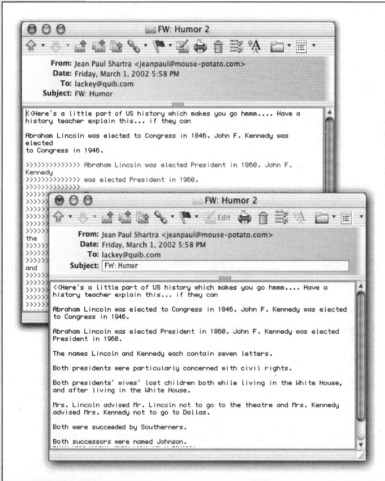

Figure 8-11:
Back left: You can see how badly text gets mangled when it's been forwarded a few times.

Front right: After using the Remove Quoting and Rewrap Paragraphs commands, the message's lines are neat and tidy. (An open email message also offers a Rewrap Paragraphs button right on the toolbar.)

Forwarding messages

Instead of replying to the person who sent you a message, you may sometimes want to *forward* the message—pass it on—to a third person.

To do so, click the Forward button in the toolbar, choose Message→Forward, or press ⌘-J. A new message opens, looking a lot like the one that appears when you reply. Once again, before forwarding the message, you can edit the subject line or the message itself. (For example, you may wish to precede the original message with a comment of your own, along the lines of: "Frank: I thought you'd be interested in this joke about Congress.") Entourage inserts one-line labels indicating what part of your message is the forwarded content, which helps eliminate confusion.

Tip: When you forward a message, Entourage puts the insertion point at the top of the message, and inserts labels—"Forwarded message" and "End of Forwarded Message"—to indicate where the forwarded message starts and stops. You can also tell Entourage to use Internet-style quote characters (">") before the forwarded text: choose Entourage→Mail & News Preferences, select the Reply & Forward pane, and check "Use quoting characters when forwarding."

All that remains for you to do is to specify who gets the forwarded message. Just address it as you would any outgoing piece of mail.

Note: If the original message contained an attachment, this time, Entourage *does* keep the attachment attached (unless you delete it first).

Redirecting messages

A *redirected* message is similar to a forwarded message, with one extremely useful difference: when you forward a message, your recipient sees that it came from *you*—just as if you'd written the whole thing yourself. But when you *redirect* a message, your recipient sees the *original* sender's name as the sender; the message bears almost no trace of your involvement. In other words, a redirected message uses you as a low-profile relay station between two other people.

Treasure this Entourage feature; plenty of email programs, including Microsoft's own Outlook and Outlook Express for Windows, don't offer a Redirect command at all. You can use it to transfer messages from one of your own accounts to another, or to pass along a message that came to you by mistake. You might use it when, for example, you, a graphic designer, receive a question from a customer about the sales tax on his bill. You could redirect it to someone in the accounting department, who could respond to it directly just by clicking Reply. You'd then be mercifully insulated from *any* ensuing discussion of sales tax.

To redirect a selected message, choose Message→Redirect, or press Option-⌘-J. Entourage presents an outgoing copy of the message for you to address. You'll notice that unlike a forwarded message, this one lacks quoting brackets. You can't edit a redirected message; the whole idea is that it ends up at its destination unaltered. If you need to make a comment to the new recipient, use Forward instead.

Note: When you redirect a message, you do leave some electronic fingerprints on it. If the recipients look at the Internet *headers* of a message you've redirected, they'll see information Entourage inserted indicating who resent the message, and there may be other clues. Entourage inserts these details both to help avoid confusion and to prevent abuse.

Printing messages

To print a message, click the Print button in the toolbar, choose File→Print, or press ⌘-P; the Entourage Print window appears. Once you've changed any necessary settings and clicked OK, the standard Print dialog box pops up, so that you can specify how many copies you want, what range of pages, and so on. Finally, click Print.

Tip: If you know you just want one copy of a message using the default print settings, choose File→Print One Copy, or press Option-⌘-P. Entourage will zap a single copy of the current message to your printer, with no need for any further dialog boxes.

Filing messages

Entourage lets you create new folders in the Folder list. Then, by dragging messages from your Inbox onto one of these folder icons, you can file away your messages into appropriate storage cubbies. You might create one folder for important messages, another for order confirmations when shopping on the Web, and so on. In fact, you can even create folders *inside* these folders, a feature beloved by the hopelessly organized: your Family folder might have subfolders for each of your siblings.

GEM IN THE ROUGH

The Entourage Email "Paper Trail"

As a sensational convenience to you, Entourage keeps track of what you've done with a message—replied, forwarded, or redirected. It displays your message's history in a yellow banner at the top of the original message, as shown here at top, identifying what was done, and when.

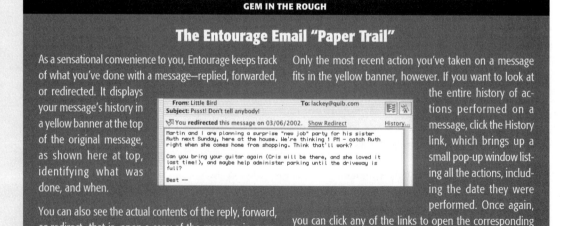

Only the most recent action you've taken on a message fits in the yellow banner, however. If you want to look at the entire history of actions performed on a message, click the History link, which brings up a small pop-up window listing all the actions, including the date they were performed. Once again, you can click any of the links to open the corresponding messages for your reference. (Note: this paper trail is also accessible via a message's Links; see page 339.)

You can also see the actual contents of the reply, forward, or redirect—that is, open a copy of the message in question—by clicking the Show link in that banner.

To create a new folder, choose File→New→Folder, press Shift-⌘-N, or choose New Folder from the New pop-up button on the Entourage toolbar. A new folder appears in the Folder list, with the imaginative name "untitled folder." Just type a new name and then press Return.

Tip: To rename a folder you've created, click it once to select it, and then click its name. Now rename the folder as you would any Macintosh icon. You can't rename Entourage's built-in folders (Inbox, Drafts, Sent Items, and so on), but your own folders are up for grabs.

You can move a message into a folder in any of three ways:

- Drag it out of the List pane onto the folder icon. You can use any part of a message's "row" in the list as a handle. You can also drag a bunch at once.

Tip: If you *Option*-drag a message into a folder, you make a copy of the message in that folder, leaving the original message where it was.

- Highlight a message in the List pane, or several, and then choose Message→Move To→Move To Folder (or press Shift-⌘-M). A window appears, listing all folders in the Folder list. Highlight the folder you want (by clicking or typing the first couple letters of its name). Then press Enter or Return (or click Move).

- Control-click a message (or one of several that you've highlighted): from the resulting contextual menu, choose Move To Folder. Once again, the Folder list appears; select the one you want, then press Return.

POWER USERS' CLINIC

Exporting and Archiving Email

Believe it or not, at some point you'll probably want to get some email *out* of Entourage. Perhaps you'd like to give a collection of messages to someone who uses a different email program (without forwarding them all), or perhaps you'd like to keep years-old correspondence around for posterity's sake, but would prefer *not* to keep it forever in Entourage's ever-growing, monolithic database. Or maybe you just want to back up some of your email separately from Entourage.

Fortunately, Entourage makes it easy to extract a bunch of messages for storage or transfer: just collect (or copy) the messages you wish to export into a single mail folder, and then drag that folder to the Mac OS X desktop. Entourage saves all the messages in a standard, text-only *.mbox* format. Virtually every email program (including Entourage)

for any Mac, Unix, or Windows machine, can open and import these files, making them ideal for transferring messages between programs. Note that Entourage doesn't include subfolders in these exports: if you want to export a group of folders, you must do so one at a time and then reorganize them when you bring them back into Entourage or another email program.

If the messages you export have attachments, Entourage includes encoded versions of those attachments in the *.mbox* file. You may not want to include attachments in your exports, and other email programs or computers may not be able to understand some of the attachments—for instance, a Mac has little use for an MS-DOS batch file. If you don't want to include attachments in your export, delete them from messages before you export them.

Tip: When you click a flippy triangle in the Folder list (or highlight a folder and press ⌘-right arrow), you get to see any folders within that folder, exactly as in the Finder's List view. You can drag folders inside other folders, nesting them to create a nice hierarchical folder structure. (You can drag a nested folder back into the list of "main" folders—just drag it to the "On My Computer" item at the top of the Folder list.)

You can also drag messages between folders. Just drag one from the message list onto the desired folder at the left side of the screen.

This can be a useful trick when applied to a message in your Outbox. If you decide to postpone sending it, drag it into any other folder (like Drafts). Entourage won't send it until you drag it *back* into the Outbox.

Flagging messages

Sometimes you'll receive an email message that prompts you to some sort of action, but you may not have the time (or the fortitude) to face the task at the moment. ("Hi there… it's me, your accountant. Would you mind rounding up your expenses for 1993 through 2001 and sending me a list by email?")

That's why Entourage lets you *flag* a message, summoning one little red flag in the Status column next to a message's name *and* next to the folder that contains it in the Folder list. There are two commands for flagging messages: Flag and Flag for Follow-Up.

- **Flag.** The little red flags are simply visual indicators that you place for your own convenience, meaning whatever you want them to mean. You can hide all the messages that *aren't* flagged by choosing View→Flagged Only (Option-⌘-O).

  To flag a message in this way, select the message (or several messages) and click the Flag button in the toolbar, choose Message→Flag, or Control-click the message's name in the list and choose Flag from the contextual menu.

- **Flag for Follow-Up.** Flag for Follow-Up shows some of the benefits of integrating an email program with a calendar. This command lets you attach a reminder to an email message. That reminder will pop up at a specified later date to remind you to do something about the message. These reminders are actually Entourage Tasks; you can read more about them in Chapter 9.

  To flag a message for follow-up, click the message and then choose Message→Flag for Follow-Up. (Alternatively, choose Flag for Follow Up from the Flag toolbar pop-up button.)

  Now a follow-up window appears, as shown in Figure 8-12; here you can specify when you want the reminder to pop up.

You can clear a flag from a message by selecting the message and then choosing Message→Clear Flag, by using the Flag pop-up button in the toolbar, or by Control-clicking the message in the list and choosing Clear Flag from the contextual menu. Note that clearing a flag does *not* delete any follow-up reminder you may have set up for the message. To do that, you need to delete the task itself (see Chapter 9).

Linking messages

Email messages can be much more valuable when they're linked to other bits of Entourage information, such as other messages, calendar events, notes, and so on—yet another payoff of having an email program with built-in calendar and address book info. For example, you can link a message to a calendar event; thereafter, you'll be able to click the link in the appropriate calendar square to consult the original message (because it contained directions, for example).

Figure 8-12:
Top: When you select a message and choose Flag for Follow-Up from the Flag button's pop-up menu, you get a window in which you can enter the details of when you should be reminded to deal with a message.

Bottom: If you set a reminder, a window will pop up at the appointed time to give you a gentle nudge.

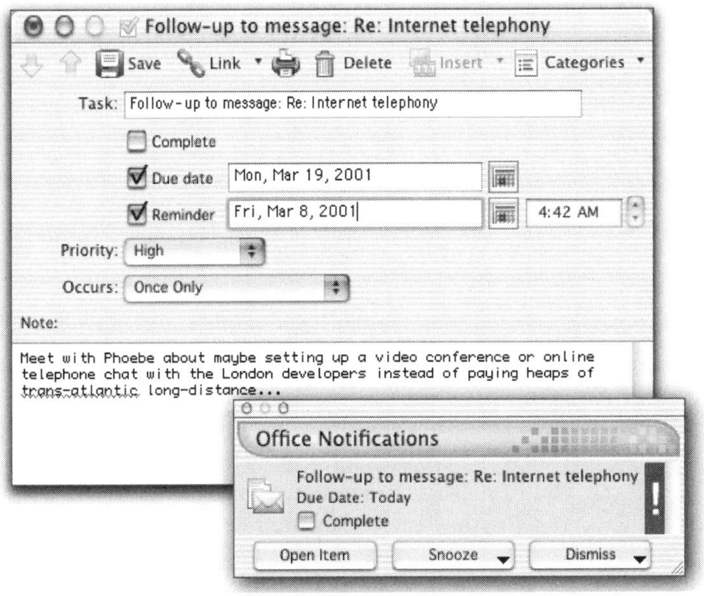

Entourage creates some links for you automatically: for instance, when you reply to a message (or forward or redirect it), Entourage automatically creates a link between the original message and your response. That's how the message history feature works (see Figure 8-12). When flagging a message for follow-up (see above), you create a reminder that links to the original message.

Chapter 11 offers full details on links. In the meantime, here's a summary that's specific to email:

In addition to responding to messages, you can link messages in three ways: by opening the links menu, creating a link to an existing item, and creating a link to a new item.

- **Open Links.** To open the Links window, choose Tools→Open Links, or click the Link button in the toolbar. In the Links window for the selected message, you can create or remove links to existing or new items. You can also open the item on the other end of a link.

- **Link to Existing Item.** You can create a link to one of seven kinds of existing Entourage info-bits: another (email) Message, a Calendar Event, a Task, a Note, a Contact (address book entry), a Group, or even a File on your hard drive. (This last feature can be extremely handy. You might link a message about the date of your Macworld Expo talk to, for example, the Word document that contains your outline.)

  To link to an existing item, choose the kind of link you want to make from the Tools→Link to Existing Item submenu, then select the item to which you want to link. You can also create such a link from the Links window.

- **Link to New Item.** You can also link a message to a Message, Calendar Event, Task, Note, Contact, or Group that you're *about* to create—that is, you can simultaneously create a link *and* the item it's linked to. This is handy when you suddenly get the inspiration to create a link, but you haven't yet created the item on the other end of that link. If a message makes you think, "Ooh, I need to remember to bring a dish to Phoebe's potluck next week!" you can create a link from that message to a new calendar item, then create the event using Entourage's calendar feature.

  To create a link to a new item, choose the kind of link (and new item) that you want to create from the Tools→Link to New Item submenu. Once you've created a link, a small chain-link icon appears in the Links column in the message list.

To remove a link, open the Links window (choose Tools→Open Links, choose Open Links from the Link pop-up button in the toolbar, or click the link column next to the message in question). Once the Links window is open, select the link, and then click the Remove Link button at the top of the window.

Prioritizing messages

You can set one of five priority levels for messages that you've received: Highest, High, Normal, Low, and Lowest. Once you've assigned priorities to your messages, Entourage can sort them so that the most important messages appear at the top.

To set a message's priority, highlight its name in the List pane and then choose from the Message→Priority menu. To sort messages by priority, click the Priority column header (the exclamation-point icon at the left side of the List pane). The first time you click, Entourage sorts your mail from lowest priority to highest; the second time, it lists them from highest to lowest importance.

Note: You're not the only one who can set a message's priority. Sometimes incoming messages have their priority already set—invariably to Highest (for those who think their messages are vital) or Lowest (for those considerate about sending out genuinely unimportant mail). You can change a message's priority once you've received it by choosing from the Message→Priority submenu.

Opening Attachments

Sending little text messages is fine, but it's not much help when somebody wants to send you a photograph, a sound recording, a Word or Excel document, and so on. Fortunately, enclosing such items as *file attachments* is one of the world's most popular email features.

When you receive an email message with an attachment, you'll notice that it often takes much longer than usual to download from the Internet. That's because attached files are typically much larger than email messages. (For more information on attaching files to send to others, see page 357.)

When you've received a message with an attachment, a small paper-clip icon appears in the attachments column at the far left of the List pane.

Unlike, say, America Online, Eudora, or Claris Emailer, Entourage doesn't store downloaded files as normal file icons on your hard drive. Instead, they're stored in the Entourage database—a big, specially encoded file on your hard drive. To extract an attached file from this mass of data, you must first open the message (either in the Preview pane or by opening the message into its own window). Now you'll see a new section in the window labeled Attachments, as shown in Figure 8-13, listing any files that came along with the message.

If you expand the flippy triangle to the left of the word Attachments, you see a list of the files, complete with their icons, plus three buttons: Open, Save, and Remove. At this point, you can proceed in any of several ways:

- Click one of the file icons (or Shift-click to select several, or click one and then press ⌘-A to highlight them all), and then click Save. The Save File dialog box appears, so that you can specify the folder in which you want to save the files on your hard drive.

- Drag a file icon (or several selected ones) clear out of the message window and onto any visible portion of your desktop, as shown in Figure 8-13.

- Double-click the attachment's icon in the message (or highlight it and click Open). If you were sent a document—a photo, Word file, or Excel file, for example—it now opens in the corresponding program (Photoshop, Word, Excel, or whatever).

Warning: After the attachment is open, if you make any changes to it, *use the File→Save As command* to save the file into a folder of your choice. Otherwise, your changes evaporate immediately.

- Highlight an icon (or several) and click Remove. You've just detached, and discarded, the file, reclaiming space on your hard drive.

Tip: It's easy to set up Entourage to save *all* incoming file attachments into a particular folder on your hard drive—or onto your desktop for easy retrieval—saving you the step of manually saving or dragging them. (This arrangement should sound familiar to America Online, Eudora, and Claris Emailer fans.)

The trick is to use the message rules described in the next section. One of them offers an option to save all file attachments (or only those from certain senders) automatically into a folder you specify.

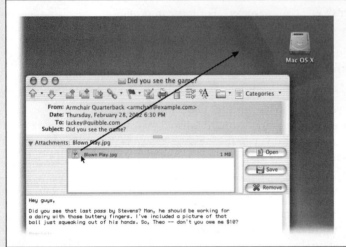

Figure 8-13:
When you receive an attachment via email, you see it represented just above the message's text. You can click the Open, Save, or Remove buttons to open, save, or remove the attachment, respectively. But dragging an attachment's icon onto your desktop takes the file out of the Entourage world and into your standard Macintosh world, where you can file it, trash it, open it, or manipulate it as you would any file.

FREQUENTLY ASKED QUESTION

Viruses by Email

I'm scared of attachments. Won't I get a virus?

Newspaper and television reporters periodically get breathless and wide-eyed about new *viruses* and *worms* (programs that have been deliberately written to gum up a computer), such as the Melissa and I Love You viruses. These little programs often come attached to, or masquerade as, ordinary files or messages sent to you—sometimes inadvertently by people you know.

When you try to open or save an attachment, Entourage warns you of the possibility of viruses and gives you an opportunity to chicken out. (Entourage *doesn't* warn you if you drag the attachment out of the message to your desktop.)

Where viruses are concerned, using a Mac is a good thing; at this writing, there isn't a single virus that runs in Mac OS X. Most viruses affect only Windows users. If someone sends you such a virus by email, it won't affect your Mac, but you could theoretically pass it along to correspondents who use Windows. (And really, aren't they suffering enough already?)

It's a good idea to delete all attachments, without opening them, from people you don't know. If you receive unexpected attachments from people you *do* know, check with them before opening any files, particularly if the message is brief or out of character, or if that person uses Windows.

Then there are *macro viruses,* written with Office's own programming language and embedded into Word and Excel documents. Here again, most such viruses do nothing on a Macintosh—but if you ever open an attached file and encounter a big, stern-sounding dialog box, click the Disable Macros button to play it safe. You've just shut down any macros that were embedded in the file, viruses or not.

When attachments don't open

Several factors may be at work if you're unable to open a file attachment. For starters, your correspondent's email program may have *compressed* or *encoded* the file to make it take less time to send. If you're having trouble getting a file to open, therefore, your first step should be to drag the attachment's icon onto that of StuffIt Expander, the free program that comes on every Macintosh hard drive. (Look in the Applications→Utilities folder.)

StuffIt Expander can gracefully decode and decompress just about any geeky Internet file, including those with file name suffixes like .sit, .cpt, .hqx, .gz, .z, .arc, .uu, and .zip (the Windows equivalent of StuffIt).

Note: Of course, Mac OS X generally hides these extensions, but you can always see a file's hidden extension by highlighting it, choosing File→Show Info, and choosing Name & Extension from the pop-up menu.

If the file still won't open, even after being decompressed, then you may be dealing with a file from a Windows PC. Some you can open; some require more work. Many, for example, open in the Mac OS X program called Preview, which you'll find in your Applications→Utilities folder.

The best clue is the three-letter *file name extension* on its name. For example:

- **.doc, .xls,** and **.ppt.** These extensions identify Microsoft Office documents: .doc is for Microsoft Word, .xls is for Excel, and .ppt is for PowerPoint. You should be able to open these documents with Office X by double-clicking them, but there may be times when you have to drag the document to the icon of the appropriate Office program.

- **.mpg.** You've been sent an MPEG movie. You can generally play these using Quick-Time Player.

- **.wmf.** You've been sent a file encoded in Windows Media Format—a Microsoft media format similar to QuickTime. You can play WMF files using the ironically named Windows Media Player for Macintosh (page 670).

- **.mp3.** MP3 files are compact, great-sounding music files. They're what Apple's iTunes and iPod are all about. If an MP3 file doesn't play when you double-click it, drag it onto the iTunes icon. (Ditto for audio files like .wav and .aif.)

- **.ra, .rm,** or **.ram.** This file is an audio, video, or streaming media item for RealPlayer. Neither QuickTime nor Windows Media Player can play these items. You can get a copy of RealPlayer at *www.real.com*, but until RealPlayer for Mac OS X is available, you'll have to play them using the older RealPlayer version in Mac OS X's Classic environment. (It doesn't always work perfectly, alas.)

- **.bmp.** This is a Windows Bitmap file. You should be able to open this type of graphic using Mac OS X's Preview program, or Word X.

- **.tif** or **.tiff**. TIFF graphics files are common in desktop publishing. (The graphics in this book, for example, are TIFF files.) If you can't open it by double-clicking, the Mac OS X Preview program can show it to you. Word can also open TIFF images.

- **.psd**. A Photoshop document. You can view these in Preview if you don't have Photoshop.

- **.exe**. This extension denotes an *executable* file for Windows—like a program on a Mac. By itself, your Mac can't run Windows programs, just as Windows computers can't run Macintosh programs. You need a program like VirtualPC (*www.connectix.com*) to run Windows programs on a Mac.

- **.bat, .pif, .scr,** or **.com**. These are other kinds of Windows programs, which you can't run on the Mac without VirtualPC. They're also, unfortunately, often associated with email-based worms and viruses. They can't harm a Mac, but delete them anyway, so that you don't pass them along accidentally to a Windows-using friend.

- **.jpg** or **.gif**. You can open these graphics files in Word, PowerPoint, Preview, or Internet Explorer. In fact, you often see these images or photographs right in the body of the email messages that brought them to you.

- **.pdf**. This downloaded item is probably a manual or brochure. It came to you as a portable document format file, better known as an Adobe Acrobat file. Entourage generally shows you a preview of the PDF file right in the email message, but you can also open the document with either Preview or the free Acrobat Reader that comes with every Mac.

- **.html** or **.htm**. A file whose name ends in .html or .htm is a Web page. In the beginning, Web pages hung out only on the Internet. These days, however, you're increasingly likely to find that you've downloaded one to your Mac's hard drive (it may be a software manual for some shareware, for example). To open the Web page, double-click in the attachment area of the message to open it in your Web browser, or drag the document to the visible area of a Web browser window, if you already have one running.

- **.vcf**. You've got yourself an electronic "business card," called a vCard, containing contact information for the sender. See page 407.

- **.rtf**. RTF stands for Rich Text Format, and indicates a formatted word processing document as described on page 64. Word X opens this kind of file with ease.

- **.wps**. This file was created using Microsoft Works, an all-in-one software suite that's something like AppleWorks. Unfortunately, Office X can't read these files: ask your correspondent to export the file as RTF, plain text, or another format if possible. For a greater feeling of self-reliance, buy a file-conversion program like MacLinkPlus (*www.dataviz.com*).

- **.wpd.** This suffix denotes a WordPerfect document. Several years ago, WordPerfect was the dominant word processing program for PCs. (The file name extension *.doc* "belonged" to WordPerfect files, in fact, until Microsoft co-opted it for use with Microsoft Word—one of many actions that caught the Justice Department's attention over the years.) Office X can't open WordPerfect files directly. Here again, ask your correspondent to export the document as RTF, HTML, or plain text.

- **.fp3** and **.fp5.** These are FileMaker Pro databases (*www.filemaker.com*).

If you were sent a file with a three-letter code not listed here, you may well have yourself a Windows file that can be opened only by a Windows program that you don't actually own. You might consider asking your correspondent to resend it in one of the more universal formats described above.

Using Message Rules

Once you know how to create folders, the next step in managing your email is to set up a series of *message rules* (or *filters*) that file, answer, or delete incoming messages *automatically* based on their contents, such as subject, address, or size. Message rules require you to think like the distant relative of a programmer, but the mental effort can reward you many times over; message rules turn Entourage into a surprisingly smart and efficient secretary.

Setting up message rules

Here's how to set one up:

1. Choose Tools→Rules.

   The Rules dialog box appears, as shown in Figure 8-14. As you can see, the tabs here let you set up different rules for each kind of email account (POP, IMAP, Hotmail), plus separate rules for newsgroups (page 363), and outgoing messages.

2. Click the tab you want to work with, and then click New.

   The Edit Rules dialog box appears.

3. Use the top options to specify how Entourage should select messages to process.

   For example, if you'd like Entourage to watch out for messages from a particular person, you would set up the first two pop-up menus to say "From" and "Contains," respectively.

   To flag messages containing *loan, $$$$, XXX, !!!!,* and so on, set the pop-up menus to say "Subject" and "Contains."

   If you click Add Criterion, you can set up another condition for this message rule. For example, you can set up the first criterion to find messages *from* your uncle, and a second that watches for messages whose subject line contains "humor." This way, only jokes passed on from your uncle get placed automatically into, say, the Deleted Items folder.

If you've set up more than one criterion, use the "Execute" pop-up menu to indicate whether the message rule should apply if *all* the conditions are true, or if *any* of them are true.

You can also set up catch-all rules that do their thing *unless* any or all criteria are met. For instance, if you're using an account purely for internal email at your company, you can set up a rule for that account that files away (or deletes) all mail *except* messages from an address containing your company's ".com" name.

4. **Specify *which* words or people you want the message rule to watch out for.**

   After you've used the two pop-up menus, a text box appears. Into this box, type the word, name, or phrase you want Entourage to watch out for—a person's name, or *XXX*, in the previous examples.

5. **In the lower half of the box, specify what you want to happen to messages that match the criteria.**

Mailing List Manager

Entourage's Mailing List Manager feature is, in essence, a specialized set of message rules. Its sole purpose is to handle incoming messages from whatever Internet mailing lists you belong to. The mailing list manager lets you easily create a set of rules to move your email messages to the appropriate folders. It also enables you to store information such as how to unsubscribe from a mailing list.

To bring up the Mailing List Manager window, choose Tools→Mailing List Manager. Click the New button to create a new mailing list rule. In the window that results, you'll be given the opportunity to enter the list's email address, and the option to have the manager move all messages (including ones that you send to the list) to a specific folder. (If a

message from a mailing list was highlighted before you began following the steps in this paragraph, Entourage fills in some of the information automatically.)

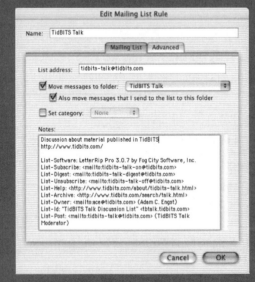

You can also have the manager set a *category* for messages from that list. If you click the Advanced tab in the Edit Mailing List Rule window, you can run each message through a whole slew of options, including "bursting" digests into individual messages, automatically marking messages from the list as "read," or even running an AppleScript script.

Finally, handling a mailing list subscription via the Mailing List Manager has another benefit: the built-in Entourage Junk Mail Filter will never treat messages from that list as spam.

If, in steps 1 and 2, you've told your rule to watch for junk mail containing *$$$$* in the Subject line, here's where you can tell Entourage to delete it or move it into, say, a Spam folder.

With a little imagination, you'll see how the options in this pop-up menu can do absolutely amazing things with your incoming email. Entourage can delete, move, or print messages; forward or redirect them to somebody; automatically save attachments into a Downloads folder that you've set up; or when you receive messages from some important person, play a sound, animate the Entourage icon in the Dock, or display a dialog box.

6. **In the very top box, name your mail rule. Click OK.**

Now the Rules dialog box appears (Figure 8-14, top). Here, you can manage the rules you've created, choose a sequence for them (those at the top get applied first), and apply them to existing messages.

Tip: Entourage applies rules as they appear, from top to bottom, in the Rules window. If a rule doesn't seem to be working properly, it may be that an earlier rule is intercepting and processing the message before the "broken" rule even sees it.

To fix this problem, try moving the rule up or down in the list by selecting it and then clicking the Move Up or Move Down buttons. You can also drag the rule to a higher or lower place in the list, or selectively turn preceding rules on or off.

Figure 8-14:
Top: Mail rules can help screen out junk mail, serve as an email answering machine, or call important messages to your attention. All mail message rules you've created appear on the Mail Rules tab. Select a rule to see what it does, and use the Move Up and Move Down buttons to specify the order in which rules should be run.

Bottom: Double-click a rule to open the Edit Rule dialog box, where you can specify what the rule does.

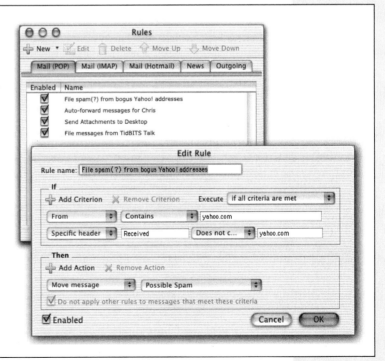

CHAPTER 8: ENTOURAGE EMAIL AND NEWSGROUPS

Sending and
Receiving Mail

Two sneaky message-rule tricks

You can use message rules for many different purposes. But here are two of the best:

- **Create a spam filter.** When spammers send junk mail, your address often doesn't appear in the To or Cc lines: it's as if they Bcc'd you on their message (see page 349). If you don't receive much mail on which you're *legitimately* Bcc'd, just make a rule that messages in which "Any recipient" "Does not contain" your email address, and have Entourage move the message to a "Possible Spam" folder. (You probably want to set these filtered messages aside rather than delete them outright: there are times it's perfectly legitimate to be Bcc'd on a message.)

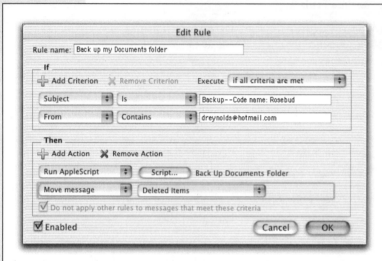

Figure 8-15:
In this example, if Entourage receives an email message with a specified subject and address—from you, for example—it launches an AppleScript script that backs up your Documents folder. You could just as easily trigger a script which updates your Web site, looks up something in a FileMaker database and sends you the results via email, or tells iTunes to play loud music to make sure your cat isn't sleeping on your keyboard—you name it.

GEM IN THE ROUGH

Using the Junk Mail Filter

The Entourage Junk Mail Filter scans your incoming messages for some telltale signs of spam (junk email), and then moves suspect mail to a folder called Junk Mail, thus keeping your Inbox relatively clean of worthless come-ons.

To use the Junk Mail Filter, choose Tools→Junk Mail Filter, and then turn on Enable Junk Mail Filter. You can select the sensitivity of the filter by sliding the sensitivity slider, and you can specify certain *domains* (companies or entities, as indicated by everything after the @ sign in email addresses) to exclude from the filter—such as stuff arriving from your work domain. Messages from addresses in your Address book are never identified as junk, and the Junk

Mail Filter never targets mailing lists you're managing via the Mailing List Manager (see page 346).

Although Microsoft isn't saying exactly what the slider controls, it's clear that it scans for "Bcc" recipients, unusual addressing, certain words in the Subject line and body of the message, and other common characteristics of spam. Even so, the Junk Mail Filter isn't perfect—even at its most sensitive setting, it doesn't catch all spam, and, conversely, sometimes flags legitimate mail as junk. But as spam filters go, it's easy to use and a great start. Give it a try—just be sure to check the Junk Mail folder periodically to rescue any "real" messages that Entourage put there by mistake.

You can then glance through the Possible Spam folder once in a while and see if there's anything there you need to read, then delete any unwanted messages. Make this one of the *last* rules in the Rules window, so that any rules for friends, work, family, and other special cases are handled *before* this rule is applied.

- **The email answering machine.** If you're going to be on vacation, turn on "Is not from a mailing list" and "Is not junk mail" in step 3 above, and then "Reply with message" in step 5. In other words, you can turn Entourage into an email answering machine that automatically sends a canned "I'm away until the 15th" message to everyone who writes you (except mailing lists and junk mailers).

Writing a Message

To create an email message in Entourage, use one of these tactics:

- Choose File→New→Mail Message.

- Press ⌘-N. (If you're using an Entourage function that has nothing to do with email—the Calendar or Tasks, for example—press Option-⌘-N instead.)

- Choose Mail Message from the New pop-up button on the toolbar.

In each case, an empty email message window appears, filled with email composition tools.

Step 1: Addressing the message

The first thing you'll see when you create a new email message is the address pane, a pop-up window with four buttons and three sections (see Figure 8-16). The fields here are labeled To, Cc, and Bcc, each of which has its own purpose:

- **To.** Most of the time, you'll type your correspondent's email address here.

- **Cc.** Cc stands for *carbon copy;* the name is a reference to the days with typewriters, when creating a copy of a document required inserting carbon paper between two sheets of typing paper. In email terms, putting someone's email address in the Cc area means, "No reply required; just thought you'd want to see this." People listed in the Cc field receive a copy of the message, but aren't the primary recipients.

- **Bcc.** A *blind carbon copy* is a secret copy. This feature lets you send a copy of a message to somebody secretly, without any of the other recipients knowing that you did so. The names in the To and Cc fields appear at the top of the message for all recipients to see, but nobody can see the names you type into the Bcc box.

  You can use the Bcc field to quietly signal a third party that a message has been sent. For example, if you send your co-worker a message that says, "Chris, it bothers me that you've been cheating the customers," you could Bcc your boss or supervisor to clue her in without getting into trouble with Chris.

  The Bcc box is useful in other ways, too. Many people send email messages (containing jokes, for example) to a long list of recipients. You, the recipient, have to scroll through a very long list of names in the To or Cc field.

But if the sender used the Bcc field to hold all the recipients' email addresses, you, the recipient, won't see any of those names at the top of the email. (Unfortunately, spammers often do something similar, so that you don't see the long list of other people who received the same junk.)

Tip: After addressing a message, you can drag the addresses back and forth among these three blanks: from the To box into the Cc line, for example.

If you want to send a message to more than one person, click the Add button and type in a second (or third, or fourth) email address, or just click in an empty area of an addressing box and start typing. As in most dialog boxes, you can jump from blank to blank in this window by pressing the Tab key (to proceed from the To field to the Cc field, for example).

You don't have to remember and type out all those email addresses, either. As you type, Entourage compares what you're typing with the names in your Address Book. If it finds a match—that is, if you've typed *zar* and your Address Book contains the name *Ed Zarynski,* for example, Entourage sprouts a list of that and any other matches. Entourage also remembers the last 150 addresses you've used that *aren't* in your address book, which can be handy when you think of something you'd like to add to a recent exchange. (You can turn this feature off in the Compose tab in Entourage→Mail & News Preferences if it bothers you.)

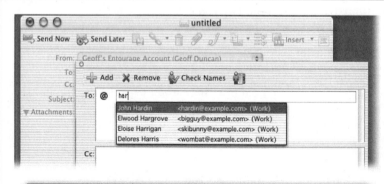

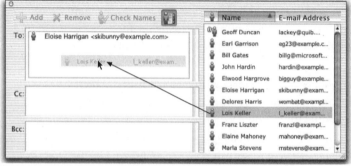

Figure 8-16:
Top: As you type an address, a pop-up menu of matching names from your Address Book appears. Click the one you want, or press the down arrow key to highlight it and then press Enter or Return.

Bottom: To use the Address Book pane, find the recipient in the list (either by scrolling or by typing the first few letters of the name). Then add this person's name to the To list by double-clicking the name (or by dragging it into the address area). You can repeat this process to add other names.

You can choose from this list of proposed addressees either by clicking a name, or by pressing the down arrow key to highlight a name, and then pressing Enter to select it. If none of Entourage's guesses are correct, just keep typing; Entourage quietly withdraws its suggestions.

Alternatively, you can access your address book just by clicking the Address Book button just above the To field (see Figure 8-16).

Tip: The tiny icon that appears in front of each email address that you've entered indicates Entourage's understanding of the address. If you see a tiny human figure, you've input an address that's in the Address Book; if you see an @ symbol, you've typed an address that's not in your Address Book. (Of course, you can always add one of these @ addresses *to* your Address Book just by Control-clicking it and choosing Add to Address Book from the contextual menu.)

A green question mark indicates Entourage doesn't understand the address, probably because it isn't a correctly formed email address and no matching names appear in your Address Book.

POWER USERS' CLINIC

Using Directory Services

You're all set to send someone an email message, when it hits you: You don't know his address.

Fortunately, several Web services (such as Bigfoot, four11, Infospace, WhoWhere, and Yahoo People Search) serve as "email phone books," and Entourage comes equipped to search Bigfoot and four11 automatically.

To capitalize on this feature, choose Tools→ Directory Services to bring up the Directory Services window, choose one of the listed Web sites (servers), enter a name or email address, and then click the Find button. If you're lucky, the person's information appears in the list below. More likely, you'll get either no results, or a huge list of possible matches. Unfortunately, the accuracy of Internet-wide directories is limited, and many people avoid being listed in them to prevent their

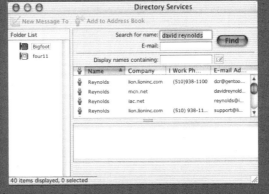

information from being "harvested" by spammers.

This feature is of far more value if you work in a company that provides its *own* email directory (via an electronic phonebook known as an *LDAP server*). In that event, choose Tools→Accounts, click the Directory Service tab, and then click the New button in the window's toolbar. The Account Setup assistant now walks you through a two-step process of entering your server's information. (Get it from your network administrator.)

While you're in the Edit Account window, you can choose which LDAP account you'd like to be your main directory by selecting the account's name and then clicking the Make Default button in the toolbar. Entourage displays your default service in bold.

Across the top of the address window are a few handy buttons. **Add** opens up a new empty row in the current addressing field, in which you can specify an additional address. The **Remove** button removes a selected recipient's row. **Check Names** is handy if you don't know somebody's email address; after typing her *name* into the Address box, click this button to consult an Internet email directory (see page 351) in hopes of turning up the email address.

Tip: You can use the Tab key to move between address fields, subject line, and the message's body text.

If you have more than one account set up in Entourage, a From pop-up menu appears above the message's addressees. Use it to choose which account you want to use from that pop-up menu.

Step 2: The Subject line

Some people, especially in the business world, get bombarded with email. That's why it's courteous to put some thought into the Subject line (use "Change in plans for next week" instead of "Hi," for example). Press the Tab key to make your cursor jump into the large message-body area. Don't make your subject too long: remember most people will see it in a list with other information like your name and the date and time you sent the message, and the subject may get compressed or truncated. If you try to send a message without a subject, Entourage will warn you this isn't a good idea, but it's not a fatal one either. You can go ahead and send it. Entourage will automatically insert "<no subject>" as a subject line.

Step 3: Composing the body

After you've addressed your message and given it a subject, it's time to fill in the message's body text. To do this, just click (or Tab into) the message area and start typing. You can use all the standard editing techniques, including selection, drag-and-drop, and the Cut, Copy, and Paste commands, to rearrange the text as you write it.

POWER USERS' CLINIC

Links in Email

The Insert Hyperlink button (under the Insert menu button on the toolbar) provides an easy way to pop Web-style links into your email. You might use it to create, for example, an email message that says, "Hey Bob! Here's the Web site I told you about: *<http://www.dumbbot.com/>*."

This pop-up menu offers you three lists of insertable links, one each culled from Internet Explorer's currently open page, its Favorites file, and its History file. When your lucky recipient opens the message, she'll be able to visit the corresponding Web page just by clicking the link, right there in the message.

Sometimes, however, you'll want to insert a link to a Web page that's *not* in your Explorer History, Favorites, or browser window. Unfortunately, to do that, you need to type out the URL yourself (or use copy and paste). Formatting your URL with those braces ("<" and ">") and the "http://" prefix ensures that your link will work in the widest range of email programs.

As you type, Entourage does something rather wonderful (or alarming, depending on your point of view): it checks your spelling as you go, using a red squiggly underline to mark questionable spelling. To check for possible alternative spellings for a suspect word, Control-click the red-squiggled word; a list of suggestions appears in a contextual menu. Choose the word you really intended, or choose Add to add the word to the Office X dictionary.

If you want to spell-check a message all at once, choose Tools→Spelling (or press Option-⌘-L) after composing it. (To turn off automatic spell checking, choose Entourage→General Preferences, click the Spelling tab, and then turn off "Check spelling as you type.")

Tip: You can use the same keyboard shortcuts in Entourage that you use in Word (such as ⌘-right arrow to move the cursor one word to the right)—a great timesaver. Just choose Entourage→General Preferences, click the General tab, and make sure that "Use Microsoft Office keyboard shortcuts for editing text" is turned on.

That same preference tab lets you make Entourage resemble Word in other ways, too. It lets you turn on automatic whole-word selection, "smart cut and paste" (spaces are automatically added or removed as necessary when you insert or delete text), and a Font menu that shows fonts in their own typefaces. Similarly, the Spelling tab in the General Preferences dialog box offers the same control over spell-checking options that Word does.

All of this should sound familiar; it's precisely the same basic mechanism that Word X employs when it looks for spelling mistakes on the fly, as described on page 83.

Tip: If you're composing a long email message, or it's one you don't want to send until later, click the Save as Draft button (⌘-S) or choose File→Save to save the message in your Drafts folder. To reopen a saved draft, click the Drafts folder in the Folder list, and then open the draft that you want to work on from the list on the right.

Step 4: Choosing a format (HTML or plain text)

When it comes to formatting a message's text, you have two choices: *plain text* or *HTML* (hypertext markup language).

Plain text means that you can't format your text with bold type, color, specified font sizes, and so on. HTML, on the other hand, lets you use formatting commands such as font sizes and bold text.

But there's a catch; some email programs can't read HTML-formatted email, and email programs that *can* handle HTML don't always handle it the same way. An HTML message that looks fine for you may be incomprehensible for someone using another email program. HTML messages can also be much larger (and therefore slower to download) than plain-text messages, especially if you include pictures, sounds, or other multimedia elements.

So which should you choose? Plain text lends a more professional, old-hand feeling to your messages—but, more importantly, it's the most compatible. Whether your recipient uses a high-end workstation, a Web browser, a cell phone, or a 20-year-old terminal in a dusty university basement, a plain-text message almost *always* gets through intact. (There are some exceptions: accented characters and language encodings may complicate the issue.)

HTML-formatted messages, on the other hand, may not arrive intact. Your recipient may see a plain-text version of the message, which Entourage includes as a courtesy, but some email programs can't even display *that* neatly. Furthermore, since a lot of junk mail is formatted with HTML, using HTML formatting may route your message into some people's Junk Mail folders.

In general, you're better off using plain text for most of your messages, and sending HTML only when you're sure your recipients can see it.

To specify which format Entourage uses for all outgoing messages (plain text or HTML), choose Entourage→Mail & News, click the Compose tab, and select a format from the "Mail format" pop-up menu.

You can also change formats on a message-by-message basis. For example, if you generally like to send plain-text messages, you can switch one particular message into HTML mode by clicking the Use HTML button to the left and just above the body text area (see Figure 8-17), or choose Format→HTML. Either action activates the HTML toolbar, which you can use to add pizzazz to your messages. This toolbar is broken up into six sections:

- **Fonts.** The two controls in this section let you choose a font for your email, and one of five type sizes: Largest, Large, Medium, Small, or Smallest.

Note: If your message's recipient doesn't have the font you specify in this toolbar section, her email program substitutes some other font. To avoid such problems, stick to common fonts like Arial, Courier, Times New Roman, or Verdana.

- **Styles.** Just as you'd expect in a word processor, you can choose Bold, Italic, Underline, or Teletype (which puts the selected text into a fixed-width font) styles for your messages.

- **Alignment.** Lets you choose left, center, or right paragraph alignment for your text.

- **Bullets and Indents.** Lets you put the selected text in a bulleted or numbered list. It also lets you set the indent level of the selected text for some good organizational formatting.

- **Color.** These two controls let you choose a text color and a background color for your email messages. You can choose from one of 16 prefab colors, or you can mix your own (see page 651).

- **Rules.** There's only one button here, the Horizontal Line button, which puts a horizontal rule (in other words, a line) at the insertion point.

Remember: less is more. If you go hog-wild formatting your email, you may make the message hard to read, especially for people using email programs that interpret the HTML codes differently than Entourage does.

Tip: All of the HTML toolbar's commands are also accessible in the Format menu.

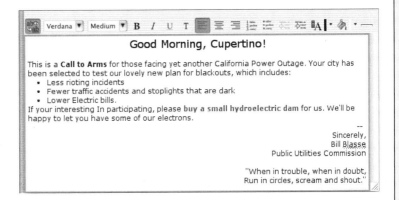

Figure 8-17:
HTML-based email lets you exercise some control over the layout of your email messages, including font, colors, and text alignment. The HTML toolbar, shown just above the message body, is similar to what you might find in a word processing program. With it, you can turn plain-Jane email into an HTML-formatted wonderland.

You can also insert pictures, sounds, or movies into HTML email messages. Type your message, place the insertion point where you'd like the item to appear, and then choose the appropriate command from the Insert pop-up button on your message's toolbar. Entourage asks you to locate and double-click the file you want to insert.

Tip: You can also drag the icons of graphics and movies right into the window of an outgoing HTML email message, where they appear at the insertion point. For sounds and background graphics, on the other hand, you must use the Insert button on the toolbar.

Note that Entourage automatically converts TIFF and PICT images into JPEG format when you add them to HTML messages. If you need your recipient to receive these files unaltered, send them as standard file attachments instead of inserting them or dragging them into the window.

Once you've inserted a media item into a message, you can't move it around except by inserting Returns and spaces in front of it. To delete a picture, sound, or movie, backspace over it, or select it and then press the Delete key. (There's no way to remove a background image once you've inserted it.)

Tip: Just as file attachments can make an email message enormous, images, sounds, and movies can mean that your message will be measured in megabytes. That's fine if your recipients all have fast connections like cable modems. But if one of them is trying to check email on the road using a modem, your ultra-cool inline images, movies, and sounds will become a giant headache.

Step 5: Adding a signature

Signatures (or "sigs") are bits of text that get stamped at the bottom of your email or newsgroup messages. Signatures began as a way to provide contact information without having to type it out in every message. But as online culture evolved, signatures became personal statements. A signature may contain a name, a postal or email address, a memorable quote, or even art composed of typed characters.

To create a signature, choose Tools→Signatures, which brings up the Signatures window. In it, you'll see something called the Standard signature. You can edit this signature by double-clicking it, or you can create any number of new signatures by clicking the New button. Either way, you get an editing window in which you can type your new signature.

Your signature can be either plain text or HTML-based, as described in the previous section, except that there's no Insert button for multimedia or hyperlinks.

Note: If you format your signature with HTML, Entourage automatically converts it to plain text when you write a plain-text message. Be sure your signature looks good in either format!

Once you've created one or more signatures, you can tack them onto your outgoing mail either always or on a message-by-message basis:

WORKAROUND WORKSHOP

The Lowdown on "Complex" Markup

If you've created Web pages using the HTML language, you're probably scratching your head as you read about Entourage HTML email features. Where are tables? Where are forms? Where is JavaScript? Heck, how do you even *embed a link* into text instead of spelling it out as an ugly URL?

The short answer is : no. Entourage's HTML features are meant to enhance typical email communication, not to produce sophisticated Web pages.

If you must send complicated HTML via email, you can create it in another program (like Adobe GoLive, Bare Bones Software's BBEdit, or even Apple's TextEdit) and then use AppleScript to embed it in an outgoing Entourage email message. There's a working example of such a script at *www.applescriptcentral.com.* (Unfortunately, simply pasting HTML from another program into an Entourage message doesn't work.)

Since you're probably not going to all this trouble for a casual message, be sure to send it to yourself as a test (and maybe also to some friends who use a variety of email programs) before setting your message loose on the world. You'll find that creating HTML that works in email programs is a different art from creating HTML for a Web site.

- **Always append a signature.** Choose Tools→Accounts. In the Accounts window, double-click the account in question. (You can have a different standard signature for each account.)

  In the resulting window, click the Options tab to reveal a pop-up menu of signatures. Select the signature that you'd like to have at the bottom of every email message created using that account. (You can always override this choice on a message-by-message basis.)

Tip: If you turn on the Random checkbox next to certain signatures, Entourage will randomly select one of these gems to grace the bottom of every email message that you send. This is the way to rotate your pithy quotes from, say, Monty Python without seeming repetitive to your correspondents.

- **Message by message.** After writing your message, choose the signature you want from the Signature pop-up button (the little pen) in your message's toolbar. Entourage pastes the signature at the location of your insertion point.

Step 6: Add any file attachments

You read about *receiving* attachments earlier in this chapter; *sending* them sometimes involves a little extra brainwork.

To attach a file or files to an outgoing email message, Microsoft, in its usual fashion, offers several different methods:

UP TO SPEED

Sig and Ye Shall Find!

As cool as signatures are, don't go overboard. Few things are more annoying than downloading a two-line message followed by a full-screen signature. On mailing lists and newsgroups, a big signature is likely to get you drummed out of town. When making signatures, follow these guidelines:

- Keep signatures to four lines of text or less, focusing on essential information.

- Consider including a hyperlink to a Web page where people can find out more about who you are and what you do.

- Avoid potentially offensive material or blatantly commercial come-ons (although a brief pointer

is OK, particularly if it's to something you're personally involved with).

- Protect your privacy: consider *not* including email addresses, phone numbers, postal addresses, and other personal data, especially when sending messages to public forums like mailing lists and newsgroups. There's no telling where that information may go or who may get their hands on it. (See "Canning Spam" on page 360.)

- If you really like flamboyant signatures for your email to your regular correspondents, great! But also create a simple, bare-bones sig just for mailing lists, newsgroups, and people outside your circle of friends.

- **Drag-and-drop.** If you can see the appropriate Finder window or item on the desktop behind the Entourage window, you can drag file or folder icons directly off the desktop and anywhere into the outgoing email message window, or to Entourage's icon on the Dock.

Tip: If you drag the *alias* of a file or folder, Entourage is considerate enough to ask you whether you mean to send the alias file itself (which will probably be worthless to your correspondent) or the file that opens when you double-click the alias.

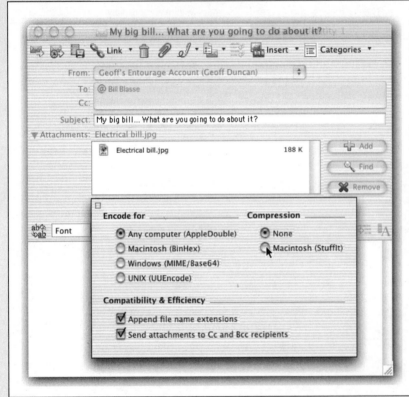

Figure 8-18:
A file's icon appears in the Attachments section of the message window; its encoding options appear below it. By clicking a couple of radio buttons and checkboxes, you can be sure that your recipients can open your attachments each and every time. The "Append file name extensions" checkbox is an incredibly valuable option; if you're sending Office files to a Windows computer and failed to add .doc, .xls, or .ppt to the end of their names, Entourage can do it for you at this stage.

- **Add button.** Click the Add Attachments button in the message's toolbar, or click the Add button in the Attachments section of the outgoing email window. Either way, the Open File dialog box appears. Navigate to, and highlight, the file or folder you want to send, and then click Choose.

- **Use a menu.** Choose Message→Add Attachments (or press ⌘-E) to do the same thing.

Once you've attached files, their names appear in the message's Attachments section, seen in Figure 8-18.

Tip: If you want to attach a certain file but you don't know where it is on your hard drive, click the Find button in the Attachments section of the message. Entourage, after first asking your permission, hands you off to Sherlock, the Mac's file-finding program. Use Sherlock to scour your hard drive for the file you want to attach. You can drag the found files out of Sherlock's "found files" list directly into your Entourage message window.

Attaching files is the easy part; knowing how to *encode* those files can be tricky. Not all computers (including the Internet computers that transmit messages) can understand Macintosh files. Furthermore, some email servers still mangle anything that *isn't* a plain-text message. Encoding your attachments is the solution to both problems.

Unfortunately, different computers recognize different file-encoding schemes. If this encoding is done improperly, the file turns into gibberish and can't be opened on the other end.

To make matters even more complicated, files can also be *compressed* (as StuffIt or Zip archives, for example) to make them smaller and reduce the amount of time it takes to send and receive them.

Fortunately, Entourage uses an encoding scheme called *AppleDouble,* which both Macs and Windows PCs can reconstitute. And it compresses your files only if you attach an entire folder (not individual files). It uses StuffIt compression in that case, which other Macs can decompress with no trouble.

There may be times, however, when you want to change these options. For example, you may want to turn on the StuffIt compression for a single large file. Or you may have trouble sending files to someone using the factory settings, so you want to try different settings.

To change encoding and compression options, click the gray encoding-summary bar just below the Attachments window (see Figure 8-18). A little pop-up window appears, where you can change both encoding and compression options:

- **Any computer (AppleDouble).** This encoding scheme flattens a Mac file into something that other kinds of computers can read, including mail servers and Windows machines.

- **Macintosh (BinHex).** This encoding method is for Mac-to-Mac transfers only. Use it only when you've tried sending a file to another Mac user using the AppleDouble setting and had no luck.

- **Windows (MIME/Base64).** This encoding method is for sending files to Windows and some Unix computers. Again, use it only when you've had no luck using AppleDouble.

- **Unix (UUEncode).** UUEncode (which stands for Unix-to-Unix Encode) is the best thing for sending to a Unix or Linux user. (It's also useful when you don't know *what* email program or operating system your recipient is using and

AppleDouble doesn't work; UUEncode has been around so long that almost any email program can open UUEncoded messages.)

- **Compression: None/Macintosh (StuffIt).** As noted above, Entourage automatically compresses your attachments when they're included in a *folder*. Only Macintosh email programs will be able to open them and turn them back into a folder on the other end; Windows users can do it, but only if they're willing to download and install the free Expander for Windows program from *www.aladdinsys.com*.

Tip: When sending a file to a Windows PC, Entourage has the potential to end your "they can't open my files" headaches forever. Just remember to follow three steps in the Encoding window shown in Figure 8-18: Use no compression; use AppleDouble encoding; and turn on the "Append file name extensions" checkbox. Of course, you still have to send your Windows-using friend a file his system can actually *open*—for instance, most Windows machines can't open AppleWorks documents, no matter what encoding you use.

FREQUENTLY ASKED QUESTION

Canning Spam

Help! I'm awash in junk email! How do I get out of this mess?

Spam is a much-hated form of advertising that involves sending unsolicited email messages to thousands of people. While there's no instant cure for spam, you can take certain steps to protect yourself from it.

1. Don't publicize your email address on the Internet—don't put it on your Web page or in your signatures, and don't allow it to be listed in any public place. Spammers have automated software robots called *trawlers* that scour every public Internet message and Web page, automatically collecting email addresses they find, and then sending spam to those addresses or selling them to other spammers.

2. Get a second email address you can use for Web sites, software registration, and mailing lists. At least if this address "leaks" to spammers, your primary address hasn't been compromised.

3. When filling out forms or registering products online, always look for checkboxes requesting

permission for the company to send you email or share your email address with its "partners." Just say no. If the company doesn't explicitly post its privacy policy on the Web site, assume *no* information you provide will be kept private.

4. Use the Entourage Junk Mail Filter (page 348).

5. Create *message rules* to filter out messages containing words and phrases most often found in spam (such as *casino, search engine placement, herbal viagra,* and so forth. (You'll find instructions in this chapter.)

6. Consider using a mail filtering service like SpamCop (*www.spamcop.net*), or asking your ISP if they can use *DNS blacklists* to prevent known spam sites from sending you junk. (Your ISP may be doing this already.)

7. If you really have a spam problem, get a new email address. Give it to people you trust. Use the old address only for junk mail, and check it for messages only infrequently.

To remove an attachment, select its icon in the expanded Attachments window (Figure 8-18) and press the Delete key (or click Remove). (*Dragging* an attachment out of the Attachments window doesn't remove it from the message. Instead, it makes a copy of the file where you drag it—unless you drag it to the Trash can in the Dock.) You can also remove all attachments in one fell swoop by choosing Message→Remove All Attachments.

Step 7: Send your email on its way

Once your message is put together properly, you can send it in any of several ways:

- Click the Send Now button in the message's toolbar.

- Choose Message→Send Message Now.

- Press ⌘-K.

- If you want to wait until the next time Entourage is connected before sending the message, choose Message→Send Message Later, press Shift-⌘-K, or click the Send Later button in the message's toolbar.

Once the message has been sent, it disappears from your Outbox, but a copy appears in the Sent Items folder for your reference. (If you're a person of steely nerve and impeccable memory, you can turn off this feature; choose Entourage→Mail & News Preferences, click the Compose tab, and turn off "Save copies of sent messages in the Sent Items folder.")

Email Netiquette

Different companies, organizations, and groups have different email cultures, so email norms might vary from place to place. But over the years, general rules of Internet etiquette—that is, netiquette—have evolved. Knowing a little netiquette not only saves you embarrassment in public forums like mailing lists, but also makes your messages more understandable.

Most of these items apply to newsgroup postings as well as ordinary email, but a few points of netiquette apply strictly to newsgroups:

- **Use your real name.** Entourage lets you enter anything you like for your name when you set up an account (see page 311). But using your real name gives you more credibility and lets your friends and correspondents more easily manage mail from you.

Note: An exception to this rule would be a newsgroup or mailing list where the privacy of participants is very important, such as online support groups. For these cases, consider using another email address managed via a separate Entourage account. The account can use whatever pseudonym (and signature) you like. (See page 316 for information on setting up multiple accounts.)

- **Write clearly.** Since email is a written medium, good writing can make you look *really* good. You don't have to be Shakespeare or even sound like a professional author. But do make sure your message includes all information your correspondent may need, check your grammar, and use Entourage's spelling checker. Also, make allowances for people whose writing seems awkward or difficult to understand: English may be the most common language on the Internet, but it's not the primary language for millions of Internet users.

- **Be civil.** Some people write things in email that they would never *dare* say to your face. No matter how offended you might be, responding in kind just makes things worse. The best response to rude email is no response at all.

- **Quote sparingly.** When quoting another message, only quote enough material so your correspondent knows what you're talking about. Quoting the entire message makes it harder for your correspondent to figure out what you're saying. You can also put your responses in between bits of quoted text, which makes it even clearer exactly what you're replying to.

- **Use blank lines.** Insert blank lines between paragraphs and quoted material in your message.

- **Put angle brackets around URLs.** If you put a Web address (URL) in a message, surrounding it with angle brackets <like this> turns it into a live, double-clickable link in a wide range of email programs.

- **Avoid all caps.** Capital letters are difficult to read on computer screens and MAKE YOU LOOK LIKE YOU'RE SHOUTING.

- **Write specific subjects.** Remember that the subject of a message is one of the few things (besides your name) your correspondents will see in a typical mailbox listing. Make your messages easy to find later by using specific subjects. "Lunch at Little John's Monday at 12:30?" is a better subject line than simply "Psst! You hungry?"

Mailing List Etiquette

The following points are particularly relevant to mailing lists:

- **Don't use HTML formatting.** There's bound to be someone—or a lot of someones—on a mailing list who can't handle, or can't abide, HTML-formatted messages. Furthermore, many mailing lists are available as *digests* where all the messages each day are sent as one large message late at night, rather than as individual messages throughout the day. HTML-formatted messages often don't come across in digests at all.

- **Don't send file attachments.** It's almost always wrong to send a file attachment to a mailing list, even if it's small. If you *must* make a file available to a mailing list, put it up on a Web or FTP site for interested members to download (Apple's iTools service is perfect for this sort of thing). Then all you have to do is put a URL in your message.

- **Keep your sig short!** Your signature should have four lines of text or less. (See page 361.)

- **Stay on topic.** Most mailing lists are devoted to a particular subject, and your messages should be reasonably "on topic" for that list. It wouldn't be appropriate to discuss sports cars on a mailing list dedicated to acoustic guitars, or ask questions about Apple's latest Mac models on a mailing list devoted to 1970's television sitcoms. On the other hand, there's probably an appropriate mailing list for almost anything you want to talk about!

- **Keep private conversations off lists.** There are times it's more appropriate to reply to a particular list member privately rather than the entire list. In those cases, just write a private email message to the person.

- **Trim the quoting down to the essential.** When you send a reply to somebody's posting, trim out all of the >quoted >portion except the part in question. Nobody needs to read the entire treatise again.

Finally, as tempting as it may be to send out flurries of advertising about your products or business using the Internet, it's a bad idea. Spam is not only illegal in many jurisdictions (meaning you can be sued), it's guaranteed to get your Internet account shut down without notice. It's fine to keep in contact with current customers via email if they've given you permission, but quite another to use the Internet as a means to harass others.

Newsgroups

Newsgroups don't necessarily contain news; in fact, they're Internet bulletin boards collectively referred to as *Usenet*. There are well over 60,000 newsgroups on every conceivable topic: pop culture, computers, politics, and every other special (and *very* special) interest. Well over 100 of them are just about the Macintosh. Fortunately, in addition to being an email and calendar program, Entourage is also a *newsreader*. You can use Entourage to read and reply to newsgroup messages almost exactly as though they were email messages.

UP TO SPEED

Newsgroups Explained

Newsgroups (also known as *Usenet*) started out as a way for people to have discussions via a bulletin-board-like system, in which a message gets posted for all to see, and anyone can reply to that posted message. These public discussions are divided into categories called *newsgroups,* which cover the gamut from miscellaneous photographic techniques to naval aviation.

These days, newsgroups have a certain reputation as a place to exchange questionable pictures, pirated software, and MP3 files with doubtful copyright pedigrees. Even so, there are tens of thousands of interesting, informative discus-

sions going on, and newsgroups are great places to get help with troubleshooting, exchange recipes, or just see what's on the minds of your fellow Internet users.

Although using newsgroups is like using email in Entourage, it's important to remember that anything you see or post in a newsgroup is public, and will probably remain so for years to come. (Sites like Google maintain searchable newsgroup archives going back to the mid-1980s, complete with email addresses!) Think before you post, especially if you have aspirations to run for Congress someday.

In fact, Entourage lets you use multiple *news servers* (bulletin-board distribution computers), subscribe to individual newsgroups, filter messages in your newsgroups using Rules, and post and read messages (complete with attachments, if needed). See Figure 8-19.

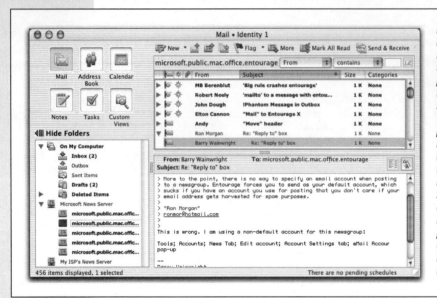

Figure 8-19:
If you've been using Entourage for email, the newsgroup portion should look familiar. It uses the same three-pane view: the Folder pane lists your newsgroups, the top-right pane lists the names of messages in a selected newsgroup, and at the bottom right, the Preview pane shows the actual text of the highlighted message.

Setting Up an Account

Setting up a new news account is similar to setting up a new email account; the adventure begins by contacting your Internet service provider and finding out its *news server address*. Depending on how your ISP runs its news service, you may also need your user name and password.

Next, choose Tools→Accounts. Choose News from the New pop-up button in the resulting Accounts window.

You can either enter news server information manually, or click the Assist Me button to have the Account Setup Assistant step you through the process of creating a news account like this:

1. **With the Account Setup Assistant open, select the email account you want to use and enter your organization.**

   Entourage needs an *email* address because every newsgroup posting has an email address associated with it.

Tip: As noted earlier, spammers use software robots to trawl newsgroup postings for "fresh" email addresses. Any email address you enter here will be targeted by junk mail.

The best way to avoid this torrent is to create a special account in Entourage just for newsgroups, making sure the email address used for that account is undeliverable. If you want your audience to be able to contact you privately for some reason, you *can* use your real email address, but insert something like NOSPAM, IHATESPAM, or REMOVETHIS somewhere into it to confuse the junk-mail address-hunting robots. That tactic isn't foolproof, but it's better than nothing.

Or use the domain *mouse-potato.com* in your bogus address–*chris@mouse-potato.com*, for example. The mouse-potato.com domain not only is unreachable, but has a delicious payoff: spammers trying to send mail to such addresses get their *own* machines pummeled with spam mail!

2. **Click the right arrow. Enter your news server address, and indicate whether or not that server requires you to log on with name and password.**

   In this step, you'll need to enter the address of your news server. Sometimes you get newsgroup access (and the necessary settings) from your ISP. If your ISP doesn't provide newsgroup access, you'll have to subscribe to a news service. They run about $10 a month, and they're generally more reliable than news servers run by ISPs. Visit *www.easynews.com, www.supernews.com,* or *www.newsguy.com* for a directory of such services.

   If you're directed to do so by your ISP, turn on Authentication and enter your user name and password.

3. **Click the right arrow. Enter your account ID and password.**

   If you told Entourage that you needed to log into your news server, you'll have to provide the details in this step. The password is optional—if you want Entourage to save it, turn on "Save password in my Mac OS keychain." If you don't enter it here, you'll have to type it every time you connect to your news server.

4. **Click the right arrow. Give your account a name.**

   You can give it any name you want, such as *Earthlink Newsgroups.*

5. **Click Finish.**

   An icon for your new account shows up in the Folder list.

Note: If you prefer to enter all of the news server particulars in one step, rather than using the multiscreen assistant, you can skip the assistant entirely, or bail out of it at any time by clicking the "Configure account manually" button in the lower part of the assistant window.

Download the List of Newsgroups

When you first click a news server icon, Entourage asks you if you want to download a list of newsgroups. Click Yes.

Entourage goes to work downloading the list, which can be quite long—tens of thousands of entries, in many cases—and takes several minutes if you connect to the Internet with a dial-up modem. Once that's done, though, you don't have to do it again. You *should* occasionally update the list, however, by selecting the server's icon in the Folder list and clicking the Update List button (or choosing View→Get New Newsgroups). New newsgroups appear on a more-or-less constant basis, and unused newsgroups sometimes even disappear.

The number (and nature) of newsgroups available on a particular server is up to its operators. For example, Entourage comes preconfigured to connect to the Microsoft News Server. Instead of carrying tens of thousands of newsgroups on every conceivable topic, the Microsoft News Server carries about 2,000 newsgroups, all related—surprise!—to Microsoft products. (Incidentally, these aren't bad places to learn about Office X programs: check out the newsgroup called *microsoft.public.mac.office.entourage*.)

Even the big ISPs rarely carry *every* available Usenet group. Furthermore, they may not keep individual newsgroup postings available for very long: the storage required to do so is enormous, and the number of people who actually *want* to read many of these newsgroups can be very small. (Honestly, do you think you'll be a regular contributor to *alt.alien.vampire.flonk.flonk.flonk*?)

Figure 8-20:
Top: After you create a newsgroup account, Entourage offers to fetch the list of every newsgroup on the server.

Bottom: Enter the text you want to look for in the newsgroup's title (such as guitar). If you turn up an appealing-sounding topic in the gigantic list beneath, select the group and click the Subscribe button in the Entourage toolbar to subscribe to it, so that Entourage will download the latest messages on that topic each time you connect.

Furthermore, many ISPs refuse to carry newsgroups that carry stolen software, music, video, and other materials. In fact, your ISP may simply deny access to the *alt.* hierarchy, which is where the most free-wheeling (and most dubious) activities take place. That's not to say *alt.** newsgroups are fundamentally bad, but if there's one you want to read (say, *alt.guitar.beginner*), you might have to ask your ISP to specifically enable it.

Caution: Like certain Web sites, plenty of newsgroups are not appropriate for children. Similarly, because newsgroups are public, spammers tend to litter newsgroups with their cheesy schemes and material many would find offensive. No one regulates newsgroups, and no one has complete control over what can and cannot be posted there.

Finding Newsgroups and Messages

If you're looking for a particular topic—guitars, for example—you can view a list of those discussions by typing in a phrase into the "Display groups containing" field at the top of the window. Entourage hides any newsgroups that *don't* match that text (see Figure 8-20).

Try different criteria—typing in *mac* will show you many Macintosh-related newsgroups, but will also turn up newsgroups devoted to Fleetwood Mac, macho trucks, and GNU emacs. Typing in *garden* shows a number of newsgroups related to gardening, but may also show newsgroups devoted to the band Soundgarden.

Reading Messages

Once Entourage has downloaded a list of available newsgroups, it's up to you to sift through them and select the discussions you want to keep up with.

Fortunately, Entourage makes it easy to follow the raging Internet discussions with a feature called *subscriptions*. To subscribe to a newsgroup, select its name in the list, and then click the Subscribe button in the toolbar. An icon for that newsgroup now appears under the server's name in the Folder list, where it will act like a nested folder.

The next time you connect to the Internet, Entourage downloads all of the messages in the discussions to which you've subscribed. (There may be just a few messages, or several hundred. They may go back only a few days or a couple of weeks, depending on how much "traffic" there is in each discussion and how long your news server keeps messages available.)

Tip: Entourage keeps copies of newsgroup messages in your Entourage database. Over time, you'll realize that most newsgroup messages are ephemeral things you don't necessarily want taking up space on your hard drive. To clean out Entourage's local cache of newsgroup messages, Control-click the name of your news server in your Folder list and choose "Clear Cache" from the contextual menu. Entourage purges its local cache of newsgroup messages. Afterward, you might want to compact the Entourage database to reclaim unused space; see page 331.

To read the actual messages in a newsgroup, either double-click its icon in the Folder list (which opens its list of messages in a new window), or click its name once in the Folder list to the left (which reveals the list of messages in the right pane of the window). Either way, Entourage downloads a list of articles in that newsgroup.

You read messages in a newsgroup exactly as you read email messages. Because newsgroups are all about discussion, choosing View→Threaded to collect messages into threads can be helpful (see page 329).

As with normal email messages, newsgroup messages that come with file attachments appear in an Attachments section inside the message; you can save those attachments just as you would email attachments. (Exercise caution with any attachment downloaded from a newsgroup.) Some particularly large attachments in newsgroups get automatically divided into multiple segments. If you're having trouble saving a multipart attachment to your hard drive, make sure that you've selected the message that contains the *first* part. Even then, you may find that joining multipart newsgroup messages isn't one of Entourage's strongest features.

Tip: To help sift through the spam that clogs newsgroups, you can set up *news rules* by choosing Tools→Rules, clicking the News tab, and then clicking the New button. Exactly as with the message rules described on page 345, you can set up rules that screen out messages from certain people, messages with certain phrases in their Subject line, and so on.

Composing, Forwarding, and Replying to Messages

Working with newsgroup messages is very similar to working with email messages. You reply to them, forward them, or compose them exactly as described earlier in this chapter (see Figure 8-21). As with email, you can use either plain text or HTML formatting, attach files, and clean up text that may have been wrapped badly somewhere along the way.

Usenet Netiquette

Although newsgroups are anarchic places, they also have traditions and general norms. Many of the points in "Email Netiquette" (see page 361) apply to composing messages for Usenet, but newsgroups have a few considerations of their own:

- **Lurk before you post.** When you read a newsgroup but don't post messages to it, you're considered a "lurker." There's no shame in lurking. In fact, you *should* lurk in a newsgroup for at least a few days, to get a sense of what topics are commonly discussed and who the most active participants are. Many newsgroups have cultures of their own—newcomers are always welcome, but it's best to avoid stepping on anyone's toes.

- **Read the FAQ and search the archive.** Many newsgroups have a FAQ ("frequently asked questions") document available on a Web site or posted periodically to the newsgroup. These documents contain the questions most often asked by newcomers to the group—and, even better, *answers* to those questions! Before posing a question you suspect may have come up before, check to see if the newsgroup has a FAQ, or search a Usenet news archive (like *http://groups.google.com*) to see if the topic has been covered recently.

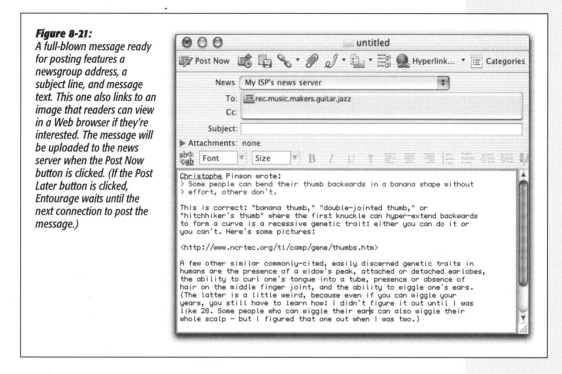

Figure 8-21:
A full-blown message ready for posting features a newsgroup address, a subject line, and message text. This one also links to an image that readers can view in a Web browser if they're interested. The message will be uploaded to the news server when the Post Now button is clicked. (If the Post Later button is clicked, Entourage waits until the next connection to post the message.)

- **Newsgroups are not billboards.** Do not post advertising to newsgroups. If you're an established member of a newsgroup, a brief announcement of something *relevant* to the group is fine—for instance, if you're a regular in a guitar-oriented newsgroup, you might mention that your little brother just released his first fingerstyle guitar CD. Similarly, a pointer in your signature to your company or your products is fine. But anything above that scale is likely to incite derisive comments or even result in abuse reports to your ISP.

- **Avoid extensive cross-posting.** Posting a message to more than one newsgroup is called *cross-posting*. It's OK to post to a handful of newsgroups if you genuinely aren't sure where your question or message is most appropriate. But widely cross-posting a message isn't much different than spamming, and so your message will be treated much like spam: derided, ignored, or even reported to your ISP.

- **Avoid HTML formatting.** Millions of people access newsgroups using old computers, old software, and slow connections. HTML-formatted newsgroup messages are frowned upon because they take longer to download and don't look good in a wide variety of newsreaders. If the major participants in a particular group all use HTML and no one objects when they do it, then posting HTML-formatted messages is probably fine. Otherwise, always use plain text.

- **Avoid "me-too" messages.** As a general rule, don't respond to messages if you're only going to agree with or restate what has just been said. (If you absolutely *must* say "I second that!" at least refrain from quoting the entire previous message in your response.)

- **Neither a troll nor a flamer be.** Tossing out provocative or insulting statements just to stir up other newsgroup participants is called *trolling*, and it's frowned upon. On the other hand, don't respond to abusive or deliberately provocative messages. You may incite a *flame war*, in which a newsgroup degenerates into increasingly vitriolic exchanges and insults. When a flame war erupts, reasonable people tend to abandon the newsgroup, sometimes never to return. If a particular person in a newsgroup always pushes your buttons, create a Rule (see page 345) so you never see newsgroup messages from that person.

Tip: Although Entourage is an OK newsgroup reader, some of its newsgroup features are limited and awkward. If you find yourself participating in Usenet newsgroups regularly, consider a separate newsreader program that offers more comprehensive features—full threading, message scoring, FAQ retrieval, and more. A good newsreader can vastly improve your Usenet experience.

You can find good lists of Mac newsreaders at *newsgroups.com* and *macorchard.com/usenet.html*—in particular, check out Thoth or one of the numerous descendents of NewsWatcher.

Mail and News Preferences

Entourage keeps track of two sets of preference settings: one covering how email and newsgroups are handled, and one handling Entourage's general behavior. The following section details the email and newsgroup options.

You can view the mail and news preferences by choosing Entourage→Mail & News Preferences or by pressing Shift-⌘-semicolon (;). This preference window, shown in Figure 8-22, is divided into five parts (via the five tabs at the top of the window): Read, Compose, Reply & Forward, View, and Proxies.

The Read tab

The controls under this tab govern what happens when you read your email, and they're divided into four parts: Messages, Languages, IMAP, and HTML. As you'll soon discover, some of them are intended exclusively for the technically minded.

- **Messages** governs what happens to open messages that you delete or file (such as whether Entourage closes the message window or opens the next message in line). You can also specify how many seconds must elapse, with a message open in front of you, before Entourage considers it as having been read, and therefore no longer displays its name in boldface type. For example, if you've set the "Mark message as read after displaying for ___ seconds" option to 3, Entourage waits three seconds before considering an open message as having been read. This feature can be useful if you like to skim through your messages, glancing for just a few seconds at each, without changing their unread status.

- **Languages** lets you select a *character set* (including non-Roman alphabet sets like Cyrillic, Greek, or Korean) for messages that arrive without a specified character set. Set this option to the character set that you read most often—usually your primary language group.

- **IMAP.** If this box is checked, deleted IMAP messages don't show up in your message lists. If this box *isn't* checked, IMAP messages marked for deletion will still be visible in their respective folders.

- **HTML** governs whether or not complex HTML coding (such as tables and forms) appears in messages that use it, and whether or not Entourage is allowed to grab images and other items from the Internet to fill in HTML-based messages. If you tend to read email when you're not connected to the Internet, disable network access for complex HTML.

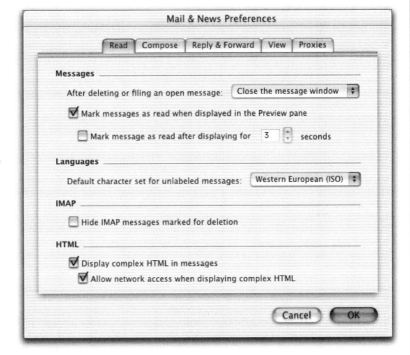

Figure 8-22:
Entourage has a separate dialog box for mail and news preferences. On the Read tab, you can specify how many seconds must elapse when a message is opened before Entourage considers read (and therefore no longer displays its name in boldface type). This feature can be useful if you like to skim through your messages without changing their unread status.

If you tell Entourage to use "complex HTML," Entourage uses technology from Internet Explorer to display those messages, which means they take more time (and more memory) to display. If you turn off complex HTML, the messages appear faster, but in a stripped-down format that is probably not what the author intended. Since you're using Mac OS X, the time and memory issues shouldn't be much of a drawback for you—after all, displaying complex HTML is useful for legitimate HTML-formatted email and newsletters you may receive. But if most of the HTML-formatted mail you receive is spam, disabling complex HTML may help you dispose of it faster.

Tip: Advertisers—and spammers—are increasingly using *Web bugs,* which are references to tiny, 1-by-1 pixel graphics that come embedded in HTML-formatted email messages. Web bugs exist purely for tracking purposes: if your email program downloads a Web bug, a corresponding entry appears in the advertiser's (or spammer's) Web server log. Now they know where and when someone viewed the message.

There's no way to tell if an HTML-formatted message contains a Web bug (at least not without examining the HTML source). But if you tell Entourage not to access the network when displaying complex HTML, you preserve a little more privacy—and deny advertisers and spammers the satisfaction of knowing they "hit" someone.

The Compose tab

This set of preferences controls what happens when you're writing messages. It's divided into three parts: General, Attachments, and Recent Addresses.

- The **General** checkboxes govern whether Entourage checks the names of your addressees against your default directory service (which is generally only useful if your company organization runs its own; see page 351) and whether or not you like to keep copies of sent messages in the Sent Items folder.

  You can also govern whether or not the HTML Formatting toolbar is visible when you're composing mail, and you can specify your preferred format for mail and news messages—plain text or HTML.

- **Attachments** lets you set up how Entourage processes file attachments—how you want such files to be compressed and encoded, and whether or not you want Windows file name suffixes added automatically.

  This dialog box also controls whether or not Entourage sends file attachments to addressees in the Cc and Bcc fields, on the assumption that you may sometimes want to send the *file* only to the primary recipients, but send the *message* to a long list of other people (whose addresses are in the Cc or Bcc fields).

- **Recent Addresses** controls whether Entourage offers to autocomplete the last 150 email addresses you've used (ones that *aren't* in your Address Book) when you're addressing messages. Some people find this feature annoying and turn it off, but others find it useful to be able to quickly re-enter email addresses without first having to create an address book entry for them.

The Reply & Forward tab

These controls govern replies and forwarded messages:

- **Include entire message in reply.** When you reply, this option adds the text of the original message, for your recipient's reference. Unless the original message is short, you'll want to edit down the original as you compose your reply.

- **Use quoting characters when forwarding.** This option adds quoting characters to each forwarded message's text. The > symbols are an Internet convention used to make it clear that *you* didn't write the bracketed text. If you turn off this box, Entourage will instead insert tags above and below the message to indicate where quoted text starts and stops.

- **Reply to messages in the format in which they were sent.** If this box is turned on, Entourage chooses the message format (HTML or plain text) according to the formatting of the *original* message. Uncheck this box to use the format you've specified on the Compose tab of the Mail & News Preferences dialog box.

- **Reply using the default account.** If this box is checked and you have more than one email account, Entourage always uses your *default* (primary) account to send replies—even if the original message was sent to a different account.

- **Mail Attribution.** If you like, Entourage can tack on some stock text that introduces a message you're answering. As you can see in the edit box, Entourage can even incorporate the sender's name and/or email address, or the date the original message was sent into this boilerplate text. As with signatures, some people get clever with these lines, coming up with introductory lines like this: "On [DATE], [NAME] is thought to have uttered:"

- **Place insertion point before quoted text.** This little checkbox puts the cursor at the *top* of the email message when you create a reply or a forwarded message. Turn this option *on* if you like your reply to appear *above* the original message text, and *off* if you like to type your reply *below* the quoted text.

Tip: On the Internet, the most accepted practice is to put replies *below* any quoted material. In the business world, however, an email culture has arisen in which replies go *above* any quoted material—thanks to the predominance of Microsoft Outlook, which comes set to do it that way.

- **News Attribution.** Like the Mail Attribution option, the News Attribution option automatically fills in some basic information when you reply to a newsgroup message. This attribution can display the message's author, the date, the time, and the article ID of the message to which you're replying.

The View tab

These controls control how Entourage displays messages, subscriptions, and quotes:

- **Show unread messages as bold.** This checkbox is responsible for displaying the names of unread messages in bold type in the message list.

- **Show messages using these colors.** Lets you choose colors (instead of bold text) to indicate which messages have been read. After turning on this box, click the color swatch next to the words "Unread and Read" to choose from a menu of 16 different colors. (Or choose the 17th option, Other, which opens the Apple Color Picker for an infinite variety of color choices.)

This can be a good option if you have a small screen or prefer a small Entourage main window: bold text is wider than normal text, so using a color to indicate unread messages can let you see more text onscreen.

- **Show Internet headers.** Turn on this box if you want to see a message's Internet *headers*—technical-looking text that details which servers the message passed through on its way to you, what attachments and encoding schemes were involved, and so on. (Even if this option is off, you can always see the headers for a particular message by choosing View→Internet Headers when you're reading it.)

- **Show attached pictures and movies in messages.** Entourage generally displays picture or movie attachments right in the message window, saving you the trouble of opening them. This option can, however, make such messages take longer to appear on the screen.

- **Toggle open threads that contain flagged messages.** If messages in a *thread* (a set of newsgroup messages on the same subject, marked by a flippy triangle) are flagged—perhaps by a Rule you've created—this option make sure that the thread is "expanded," so that you don't miss seeing the flags it contains.

- **Show newsgroups and IMAP folders using these colors.** When checked, this option lets you color-code the names of newsgroups and IMAP mail folders to which you've subscribed.

- **Color Quoting.** In this multihued box, you can change the color given to various levels of text quoting—levels one through four, at least.

For example, suppose you write to your boss: "How does it look?" She writes back to you, "How does WHAT look?"—and you see your own original query bracketed (>) and in blue type. When you reply to her, your original question now appears with *double* brackets (>>) and in the second-level color you choose here. This color-coding can make it simpler to follow a protracted discussion taking place via email or a newsgroup.

Anything higher than level-four quoted text takes on the same color as level-four quoting. To change a color, click one of the text strings in the box and select a new color from the menu that pops up.

The Proxies tab

Proxy servers are, in part, a security measure to keep unauthorized people out of your network's computers—including yours. If you use proxy servers to access the Internet (you know who you are), you can use these controls to specify how Entourage accesses those proxies. You can also list host addresses that should be accessed *without* going through your proxy servers; this can be handy for accessing Web sites and other resources within your business or organization.

If your organization uses proxy servers but you don't know how to configure these settings, contact your network administrator.

Entourage Calendar and Tasks

I f it weren't for its Calendar and Tasks features, Entourage would be little more than Outlook Express, Microsoft's free email program. But thanks to these functions, Entourage makes a very good time manager indeed.

The best part about all of this is that these data bits are smoothly integrated with Entourage's email and address-book features, so that you can pull off software stunts like inviting people (via email) to meetings that you schedule (on the calendar), all without leaving the program.

The Calendar

You can open the Entourage calendar either by clicking the Calendar icon in the upper left of the Entourage main window, choosing View→Go To→Calendar, or pressing ⌘-3. No matter how you open it, your calendar shows up with all scheduled events listed on the appropriate days at the appropriate times (see Figure 9-1). In fact, it can display anything from a single day to six weeks on a single screen.

Actually, you get two different calendars. In addition to the main one, there's a miniature overview calendar in the lower-left corner. (Drag the divider bar above the overview calendar to dictate the number of months it shows.)

Working with Views

Entourage offers two kinds of views: a *month view,* which looks like every wall calendar you've ever seen, and a *column view,* in which you see up to seven days' worth of events displayed as vertical time lines (see Figure 9-3).

Displaying days, weeks, and months

To control what the main calendar window shows, use the following buttons on the Entourage toolbar or commands on the Calendar menu:

Views   Toolbar

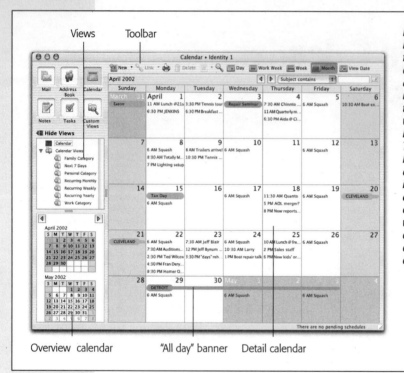

Figure 9-1:
Entourage's Calendar function provides an overview of adjacent months and a big view of the current month. You can also display the current week, work week, or day, in which case Entourage also displays a Task list for that time frame. Holidays and other special days (which you have to import from a separate file) appear in the large detail calendar. At the top of the window, Entourage offers a calendar-specific toolbar for easy access to common commands.

Overview calendar   "All day" banner   Detail calendar

- **Day** shows the appointments for a single day in the main calendar area, broken down by time slot.

- **Work Week** shows five columns, representing the workdays of the current week.

- **Week** fills the main display area with seven columns, reflecting the current week (including Saturday and Sunday).

Tip: If you enjoy an eccentric work schedule, you can redefine which days constitute your work "week" by choosing Entourage→General Preferences, selecting the Calendar tab, then changing the days-of-the-week checkboxes. When you choose "Work week" using the toolbar or the Calendar menu, Entourage will be happy to display columns for only Tuesday, Thursday, and Friday (or whichever days you work).

- **Month** shows the current month in its entirety.

- **List,** unlike the other views, doesn't offer a vertical grid of time slots. Instead, it offers a simple list of events scheduled for the current day (or days), as shown at top in Figure 9-3. Unlike the other views, List view isn't available via the toolbar, but you can choose it from the Calendar menu or by Control-clicking anywhere in the detail calendar area and choosing List from the resulting contextual menu.

Figure 9-2:
When you drag the cursor across a set of dates in the overview calendar, the main calendar shows nothing but those days. You can select as many as six weeks' worth using this method (compare with Figure 9-1). Just drag from the first date to the last date you want to see—you can even drag across months. Boldface numbers in the overview calendar indicate dates on which you have something scheduled.

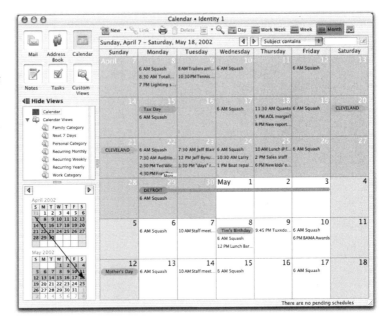

You can also determine which days show up in the detail calendar by selecting them in the overview calendar at the lower left of the Entourage main window. For example, to make the calendar show nothing but an important three-day stretch, simply drag the cursor across those three calendar squares in the mini calendar at lower left (Figure 9-3).

Tip: Entourage provides a quick way to access the current day's date—choose Calendar→Go to Today, or press ⌘-T. If you're in month view, the command displays the current month with today's date selected; otherwise, Go to Today displays information for only the current date, regardless of the view you were using.

Recording Events

Most of Entourage's calendar is pretty intuitive. After all, with the exception of one unfortunate Gregorian incident, we've been using calendars successfully for centuries.

In many ways, Entourage's calendar is not so different from those analog versions we leave hanging on our walls for months past their natural life span. But Entourage offers several advantages over paper calendars. For example:

- Entourage can automate the process of entering repeating events, such as weekly staff meetings or gym workout dates.

- Entourage can give you a gentle nudge (with a reminder in a pop-up dialog box) when an important date is approaching.

- Entourage can automatically send email to other people to let them know about important meetings. (Let's see one of those "Hunks of the Midwest Police Stations" calendars do *that*!)

You can record an appointment using any of several methods, listed here in order of decreasing efficiency:

- When viewing a column view, drag vertically through the time slots that represent the appointment's duration, and then double-click within the highlighted area (see Figure 9-4).

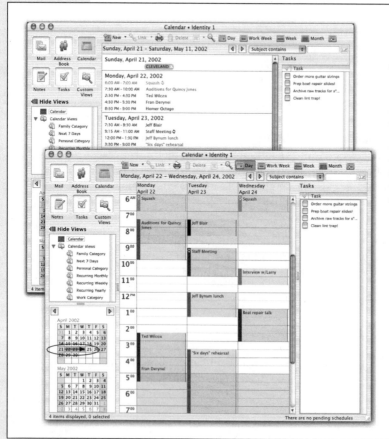

Figure 9-3:

Top: Entourage can display its detail calendar in one of five prefab formats: Day, Week, Work Week, Month, or List (shown here).

Bottom: You can also select an arbitrary number of days and weeks in the overview calendar for display in the detail calendar, as shown by the circled arrow here. This example shows three days; Figure 9-2 showed six weeks.

- Using either of the month views, double-click the appropriate date.

- Click the New toolbar button.

- Choose File→New→Calendar Event (or press ⌘-N).

In each case, Entourage brings up an untitled new calendar event window, depicted in Figure 9-4. Here's an unusually elaborate example of how you might enter an appointment:

Figure 9-4:
You can open this New Event window by double-clicking a highlighted swath of hours on any column view (background, left).

With the help of the new calendar event window, shaping an event to do exactly what you want is easy enough. By twiddling a few of these knobs and buttons, you can change a ten-minute event into an all-week extravaganza—and you can invite all of your closest friends and co-workers.

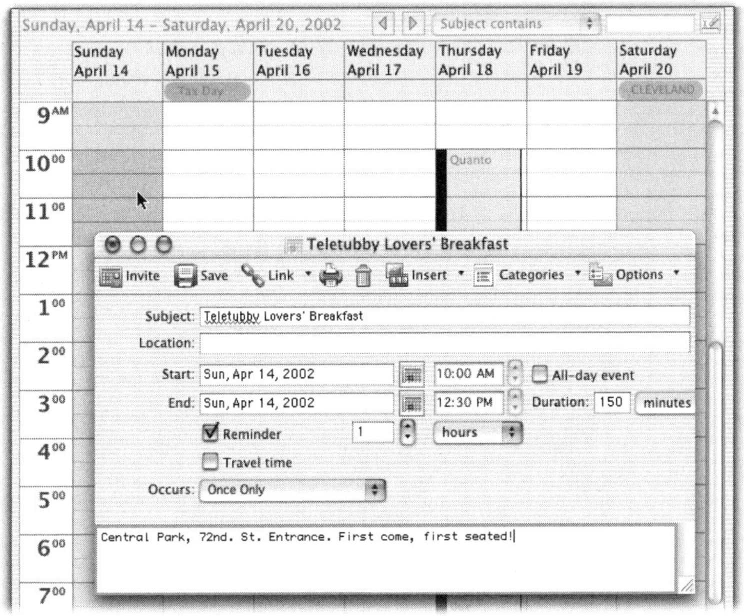

1. **Type a name for this appointment into the Subject line.**

   For example, you might type *Fly to Phoenix.*

2. **Press Tab to jump to the Location field. Specify where this event is to take place.**

   This field makes a lot of sense; if you think about it, almost everyone needs to record *where* a meeting is to take place. You might type a reminder for yourself like *My place,* a specific address like *212 East 23,* or some other helpful information like a contact phone number or flight number.

   You can also leave this field empty if it's not especially pertinent to the appointment you're recording.

3. **Press Tab. Specify the starting date, if necessary.**

   If you began this entire exercise by double-clicking a date in Entourage's month view, or by dragging through time slots on one of the Entourage calendar displays, then skip this step, since Entourage has automatically filled in the date you indicated.

   Otherwise, you can change the date here in either of two ways. First, you can edit the date displayed here, using almost any format—*12/12/02, 4-4-03,* or *Nov 14*— to specify the date. (If you omit the year, Entourage assumes you mean this year.)

Note: Entourage understands certain ways that people type dates, but stumbles badly on others. For instance, if you type out the whole name of a month without specifying a year—like *March 15* or *November 28*—you'll get some pretty wacky results. Make sure Entourage interprets your dates the way you intended!

   Or you may prefer to click the tiny calendar button next to the Starting Date field. A mini calendar window appears; move to the month you want by clicking the arrows at the top, and then click the date you want (or the Today button) to close the mini-calendar. You've successfully filled in the Starting Date and Ending Date fields.

Tip: When editing a date, pressing the + key moves the date one day forward, and pressing – moves the date one day backward. The + and – keys on the numeric keypad work great for this. When using a laptop, remember to press Shift to get the + key instead of =.

---

4. **Press Tab. Specify the ending date.**

   Most events, thank goodness, start and end on the same day. Entourage saves you time by making that assumption, and setting both Starting and Ending dates to match. (The only time you have to type the ending date manually is if it's later than the starting date.) Entourage lets you type an ending date earlier than the starting date for an event, but complains only when you actually try to save the event.

5. **Turn off the "All day event" checkbox, if necessary, and then specify the starting and ending *times.***

   If you opened this dialog box by dragging through time slots on the Entourage calendar, then skip this step. Entourage has already filled in the starting and ending times for you.

   Otherwise, turn off "All day event" (unless, of course, this event really will last all day; we've all had meetings like that). Doing so prompts the starting- and ending-time boxes to appear for the first time. You can adjust the times shown here by typing, clicking buttons, or a combination. For example, start by clicking the hour, then increase or decrease this number by clicking either the arrow buttons or by pressing your up and down arrow *keys.* (Of course, you can also type a number; you may need to preface numbers less than ten with a zero.) Press Tab to highlight the minutes, and repeat the arrow buttons-or-keys business. Finally, press Tab to highlight the AM/PM indicator, and type either *A* or *P* to change it, if necessary. (You can also press the up or down arrow keys or the Space bar to toggle between AM and PM.)

Continue pressing Tab to highlight the ending-time field.

By now, you're probably exhausted just *reading* about all the steps required to set up, say, a lunch meeting. That's why it's usually quicker to begin the appointment-entering process by dragging vertically through an Entourage calendar column display; this spares you from having to specify the date and time.

6. **Use the Occurs pop-up menu if an event will recur according to a predictable schedule.**

The Occurs pop-up menu contains common options for recurring events: once a week, on a particular day of every month, on a particular day each year, every day, or every weekday. You can select any of these items, or move immediately to the Custom option, which opens the Recurring Event window (Figure 9-5). Use the Recurring Event window to indicate how often the event recurs (daily, weekly, monthly, or yearly). Once you've clicked the appropriate button, an additional set of controls appears, offering such plain-English variations as "Every January 14," "The second Tuesday of January," "The third Tuesday of every __ months," and so on.

Figure 9-5:
If you've indicated a Weekly repeat, you can specify that this event takes place more than once a week by turning on the days-of-the-week checkboxes. This event—a gym workout—takes place Monday, Wednesday, and Friday of each week.

The bottom part of the box lets you indicate how long this event will keep repeating. If you click "No end date," you'll be stuck with seeing this event repeating on your calendar until the end of time (a good choice for recording, say, your anniversary—especially if your spouse consults the same calendar). You can also turn on "End after ___ occurrences," a useful option for car payments provided you know how many more you have to make. You can also turn on "End by", and specify a date that will cut off the repetitions; use this option to indicate the last day of school, for example.

Click OK when you've finished setting up how events will repeat. To the right of the Occurs pop-up menu, there should be a plain-English summary of the options you set up.

7. Set up a reminder, if you like.

The Reminder section of the dialog box lets you set up a reminder that will pop up on your screen when the time for your reminder passes. (Office Notifications must be turned on for reminder windows to pop up; for more about Office Notifications, see page 397.) You can specify how much advance notice you want for this particular appointment. For your favorite TV show, you might set up a reminder only five minutes before air time; for an important birthday, you might set up a two-day warning to allow yourself enough time to buy a present; and so on. (Entourage starts out proposing 15 minutes in advance for every reminder; you can change this default setting in the Calendar tab under Entourage→General Preferences.)

If the event requires a little planning for travel, turn on "Add travel time" and then enter the amount of cushion that you want to leave yourself for traffic and the like.

Figure 9-6:
All reminders for an event or task are handled by the Office Notifications program, which is installed with every Office X program. When a reminder comes due, Office Notifications pops a reminder window in front of whatever else is on your screen. You can open the associated item directly (whether a calendar event, email message, Word document, or a task), dismiss the reminder (just make it go away), or snooze the reminder (tell it to go away now, but come back later).

8. Press Tab. In the white, empty Notes area, type or paste any helpful text.

Here's your chance to customize your calendar event. You can add any text that you like in the notes area—driving directions, contact phone numbers, a call history, or whatever. Several pages' worth of information can fit here.

If you choose to use the invitation feature described on page 386, the text you place here will be included in the email invitations you send out.

Tip: In the Notes area, you can use the Insert Hyperlink button on the event's toolbar to insert a URL from your Internet Explorer browser, History, or Favorites—just like you can in an email message.

---

9. **Specify a category for this appointment, using the pop-up menu at the right end of the toolbar.**

   See page 428 to read more about categories. For now, it's enough to note that Entourage's color-coded categories are helpful in distinguishing your calendar events at a glance. Family events might show up in blue, for example, and work events in red.

Note: The date book program on Palm palmtops doesn't offer a Category feature, so the categories you assign in Entourage won't show up on your handheld.

---

10. **Click Save (or press ⌘-S), then close the event window (by pressing ⌘-W, for example).**

    Your newly scheduled event now shows up on the calendar, complete with the color coding that corresponds to the category you've assigned. (In Month views, the *text* of the event itself reveals the color; in column views, the *block of time* occupied by the event reflects its category color.) Appointments that last longer than one day (such as vacations) appear as category-colored banners that stretch across squares on the month view; in column views, they appear just beneath the date at the top of the column (see Figure 9-7).

Figure 9-7:
After you've created your event, it dutifully appears in your daily calendar nestled among your other calendar events. This column view shows all-day events (or banner events) at the top of the calendar, above the start of your day. Then, each event shows up as a colored rectangle in the column. If an event has a reminder, a small alarm clock icon appears in the box; if the event is recurring, it shows two arc-shaped arrows in a yin-yang arrangement.

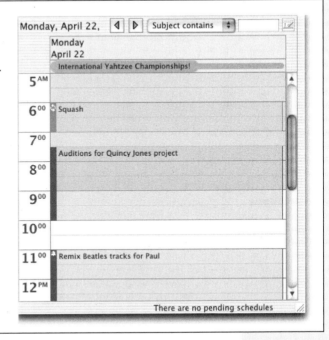

What to Do with an Appointment

Once you've entrusted your agenda to Entourage, you can start putting it to work. Microsoft Office is only too pleased to remind you (via pop-up messages) of your events, to reschedule them, to print them out, and so on. Here are a few of the possibilities.

Editing Events

To edit a calendar event, open its event window either by double-clicking its name on the calendar or by highlighting it and choosing File→Open Event (⌘-O). The calendar event pops up in its window, exactly as shown in Figure 9-4. Alter any of its settings as you see fit.

Tip: When changing only an appointment's category, bypass the event dialog box. Instead, just Control-click the appointment's block or its name, and choose Categories from the resulting contextual menu.

You don't have to bother with this, however, if all you want to do is reschedule an event, as described next.

Rescheduling Events

If an event in your life gets rescheduled to a new date that's currently visible on the screen, then you can simply drag it to that new date to officially reschedule it (see Figure 9-8).

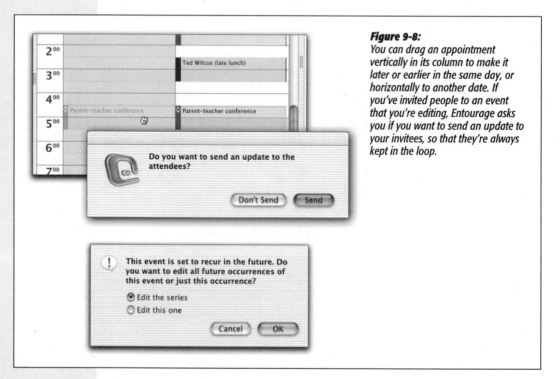

Figure 9-8:
You can drag an appointment vertically in its column to make it later or earlier in the same day, or horizontally to another date. If you've invited people to an event that you're editing, Entourage asks you if you want to send an update to your invitees, so that they're always kept in the loop.

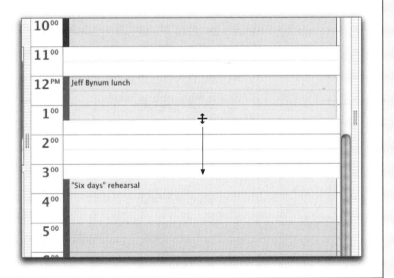

Alas, Entourage doesn't let you copy, cut, or paste calendar events. If something is postponed for, say, a month or two (that is, to a calendar "page" that would require scrolling), you have no choice but to double-click its name and then edit the Starting and Ending dates or times.

Note: When rescheduling a recurring event, Entourage applies the change *only* to the event you've moved, leaving the rest of the recurring events intact. If you want to change the time or date of the whole series, open the event for editing. Only then does Entourage ask whether you want changes applied to just the event you opened, or all the recurring events.

Lengthening or Shortening Events

If a scheduled meeting becomes shorter or your lunch hour becomes a lunch hour-and-a-half (in your dreams!), changing the length of the representative calendar event is as easy as dragging the top or bottom border of its block in any column view (see Figure 9-9).

Figure 9-9:
You can resize any Entourage calendar event just by dragging its border. As your cursor touches the top or bottom edge of a calendar event, it turns into a horizontal line with arrows above and below. You can now drag the event to make it encompass more or less time on your calendar.

Printing Events

Entourage has a great way of committing your calendars to paper. To get there, click the Print toolbar button, choose File→Print, or press ⌘-P.

In this window, you can exercise some control over how Entourage prints your calendar by changing the control settings: Print, Start and End dates, Layout, and Form:

- The **Print** pop-up menu presents four options regarding what to print: a Daily Calendar, a Calendar Event List, a Weekly Calendar, and a Monthly Calendar (see Figure 9-10).

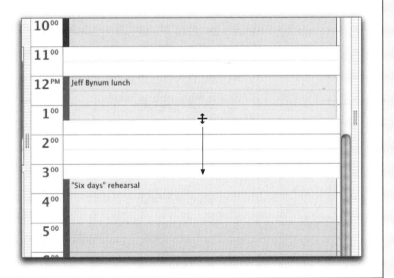

• **Start** and **End** let you specify start and end dates for the printout.

• **Layout** lets you choose which portions of the calendar to print: Events, Tasks, or All-day events. It also lets you specify whether *cutting lines* (for trimming your pages to fit a day planner), notes, and page numbers are printed. You can opt to have "punch holes here" indicators printed on each sheet, for use with daily planners (described next).

• **Form.** If you use a paper-based, binder-style day planner (such as a Franklin Covey or Day Runner) you're in luck. Entourage lists canned layouts for these popular formats in the Forms pop-up menu.

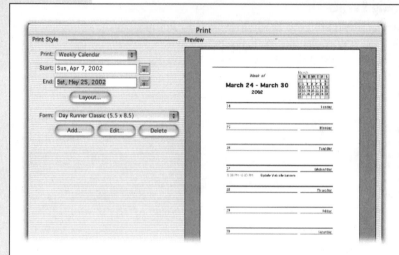

Figure 9-10:
Entourage's special Print window pops up before the Mac OS X Print dialog box, letting you set some powerful printing options for Entourage calendars. You can even shape them to fit paper planners, as shown here. If your planner brand isn't listed in the Form section, click Add Form to set the margins so that they fit your planner.

Deleting Events

To delete an appointment, first select it, then either click the Delete button in the toolbar, choose Edit→Delete, press ⌘-Delete, or simply press the Delete key. In the confirmation dialog box, click Delete (or press Enter).

Tip: If you delete a recurring event (like a weekly meeting), Entourage asks if you want to delete just that particular instance of the event or the whole series.

Sending Invitations

At last it's time for you to harness the power of your combined calendar/email/address-book program. If you click the Invite button in an event window (see Figure 9-4), Entourage sprouts an Invite field. Use it like the To field in an email message, as described in Chapter 8; that is, specify the email addresses of anyone that you'd like to invite to the event. If they're already in Entourage's address book (Chapter 10), you save a lot of time, thanks to the pop-up menu of addresses that match the few letters you've typed.

To compose the actual invitation, use the blank white notes area at the bottom of the Event dialog box (see Figure 9-4); this is the message your invitees will see.

Sending the invitation

Once an invitation becomes part of an appointment, the toolbar sports these three new buttons:

- **Send Now** sends an email message to everyone on the guest list (complete with the subject, location, and any notes).

- **Send Later** adds outgoing email messages to your Outbox without actually sending them. They won't get broadcast until you use the Send & Receive command, as described in Chapter 8.

- **Cancel Invitation** deletes any invitations in your Outbox that you haven't sent yet. It also sends cancellation messages via email to attendees you've already invited.

Receiving an invitation

If you're on the receiving end of one of these meeting summonses, but you don't use Entourage (or another *iCalendar-aware* email program) as your email program, you get a note like the one shown in Figure 9-11.

But if you're using Entourage as your email program, a special thrill awaits: The invitation inserts *itself* into your calendar, complete with times and reminders (Figure 9-12). You even get a yellow banner in the email message window that lets you respond to the invitation by clicking either the Accept, Decline, or Accept Tentatively button in the toolbar. (Links with the same functions also appear in the yellow banner at the top of the email message.)

Clicking any of these buttons sends an email message *back* to the sender, whose copy of Entourage now offers even more surprises.

Figure 9-11:
If you're using Eudora (or another email program that is not Entourage), invitations sent to you from Entourage look like ordinary email messages.

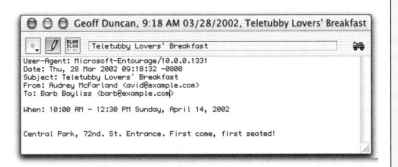

```
Geoff Duncan, 9:18 AM 03/28/2002, Teletubby Lovers' Breakfast

Teletubby Lovers' Breakfast

User-Agent: Microsoft-Entourage/10.0.0.1331
Date: Thu, 28 Mar 2002 09:18:32 -0800
Subject: Teletubby Lovers' Breakfast
From: Audrey McFarland <avid@example.com>
To: Barb Bayliss <barb@example.com>

When: 10:00 AM - 12:30 PM Sunday, April 14, 2002

Central Park, 72nd. St. Entrance. First come, first seated!
```

Receiving RSVPs for your invitation

Now suppose you're the person who sent the original invitation. As your invitees reply to your note, one of two things may happen:

- If you sent the invitation to somebody who doesn't use Entourage, you'll simply receive an uninspired email message that says, for example, "OK, I'll be there."

    After reading this reply, double-click the event on your calendar that represents the get-together. In the event window, you'll see a yellow banner across the top of the message indicating that you've sent invitations. It also contains a "View Attendee Status" link. When you click the link, a floating window appears that lists all the people you invited, complete with a pop-up menu that lets you track their responses: No Response, Accepted, Tentative, or Decline (see Figure 9-12). Use the pop-up menu to update the list, according to the reply you just received.

- If you sent the invitation to somebody who *does* use Entourage, life is sweet indeed. The program *automatically* updates the Attendee Status window, based on the button that your prospective guest clicked (Tentative, Accept, or Decline) upon receiving the invitation.

Whenever you change the specifics of a calendar appointment about which you've sent invitations (such as its date), Entourage offers to send an updated email message to the guests. The buttons in the upper-left corner of the event dialog box now read Send Update and Send Later.

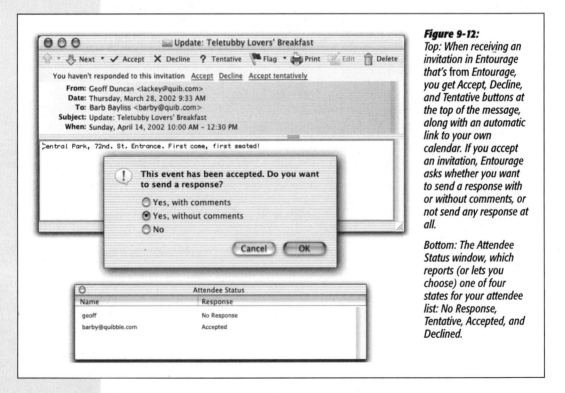

Figure 9-12:
Top: When receiving an invitation in Entourage that's from Entourage, you get Accept, Decline, and Tentative buttons at the top of the message, along with an automatic link to your own calendar. If you accept an invitation, Entourage asks whether you want to send a response with or without comments, or not send any response at all.

Bottom: The Attendee Status window, which reports (or lets you choose) one of four states for your attendee list: No Response, Tentative, Accepted, and Declined.

Adding Holidays

Your Entourage calendar doesn't come with any holidays listed. In marketing a customizable calendar that can reflect the holidays of different countries, cultures, or religious beliefs, Microsoft didn't presume to know which canned events you'd want to add. Fortunately, it's easy enough to tell Entourage what you want.

UP TO SPEED

iCalendar: An iProgram Steve Jobs Didn't Dream Up

Entourage's invitations use iCalendar, a format developed in part by Microsoft, Lotus, Netscape, and others in 1998. The idea was to provide a common way for applications to exchange calendar and scheduling data.

Unfortunately, not all programs understand iCalendar, even those from major software companies. Although invitations and acknowledgements usually work fine among Entourage users, you may find they don't work well with Netscape Communicator, Palm Desktop, and even Microsoft's own Exchange and Outlook products. (That last incompatibility is a shocker, considering that Outlook has its own, apparently identical feature.)

Support for iCalendar may improve over time, but you may discover that certain correspondents are confused by invitations you send, or that you have to manually handle their responses.

To import a set of holidays into Entourage's calendar, choose File→Import. Entourage's Import assistant opens, and asks whether you want to import information from a program, import information from a text file, or import holidays. Choose "Import holidays" and click the right arrow.

Now Entourage presents a list of more than 40 countries and religions for which you can import holidays (see Figure 9-13). Turn on the checkboxes next to the countries or religions whose holidays you want imported, and click OK. Those holidays now appear in your Entourage calendar.

Figure 9-13:
To add holidays to your Entourage calendar, just turn on the checkboxes next to the countries or religious holidays that you want to bring in, then click OK. Entourage takes care of the rest. You can import one, some, or all of these holidays, if you like. As a convenience, Entourage labels them with the category called, as you might expect, Holidays.

Note: The holiday data that Entourage imports may contain significant days that aren't technically holidays. For example, if you import United States holidays, "Tax Day" (April 15) winds up on your calendar—an example of a special day that you may observe, but probably don't *celebrate*.

POWER USERS' CLINIC

Your Very Own Holidays

The Holidays file isn't massively difficult to decipher. If you visit your Applications→Microsoft Office X→Office folder, you'll see a SimpleText file called Holidays. If you open it in a text editor or Word X, you'll discover that it's just a simple list of holidays in this format:

Father's Day,2000/6/18

Father's Day,2001/6/17

Father's Day,2002/6/16

Father's Day,2003/6/15

Each country, region, or religion is preceded by a bracketed title and a number indicating the number of entries for the category. In other words, it's easy enough to create Holiday files of your own.

First, make a copy of the Holidays file in the Finder, and rename it something like "My Holidays." Then open your file in Word X; delete the existing text; and type the name of each holiday, followed by a comma, no space, then the date (in year/month/day format); press Return and type the next holiday the same way.

When you're finished, type a category name and the total count at the top of the file (use the default Holidays file as an example), and then save it as a *text only* file. Finally, choose File→Import, select Import Holidays, and open your customized Holiday category just as you would any other.

You can use this trick to set up a file containing any number of occasions—corporate events for the year, a softball league game schedule, church social meetings, the birthdays of your favorite rock stars, etc.—so that your colleagues can import them into their own calendars.

Saving Calendars as Web Pages

One of the calendar module's best features is its capability to save your calendar as a Web page. You can make your calendar available to a select few (perhaps via Mac OS X's built-in Web Sharing), or you can post the result on the Internet for all to see. For example, you might use this feature to post the meeting schedule for a group or club that you manage, or to make clear the agenda for a series of upcoming financial meetings that all of your co-workers will need to consult.

Note: There's no way to include only certain categories on a Web-published calendar, so that only your corporate appointments are publicized but not your private ones. You can, of course, maintain a separate calendar under a different Entourage *identity* (see page 420) for this purpose.

Begin by choosing File→Save As Web Page. The Save as Web Page window appears (Figure 9-14). Here, you customize how your saved calendar is going to look and work. For example, you can specify:

- **Start and End dates.** This option prevents you from saving an entire century's calendar in HTML form.

- **Include event details.** Use this option if you want your Web page to include the notes that you may have entered in a calendar event's Notes area.

- **Use background graphic.** Turn on this box if you want your Web page calendar superimposed on a picture. Then click the Choose button to the right. You'll then be asked to select a graphics file from your hard drive.

Tip: To avoid the ridicule and wrath of your audience, use the graphics feature with caution. Choose only an extremely light, low-contrast image, so that the text of the calendar is still legible when superimposed over it. If possible, choose a graphic image that's roughly the same size as the calendar, too, so Entourage doesn't stretch out of shape. Also remember that downloading an enormous background image over a modem is no one's idea of a good time.

- **Web page title.** The text you enter in this box will appear as the Web page's title.

- **Open saved Web page in browser.** If this box is turned on, Entourage will open the newly saved calendar in your Web browser just after saving it, so that you can make sure it wound up the way you intended.

Once you've set your options, click Save.

Next, in the Save dialog box, name the calendar file (suppose it's *Summer Schedule*). Select a folder location on your hard drive, then click Save. Entourage creates two new icons on your hard drive—an HTML file called Summer Schedule.htm, and a folder called Summer Schedule. The folder contains a bevy of graphics and HTML files that comprise your calendar.

POWER USERS' CLINIC

Your Mac as Web Server

If you have a full-time Web connection, such as a cable modem or DSL service, you can use the Mac's own Web Sharing feature to post your calendar for the entire online world to see. A complete discussion of this feature awaits in *Mac OS X: The Missing Manual,* but here's a summary.

Open the Mac OS X System Preferences, select the Sharing pane, click the File & Web tab, and the Start button under Web Sharing. Make a note of the IP address displayed in the lower part of the File & Web tab: It might be a name (like *mymac.example.com)* or a series of numbers (like *127.0.0.1).*

Next, return to the Finder and open your Home folder (Option-⌘–H). In your Home folder, you'll find a folder called Sites. Drag your calendar file and folder into it.

To view your calendar, open a Web browser and enter a URL in this form:

<http://192.168.1.11/~chris/SummerSchedule.htm>

Of course, for *192.168.1.11,* substitute the actual address you noted in the File & Web tab, replace *chris* with your Mac OS X account name (preceded by a ~), and replace *SummerSchedule.htm* with the name of the calendar file Entourage created.

When you press Enter, your Web browser connects to your own Mac to call up the calendar. (If you don't get your calendar, go through the steps again to verify that everything works.)

If you chose "Open saved Web page in browser" (Figure 9-14), your newly saved calendar now appears. Review it for accuracy, and marvel that it offers live links; clicking an item brings up details about it in the right-hand frame of the Web page (Figure 915).

Note: The Web pages created by Entourage exploit such advanced Web-browser features as frames, style sheets, and JavaScript. Not surprisingly, they tend to behave best using Microsoft's Internet Explorer browser.

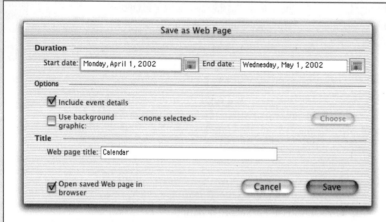

Figure 9-14:
When you save your calendar as a Web page, you can control what dates are saved for the Web and what information is included. You're welcome to give your Web page a title more imaginative than Calendar.

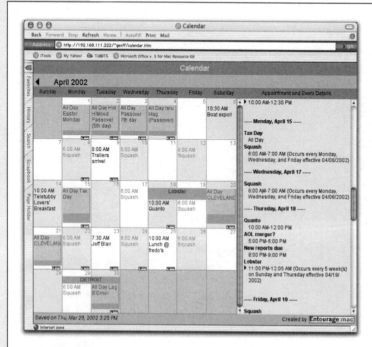

Figure 9-15:
When saved as a Web page, Entourage calendars retain most of their pertinent details, such as events, times, and even notes associated with those events.

If you've attached a note to an event, you can click a small flippy triangle next to that event to reveal the note.

You can save everything from a day to many months as Web pages; that way, you can keep those who need to know in the know.

If the file looks good, the final step is to upload the Web page to a Web server so others may see it. Of course, this step requires you to have a Web site. The easiest way to secure one is through Apple's free HomePage service (visit *www.apple.com /itools* for instructions). You can also contact your Internet service provider to find out how much Web space your account grants you and what steps are required to post new Web pages there.

Tasks

Entourage's Tasks feature lets you make a To Do list, all the while helping you along with gentle reminders, if you so desire. And, like just about every other item in Entourage, Tasks can be linked to email messages, calendar events, and even to other tasks.

The Tasks Module

You can put Entourage into Task mode either by clicking the Tasks icon at the upper left, choosing View→Go To –> Tasks, or pressing ⌘-5. You get a simple list of tasks, complete with due dates and categories (see Figure 9-16).

There are five columns to the left of the tasks' names:

- **Links** (indicated by a tiny chain-link icon) shows if the task is linked to any other item, such as a message or a calendar event (see page 426).

- **Status** (indicated by a tiny checkmark icon) shows a checkbox, which you can turn on when the task is complete (or sooner, if you just need a bright spot in your day).

- **Priority** (indicated by a tiny exclamation point) is the same as the priority column found in Mail—Highest, High, Normal, Low, and Lowest. It helps you prioritize what you really *should* be working on.

- **Recurring** (indicated by a double arrow) shows, at a glance, whether the task is a one-time deal or something you must contend with on a continuing basis.

- **Reminder** (indicated by a tiny alarm clock) shows a similar alarm-clock icon if you've set a reminder for a particular task—in other words, it's a reminder of your reminder.

- You specify the **Task** name, **Due Date,** and **Categories** when you type in your to-do list, described next.

Note: If you've used the Flag for Follow Up feature (in Word, Excel, PowerPoint, or Entourage's Mail) to remind you to return to a document or message, those follow-ups appear as items in Entourage's Task list. You can edit and manage them as you would any other task.

Creating Tasks

To create a new Task in Entourage, you take your pick of the usual array of options:

- Choose File→New→Task.

- If the Tasks icon is selected in the upper left of the Entourage widow, press ⌘-N.

- Click the New toolbar button. (If you're not already viewing your to-do list, choose Task from the New pop-up button.)

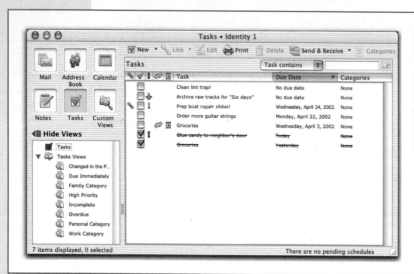

Figure 9-16:
Entourage's Tasks toolbar includes common Entourage commands listed across the top, and a filter box so you can quickly sift through your busy life for just the task you want.

The new task window appears (Figure 9-17). Conduct your task-recording business like this:

1. **Type a name for the task.**

   This will be the title that appears in your task list. You can probably come up with something more illuminating than *untitled*.

2. **Change its priority, if you like.**

   If you take a moment to categorize your tasks this way, you'll be able to sort your task list by priority.

3. **Specify a due date for this item, if you like.**

   Turn on "Due date" and enter a deadline date. Feel free to use any of the same date-setting tricks described on page 380.

   There's only one difference between a dated to-do item and one that doesn't have a due date: When the specified date goes by, an "expired" to-do item shows up in boldface in the Tasks window. If you double-click it, you'll see "Overdue" next to an attention-getting light bulb icon at the top of the task's description window.

4. **If this to-do item reflects a recurring headache, such as a weekly staff meeting, use the options in the Occurs pop-up menu.**

   You'll be able to specify an event that recurs daily, weekly, monthly, or yearly. Use the Occurs options here exactly as those described for events on page 381.

5. **Set up a reminder, if you like.**

   Turn on the Reminder checkbox, and set a date and time for the reminder to get in your face—in the form of a pop-up dialog box displayed by the Office Notifications program. (See page 397 for more on reminders.)

6. **Make notes for more information.**

   Tab to the Note box to type, or paste, text that helps describe your task.

7. **Click Save (or press ⌘-S).**

   If you're finished entering tasks, you can close the window (press ⌘-W). Otherwise, change the text and options in the dialog box to create another to-do list, starting over at step 1.

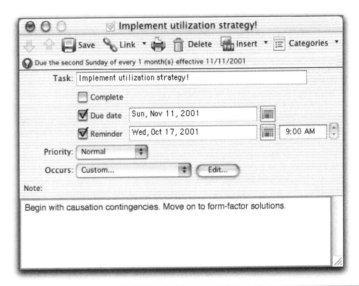

Figure 9-17:
The new task window lets you create, edit, print, and delete tasks; you can also set all of a task's particulars. Note the strip across the top, which denotes a recurring to-do item.

Other Task Tricks

Once you've recorded some to-do items, you can manipulate them in ways that should be familiar if you've used the Entourage calendar.

Editing a task

Change a task's name by selecting the task, clicking the task's name, and then waiting about one second for the editing box to appear. Type a new name and then press

Enter or Return. Similarly, you can change its category by clicking in the Categories column; a pop-up menu of your categories appears.

You can change a task's priority, repeat status, and so on, by double-clicking its name in the Tasks window (or by highlighting it and pressing ⌘-O, or choosing File→Open Task). The dialog box shown in Figure 9-17 reappears, allowing you to change any aspect of a task and save it again.

Checking off a task

After finishing a task, you can celebrate by turning on its checkbox in your list. Once you do so, Entourage puts a line through the task to give you the satisfaction of crossing it off your list. If a task's window is open, you can also turn on the Complete checkbox and then close the window.

Note: Your to-do items don't show up as separate items in the Entourage Calendar. However, you can activate a separate Tasks pane at the far right of the Calendar window so that at least your tasks and calendar appear side-by-side. Just choose View→Tasks Pane while using any calendar view.

Deleting a task

To delete a task, click it in the task list and then either click the Delete button, press ⌘-Delete or the Delete key, or choose Edit→Delete Task. (You'll be asked to confirm the deletion. That's fortunate, because no Undo command is available, and the deleted task doesn't go into the Deleted Items folder; it's gone forever.)

Tip: You can select multiple tasks (in preparation for deleting them en masse, for example) just as you would email messages: using either the Shift-clicking or ⌘-clicking tricks described in the box on page 330.

Printing tasks

It's easy enough to print out a list of your to-dos. To print only some of them, start by highlighting the ones you want (see the preceding tip).

Now click the Print button in the toolbar, or choose File→Print (⌘-P). This triggers the custom Entourage Print window, which lets you choose which tasks to print (all tasks, selected tasks, tasks due today or this week, and so on), what style you want to use for printing them, and whether you want to print those pages on standard paper or special Franklin Covey planner or Day Runner paper.

When you finally click OK, your printer's standard Print dialog box appears. You're on your way to a hard copy reminder of the errands and chores that await you.

Linking tasks

Linking tasks to other Entourage items is a great use of the Links function (see Chapter 11), since it lets you draw connections between tasks that you're working on and any email messages, calendar events, or contacts that might be related to the task. When you have a task's window open, you can create a link with the click of a Links button, which opens the Links window. If you use the Links button as a menu, your choices let you link that task either to an existing Entourage item or to a new one that's created on the spot.

Office Notifications

After you've set up a reminder for an appointment or task in Entourage (or via the Flag for Follow Up feature in any Office X program), Office X will display handy on-screen alerts when your items come due. You can instruct these alerts to go away or to come back later, or you can use them for quick access to appropriate appointments, documents, or messages.

Office X uses a small add-on program called Office Notifications to perform the alerting. (It's in the Microsoft Office X→Office folder, if you're curious.) When an alert comes due, Office Notifications appears as a separate item in the Mac OS X Dock. When you've dealt with any pending items, Office Notifications vanishes, re-appearing when it's time for the next reminder or follow-up.

It might sound complicated to deal with yet another program to handle alerts and notifications, but Office Notifications is straightforward. First, you can manage everything about alerts and notifications within Entourage, so you don't really feel like you're using a separate program. Second, using a separate tiny program to handle alerts and notifications means these alerts work *all the time,* even when no Office X programs are running. This is a big improvement over Office 2001, where your reminders popped up only when an Office program was running. (Of course, you can disable Office Notifications any time, if you don't want to be interrupted during an air guitar solo or while keeping earth safe for humanity.)

Tip: If you use Microsoft's MSN Messenger and Passport services, Office Notifications can also tie in Microsoft's .NET Alerts. For instance, a shipping company might use .NET Alerts to provide status updates on a package, a bank might notify you of deposits to your account, or an auction site might let you know that an item you've always coveted is up for sale.

You can't manage .NET Alerts within Entourage. Typically, you sign up for (and configure) .NET services via a service provider's Web site and set your contact preferences using Microsoft Passport. However, you do *not* need MSN Messenger or a Passport to use Office Notifications, as described here.

The Notifications Window

When a reminder, task, or item you've flagged for follow-up comes due, the Office Notifications window appears in front of any other programs, a sound plays, and the name of the item appears. If more than one item is due, the Office Notifications window lists them all. Figure 9-18 shows three different kinds of notifications: a reminder, a Microsoft Word document flagged for follow-up, and a task set up in Entourage. The Office Notifications window also has three buttons across the bottom: Open Item, Snooze, and Dismiss. Snooze and Dismiss also act as pop-up menus; their options are covered below.

Alerts show three basic items:

- **An icon.** An alert's icon indicates where the alert came from. For example, a reminder about an appointment displays a calendar icon (like the top item in Figure 9-18), and a flagged Microsoft Word document appears with a Word document icon (like the middle item in Figure 9-18).

- **A title.** The Alert's title is the subject of the appointment or task you set up, or it indicates the title of the document or message you flagged.

  Flagged documents also have a blue, underlined link, which you can click to open the flagged document immediately. Opening a flagged document or message does not dismiss or snooze the alert in Office Notifications (see next page); it just brings the flagged item front and center for you to act on, so you don't first have to hunt around your mail folders (or your hard drive).

Figure 9-18:
Here, Office Notifications shows three items: a reminder of a calendar event that's due in 10 minutes, a Microsoft Word document that's flagged for followup, and an overdue item on Entourage's Task list.

- **A due date.** Office Notifications also shows the item's due date or, for reminders of pending calendar items, how much time remains until the event. (For instance, the "Ship Demo CDs!" item in Figure 9-18 is due in 10 minutes.) If an item is past due (like the last item in Figure 9-18), Office Notifications shows "(Overdue)" in red next to the due date.

Tasks and flagged documents also have a checkbox you can use to mark an item as complete. This checkbox actually performs two functions in one easy step: indicates that you're finished with an item *and* dismisses the alert box.

Acting on Notifications

When a notification appears, it can be processed in one of three ways: open it, snooze it, or dismiss it.

- **Open Item.** Double-clicking an item opens the corresponding task, calendar entry, or mail message in Entourage. (If an item is already highlighted, you can also click the Open Item button.)

The Open Item button does *not* open any documents you may have flagged for follow-up. Instead, it opens the Entourage *task* that marks the follow-up, so that you can change the time, category, or other information associated with the task.

Tip: You can select multiple items in the Office Notifications window just by Shift-clicking to select a range of items, or by ⌘-clicking to choose non-adjacent items in the list—exactly as in the Finder or in the Entourage email module. At that point, the Open Item button opens *all* the corresponding calendar items or tasks in Entourage, letting you see, edit, or dispose of a bunch of related items all at once.

Figure 9-19:
Use the Snooze pop-up menu to specify when you'd like an alert to reappear. Some of the choices are obvious—come back in ten minutes, two hours, three days, and so on—but some choices (like "15 minutes before start" and "End of the day") are nicely flexible.

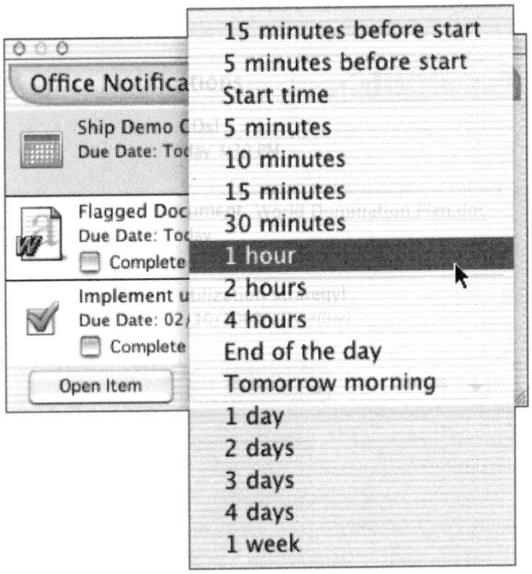

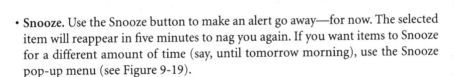

- **Snooze.** Use the Snooze button to make an alert go away—for now. The selected item will reappear in five minutes to nag you again. If you want items to Snooze for a different amount of time (say, until tomorrow morning), use the Snooze pop-up menu (see Figure 9-19).

- **Dismiss.** Click Dismiss to make a selected alert go away, never to be seen again.

If you want to Dismiss all the items shown by Office Notifications, choose Dismiss All from the Dismiss pop-up button. All the current alerts are dismissed (although no documents or tasks get marked as completed).

- **Mark as Complete.** Use the Complete checkbox on tasks and flagged items to indicate you're finished with the task or item you flagged. Unlike other elements appearing with individual alert items, turning on the Complete checkbox both marks the task as completed *and* dismisses the alert, so that the item disappears from Office Notifications.

Note: Watch out—the program doesn't allow enough time to *un*check the box if you make a mistake. If you turn on the Complete checkbox on an item that you really *aren't* done with, you must return to Entourage's Task list, where the item appears with a line through its name. To "uncomplete" an item, turn off the Complete checkbox in the Status column (and set up another reminder, if you like).

Configuring Office Notifications

Office Notifications is a simple program, generally keeping out of sight until the moment when you want to be reminded about something. You can change only two settings: whether the program is enabled or disabled and whether or not an alert sound plays when an item comes due.

Turn Office Notifications On or Off

Sometimes you might not want Office Notifications to display alerts onscreen, even if something comes due. For instance, you may be using your Macintosh to give a demo or presentation to clients—or to save the planet from extraterrestrial insect hordes. (We all have our priorities.)

Here are the two ways to turn off Office Notifications:

• In Entourage, choose Entourage→Turn Off Office Notifications.

• If Office Notifications is already on your screen, click its window once to ensure it's the frontmost program, and then choose Office Notifications→Turn Off Office Notifications.

Turning Office Notifications back on again is almost identical:

• In Entourage, choose Entourage→Turn On Office Notifications

• If Office Notifications is on your screen, click its window once to make it the frontmost program, and then choose Office Notifications→Turn On Office Notifications.

Turn Office Notification Sounds On or Off

Office Notifications generally plays a sound when an alert appears. If you don't want to hear these sounds, turn them off by choosing Office Notifications→Turn Off Sounds. Alternatively, choose Entourage→General Preferences, select the Notification tab, and then turn off the checkbox next to "Reminder sound." To turn the sound back on, just turn the "Reminder sound" checkbox back on.

CHAPTER

10

Entourage Address Book and Notes

Microsoft clearly hopes that Entourage will be the only personal information manager you'll ever need. As proof, it offers a built-in Rolodex function that serves as a master name/address/phone number/photo gallery/
email address book for Office X, and a Notes module that lets you write pithy comments about everybody you know.

But make no mistake: the names, numbers, and comments you store in these programs don't just sit there, locked away in a stand-alone database. In fact, you'll often
consult your electronic little black book from within the *other* Office programs.

For example, once your Address Book contains a few names, Entourage can
autocomplete addresses as you start typing in the To field of email messages. It can
also fetch the phone numbers of people you're inviting to events that you schedule
in Entourage's calendar. You can also easily include address book information in
Word, Excel, or PowerPoint.

Address Book

The Address Book isn't a separate application that you double-click when you want
to look up something; it's just one module of Entourage. You view it by clicking the
Address Book icon in the upper left of Entourage's main window, by choosing
View→Go To→Address Book, by pressing ⌘-2 (and probably in dozens of other
ways).

Tip: As with email in Entourage, you can opt to view your address book either as a single pane of the Entourage screen, as shown in Figure 10-1, or in a window of its own. To do the latter, Control-click the Address Book icon in the Entourage main window and choose Open Address Book in New Window from the contextual menu that appears.

A Tour of Address Book World

The Address Book interface parallels Entourage's email view, which shows a list of messages above, the body of the highlighted message below. In the Address Book, when you click someone's name in the list above, you get a detailed view beneath. Sometimes you'll have recorded only a name; sometimes you'll have gone whole-hog, recording that person's mailing addresses, anniversary, astrological sign, and so on.

You also manipulate the Address Book list view exactly as you do with email. For example, you navigate the list and highlight selected names exactly the same way (see page 330). And you manipulate the various columns of address information just as you would with email messages. The columns give you at-a-glance information about your acquaintances—whether they have any links or flags, the person's name, company, phone numbers, email address, and category.

Tip: Entourage can show you over 40 columns of information about each person in your address book. Unless you have either (a) a 70-inch monitor, or (b) some kind of weird obsession with detail, you can probably get by with a subset of these. To specify which columns show up in the list view, select them from the View→Columns submenu.

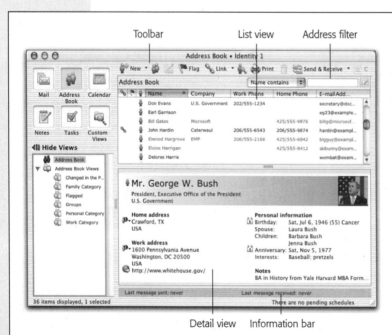

Toolbar   List view   Address filter

Detail view   Information bar

Figure 10-1:
Much like the Entourage Mail module, the Address Book window has a Preview pane showing a list up top, detailed information down below. It reveals the last time you sent a message to—or received a message from—the person whose name is highlighted, along with a plethora of other information. Like the Mail and News modules, the Address Book module has a quick-find filter in the upper-right corner. To find a certain person's information quickly, type a few letters of his name into this box. Entourage instantly hides all names that don't match what you typed.

Creating Contacts

Suppose you're already looking at your Address Book list. To open a new "Rolodex card" for somebody you know—a new *contact,* in Address Book lingo—click the New button or press ⌘-N. (If you're *not* already in Address Book view, choose File→New→Contact, or choose Contact from the New pop-up button.)

Entourage presents the Create Contact window (Figure 10-2). You can use this window to enter basic data about new contacts, such as names, addresses, email addresses, and phone numbers.

Tip: If someone has sent you contact information via email using a vCard (usually appearing as an email attachment with a ".vcf" extension), you can drag the vCard directly to Entourage's address list. Entourage creates a new contact record for you automatically. See page 407 for more details.

Three of the fields—email, the address field, and one of the phone fields—have pop-up menus next to them for labeling the information you've recorded. You can use these to specify whether the address or email address you've just typed in is home or work, or whether a phone number is mobile, fax, or whatever.

It's not necessary to click inside each field before typing into it. As in any dialog box, you can press Tab to move the cursor to the next field (from the First Name to Last Name field, for example), or Shift-Tab to jump back to the *previous* field.

Tip: Don't bother with parentheses and hyphens in phone numbers: Entourage adds them for you. You'll find the controls for turning this feature on and off (and specifying the punctuation you prefer) by choosing Entourage→General Preferences and clicking the Address Book tab.

In an unusual, uncharacteristic Microsoftian feature lapse, Entourage doesn't automatically capitalize names. Nor is there any way to use information in a previously created contact as a starting point for a new contact. In other words, if you know 30 people who work for Microsoft and you want to enter their contact information in Entourage, you'll have to type (or paste) *Microsoft* 30 times.

Tip: Although Entourage may be lacking some built-in timesaving features, it is *scriptable.* If you're familiar with AppleScript, you can create a simple script that handles such repetitive tasks automatically. Easier yet: If you're familiar with the Web, you can download some excellent, ready-to-run Entourage scripts from *www.applescriptcentral.com.*

Once you've filled out the information in this window, you can click any of three buttons (unfortunately, none have keyboard shortcuts, so data entry involves a lot of mouse-groping):

- **Save & Close.** Entourage stores your info, nods politely, and takes you back to the master Address Book screen.

- **Save & New.** Entourage adds the person's info to its database, and then empties all of the fields in the dialog box, making them ready for you to enter the next person's contact specifics.

- **More.** This button expands the form into the long form (Figure 10-2), which has places for exhaustive information on your contacts.

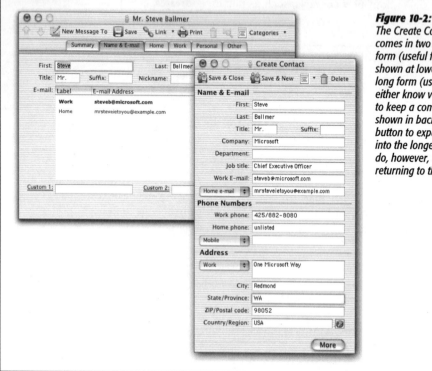

Figure 10-2:
The Create Contact window comes in two flavors—the short form (useful for casual contacts, shown at lower right) and the long form (useful for people you either know very well, or need to keep a complete dossier on, shown in back). Click the More button to expand the short form into the longer one. (Once you do, however, there's no returning to the simpler form.)

The long form

If you click the More button at the bottom of the window, you've moved into *long-form* country. While the short-form window is great when all you need in a contact is a person's name, address, email address, and phone number, the long form turns Entourage into a giant personal information database, in which you can enter a contact's birthday, astrological sign, and even a photo.

Tip: You open the expanded version of the Contact dialog box whenever you double-click an existing contact in your address book. You can also reach the expanded form by highlighting a name and pressing ⌘-O or choosing File→Open Contact.

The long form has its own toolbar. Most of its commands are familiar (Save, Print, Delete, and so on), but a few deserve special mention:

- **New Message To.** Creates a new email message addressed to the currently open contact.

- **Find Related.** With one click, this button has Entourage round up all email messages that you've sent to or received from this person (and haven't yet deleted).

Bug alert: The expanded contact dialog box isn't resizable in Entourage X, and the Find Related button can disappear behind the Category button at the far right of the toolbar. In most cases, opening and then closing the Category menu forces Entourage to redraw the Toolbar and make the Find Related button reappear.

- **Categories.** Lets you choose a category for the currently open contact (see page 428).

This long form window also sports six tabs along the top that you can use to enter and view more information about the currently open contact:

- **Summary tab.** Shows all of the information that you've entered about the person. If you haven't entered any contact information yet, this window is blank. The bottom of the Summary tab also displays when you last sent or received a message from the contact.

- **Name & E-mail tab.** Lets you enter complete naming information about your contact, including a title, nickname, and suffix, if any. It also lets you enter a slew of email addresses.

Note: Curiously, Entourage doesn't directly offer a place for middle names or initials. You'll just have to enter them as part of the First Name. (Just watch out if you use your Address Book to fuel a mail merge!)

This window also offers *custom fields*—Custom 1 and Custom 2—where you can store other kinds of information about this contact's name and email addresses, such as what email address a person prefers to use while on vacation.

Tip: If you use one of this person's email addresses most of the time, select it and click the Make Default button to the right of the E-mail field. From now on, when you type that person's email address in a new message, Entourage will suggest that address alone as the primary address.

- **Home tab.** Shows the person's home address, Web page, and telephone numbers, along with two more custom fields—Custom 3 and Custom 4—where you can enter your own kinds of data (perhaps the person's garage color or favorite lawn fertilizer).

If you turn on the Default Address checkbox in this window, this address becomes the *default* address for that contact, the one that Entourage goes to first when you don't have a choice of addresses—for example, when you choose Contact→Map Address.

- **Work tab.** Shows the contact's work address, employer's Web page, and work telephone numbers. It also includes the contact's company, job title, and department. Once again, you get a couple of custom fields—Custom 5 and Custom 6—to handle any extra information.

- **Personal tab.** Here, you can enter your contact's birthday. It's worth typing in a couple of friends' birthdays, if only to see the raw, seething power of Microsoft software at work: Entourage automatically calculates the astrological sign and age for your pal, saving you the math.

  There's also room here for recording a spouse's name, the names of any children, your contact's anniversary, and any interests of note.

  You can probably guess the function of the "Drag an drop image here" box. Yes, it's a place to paste in, or drag in, a graphics file that depicts this person for handy visual reference.

Tip: The tiny calendar icon to the right of the Birthday and Anniversary fields is a pop-up menu. It offers commands that summon a pop-up calendar for easier date selection, inserting today's date, or adding a birthday or anniversary to your Entourage calendar so that you don't forget to buy a gift.

- **Other tab.** Lets you enter notes about your contact, and provides still more custom fields—Custom 7 and Custom 8, plus Custom Date 1 and Custom Date 2—to provide places for any data that Microsoft may have missed.

Tip: To change the name of a custom field, click it and type in a new field name in the window that results. Click OK or press Enter—but note that you're changing this field's label for *all* "cards" in your Address Book.

When you finish entering all of this information about your contact, you'll have quite an impressive dossier. Click Save (or press ⌘-S) to commit it to your hard drive. (Entourage also saves changes to contact information automatically if you close the contact window.)

GEM IN THE ROUGH

The Illustrated Rolodex

If you have a digital photo of one of your contacts, you can drag the graphics file right out of a Finder window or a Web browser and into the well at the Personal tab's right edge. Entourage accepts most standard graphics formats—even Photoshop files.

You can use any size picture, but keeping it small is wise from a disk-space and memory perspective. After all, does your address book really *need* an 8 x 10 image of your boss?

Tip: When you're processing email, you can add someone's email address to your Address Book without having to bother with all of the dialog-box shenanigans described in this section. Whenever you're looking at an open email message—or even a closed one in a list of messages—Control-click the sender's email address and choose Add to Address Book from the contextual menu. Entourage instantly creates a new Address Book entry for that person, featuring the email address and the person's name (if they supplied it with the email message). Adding the other details is up to you.

To add information from a *directory service* search (see page 351), select the address in the search results window and click the Add to Address Book button.

Working with vCards

You've probably received plenty of email messages that come with strange little files attached whose names end in *.vcf*—but unless you pay very close attention to Internet standards, you may not know what they are.

They're vCards, which were invented as a way of exchanging business-card information via email, sweeping away the drudgery of manual input forever. Although they sound like a good idea, vCards haven't really caught on, primarily because they're typically incomplete and poorly implemented (most people don't enter all of the pertinent information). Furthermore, they litter your hard drive with annoying attachments. Entourage is one of the few Mac programs that can understand vCards at all.

To pull the information out of a vCard and into the Entourage Address Book, drag the .vcf attachment onto your open Address Book, as shown here. The contact information nestles itself nicely among your other contacts. If the .vcf file is on your hard drive (rather than attached to an email message), drag it into your Address Book window instead.

To *send* contact information as a vCard (which could be either your own electronic business card or any of your contacts'), drag a name from your open Address Book (or an entire *row* in a list view) anywhere onto a waiting email message. (Alternatively, highlight a name in your Address Book and then choose Contact→Forward as vCard.) Either way, your outgoing message now displays the .vcf file attached. If you want to create individual vCard files, just drag contacts from your Address Book to the Mac OS X desktop.

When using vCards, remember there's no way to choose what information Entourage includes in a vCard: nearly *everything* goes in, including birthdays, notes, complete home and work contact info, and even a photo if you've entered one. (A photo may make the vCard enormous, and in any case is only likely to get through to other Entourage users.) So before you send a person's vCard to someone else, be certain it's appropriate to send along everything you have recorded about the contact.

Your correspondent will be able to incorporate that Address Book "card" into her own address book, and will appreciate your timesaving gesture—if she's even heard of vCards, that is.

Opening, editing, and deleting contacts

To edit a contact you've already entered into Entourage, double-click the appropriate row of the Address Book list, or click once and then choose File→Open Contact (⌘-O). Entourage presents the Summary window shown in Figure 10-3. Click the appropriate tab to edit the details on it, just as you did to begin with.

If someone is no longer part of your life—or you wish it were so—click the Delete button in the toolbar, choose File→Delete Contact (⌘-Delete), or just press the Delete key if the contact is selected in the list view. Entourage asks if you're sure you know what you're doing (there's no way to undo such a deletion).

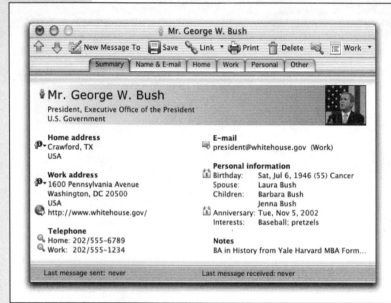

Figure 10-3:
Once you've gone through the trouble of entering complete information about your contact, you'll know more than you probably should. Click the Summary tab to gaze admiringly at the expansive data screen.

Creating groups

As you might expect, *groups* are collections of contacts. They make it easy to send an email message to everyone in a group in one fell swoop—just address it to the group instead of entering a bunch of single email addresses.

Here are three fascinating tidbits about groups:

• You can enter an email address into a group without having to enter it first as an independent Address Book card.

This feature may come back to haunt you, however. You may one day start to address an email message by typing *McGi*, frustrated that Entourage refuses to complete *McGillicuddy*, even though you're certain you entered Bob McGillicuddy into the Address Book. What's probably happened is that you entered old Bob only into a group without first creating an independent address book card for him. (People whose names exist only in a group aren't eligible for Entourage's AutoComplete feature.)

- Someone can be a member of more than one group.

- A group can be a part of another group.

To create a new group when you're viewing the Address Book, click the New Group toolbar button. (In other views, choose File→New→Group, or choose Group from the New pop-up button.)

Now the Group window appears. Once you've typed in a name *(Design Dept., Newsletter List,* or *Pass Jokes On,* for example), creating a group is easy. You can add people's names to the group by dragging them in from the Address Book window (Figure 10-4).

If you'd rather type than drag, you can type an email address from your Address Book (which Entourage automatically completes for you), or you can enter a completely new email address as part of the group. Simply click the Add button on the toolbar, which adds a blank space in the group, ready for you to type in an email address.

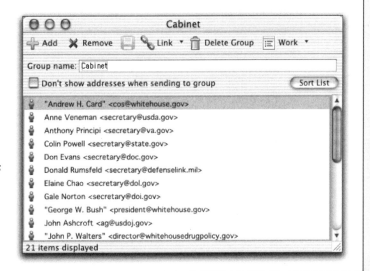

Figure 10-4:
By dragging addresses to a group window, you can quickly create a group. Turn on "Don't show addresses when sending to a group" to protect the privacy of members of that group. That way, the individual email addresses won't show on the message; however, your own address will appear on both the From and To lines of the message. This configuration, unfortunately, makes the message vulnerable to certain spam filters, including, ironically, Entourage's own Junk Mail Filter.

Importing Contacts

If you haven't used Entourage before, there's a good chance that, if you keep your addresses on the Mac at all, it's in another program, such as Now Contact, Palm Desktop, Claris Organizer, or even Netscape Communicator. "No problem," says the ever-confident Microsoft. Entourage can import contact information from these programs and several more.

Furthermore, if your little black book is stored in something like a FileMaker Pro database, an Excel spreadsheet, or some obscure off-brand address software, Entourage can grab contact information from a *tab-* or *comma-delimited text file.* Most databases, and many address book programs, can save their contents in these intermediary formats, precisely to make it easier for you to transfer your life from one such program to another. If you were to open up one of these files in a word processor, you'd see that each piece of information is separated by a press of the Tab key (Bob→Smith→23 Main Street→Chicago, and so on) or a comma, and that each "card's" information is separated by a press of the Return key.

It's in Microsoft's best interest to make sure that Entourage can bring in as many formats as possible, because switching over to a new email or contact management program is not a trivial endeavor.

The Import Assistant

Fortunately, importing contacts from another program into Entourage *is* relatively trivial. Just choose File→Import to bring up the Import Assistant, which walks you through the process.

Note: The File→Import command is the first step in importing contacts, mail messages, *and* calendar events, so you may see some references to those other data types on the Import Assistant's screens.

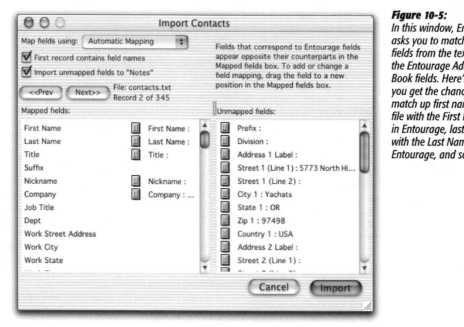

Figure 10-5:
In this window, Entourage asks you to match up the fields from the text file with the Entourage Address Book fields. Here's where you get the chance to match up first names in the file with the First Name field in Entourage, last names with the Last Name field in Entourage, and so on.

In the first window, you're asked whether you want to import information from one of nine programs—Entourage 2001, Outlook Express, Qualcomm Eudora, Netscape Communicator, Claris Emailer, Now Contact, Now Up-To-Date, Claris Organizer, or Palm Desktop—or from a special text file (tab- or comma-delimited). This process may feel familiar; it's the same Import Assistant you saw when setting up Entourage for the first time.

If you choose to import information from one of these nine programs, Entourage asks you what information you would like to grab—such as contacts or calendar events—and then proceeds to inhale that information.

If, on the other hand, you choose to import contacts from a text file, Entourage asks you for the location of that text file. Then it opens the Import Contacts window (see Figure 10-5).

To align the fields in the list so that they match up with the corresponding tidbits of address info, drag them up or down, using the ribbed rectangular handle that appears on each line. If there are *unmapped* fields—fields from your older address book software that Entourage isn't sure *what* to do with—you can drag them from the "Unmapped fields" section into the proper place on the left side of the window.

Once you've lined up all the fields correctly, click Import (or press Enter) to bring your social circle into its new software home.

Exporting Contacts

Exporting Entourage's contacts is a lot simpler than importing them, because Entourage offers but one option for export—the time-honored tab-delimited text file. When the day comes that you want to bring your little black book into some other database or address program, choose File→Export Contacts, choose a folder location for the file, and then click Save.

WORKAROUND WORKSHOP

Cross-platform Contact Imports

If you're moving an address book from a Windows-based program to Entourage, you won't encounter much trouble. Just export the contact list as a tab-delimited text file, which you can transfer to the Mac via network, email attachment, or disk. Then, in Entourage, choose File→Import and proceed exactly as described on these pages.

To move contacts in the opposite direction–from Entourage to a PC–export your contacts as a tab-delimited file, and then hand them off to your PC. Don't forget to append the required Windows suffix .txt to the end of your file's name. Also, when naming the file, use standard let-

ters and numbers; Windows doesn't accept such wacky characters as the vertical bar (|) or the asterisk (*).

Finally, note that the invisible character that ends each line in a text file is different in Mac OS 9, Mac OS X (and other Unix operating systems), and Windows. If a Windows program doesn't understand your text file, you may have better luck if you send it to the Windows machine via email (which should convert the line endings), or switch the file to Windows line endings using a program like the free BBEdit Lite *(www.barebones.com)* or the text-processing utilities you can find at *www.versiontracker.com.*

Using Contacts

Once your Address Book is brimming with people, it's time to actually *do* something with all that data. Besides providing email addresses for Entourage mail, you can put all those names and numbers to work in Word, Excel, or PowerPoint. Here are a few of the ways you can reap the benefits of your Address Book:

Sending email to someone

Chapter 8 covers the various ways you can address a piece of outgoing email from within the email portion of Entourage. But you can also summon a preaddressed piece of outgoing email from within the Address Book itself. For example:

- Click a name in the Address Book and choose Contact→New Message To.

- Control-click someone's name and then choose New Message To from the contextual menu that pops up.

Either way, Entourage whips open a new email message addressed to that lucky individual.

Flagging a contact

Flagging someone's name can be useful in a number of different situations. For example, flagged contacts bubble up to the top of a list when you sort it accordingly (by clicking the Flag column in the Address Book list); this makes flags an excellent way to denote important contacts. And when you print your contacts, you can print just the flagged ones.

To plant that little red flag to the left of a contact, select the contact and choose Contact→Flag.

To get rid of flags, select the corresponding rows of the Address Book and then choose Contact→Clear Flag.

Using contacts in Word

Suppose you're writing a letter to someone listed in your Address Book. As you start to type the person's name in Word, a floating yellow AutoText balloon appears, as shown in Figure 10-6, showing the contact's full name. If Word has correctly guessed what you're trying to do, press the Return key while the autotext balloon is showing. Word obligingly completes the person's name for you.

If you *don't* intend to type a name—that is, if you've typed *will*, but Word's autotext balloon proposes William Shakespeare (a name it found in your Address Book), just continue typing without pressing Return. The box goes away. (This behavior is part of Word's AutoCorrect feature, described on page 96.)

As Figure 10-6 points out, you can Control-click an inserted person's name if you'd like to add her phone number, mailing address, and so on. The resulting contextual menu gives you several choices:

- **Open Contact.** Opens the contact into its own window, where you can get more information or even edit the contact info, without having to launch Entourage.

- **Update Contact.** You'd use this command when editing a Word document you wrote some time ago. The command consults the Entourage Address Book and updates the name, number, or address (if it's been changed in Entourage since you first created the Word document).

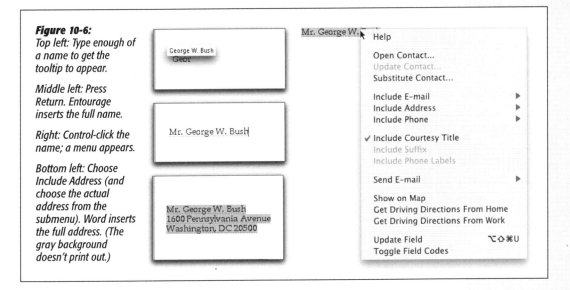

Figure 10-6:
Top left: Type enough of a name to get the tooltip to appear.

Middle left: Press Return. Entourage inserts the full name.

Right: Control-click the name; a menu appears.

Bottom left: Choose Include Address (and choose the actual address from the submenu). Word inserts the full address. (The gray background doesn't print out.)

- **Substitute Contact.** Brings up your contact list, so that you can substitute a different person's information. You might use this command when, for example, sending an existing letter out to a different person.

- **Include E-mail, Include Address, Include Phone.** Pastes the contact's email address, postal address, or phone number into the document. These commands are only available if, in fact, you've specified that information in Entourage.

Note: Office applications only draw contact information from the currently active Entourage *identity* (more on identities in Chapter 11).

This auto-insert feature isn't the only example of Entourage/Word integration. You also encounter it when doing a Mail Merge in a Word document, as described on page 254.

Five Very Impressive Buttons

When you're viewing the expanded address book screen for somebody in your Address Book, Entourage offers five buttons that let you harness the data you've input in clever ways. These five icons appear in the contact's Summary tab, among other places. Here's a look at what they do, in the order in which you see them illustrated in Figure 10-7:

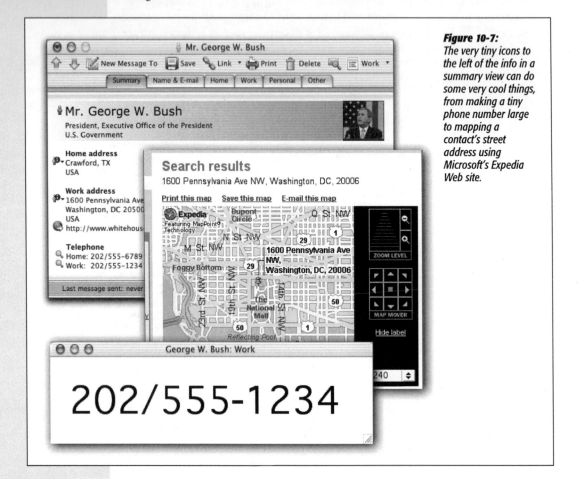

Figure 10-7:
The very tiny icons to the left of the info in a summary view can do some very cool things, from making a tiny phone number large to mapping a contact's street address using Microsoft's Expedia Web site.

- The **information** icon sits to the left of every street address. It hides a menu that, when clicked, offers to consult the Internet for a map of, or driving directions to, the selected address (or, less glamorously, to copy the address to the Clipboard, ready for pasting into a letter you're writing in a word processor). Not surprisingly, Entourage only uses mapping services from Expedia, a Microsoft Web site.

- The globe-like **Web page** icon appears next to any URLs (Web addresses) you've entered onto somebody's "card." When you click this button, your Web browser opens the associated Web page.

- When you want to dial a contact's telephone number, click the small **magnifying glass** icon to the left of it. Doing so doesn't *dial* the phone for you. It does, however, magnify that telephone number so that it's big enough to see from several feet away (Figure 10-7).

- The **message** icon sits next to the contact's email address. When you click it, Entourage creates a new email message addressed to that contact.

- The **calendar** icon appears to the left of the Birthday and Anniversary fields. Clicking it adds a recurring event to your Entourage calendar—handy insurance against missing important birthdays or anniversaries.

Printing the Address Book

Thanks to some fine attention to detail by the Entourage programmers, you can print the Address Book in a variety of formats, specifying just the details you want to have on paper.

Start by clicking the Address Book icon at the upper left of the Entourage main window. Then choose File/Print, which brings up the Print window (Figure 10-8). In addition to a print preview, it offers four small sections:

- **Print.** This pop-up menu lets you select what to print: All Contacts, Flagged Contacts, or Selected Contacts (that is, names you've highlighted by clicking, Shift-clicking, or ⌘-clicking, as described on page 330).

- **Style.** This pop-up menu lets you choose whether you want to print a full address book (with lots of contact information per page) or a simple phone number list.

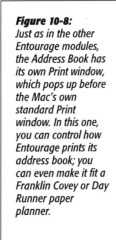

Figure 10-8:
Just as in the other Entourage modules, the Address Book has its own Print window, which pops up before the Mac's own standard Print window. In this one, you can control how Entourage prints its address book; you can even make it fit a Franklin Covey or Day Runner paper planner.

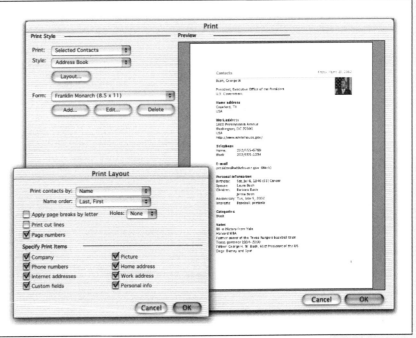

- **Layout.** The Layout button opens the Print Layout window, in which you can specify how contacts are sorted, whether first names or last names are printed first, whether cut lines and punch holes are printed, and what other bits of contact information are printed (such as company name and personal information).

- **Form.** If you use a Franklin Covey or Day Runner paper planner, you can choose a template from this pop-up menu, corresponding to the most popular precut paper types that are available at office-supply stores. You can also use the *Add form*, *Edit form*, and *Delete form* buttons to create and delete your own paper designs.

The Note Pad

The oft-ignored Notes section is a great place for storing random thoughts and odd things that you want to write down. You can attach a note to any other Entourage element, making them ideal for tasks like these:

- Typing in the driving directions to an event you've added to your calendar.

- Adding a record of a follow-up phone call you had with a given contact to an email message.

- Adding phone-call details, physical descriptions, or Web site address to somebody's card in your Address Book.

Notes, despite their plain appearance, are incredibly flexible and can be used anywhere text is needed.

Figure 10-9:
The Notes window is nothing more than a list of notes. The familiar blank (usually labeled "Title contains") at the upper-right corner of the screen helps you filter your thousands of memos down to just a few. Oddly enough, Entourage doesn't offer a Preview pane for notes at the bottom of the main window, as it does with email messages and Address Book entries.

Notes Mode

To put Entourage into Notes mode, click the Notes icon in the upper left of the Entourage main window, or choose View→Go To→Notes (⌘-4). The right side of the Entourage main window switches over to the Notes feature, as shown in Figure 1-9.

Creating Notes

To create a new note once you're viewing the Notes list, click the New button or press ⌘-N. (If you're not already in Notes view, choose File→New→Note, or choose Note from the New pop-up button.)

You get the untitled note window shown in Figure 10-10. Type a title for the note, press Tab, and then type the body of the note into the lower, larger box (driving directions, an order number, or whatever).

As you go, don't miss the formatting toolbar that lets you add colors, fonts, and other visual spice to a note. These formatting controls offer the same HTML capabilities as email messages, which means that you can paste a formatted note into an email message when the day comes where you'd find that necessary. You can also paste—or drag—formatted text from another application (say, a Word document) into a note and have the text retain much of its formatting. Notes can also contain hyperlinks, pictures, sounds, movies, background images, and so on. Although Notes are mostly intended to help organize small bits of text and information, they can be quite large, holding hundreds of kilobytes of text if necessary.

Once you've typed your note (or pasted text into it), just close the window, or click Save, or choose File→Save, or press ⌘-S. Your note's title now shows up in the Notes list.

To delete a note, highlight its name in the list and then click the Delete button in the toolbar, or choose Edit→Delete, or press ⌘-delete.

Tip: By far one of the best things about Notes is the ability to link them to other Entourage elements (calendar appointments, for example). Don't miss the discussion of Links that begins on page 426.

Figure 10-10:
Notes provide a resting place for all of those things that should be attached to other Entourage items, but for which there are no proper categories.

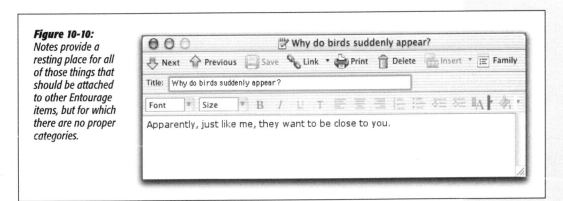

Printing Notes

To print a note, choose File→Print, or click the Print button in the toolbar. Entourage puts up the Print window for Notes, in which you can choose to print all notes or just the selected ones. You can also specify how those notes are laid out (cut lines, page numbers, and so on) and whether any pictures in your notes get printed. Finally, you can select whether the notes should be printed in a format that works with Franklin Covey or Day Runner planners, or even add your own form to that list with a click of the "Add form" button.

Advanced Entourage

Although the last three chapters have plumbed the depths of Entourage's primary modules, this vast program has even more power up its software sleeve. This chapter shows you a few more ways to harness the program's seething mass of muscle, including:

- **Searching.** How to find a particular scrap of information in the Entourage haystack of events, messages, and contacts.

- **Linking.** How to link bits of data to each other, forming a useful web of interrelated events.

- **Customizing.** How to play with the program's views and preferences, the better to tailor the program to your liking.

Palm Synchronization

This would also be the chapter, by the way, where you'd read about Entourage's remarkable capability to synchronize the information in its Categories, Address Book, Notes, Calendar, and Task modules with the corresponding programs on Palm organizers (or compatibles from Sony, Handspring, and so on). Imagine the convenience of carrying the Mac-based details of your life around in your pocket! Unfortunately, as this book goes to press, that's not yet possible in Entourage X.

The problem isn't making the Mac sync with a Palm—it's making Microsoft sync with Palm Computing. The latter didn't finish the Mac OS X version of its synchronization software in time for Microsoft to include it in the original release of Office X—or even the June 2002 update to Office X (page 12).

Microsoft promised to put the Palm synchronization feature back into Entourage by the end of summer 2002, and to make it work as least as well as it did in Office 2001. That was, alas, too late for this book's date with the printer.

Once that great moment comes, however, you'll find a free, downloadable insert to this chapter that covers the Palm-syncing feature step-by-step. (To find it, visit *www.missingmanuals.com,* and then click the "Missing CD-ROM" icon.)

Tip: If you're lucky enough to own an Apple iPod music player, you don't need a Palm organizer just to carry your little black book around in your pocket. You can transfer your contact list right to the iPod, where you can scroll through it using the new Contacts menu (latest iPod software update required). All you need is the AppleScript program called Entourage to iPod. It's a free download from the Apple Web site or from *www.missingmanuals.com.*

Multiple Identities

Trying to master every last feature of Office X could drive almost anyone to developing multiple identities.

When Microsoft refers to multiple identities, however, it's talking about an Entourage feature that lets several members of a family, school, or work circle use the same program on the same Mac—but maintain independent calendars, email accounts, mailing list info, rules, messages, preferences, signatures, to do lists, address books, and so on.

You'll find reference to these *identities* throughout the Office X suite. For example, the currently selected Entourage identity is the source of names for the AutoText feature in Word described on page 98. (That's also why you can't edit or switch identities while Word, Excel, or PowerPoint are open. They depend on the currently active Entourage identity for some information.)

To some extent, of course, Mac OS X makes the Identities feature obsolete. After all, everyone who shares a Mac OS X machine generally signs in with a name and password as it is—and therefore each person's mail, calendar, and other information is *already* separate. Still, there's nothing to stop you from using Identities on Macs where the user-accounts feature isn't turned on (because it's just you and a spouse, say, with no secrets from each other), or when you want to create different identities for *yourself* (a Work and a Home collection of email, for example). For more detail on handling multiple users and identities, see the box on page 420.

Creating a New Identity

When you first set up Entourage, you get a single identity. (Of course, you can have multiple email *accounts* within that identity.) To create a new identity, proceed like this:

1. **Quit all Microsoft Office programs except Entourage. In Entourage, choose Entourage→Switch Identity (Option-⌘-Q).**

   (Just be careful not to hit *Shift-⌘-Q*, which logs you off your Mac!)

   Entourage asks you if you really want to switch identities.

2. **Click Switch.**

   The identity management window opens (Figure 11-1). In this window, you can create, rename, or delete a selected identity (or quit Entourage). Be careful before you delete an identity. Once an identity's gone, you can't retrieve any of its information.

Tip: If you turn on "Show this list at startup," Entourage will offer a tidy list of identities each time you start up the program, making it easy to specify which identity to use for that session.

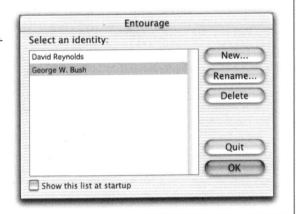

Figure 11-1:
Any identities that you create in Entourage show up in this window. Use the three buttons along the right-hand side to create, edit, or delete those identities.

3. **Click New.**

   The small New Identity window pops up.

4. **Type a name for your new identity.**

   Choose a descriptive name for the new identity.

5. **Follow the Setup Assistant.**

   Once you've chosen a name for your new identity, Entourage asks you if you want it to be your default email program. Your reply here actually changes a system-wide setting in Mac OS X, so this choice will apply to *all* your Entourage identities.

After you choose Yes or No, Entourage walks you through the Setup Assistant to create your new identity—a process very similar to what you did when you first set up Entourage (see Chapter 8). When you're done, Entourage opens its main window, displaying that familiar "Welcome to Entourage" mail message in your new Inbox.

Finding Messages

In a short time—shorter than you might think—you'll collect a lot of email messages, contacts, and other Entourage items. Trying to find a particular morsel of information just by browsing becomes impractical. ("I remember reading something about a good deal on Mac memory in some mailing-list posting just last week. Now where the heck did I file it?…")

Fortunately, Entourage includes a powerful (if slow) search feature that can help you find what you're looking for. Even better, you can save these searches as Custom

---

UP TO SPEED

Identities vs. Multiple Users in Mac OS X

Identities are for convenience, not security—that is, they're not guarded by passwords. Anyone sitting in front of your Mac can switch between your Entourage identities at will, read your email, modify or delete your contacts, calendar items, or even delete your identity altogether.

To protect your data with a password, you should set up individual accounts for each person who uses your Mac, instead of using Entourage identities. At its core, Mac OS X is a multiuser operating system, and each account holder has his own desktop, Documents folder, programs, bookmarks, music and picture collections, and more, all of which can be protected from other people who use the same machine. You set up user accounts in the →System Preferences→Users panel. See your Mac OS X help for more details.

If you've already set up identities in Entourage *before* you've created Mac OS X user accounts, more work is involved.

Each identity that you've created is represented by its own folder in the Home→Documents→Microsoft User Data→Office X Identities folder of whomever first set up Mac OS X.

To straighten out your folder setup, you can move the identities to other Mac OS X users. First, log in as the Mac OS X user who has the Entourage identities you want to move. Find the appropriate identity folders within your Office X Identities folder, and then drag (or copy) them to your Home→Public folder.

Next, have other account holders log in. Once they've done so, they can navigate to your Public folder and copy the appropriate identity folders to their *own* Home→Documents→Microsoft User Data→Office X Identities folders. The next time each person opens Entourage, the copied identity will be in place, revealing only that person's email, calendar, and so on.

views so you can use them again later—a handy timesaver if you find yourself often performing similar searches.

The Find Window

To do a basic search, choose Edit→Find (⌘-F), or click the Find button in the upper-right corner of the main window. Either way, the Find window appears (Figure 11-2). Although the basic Find window is small, it offers a wealth of search features. For example:

- In the Find box, type the word or phrase that you're searching for.

- Click "Current item" to search for the specified phrase within the currently selected item (such as a message or note).

- Use the pop-up menu to search for the phrase within just one facet of Entourage: Messages (your email), Contacts (your addresses), Calendar Events, Tasks, or Notes. If you can't even remember which of these features contains the elusive message, you can choose All Items—but be prepared to rent a video during the time Entourage will take to search its entire multimegabyte database.

- If you turn on "Search subjects, titles, and names only," Entourage restricts its search to just those things, *greatly* speeding up the search. Now, instead of having to "read" every word of every message, address, and set of driving directions, for example, Entourage can just skim their titles.

- Click More Options to open the Advanced Find window, described next.

After specifying how and where you want to search, click Find or press Return. Entourage begins its quest.

Figure 11-2:
The basic Find function in Entourage is a simple window with a single text field and a couple of controls to help you narrow your search. Use this feature when you're searching for a single item that you're pretty sure is in a specific message or location.

Once the search is wrapped up, the results appear in a Search Results window. It looks very much like an email folder window, with a small set of columns indicating an item's type and status, columns for Title, Date, and Category, plus a standard Entourage toolbar along the top of the window. If your search turns up lots of results, you can sort the found items by any of these criteria, just as you'd sort your Inbox window.

Advanced Find

Suppose you want to search for a message containing the term "Rosebud" from your friend c_kane@example.com—a message that came with an attached file. Performing such a pinpoint, multiple-criteria search would be impossible using the Find methods described so far.

The Advanced Find dialog box, on the other hand, lets you build complex searches like this one with just a few pop-up menus.

To use Advanced Find, choose Edit→Advanced Find, press ⌘-F, or click More Options in the Find window. As shown in Figure 11-3, the resulting mega-Find dialog box is divided into three sections:

- **Item Types.** Using the checkboxes in this section, you can select any combination of Messages, Contacts, Calendar events, Tasks, or Notes to search. If you're willing to wait for a lengthy search, you can click All Items to turn them all on.

- **Location.** This section lets you confine the search to the email folder listed in the "Only in this folder" pop-up menu—a great timesaver. If you turn on "Search subfolders," Entourage also searches through the folders *within* the selected folder, if any. (These options apply only to mail and newsgroup messages, not calendar items, tasks, and so on.)

- **Criteria.** This is the heart of Advanced Find's power, where you specify exactly what you are—or are not—looking for. Using the pop-up menus, you can choose any of 25 different characteristics for the email message or other Entourage tid-

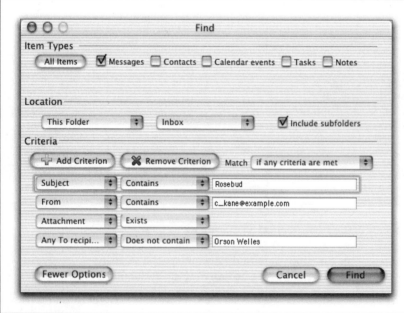

Figure 11-3:
If you happen to be looking for messages with the subject of Rosebud sent from c_kane@example.com, but you want only the ones with attachments that weren't sent to that busybody Orson Welles, then Entourage's Find window can handle what you want.

bit you're looking for: who it's from, whether there was an attachment, whether it's junk mail, its category or status, and so on.

Once you've selected a criterion from the first pop-up menu at the left, use the second pop-up menu to tell Entourage what it is about that criterion that you're looking for, such as a subject that does not end with "izza." (Figure 11-3 shows an example.)

As if these controls didn't let you be specific enough, you can layer on additional criteria by clicking the Add Criterion button. Each time you do so, you get a new row of pop-up menus to further refine your search. See Figure 11-3 for an example. If you're into logic puzzles, you can also use the Match pop-up menu to indicate whether you want to see search results that match any of your criteria, all criteria, or none of the criteria.

POWER USERS' CLINIC

Custom Views

After you've performed a search, the results appear in a Search Results window. If you save the search results window as a custom view, you in effect save the search itself, enabling you to repeat the same search over and over without the work of opening the Find window.

For example, you could set up a custom view that rounds up only the messages that are less than a week old, from your boss, with a subject line pertaining to your current project.

To save a custom view, perform a search using either Find or Advanced Find, and then choose File→Save As Custom View (or click the Save As Custom View button in the search results window toolbar). This brings up a window that looks like the Advanced Find window, except that it has room for you to name your search. Give it a name ("Baxter Project Emails," for example) and click OK. Your search now appears with its own icon in a section of Entourage's Custom Views function, as shown here.

Entourage comes with dozens of prefab custom views, sorted into categories based on their search criteria: Mail Views, Address Book Views, Calendar Views, and so on. A special category called Combined Views contains searches that span more than one Entourage function, like one that hunts through both tasks and calendar items. The canned views look for contacts in certain categories, for messages received today, and so on.

To perform one of the searches described by a custom view, just click its name; Entourage automatically shows the matching items on the right side of the main window, temporarily hiding all others. Custom views you create yourself (such as "Budapest" or "Anniversary Msgs & Events" illustrated here) appear in categories related to what they search: if your custom view searches email and newsgroup messages, it'll appear under Mail Views, and so on.

Find Related

Entourage has another way of searching for items—the Find Related command. It lets you find all email messages to or from an individual person in one fell swoop—a handy technique when there are hundreds or thousands of messages in your message list, and you're trying to find the messages that constituted a particular correspondence.

To use this feature, open your address book. Click the name of a person listed, and then choose Edit→Find Related. Entourage searches for any messages sent to or received from that person. The results appear in a Search Results window, which you can save as a custom view, if you like.

Links

The Link command lets you weave your own web of connections between Entourage items. You might use it to connect, for example, someone in your address book to a specific calendar event *and* to all of the messages sent to and from that person *regarding* that calendar event, for example.

Once you've set up such a link, you can use it to quickly open the event to which it's linked. When you've linked an item, a small link icon appears in the item's listing in Entourage's main window. To open a link, click the link icon and select a linked item from the menu that pops up (see Figure 11-4).

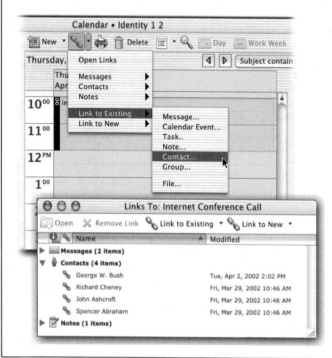

Figure 11-4:
Top: To create a link, choose from the Links pop-up button on the toolbar. Bottom: After you've created a link, you can use the Link button as a menu, or click it to open a separate window showing all linked items. The submenus list the different categories of linked items you may have set up. In this example, you can jump directly from the Links window to the contact window of any of the four people who'll be coming to the meeting, as well as the messages and notes linked to the meeting.

You create a link like this:

1. **Highlight the item that you want to create a link for.**

   For example, click the name of an email message, click an item on your calendar, or highlight the name of one of your to-do items.

2. **To create a connection with a piece of information that's already in Entourage, choose from the Tools→Link to Existing submenu. When the Link Maker window opens, find the Entourage item you want to link to and *drag its name* directly on top of the Link Maker window, as shown in Figure 11-5.**

   You may first have to click one of the other icons in the Folder list, such as the Calendar or Notes icon—whatever's necessary to reveal the appropriate list. (You can also choose the Link to Existing command from the Link pop-up button on the Entourage toolbar.)

Tip: You can even drag *files from your hard drive* into the Link Maker window, directly from the Finder (if you can see it). In effect, Entourage is giving you the option to set up any calendar item, address book entry, or email message, for example, as a launching bay for the appropriate items on your Mac, such as Word documents. You can open the file as described under "Using Links" on page 428.

If you want to link your original item to more than one other bit of information, that's fine. Just keep dragging items into the Link Maker window. Entourage automatically creates the links as you go; you'll see "Link Created" appear briefly in the "Link To" area of the Link Maker window.

Figure 11-5:
The top of the window—the Link from section—displays the item that was selected when you began the procedure. The bottom portion of the window—the Link to section—is where you drag other items, such as messages, contacts, or notes, to create links.

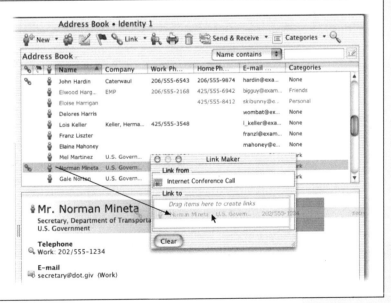

---

3. **If, instead, you want to link to an empty, brand-new Mail Message, News Message, Calendar Event, Task, Note, Contact, or Group, choose from the Tools→Link to New submenu.**

(Here again, you can also use the Link pop-up button on the Entourage toolbar to produce the Link to New submenu.)

Entourage creates the corresponding tidbit (email message, calendar event, or whatever) right away and lets you fill in the details on the fly. When you save the new item, Entourage automatically forges the link. For example, if you link somebody's address book card to a new mail message, Entourage creates a new mail message for you to address and fill out.

Using Links

Once you've created links to a particular Entourage item, a tiny chain-link icon appears next to its name. At this point, you can view a pop-up list of its links. By choosing one of them, you instantly open the Link item.

To view this pop-up list of links, use one of these techniques:

- Click the chain-link icon that appears next to its name and use it as a menu.
- Highlight an item that displays the chain-link icon, and then use the Link pop-up button on the Entourage toolbar as a menu, as in Figure 11-4.
- Highlight an icon that shows the chain-link icon and then choose Tools→Open Links.

This last technique opens the Links window, which lets you go beyond simply opening link items. Its toolbar buttons—Open, Remove Link, Link to Existing Item, or Link to New Item—let you open the item to which the link leads, remove a link, or create a link to new or existing item, respectively.

Tip: By the way, if all of this linking business sounds like it creates more busywork than it eliminates, you can ignore Links completely. You wouldn't be alone.

Categories

Categories are labels that you can apply to just about any Entourage item. They're designed to let you apply an organizational scheme to a group of items that may not have much in common.

For example, you can define a category related to a trip that you're taking, or to a certain work project, and apply that category to dissimilar Entourage information bits (calendar, email, and to-do items, for example). Each category can have its own color, making it easy to identify at a glance. Categories, in other words, are a convenient, easy-to-use means of helping you organize and keep track of your Entourage information.

Setting Up Categories

Entourage comes with eight prefab categories—Family, Friends, Holiday, Junk, Personal, Recreation, Travel, and Work. If you import holidays into Entourage—see page 389—they show up in a category of their own.

You can also create new categories, of course. To do so, choose Edit Categories from the Categories pop-up button on the toolbar, or choose Edit→Categories→Edit Categories. Either way, you now face the Edit Categories window (Figure 11-6). To create a new category, click New and type the name you want. Entourage assigns a color to your new category, but you can choose any of the thirteen colors listed on the pop-up menu, or choose Other to mix your own color.

You can also delete a category: Click its name and then click Delete.

Tip: The Categories window has one other nifty feature: the Find Items in Category button. Select a category for which you'd like to search for items, and then click this button. Entourage shows you a tidy listing all of the items in your Entourage world—messages, tasks, and so on—that have been assigned to that category.

Figure 11-6:
Top: Entourage lets you create any number of your own categories, which you can then apply to Entourage items of any kind—including folders in your email box.

Bottom: To assign multiple categories to an item, open the Assign Categories window and then turn on the checkboxes next to the categories you want to assign. Once you've done so, click OK; Entourage assigns all checked categories to the selected items.

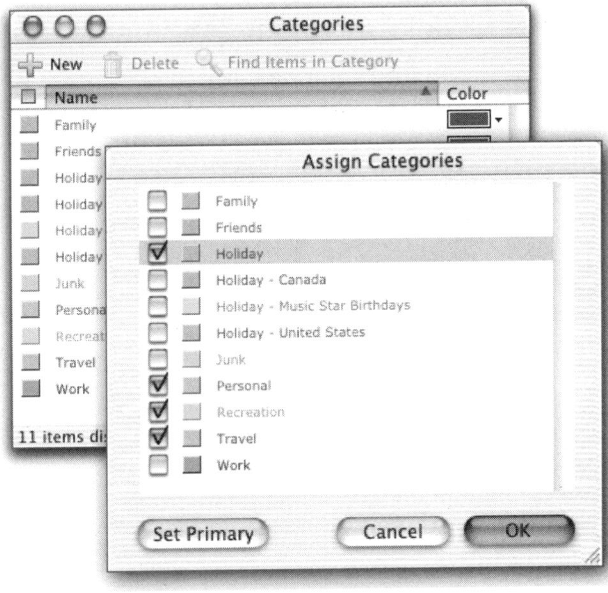

Assigning a Category

To apply a category to an Entourage item—an email message, calendar event, task, note, news message, contact, or even an item in the email Folder list—highlight it. (You can highlight a lot of them at once, if that's what you want to do.) Use the

Categories pop-up button in the toolbar or the Edit→Categories submenu to choose a category. Entourage assigns the category to the selected item for you and changes its color accordingly.

Tip: The main window for certain kinds of Entourage information, including email messages, tasks, notes, and the Address Book, includes a column called Categories. One of the easiest ways to apply a category to an item is to click in this column, if it's showing; a pop-up menu of your categories appears.

You can even place an individual Entourage item into more than one category. To do so, click the Categories button (or press ⌘-comma) to bring up the Assign Categories window (Figure 11-10), in which you can assign as many categories as you want by turning on the appropriate checkboxes. For instance, a note with flight information might pertain to both the Travel and Work categories. (You can do the same thing by choosing Edit→Categories→Assign Categories.)

Checking Your Spelling

In parts of Entourage that involve lots of text (such as notes and mail messages), you can ask Entourage to check your spelling for you. Although Entourage can do this on the fly by marking suspect words with a red squiggly underline, it also has a more traditional spell checker at its disposal.

To use Entourage's spell checker, open the note or message that you want to check and then choose Tools→Spelling (option-L). The procedure works much as it does in Word (see Figure 11-7), and in fact relies on the same spelling dictionaries.

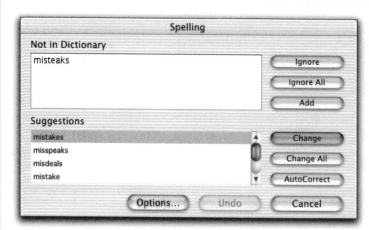

Figure 11-7:
Entourage's Spelling window flags questionable words; you click the buttons on the right to ignore, add, or correct those words. The Options button at the bottom is a direct link to the Spelling preferences, in which you can control aspects of how spell checks are conducted.

The Script Menu

There's no more conspicuous badge that Microsoft has gotten Macintosh religion than its embrace of AppleScript, the Macintosh-only programming language. As a happy result, even advanced-beginner programmers can automate the Office programs with custom features.

Like its sibling Outlook Express, Entourage has some impressive AppleScript capabilities. (In fact, Entourage is the only Office program that *doesn't* exploit Microsoft's own programming language, Visual Basic for Applications.) It even has a Script menu that houses several AppleScript scripts, which add useful features like:

- **Create Event from Message.** When you highlight an email message and choose this command, Entourage creates a new calendar event based on the message. All you have to do is fill in a few details. Even better, the event is automatically linked to the original message.

- **Insert Text File.** When you choose this command, Entourage opens the Choose a File dialog box, so that you can locate a text file to insert into the body of a message. This feature can be handy when you want to send quick, canned responses from time to time.

- **Save Selection.** Here's a great way to save some critical information that's been emailed to you into its own text file on your desktop. Highlight some text, choose Script→Save Selection, and then provide a file name and location when Entourage asks for it.

The best thing about this menu, however, is that you can add your own scripts to it. (Of course, writing such scripts requires some familiarity with programming AppleScript.) Save such scripts as compiled scripts (not text files or applets), and then drop them into your Home→Documents→Microsoft User Data folder→Entourage Script Menu Items folder. They'll show up in the Entourage Scripts menu the next time you run the program.

POWER USERS' CLINIC

Adding a Shortcut Key to Script Menu Items

You can add a keyboard shortcut for any script in the Entourage Script Menu Items folder.

First, locate the file's icon in the Finder. (You'll find it in your Home→Documents→Microsoft User Data folder→Entourage Script Menu Items folder.) Onto the end of its file name, just tack a backslash (\), the letter *c*, and then the Control-key that you'd like to use. For example, to add the shortcut key equivalent Control-A to an archive email

script, add the following text to the end of its file name: |*c*A. (That first character is a backslash.) You can't assign the ⌘ key for this purpose—only the Control key.

The next time you pull down the Script menu in Entourage, you'll see your key combo (represented by the ^ symbol, which designates the Control key, and the key that you chose) next to the script's name.

If you aren't an AppleScript programmer, you can still capitalize on this feature by downloading scripts that other people have written. For example:

- At *www.mattridley.com/products/applescript/,* you'll find lots of information about using AppleScript with Entourage, along with several scripts available for download.

- You can also visit Allen Watson's iDisk at *http://homepage.mac.com/allenwatson/* for more Entourage scripts for all Entourage modules.

- Paul Berkowitz has scripts available for download at *http://homepage .mac.comberkowit28.*

- You can also find a hearty collection of Paul Berkowitz's Entourage scripts at *www.applescriptcentral.com.*

3

Part Three: Excel

CHAPTER
12

Basic Excel

The best ad Microsoft ever ran for Excel went like this: "99% of spreadsheet users use Microsoft Excel. What are we doing wrong?" It was good because it was true; Excel is the biggest thing going when it comes to hard-core business programs. But Microsoft still seems determined to keep finding ways to make it better, warming the hearts of accountants and statisticians the world over.

Excel X offers a modest new feature list, but that's OK—Mac OS X compatibility is quite a hefty feature all by itself. Excel's development team *carbonized* the program, meaning they adapted it to look and work like a genuine Mac OS X program. That's good news for the charts and graphs that Excel makes, which now capitalize on the gorgeous visual effects offered by Mac OS X's graphics software.

Spreadsheet Basics

You use Excel, of course, to make a *spreadsheet*—an electronic ledger book composed of rectangles, known as *cells*, laid out in a grid (see Figure 12-1). As you type numbers into the rectangular cells, the program can automatically perform any number of calculations on them.

Opening a Spreadsheet

A new Excel document, called a *workbook,* is made up of several pages called *worksheets.* (More on the workbook/worksheet distinction in Chapter 14.) Each worksheet looks a great deal like a traditional spreadsheet, with lettered columns and numbered rows. The letters and numbers provide a quick way to refer to the cells in the grid—it's a lot like the game Battleship. (In fact, with a lot of time and some sophisticated programming skills, you could even *play* Battleship using Excel.)

You can create a plain-Jane Excel workbook by selecting File→New Workbook (⌘-N), or you can use the Office Project Gallery (File→Project Gallery). The Project Gallery lists preformatted spreadsheets, complete with formulas already inserted. If you happen to find a template that fits what you're trying to do, such as planning a budget, the Gallery can be a real timesaver. (See page 15 for more on the Project Gallery.)

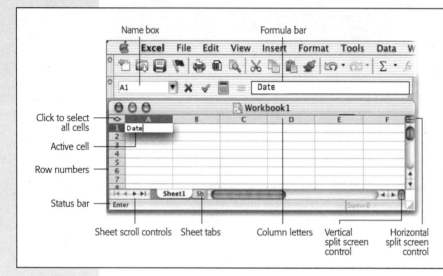

Figure 12-1:
Excel X matches Mac OS X. It has the new Close, Minimize, and Zoom buttons, rounded edges on the top corners, and jelly-bean-like split boxes and scroll bars. In the status area at the bottom left, Excel tells what it thinks is happening—in this case, the active cell (A1) is being edited.

Tip: You can also open an existing document by choosing from the list of recent files at the bottom of the File menu. If you'd rather Excel not keep track, you'll find the "Recently used file list" control by choosing Excel→Preferences→General panel. This is also the place to change how *many* recent files show up in the File menu.

Each worksheet can grow to huge proportions—256 columns wide (labeled A, B, C…AA, AB, AC…all the way to IV), and 65,536 rows tall (see Figure 12-2). Furthermore, you can get at even more cells by using other worksheets in the workbook—switch to them by clicking the tabs at the bottom left. You can add many more sheets to a workbook, too, if you need them, by choosing Insert→Worksheet. (This command inserts a new worksheet *before* the currently active worksheet.)

In total, you can have billions of cells in a single Excel document. The only company that needs more space than *that* for its accounting is Microsoft.

Tip: To rename a worksheet, double-click the sheet's name (it's on the tab on the bottom) and type in a new one. Sheet names can be as long as 31 characters.

Each cell acts as a container for one of two things: data or a formula. *Data* can be text, a number, a date, or just about anything else you can type. A *formula*, on the other hand, does something with the data in *other* cells—such as adding together the numbers in them. (More on formulas later in this chapter.)

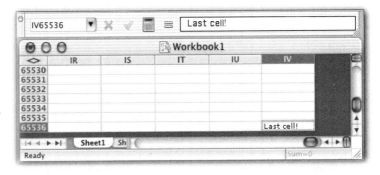

Figure 12-2:
You can't scroll all the way to cell IV65536 in a new spreadsheet, but as you fill in cells at the outer edges of what you can see, Excel automatically tacks on new chunks of empty rows and columns. Or, to make a hyperspatial leap to the lower right corner, enter IV65536 in the Name box on the left side of the Formula bar.

Excel refers to cells by their coordinates, such as B23 (column B, row 23). A new spreadsheet has cell A1 selected (surrounded by a thick border)—it's the *active* cell. When you start typing, the cell pops up slightly, apparently hovering a quarter-inch above your screen's surface. Whatever you type appears in both the active cell and the Edit box on the right side of the Formula bar (see Figure 12-1). When you finish typing, you can do any of the following to make the active cell's new contents stick:

- Press Return, Tab, Enter, or an arrow key.
- Click another cell.
- Click the Enter button in the Formula bar.

Tip: If you keep landing in this "in-cell editing" mode accidentally, choose Excel→Preferences→Edit panel, turn off "Edit directly in cell," and click OK. Now you can edit cell contents only in the Edit box on the Formula bar.

Data Entry

Working in an Excel sheet is simple, at its heart: You enter data or a formula into a cell, move to the next cell, enter more information, and so on. Before entering data in a cell, you must first *select* the cell. Clicking is the easiest method; after you click a cell, the cell border thickens and the cell does that popping-up thing.

To select a cell far away from the current active cell, enter the cell's *address* (the column letter followed by the row number) in the Name box on the Formula bar (see Figure 12-2). Or choose Edit→Go To, which brings up a dialog box in which you can enter the address of the lucky cell in the Reference field.

But the fastest means of getting from cell to cell is to use the keyboard. Excel is loaded with keyboard shortcuts that make it easy to plow through an entire sheet's worth of cells without having to touch the mouse. Here are the navigation keystrokes that make data input easier:

Keypress	What Happens
Arrow key	Selects a different cell—the next one above, below, to the left, or to the right of the current one.
Shift-arrow key	Selects the current cell *and* the one above, below, to the left, or to the right. Hold the Shift key down and press the arrow key more than once to extend the selection.
Option-left arrow, -right arrow	Makes the previous or next *sheet* in the workbook active.
Control-arrow key	*Moves* the active cell to the next non-empty cell in the direction indicated by the arrow key.
Return	Accepts the entry and moves the active cell down one row.
Shift-Return	Accepts the entry and moves the active cell up one row.
Tab	Accepts the entry and moves the active cell right one column.
Shift-Tab	Accepts the entry and moves the active cell left one column.
Control-Option-Return	Starts a new line within the same cell.
Control-Return	Fills each selected cell with the same entry. (First select the cell range, type the data that you want repeated in each cell, and then hit Control-Return to fill all of the cells.)
Esc	Cancels an entry (although this doesn't always work).
Control-D	Fills the active cell with the contents of the cell directly above it.
Control-R	Fills the active cell with the contents of the cell directly to the left of it.
Control-'	Fills the active cell with the *formula* in the cell directly above it.
Control-;	Enters the current date.
Control-Shift-:	Enters the current time.

Tip: Return doesn't have to select the next cell down; it can select any of the four neighboring cells, or do nothing at all. You change what the Return key does in the Excel→Preferences→Edit panel.

A quick glance at that table should confirm the bad news to Excel users who haven't upgraded in a while. Back in Excel 2001, Microsoft changed the Excel 98 keystrokes for some of the most important editing commands as part of an effort to make all Office programs use more consistent keystrokes, and those changes are still present in Excel X. Combinations that used to involve the ⌘ key, such as ⌘-D for Fill Down and ⌘-I for Insert Cells, now require the Control key instead.

In Excel 2001, you were stuck with these changes. In Excel X, fortunately, you're allowed to change the program's keystrokes back to their old assignments—or anything you like. See page 633.

UP TO SPEED

Window Tricks

Because spreadsheets can be wide, sprawling affairs, Excel is filled with window-manipulation tools that let you control how the program uses your precious screen real estate.

For example, when you need to see a few more rows and columns, choose View→Full Screen. Excel hides all of its toolbars, status bars, and other non-essential detritus. Your cells fill your monitor. Choose View→Full Screen again (or click Close Full Screen on the tiny, one-button toolbar) to bring back the bars.

Another example: As shown here, Excel's scroll bars offer vertical and horizontal *split boxes*, which you can double-click or drag to split a sheet into independently scrolling sections, as shown here. (Note the discontinuity in the let-tering and numbering of rows and columns in this illustration; these panes have been independently scrolled.) To remove the split, just double-click the split box or the *split bar* that separates the panes. (Or choose Window→ Remove Split.)

You don't have to split the window if all you want to do is keep the row and column names in view while scrolling the rest of the document, however. Excel offers a much more streamlined means of locking the column and row labels:

Click in the cell just below and to the right of the row/column label intersection, and then choose Window→Freeze Panes. Now scrolling affects only the body of the spreadsheet; the row and column labels remain visible.

Kinds of Data

You can enter four kinds of data into an Excel spreadsheet (not including formulas, which are described beginning on page 453): numbers, text, dates, or times. Most of the time, entering data is as straightforward as typing, but there are exceptions.

Numbers

• There are only 21 characters that Excel considers numbers: 1 2 3 4 5 6 7 8 9 0 . , ( ) + - / $ % e and E. Anything else is treated as text, which is ineligible for performing most calculations. For example, if Excel sees *three point one four* in a cell, it "sees" a bunch of typed words with no numerical value; when it sees *3.14*, it sees a number.

• Depending on the formatting of the cell in which you're entering numbers, Excel might try to do some work for you. For example, if you've applied *currency formatting* to a cell (see page 486), Excel turns *3/2* into $1.50. But if you've formatted the same cell as a date, Excel turns *3/2* into a date—March 2 of the current year.

• If the number you've entered is longer than eleven digits (such as *12345678901112*), Excel converts it to scientific notation (*1.23457E+13*).

Text

• Text can be any combination of characters: numbers, letters, or other symbols.

• To make Excel look at a number as if it were a string of text (rather than a number with which it can do all kinds of mathematical wizardry), you must format the cell as a text-based cell. Just select the cell and choose Format→Cells. Click the Number tab and then select Text from the Category list. Click OK.

Dates

• You can perform math on dates, just as though they were numbers. The trick is to type an equal sign (=) into the cell that will contain the answer; then enclose the dates in quotation marks and put the operator (like + or *) between them. For example, if you click a cell, type *="4/1/2002" -"3/2/1965"*, and then press Enter, Excel will fill the cell with 13544, the number of days between the two dates.

This math is made possible by the fact that dates in Excel *are* numbers. Behind the scenes, Excel converts any date you type into a special date serial number, which is composed of a number to the left side of a decimal point (the number of days since January 1, 1904) and a number on the right (the fraction of a day).

• When entering dates, you can use either a slash or a hyphen to separate months, days, and years.

Warning: Usually it's OK to format date and time numbering at any time. However, you may avoid occasional obscure problems by applying date or time formatting *before* you enter the data in the cell.

Times

• Excel also treats *times* as numbers—specifically, as the fractional part of a date serial number, which is a number representing the number of days since midnight on January 1, 1904.

- Excel bases times on the 24-hour clock, or military time. To enter a time using the 12-hour clock, follow the number with an *a* or a *p*. For example, to Excel, *9:34* always means 9:34 a.m., but *9:34 p* means 9:34 p.m. (*21:34* also means 9:34 p.m., but it appears in the spreadsheet the way you typed it—as 21:34.)

- As with dates, you can perform calculations on times by entering an equal sign and then enclosing the times in quotation marks and typing the separator in the middle. For example, *="9:34"-"2:43"* gives you 0.285416667, the decimal fraction of a day between 2:43 a.m. and 9:34 a.m. (If you format the cell with time formatting, as described on page 488, you instead get 6:51, or six hours and 51 minutes' difference.)

WORKAROUND WORKSHOP

When Excel Formats Numbers as Dates

If you enter what looks like a date to Excel (say, *May 3, 1999*), and then later, in the process of revising your spreadsheet, enter a number containing a decimal (such as 23.25), Excel converts your decimal into a date. (23 becomes January 24, 1904).

What's going on?

All cells start out with a generic format. But when you enter what Excel interprets as a date or time, Excel automatically applies date or time formatting. In this example, when Excel interpreted the first entry as a date, it applied *date formatting* to the cell.

Later, when the first entry was replaced with a decimal number, Excel *retained* the date formatting–and merrily displayed the number as a date. You don't have to let Excel guess at what format you want, though. Take charge! Select the cells in question and choose Format→Cells. Use the Number tab to select the appropriate format, and your troubles are over.

Similarly, to keep Excel from turning two numbers separated by a forward slash into a date, and keep it as a fraction instead, put a 0 and a space in front of the fraction (enter *0 1/4*). Excel now understands that you intended to enter a fraction.

Tedium Savings 1: AutoComplete

Excel X is teeming with features designed to save you typing. The first, *AutoComplete*, comes into play when you enter repetitive data down a column. Find out more in Figure 12-3.

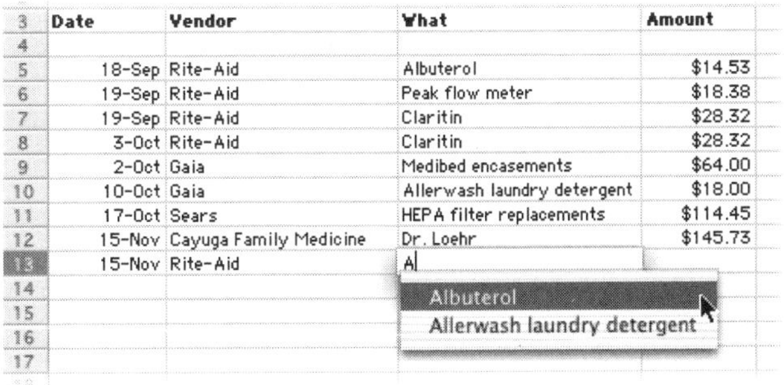

Figure 12-3:
Excel's AutoComplete function watches as you type in a given cell; if your entry looks as though it may match the contents of another cell in the same column, Excel offers a pop-up menu of those possibilities. To select one, press the down arrow until the entry you want is highlighted, and then press Enter. Alternatively, just click the entry in the list. Either way, Excel finishes the typing work for you.

	Date	Vendor	What	Amount
3	Date	Vendor	What	Amount
4				
5	18-Sep	Rite-Aid	Albuterol	$14.53
6	19-Sep	Rite-Aid	Peak flow meter	$18.38
7	19-Sep	Rite-Aid	Claritin	$28.32
8	3-Oct	Rite-Aid	Claritin	$28.32
9	2-Oct	Gaia	Medibed encasements	$64.00
10	10-Oct	Gaia	Allerwash laundry detergent	$18.00
11	17-Oct	Sears	HEPA filter replacements	$114.45
12	15-Nov	Cayuga Family Medicine	Dr. Loehr	$145.73
13	15-Nov	Rite-Aid	Al	
14			Albuterol	
15			Allerwash laundry detergent	
16				
17				

Tedium Savings 2: AutoFill

Excel's AutoFill feature can save you hours of tedious typing, thanks to its ingenious ability to fill miles of cells with data automatically. The Edit→Fill submenu is especially useful when you're duplicating data or typing items in a series (such as days of the week, months of the year, or even sequential apartment numbers). It has seven options: Down, Right, Up, Left, Across Worksheets, Series, and Justify.

Here's how they work. In each case, as shown in Figure 12-4, suppose you've started the process by typing data into a cell and then highlighted a block of cells beginning with that cell:

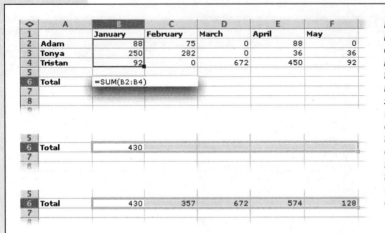

Figure 12-4:
Excel can quickly fill a range of cells with numbers and text, but filling a range of cells with formulas is where AutoFill really shines. Suppose you've set up a formula in cell B6 (top), which adds the contents of column B. Select cells B6 through E6 (center) and then choose Edit→Fill→Right. Excel fills cells C6 through E6 with the same Sum formula (bottom), which totals the columns above them.

- **Down, Up.** Fills the selected block of cells with whatever's in the top or bottom cell of the selected block. You might use one of these commands when setting up a series of formulas in a column that add a row of cells.

- **Right, Left.** Fills the selected range of cells with whatever's in the leftmost or rightmost cell. For example, you'd use this feature when you need to put the same total calculation at the bottom of 23 different columns. Figure 12-4 shows a common example.

- **Across Worksheets.** Fills the cells in other sheets in the same workbook with the contents of the selected cells. For example, suppose you want to set up worksheets that track inventory and pricing over different months in different locations, and you want to use a different worksheet for each location. You can fill in all of the general column and row headings (such as part numbers and months) across worksheets with this command.

To make this work, start by selecting the cells whose contents you wish to copy. Then select the sheets you want to fill by Shift-⌘-clicking the sheet tabs at the bottom of the window. (If you can't see all the tabs easily, drag the slider between the tabs and the horizontal scroll bar. When you drag it to the right, the scroll bar shrinks, leaving more room for the tabs.)

Choose Edit→Fill→Across Worksheet. A small dialog box (see Figure 12-5) asks whether you want to copy data, formulas, or both across the selected worksheets. Make your choice by clicking one of the radio buttons, and then click OK.

Figure 12-5:
You can copy into other worksheets: **All** *(both the formulas and data),* **Contents** *(just the data in the worksheet), or* **Formats** *(just the formulas in the worksheet).*

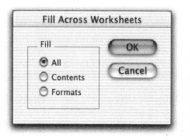

- **Series.** Fills the selected cells with a *series* of increasing or decreasing values based on the contents of the topmost cell (if the selected cells are in a column) or the leftmost cell (if the cells are in a row).

For example, suppose you're about to type in the daily statistics for the number of dot-com startups that went out of business during the first two weeks of 2002. Instead of having to type fourteen dates into a row of cells, you can let Excel do the grunt work for you.

Enter *1/1/2002* in a cell. Then highlight that cell and the next thirteen cells to its right. Now choose Edit→Fill→Series. The Series window appears, in which you specify how the fill takes place. You could make the cell labels increase by months, years, every other day, or whatever. Click OK; Excel fills the cells with the date series 1/1/2002, 1/2/2002, 1/3/2002, and so on.

Tip: The above example reflects the way Americans write dates, of course. If you use a different system for writing dates (perhaps you live in Europe or Australia), and you've used the Mac's International preference pane (in the Finder, choose →System Preferences) to specify that you like January 14, 2002 written *14/1/2002*, Excel automatically formats dates the way you like them. (Non-U.S. Excel fans may find other glitches in Excel's handling of date calculations, however.)

The other options in this dialog box include Linear (adds the amount in the Step field to each successive cell's number), Growth (*multiplies* by the number in the Step field), and AutoFill (relies on the lists described in the next section).

- **Justify.** Spreads the text in a single cell across several cells. You'd use this function to create a heading that spans the columns beneath it.

If the cells are in a row, this command spreads the text in the leftmost cell across the selected row of cells. If the cells are in a column, it breaks up the text so that one word goes into each cell.

Using the Fill handle

You don't have to use the Edit→Fill submenu to harness the power of Excel's AutoFill feature. As a timesaving gesture, Microsoft also offers you the *fill handle* (see Figure 12-6), a small square in the lower right of a selection rectangle. It lets you fill adjacent cells with data, exactly like the Fill commands—but without a trip to a menu and a dialog box.

To use it, select the cells that contain the data that you want to duplicate or extend, then drag the tiny fill handle across the cells where you want the data to be, as shown in Figure 12-6. Excel then fills the cells, just as though you'd used the Fill Down, Right, Up, or Left command. (To fill a series, Control-click the handle and choose an option from the contextual menu.)

Tip: Excel can perform some dramatic and complex fill operations for you if you highlight *more than one* cell before dragging the fill handle.

Suppose, for example, that you want to create a list of *every third* house on your street. Enter *201 Elm St.* in the first cell, then *204 Elm St.* in the next one down. Highlight both of them, then drag the fill handle at the lower-right corner of the second cell downward.

Excel cleverly fills the previously empty cells with *207 Elm St., 210 Elm St., 213 Elm St.,* and so on.

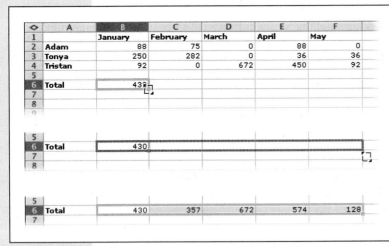

Figure 12-6:
The fill handle provides a smarter alternative to the Edit→Fill submenu. To use it, select the cell containing the formula or values you want to replicate (top). Drag the tiny fill handle at the lower right corner of the selection across the cells you want to fill (middle). Excel duplicates the formula intelligently so that it totals the columns appropriately (bottom).

What's more, the fill handle can do *smart filling* that you won't find on the Edit→Fill submenu. For example, if you type *January* into a cell and then drag the fill handle across the next bunch of cells, Excel fills them with February, March, and so on; ditto for days of the week.

In fact, you can teach Excel about any other sequential lists you use regularly in your line of work (NY Office, Cleveland Office, San Diego Office, and so on). Just choose Excel→Preferences→Custom Lists panel; click Add and then type the series of items in order, each on its own line. Click OK; the AutoFill list is ready to use.

FREQUENTLY ASKED QUESTION

Invasion of the ######s

A few of my numbers have been replaced by ##### symbols. Do I have a virus?

A string of number signs in a cell means, "The cell isn't wide enough to show whatever text or number is supposed to be here. Widen the column—or use a smaller font—if you ever hope to see your numbers again."

As noted later in this chapter, the quickest way to fix the problem is to double-click the *divider line* between the gray column-letter headings—the one to the right of the column containing the ######s. Excel instantly makes the column wide enough to show all the numbers inside of it.

That's not the only error notation you may see in a cell, by the way. Excel may also react to faulty formulas by showing, for example, *#DIV/0!* (your formula is attempting to divide a number by zero, which is a mathematical no-no); *#VALUE!* (you've used unavailable data in a formula, by referring to an empty cell, for example); *#REF* (a bogus cell reference); and so on. For a complete table of these error codes, choose Help→Search Excel Help and search for *error values*.

Selecting Cells (and Cell Ranges)

Selecting a single cell in Excel is easy; just click the cell to select it. Often, though, you'll want to select more than one cell—in readiness for copying and pasting, making a chart, applying boldface, or using the Fill command, for example. Figure 12-7 shows you all you need to know for your selection needs.

- **Select a single cell.** To select a single cell, click it, or enter its address in the Name Box (which is shown in Figure 12-1).

- **Select a block of cells.** To select a rectangle of cells, just drag diagonally across them. You highlight all of the cells within the boundaries of the imaginary rectangle you're drawing. (Or click the cell in one corner of the block and then Shift-click the cell diagonally opposite.)

- **Select a noncontiguous group of cells.** To select cells that aren't touching, ⌘-click (to add individual independent cells to the selection) or ⌘-drag across cells (to add a block of them to the selection). Repeat as many times as you like; Excel is perfectly happy to highlight random cells, or blocks of cells, in various corners of the spreadsheet simultaneously.

- **Select a row or column.** Click a row or column *heading* (the gray label of the row or column).

- **Select several rows or columns.** To select more than one row or column, *drag through* the gray row numbers or column letters. (You can also click the first one, then Shift-click the last one. Excel highlights everything in between.)

- **Select noncontiguous rows or columns.** To select two or more rows or columns that aren't touching, ⌘-click, or ⌘-drag through, the corresponding gray row numbers. You can even combine these techniques, highlighting first rows, then columns, forming intersecting swaths of highlighting.

- **Select all cells.** Press ⌘-A to select every cell on the sheet—or just click the gray, far upper-left rectangle with the diamond in it.

Tip: To select within the *contents* of a cell, double-click the cell and then use the I-beam selection tool to select the text that you want.

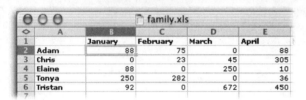
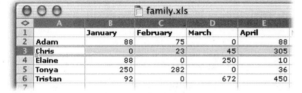
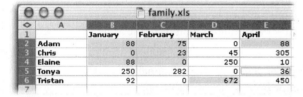
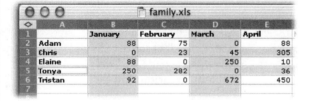

Figure 12-7:
You can highlight spreadsheet cells, rows, and columns in various combinations.

Top: Click a cell (or arrow-key your way into it) to highlight just one cell.

Second from top: Click a row number (4, in this case) to highlight an entire row. Third from top: Drag to highlight a rectangular block of cells; add individual additional cells to the selection by ⌘-clicking.

Bottom: ⌘-click row headings and column headings to highlight intersecting rows and columns.

Moving Things Around

Once you have selected some cells, you can move their contents around in various ways—a handy fact, since few people type everything in exactly the right place the first time.

Cutting, copying, and pasting

Just as in any other Mac application, you can use the Edit menu commands—Cut (⌘-X), Copy (⌘-C), and Paste (⌘-V)—to move cell contents around the spreadsheet—or to a different sheet or workbook altogether.

But unlike other Mac applications, Excel doesn't appear to cut your selection immediately. Instead, the cut area sprouts a dotted, *moving border*, but otherwise remains unaffected. It isn't until you select a destination cell or cells and select Edit→Paste that the cut takes place (and the shimmering stops).

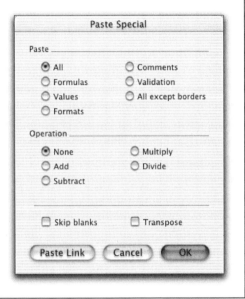

Figure 12-8:
The Paste Special command lets you paste formulas, comments, and formatting independently. The Operations options let you perform a mathematical operation as you paste, such as adding what you've copied to the contents of the cells you're pasting over.

POWER USERS' CLINIC

The Difference Between Cut and Copy

When you use the Cut command on *formulas*, you paste *relative* cell references; when you *copy* a formula, you paste *absolute* references. Page 463 defines these concepts.

For example, if the formula in cell A1 was *=SUM(B1:B4)* when you copied it, the pasted formula in cell A10 changes to say *=SUM(B10:B13)*—the cell references have been offset nine cells down, to reflect the distance between the formula's original cell and its copy. Because you're placing a *copy* of the formula in a new place, the cells to which the formula refers should be offset by the same amount—which

is handy for filling in a spreadsheet that has lots of similar formulas in different locations.

To avoid this shift in pasted formulas, you can make the cell references *absolute* by putting a dollar sign in front of each cell address that you don't want to change.

In the example above, if you always want a SUM function to refer to cells B1 through B4, even after it's been copied and pasted, change the formula to read *=SUM($B$1:$B$4)*. That'll make sure that *everything* stays in place.

Tip: Press the Esc key to make the animated dotted lines stop moving, without otherwise affecting your copy or cut operation. One more piece of advice: Check the status bar at the bottom of the window to find out what Excel thinks is happening ("Select destination and press ENTER or choose Paste," for example).

Paste Special

The Edit→Paste Special command summons a dialog box that interviews you about *how* and *what* to paste. For example, you may decide to paste the formulas contained in the material you copied so that they continue to do automatic math—or only the *values* (the results of the calculations as they appear in the copied material).

Tip: This dialog box also contains the mighty Transpose checkbox, a tiny option that can save your bacon. It lets you swap rows-for-columns in the act of pasting, so that data you'd input in columns winds up in rows, and vice versa.

Drag-and-drop

Excel also lets you grab a selected range of cells and drag the contents to a new location. To do this, select the cells you want to move, then point to the thick border on the edge of the selection, so that the cursor changes into a little hand that grabs the cells. You can now drag the selected cells to another spot on the spreadsheet. When you release the mouse button, Excel moves the data to the new location, exactly as though you'd used Cut and Paste.

There are a few keys that, if held down, modify how dragging and dropping items in Excel works:

- **Option.** If you hold down the Option key, Excel *copies* the contents to the new location, leaving the originals in place.

- **Shift.** Normally, if you drag cells into a spreadsheet area that you've already filled in, Excel asks you if you're sure you want to wipe out the cell contents that were already there. If you Shift-drag cells, however, Excel creates enough new cells to make room for the dragged contents, shoving aside (or down) whatever cell contents were already there to make room.

- **Option and Shift.** Holding down both the Option *and* Shift keys as you drag copies the data *and* inserts new cells for it.

- **Control.** Control-dragging yields a menu of eleven options when you drop the cells. This menu lets you choose whether you want to move the cells, copy them, copy just the values or formulas, create a link or hyperlink, or shift cells around. It even lets you cancel the drag.

Inserting and Removing Cells

Suppose you've just completed your spreadsheet cataloging the rainfall patterns of the Pacific Northwest, county by county, and then it hits you: You forgot Coos County in Oregon. Besides the question of how you could possibly forget Coos County, the larger question remains: What do you do about it in your spreadsheet? Delete the whole thing and start over?

Fortunately, Excel lets you insert new, blank cells, rows, or columns into existing sheets through the Insert menu. Here's how each works.

- **Cells.** The Insert→Cells command summons the Insert dialog box. It lets you insert new, blank cells into your spreadsheet, and lets you specify what happens to the cells that are already in place—whether they get shifted right or down. See Figure 12-9.

> **Tip:** Longtime Excel fans should note that the keystroke for Insert Cells is now Control-I, not ⌘-I.

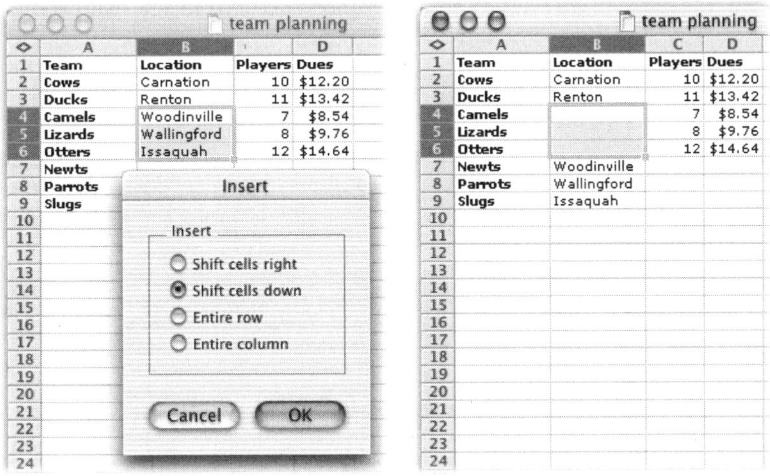

Figure 12-9:
When you select cells and then choose Insert→Cells, Excel asks where you want to put the new cells (left). The two buttons at the bottom let you insert entire rows or columns. Excel will then insert the same number of cells as you have selected in the location selected, and will move the previous residents of those cells in the direction that you specify (right).

- **Rows.** If you choose Insert→Rows, Excel inserts a new, blank row above the active cell.

> **Tip:** If you select some cells before using the Insert→Cells command, Excel inserts the number of rows equal to the number of rows selected in the range. That's a handy way to control how many rows get added—to add six blank rows, highlight six rows, regardless of what's in them at the moment.

- **Columns.** If you choose Insert→Columns, Excel inserts a new blank column to the left of the active cell. If you've selected a range of cells, Excel inserts the number of columns equal to the number of columns selected in the range.

Find and Replace

Exactly as in Word, Excel offers both a Find function, which helps you locate a specific spot in a big workbook, and a Replace feature that's ideal for those moments when your company gets incorporated into a larger one, requiring its name to be changed in 34 places throughout a workbook. The routine goes like this:

1. **Highlight the cells you want to search.**

   This step is crucial. By limiting the search range, you ensure that your search-and-destroy operation won't run rampant through your spreadsheet, changing things you never suspect are being changed.

2. **Choose Edit→Find. In the resulting dialog box, specify what you want to search for, and in which direction (see Figure 12-10).**

   You can use a question mark (?) as a stand-in for a single character, or an asterisk (*) to represent more than one character; in other words, typing *P*ts* will find cells containing "Profits," Prophets," and "Parakeets."

   The "Find entire cells only" checkbox means that Excel will consider a cell a match for your search term only if its entire contents match; a cell that says "Annual profits" isn't considered a match for the search term "Profits."

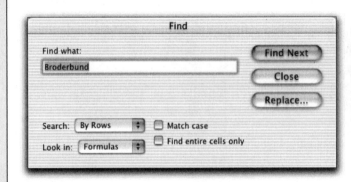

Figure 12-10:
Using the Search pop-up menu, you can specify whether Excel searches the highlighted cells from left to right of each row ("By Rows") or down each column ("By Columns"). Use the "Look in" pop-up menu to specify which cell components are fair game for the search: formulas, values (that is, the results of those formulas, and other data you've typed into the cells), or comments.

3. If you intend to *replace* the cell contents (instead of just finding them), click Replace; type the replacement text into the "Replace with" box. Click Find Next (or press Return).

   Each time you click Find Next, Excel highlights the next cell it finds that matches your search phrase. If you click Replace, you replace the text with the "Replace with" text. If you click Replace All, of course, you replace *every* matching occurrence in the selected cells. Use caution.

Erasing Cells

"Erase," as any Enron staff member can attest, is a relative term. In Excel, the Edit→Clear submenu lets you strip away various kinds of information without necessarily emptying the cell completely. For example:

- **Edit→Clear→All** truly empties the selected cells, restoring them to their new-spreadsheet, unformatted condition. (Control-B does the same thing.)

- **Edit→Clear→Formats** leaves the contents, but strips away formatting (including both text and number formatting).

- **Edit→Clear→Contents** empties the cell, but leaves the formatting in place. If you then type new numbers into the cell, they take on whatever cell formatting you'd applied (bold, blue, Currency, and so on).

- **Edit→Clear→Comments** deletes only any electronic yellow sticky notes (see page 562).

None of these is the same as Edit→Delete, which actually chops cells out of your spreadsheet and makes others slide upward or leftward to fill the gap. (Excel asks you which way you want existing cells to slide.)

Tutorial 1: Entering Data

If you've never used a spreadsheet before, the concepts described in the previous pages may not seem to make sense until you've applied them all in practice. This tutorial, which continues in a second lesson on page 460, may help.

Suppose that you, former billionaire CEO of a dot-com startup, have just gone bankrupt. As the vulture-like office equipment repossession guys begin to pack up your desks and chairs, you whip out Excel to see if you can figure out how it all went wrong.

1. **Create a new spreadsheet document by choosing File→New (⌘-N).**

   Excel fills your screen with the spreadsheet grid; the first cell, A1, is selected as the active cell.

2. **Begin by typing the title of your spreadsheet in cell A1.**

   Profit and Loss Statement: Riches, Ruin, and Recovery might be a good choice. As you type, the characters appear in the cell and in the Edit box in the Formula bar.

3. **Press Return three times.**

   Excel inserts the contents of the Edit box into cell A1 and moves the active cell frame down a couple of rows, selecting cell A4.

4. **Type *January*.**

   You need to track expenses over time, so to track the project by calendar year, name the first column January. You could now tab to the next cell, enter *February*, and work your way down the spreadsheet—but there's an easier way.

   As noted earlier, Excel can create a series of months automatically for you, saving you the effort of typing *February, March,* and so on—you just have to start it off with the first entry or two.

5. **Click once outside cell A4 to get out of entry mode, and then click cell A4 again to select it.**

6. **Carefully click the tiny square at the lower-right corner of the highlighted cell; drag directly downward through 11 more cells.**

   Pop-out yellow tooltips show what Excel is filling into the cells through which you're dragging. They let you know when you've gone too far; when the tooltip says *December,* stop.

   Excel highlights the cells you dragged through. Figure 12-11 illustrates this step.

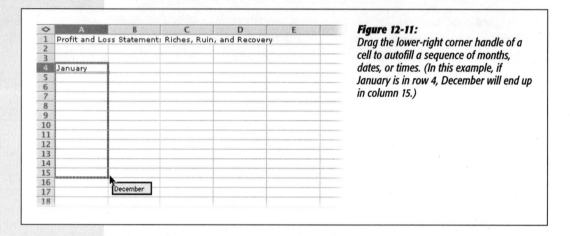

Figure 12-11:
Drag the lower-right corner handle of a cell to autofill a sequence of months, dates, or times. (In this example, if January is in row 4, December will end up in column 15.)

Now it's time to add the year headings across the top.

7. **Click cell B3 to select it. Type *1998.* Press Tab, type *1999,* then press Enter.**

   You'll use the same AutoFill mechanism to type in the next four years' names for you. But just dragging the tiny square AutoFill handle on the 1998 cell wouldn't work this time, because Excel wouldn't know whether you want to fill *every* cell with "1998" or to add successive years. So, you've given it the first *two* years as a hint.

8. **Drag through the 1998 and 1999 year cells. Carefully click the tiny square at the lower-right corner of the 1999 cell; drag directly to the right through three more cells.**

   Excel automatically fills in *2000, 2001,* and *2002,* using the data in the first two cells to establish the pattern.

   If you like, you can now highlight the year row, the month column, or both, and then press ⌘-B to make them boldface (see Figure 12-12); Chapter 13 offers much more detail on formatting your spreadsheets.

   Now that the basic framework of the spreadsheet is in place, you can begin typing in actual numbers.

9. **Click cell B4, January 1998. Enter a figure for your January income.**

You didn't make much money in January, and the first year was slow, so you were living off credit cards at the time; $250 might be about right. Leave off the dollar sign—just type *250*.

Figure 12-12:
You can make the headings stand out from the data you'll soon put in the cells by changing the font style and alignment (see Chapter 13). In this example, you've finished typing in the numbers, as described in steps 9 through 12.

	A	B	C	D	E	F	C
1	Profit and Loss Statement: Riches, Ruin, and Recovery						
2							
3		1998	1999	2000	2001	2002	
4	January	250	1290	44000	17890	-33	
5	February	272	1484	18000	10870	25	
6	March	689	211344	265987	9506	156	
7	April	342	234560	300877	8502	3299	
8	May	291	222000	275280	4566	4500	
9	June	980	322401	234654	2345	4522	
10	July	810	342356	42356	40	3901	
11	August	879	353399	23456	-88	5677	
12	September	985	367000	455080	-1600	12345	
13	October	650	37500	46500	-2402	65777	
14	November	792	40020	500872	-4600	88992	
15	December	946	4490880	456001	-5899	84332	
16							
17							
18							

10. **Press Return (or the down arrow key).**

Excel moves the active cell frame to the next row down.

11. **Type another number to represent your income for February; press Return. Repeat steps 9 and 10 until you get to the bottom of the 1998 column.**

For this experiment, the exact numbers to type don't much matter, but Figure 12-12 shows one suggestion.

12. **Click in the January 1999 column (C4); fill in the numbers for each month, pressing Return after each entry. Repeat with the other years.**

Remember to type extremely high numbers in the 1999 and 2000 columns (when venture capitalists poured money into your company), and equally huge negative numbers (each preceded by a minus sign) for the 2001 column, as the technology recession hit. Increase the numbers again in 2002, since business picked up once your advertisers realized that you weren't going down with the dot-com ship—not yet anyway.

You've successfully populated your spreadsheet with data; choose File→Save to preserve and name the document. You'll return to it later in this chapter—after you've read about what Excel can *do* with all of these numbers.

Formula Fundamentals

Without *formulas*, Excel would be just glorified graph paper. With them, Excel becomes a number-crunching powerhouse worthy of having its own agent. Excel formulas do everything from basic arithmetic to complex financial analysis. You can even use formulas to switch the capitalization of text, remove all nonprintable characters from a text string, and probably vacuum the living room.

Basic Calculations

A *formula* in a cell can perform calculations on other cells' contents. For example, if cell A1 contains the number of hours in a day, and cell A2 contains the number of days in a year, then you could type =A1*A2 into cell B3 to find out how many hours there are in a year. (In spreadsheet lingo, you'd say that this formula *returns* the number 8670.)

After typing the formula and pressing Enter, you'd see only the mathematical answer in cell B3; the formula itself is hidden, though you can see it in the Formula bar if you click the cell again (see the extreme example in Figure 12-13).

Tip: Your formulas don't have to remain invisible until clicked. To reveal formulas on a given sheet, press Control-' (the key in the upper-left corner of most keyboards). This command toggles the spreadsheet cells so that they show formulas instead of results. (Excel widens your columns considerably, as necessary, to show the formulas.) To switch things back to the way they were, press Control-' again.

You can consider that keystroke a shortcut for the official way to bring formulas into view: Choose Excel→Preferences→View panel. Under Window options, click Formulas; click OK. Repeat the procedure to restore the results-only view.

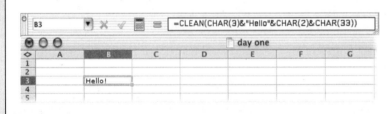

Figure 12-13:
A fairly complex formula may be hiding behind a simple cell display.

Formulas do math on *values*. A value is any number, date, time, text, or cell address that you feed into a formula. The math depends on the *operators* in the formula—symbols like + for addition, – for subtraction, / for division, * for multiplication, and so on.

To enter a simple formula that you know well, just select the cell and then click the Edit box in the Formula bar, which is shown in Figure 12-1. The cursor appears simultaneously in the cell and in the Edit box, signaling that Excel awaits your next move.

Your next move is to type an equal sign (=), since every formula starts with one (see Figure 12-13). Then type the rest of the formula using values and operators. When you want to incorporate a reference to a particular cell in your formula, you don't actually have to type out *B12* or whatever—just *click* the cell in question.

Tip: If you mess up while entering a formula and want to start fresh, click the Cancel button on the Formula bar. (It looks like an X.)

To complete a formula, click the Enter button on the Formula bar (it looks like a checkmark) or press Enter. Pressing Return or Tab also works.

Functions

When you tire of typing formulas (or, let's be honest, when you can't figure out what to type), you can let Excel do the brainwork by using *functions*. (You can also accelerate formula entry through the Calculator, described in this chapter.)

The AutoSum button

You don't need access to Microsoft's reams of focus-group studies to realize that the most commonly used spreadsheet function is *adding things up*. That's why Excel comes equipped with a toolbar button that does nothing but add up the values in the column directly above the active cell; Figure 12-14 shows the idea. (The tutorial that resumes on page 460 also shows why AutoSum is one of the most important buttons in Excel.)

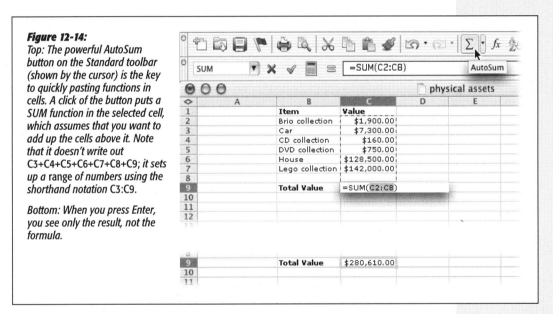

Figure 12-14:
Top: The powerful AutoSum button on the Standard toolbar (shown by the cursor) is the key to quickly pasting functions in cells. A click of the button puts a SUM function in the selected cell, which assumes that you want to add up the cells above it. Note that it doesn't write out C3+C4+C5+C6+C7+C8+C9; it sets up a *range* of numbers using the shorthand notation C3:C9.

Bottom: When you press Enter, you see only the result, not the formula.

The flippy triangle to the right of the AutoSum button reveals a menu with a few other extremely common options, such as:

- **AVERAGE.** Calculates the average (the arithmetic mean) of the numbers in the column above the active cell. For example, if you fill a cell with =*AVERAGE(2,4,4,5)* and press Enter, you'll get the answer 3.75.

- **COUNT.** Tells you *how many* cells in a selected cell range contain numbers; COUNT can also tell you how many times a specific number appears in a selected set of cells.

- **MAX** and **MIN.** Shows the highest or lowest value of any of the numbers referred to in the function. If you enter *=MAX(34,23,95,34)*, you'll get 95.

A sixth pop-up menu command reads More Functions. When selected, More Functions brings up the Paste Function dialog box, described shortly.

Tip: After you click the AutoSum button (or use one of its pop-up menu commands), Excel assumes that you intend to compute using the numbers in the cells just *above* or *to the left of* the highlighted cell; it indicates, with a moving border, which cells it intends to include in its calculation.

But if it guesses wrong, simply grab your mouse and drag through the numbers you *do* want computed. Excel redraws its border and updates its formula. Press Enter to complete the formula.

The Anatomy of a Function in a Formula

Like Web-page addresses, formulas have a regular form. If you understand that anatomy, you'll find working with formulas much easier.

The first element in a formula is the equal sign (=), which signals to Excel that what follows is a formula, not plain old data. Next comes the function name, like *SUM*. After the function name comes a left parenthesis, which tells Excel that the function's *arguments* are coming next.

Arguments in this case have nothing to do with cranky accountants, and everything to do with telling the function *what values to process*. Some functions have one argument; others have more. To use more than one argument,

separate them with commas. Finally, finish the function with a closing parenthesis.

For example, the formula *=SUM(B2,B4:B8,20)* adds the contents of cells B2,B4, B5, B6, B7, and B8, and then adds 20.

Given the many functions and operators Excel provides, you can do more number crunching in an hour with Excel than you probably did in your entire grade-school experience. (Unless, of course, you used a computer *during* grade school, in which case may have already programmed Excel to play Battleship.)

Looking up functions

Whipping up the sum or average of some cells is only the beginning. Excel is also capable of performing the kinds of advanced number crunching that can calculate interest rates, find the cosine of an arc, and so on. There are probably two or three people, in fact, who have most of these functions memorized.

Fortunately, you don't have to remember how to write each function; save that brainpower for figuring out what to have for lunch. Instead, you can use Excel's Paste Function dialog box to look up the exact function that you need. To call up the Paste Function dialog box, choose Insert→Function, or click the Paste Function button on the Standard toolbar.

Note: When the Paste Function dialog box appears, the Office Assistant—if it's visible—offers to help with any function you select. (See page 686 for more on this little animated Help character.) You can safely ignore the Assistant; it hides its offer and goes away when you click OK or Cancel.

In the Paste Function dialog box, you'll see two panels: the left panel lists the function *categories* (nine of them, plus two special categories at the top of the list); the right panel lists the individual functions in the selected category (see Figure 12-15).

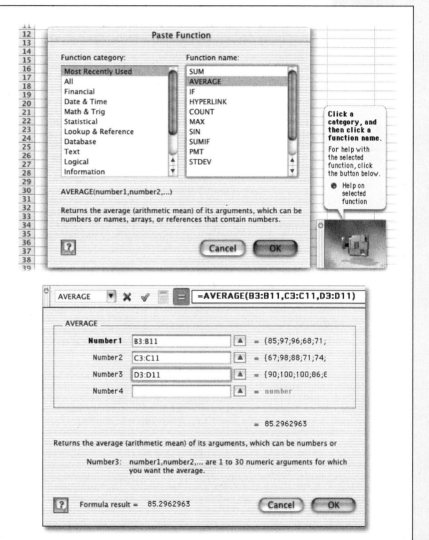

Figure 12-15:
Top: First, select a category in the left panel, and then pick a function from the right panel. Excel describes the selected function in the space below the panels. Once you have the right function (such as the Average function when you're building a grade book), click OK; Excel pastes the function into the selected cell.

Bottom: Next, Excel pops up the Formula palette, in which you can fine-tune your function's arguments—the values that the function uses to do its calculations.

Using the Calculator to assemble formulas

What with all the operators, parentheses, cell addresses, functions and such, all of which must be entered in exactly the correct order, assembling a formula can be a painstaking business.

Fortunately, the Calculator centralizes formula creation. It has a lot of the standard buttons that you might find on a pocket calculator, plus parentheses buttons, an IF button (to insert an IF statement), and a SUM button (to insert a SUM function). As shown in Figure 12-16, the window also has three fields: a large one up top that displays the current formula (and that also lets you type your own formula, if you're so inclined) and two smaller ones below it, which show the answer to the formula and the cell where the formula is located.

To use the Calculator, click the Calculator button in the Formula bar (just to the right of the X and the checkmark). To create a formula, click the calculator's buttons as you would on a real calculator. As you build your formula with the various calculator buttons, the formula shows up in the top window, and the result of the calculation shows up in the Answer field.

If you want to access other functions (besides the IF and SUM functions), click More. This brings up the Paste Function dialog box (Figure 12-15), which gives you access to every one of Excel's functions.

Once you've built your formula, click OK to paste it into the spreadsheet. (And don't let your friends who use Excel for Windows see this; they don't have this feature.)

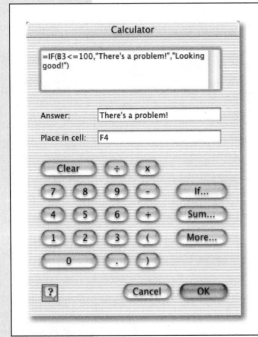

Figure 12-16:
The Calculator lets you build a formula with just a few button clicks—in this case, an IF statement that presents different messages depending on the value of B3. Once the formula is perfected, click OK to insert it into the spreadsheet.

Tip: If you need a little help with a balky formula that you've already entered (perhaps you haven't gotten its syntax just right), select the cell and then click the Edit Formula button in the Formula toolbar. This brings up the Formula palette (a relative of the Calculator), which shows the formula's possible arguments and lets you know how they should be used. It's like having a friendly Excel nerd in your Mac.

Order of Calculation

Anyone who managed to stay awake in algebra knows that you get different answers to an equation depending on how its elements are ordered. So it's important for *you*, the purveyor of fine Excel formulas, to understand the order in which Excel calculates its values.

If a formula is spitting out results that don't jibe with what you think ought to be the answer, consult the following table. Excel calculates the operations at the top of the table first, working its way down until it hits bottom. For example, Excel computes cell references before it tackles multiplication, and it does multiplication before it works on a "less than" operation.

Excel's Calculation Order
Computed first

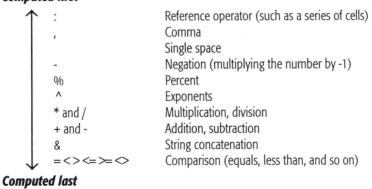

:	Reference operator (such as a series of cells)
,	Comma
	Single space
-	Negation (multiplying the number by -1)
%	Percent
^	Exponents
* and /	Multiplication, division
+ and -	Addition, subtraction
&	String concatenation
= < > <= >= <>	Comparison (equals, less than, and so on)

Computed last

For example, Excel's answer to =2+3*4 is not 20. It's 14, because Excel performs multiplication and division within the formula *before* doing addition and subtraction.

You can exercise some control over the processing order by using parentheses. Excel calculates expressions within ( ) symbols before bringing the parenthetical items together for calculation. For example, the formula =(C12*(C3-C6)) subtracts the value in C6 from the value in C3 and multiplies the result by the value in C12. Without the parenthesis, the formula would read =(C12*C3-C6), and Excel would multiply C12 by C3 and *then* subtract C6—a different formula entirely.

Tip: Excel does its best to alert you to mistakes you make when entering formulas manually. For example, if you leave off a closing parenthesis (after using an open parenthesis), Excel pops up a dialog box suggesting a fix.

Tutorial 2: Yearly Totals

Suppose you've entered a few numbers into a spreadsheet, as described in the tutorial earlier in this chapter. Now it's time to put these numbers to work. Open the document shown in Figure 12-12.

Now that it has some data to work with, Excel can do a little work. Start with one of the most common spreadsheet calculations: totaling a column of numbers. First create a row for totals.

1. **Click cell A17 (leaving a blank row beneath the month list). Type** *Total.*

   This row will contain totals for each year column.

2. **Click cell B17, in the Total row for 1998. Click the AutoSum button on the Standard toolbar.**

   In cell B17, Excel automatically proposes a *formula* for totaling the column of numbers. (It's =*SUM(B3:B16)*, meaning "add up the cells from B3 through B16.") The moving border shows that Excel is prepared to add up *all* of the numbers in this column—including the year label *1998!* Clearly, that's not what you want; don't press Enter yet.

3. **Drag through the numbers you** *do* **want added: from cell B4 down to B15. Then press Enter.**

   Excel adds up the column.

   Now comes the real magic of spreadsheeting: If one of the numbers in the column *changes*, the total changes automatically. Try it:

4. **Click one of the numbers in column B, type a much bigger number, and then press Enter.**

   Excel instantly updates 1998's total to reflect the change.

Tip: The AutoSum feature doesn't have to add up numbers *above* the selected cell; it can also add up a *row* of cells. In fact, you can even click the AutoSum button and then drag through a *block* of cells to make Excel add up all of *those* numbers.

You *could* continue selecting the Total cells for each year and using AutoSum to create your totals. Instead, you can avoid repetition by using the Fill command described earlier in this chapter. You can tell Excel to create a calculation similar to the 1998 total for the rest of the columns in the spreadsheet.

5. **Starting with the cell containing the 1998 total (B17), drag to the right, all the way over to the 2002 column (F17).**

   You've highlighted the range of cells for column totals, as shown in Figure 12-17.

6. Choose Edit→Fill→Right.

You could have bypassed steps 5 and 6 simply by dragging the lower-right corner handle of cell B17, using the AutoFill process described on page 442.

Either way, Excel copies the contents of the first cell and pastes it into every other cell in the selection. In this example, the first cell contains a *formula*, not just a total you typed yourself. But, instead of pasting the exact same formula, which would place the 1998 total into each column, Excel understands that you want to total each column, and enters the appropriate formula in each cell of your selection. The result is yearly totals calculated right across the page.

Finally, to make the yearly totals in the tutorial example more meaningful—and see just how much money you actually made—calculate an overall total for the spreadsheet.

Figure 12-17:
Top: To total all of the columns in the spreadsheet quickly, drag from the cell containing the total for the first column (B17) all the way over to the last cell in the row that you need a column total for.

Bottom: When you choose Edit→Fill→Right, Excel creates a total for each of the selected columns.

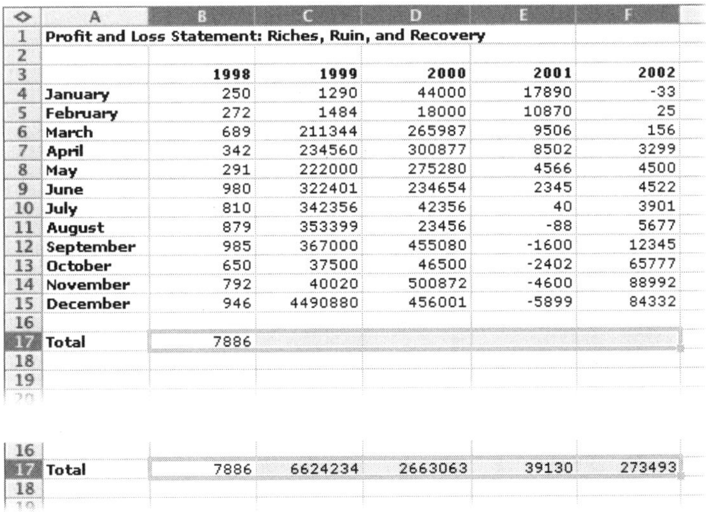

	A	B	C	D	E	F
1	Profit and Loss Statement: Riches, Ruin, and Recovery					
2						
3		1998	1999	2000	2001	2002
4	January	250	1290	44000	17890	-33
5	February	272	1484	18000	10870	25
6	March	689	211344	265987	9506	156
7	April	342	234560	300877	8502	3299
8	May	291	222000	275280	4566	4500
9	June	980	322401	234654	2345	4522
10	July	810	342356	42356	40	3901
11	August	879	353399	23456	-88	5677
12	September	985	367000	455080	-1600	12345
13	October	650	37500	46500	-2402	65777
14	November	792	40020	500872	-4600	88992
15	December	946	4490880	456001	-5899	84332
16						
17	Total	7886				
18						
19						

	A	B	C	D	E	F
16						
17	Total	7886	6624234	2663063	39130	273493
18						

7. Click cell E19 and type *Grand Total*. Press Tab twice.

Excel moves the active cell to G19.

To calculate a lifetime total for the spreadsheet, you need to tell Excel to add together all the yearly totals.

8. Click the AutoSum button on the Standard toolbar.

In this case, the cells to be added aren't lined up with the Grand Total cell, so the AutoSum button doesn't work quite right; it says only *=SUM()*, with nothing in the parentheses. You need to tell Excel what to put into those parentheses:

9. **Drag across the yearly totals (from B17 through F17).**

   As you drag across the cells, Excel inserts the cell range within the parentheses. In this example, the function now reads, =SUM(B17:F17)—in other words, "add up the contents of the cells B17 through F17, and display the result."

10. **Press Enter.**

    Excel performs the calculation and displays the result in cell G19, the grand total for the life of your startup.

Named ranges

As you create formulas, you may find yourself referring over and over to the same cell or range of cells. For example, in the profit and loss spreadsheet (see figures 12-12 and 12-17), you may need to refer to the Grand Total in several other formulas. So that you don't have to repeatedly type the cell address or click to select the cell, Excel lets you give a cell, or range of cells, a *name*. After doing so, you can write a formula in the form of, for example, = *Grand Total – Taxes* (instead of =G19 - F27).

To create a named cell or range, simply select the cell or range, and in the Name box at the upper-left corner of the Formula bar, type the name you want, then press Enter (see Figure 12-18).

Note: No spaces are allowed. Furthermore, as you would expect, no two names can be the same, and Excel considers upper- and lowercase characters to be the same, so *profit* is the same as *PROFIT*.

Other requirements: the first character of a name must be a letter (or an underscore), names can't contain punctuation marks (except periods) or operators (+, =, and so on), and they can't take the form of a cell reference (such as B5) or a function (such as SUM()).

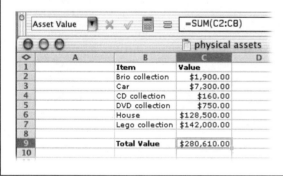

Figure 12-18:
To name a cell, select it, type the name in the Name Box, then hit Return. Your named cell will now show up in the Name Box pop-up menu; in the future, you can select that cell by selecting the name from the pop-up menu. (Using this same technique, you can also name cell ranges.)

From now on, the cell's or range's name appears in the Name Box pop-up menu. The next time you want to go to that cell or range or use it in a formula, you need only select it from this pop-up menu. Excel displays the name instead of the cell address whenever you create a formula that refers to a named cell.

If you need to change or remove a name, choose Insert→Names→Define to display the Define Names dialog box. From there, you'll find it easy to delete, create, or apply names.

Tip: You can use named cells as a quick way to navigate a large spreadsheet. By naming cells at key points in the spreadsheet, you can select them from the Name Box pop-up menu and jump to the corresponding cells.

References: Absolute and relative

When you create a formula by typing the addresses of cells or by clicking a cell, you've created a *cell reference*. Excel generally considers cell references in a *relative* way—it remembers those cell coordinates by position relative to the selected cell, not as, for example, "B12." For example, a relative reference thinks of another cell in the spreadsheet as "three rows above and two columns to the left of this cell" (see Figure 12-19).

Relative references make it possible for you to insert a new row or column into your spreadsheet without throwing off all of the formulas you've already stored. They make the Fill Right command possible, too. They also make formulas portable: When you paste a formula that adds up the two cells above it into a different spot, the pasted cell adds up the two cells above *it* (in its new location).

The yearly totals in Figure 12-17 work this way. When you "filled" the Total formula across to the other cells, Excel pasted *relative* cell references into all those cells that say, in effect, "display the total of the numbers in the cells *above this cell.*" That way, each column's subtotal applies to the figures in that column. (If Excel instead pasted absolute references, then all the cells in the subtotal row would show the sum of the first year column.)

Figure 12-19:
Top: The formula in cell D5 calculates the sales tax for the item priced in C5. The sales tax rate is stored in C1. Therefore, the formula in D5 multiplies the price (C5) by an absolute reference to the sales tax rate (expressed $C$1). When you copy this formula to other cells in column D, it always refers to the fixed cell C1.

Bottom: If you press ⌘-' (that's the upper-left keyboard key), Excel displays the formulas right in the cells, making it easy to see how the absolute references remain the same and the relative references change.

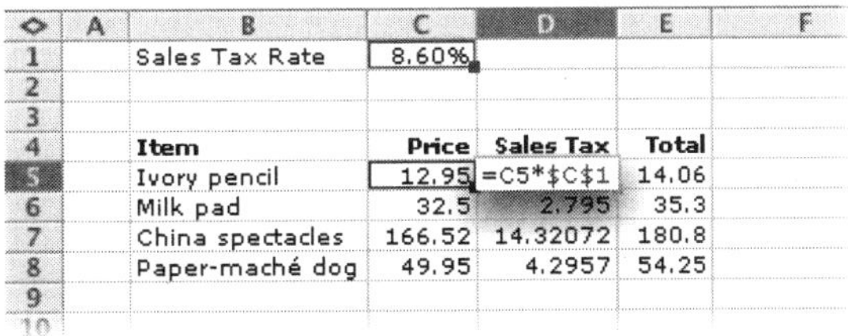

	A	B	C	D	E	F
1		Sales Tax Rate	8.60%			
2						
3						
4		Item	Price	Sales Tax	Total	
5		Ivory pencil	12.95	=C5*$C$1	14.06	
6		Milk pad	32.5	2.795	35.3	
7		China spectacles	166.52	14.32072	180.8	
8		Paper-maché dog	49.95	4.2957	54.25	
9						
10						

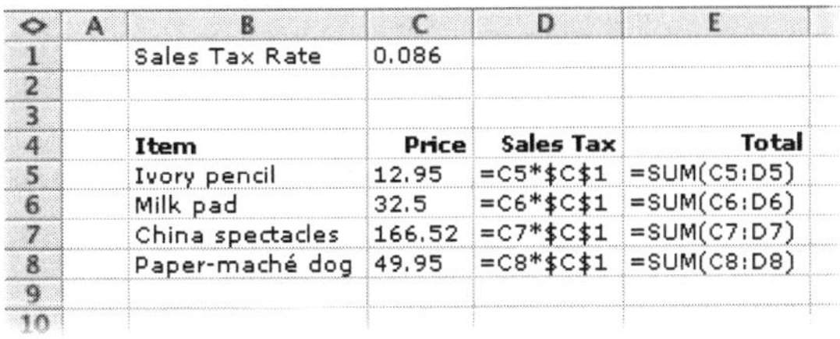

	A	B	C	D	E
1		Sales Tax Rate	0.086		
2					
3					
4		Item	Price	Sales Tax	Total
5		Ivory pencil	12.95	=C5*$C$1	=SUM(C5:D5)
6		Milk pad	32.5	=C6*$C$1	=SUM(C6:D6)
7		China spectacles	166.52	=C7*$C$1	=SUM(C7:D7)
8		Paper-maché dog	49.95	=C8*$C$1	=SUM(C8:D8)
9					
10					

Absolute references, on the other hand, refer to a specific cell, no matter where the formula appears in the spreadsheet. They can be useful when you need to refer to a particular cell in the spreadsheet—the one containing the sales tax rate, for example—for a formula that repeats over several columns. Figure 12-19 gives an example.

You designate an absolute cell reference by including a $ in front of the column and/or row reference. (For the first time in its life, the $ symbol has nothing to do with money.) For example, $A$7 is an absolute reference for cell A7.

You can also create a *mixed reference* in order to lock the reference to *either* the row or column—for example, G$8, in which the column reference is relative and the row is absolute. You might use this unusual arrangement when, for example, your column A contains discount rates for the customers whose names appear in column B. In writing the formula for a customer's final price (in column D, for example), you'd use a *relative* reference to a row number (which is different for every customer), but an *absolute* reference to the column (which is always A).

Tip: Here's a handy shortcut that can save you some hand-eye coordination when you want to turn an absolute cell reference into a relative one, or vice versa: First, select the cell that contains the formula. In the Formula bar, highlight only the cell name you'd like to change. Then press ⌘-T. This keystroke makes the highlighted cell name cycle through different *stages* of absoluteness—for example, it changes the cell reference B4 first to $B$4, then to B$4, then to $B4, and so on.

Excel, the List Maker

After spending years loading up Excel with advanced number-crunchy features like pivot tables, database queries, and nested formulas, in 1999 Microsoft decided to step back and conduct some studies to see how its customers were enjoying their NASA-caliber spreadsheet program.

And what were 60 percent of Excel users doing with all this power?

Making lists.

That's right—most people use the software that drives uncounted businesses and statistical analyses for nothing more than building lists of phone numbers, CD collections, and so on.

That's why Microsoft, which never met a feature it didn't like, added to Excel 2001 the Macintosh-only List Manager, which makes building and manipulating lists easy (Figure 12-20). Excel does this by creating something called a *list object,* which is nothing more than a simple database. It's made up of rows (which are the same as database *records*—that is, the individual "rolodex cards" of an address database) and columns (which are like the *fields* in a database record—that is, the address, city, zip code, and other bits of information). These rows and columns are contained inside a list frame.

The List Manager offers a number of features that improve upon using regular spreadsheet cells to store your lists (and upon Excel *databases*, as they were called in some previous versions):

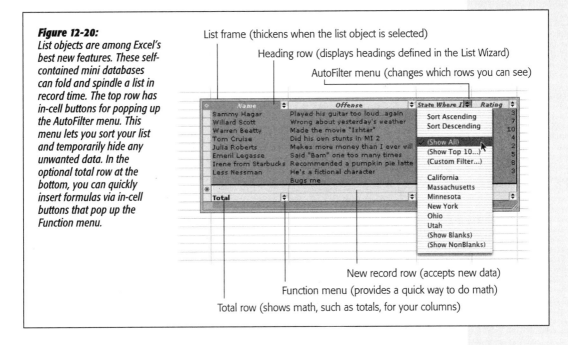

Figure 12-20:
List objects are among Excel's best new features. These self-contained mini databases can fold and spindle a list in record time. The top row has in-cell buttons for popping up the AutoFilter menu. This menu lets you sort your list and temporarily hide any unwanted data. In the optional total row at the bottom, you can quickly insert formulas via in-cell buttons that pop up the Function menu.

List frame (thickens when the list object is selected)

Heading row (displays headings defined in the List Wizard)

AutoFilter menu (changes which rows you can see)

New record row (accepts new data)

Function menu (provides a quick way to do math)

Total row (shows math, such as totals, for your columns)

- The list frame, a special border that appears when you click a list object, clearly outlines your data. You don't have to wonder which cells are meant to be part of the list.

- Excel keeps the column headings of a list completely separate from the data beneath them; they won't disappear or get sorted into the rows of the list itself, as might have happened outside a list object.

- You always get an empty record row at the bottom of the list, making it easy to add a new record; just click in the row and type.

- Lists have pop-up AutoFilter menus that make it simple to sort their rows or even *filter* them (so that only certain rows remain visible).

- Unlike Excel databases of old, you can have more than one list per spreadsheet.

The List Manager feature, in other words, is ideal for tasks like these:

- Build a list of all of the DVDs in your vast collection and sort them by genre, rating, number of stars in reviews, whether discs have director's commentaries—the possibilities are endless.

- Create a restaurant list for every city you visit, complete with names, categories, comments, and telephone numbers. When leaving for a trip to Detroit, you can filter that list so that it shows only the names of eateries in Detroit.

- Make an inventory list, with prices, part numbers, and warehouse location; you can later add a column to that list when you remember that you should have included something to indicate availability. Plus, you can format your list with alternating row colors that retain proper alternating colors when you add that new column.

Just try *any* of these tricks with a plain spreadsheet and you'll soon be sobbing in frustration.

Building Your List—The List Wizard

Excel's List Wizard walks you through building a list. Here's how to build a new list from scratch—in this example, an enemies list in the style of former president Nixon.

Tip: To build a list object out of an existing list, first select all of the cells that make up your existing list, and then choose select Insert→List. The List Wizard walks you through turning your ersatz list into the real deal.

---

1. **In a new spreadsheet, click where you want the list to be.**

   You can always move it later.

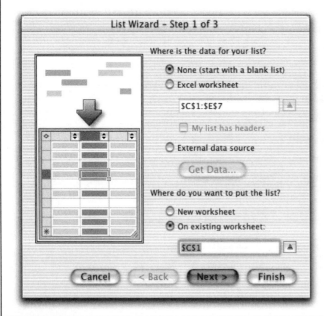

Figure 12-21:
The first step in the List Wizard has three options for data sources for your lists: none (meaning you'll enter the data as you go along), Excel worksheet (use this to convert a selection into a list), and External data source (which lets you access a database via Microsoft Query for Excel X and ODBC— more on page 537). As for where the list goes, you can specify a location in the worksheet currently open, or you can tell Excel to create a whole new sheet for your list to call home.

2. **Choose Insert→List.**

Excel presents the List Wizard (see Figure 12-21). The first screen asks you for the location of the data for your list and where you want the list to appear. Leave the data location radio button set to None (in this example, you'll be typing in the data *after* setting up the table), and leave the list location radio button set to "On existing worksheet."

3. **Click Next.**

Now the List Wizard wants you to specify the columns for your list. If you've ever used FileMaker Pro or another database program, you should be familiar with this process—it's very similar to the one used to create fields for a database file.

The enemies list will include four columns: Name, Offense, State Where Incident Occurred, and Rating.

Figure 12-22:
The second step of the List Wizard looks like a database field definition dialog box, and for good reason—Excel lists are databases, at heart. In this step, you can create as many or as few columns as your list needs and specify settings for each column.

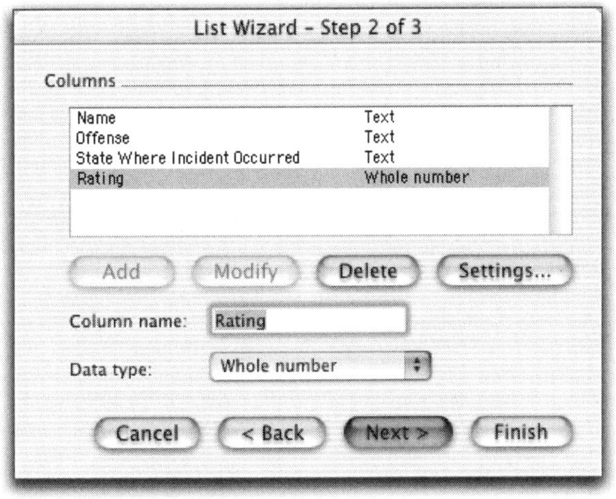

4. **Type *Name* into the Column name field.**

The List Wizard lets you classify each column as one of ten data types, such as numbers, text, or dates. It even lets you set a column to be *another* list or a calculated value, which lets you bring formulas into your lists.

5. **From the "Data type" pop-up menu, choose Text; click Add.**

Excel adds the Name column to its list.

6. **Type *Offense,* then click Add; type *State Where Incident Occurred,* then click Add.**

The "Data type" pop-up menu remains set to the correct setting—*Text*—throughout this column building procedure. The last column, however, will be a number.

7. **Type** *Rating;* **change the "Data type" pop-up menu to read Whole Number. Click Add.**

Once you've created a column, you can click its name and then click the Settings button to bring up the Column Settings dialog box. Here, you can change the settings for the column (including its name and data type). You can also specify a *default* value for it—that is, each time you add a new row to your list, Excel will fill in a canned entry for this row automatically. If most of your CDs are jazz recordings, for example, your CD-database list might contain a Category column with *Jazz* set up to be the default value for each new recording you add to your list. (For the CDs in different categories, you could always type in something different.)

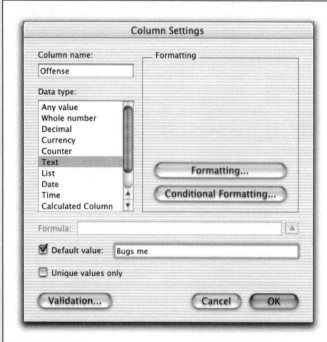

Figure 12-23:
The Column Settings dialog box contains much of the power behind Excel's lists. Here you can set a column's data type, whether the data entered in a column has to be a specific kind of data, and how that data is formatted. The Conditional Formatting button is the key to some of the graphic power of lists, letting you specify changes in appearance depending on how the data in the column changes.

Column Settings also offers a checkbox called "Unique values only." If you use this option, Excel requires that whatever you type into this list column is *unique* (not duplicated in the list)—for example, a serial number.

Suppose you turn this on for the Title field in a CD list, for example. When somebody tries to enter the name of a CD that has already been cataloged, Excel will beep, alert them that this column is supposed to contain unique values, and refuse to budge until the entry is changed.

You can also format cells using two handy buttons. By clicking the Formatting button, you bring up Excel's Format Cells dialog box, in which you can set up this column's type and formatting characteristics: number formatting; text alignment, rotation, and indentation; font size, style, and color; cell borders; fill patterns and colors; and whether a cell is locked or hidden. (The first half of Chapter 13 offers much more on these possibilities.)

The Conditional Formatting button, on the other hand, brings up the Conditional Formatting dialog box, in which you can set a series of rules to change a cell's formatting *automatically* depending on what's happening in the cell. This feature can do things like make positive numbers in your Profits column appear in green, and losses in red. (More on conditional formatting in Chapter 13.)

Finally, Column Settings offers a Validation button. It summons a powerful window called Data Validation, where you can specify limits for the text or numbers typed into each cell in this column—and what happens if somebody disregards the limits. Figure 12-24 shows the procedure.

When you're finished with the Column Settings dialog box—if, indeed, you opened it at all—click OK. You return to the wizard.

Figure 12-24:
The Data Validation window has three tabs.

Top: Settings lets you set up what kind of data should be entered in a given column, like numbers only or text of a specific length.

Middle: Input Message lets you create an alert message that will appear when a cell in the column is selected.

Bottom: Error Alert lets you tell Excel what kind of angry error message to display if someone tries to enter data that doesn't fit what you had in mind. You also get to choose which icon is shown in the error alert: a stop sign, a caution sign, or an exclamation point in a speech bubble.

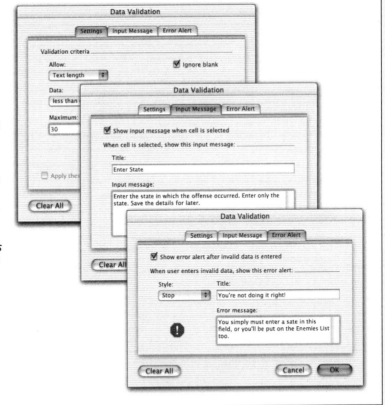

---

8. **Click Next to continue.**

   Finally—step 3 of 3 (at least according to the List Wizard). In this near-final step, you name the list, choose to show the totals row, and control whether the list's visuals—its display of pop-up menu controls and such, that is—appear.

   Of particular interest here is the "Autoformat list after editing" checkbox; if you turn it on and then click AutoFormat, you're offered a list of sixteen preset formats (color and accent schemes) for the list, as shown in Figure 12-25.

   If you turn on "Show totals row," Excel will add a row at the bottom of your list that automatically keeps a running total (or count, or average) of the numbers above it; see page 473 for details.

   This list, however, doesn't require a total row, so leave the "Show totals row" box turned off.

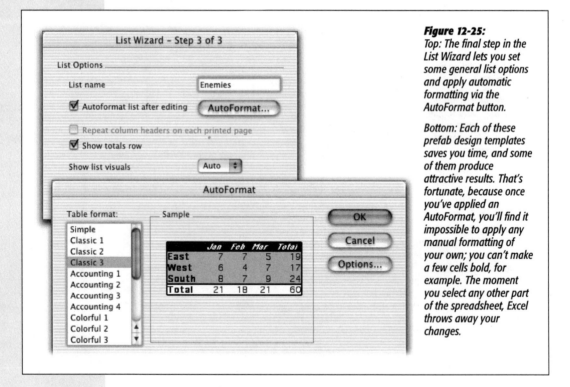

Figure 12-25:
Top: The final step in the List Wizard lets you set some general list options and apply automatic formatting via the AutoFormat button.

Bottom: Each of these prefab design templates saves you time, and some of them produce attractive results. That's fortunate, because once you've applied an AutoFormat, you'll find it impossible to apply any manual formatting of your own; you can't make a few cells bold, for example. The moment you select any other part of the spreadsheet, Excel throws away your changes.

9. **Click Finish.**

   You return to your spreadsheet, where a newborn list appears.

You're done with the List Wizard, but not with the list; it needs some touching up. By widening the columns, you can make room for column entries that are extra long. And although Excel has thoughtfully provided a place for a new column, you may want to hide it by dragging its right edge to the left. (If, by some chance, you need to add a column to your list later, you can click the Insert Column button in the List toolbar.)

Congratulations—you've just made an enemies list! To populate it with information, click the upper-left cell and type the first person's name. Press Tab after you fill in each cell, or Return whenever you want to jump down to the next row. The list frame grows automatically to accommodate your growing stack of rows.

As you go, you may note that AutoComplete works in list objects as well as in regular worksheets—Excel may sprout a pop-up list as you enter information into a cell. The list consists of entries you've added to the column that begin with the same characters you've typed in the cell. If a sprouted list contains an entry you want to reuse, just click the entry (or press the down arrow until you highlight the desired entry and then press Enter); Excel fills in the cell you were editing, saving you some typing.

Note: Excel offers a list of entries you've used in the column *even* if you've turned on the "Unique values only" option for the column. It just goes to show you: Even smart software can be pretty simple-minded.

What to Do with a List

An Excel list is a dynamic, living object that has more in common with a database than it does with a regular pencil-and-paper list. Here are some basic things that you can do with a list, just to get you on the road to your personal list-making nirvana. For many of these tricks, you'll need the List toolbar. It generally opens when you click a list so that its frame appears; if you don't see it, choose View→Toolbars→List.

Add a row or column

To add a row to a list, select a cell or cells in the row *below* where you want the new row to appear, then click the Insert Row button on the List toolbar. To insert a column in a list, select a cell or cells *to the right* of where you want the new column to appear, then click the Insert Column button. The new column appears to the left of the selected cell or cells. You can also get to either of these insert commands by choosing Insert→Row or Insert→Column from the List pop-up button in the List toolbar.

Note: Excel calls inserting a row in a list *inserting a row* (or a *record*), and it calls inserting a column in a list *inserting a field*.

Delete a row or column

To delete a row or column, select a cell or cells in the row or column you want to delete, and then choose Delete→Row or Delete→Column from the List pop-up button in the List toolbar.

When you delete a column or row in a list that you've formatted with an alternating colored-row scheme using AutoFormat, Excel automatically reshades all of the rows and columns so that they're still alternating—something that you'd have to do by hand if you tried this in a spreadsheet without the list feature.

Rearrange a row or column

To move an entire row to a new location, select it by moving the cursor over the list border to the left, and then click to select the row (as shown in Figure 12-26). Now move the row by dragging it by one of its borders, as if it were a range of cells (the cursor should look like a hand). Moving an entire column works the same way: Select it by moving the cursor over the list border until it changes shape (Figure 12-26), and then click to select the column. You can now move the column by dragging one of its borders.

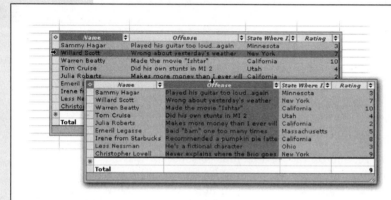

Figure 12-26:
Top: To select a row in a list, click at its left border (the cursor turns into an arrow when you're in the right spot).

Bottom: To select a column, use the same technique: Click at the top of the column.

Sort and filter the list

You can pop up the AutoFilter menu on the right side of each column heading to *sort* your list (change the order of your records) and *filter* it (choose which records to show and which to conceal). Figure 12-20 shows the menu.

Note: If the in-cell buttons for the AutoFilter menu don't appear in the top row when you click the list, check the List toolbar and turn on Visuals and AutoFilters.

Slicing and dicing your list is easy with the three-part AutoFilter menu. Choose commands from the top part to sort the list based on the entries in that column in ascending or descending order. The middle part lets you filter the list using three different commands: Show All reveals all items in the list, Show Top 10 shows the top 10 items or percent (for numerical items only), and Custom Filter lets you build your own filter. The bottom part lists the unique entries in the column; if there are duplicate entries, Excel shows only one of each.

Tip: For more advanced sorting, select Sort from the List pop-up button in the List toolbar. The Sort dialog box lets you choose three criteria by which to sort your list, much as you might do with a database.

POWER USERS' CLINIC

Building a Custom List Filter

By selecting Custom Filter from the pop-up AutoFilter menu, you open up the·Custom AutoFilter dialog box, where you can build your own filter. In it, you can set up a rule for what data is shown with some simple operations and logical statements.

For example, you can show all data that's greater than a certain value or contains the word *blue*. The Custom

AutoFilter understands *wild card* characters, too. That is, you can insert a question mark (?) to mean "any typed character," or an asterisk (*) to represent any number of any characters. Although AutoFilter offers only two fields that you can define and only two logical operators (and, or), you can use these in combination to build some complex filters indeed.

Use the total row

A great feature in Excel's List Manager is the total row—which you can use by turning on the "Show totals row" checkbox in step 3 of 3 in the List Wizard. (You can also hide or show it by clicking the Total Row button in the List toolbar.)

The total row appears at the bottom of the list. If the rightmost column of your list contains number fields, Excel automatically adds up its contents and shows the re-

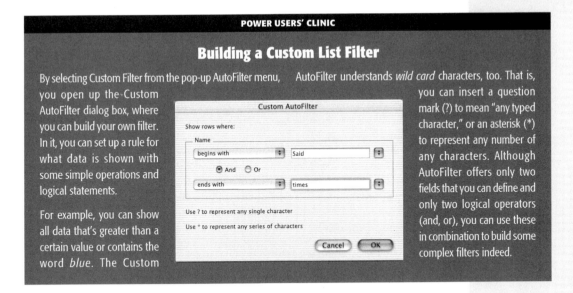

Figure 12-27:
To quickly add a formula to a cell in the total row, click the cell to activate its pop-up menu. Choose a function from the menu, or choose Other to bring up the Paste Function dialog box, where you can noodle over Excel's entire function collection.

sult in the rightmost total row cell; if not, Excel counts the number of occupied rows showing in your list and shows that result in the cell instead. (You can change this function using the pop-up Function menu that becomes available when you click the rightmost cell in the total row.)

But you're not limited to placing a formula beneath the rightmost column. Using the Function pop-up menu in each cell of the total row, you can summon a variety of functions (see Figure 12-27). If you'd rather, you can choose Other and then work in the Paste Function dialog box to concoct your own, even more complex formula. (You can even enter any formula you like using the Formula bar, and that formula needn't have *anything* to do with the items in the list.)

Move or delete the whole list object

To move or delete a list object, you must first select it. To perform this surprisingly delicate operation, click the list to make its frame appear. Then position the cursor carefully over the upper-left corner of the frame until the cursor turns into a hand. With the hand cursor, click the upper-left corner to select the entire list object. Now you can:

- Delete the list by choosing Edit→Clear→All.

- Move the list by choosing Edit→Cut. Then click where you want the upper left cell of the list to move to, and choose Edit→Paste. Excel moves the list to the new location. (You can move the list elsewhere on its worksheet, or switch to a different sheet in the workbook by clicking a tab at the bottom of the window.)

Caution: Microsoft recommends that a list object containing more than fifty rows should go on its own worksheet all by itself. A worksheet holding nothing but a list object is called a *listsheet.*

The List Menu

The List toolbar gives you access to some of Excel's most powerful list-related features. Most of its buttons relate to features you already encountered during your list construction.

But take special note of the List pop-up button, which is rife with useful commands. Some of them (Insert, Delete, Clear Contents) are self-explanatory. A few others could stand clarification:

- **Sort.** Opens the advanced Sort dialog box, in which you can sort your list by up to three criteria (by Company, for example, and then alphabetically within each company group).

- **Filter.** AutoFilters are the canned filtering options that appear when you open the pop-up menu atop any column (such as Ascending, Descending, Top 10, and so on). Using this Filter command, however, you can choose AutoFilter to turn *off* the pop-up menu controls, thus removing your option to use those canned filters. (The other commands in this submenu apply to old-style Excel databases, not to list objects.)

- **Form.** Calls up the Data Form, which lets you work with your list in a database-like environment.

- **Chart.** Turns your list into a chart, as described in Chapter 13.

- **PivotTable Report.** Opens the PivotTable Wizard to help you turn your list into a PivotTable (see Chapter 13).

- **Remove List Manager.** Converts the list back into a block of ordinary cells.

- **Refresh Data.** Grabs fresh data from the list's external data source, if it has one (see page 537).

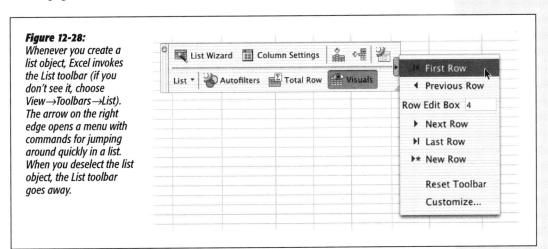

Figure 12-28:
Whenever you create a list object, Excel invokes the List toolbar (if you don't see it, choose View→Toolbars→List). The arrow on the right edge opens a menu with commands for jumping around quickly in a list. When you deselect the list object, the List toolbar goes away.

Formatting and Charts

When you start entering information in an Excel spreadsheet, your text appears in crisp, 10-point Verdana type. But too much of any font on a background resembling graph paper can look drab, so Excel comes packed with formatting tools that take spreadsheets from blah to brilliant.

For starters, Excel offers a broad selection of fonts, colors, and borders to make your sheets stand out. Excel can also import pictures and movies (either clip art provided by Microsoft or images of your own), and you can even use Excel's drawing tools to create your own works of art.

Excel is also expert, of course, at turning your dull numbers into lively charts and graphs—for many people, that's the whole point of typing in all those numbers in the first place.

This chapter covers all of these visual aspects of Excel, including the payoff moment of printing out your beautifully formatted spreadsheets.

Formatting Worksheets

When it comes to spreadsheets, the term *formatting* covers a lot of ground. It refers to the size of the cell, how its borders look, what color fills it, how the contents of the cell are formatted (with or without dollar signs, for example)—anything that affects how the cell looks.

There are two ways to add formatting to your spreadsheet: by using Excel's automatic formatting capabilities or by doing the work yourself. Odds are, you'll be using both methods.

Automatic Formatting

If you're not interested in hand-formatting your spreadsheets—or you just don't have the time—Excel's AutoFormat tool is a quick way to apply formatting to your sheets. It instructs Excel to study the layout and contents of your spreadsheet and then apply colors, shading, font styles, and other formatting attributes to make the sheet look professional.

Note: AutoFormat is best suited for fairly boring layouts: column headings across the top, row labels at the left side, totals at the bottom, and so on. If your spreadsheet uses a more eccentric layout, AutoFormat may make quirky design choices.

FREQUENTLY ASKED QUESTION

Changing the Default Fonts

How do I change the default font and other formats?

Ah, you've been reading Microsoft's Top Ten Tech Calls list, haven't you?

Whether you want a funky new font to lighten up your serious number crunching, or you want to switch back to the Geneva 9-point font of Office versions gone by, a quick trip to the Edit→ Preferences→General panel will solve your problem. After you change the standard font and size (the controls are right in the middle of the General panel) and click OK, Excel displays a warning message, noting that you must quit and restart Excel before the new formatting takes effect in new spreadsheets.

To apply the changes to *old* spreadsheets, press ⌘-A to select the entire sheet, and then change the formatting in the Format→Cells→Font tab (shown here).

To make broader changes, you can modify the Normal style (page 493) or create a *template*—a generic document that

can be used over and over to start new worksheets. Because a template can hold formatting and text, it's a great base for a spreadsheet that you redo regularly (such as a monthly report).

To create a template, use a new worksheet or a copy of one that already looks the way you like it. You can select the entire sheet or specific sections of it, apply formats (as described in this chapter), and even include text (column headings you'll always need, for example). When you finish formatting the sheet, choose File→ Save As. In the Save dialog box, enter a name for the template in the "Save As" field, and then choose Template from the Format menu. Excel gives your file an .xlt extension and switches the Where pop-up menu to "My Templates." Click Save.

Back in Excel, close the template spreadsheet.

Thereafter, whenever you'd like to open a copy of the template, choose File→Project Gallery. Click the My Templates category, click your template, and click OK.

To use the AutoFormat feature, select the cells you want formatted, and then choose Format→AutoFormat. The AutoFormat dialog box appears, complete with a list of formats on the left. By clicking each one in turn, you'll see (in the center of the dialog box) that each one is actually a predesigned formatting scheme for a table-like makeover of the selected cells (see Figure 13-1).

On the right is a button labeled Options, which lets you control the formatting elements that will be applied to the selected cells.

Once you've selected an AutoFormat option (and made any tweaks to the applied formats), click OK. Excel goes to work on the selected cells. If you don't care for the results, you can always undo them with a quick ⌘-Z.

Figure 13-1:
The AutoFormat dialog box is your window into making your spreadsheets more readable—and more attractive. Each scheme may include font selections; shadings for table rows; background patterns; adjustments to the height and widths of the cells; cell alignment; divider lines to segregate the bottom total row; and so on. Click Options to see the checkboxes at the bottom, which refine the selected format.

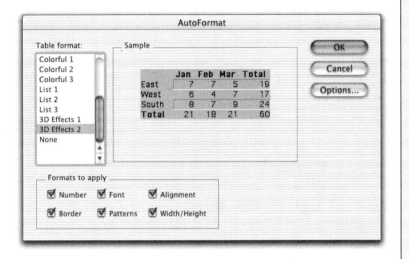

The Format Painter

Another way to quickly apply formatting to a group of cells is the Format Painter. Suppose you've painstakingly applied formatting—colors, cell borders, fonts, text alignment, and the like—to a certain patch of cells. Using the Format Painter, you can copy the formatting to any other cells.

Figure 13-2:
The Format Painter can take everything but the data from the cells on the left, and apply it to the cells on the right.

To start, select the cell or cells that you want to use as an example of good formatting. Then click the Format Painter button (the little paintbrush) on the Standard toolbar. Now move the cursor over the spreadsheet so that it changes to look like a + sign and a paintbrush.

Next, drag the cursor over the cells you'd like to change to match the first group. Excel applies the formatting—borders, shading, font settings, and the like—to the new cells (Figure 13-2).

Formatting Cells by Hand

If the AutoFormat feature is a bit too canned for your purposes, you can always format the look of your spreadsheet manually.

When formatting cells manually, it's helpful to divide the task up into two concepts—formatting the cells themselves (borders and backgrounds), and formatting the *contents* of those cells (what you've typed).

Conditional Formatting

Cell formatting doesn't have to be static. With Conditional Formatting, you can turn your cells into veritable chameleons, changing colors or typography on their own, based on their own contents.

By far the most common example is setting up income-related numbers to turn bright red when they go negative, as is common in corporate financial statements. Another common example is using this feature to highlight in bold the sales figures for the highest-earning salesperson listed in a column.

To use conditional formatting, select the cell or cells that you want to change on their own, and then choose Format→Conditional Formatting. In the Conditional Formatting dialog box, set up the conditions that trigger the desired formatting changes.

For example, to set up a column of numbers so that they'll turn red when negative, use the first pop-up menu to choose "Cell Value Is" and the second to choose "less than."

Finally, type *0* into the text field, as shown here. Then click Format to specify the typographical, border, and pattern changes you want to see if a highlighted cell's contents fall below zero. For example, in the Font tab, choose red from the Color pop-up menu and Bold from the Font Style list. Click OK.

By clicking the Add button at this point, you can even add a second set of conditions to your cells. For example, you might want your monthly income spreadsheet to show numbers over $10,000 with yellow cell shading.

You can apply up to three conditions to the same selection, but if more than one condition applies, Excel uses only the first one.

The dialog box previews how your cells will look if a condition is met. If everything looks right, click OK. You return to the spreadsheet, where numbers that meet your conditions now display their special formatting.

Changing cell size

The factory setting for the size of a cell is 13 *points* high by 10 average-width *characters* wide. That's right——the units used to measure cell height are different than the ones used to measure cell width. A row can range from 0 to 409 points tall; a column can range from 1 to 255 characters wide.

There are several ways to set a cell's height and width. Here's a rundown.

- **Dragging the borders.** Obviously, you can't enlarge a single cell without enlarging its entire row or column; Excel has this funny way of insisting that your cells remain aligned with each other. Therefore, you can't resize a single cell independently—you can only enlarge its entire row or column.

  To adjust the width of a column, drag the divider line that separates its *column heading* from the one to its right, as shown in Figure 13-3; to change the height of a row, drag the divider line between its row and the one below it. In either case, the trick is to drag *in the row numbers or column letters.* Your cursor will look like a double-headed arrow if you drag in the right place.

Note: Excel adjusts row heights automatically if you enlarge the font or wrap your text.

Figure 13-3:
Changing the width (left) of a column or height (right) of a row is as simple as dragging its border in the column letters or row numbers. A small yellow box pops up as you drag, continually updating the exact size of the row or column. If you select multiple columns or rows, dragging a border changes all of the selected columns or rows.

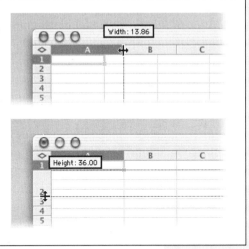

- **Menu commands.** For more exact control over height and width adjustments, choose Format→Row→Height, or Format→Column→Width. Either command pops up a dialog box in which you can enter the row height or column width by typing numbers on your Mac's keyboard. (If you've really made a mess of things, then just restore the highlighted columns to their original widths by choosing Format→Column→Standard Width.)

• **Auto sizing.** For the tidiest spreadsheet possible, highlight some cells and then choose Format→Row→AutoFit, or Format→Column→AutoFit Selection. Excel readjusts the selected columns or rows so that they are exactly as wide and tall as necessary to contain their contents, but no larger. That is, each column expands or shrinks just enough to fit its longest entry.

Tip: You don't have to use the AutoFit command to perform this kind of tidy adjustment. You can also, at any time, make an individual row or column precisely as large as necessary by double-clicking the divider line between the gray row numbers or the gray column letters. (The column to the *left* of your double-click, or the row *above* your double-click, gets resized.) When using this method, there's no need to highlight anything first.

Cell borders and colors 1: The Format Cells Window

The light gray lines that form the graph-paper grid of an Excel spreadsheet are an optical illusion. They exist only to help you understand where one column or row ends and the next begins, but they don't print out (unless you want them to; see page 517).

If you'd like to add solid, printable borders to certain rows, columns, or cells, Excel offers three different methods: the old, slightly stale Format Cells dialog box, the whiz-bang Borders and Shading section of the Formatting palette, and the very similar Border Drawing *toolbar*. All techniques let you control how lines are added to the

Hiding and Showing Rows and Columns

There are any number of reasons why you may want to hide or show certain columns or rows in your spreadsheet. Maybe the numbers in a particular column are used in calculations elsewhere in the spreadsheet, but you don't need them taking up screen space. Maybe you want to preserve several previous years' worth of data, but don't want to scroll through them. Or maybe the IRS is coming for a visit.

In any case, it's easy enough to hide certain rows or columns. Start by highlighting the rows or columns in question. (Remember: To highlight an entire row, click its gray row number; to highlight several consecutive rows, drag vertically through the row numbers; to highlight nonadjacent rows, ⌘-click their row numbers. To highlight certain columns, use the gray column letters at the top of the spreadsheet in the same way.)

Next, choose Format→Row→Hide, or Format→Column→Hide. That's all there is to it: The column or row disappears completely, leaving a gap in the numbering or letter sequence at the left or top edge of the spreadsheet. The row numbers or column letters surrounding the hidden area turn blue.

Making them reappear is a bit trickier, since you can't exactly highlight an invisible row or column. To perform this minor miracle, use the blue-colored row numbers or column headers as clues. Select cells on *either side* of the hidden row or column. Then choose Format→Row→Unhide, or Format→Column→Unhide.

Alternatively, you can also select a hidden cell (such as B5) by typing its address in the Name box on the Formula bar, and then choosing Format→Row→Unhide, or Format→Column→Unhide.

cell's edges, but only the Formatting palette and the toolbar let you change borders and shading without first opening a dialog box to make the changes.

To add cell borders using the time-honored Format Cells command, highlight some cells and then choose Format→Cells (or press ⌘-1). The Format Cells dialog box appears; now click the Border tab to show the border controls. In this tab, you'll see three sections: Presets, Border, and Line (see Figure 13-4).

1. **If you don't want to use the default line style and color, choose new ones in the Line section.**

   Excel loads your cursor with your desired style and color.

2. **If one of the preset options appeals to you, click it. To border all cells in your selection, click Outline and Inside.**

   If you change your mind, click None to remove the option. Excel previews your work in the Border section.

3. **To apply custom borders, use the buttons that surround the preview in the Border section, or click directly between the guides in the preview.**

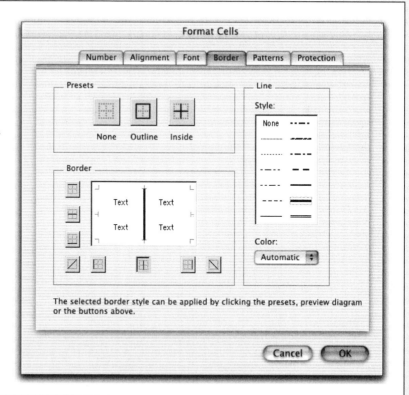

Figure 13-4:
Clicking in the preview area inside the Border section allows you to place borders where you want them. First, select the style of line on the right side, and then click in the preview area to place the line—if you do it the other way around, you'll get the line style that was selected for the last line drawn. If the preview makes you dizzy, use the Presets buttons above or try the eight buttons around the left and bottom edges of the preview area to draw your horizontal, vertical, and diagonal borders. .

To change a line style, reload the cursor with a new style from the Line section and then click the borders in the preview area you wish to change.

If you mess up, click None in the Presets area to start again.

4. **Once the borders look the way you'd like, click OK.**

Excel applies the borders to the selection in your spreadsheet.

Cell borders and colors 2: The Formatting Palette

To use Excel's Formatting Palette to draw borders, select the cells you want to work with, and then open the Borders and Shading portion of the palette.

Tip: If you don't see the Formatting Palette, choose its name from the View menu. And if you don't see the Borders and Shading controls once the palette is open, click the Borders and Shading triangle to bring them into view.

In this section of the palette, you'll see six controls that help you box in your cells and apply colors and patterns (Figure 13-5).

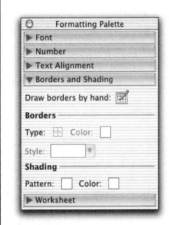

Figure 13-5:
The Formatting Palette is one of the best things to come to Excel in a long time—and the Borders and Shading section makes adding borders to your spreadsheet painless. Click the flippy triangle to the left of "Borders and Shading" on the palette to show or hide the controls.

Here's what each control does.

- **Type.** The button itself indicates the kind of border you've already applied to the selected cells; if you haven't applied a border, the icon on the button is a faint, dotted-line square. In any case, click it to open a pop-out palette of eighteen different border styles, covering most conceivable border needs. The first twelve borders are standard fare, mostly outlines and single lines. The last six styles show more variety; some put borders on two sides of a selection or include thicker borders on one side. (If you point to one of these border styles without clicking, a yellow pop-up tooltip offers a plain-English description of its function.)

This pop-up palette should be your first stop; some of the other palettes described here aren't even available until you've first selected a border type.

- **Style.** Choose a line style, including dotted lines and thick lines.

- **Color.** This button lets you choose from one of 40 preset line colors. Note that you can also leave the line color set to Automatic (which usually means black) if you choose, but you can't mix your own line color.

- **Pattern.** Instead of changing the style of *line* that surrounds the selected cells, this button offers patterns with which to fill the selected cells' *backgrounds*. (The bottom half of this menu specifies the color that Excel will use to draw the black areas of the displayed patterns. You'll probably find that most of the patterns make your cell contents illegible, unless you also select a very light color for the fill.)

"Automatic," by the way, means "no pattern."

- **Fill color.** Clicking this button reveals options for 40 preset fill colors for your cell backgrounds. Here again, use this option with caution; unless you also change the text color to something bright, you should use only very light colors for filling the cell backgrounds. (To change which colors appear here, choose Excel→ Preferences→Color panel and then click Modify.)

- **Draw borders by hand.** Clicking Draw Border brings up the Border Drawing toolbar, a mosquito of a toolbar with five unlabeled buttons. (Point to each without clicking to reveal its pop-up yellow label.)

The first one, Draw Border, pops up so you can choose between two modes: Draw Border and Draw Border Grid. The Draw Border tool lets you create a border that encloses an otherwise unaffected block of cells just by dragging diagonally in your spreadsheet; the border takes on the line characteristics you've specified using the other tools in the toolbar. The Draw Border Grid tool works similarly, except that it doesn't draw one master rectangle; instead, it adds borders to every cell *within* the rectangle that you create by dragging diagonally, "painting" all four walls of every cell inside.

POWER USERS' CLINIC

Protecting the Spreadsheet Cells

Excel's Format Cells dialog box is a real workhorse when it comes to applying a bunch of formatting changes to a sheet. The first five of its tabs—Number, Alignment, Font, Border, and Patterns—let you exercise pinpoint control over how your spreadsheet—both cells and text—looks and feels, as described in this chapter.

The last tab—Protection—is the exception to the formatting rule. The Protection tab has only two options, presented as checkboxes: Locked and Hidden. These two options let you protect selected cells from changes or hide formulas from view.

But be warned: Neither of these options takes effect unless you also protect the sheet through the Protection feature, which is nestled in the Tools menu.

To erase borders from the spreadsheet, click Erase Border and then drag across any unwanted borders (or those painted in by mistake). Press Esc to cancel the eraser cursor. (The middle button, Merge Cells, is described on page 491.)

Tip: You can tear palettes off the Formatting Palette, which makes for easy access if you need to get to their functions frequently. To do so, click the Font Color button, for example, and then click the double-dotted line at the top of the pop-out. The Font Color palette "tears off" and becomes a palette unto itself.

Changing How Text Looks

Borders and fills aren't the only things that you can change to make your sheets look their best; Excel gives you a great deal of control over how your text looks, as well. The text controls in Excel are divided into three major categories: number formatting, font control, and text alignment.

Adding number formats

Number formats in Excel add symbols, such as dollar signs, decimal points, or zeros, to whatever raw characters you've typed—usually numbers, but certain kinds of text are eligible, too. For example, if you apply Currency formatting to a cell containing *35.4*, it appears in the spreadsheet as $35.40; if you apply Percentage formatting, it becomes 3540.00%.

What may strike you as odd, especially at first, is that this kind of formatting doesn't actually change a cell's contents. If you double-click the aforementioned cell that says $35.40, the trappings of currency disappear instantly, leaving behind only the *35.4* that you originally entered. All number formatting does is put the niceties in numbers to make them easier to read. (The exception: dates and times. Date and time formatting may change the actual contents of these cells, as described on page 440.)

To apply a number format, select the cells on which you want to work your magic, and then select the formatting that you want to apply. Excel comes prepared to format numbers using eleven broad categories of canned formatting. You get at them in any of three ways:

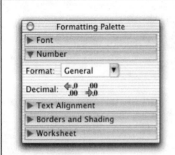

Figure 13-6:
The Number section of the Formatting Palette provides quick access to common number formatting options via the Format pop-up menu. It also lets you increase or decrease the number of decimal places shown by clicking the Increase Decimal or Decrease Decimal buttons.

- The Format pop-up menu in the Number section of the Formatting Palette (better known as "the easy way"), as shown in Figure 13-6.

- The Format Cells dialog box that appears when you choose Format→Cells (or Control-click some cells and choose Format Cells from the contextual menu).

- The old Formatting toolbar (choose View→Toolbars→Formatting). The new Formatting Palette is light-years more flexible, so if you have the screen space for it, you can safely ignore the Formatting toolbar. (Unless you, as a diehard Excel 98 fan, have a raging antipathy toward change, that is.)

Each method offers the same broad categories of formatting; however, options in the Formatting Palette are far fewer. Instead, they apply the most popular choice (for example, $ signs when you choose the currency formatting) without asking your opinion. The Format Cells dialog box, on the other hand, offers more control over each format, along with a little preview of the result.

The following descriptions identify which additional controls are available in the Format Cells dialog box:

- **General.** This option means "no formatting." Whatever you type into cells formatted this way remains exactly as is.

- **Number.** This control formats the contents as a generic number, automatically adding commas and two decimal places.

  Format Cells dialog box extras: You have the option to specify exactly how you want negative numbers to appear, how many decimal places you want to see, and whether or not a comma should appear in the thousands place.

- **Currency.** A specific kind of number format, the Currency format adds dollar signs, commas, decimal points, and two decimal places to numbers entered in the selected cells.

  Format Cells dialog box extras: You can specify how many decimal places you want to see. You also get a Currency Symbol pop-up menu that offers a list of hundreds of international currency symbols, including the euro. You can also set how Excel should display negative numbers.

Tip: The Currency setting in the Formatting Palette applies dollar formatting only if that's the currency you've typed in the Numbers tab of the International panel of the Mac's System Preferences program.

- **Accounting.** A specific kind of *currency* format, the Accounting format adds basic currency formatting—a $ sign, commas in the thousands place, and two decimal places. It also left-aligns the $ sign and encloses negative numbers in parentheses.

  Format Cells dialog box extras: You can opt to use a different currency symbol and indicate how many decimal places you'd like to see.

- **Date.** Internally, Excel converts the number in the cell to a date and time *serial number* (see page 440) and then converts it to a readable date format, such as 11/2.

  Format Cells dialog box extras: You can specify what date format you want applied, such as 11/2/02, November-02, or 14-Nov-2002.

- **Time.** Once again, Excel converts the number to a special serial number and then formats it in a readable time format, such as 1:32.

  Format Cells dialog box extras: The dialog box presents a long list of time formatting options, some of which include both the time and date.

- **Percentage.** This displays two decimal places for numbers and then adds percent symbols; the number 1.2, for example, becomes 120%.

  Format Cells dialog box extras: You can indicate how many decimal places you want to see.

- **Fraction.** This option converts the decimal portion of a number into a fraction. (People who still aren't familiar with stock-market statistics represented in decimal form will especially appreciate this one.)

  Format Cells dialog box extras: You can choose from one of nine fraction types, some of which round the decimal to the nearest half, quarter, or tenth.

- **Scientific.** The Scientific option converts the number in the cell to scientific notation, such as 3.54E+04 (which means 3.54 times 10 to the fourth power, or 35,400).

  Format Cells dialog box extras: You can specify the number of decimal places.

Figure 13-7:
Here's how the eleven different number formats make the number 35396.573 look. Some of the differences are subtle, but important. The contents of Text formatted cells are left-justified, for example, and the Number format lets you specify how many decimal places you want to see. Date and Time formats treat any number you specify as date and time serial numbers—more a convenience for Excel than for you.

- **Text.** This control treats the entry in the cell as text, even when the entry is a number. The contents are displayed exactly as you entered them. The most immediate change you'll discover is that the contents of your cells are left-justified, rather than right-aligned as usual. (No special options are available in the Format Cells dialog box.)

- **Special.** This option formats the numbers in your selected cells as postal Zip codes. If there are fewer than five digits in the number, Excel adds enough zeros to the beginning of the number. If there's a decimal involved, Excel rounds to the nearest whole number. And if there are more than five digits, Excel leaves the additional numbers alone.

  Format Cells dialog box extras: In addition to Zip code format, you can choose from several other canned number patterns: Zip Code + 4, Phone Number, and Social Security Number. In each case, Excel automatically adds parentheses or hyphens as necessary.

- **Custom.** The Custom option brings up the Format Cells dialog box, where you can create your own number formatting, either starting with one of 39 preset formats or writing a format from scratch using a small set of codes. For example, custom formatting can be written to display every number as a fraction of 1,000— something not available in the Fraction formatting.

Add or remove decimal places

To add or remove decimal places, turning *34* and *125* into *34.00* and *125.00,* for example, click the Decimal buttons in the Formatting Palette, as shown in Figure 13-6. Each click on the Increase Decimal button (on the left) adds decimal places; each click on the Decrease Decimal button (on the right) decreases the level of displayed precision by one decimal place.

Changing fonts

Excel lets you control the fonts used in its sheets via the Font portion of the Formatting Palette. As always, the Macintosh instructions are (1) highlight what you want to format, and (2) apply the formatting, in this case using the Formatting Palette.

Of course, you can highlight the cell or cells you want to format using any of the techniques described on page 445. But when it comes to character formatting, there are additional options; Excel actually lets you apply different fonts and font styles *within* a single cell. The trick is to double-click the cell and then use the I-beam cursor—carefully—to select just the characters in the cell that you want to work with. As a result, any changes you make in the Formatting Palette affect only the selected characters.

Once you've highlighted the cells or text you want to change, open the Fonts section of the Formatting Palette (Figure 13-8) to reveal its four main controls:

- The **Name** pop-up menu lets you apply any installed font on your Mac to the highlighted cell or cells.

Tip: If your Mac has numerous fonts installed, you may find it faster to specify your desired font by typing its name in the Name field rather than using the pop-up menu. (Unfortunately, you must type the entire font name before pressing Return; you can't type simply *pal* to indicate Palatino, as you can in Word.)

- The **Size** pop-up menu lets you choose from nine commonly used font sizes (9 point, 18 point, and so on); if the size you want isn't listed, type a number into the Size field and then press Enter or Return. (Excel accommodates only whole- and half-number point sizes; if you type in any other fractional font size, such as 12.2, Excel rounds it to the nearest half-point.)

- The **font style** item offers buttons for applying bold, italic, underline, or strikethrough (or any combination).

Tip: You can apply or remove these font styles to selected characters or cells without even visiting the Formatting Palette; just press ⌘-B for bold, ⌘-I for italic, ⌘-U for underline, or Shift-⌘-hyphen for strikethrough. In fact, you can use keyboard shortcuts to apply shadow and outline styles, which don't even appear in the Formatting Palette (probably because they look terrible). Try Shift-⌘-W for shadowed text, and Shift-⌘-D for outlined text.

- Finally, the **font color** control lets you choose from one of 40 different text colors for the selected text, cell, or cells.

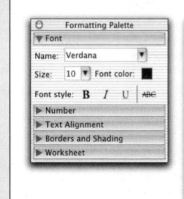

Figure 13-8:
Left: By tweaking the controls in the Font section of the Formatting Palette, you can quickly create your own custom text look.

Right: The Text Alignment section of the Formatting Palette provides precise control over how text fills a cell; it can even be used to join cells together.

Aligning text

Ordinarily, Excel automatically slides a number to the right end of its cell, and text to the left end of its cell. That is, it right-justifies numbers, and left-justifies text. (*Number formatting* may override these settings.)

But the Formatting Palette offers far more control over how the text in a cell is placed. In the Text Alignment section of the palette (Figure 13-8, right), you'll find enough controls to make even a hardcore typographer happy:

- **Horizontal** affects the left-to-right positioning of the text within its cell. Click one of the four buttons to specify left alignment, centered text, right alignment, or full justification. You probably won't see any difference between the full justification and left-alignment settings unless there's more than one line of text within the cell. (And speaking of full justification, note that it wraps text within the cell, if necessary, even if you haven't turned on the text wrapping option.)

- **Indent** controls how far text should be indented from the left edge of its cell. Each time you click the up arrow button, Excel slides the text approximately two character widths to the right; you can also click in the Indent field and type a number, followed by Enter or Return.

  It's especially important to use this control when you're tempted to indent by typing spaces or pressing the Tab key. Those techniques can result in misaligned cell contents, or worse.

- **Vertical** aligns text with the top, middle, or bottom of a cell. If the cell contains more than one line of text, you can even specify full vertical *justification,* which means that the lines of text will be spread out vertically enough to fill the entire cell.

- **Orientation** rotates text within its cell—you can make text run "up the wall" (rotated 90 degrees), slant at a 45-degree angle, or form a column of right-side-up letters that flow downward. You might want to use this feature to label a vertical stack of cells, for example.

- **Wrap text** affects text that's too wide to fit in its cell. If you turn it on, the text will wrap onto multiple lines to fit inside the cell. (In that case, the cell grows taller to make room.) When the checkbox is turned off, the text simply gets chopped off at the right cell border (if there's something in the next cell to the right), or it overflows into the next cell to the right (if the next cell is empty).

- **Shrink to fit** attempts to shrink the text to fit within its cell, no matter how narrow it is. If you've never seen one-point type before, this may be your opportunity.

- **Merge cells** causes two or more selected cells to be merged into one large cell (described next).

Merging cells

Every now and then, a single cell isn't wide enough to hold the text you want placed inside—the title of a spreadsheet, for example, or some other heading. For example, the title may span several columns, but you'd rather not widen a column just to accommodate the title.

The answer is to *merge cells* into a single übercell. This function removes the borders between cells, allowing whatever you put in the cell to luxuriate in the new space. You can merge cells across rows, across columns, or both.

To merge two or more cells, select the cells you want to merge, ensure the Text Alignment portion of the Formatting Palette is open, and then turn on the Merge Cells checkbox, shown in Figure 13-9.

Warning: Merging two or more cells containing data discards *all* of the data except whatever's in the upper-left cell.

All-Star Team Scores

Team	Score	Score	Score
Tarantulas	9	4	0
Slugs	3	1	4
Cows	2	1	1
Shovels	8	3	3
Compasses	8	5	3

All-Star Team Scores

Team	Score	Score	Score
Tarantulas	9	4	0
Slugs	3	1	4
Cows	2	1	1
Shovels	8	3	3
Compasses	8	5	3

Figure 13-9:
Because Excel treats merged cells as one big cell, you can align the contents of that cell any way you'd like; you don't have to stick to the grid system imposed by a sheet's cells. One typical use for this is centering a title over a series of columns. Without using merged cells, centering doesn't do the job at all (top). When you merge those cells together and apply center alignment, the title is happily centered over the table, though you may need to patch up border formatting for your merged cell (bottom).

To unmerge merged cells, select the cells and turn off the Merge Cells checkbox; the missing cell walls return. Note, however, that although the combined space returns to its original status as independent cells, whatever data was discarded during the merge process doesn't return.

You can also merge and unmerge cells by using the Format Cells dialog box. To do this, select the cells to merge, then choose Format→Cells (or Control-click the cells and choose Format Cells from the contextual menu). In the Format Cells dialog box, click the Alignment tab, and then turn on (or turn off) the Merge cells item in the Text control section.

Adding Pictures and Movies

Although you probably won't want to use Excel as a substitute for Photoshop (and if you do, you need licensed help), you *can* add graphics and even movies to your sheets and charts. Plus, if you're artistically inclined (or unwilling to heed the warnings of your high school art teacher), you can use Excel's drawing tools to create your own art.

When using Excel for your own internal purposes—analyzing family expenditures, listing CDs, and so on—the value of all this graphics power may not be immediately apparent. But in the business world, you may appreciate the ability to add clip art, fancy legends, or cell coloring (for handouts at meetings, for example); you can even add short videos explaining how to use certain features of your spreadsheet.

Adding pictures

To summon the Picture toolbar, use the Insert→Picture submenu, which has six options. Here's a summary:

Making Your Own Styles

If you format spreadsheet cells in the same ways over and over again, you can save a lot of time and tedium by defining a particular set of formatting attributes as a *style*.

Exactly as in Word (see page 141), a style is a canned set of formatting characteristics, which you can apply to a selection with just a couple of clicks, saving time and ensuring consistency. Excel comes with a few preset styles, but there's room for more.

To create your own style the quick way, apply any of the formatting characteristics described in this chapter to a selected cell or block of cells. Now choose Format→Style, which calls up the Style dialog box. Enter a new style name. You'll see that Excel has already recorded the formatting exhibited by the selected cells: the number format, the text alignment, the font, the border, the cell pattern, and the cell protection. If you're happy with the formatting, click the Add button on the right.

Or, if you want to further change any of the settings, click Modify to summon the Format Cells dialog box. In fact, if

you failed to highlight some already-formatted cells before choosing Format→Style, this is how you would define your style characteristics from scratch.

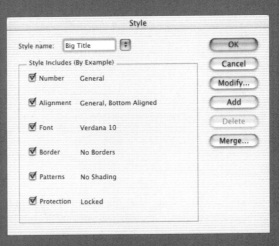

To apply a style to selected cells in the spreadsheet, choose Format→Style. In the Style dialog box that appears, select the style name you want to apply, and then click OK. You'll see your canned formatting applied to the selected cells.

Excel doesn't offer nearly as many ways to apply styles as Word does; style sheets simply aren't as critical in spreadsheet formatting as they are in word processing. For example, you can't associate a particular keystroke with a certain style, unless you create a macro for the task (see page 563).

Still, there is a Style pop-up menu, which is easier to use than burrowing into the Format→Style dialog box. However, you have to add it to one of your toolbars manually, using the Tools→Customize command as described on page 630.

- **Clip Art.** This command brings up the Microsoft Clip Gallery, a database containing hundreds of images in over 40 categories. You can also search for specific images using the built-in search feature.

- **From File.** Using this option, you can import into your sheet any graphic file format that QuickTime understands, including EPS, GIF, JPEG, PICT, TIFF, or Photoshop.

- **AutoShapes.** Choose this command to summon the AutoShapes toolbar, from which you can insert many different automatically generated shapes—arrows, boxes, stars and banners, and so on.

- **Organization Chart.** When you choose this menu item, Excel launches the MS Organization Chart application, which lets you create a corporate-style organizational chart with ease. (This kind of chart, which resembles a top-down flowchart, is generally used to indicate the hierarchy of employees in an organization. But it's also a great way to draft the structure of a Web site.)

- **WordArt.** Using the WordArt menu command, you can apply some wild effects to type, including 3D effects, gradients, shadows, or any combination.

- **From Scanner or Camera.** Excel can use Photoshop or TWAIN drivers to access images directly from a scanner or camera. Choosing this option leads you through a series of steps that help you import images. (Of course, most Mac OS X fans have set up iPhoto or Image Capture to open automatically when a camera is plugged in, thus getting to your pictures before Excel can.)

Each of these graphics types is described more completely in Chapter 18.

Tip: QuickTime movies can be added to an Excel spreadsheet by choosing Insert→Movie.

Charts

To paraphrase the old saying, "a graph is worth a thousand numbers." Fortunately, Excel can easily turn a spreadsheet full of data into a beautiful, colorful graphic, revealing patterns and trends in the data that otherwise might be difficult or impossible to see.

The keys to making an effective chart are to design your spreadsheet from the beginning of charthood, and then to choose the right chart type for the data (see Figure 13-10).

Note: If you've read the reviews of Excel X—or its marketing materials—you may be pretty excited about making charts with transparent fills, one of the few truly new features. Reserve judgment, however, until you've read page 507.

Making a chart in Excel is easy, especially if you take advantage of the program's Chart Wizard, a four-screen "interview" that walks you through the process of creating a chart from the data you select.

Step 1: Select the Data

The first step is to select the data that you want to chartify; select the cells worth including exactly the way you'd select cells for any other purpose (see page 445).

Although it sounds simple, knowing which cells to select in order to produce a certain charted result can be difficult—almost as difficult as designing the sheet to be charted in the first place. Think about what you want to emphasize when you're charting, and then design your spreadsheet to meet that need.

Here are a few tips for designing and selecting spreadsheet cells for charting:

• When you're dragging through your cells, include the labels you've given to your rows and columns. These labels will be incorporated into the chart.

• Don't select total cells unless you want them as part of your chart.

• Give each part of the vital data its own column or row. For example, if you want to chart regional sales revenue over time, create a row for each region, and a column for each unit of time (month or quarter, for example).

Figure 13-10:
Here's an example of the importance of choosing the right chart to match your data. Both charts use the same set of data, but the area chart on the top is appropriate for the kind of data presented. Conversely, the doughnut chart below is the wrong way to present this information. All you get is a rainbow of colors that fails to communicate any useful information.

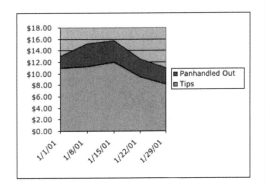

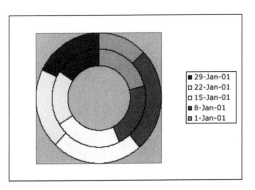

- It's usually easier to put the *data series* (see the sidebar box on the next page) into columns rather than rows, since we tend to see a list of data as a column. Furthermore, the numbers are closer together.

- Keep your data to a minimum. If you're charting more than twelve bars in a bar chart, consider merging some of that data to produce fewer bars. For example, consolidating a year's worth of monthly sales data into quarterly data uses four bars instead of twelve.

- Keep the number of data series to a minimum. If you're charting more than one set of data (such as gross revenues, expenses, and profits), avoid trying to fit six different data series on the same chart. Use no more than three to avoid hysterical spreadsheet confusion. (A pie chart can't have more than *one* data series.)

- Keep related numbers next to each other. For example, when creating an XY chart, use two columns of data, one with the X data and one with the Y data.

- You can create a chart from the data in nonadjacent cells. To select the cells, hold down the ⌘ key while clicking or dragging through the cells to highlight them, as described on page 445. When you finally choose Insert→Chart (or click the Chart Wizard button in the Standard toolbar), Excel knows exactly what to do.

Step 2: Choose a Chart Style

When you choose Insert→Chart, the first screen of the Chart Wizard appears (Figure 13-11). Your first challenge is to choose the kind of chart that's appropriate for the data at hand; don't use a Pie or Doughnut chart to show, say, a company's stock price over time (unless it's a bakery).

Understanding Data Series

To master Excel charts, you'll have to first master the concept of a *data series*. Put simply, a data series is a group of numbers or data points that encompasses a single row or column of numbers from a spreadsheet (such as monthly revenues). In a simple bar or column chart, Excel turns each data series into its own set of bars or columns and assigns a different color to each.

For example, suppose you have a chart with two data series—that is, the numbers begin life as two spreadsheet columns, as shown here with Rev-

enue and Profit columns. When you create the chart, each month's revenue might show up as a blue bar, and each month's expenses as a green bar. Each set of like-colored bars came from the same data series.

One more tip: When you make a chart from a selection of cells, whichever there is fewer of—rows or columns—becomes the data series. You can always switch this arrangement, swapping the horizontal and vertical axes of your chart, once the chart is born.

	Revenue	Profit
Jan	143	52
Feb	232	88
Mar	188	79

Here are your options, each of which may offer several variations. Note that the illustrations accompanying these descriptions reveal which cells were highlighted to produce the charted results shown.

Figure 13-11:
When you click the "Press and Hold to View Sample" button without releasing the mouse button, Excel displays, in the area originally occupied by all the little example graphs, a miniature version of the actual graph you're about to create, using your own data. It's important to use this button to make sure that the chart type you've chosen is the right one for what you're doing. In most cases, you can tell immediately if the graph Excel is about to produce looks anything like the one you envisioned.

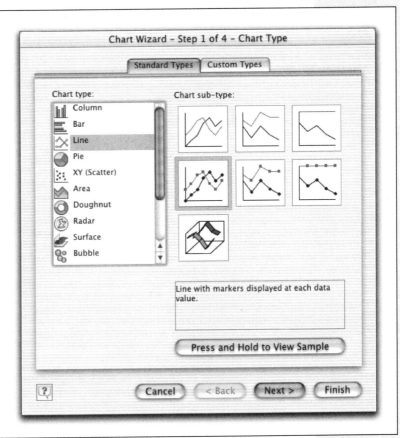

• **Column** charts are ideal for illustrating the data that changes over time—each column might represent, for example, sales for a particular month. As you'll see in the dialog box when you click Column, Excel offers seven variations of this chart type. Some are two-dimensional, some are

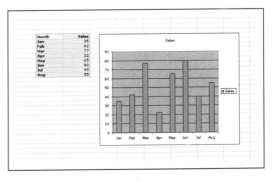

three-dimensional, some are stacked, and so on. (Stacked-column charts reveal totals for subcategories each month. That is, the different colors in each column might show the sales for a particular region, while three-dimensional charts can impart even more information—sales over time plotted against sales region, for example.)

• **3-D Column** charts let you compare two sets of data. In this example, check out the transparent fill applied to the front data series (Wands), which makes it easier to see the rear series (Hats). Transparent fills are new in Excel X, and enjoy more coverage on page 507.

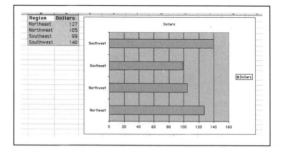

• **Bar** charts, which resemble column charts rotated 90 degrees clockwise, are as good as column charts for showing comparisons among individual items— but bar charts generally aren't used to show data that changes over time. Again, you can choose (in the right side of the dialog box) stacked or three-dimensional bar chart variations.

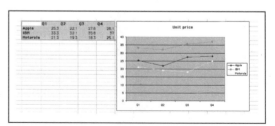

• **Line** charts help depict trends over time or among categories. The Line sub-type has seven variations; some show the individual points that have been plotted, some show only the line between these points, and so on.

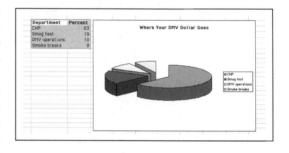

• **Pie** charts are great for showing how parts contribute to a whole, especially when there aren't very many of these parts. For example, a pie chart is extremely useful in showing how each dollar of your taxes is spent on various government programs, or how much of your diet is composed of, say, pie. The Pie subtype has six variations, including "exploded" views and three-dimensional ones.

- **XY (Scatter)** charts are common in the scientific community; they plot clusters of data points, revealing relationships among points from more than one set of data.

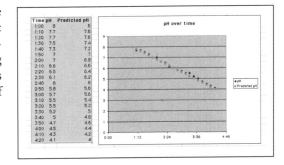

- **Area** charts are useful for showing both trends over time or across categories *and* how parts contribute to a whole. **3-D area** charts, of course, are even better when you want to compare *several* data series, especially if you apply a transparent fill to reduce the problem of one series blocking another. Once again, however, check out page 507, which explains an important printing bug and provides a few tips.

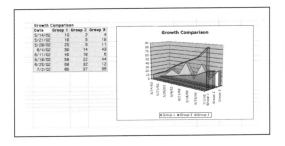

- **Doughnut** charts function like pie charts, in that they reveal the relationships of parts to the whole. The difference is that the various rings of the doughnut can represent different data sets (data from different years, for example).

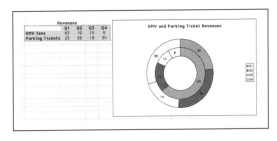

- **Radar** charts exist for very scientific and technical problems. A radar chart features an axis rotated around the center, polar-coordinates style, in order to connect the values of the same data series.

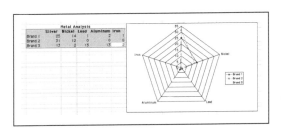

- **Surface** charts act like complicated versions of the Line chart. It's helpful when you need to spot the ideal combination of different sets of data—the precise spot where time, temperature, and flexibility are at their ideal relationships, for example. Thanks to colors and

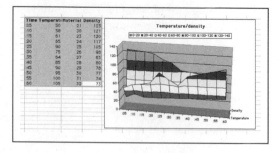

shading, it's easy to differentiate areas within the same ranges of values.

- **Bubble** charts are used to compare three values; the first two values form what looks like a scatter chart, and the third value determines the size of the "bubble" that marks each point.

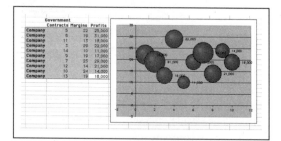

- **Stock** charts are used primarily for showing the highs and lows of a stock price on each trading day, but it's also useful for indicating other daily ranges (temperature or rainfall, for example).

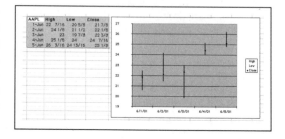

- **Cone, Cylinder, and Pyramid** charts are simply variations on basic column and bar charts. The difference is that, instead of a rectangular block, either a long, skinny cone, narrow cylinder, or a triangular spike (pyramid) represents each column or bar.

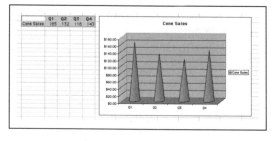

Note: If none of these chart types is exactly what you're looking for, Excel isn't finished with you yet. By clicking the Custom Types tab, you can choose from another 20 chart types, or even define your own. This tab is described in the next section.

After selecting your preferred chart type, click the Next button to continue.

Step 3: Set up Your Rows or Columns

On the next Chart Wizard screen (which Excel terms "Step 2 of 4 – Chart Source Data"), specify exactly which cells of your spreadsheet you want to graph. If you were wise, of course, you began this entire exercise by highlighting the appropriate cells in the spreadsheet.

But if you forgot, or you're some kind of iconoclast, you can do it now. One way is to edit the contents of the "Data range" field, where the spreadsheet, starting cell, and ending cell are represented with absolute cell references (see page 463).

The easier way to do it is to click the cell-selection triangle icon to the right of the "Data range" field. This icon, wherever it appears in Excel, always means, "Collapse this dialog box and get it out of my way, so that I can see my spreadsheet and make a selection." (Figure 13-12 illustrates the procedure.)

Tip: You don't have to collapse the Chart Wizard in order to change the data range. Any clicking or dragging in the spreadsheet will be reflected in the Data range field, whether the dialog box is collapsed or not.

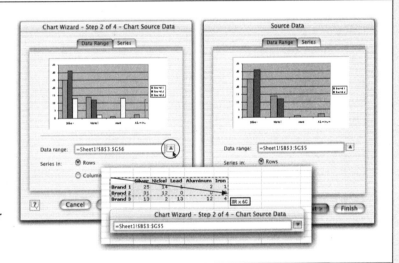

Figure 13-12:
Left: The cell-selection icon (circled) pops up in dozens of Excel dialog boxes.

Middle: When you click it, Excel collapses the dialog box, permitting access to your spreadsheet. Now you can select a range by dragging.

Right: Clicking the cell-selection triangle again returns you to the dialog box, which uncollapses and displays, in Excel's particular numeric notation, the range you specified.

This is also your opportunity to swap the horizontal and vertical axes of your chart, if necessary. (The preview on the first Chart Wizard screen should have provided an early warning that you might have your X and Y axes mixed up.)

If that preview looked all wrong, swap the horizontal and vertical dimensions of your chart by clicking the Rows or Columns radio button, whichever contains the data series.

Step 4: Add More Series

The other tab here is the Series tab, which you can use to tweak the data series included in your chart (see Figure 13-13). If things look good, click Next to continue.

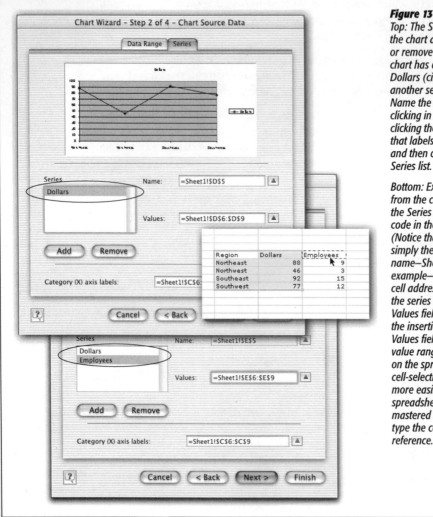

Figure 13-13:

Top: The Series tab previews the chart and lets you add or remove a series. Here, the chart has one series, called Dollars (circled). To add another series, click Add. Name the new series by clicking in the Name field, clicking the spreadsheet cell that labels the series (inset), and then clicking once in the Series list.

Bottom: Excel adds the text from the cell you clicked to the Series list and inserts a code in the Name field. (Notice that this code is simply the worksheet name—Sheet1 in this example—and the absolute cell address). Finish adding the series by filling in the Values field. Once you place the insertion point in the Values field, indicate the value range by selecting it on the spreadsheet (click the cell-selection triangle to more easily view the spreadsheet), or (if you've mastered Excel geek talk) type the coded range reference.

Step 5: Design the Chart

When it comes to customizing your chart, this Chart Wizard screen ("Step 3 of 4 – Chart Options") is the big one (Figure 13-14). Its six tabs let you change the look of every conceivable chart element, including the chart and axes titles, how gridlines are displayed, where the legend is placed, how data is labeled, and whether the spreadsheet cells used to make the chart are displayed. For example:

- The **Titles** tab lets you enter names for your chart's title, its X axis, its Y axis, and second X and Y axes (if you have them). These names appear as parts of the chart.

- The **Axes** tab allows you to specify whether the X axis is a *category* axis (that is, whether it displays the label you've assigned each group of data series in the chart), or whether it's a time scale, depicting change over time.

- The **Data Table** tab lets you choose whether your chart shows the actual data that was used to build your chart, along with the chart itself. If you answer in the affirmative, this data appears in a series of cells below the chart itself. Check "show legend keys" to make Excel show how each data series appears on the chart. You can see this helpful option in the preview on the Data Table tab.

Keep an eye on the preview on the right side of the wizard to see how your chart is shaping up. Once you've made settings to your heart's content, click the Next button to continue.

Figure 13-14:
This big tabbed screen holds a lot of the controls that you can use to customize your chart. Each tab area controls a different aspect of the chart's look.

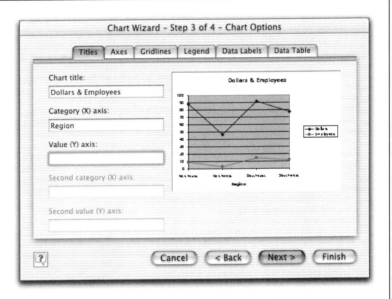

Step 6: Tell Excel Where to Put It

The final Chart Wizard screen asks where you want the chart to wind up:

- **As new sheet:** Your chart will occupy a new worksheet, called a chart sheet, in the current workbook document. Use this option when what you really wanted all along was a chart, and plugging the numbers into a spreadsheet was just a scratchpad for the chart's benefit.

• **As object in:** You will create an embedded chart—a chart floating as a graphic object right in your spreadsheet. (Use the pop-up menu to identify which worksheet you want the chart to appear in.) Use an embedded chart when you want your flashy graphics next to their data source.

Either way, charts remain linked to the data from which they were created, so if you change the data in those cells, the chart updates itself appropriately.

After making your selection, click the Finish button to make Excel place your chart.

Step 7: Tweak the Chart to Perfection

As is so often the case, the wizard is only the beginning. Once the chart has appeared on the screen, hundreds of flexible formatting options are now available to you.

Before redesigning the various pieces of your chart, however, it may be worthwhile to learn their anatomical names:

• **Legend.** The *legend* is the key that tells you what the chart's elements represent—its lines, pie slices, or dots. It's just like the legend on a map.

• **Axes.** An *axis* is the "ruler," either horizontal or vertical, against which Excel charts your data. The horizontal line that forms the floor of the chart is called the X axis; the vertical one that forms the "left wall" is the Y axis.

• **Axis labels.** This term may refer either to the tick mark labels ("January, February, March…") or to the overall label of the horizontal or vertical scale of your chart ("Income, in millions" or "Months since inception," for example).

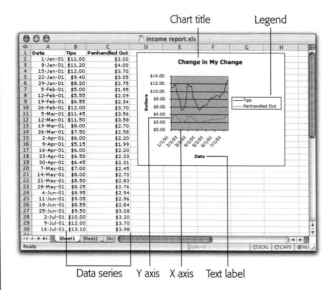

Chart title   Legend

Data series   Y axis   X axis   Text label

Figure 13-15:
Here's how a typical line chart breaks down into its parts. The X axis represents the dates in column A, and the Y axis represents the value of the numbers in columns B and C in dollars—in other words, columns B and C are each a data series. The text headers at the top of columns B and C are the series names, which Excel uses in the legend.

When modifying your chart, start with the most urgent matters:

- **Move the chart** by dragging it around on a sheet.

- **Delete some element of the chart** (such as the legend) by clicking it and then pressing the Delete key.

- **Resize the chart** by dragging any of the black square handles at its corners and edges. (If you don't see them, the chart is no longer selected. Click any blank white area inside the chart to select it.)

- **Reposition individual elements *in* the chart** (the text labels or legend, for example) by dragging them.

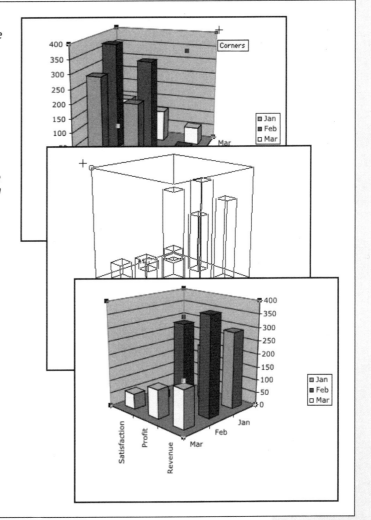

Figure 13-16:
Top: Rotating a 3-D chart is one of the flashiest Excel features; more practically, it lets you put your chart in the best possible light. To rotate a chart, drag a corner square (a tiny square visible in an active chart).

Middle: The chart rotates as a wireframe cube. You can press ⌘ at any time to see wire frames of the series objects inside the chart.

Bottom: When you release the mouse button, the chart appears, once again fleshed out, in its newly rotated position.

- **Convert a chart sheet into an embedded chart (or vice versa)** by selecting the chart and then choosing Chart→Location and making the appropriate choice in the resulting dialog box.

- **Rotate a 3D chart** by clicking inside the actual graph to produce its corner handles, and then dragging one of those corner handles vertically or horizontally. As shown in Figure 13-16, you see a wireframe representation of the chart while you're dragging. When you release the mouse, the chart redraws itself at the new angle that you specified.

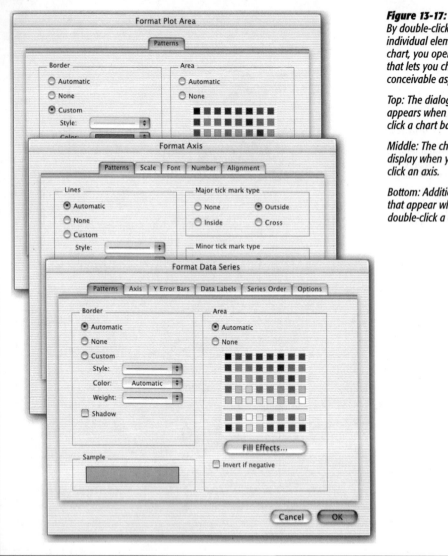

Figure 13-17:
By double-clicking the individual elements in a chart, you open a dialog box that lets you change every conceivable aspect of them.

Top: The dialog box that appears when you double-click a chart background.

Middle: The choices that display when you double-click an axis.

Bottom: Additional choices that appear when you double-click a chart bar.

Or, for a less free-form approach to chart rotation, choose Chart→3-D View and enter numbers in the various configuration fields, or click the various buttons to step through different views. (If you're rotating a chart in order to reveal a hidden data series, you can also format the blocking data series with a partially transparent fill. Learn more in the following section.)

- **Move series in a 3-D chart** to put smaller series in front of larger ones. Start by double-clicking any data series to open the Format Data Series dialog box, and then click the Series Order tab. Watch the preview in the dialog box as you click Move Up and Move Down.

Many different specialized Format dialog boxes await your investigation, too (see Figure 13-17). To open the dialog box, just double-click the pertinent piece of the chart. For example, when working with a simple bar chart:

- **Change the border or interior color** of the chart by double-clicking within the body of the chart.

- **Change the font, color, or position of the legend** by double-clicking it.

- **Change the scale, tick marks, label font, or label rotation of the axes** by double-clicking on their edges or slightly outside their edges.

- **Change the border, color, fill effect, bar separation, and data label options of an individual bar** by double-clicking it. You can even make bars partially transparent, revealing hidden series at the rear, as described in the next section.

You'll also notice that when a chart is selected, the Formatting Palette offers specialized formatting controls borrowed from the Chart Wizard; using the palette, you can change the chart type, gridline appearance, legend placement, and so on. And if you still haven't found your preferred method of formatting a finished chart, you can use the Chart toolbar (View→Toolbars→Chart). It offers a pop-up menu listing the various chart components that you can edit by double-clicking (such as Corners, Floor, Legend, and Series Axis).

Tip: You can copy a selected chart into another program either by dragging it or by using the Copy and Paste commands in the Edit menu.

Transparent Bars

It's the single most heavily advertised new feature in Excel X: chart transparency. For the first time, individual bars of a chart can be partially or completely see-through, making it much easier to display 3-D graphs where the frontmost bars would once have obscured the back ones.

You can apply transparent fills to most chart types, but their see-through nature makes the most sense in charts with at least two data series, where the front series blocks a good view of the rear (Figure 13-18, top).

Begin applying a transparent fill to a data series by double-clicking the series (the bar or column, for example). In the resulting Format Data Series dialog box, click the Patterns tab and then click Fill Effects. Now, in the Gradient tab, you can adjust the transparency of the series using the sliders (Figure 13-18, middle).

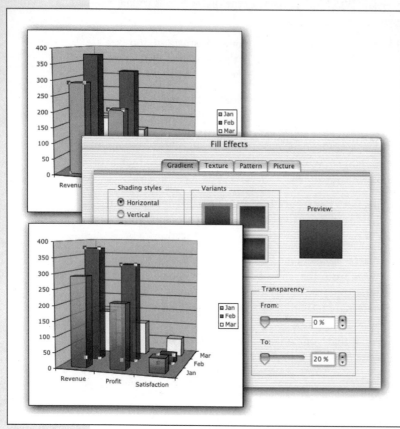

Figure 13-18:
This simple transparent-chart example illustrates how big a difference a little transparency can make. Just compare the opaque bars (top) with the see-through ones (bottom). You can even vary the amount of transparency along the bars' lengths. For example, the darker, middle bars go from 0% to 20% transparency, bottom to top; the frontmost ones are 20% transparent from top to bottom. The two Transparency sliders shown in the middle dialog box make it all possible.

To format a multi-series 3-D chart for maximum Wow factor, you may also wish to rotate it (drag a corner handle to spin the chart, or choose Chart→3-D View) or change the series order (double-click a series and work in the Series Order tab).

The Non-Printing Bug

If you have certain early versions of Office X and Mac OS X, you may encounter the Transparency Glitch, in which transparent bars (like those shown in Figure 13-18) look perfect onscreen but print out looking all too solid.

You have two choices: Update at least to Mac OS X 10.2 and Office X 10.1.4, or make a *screen capture* of the chart (also called a screenshot) and print *that*.

Printing a screenshot is a lame and low-resolution workaround. But it may be all you've got.

Here's how to do it: Press Shift-⌘-4, drag your new crosshair cursor diagonally across the portion of the screen that you'll want to print, and release the button. You hear a camera-shutter sound, and a new file called Picture 1 appears on your desktop. Print it.

Advanced Charting

The Chart Wizard suffices for almost every conceivable kind of standard graph. But every now and then, you may have special graphing requirements; fortunately, Excel can meet almost any charting challenge that you put before it—if you know how to ask.

Error bars

On some charts—such as those that graph stocks and opinion polls—it's helpful to graph not only the data, but also the range of movement or margin of error that surrounds the data. And that's where *error bars* come in. Error bars let you specify a range around each data point displayed in the graph, such as a poll's margin of error (Figure 13-19).

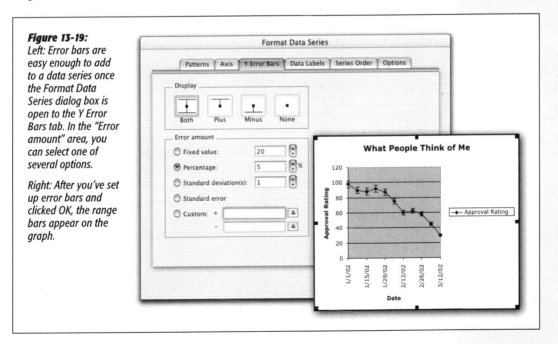

Figure 13-19:
Left: Error bars are easy enough to add to a data series once the Format Data Series dialog box is open to the Y Error Bars tab. In the "Error amount" area, you can select one of several options.

Right: After you've set up error bars and clicked OK, the range bars appear on the graph.

To add error bars to a chart, first select the data series (usually a line or bar in the chart) to which you want to add error bars. Choose Format→Selected Data Series (or double-click the selected line or bar) to bring up the Format Data Series dialog box. To add error bars along the Y axis—the usual arrangement—click the Y Error Bars tab; then choose display and error amounts for your bars. Click the OK button to add the error bars to your data series. If you want to remove them later, open the Format Data Series dialog box and set the Display to None.

Note: You can add error bars to 2-D area charts, bar charts, bubble charts, column charts, line charts, and scatter charts. In fact, X-axis error bars can even be added to scatter charts. (You'll see this additional tab in the Format Data Series dialog box.)

Trend lines

Graphs excel at revealing *trends*—how data is changing over time, how data probably changed over time before you started tracking it, and how it's likely to change in the future. To help with such predictions, Excel can add *trend lines* to its charts (Figure 13-20). Trend lines use a mathematical model to help accentuate patterns in current data and to help predict future patterns.

Note: You can use trend lines only in unstacked 2-D area charts, bar charts, bubble charts, column charts, line charts, scatter charts, and stock charts.

To add a trend line to your chart, click to select one of the data series in the chart—typically a line or a bar—and then choose Chart→Add Trendline. This opens the Add Trendline dialog box, which has the tabs Type and Options.

The Type tab lets you choose one of these trend-line types:

- **Linear**. This kind of trend line works well with a graph that looks like a line, as you might have guessed. If your data is going up or down at a steady rate, a linear trend line is your best bet, since it closely resembles a simple straight line.

- **Logarithmic**. If the rate of change in your data increases or decreases rapidly and then levels out, a *logarithmic* trend line is probably your best choice. Logarithmic trend lines tend to have a relatively sharp curve at one end and then gradually level out. Logarithmic trend lines are based on logarithms, a mathematical function.

- **Polynomial**. A *polynomial* trend line is great when graphed data features hills and valleys, perhaps representing data that rises or falls in a somewhat rhythmic manner. Polynomial trend lines can also have a single curve that looks like a camel's hump (or an upside-down camel's hump, depending on your data.) Polynomial trend lines are based on polynomial expressions, familiar to those who've spent some time in a high school algebra class.

- **Power.** If the graphed data changes at a steady rate, as in an acceleration curve, a *power* trend line is the way to go. Power trend lines tend to curve smoothly upward.

- **Exponential.** If, on the other hand, the graphed data changes at an ever-increasing or decreasing rate, then you'd be better off with an *exponential* trend line, which also looks like a smoothly curving line.

- **Moving Average.** A *moving average* trend line attempts to smooth out fluctuations in data, in order to reveal trends that might otherwise be hidden. Moving averages, as the name suggests, can come in all kinds of shapes. No matter what the shape, though, they all help spot cycles in what might otherwise look like random data.

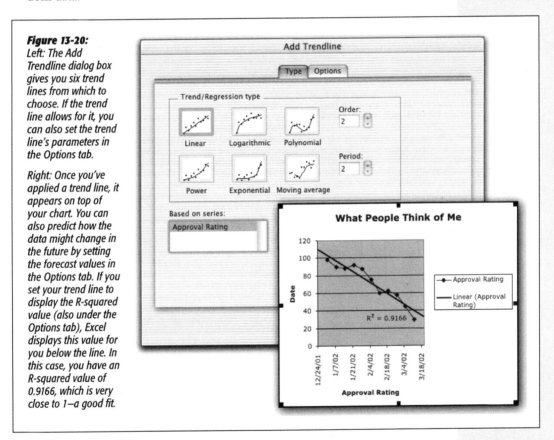

Figure 13-20:
Left: The Add Trendline dialog box gives you six trend lines from which to choose. If the trend line allows for it, you can also set the trend line's parameters in the Options tab.

Right: Once you've applied a trend line, it appears on top of your chart. You can also predict how the data might change in the future by setting the forecast values in the Options tab. If you set your trend line to display the R-squared value (also under the Options tab), Excel displays this value for you below the line. In this case, you have an R-squared value of 0.9166, which is very close to 1—a good fit.

The Options tab, on the other hand, lets you name your trend line, extend it beyond the data set to forecast trends, and even display the R-squared value on the chart. (The R-squared value is a way of calculating how accurately the trend line fits the data; you statisticians know who you are.)

Incidentally, remember that trend lines are just models. As any weather forecaster, stockbroker, or computer-company CEO can tell you, trend lines don't necessarily predict *anything* with accuracy.

The One-Step Chart

If you want an insta-chart without having to futz around with the Chart Wizard, there's an incredibly easy way to do it. Just select the data you want in the chart and then press F11. Excel instantly creates a standard chart, in its own document window, made from that data.

There's also a Default Chart toolbar button that creates, with a single click, a chart embedded in your spreadsheet. This button isn't on the standard toolbar, however. To add it to one of your toolbars, follow the instructions on page 630.

Because Excel uses a *default* chart type to create this insta-chart, it's helpful to know how to change that default. To do so, first select a chart, choose Chart→Chart Type, and then, in the Chart Type dialog box, click the "Set as Default Chart" button. When Excel asks if you really want to do this, click Yes. Then click OK to finish up.

Printing Worksheets

Now that you've gone through the trouble of making your sheets look their best with killer formatting and awe-inspiring charts, the next logical step is printing them out.

Print Preview (Microsoft's)

Excel comes with a print-preview function that can save you frustration and time, as well as an old-growth forest that would otherwise be harvested for the sake of your botched spreadsheet printouts. What's a little strange is that Mac OS X, of course, comes with its *own* print-preview function with slightly different features. Ah, well—if one is good, two must be better.

To use Excel's print preview, choose File→Print Preview, which puts Excel into Print Preview mode (Figure 13-21). In this specialized view of the currently selected sheet, you can see how your data will look when divided up onto several sheets of paper. Use the Print Preview toolbar to tweak how your sheet prints. Here's a quick look at the toolbar buttons.

- **Setup.** This button opens the Page Setup dialog box, as described on page 514.

- **Print.** This button opens up the Print dialog box, where you can set your print options and send your sheet to the printer.

- **Zoom.** Click the Zoom button to magnify or reduce the preview, giving you a closer look at the cell contents that may be chopped off at the edge of the page. The Zoom button provides quick toggle action for reducing and enlarging the overall page; to enlarge a particular area, click the area with the cursor instead.

- **Prev, Next.** If your spreadsheet is too big for a single sheet of paper, these buttons show you the previous page, or next page, of the preview.

- **Margins.** Click this button to show or hide dotted lines and little black handles, representing the margins of your page. You can drag them to adjust the sizes of your margins. For example, if your spreadsheet is only slightly too big to fit on a page, shrinking the margins might make just enough room to accommodate the whole thing.

- **Page Break Preview.** Microsoft is justifiably proud of this feature. When you click this button, you enter Page Break Preview mode, where thick blue-dotted lines indicate how Excel plans to divide your spreadsheet onto multiple pages (Figure 13-21). (If your spreadsheet doesn't require multiple pages, the Page Break Preview button is dimmed and unavailable.)

Tip: To check out your page-break preview without doing a print preview first, just choose View→Page Break Preview at any time.

Figure 13-21:
A disaster waiting to print. This printout will be chopped off in mid-chart. Fortunately, by choosing File→Print Preview before actually printing the spreadsheet, you get a chance to see how it's going to spill over onto two sheets–and you get the chance to correct it by using the Print Preview controls.

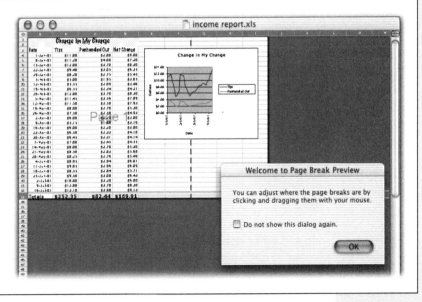

Suppose you've resigned yourself to the fact that your spreadsheet is too big for a single sheet—but Excel is cutting it off at a really bad place, such as just before the December sales-figure column. The beauty of Page Break Preview is that you can drag the blue-dotted lines up, down, left, or right to redefine where the page breaks fall. After each drag, Excel automatically shrinks or enlarges the contents of the affected pages to accommodate your page-break preferences. (All things in moderation, however; with this feature it's possible to force Excel to shrink the numbers in your cells to the size of atoms.)

To exit Page Break Preview mode, choose View→Normal.

- **Close.** This button closes the Print Preview window and returns you to your regularly scheduled spreadsheet.

- **Help (?) icon.** The question-mark button opens Microsoft Office Help to the topic of Print Preview.

Tip: To print just a certain portion of your spreadsheet, select the cells that you want to print and then choose File→Print Area→Set Print Area. This tells Excel to print only the selected cells. To clear a custom print area, select File→Print Area→Clear Print Area.

Print Preview (Apple's)

As in any Mac OS X-compatible program, you turn a document into a print-preview file by choosing File→Print and then, in the Print dialog box, clicking the Preview button at the bottom. Your Mac fires up the Preview program, where you see the printout-to-be as a graphic. Use the commands in the Display menu to zoom in, zoom out, scroll, and so on.

The best part, though, is the File→Save As PDF command. It turns your printout into an electronic document—a PDF or Acrobat file—that you can send to almost anyone with a computer, so they can open, read, search, and print your handiwork. (The software they need is the free Acrobat Reader program.)

Page Setup

Excel's Page Setup dialog box (Figure 13-22) is far more comprehensive than the Page Setup that appears when you choose File→Page Setup in TextEdit, for example. In it, you can control how pages are oriented, how spreadsheets fit on a page, the print quality, the margins, how headers and footers are printed, and the order in which pages are printed.

Page tab

In the Page tab, you can change the orientation of each page (Portrait for the usual up-and-down style or Landscape for a sideways style), reduce or enlarge the printout by a certain percent, or—using the "Fit to" radio button—force the spreadsheet to fit onto a certain number of printed pages. (Using this control, of course, affects the printout's type size.) If you don't want the pages of your spreadsheet numbered 1, 2, and so on, then type a different number into the "First page number" field; that's how you force Excel to number the pages beginning with, say, 5 on the first printed sheet.

Tip: Setting the starting page number in the Page tab won't make page numbers appear on your sheets; you must also initiate page numbering in the Header/Footer tab. The easiest technique is to choose a page number option from the Header or Footer pop-up menu.

An Options button on the right brings up the more familiar Page Setup dialog box for your printer, in which you can set more of your printer's options (such as paper size).

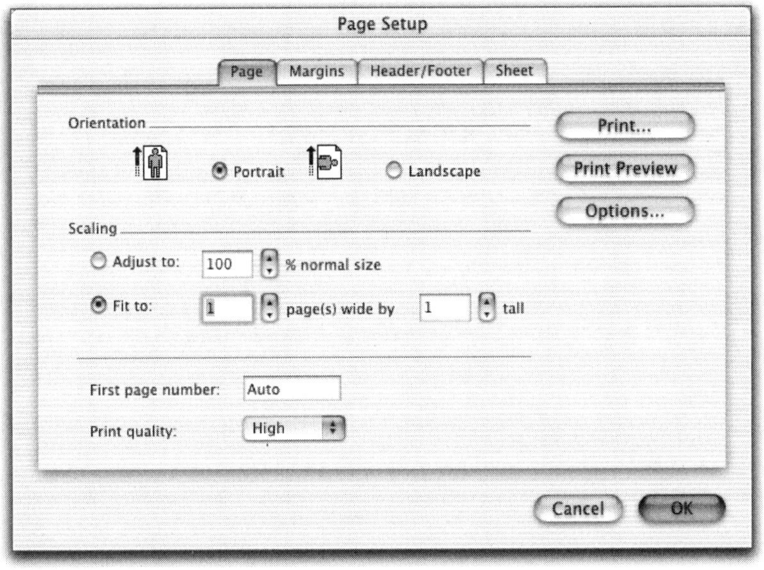

Figure 13-22:
The Page tab of the Page Setup dialog box is where to start if you want a spreadsheet to print on one page. A click in the "Fit to" radio button (in the Scaling area) automatically adjusts your spreadsheet's print size to fit on a sheet of paper. If you want it to fit on more than one sheet, adjust the numbers in the "Fit to" area.

Margins tab

The Margins tab (Figure 13-23, top) lets you specify the page margins for your printout (and for the header and footer areas). You can also tell Excel to center the printout on the page horizontally, vertically, or both. The Options button, once again, summons the standard Page Setup dialog box for your printer.

Header/Footer tab

If you want something printed on the top or bottom of every page (such as a title, copyright notice, or date), it's time to visit the Header/Footer tab (Figure 13-23, bottom).

Here, you can use the Header or Footer pop-up menu to choose from a selection of prepared headers and footers—"Page 1 of 7," "Confidential," and so on.

If the header or footer message you want isn't there, click the Custom Header or Custom Footer buttons to bring up a customization dialog box. In it you can enter your own header or footer text; click the Font button to format the text; and use the remaining buttons to insert placeholder codes for the current page number, the total number of pages, the current date, the current time, the file name, and the tab name.

You can combine these codes with text that you type yourself. For example, in the "Center section" box, you could type, *CD Collection Status as of,* and then click the fourth icon. Excel inserts the code *&[Date};.* Now whenever you print this document, you'll find, across the top of every page, "CD Collection Status as of 9/15/02," or whatever the current date is.

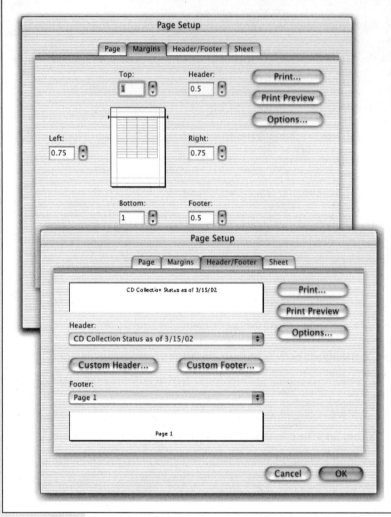

Figure 13-23:
Top: The Margins portion of the Page Setup window gives you power over your sheet's margins when printed, naturally. It lets you set top, left, right, and bottom margins, and it gives you the chance to determine how much top and bottom space is left over for headers and footers—useful if you have particularly large headers and footers. The checkboxes at the bottom of the box let you set how— and whether—your printouts are centered on the page.

Bottom: The Header/Footer part of the Page Setup dialog box is where you can set text to be printed on the top or bottom—or both—of every page.

Sheet tab

The last section of the Page Setup dialog box, called Sheet, offers yet another way to specify which portions of the sheet are to be printed (Figure 13-24). You can type starting and ending Excel coordinates into the "Print area" box (separated by a colon), click the striped-triangle icon to return to the spreadsheet to select a region, or you can highlight the cells you want printed.

Tip: If fields are dim in the Sheets tab, they can be accessed by closing the Page Setup dialog box, closing print preview, and then choosing File→Page Setup.

You'll also find the following in the Sheet tab:

- **Rows to repeat at top, Columns to repeat at left.** If you've carefully typed the months of the year across the top of your spreadsheet, or product numbers down the left side, you'll have a real mess on your hands if the spreadsheet spills over onto two or more pages. Anyone trying to read the spreadsheet will have to refer all the way back to Page 1 just to see the labels for each row or column.

  Excel neatly avoids this problem by offering to _reprint_ the column or row labels at the top or left side of _each_ printed page. To indicate which row or column contains these labels, click in the appropriate "Print titles" field, and then click the desired row number or column heading directly in the spreadsheet. Or click the triangle icon just to the right of each field; this more effectively shrinks the dialog box and more easily selects the repeating cell range.

- **Grid lines, Row and column headings.** It's too bad that the answer to one of the world's most frequently asked spreadsheet questions—"How do I get the grid lines to print?"—is buried in the fourth tab of a buried dialog box.

Figure 13-24:
The Sheet portion of the Page Setup window lets you set a print area (if you haven't already done so). You can also specify that certain rows repeat at the top of each page and/or columns repeat on the left of each page. It gives you five print-quality options, and it enables you to control whether pages are printed down and then over, or over and then down.

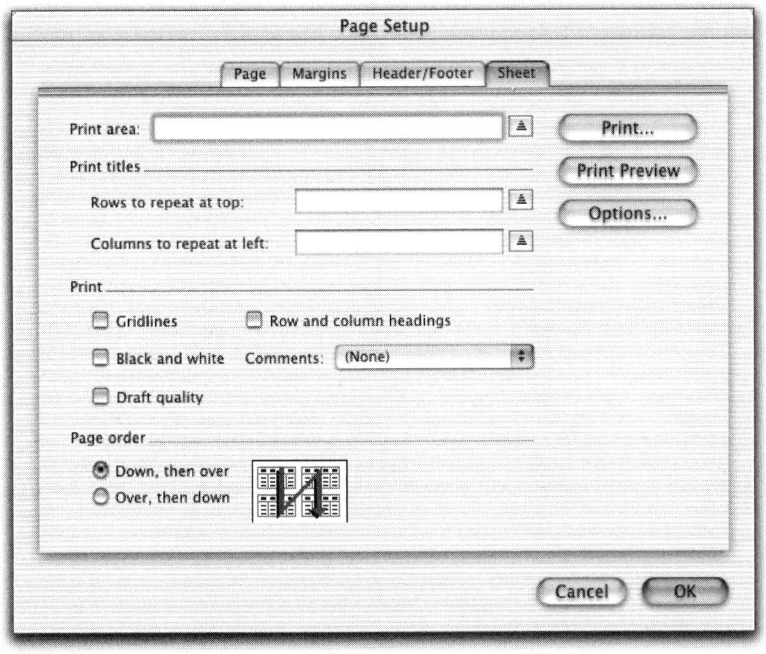

In any case, this tab should clarify everything. Excel never prints grid lines or the gray row and column headings unless you turn on their corresponding checkboxes here.

- **Black and white, Draft quality.** Use these two checkboxes when you're in a real hurry. Draft quality speeds up printing by omitting graphics and some formatting. "Black and white" means that your printer won't bother with time-consuming color, even if color appears in the spreadsheet.

- **Comments.** Use this pop-up menu to specify where *comments* (see page 562) appear on the printout—on its last page, or right where you put them in the spreadsheet itself.

- **Page order.** Use these controls to control whether Excel prints a multiple-page spreadsheet column by column (of pages), or row by row .

Advanced Spreadsheeting

I f you've mastered enough of Excel to input numbers, perform calculations, create charts and graphs, and log your CD collection using the List Manager, then congratulations—you already have far more spreadsheet ability than most people.

If, on the other hand, you're the kind of person who uses Excel more than a word processor, whose business depends on the flow of numbers, projections, and calculations, there's still more to learn. This chapter covers the eerie realms of power Excel, where several people can work on the same spreadsheet simultaneously over the network, files can connect to databases or even the Web for their information, and Excel can be programmed to function by itself.

Workbooks and Worksheets

A *workbook* is an individual Excel file that you save on your hard drive. Each workbook is made up of one or more *worksheets*, which let you organize your data in lots of complex and interesting ways. Try thinking of a workbook as a bound ledger with multiple paper worksheets. Although most of the work you do is probably in an individual sheet, it's often useful to store several spreadsheets in a single workbook document—for the convenience of linking multiple Excel worksheets.

Working with Multiple Worksheets

Although it doesn't offer quite the heart-pounding excitement of, say, the List Manager, managing the worksheets in a workbook is an important part of mastering Excel. Here's what you should know to get the most out of your sheets.

Tip: Several of the techniques described here involve selecting more than one worksheet. To do so, ⌘-click the tabs of the individual sheets you want—or click the first in a consecutive series, then Shift-click the last.

- **Adding sheets.** Every Excel workbook starts out with three sheets, bearing the inspired names Sheet1, Sheet2, and Sheet3. (You can set the number of sheets in a new workbook in Excel→Preferences→General panel.)

   To add a new sheet to your workbook, choose Insert→Worksheet, or Control-click one of the tabs at the bottom of the worksheet and choose Insert from the contextual menu. A new sheet appears *to the left* of the currently selected sheet, and it's named Sheet4 (or Sheet5, Sheet6, and so on).

Tip: To insert multiple sheets in one swift move, select the same number of sheet tabs that you want to insert and *then* choose Insert→Worksheet. For example, to insert two new sheets, select Sheet1 and Sheet2 by Shift-clicking both tabs, and then choose Insert→Worksheet. Excel then inserts Sheet4 and Sheet5 (yes, to the *left* of Sheet1).

POWER USERS' CLINIC

Adding Background Pictures to Sheets

Every now and then, it's easy to feel sorry for Microsoft programmers; after umpteen revisions, what possible features can they add to Excel? They must rack their brains, lying awake at night, trying to figure out what else they can invent.

Surely, the ability to add a graphics file as a background image behind your cell grid is an idea that sprang from just such a late-night idea session.

Start by choosing Format→Sheet→ Background. An Open dialog box pops up, in which you can choose the graphics file (JPEG, GIF, Photoshop, and so on) that you want to use as a background. Once you've selected it and clicked Open, the im-

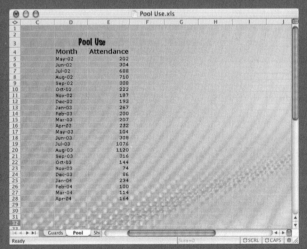

age loads as the spreadsheet's background. If the image isn't large enough to fill the entire worksheet, Excel automatically *tiles* it, placing copies side-by-side until every centimeter of the window is filled.

Clearly, if this feature is ever successful in improving a worksheet, it's when the background image is extremely light in color and low in contrast. Most other images succeed only in rendering your numbers and text illegible.

If, after adding an image to a sheet, you decide that it makes things much, much worse, choose Format→Sheet→Delete Background. Your normal white Excel sheet background returns.

- **Deleting sheets.** To delete a sheet, click the doomed sheet's tab (or select several tabs) at the bottom of the window, and then choose Edit→Delete Sheet. (Alternatively, Control-click the sheet tab and choose Delete from the contextual menu.)

Warning: You can't bring back a deleted sheet. The Undo command (Edit→Undo) doesn't work in this context.

- **Hiding and showing sheets.** Instead of deleting a worksheet forever, you may find it helpful to simply hide one (or several), keeping your peripheral vision free of distractions while you focus on the remaining ones. To hide a sheet or sheets, select the corresponding worksheet tabs at the bottom of the window, then choose Format→Sheet→Hide. To show (or *unhide*, as Excel calls it) sheets that have been hidden, choose Format→Sheet→Unhide; this brings up a list of sheets to show. Choose the sheet that you want to reappear, and click OK.

Note: You can unhide only one sheet at a time.

- **Renaming sheets.** The easiest way to rename a sheet is to double-click its tab to highlight its name, and then type the new text (up to 31 characters long). Alternatively, you can select the tab of the sheet you want to rename and then choose Format→Sheet→Rename; you can also Control-click the sheet tab and choose Rename from the contextual menu.

- **Moving and copying sheets.** To move a sheet (so that, for example, Sheet1 comes after Sheet3), just drag its tab horizontally; a tiny black triangle indicates where the sheet will wind up, relative to the others, when you release the mouse. Using this technique, you can even drag a copy of a worksheet into a different Excel document.

Tip: Pressing Option while you drag produces a copy of the worksheet. (The exception is when you drag a sheet's tab into a different workbook; in that case, Excel copies the sheet regardless of whether the Option key is held down.)

As usual, there are other ways to perform this task. For example, you can also select a sheet's tab and then choose Edit→Move or Copy Sheet, or Control-click the sheet tab and choose Move or Copy from the contextual menu. In either case, the Move or Copy dialog box pops up. In it, you can specify which open workbook the sheet should be moved to, whether the sheet is copied or moved, and where you want to place the sheet relative to the others.

- **Scrolling through sheet tabs.** If you have more sheet tabs than Excel can display in the bottom portion of the window, you can use the four tab scrolling buttons to scoot between the various sheets (see Figure 14-1). Another method is to Control-click any tab-scrolling button and then choose a sheet's name from the contextual menu.

- **Showing more or fewer sheet tabs.** The area reserved for Sheet tabs must share space with the horizontal scroll bar. Fortunately, you can change how much area is devoted to showing sheet tabs by dragging the small, gray, vertical tab split bar that sits between the tabs and the scroll bar. Drag it to the left to expand the scroll bar area (and hide worksheet tabs if necessary); drag it to the right to reveal more tabs.

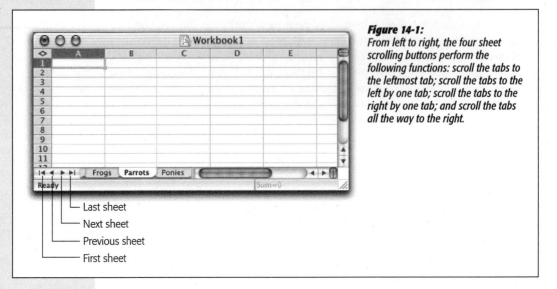

Figure 14-1:
From left to right, the four sheet scrolling buttons perform the following functions: scroll the tabs to the leftmost tab; scroll the tabs to the left by one tab; scroll the tabs to the right by one tab; and scroll the tabs all the way to the right.

Sharing a Workbook

With a little preparation, several Excel users on the same network can work on a single worksheet at the same time. (If you want to share a workbook, but prevent others from accessing it, read about protection on page 524 first. Bear in mind, some protection commands must be applied *before* you turn on sharing.) To share a workbook, choose Tools→Share Workbook, which brings up the Share Workbook dialog box. On the Editing tab (Figure 14-2), turn on "Allow changes by more than one user at the same time." Click the Advanced tab for the following options:

- **Track changes.** This section lets you set a time limit on what changes are tracked (see "Tracking Changes" on page 525). If you don't care what was changed 61 days ago, you can limit the tracked changes to 60 days. You can also tell Excel not to keep a change history at all.

- **Update changes.** Here, you specify when your view of the shared workbook gets updated to reflect changes that others have made. You can set it to display the changes that have been made every time you save the file, or you can command it to update at a specified time interval.

If you choose to have the changes updated automatically after a time interval, you can set the workbook to save automatically (thus sending your changes out to co-workers sharing the workbook) and to display others' changes (thus receiving changes from your co-workers' saves). Or you can set it not to save your changes, and just to show changes that others have made.

- **Conflicting changes between users.** This section governs whose changes "win" when two or more people make changes to the same workbook cell. You can set it so that you're asked to referee (which can be a *lot* of work), or so that the most recent changes saved are the ones that win (which can be risky). Clearly, neither option is perfect. Since each person can establish settings independently, it might be worth working out a unified collaboration policy with your co-workers.

- **Include in personal view.** These two checkboxes—Print settings and Filter settings—let you retain printing and filtering changes that are independent of the workbook. These checkboxes can be set independently by anyone who opens the workbook.

When you click OK, Excel prompts you to save the workbook—if you haven't already. Save it on a networked disk where others can see it. Now, anyone who opens the workbook from across the network opens it as a shared book.

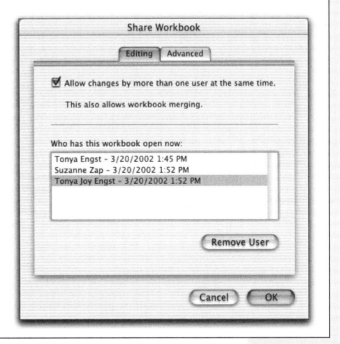

Figure 14-2:
The Share Workbook dialog box reveals exactly who else is using a shared workbook. If you worry that one of your fellow network citizens is about to make ill-advised changes, click her name and then click Remove User. Your comrade is ejected from the spreadsheet party. If she tries to save changes to the file, she'll get an error message explaining the situation. You should also note that there's little security in shared workbooks. As you can see, the same user is logged in and able to make changes from two different Macs at the same time. Of course, if you password-protect the sheet before sharing it, you'll achieve a basic, keeping-honest-people-honest level of security.

Shared workbooks have some limitations, detailed in the online help topic, "Limitations of shared workbooks." Here's a summary of things that you *can't* do with a shared workbook:

- Assign, change, or delete a password that protects a worksheet.

- Create, edit, view, or assign *macros* (see page 563).

- Insert charts, hyperlinks, objects, or pictures.

- Make or change PivotTables, or make or refresh data tables (page 542).

- Merge, insert, or delete blocks of cells; delete worksheets.

- Use automatic subtotals or drawing tools.

- Use or create conditional formats or data validation.

- View or edit *scenarios* (page 549).

Protecting the spreadsheet

Fortunately, there's no need to give everyone on the network unfettered access to your carefully designed spreadsheet. You can protect your spreadsheet in several ways, as described here, and your colleagues can't turn off these protections without choosing Tools→Unprotect Sheet (or Unprotect Workbook)—and *that* requires a password (if you've set one up).

- **Protect a workbook from changes.** Choose Tools→Protection→Protect Workbook, which brings up the Protect Workbook dialog box. By turning on Structure and/or Windows, you can protect the workbook's *structure* (which keeps its sheets from being deleted, changed, hidden, or renamed) and its windows (which keeps the workbook's windows from being moved, resized, or hidden). Both of these safeguards are especially important in a spreadsheet you've carefully set up for onscreen reviewing. You can also assign a password to the workbook so that if a user wants to turn *off* its protection, he must know the password.

- **Protect a sheet from changes.** Choose Tools→Protection→Protect Sheet to bring up the Protect Sheet dialog box. Turn on the Contents checkbox to protect all *locked* cells in a worksheet (described next), as well as formats in a chartsheet. Turn on Objects to prevent changes to graphic objects on a worksheet, including formats of all charts and comments. Finally, turn on the Scenarios checkbox to keep *scenario* definitions (page 549) from being changed.

  The bottom of the dialog box lets you assign a password to the worksheet; this password will be required from anyone who attempts to turn off the protections you've established.

- **Protect individual cells from changes.** Excel automatically formats all cells in a new worksheet as locked, so if you protect the contents of a sheet you've been working in, all the cells will be rendered unchangeable. If you want *some* cells in a protected sheet to be editable, you must unlock them while the sheet is unprotected. Unlock selected cells by choosing Format→Cells. In the resulting dialog box, click the Protection tab, turn off the Locked checkbox, and then click OK.

- **Require a password to open a workbook.** Open the workbook you want to protect and choose File→Save As (or, if you've never saved this workbook before, choose File→Save). In the Save dialog box, click Options. In the resulting dialog box (Figure 14-3), enter one password to allow opening of the file and another to allow file modification.

Warning: Remember these passwords. If you forget them, there's no way to recover them; it's possible to lock yourself out of your own workbook.

Figure 14-3:
Entering a password in the top text box prevents others from opening your workbook without the password. If you specify only the second password, people can open the file, but can't make changes without the password.

- **Hide rows, columns, or sheets.** Once you've hidden some rows, columns, or sheets (page 521), you can prevent people from making them reappear by choosing Tools→Protection→Protect Workbook. Turn on Structure and then click OK.

- **Allow selection of only certain parts of a worksheet.** If you're a programmer with serious knowledge of macros and Visual Basic, you can use the EnableSelection property to keep specific cells from being selected by other people. Although you can play with changing this property from NoRestriction to UnlockedCells in the VisualBasic Editor (which keeps you from selecting cells that are locked), to actually *implement* this change into a worksheet requires writing code in Visual Basic.

- **Protecting a shared workbook.** To protect a shared workbook, choose Tools→Protection→Protect Shared Workbook, which brings up the Protect Shared Workbook window. This window presents you with two protection choices. If you turn on "Sharing with track changes" and enter a password, you prevent others from turning off change tracking—a way of looking at who makes what changes to your workbook. Turning on this checkbox *also* shares the workbook, as detailed previously.

Tracking Changes

When people make changes to your spreadsheet over the network, you aren't necessarily condemned to a life of frustration and chaos, even though numbers that you input originally may be changed beyond recognition. Exactly as in Word, Excel offers a *change tracking* feature that lets you see exactly which of your co-workers made what changes to your spreadsheet and on a case-by-case basis, approve or eliminate them. (The changes, not the co-workers.)

To see who has been tip-toeing through your workbook, choose Tools→Track Changes→Highlight Changes, which brings up the Highlight Changes dialog box (Figure 14-4). In it, you can choose how changes are highlighted: by time or by person making the changes. To limit the revision tracking to a specific area on the worksheet, click the triangle icon at the right of the Where field, select the area, and then click the triangle again.

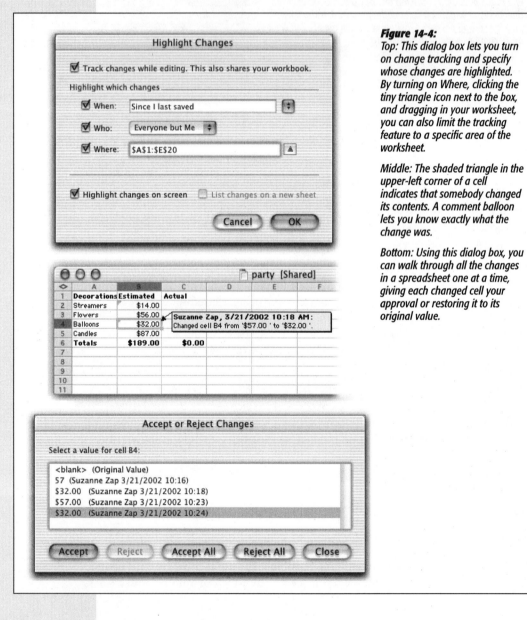

Figure 14-4:
Top: This dialog box lets you turn on change tracking and specify whose changes are highlighted. By turning on Where, clicking the tiny triangle icon next to the box, and dragging in your worksheet, you can also limit the tracking feature to a specific area of the worksheet.

Middle: The shaded triangle in the upper-left corner of a cell indicates that somebody changed its contents. A comment balloon lets you know exactly what the change was.

Bottom: Using this dialog box, you can walk through all the changes in a spreadsheet one at a time, giving each changed cell your approval or restoring it to its original value.

As life goes on with this spreadsheet on your network, changes made by your co-workers appear as a triangular flag at the upper-left corner of a cell or block of cells (Figure 14-4, middle).

Once you've reviewed the changes, you may decide that the original figures were superior to those in the changed version. At this point, Excel offers you the opportunity to analyze each change; if you think the change was an improvement, you can accept it, making it part of the spreadsheet from now on. If not, you can reject the change, restoring the cell contents to whatever was there before your network comrades got ambitious.

To perform this accept/reject routine, choose Tools→Track Changes→Accept or Reject Changes. In the Select Changes to Accept or Reject dialog box, you can set up the reviewing process by specifying which changes you want to review (according to when they were made, who made them, and where they are located in the worksheet). When you click OK, the reviewing process begins (Figure 14-4, bottom).

Merging Workbooks

In many work situations, you may find it useful to distribute copies of a workbook to several people for their perusal and then incorporate their changes into a single workbook.

Performing this feat, however, requires some preparation—namely, creating a shared workbook (see the previous section), and then configuring the workbook's *change history*. You'll find this option by choosing Tools→Share Workbook and then clicking the Advanced tab (Figure 14-5). The number that you specify in the "Keep change history for" box determines how old changes can be before they become irrelevant.

POWER USERS' CLINIC

Unbinding Windows Binder Documents

To the relief of many, the document formats for Word, Excel, and PowerPoint are identical on the Mac and on Windows; you don't have any conversion to do when sending a document from one kind of computer to the other. That's not to say, however, that Office is identical on both platforms. For example, Office for Windows doesn't come with Entourage, and Office for the Mac doesn't let you make *Binders*.

Binders are specialized holder files capable of containing a mix of Excel workbooks, Word files, and PowerPoint documents. Windows users can pass them from PC to PC, edit the documents, and pass them on again.

While those documents are in a Binder, you can't work with them on the Macintosh. In the past, Microsoft provided a solution: the Unbind utility, which came in the Value Pack with Macintosh versions of Office.

Microsoft did not provide Unbind with Office X (and does not plan to), so if you find yourself in a bind over a Binder, the best you can do is track down a computer with Office 2001 whose owner is willing to help you. With a copy of Unbind at your disposal, you can bust open a Binder file by double-clicking Unbind's icon and then locating and opening the Binder file in the Open dialog box that pops up. Unbind splits apart the Binder file and saves each distinct Excel, PowerPoint, and Word file in the same folder. (Unfortunately, there's no way to rebind a binder file on the Mac.)

The theory behind this feature contends that you'll stop caring about changes that are older than the number of days that you set. (Tracking changes forever can bloat a file's size, too.)

Once you've prepared your workbook, distribute it via email or network. Ask your colleagues to make comments and changes and then return their spreadsheet copies to you (within the time limit you specified, as described in the previous paragraph). Collect all of the copies into one place. (You may need to rename the workbooks to avoid replacing one with another, since they can't occupy the same folder if they have the same names.)

Now open a copy of the shared workbook and choose Tools→Merge Workbooks, which brings up an Open dialog box. Choose the file you want to merge into the open workbook, and then click OK. This process must be repeated for every workbook you want to merge.

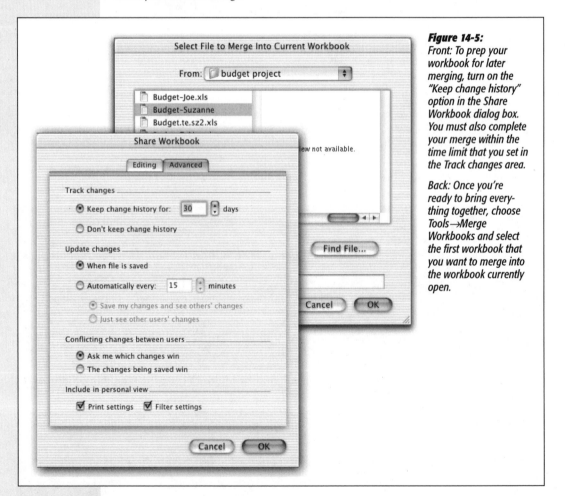

Figure 14-5:
Front: To prep your workbook for later merging, turn on the "Keep change history" option in the Share Workbook dialog box. You must also complete your merge within the time limit that you set in the Track changes area.

Back: Once you're ready to bring everything together, choose Tools→Merge Workbooks and select the first workbook that you want to merge into the workbook currently open.

Exporting Files

Every now and then, it can be useful to send your Excel data to a different program—a database program, for example, or AppleWorks (if you're collaborating with somebody who doesn't have Office). Fortunately, Microsoft engineers have built in many different file formats for your Excel conversion pleasure.

To save your Excel file in another file format, choose File→Save As; then select the file format you want from the Format pop-up menu. Here are a few of the most useful options in that pop-up menu.

Tip: When swapping files with someone who has an earlier version of Excel, save your workbooks in one of the earlier Excel file formats listed in the Format pop-up menu; you'll find formats that go all the way back to Excel 2.2. Be warned, however, that certain kinds of information may not survive the transition. For example, such recently added elements as in-cell font changes, graphics-file backgrounds, and Lists didn't exist in earlier Excel versions.

Text (Tab delimited)

The *tab-delimited* file format provides an often used way of getting your Excel sheets into other spreadsheets or databases (AppleWorks, FileMaker, non-Microsoft word processors, and so on). It saves the data as a text file, in which cell contents are separated by a "press" of the Tab key, and a new row of data is denoted by a "press" of the Return key.

Saving a file as a tab-delimited text file saves only the currently active worksheet, and it doesn't keep formatting or graphics.

Template

The Template file format is a special kind of Excel file that works like a stationery document: When you open a template, Excel automatically creates and opens a *copy* of the template, complete with all of the formatting, formulas, and data that were in the original template. If you use the same kind of document over and over, templates are a great way to save yourself some time. (For more on Excel templates, see page 478.)

To save an Excel workbook as a template, choose File→Save As and then select Template in the pop-up menu of the Save window. Excel proposes storing your new template in the Microsoft Office X→Templates→My Templates folder on your hard drive.

Tip: Any templates created this way appear in the My Templates portion of the Project Gallery (see page 15).

Web page

Where would a modern software program be without the ability to turn its files into Web pages?

Sure enough, Excel can save workbooks as Web pages, complete with charts, and with all sheets intact. In the process, Excel generates the necessary HTML files and converts your graphics into Web-friendly file formats (such as GIF). All you have to do is upload the saved files to a Web server to make them available to the entire Internet (see page 304). Once you've posted them on the Internet, others can look through your worksheets with nothing but a Web browser, ideal for posting your numbers for others to review. That's the only thing they can do, in fact, since the cells in your worksheet aren't editable.

Tip: Technically, Excel converts your documents into Web pages using the more modern XML language, which permits greater formatting flexibility than standard HTML. Unfortunately, not all Web browsers understand XML, so some of your audience may not see exactly what you intended.

To save a workbook as a Web page, choose File→Save As, and then choose Format→Web Page. At this point, the bottom of the Save window offers some powerful options that control the Web page creation process:

- **Workbook, Sheet, Selection.** Using these buttons, specify how much of your workbook should be saved as a Web page—the whole workbook, the currently active sheet, or just the selected cells. (If you choose Workbook, all of the sheets in your workbook will be saved as linked HTML files; there'll be a series of links along the bottom that look just like your sheet tabs in Excel. Here again, though, these features won't work smoothly for everyone, because not all Web browsers understand JavaScript and frames, which these bottom-of-the-window tabs require.)

- **Automate.** This button brings up the Automate window, which lets you turn on a remarkable and powerful feature: Every time you save changes to your Excel document, or according to a complex schedule that you specify, Excel can save changes to the Web-based version automatically. Of course, you'll still be responsible for posting the HTML and graphics files to your Web server.

  To set up a schedule, click "According to a set schedule" and then click Set Schedule. In the Recurring Schedule window, set the Web version to be updated daily, weekly, monthly, or yearly. You can also specify the day of the week, as well as a start and end date for automatic updating.

- **Web Options.** The Web Options dialog box lets you assign appropriate titles and keywords to your Web pages. (The title appears in the title bar of your visitors' browser windows and in search results from search engines like Yahoo and Google; search engines also sometimes reference these keywords.)

  On the Pictures tab, you can also turn on *PNG (Portable Network Graphics) graphics,* which makes smaller graphics that download more quickly. Unfortunately, not all Web browsers can display this relatively new graphics format, so leave this option unchecked unless you're *sure* that all of the Web browsers used to view your Web-based spreadsheet are PNG-savvy. (Most recent browsers are.)

Finally, these controls can be used to specify the *target monitor size;* that is, what's the smallest monitor size your visitors will be using? Your answer to this question is important, because it will determine the width of Excel's finished Web pages. If you spew out Web pages with broad dimensions, your visitors will have to do a lot of scrolling; if you set the dimensions too small, Excel will do its best to cram the graphics and text into the smaller area. If necessary, Excel can spread out a spreadsheet's contents to maintain the same layout as the original, even if you've asked it to keep pages small.

Tip: You can test the workbook-saved-as-Web-page by dropping the HTML file on your Web browser's icon.

Spreadsheet properties

Excel gives you the chance to attach additional information to your files through something called *properties*. To call up the Properties dialog box for a worksheet, select File→Properties. In the resulting dialog box, you'll see five tabbed subject areas with all kinds of information about your file.

- **General.** This subject area tells you the document type, its location, size, when it was created and last modified, and whether it's read-only or hidden.

- **Summary.** This feature lets you enter a title, subject, author, manager, company, category, keywords, comments, and a hyperlink base for your document.

- **Statistics.** This tab shows when a document was created, modified, and last printed, as well as who last saved it. It also displays a revision number and the total editing time on the document.

- **Contents.** Here, you'll see the workbook's contents—mostly, the worksheets embedded in it.

- **Custom.** Finally, this tabbed area lets you enter any number of other properties to your workbook by giving the property a name, a type, and a value. You can enter just about anything here.

Filling out these fields isn't just good typing exercise; the information you specify here pays off handsomely when you later want to search your hard drive for a particular Excel document. When you choose File→Open and then click Find File, you get the Office X Search dialog box. By clicking Advanced Search, you can search your machine for all Excel documents with certain keywords or created by a certain author, even if you can't remember the file's name or location.

Advanced Formula Magic

Chapter 12 covers the fundamentals of formulas—entering them manually, using the Calculator, and so on. The following section dives deeper into the heart of Excel's power—its formulas.

Note: There's a difference between formulas and *functions*. A *formula* is a calculation that uses an arithmetic operator (such as *=A1+A2+A3+A4+A5*), while a *function* is a canned formula that saves you the work of creating a formula yourself (such as *=SUM(A1:A5)*).

Because there's no difference in how you *use* them, this chapter uses the terms interchangeably.

Nested Formulas

A *nested* formula is a formula that's used as an argument to another formula. For example, in the formula *=ABS(SUM(A1:A3))*, the formula *SUM(A1:A3)* is nested within an absolute-value formula. When interpreting this formula, Excel first adds the contents of cells A1 through A3, and then finds the absolute value of that result—that's the number you'll see in the cell.

Nested formulas keep you from having to use other cells as placeholders; they're also essential for writing compact formulas. In some cases (such as with the IF function), nesting lets you add real sophistication to your Excel spreadsheets by having Excel make decisions based on formula results.

The Formula Palette

The Formula Palette is a quick way of building powerful mathematical models in your spreadsheets. When activated, the Formula Palette shows every imaginable aspect of a formula: the value of the cells used in it, a description of what the formula does, a description of the arguments used in the formula, and the result of the formula.

To use the Formula Palette, click the Edit Formula button (which looks like a bold = sign) in the Formula bar. When the Formula Palette pops up (Figure 14-6), it shows one of two things:

- If the currently active cell doesn't contain a function, the Formula Palette turns into a small pane displaying the formula result. The result updates itself as you create or edit the formula.

- If the currently active cell contains a function, or if you type a function into your formula, the Formula Palette opens fully and tries to help you with the function.

Once the Formula Palette appears, you can use it to construct your formula without typing it blindly. It provides a text box for each function parameter. Typing the parameter in the text box effectively inserts it into its proper place in the formula . You can also click the small cell-selection triangle by each parameter box for easy cell-dragging, as described on page 501.

As you fill out the formula in the Formula Palette, the formula's result appears in the bottom of the palette. When you're done creating the formula in the Formula Palette, click OK to paste it into the cell.

Although the Formula Palette might seem like overkill when it comes to simple formulas (such as a SUM), it's a big help when you're dealing with a more complex formula. It outlines the parameters that the formula is expecting and gives you places to plug in those parameters.

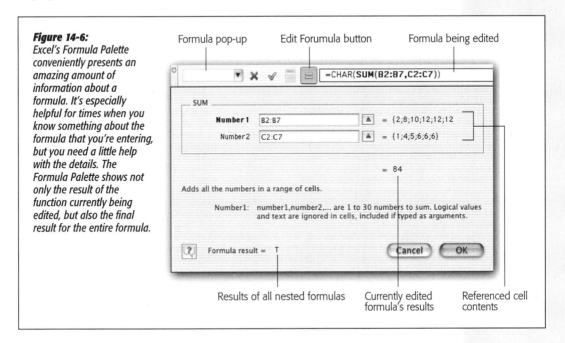

Figure 14-6:
Excel's Formula Palette conveniently presents an amazing amount of information about a formula. It's especially helpful for times when you know something about the formula that you're entering, but you need a little help with the details. The Formula Palette shows not only the result of the function currently being edited, but also the final result for the entire formula.

Formula pop-up   Edit Forumula button   Formula being edited

=CHAR(SUM(B2:B7,C2:C7))

SUM

Number 1   B2:B7   = {2;8;10;12;12;12

Number 2   C2:C7   = {1;4;5;6;6;6}

= 84

Adds all the numbers in a range of cells.

Number1:   number1,number2,... are 1 to 30 numbers to sum. Logical values and text are ignored in cells, included if typed as arguments.

Formula result =   T   Cancel   OK

Results of all nested formulas   Currently edited formula's results   Referenced cell contents

Circular References

If you create a formula that, directly or indirectly, refers to the cell *containing* it, beware of the *circular reference*. This is the spreadsheet version of a Mexican stand-off: The formula in each cell depends on the other, so neither formula can make the first move.

For example, suppose you type into cell A1, the formula *=SUM(A1:A6)*. This formula asks Excel to add cells A1 through A6 and put the result in cell A1—but since A1 is included in the range of cells for Excel to add, things quickly get confusing. To make matters worse, a few specialized formulas actually *require* that you use formulas with circular references. Now, imagine how difficult it can be to disentangle a circular reference that's *inside* a nested formula that *refers* to formulas in other cells—it's enough to make your teeth hurt. Fortunately, Excel can help.

For example, when you enter a formula containing a circular reference, Excel immediately interrupts your work with a dialog box that explains what's happening. You may enter a formula that doesn't itself contain a circular reference, but that completes a circular reference involving a group of cells. Or the formulas in two different cells might refer to each other in a circular fashion, as shown in Figure 14-7.

To leave the formula as is, click Cancel. For help, click OK, which brings up a Microsoft Office Help window loaded with directions and the Circular Reference toolbar. (Excel also overlays circles and skinny arrows on the cells of your spreadsheet.)

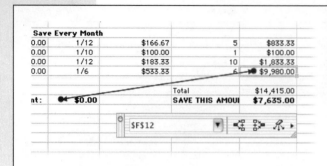

Save Every Month

0.00	1/12	$166.67	5	$833.33
0.00	1/10	$100.00	1	$100.00
0.00	1/12	$183.33	10	$1,833.33
0.00	1/6	$533.33	6	$9,980.00
		Total		$14,415.00
nt:	$0.00	SAVE THIS AMOUI		$7,635.00

$F$12

Figure 14-7:
Double-click the skinny arrow to jump to the next cell involved in the circular reference, or click the buttons on the toolbar. With these tools, Excel reveals the various cells involved in the circular reference; eventually, you should be able to understand the problem (and correct it, if necessary).

Iterations

On the other hand, certain functions (mostly scientific and engineering) *need* circular references to work properly. For example, if you're doing a bit of goal-seeking (page 547), you can use circular references to plug numbers into a formula until the formula is equal to a set value.

In these cases, Excel must calculate formulas with circular references repeatedly, because it uses the results of a first set of calculations as the basis for a second calculation. Each such cycle is known as an *iteration*. For example, suppose you want to figure out what value, when plugged into a formula, will produce a result of 125. If your first guess of 10 gives you a result of 137 when plugged into the formula, a circular reference can use that result to *adjust* your guess (say, reducing it to 9.5), then making a second pass at evaluating the formula. This second pass is a second iteration. If 9.5 doesn't do the trick, Excel can make a third iteration to get even closer, and so on, until it reaches a level of accuracy that's close enough.

To turn iteration on (and set some of its parameters), choose Excel→Preferences; click Calculation. In the Calculation panel, turn on Iteration, and change the number of iterations and a maximum change value, if you like. By default, Excel stops after 100 iterations, or when the difference between iterations is smaller than 0.001. If you make the maximum number of iterations larger or the maximum change between iterations smaller, Excel produces more accurate results, although it also needs more time to calculate those results.

Connecting to Other Workbooks

Formulas don't have to be confined to data in their own "home" worksheet; they can be linked to cells in other worksheets in the same workbook, or even to cells in other Excel documents. That's a handy feature when, for example, you want to run an analysis on a budget worksheet with your own set of Excel tools, but you don't want to re-enter the data in your workbook or alter the original workbook.

To link a formula to another sheet in the same workbook, start typing your formula as you normally would. When you reach the part of the formula where you want to refer to the cells in another worksheet, click the sheet's tab to bring it to the front. Then select the cells that you want to appear in the formula, just as you normally would when building a formula. When you press Enter after clicking or dragging through cells, Excel instantly takes you back to the sheet where you were building the formula. In the cell, you'll find a special notation that indicates a reference to a cell on another sheet. For example, if a formula on Sheet 3 takes the sum of I1 through I6 on Sheet 1, the formula looks like this: =SUM(Sheet1!I1:I6).

TROUBLESHOOTING MOMENT

Keeping Track of References

The problem with referring to other workbooks in formulas is that things change—and cause confusion. Suppose, for example, that one Excel workbook, Document A, contains a formula reference to a cell in Document B. But if somebody renames Document B, renames the disk it's on, or moves the file to a different folder, Excel can't find Document B. The link to the external workbook is broken.

When you try to update those references, Excel will tell you that it can't find the sheet that contains the data it needs. It'll also put up an Open dialog box, asking you to locate the missing data. Now all you need to do is navigate to Document B—even if it has a new name or it's on a new hard drive—and click OK. Excel fixes the reference so that everything works normally.

For the curious (or masochistic), there's a manual way to fix such a broken link, too. Click the cell with the external reference; the formula—complete with the external reference—appears in the Formula bar. Inside the formula, there's a series of names with colons and brackets, as shown in the illustration here.

Think of this *path notation* as a street map to the location of the external file on your hard drive. The first phrase after the left parenthesis and single quote is the name of the hard drive (*Lindy*, in this illustration). Then come a series of folder names separated by colons; in this illustration, the file is in the tonya *user directory*, in the Documents folder, and then in a folder called *Information*. Finally, you'll find the file's name (*ReportInfo*, in this example) inside the brackets.

The phrase to the right of the right bracket identifies one worksheet name inside the file *(Sheet1)*; after that, there's another single quote and an exclamation point, which marks the end of the external reference. Then, finally, there's the name of the cell (expressed as absolute cell references with $ signs, as described on page 463) used in the formula.

Armed with this information, you can repair a broken external cell reference. If you renamed the hard drive, correct the problem by changing the first name in the list to match the new hard drive name. If you've changed the folder location of Document B, you can correct the situation here by typing the proper folder path. If you've renamed Document B, simply enter the new file name in the space between the brackets.

Formula bar content:
```
A8                              =B7+'Lindy:Users:tonya:Documents:
                                Information:[ReportInfo]Sheet1'!$A$9
```

To link a formula in Document A to cells in another workbook (Document B), the process is almost identical. Start typing the formula in Document A. Then, when it's time to specify the cells to be used in the formula, open Document B. Select the cells you want to use by clicking or dragging; when you press Enter, they appear in the formula. Excel returns you to the original document, where you'll see the Document B cells written out in a *path notation* (see the Tip below).

Once you've set up such a cell reference, Excel will automatically update Document A each time you open it with Document B already open. And if Document B is closed, Excel asks if you want to update the data. If you say yes, Excel looks into Document B and grabs whatever data it needs. If somebody has changed Document B since the last time Document A was opened, Excel recalculates the worksheet based on the new numbers.

Tip: If you want Document A updated automatically whenever you open it (and don't want to be interrupted with Excel's request to do so), choose Edit→Preferences, click Edit, and then *turn off* "Ask to update automatic links." Excel now automatically updates the link with the data from the last saved version of Document B.

Auditing

Every now and then, you'll find a formula whose cell references are amiss. If the formula references another formula, tracing down the source of your problems can be a real pain. Excel's Auditing tools can help you access the root of formula errors by showing you the cells that a given formula references and what formulas reference a given cell. Brightly colored *tracer arrows* appear between cells to indicate how they all relate to each other.

The key to correcting formula errors is the Tools→Auditing menu item, which has five submenu choices:

- **Trace Precedents** draws arrows from the currently selected cell to any cells that provide values for its formula.

- **Trace Dependents** draws arrows from the currently selected cell, showing which *other* formulas refer to it.

- **Trace Error** draws an arrow from an active cell containing a "broken" formula to the cell or cells that caused the error.

- **Remove All Arrows** hides all the auditing arrows.

- **Show Auditing Toolbar** hides or shows the Auditing Toolbar. This toolbar's buttons turn on (and off) the kinds of arrows described in the previous paragraphs, all in an effort to help you trace how formulas and cells relate with each other.

Working with Databases

Excel has much in common with database programs. Both kinds of software keep track of a list of *records* (like cards in a card catalog—or rows of a spreadsheet), and let you browse through those records and even perform some calculations on them. No wonder Excel is so adept at incorporating database files into its spreadsheets; Excel X can access data in Web pages and FileMaker Pro databases, and may be able to use *open database connectivity* to access data from additional databases. Open database connectivity, usually called ODBC (pronounced "oh-dee-bee-see"), is a standard set of rules for transferring information between databases, even if the databases are in different programs from different companies.

Fetching FileMaker Pro Data

Excel can import data from FileMaker Pro databases directly into its worksheets—no muss, no fuss, no messy translation workarounds.

Here's how to go about it.

Note: Excel can only work with FileMaker databases if you actually *have* FileMaker on your Mac. Also, if you run Excel X version 10.0.0, the database itself must be on your Macintosh. Excel X as updated by Service Release 1 (page 12) can access databases on a networked server.

Step 1: Import the database

A FileMaker Pro database can be imported in either of two ways. First, you can bring the data into Excel once, where you continue to work on it (this is called a *one-time* import). Second, the data can remain connected to FileMaker, and updates itself in Excel when it's updated in FileMaker (this is called an *updating* import).

GEM IN THE ROUGH

Open Database Connectivity (ODBC)

Previous versions of Excel could access data from ODBC databases, which are standard in many corporations. But Excel X version 10.0.0 cannot. Although Microsoft *Carbonized* (updated) most of Office for Mac OS X, a few components didn't make the shipping deadline, with the ODBC–related components falling into that group. (This discussion applies to non-FileMaker databases. Excel-to-FileMaker links work just fine in every version of Office X.)

Microsoft began to provide ODBC features with Excel X version 10.1.0. If you don't have that version or a later one, install Service Release 1 from the Mactopia Web site at *www.mactopia.com.* Excel X version 10.1.0 provides bare-bones ODBC support—it can refresh existing database queries. But you must jump through two hoops to do your refreshing.

First, since you can't create *new* queries in Excel X, you must make them in a different version of Excel, such as Excel 2001, and then open the query-containing worksheet in Excel X.

Second, to make those queries work, you must install a driver for the database you want to query. Microsoft doesn't supply drivers to Office X customers; instead, you must purchase a driver from another company, such as OpenLink Software (*www.openlinksw.com*).

Excel X version 10.1.0 also comes equipped with the necessary smarts to use Microsoft Query for Excel X–software that puts a graphical user interface on the task of creating queries. With Microsoft Query for Excel X, you can finally create and modify queries in Excel X, if you have the driver installed, that is.

Once you've rounded up and installed all the required ODBC software, you can get started with ODBC by investigating the commands listed on the Data→Get External Data submenu and playing with the External Data toolbar (View→Toolbars→External Data).

- **For a one-time import,** which puts data into Excel as a *list sheet* (a sheet containing nothing except a list object, as described on page 464), choose File→Open, then navigate to, and double-click, the FileMaker file's icon in the Open dialog box.

  Alternatively, in the Finder, simply drag the icon of your FileMaker file onto the Excel icon. (Try this procedure twice if it doesn't work completely on the first attempt.) Either way, if you make changes in FileMaker and want the changed data to come into Excel, you must reimport the entire database.

- **For an updating import,** which places data in an Excel worksheet and lets you control how often cells update to reflect changes made in FileMaker, choose Data→Get External Data→Import from FileMaker Pro. (You must have a workbook open in Excel for this menu option to be available.)

In either case, an amazing thing happens: Excel now triggers FileMaker Pro to launch automatically, opening the specified database.

Then the FileMaker Import Wizard window appears. On the first screen, specify which of the FileMaker file's fields you want to import (Name, Address, Phone, or whatever). You can also specify the fields and layout you want, as shown in Figure 14-8.

Click Next to continue.

Figure 14-8:
If one of the FileMaker file's layouts contains the fields you want, select its name from the Layouts pop-up menu; otherwise, leave the pop-up menu set to All Fields. Next, choose the fields you want by double-clicking each in the "Available fields" pane on the left. (Move all fields at once by clicking the >> button between the two panes.) This action adds each selected field to the pane on the right. You can also rearrange the order of the fields in the right-hand list by clicking one and then clicking the up and down arrow buttons on the right.

Step 2: Choose only the data you want

The next screen in the FileMaker Import Wizard offers to *filter* (screen out) the records that you import into your Excel workbook (see Figure 14-9). The Wizard lets you specify three criteria to help eliminate unwanted data from the import process. (If you want *all* of the data, skip this step by clicking Finish.)

Click Finish to continue. Excel commences importing the data from your FileMaker file.

Note: This process may take a long time (depending, in part, on how much data you're importing); because there's no progress bar, spinning cursor, or any other sign that Excel is working, you might assume that the program has crashed. Be patient and don't switch out of Excel; the program is communicating with the database and constructing the spreadsheet.

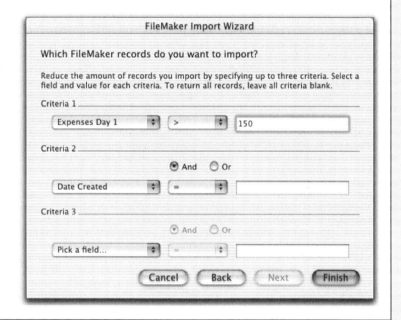

Figure 14-9:
Suppose you want to import only the records in which the expenses on Day 1 were greater than 150, so that you can focus on big spenders in the company. Set the Criteria 1 pop-up menu to Expenses Day 1, set the middle pop-up menu to >, and type 150 into the final field. After filling in Criteria 1, you can set up additional criteria in the Criteria 2 and Criteria 3 areas.

If you began this process by choosing File→Open, you're all set; Excel produces a new listsheet, a worksheet with the database's contents embedded in it as a list object. Listsheets also display the List toolbar.

If, on the other hand, you chose Data→Get External Data→Import from FileMaker Pro, Excel now asks you exactly where you'd like the imported data to be placed; you can specify a cell or opt to create a new worksheet (Figure 14-10).

After telling Excel where and how to place the data, click Finish. Excel imports the data and shows the External Data toolbar, and if you turned on the "Use List Manager" checkbox in the properties section of the FileMaker Import Wizard, it also shows the List toolbar. The External Data toolbar lets you quickly change options on incoming database information, set special query criteria, and refresh data from a database.

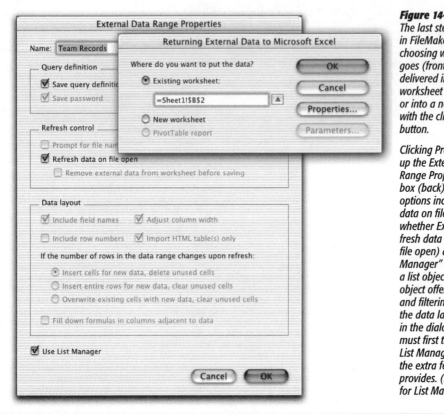

Figure 14-10:
The last step in bringing in FileMaker Pro data is choosing where the data goes (front). It can be delivered into the worksheet currently open or into a new worksheet with the click of a radio button.

Clicking Properties brings up the External Data Range Properties dialog box (back), whose options include "Refresh data on file open" (sets whether Excel receives fresh data every time the file open) and "Use List Manager" (puts data into a list object). The list object offers easy sorting and filtering. But to use the data layout controls in the dialog box, you must first turn off "Use List Manager" and forgo the extra features that it provides. (See page 464 for List Manager info.)

TROUBLESHOOTING MOMENT

"Microsoft Office is not able to run FileMaker Pro at this time."

You may encounter this error message when attempting to open a FileMaker database into Excel. Of course, there are many reasons why Office might not be able to run FileMaker—it's not installed, it's compressed, or it's out on a lunch break. You can solve the problem, though, by launching FileMaker on your own. (You can launch FileMaker by double-clicking its icon in the Finder.)

If you don't have FileMaker 5.5 or later, your Macintosh will first launch the *Classic environment* (Mac OS X's "Mac OS 9 simulator") and then open FileMaker in Classic mode. After launching FileMaker, try to open the database again from Excel.

Grabbing Data from the Web

If pulling data from a database isn't exciting enough, Excel can also grab data from certain Web sites (and FTP, Gopher, or intranet sites).

Excel comes with four canned Web queries that help demonstrate the power of this little-known feature:

- **MSN MoneyCentral Currencies.** This query grabs the current currency value for more than 50 countries on an open exchange. Check it before you head out on an international trip, so you'll know how much you're being gouged at the currency-exchange counter.
- **MSN MoneyCentral Major Indices.** This query grabs data for around 20 stock exchanges, including the Dow, S&P 500, FTSE 100, and NASDAQ.
- **MSN MoneyCentral Stock Quotes.** This query looks up data including last value, close value, volume, and change for a stock symbol you specify. (If you're among the thousands of people who use Excel to track your stock market holdings, behold the dawn of a new era—you no longer need to type in the latest stock prices. Your software can do it automatically.)
- **Get More Web Queries.** This last Web query is the most interesting. It grabs a list of saved Web queries and puts them into a sheet. This list has links to many more Web Queries, which include more stock and currency quotes, plus a mortgage calculator and interest-rate finder.

Tip: This list changes from time to time, so it's a good idea to refresh it occasionally to see what's new.

To use one of these predesigned Web queries, choose Data→Get External Data→Run Saved Query, which brings up an Open dialog box. Double-click one of the queries listed here. (You can find the saved queries in the Microsoft Office X→Office→Queries folder.)

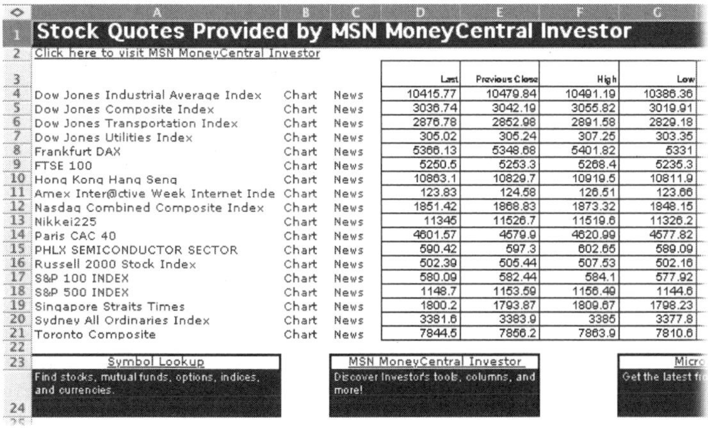

Stock Quotes Provided by MSN MoneyCentral Investor

Click here to visit MSN MoneyCentral Investor

			Last	Previous Close	High	Low
Dow Jones Industrial Average Index	Chart	News	10415.77	10479.84	10491.19	10386.36
Dow Jones Composite Index	Chart	News	3036.74	3042.19	3055.82	3019.91
Dow Jones Transportation Index	Chart	News	2876.78	2852.98	2891.58	2829.18
Dow Jones Utilities Index	Chart	News	305.02	305.24	307.25	303.35
Frankfurt DAX	Chart	News	5366.13	5348.68	5401.82	5331
FTSE 100	Chart	News	5250.5	5253.3	5268.4	5235.3
Hong Kong Hang Seng	Chart	News	10863.1	10829.7	10919.5	10811.9
Amex Inter@ctive Week Internet Inde	Chart	News	123.83	124.58	126.51	123.66
Nasdaq Combined Composite Index	Chart	News	1851.42	1868.83	1873.32	1848.15
Nikkei225	Chart	News	11345	11526.7	11519.6	11326.2
Paris CAC 40	Chart	News	4601.57	4579.9	4620.99	4577.82
PHLX SEMICONDUCTOR SECTOR	Chart	News	590.42	597.3	602.65	589.09
Russell 2000 Stock Index	Chart	News	502.39	505.44	507.53	502.16
S&P 100 INDEX	Chart	News	580.09	582.44	584.1	577.92
S&P 500 INDEX	Chart	News	1148.7	1153.59	1156.49	1144.6
Singapore Straits Times	Chart	News	1800.2	1793.87	1809.67	1798.23
Sydney All Ordinaries Index	Chart	News	3381.6	3383.9	3385	3377.8
Toronto Composite	Chart	News	7844.5	7856.2	7863.9	7810.6

Figure 14-11: *Using the saved MSN MoneyCentral Major Indices Web query, you can call up current information on a number of major stock market indices directly in your Excel worksheet. Now all you need is some serious cash to be an international tycoon.*

Excel then asks you where in the spreadsheet you want to put the information that it downloads from the Web (this modest dialog box calls itself Returning External Data to Microsoft Excel). After you select a location and click OK, Excel connects to the Internet, downloads the information, and inserts it into the spreadsheet.

Note: Excel may ask you if you want to accept *cookies* while importing Web-based data. (Cookies are small text files that Web sites place on your hard drive as preference files.) Excel, Entourage, and Internet Explorer all share a common cookies file; Excel is simply obeying the cookie-alert messages you've set up using the preferences settings in Internet Explorer.

Importing Data from a Text File

Databases and the World Wide Web both make great data sources, but sometimes you just want to pull some information out of a text file and into your Excel worksheet. Here's how to do it.

Choose Data→Get External Data→Import Text File; in the resulting Open dialog box, navigate to, and double-click, the text file that you want to import. The Text Import Wizard walks you through a three-step process to bring the data from the text file into the currently open worksheet.

Opening the Excel Toolbox

Like a good piece of Swiss Army Software, Excel provides tools that go beyond the basics. Using features like PivotTables, Scenarios, and Goal Seeking, Excel lets you look at your data in new and interesting ways.

Making a PivotTable

A *PivotTable* is a special spreadsheet entity that helps summarize data into an easy-to-read table. You can rotate the table's rows and columns (thus the name PivotTable) to achieve different views on your data. PivotTables let you quickly plug different sets of numbers into a table; Excel does the heavy lifting of arranging the data for you.

PivotTables are useful when you want to see how different but related totals compare, such as how a retail store's sales per department, category of product, and salesperson relate. They let you build complicated tables on the fly by dragging various categories of data into a pre-made template. PivotTables are especially useful when you have a large amount of data to wade through, partially because Excel takes care of subtotals and totals for you.

Here's how to create a PivotTable from data in an Excel sheet.

Step 1: Choose the data source

Suppose, for example, that you're a TV advertiser trying to decide which cable TV cult-hit show should be the beneficiary of your advertising dollars. You have a spreadsheet that shows three days' worth of data on five different shows (such as each show's ranking, number of viewers for the day, and ad revenues). But you can't yet see the trends that identify which shows reach the largest number of people for the least dollars while achieving the highest ranking in the ratings. A PivotTable, you realize, would make the answer crystal clear.

Select a cell in the data range from which you want to create a PivotTable. Choose Data→PivotTable Report, which brings up the PivotTable Wizard. This will walk you through the process of creating a PivotTable in three steps.

In the first step, locate the data from which you want to create a PivotTable. Your choices include an Excel list, multiple consolidation ranges (which use ranges from one or more worksheets), and another PivotTable. If you've installed the necessary ODBC-related software (see page 537), you can also use data from an external data source.

In this example, you want to create a PivotTable from existing data in an Excel sheet. Choose "Microsoft Excel list or database"; click Next to continue.

Step 2: Choose the cells

This PivotTable Wizard asks for the cell range that you want to use in your PivotTable. Excel—bless its digital heart—takes its best guess, based on the active cell when the Wizard was invoked. If that range is *not* correct, type the range you want in the Range field or use the cell-selection triangle (see page 501) to select the range yourself. Click Next to continue.

Step 3: Direct the PivotTable

Finally, Excel asks where you want to place your new PivotTable. You can put it either in a new worksheet or in an existing worksheet at a specific location. Because this table is relatively small, place it in the same worksheet as the source data.

This last screen offers two additional buttons for your customization pleasure:

- The **Layout** button opens the Layout window, in which you can exercise some control over how the PivotTable is laid out.

- The **Options** button opens the Options window, in which you can choose to include grand totals, to preserve cell formatting, and how you want data sources handled.

To finish your PivotTable, click Finish.

Step 4: Pivot

At this point, Excel has dropped a blank PivotTable into the specified location, but there's still no data in it. To help with the data-insertion process, Excel opens the PivotTable toolbar, which you can use to add elements to your blank slate.

The bottom of the PivotTable toolbar shows a few names that coincide with the column names in your original data (Figure 14-12); these are called *field names*. To complete your PivotTable, you need to drop these field names onto the row axis (the column on the left), the column axis (the row across the top), or the data field (the big empty space in the center). A different table will form, depending on which data fields you drop on which axes.

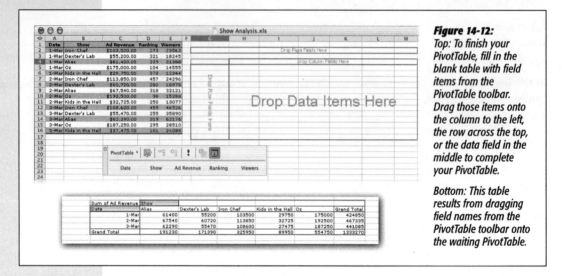

Figure 14-12:
Top: To finish your PivotTable, fill in the blank table with field items from the PivotTable toolbar. Drag those items onto the column to the left, the row across the top, or the data field in the middle to complete your PivotTable.

Bottom: This table results from dragging field names from the PivotTable toolbar onto the waiting PivotTable.

Step 5: Build the table

As the advertising buyer, suppose you want to build a table that shows how much ad revenue each show took in on each of three days. Drag the Date field name onto the Row Field area, the Show field name onto the Column Field area, and the Ad Revenue field name onto the data area.

As depicted in Figure 14-12, Excel builds a table that displays how much ad revenue each show took in, and adds the totals for each show at the bottom and for each day at the right.

Step 6: Massage the data

Now that you've created your simple PivotTable, you can quickly rearrange it by dragging field names to different areas in the PivotTable, or you can add a new dimension by dragging yet another field name (in the case of the ad buyer, the number of viewers) onto the table. If you add a new field to the data area, Excel divides each row into two, showing how the data for each date interrelate. The more field names you drag into the data area, the more complex your table becomes, but the more chance you'll have to spot any trends. Field names can also be added to the row and column axes for an entirely different kind of table.

Analyzing Your Data

PivotTables aren't the only way to analyze your Excel data. In fact, if you're the type who loves to pose "what if" questions, then Excel has a few tools for you: *data tables, goal seek, scenarios,* and the *Solver.*

Data tables

Data tables let you plug several different values into a formula to see how they change its results. They're especially useful, for example, when you want to understand how a few different interest rates might affect the size of a payment over the life of a five-year loan.

Figure 14-13:
These three PivotTables were created using the same data source—the only difference is that the fields from the PivotTable toolbar were dragged to different areas on the blank PivotTable.

In the case of the complicated PivotTable (bottom), two different fields were dragged to the same axis. Exercise this option with caution, since dragging multiple fields to the same axis can quickly render a PivotTable unread-able.

Date	Data	Show Alias	Dexter's Lab	Iron Chef	Kids in Hall	Oz	Grand Total
3/1/02	Sum of Ad Revenue	61400	55200	103500	29750	175000	424850
	Sum of Viewers	31388	18245	23563	12344	14555	100095
3/2/02	Sum of Ad Revenue	67540	60720	113850	32725	192500	467335
	Sum of Viewers	32121	18978	24296	13077	15288	103760
3/3/02	Sum of Ad Revenue	62290	55470	108600	27475	187250	441085
	Sum of Viewers	62176	35890	46526	24088	28510	197190
Total Sum of Ad Revenue		191230	171390	325950	89950	554750	1333270
Total Sum of Viewers		125685	73113	94385	49509	58353	401045

Date	Data	Show Alias	Dexter's Lab	Iron Chef	Kids in Hall	Oz	Grand Total
3/1/02	Sum of Ad Revenue	61400	55200	103500	29750	175000	424850
	Sum of Viewers	31388	18245	23563	12344	14555	100095
	Sum of Ranking	239	321	273	378	104	1315
3/2/02	Sum of Ad Revenue	67540	60720	113850	32725	192500	467335
	Sum of Viewers	32121	18978	24296	13077	15288	103760
	Sum of Ranking	318	280	457	250	98	1403
3/3/02	Sum of Ad Revenue	62290	55470	108600	27475	187250	441085
	Sum of Viewers	62176	35890	46526	24088	28510	197190
	Sum of Ranking	319	255	455	101	295	1425
Total Sum of Ad Revenue		191230	171390	325950	89950	554750	1333270
Total Sum of Viewers		125685	73113	94385	49509	58353	401045
Total Sum of Ranking		876	856	1185	729	497	4143

Date	Data	Ranking	Show Alias	Dexter's Lab	Iron Chef	Kids in Hall	Oz	Grand Total
3/1/02	Sum of Ad Revenue	104					175000	175000
		239	61400					61400
		273			103500			103500
		321		55200				55200
		378				29750		29750
	Sum of Viewers	104					14555	14555
		239	31388					31388
		273			23563			23563
		321		18245				18245
		378				12344		12344
3/1/02	Sum of Ad Revenue		61400	55200	103500	29750	175000	424850
3/1/02	Sum of Viewers		31388	18245	23563	12344	14555	100095
3/2/02	Sum of Ad Revenue	98					192500	192500
		250				32725		32725
		280		60720				60720
		318	67540					67540
		457			113850			113850
	Sum of Viewers	98					15288	15288
		250				13077		13077

Data tables come in two flavors: one-variable tables (in which you can change one factor to see how data is affected) and two-variable tables (in which you can change two factors). The hardest part about using a data table is setting it up. You'll need to place the formula, the data to substitute into the formula, and an *input cell* that will serve as a placeholder for data being substituted into the formula.

To create a one-variable table, arrange the data in your cells so that the items you want plugged into your calculation (the interest rate, for example) are in a continuous row or column; then proceed as shown in Figure 14-14. If you choose a row, type the formula you want used in your table in the cell that's *one column to the left* of that range of values, and one row below it. If you choose a column, type the formula in the row above the range of values, and *one row to the right* of it. Think of the values as row or column heads, and the formula's location as the heading of an actual row or column in your soon-to-be-formed table. You'll also need to decide on the location of your input cell; it should be outside this table.

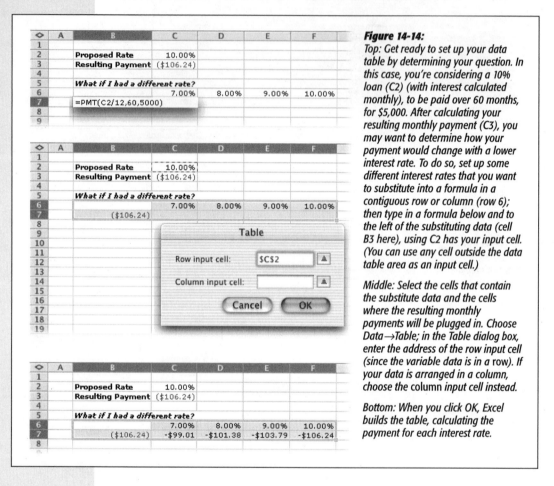

Figure 14-14:

Top: Get ready to set up your data table by determining your question. In this case, you're considering a 10% loan (C2) (with interest calculated monthly), to be paid over 60 months, for $5,000. After calculating your resulting monthly payment (C3), you may want to determine how your payment would change with a lower interest rate. To do so, set up some different interest rates that you want to substitute into a formula in a contiguous row or column (row 6); then type in a formula below and to the left of the substituting data (cell B3 here), using C2 has your input cell. (You can use any cell outside the data table area as an input cell.)

Middle: Select the cells that contain the substitute data and the cells where the resulting monthly payments will be plugged in. Choose Data→Table; in the Table dialog box, enter the address of the row input cell (since the variable data is in a row). If your data is arranged in a column, choose the column input cell instead.

Bottom: When you click OK, Excel builds the table, calculating the payment for each interest rate.

If you use Excel to do the same table, be sure to tell it to compute the size of a payment based on different interest rates *and* a different number of total payments. This is called a two-variable data table, and it's created in much the same way as a single-variable data table.

To create a two-variable table, enter a formula in your worksheet that refers to the *two* sets of values plugged into the formula; proceed as shown in Figure 14-15.

Goal seek

When you know the answer that you want a formula to produce but you don't know the values to plug into the formula to *get* that answer, then it's time for Excel's *goal seek* feature.

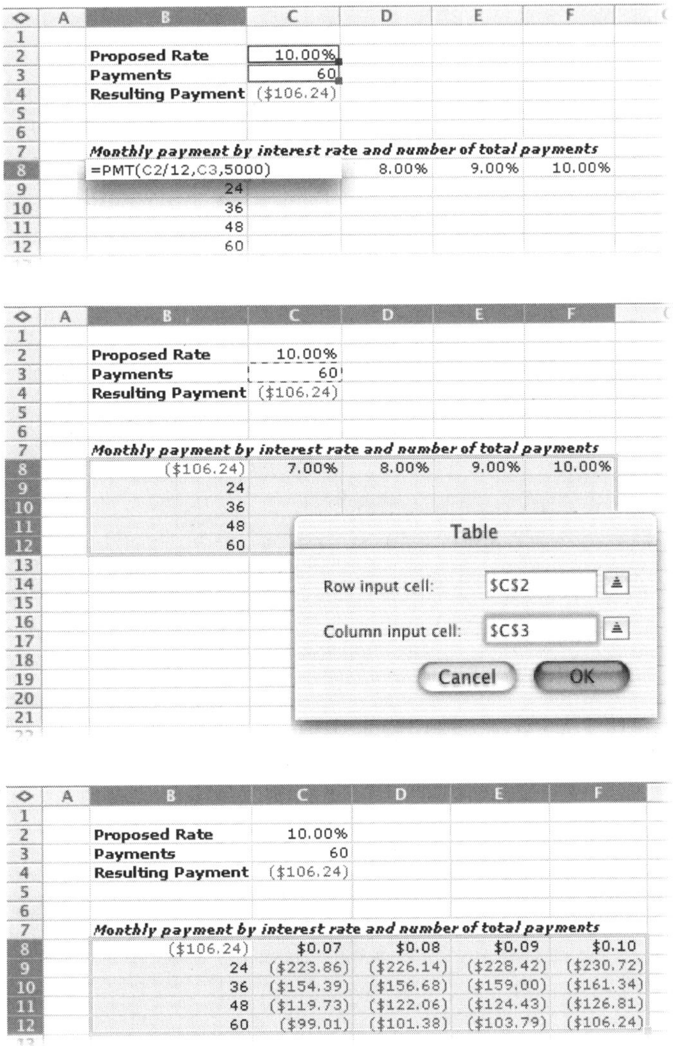

Figure 14-15:
Top: In a two-variable data table, one set of data serves as one axis, and the second set serves as the second axis. The formula sits in the upper-left corner (B8), and it refers to two input cells outside of the table (C2 and C3). Enter one set of values in a column starting just below the formula, and the second set of values in a row starting just to the right of the formula.

Middle: Select the range of cells containing the formula and all of the input values that you just entered, and choose Data→Table. Enter the addresses for the row input cell and the column input cell.

Bottom: Click OK; Excel creates a beautiful table of payments based on how two variables interact.

To use it, choose Tools→Goal Seek. In the resulting dialog box (Figure 14-16), fill in the following three fields:

- **Set cell.** Specifies which cell to start from—the cell containing the formula you're using to seek your goal. For example, Figure 14-16 illustrates a mortgage calculation. The Set cell (the lower-right cell), which shows the monthly payments, would be H30. The purpose of this exercise is to find a monthly income that would make the mortgage payment possible.

- **To value.** Specifies the value that you want to see in that cell. In the example of Figure 14-16, the To value is $1,300; that's the amount that the two-story house down the street would cost per month.

- **By changing cell.** Tells Excel which cell it can tinker with to make that happen. The key cell in Figure 14-16 is C6, your monthly income. You want to know how much your salary would have to go up to afford that kind of mortgage payment.

Click OK to turn Excel loose on the problem. It reports its progress in a Goal Seek Status dialog box, which lets you step Excel through the process of working toward your goal. There are a couple of caveats: You can select only single cells, not ranges, and the cell you're tweaking must contain a value, not a formula.

Tip: Another way to conduct a little goal-seeking is to fiddle with a chart. First, set up a chart of the data, and then link a couple of cells with the Tools→Goal Seek function. That way, when you resize an element (such as a bar in a bar chart), the value in the cell represented by that element changes automatically. The Goal Seek dialog box pops up, giving you the opportunity to seek the new value.

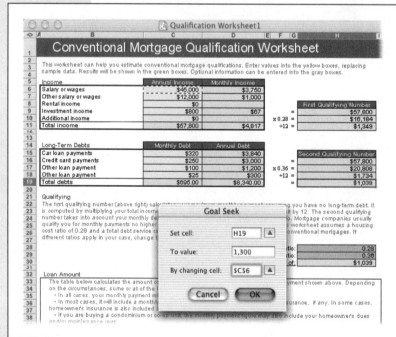

Figure 14-16:
By letting Excel retool the reported income on a mortgage qualification sheet via its Goal Seek function, you'll know how much extra cash to ask for in your next performance evaluation in order to afford that nice house down the street. (You can use this same worksheet by choosing File→Project Gallery. In the Project Gallery, click the Home Essentials flippy triangle and click Finance Tools. Finally, click Qualification Worksheet.)

Scenarios

Scenarios are like little snapshots, each containing a different set of "what if" data plugged into your formulas. Because Excel can memorize each set and recall it instantly, scenarios help you understand how your worksheet model is likely to turn out given different situations. (You still have to enter the data and formulas into your spreadsheet before you play with scenarios, though.) In a way, scenarios are like saving several different copies of the same spreadsheet, each with variations in the data. Being able to quickly switch between scenarios lets you run through different situations without retyping any numbers.

To create a scenario, choose Tools→Scenarios to bring up the Scenarios Manager, in which you can add, delete, edit, and merge different scenarios as shown in Figure 14-17.

Figure 14-17:
In the Scenario Manager dialog box (lower right), you can switch between saved scenarios, add new ones, edit existing ones, merge scenarios from other worksheets into the Scenarios list, or even summarize your scenarios to a standard summary or PivotTable. The Scenarios list displays all of the scenarios that you've created and saved, and by selecting a scenario and clicking a button, you can do wonderful things with it (upper left).

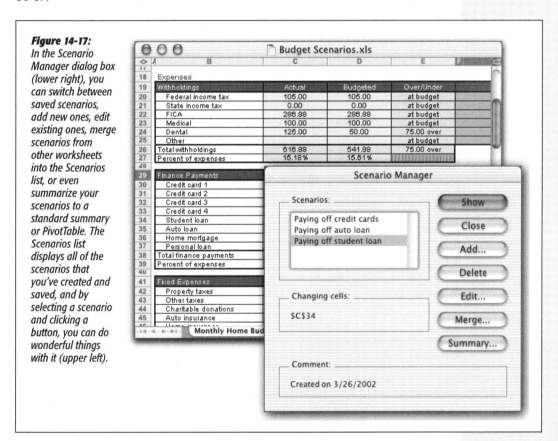

The list box on the left side shows all of the scenarios that you've saved. By selecting a scenario and then clicking a button on the right, you can display your scenarios in your spreadsheet, or even make a summary. Here's what each does:

- **Show.** The Show button lets you switch between scenarios; just select the scenario you want to view, and then click Show. Excel changes the spreadsheet to reflect the selected scenario.

- **Close.** This button simply closes the Scenario Manager.

- **Add.** Click this button to design a new scenario, courtesy of the Add Scenario dialog box (Figure 14-18). It lets you name your scenario and specify the cells you want to change (you can either enter the cell references or select them with the mouse). Excel inserts a comment regarding when the scenario was created. This comment can be edited to say anything you like, making it a great place to note exactly what the scenario affects in the spreadsheet.

After clicking OK, you're taken to the Scenario Values dialog box, in which you enter new values for the cells you specified in the previous window. Once you're done entering your new values, click OK. The new scenario appears in the Scenario Manager.

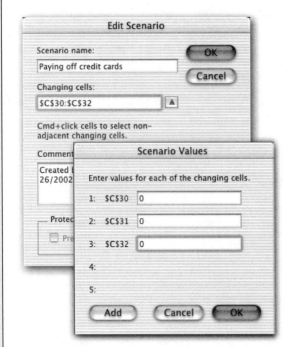

Figure 14-18:
Top left: Clicking Add in the Scenario Manager (Figure 14-17) calls up the Add Scenario dialog box, shown here. (It changes to say Edit Scenario when you fill in the Changing cells field.) In this box, you name your scenario and tell Excel which cells to change when showing it.

Bottom front: Once you click OK, you see the Scenario Values dialog box, in which you enter the new values for the cells that you specified in the previous window.

- **Delete.** This button deletes the currently selected scenario.

- **Edit.** The Edit button opens the Edit Scenario dialog box, which looks just like the Add Scenario box. Use this box to adjust a previously saved scenario.

- **Merge.** This command merges scenarios from other worksheets into the Scenario list for the current worksheet. To merge scenarios, open all of the workbooks that contain scenarios that you want to merge, and then switch to the worksheet where you want the merged scenarios to appear. This is your destination worksheet for the merge.

  Open the Scenario Manager (Tools→Scenarios) and click Merge; proceed as shown in Figure 14-19.

Tip: When you're merging scenarios, make sure that your destination worksheet is the same as all of the scenarios. Otherwise, merged data will still appear in the proper cells, but if those cells aren't properly placed or formatted, it'll look all wrong.

Figure 14-19:
Top: A summary report shows all of the scenarios in your worksheet. Click the + and – buttons in the margins to expand and contract rows.

Bottom: To merge several scenarios into one worksheet, click Merge in the Scenario Manager, select the workbook that has the scenarios to merge, then select the sheet that contains the actual scenarios.

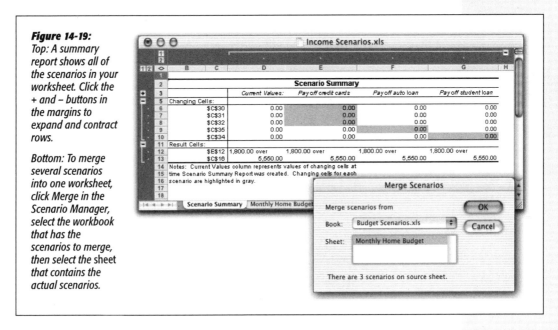

- **Summary.** When you click the Summary button, the Scenario Summary dialog box appears. It has two radio buttons: one for a standard summary (which creates a table) and one for a PivotTable summary (a PivotTable of your changes *really* lets you tweak the numbers). Figure 14-19 shows a standard summary, complete with buttons for expanding and contracting the information.

Solver

Excel's Solver builds a spreadsheet model that works by adjusting the values of some of the sheet's cells; it's a great tool for such tasks as balancing a complicated budget. In practice, it's similar to goal-seeking, only more powerful.

Note: This command appears in the Data menu only if you've installed it using the Value Pack installer described on page 681. Install Solver from the Excel Add-ins category and Solver Examples from the Programmability category.

To use the Solver, choose Tools→Solver. In the Solver Parameters dialog box (Figure 14-20), you can tell the Solver what its target solution is, what cells it can change, and some rules to adhere to while it's working toward its solution. By entering the right cell references and clicking the buttons, you can have Excel tweak your worksheet to reflect a reality that you hope (or fear) will come true. Here are the functions of each field; go through the first few fields from top to bottom to enter your information.

- **Set Target Cell.** This cell contains the value that you want to solve for. Type in the cell reference, or click it to enter it automatically.

- **Equal To.** These three radio buttons let you set a goal for the solver. This is the value that you want to end up in the target cell after the solver has done its work.

- **By Changing Cells.** This is where you tell Excel which cells are fair game to change while looking for a solution. You can also click Guess, which will tell Excel to examine the spreadsheet and take its best guess as to which cells to change.

- **Subject to the Constraints.** This field, with Add, Change, and Delete buttons, lets you enter conditions that the solver has to follow when coming up with a solution. When you click Add, a dialog box appears in which you can tell Solver to keep certain cells within a certain value range. This is important because without adding constraints, Solver could use values that theoretically solve the problem but don't work in the real world. You can use the Change button to edit an existing constraint, or select a constraint and hit Delete to get rid of it.

Once you enter a constraint (or several), you can use the five buttons on the right—Solve, Close, Options, Reset All, and Help—to further refine or continue your work.

- **Solve.** This is the Go button. When you click it, Solver goes to work on your problem.

- **Close** closes Solver Parameters without looking for a solution.

- **Options** opens the Solver Options dialog box, in which you can get very specific about how Solver goes about its task. You can set a time limit, an iteration limit, and tell it how precise to be, plus you can load and save these Solver models for use later. This window also lets you control the intricacies inherent in the Solver, such as whether it uses a linear model for its changes, and how it handles estimates, derivatives, and searches. (Don't miss the Help button. You may need it.)

- **Reset All.** This resets the items in the Solver Parameters window so you can start over.

- **Help.** This button opens Excel's help system to the entry for the Solver Parameters dialog box.

Once you click Solve, Solver will go about its business, plugging new numbers into the spreadsheet. It will then put up a Solver Results dialog box, which lets you change your spreadsheet back to the way it was or keep the Solver results. You can also save the Solver's changes as a scenario in your worksheet, if you like.

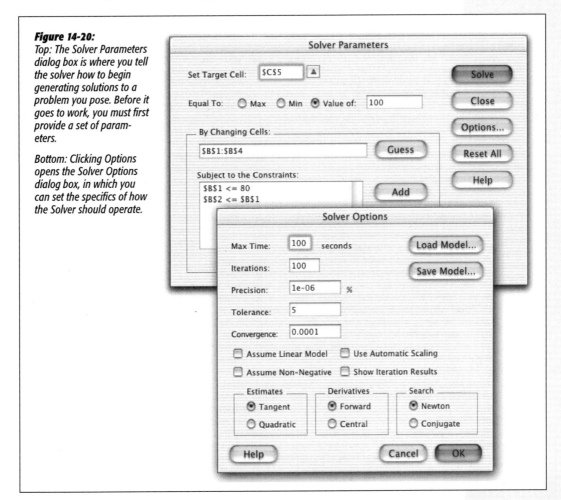

Figure 14-20:
Top: The Solver Parameters dialog box is where you tell the solver how to begin generating solutions to a problem you pose. Before it goes to work, you must first provide a set of parameters.

Bottom: Clicking Options opens the Solver Options dialog box, in which you can set the specifics of how the Solver should operate.

Tapping the Data menu

PivotTables and databases are some of the most powerful elements found in the Data menu; but a few other commands in the Data menu let you perform additional tricks with your data.

- **Sort.** This powerful menu command lets you sort selected data alphabetically or numerically. You can perform several levels of sorting, just as you can when sorting database items—for example, sort by year, then by month *within* each year. As shown in Figure 14-21, the beauty of the Sort command is that it sorts entire *rows,* not just the one column you specified for sorting.

Tip: Clicking "Header row" avoids sorting the top-row column labels into the data—a common problem with other spreadsheet software. Excel leaves the top row where it is, as shown in Figure 14-21.

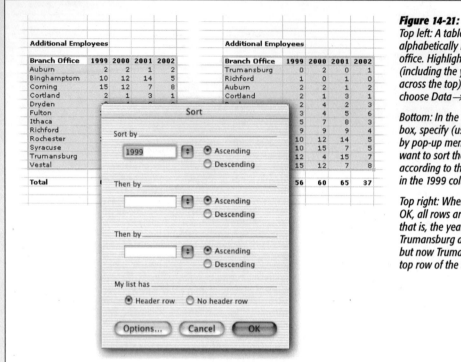

Figure 14-21:
Top left: A table sorted alphabetically by branch office. Highlight the table (including the year labels across the top), and then choose Data→Sort.

Bottom: In the Sort dialog box, specify (using the Sort by pop-up menu) that you want to sort the rows according to the numbers in the 1999 column.

Top right: When you click OK, all rows are sorted; that is, the year totals for Trumansburg are the same, but now Trumansburg is the top row of the table.

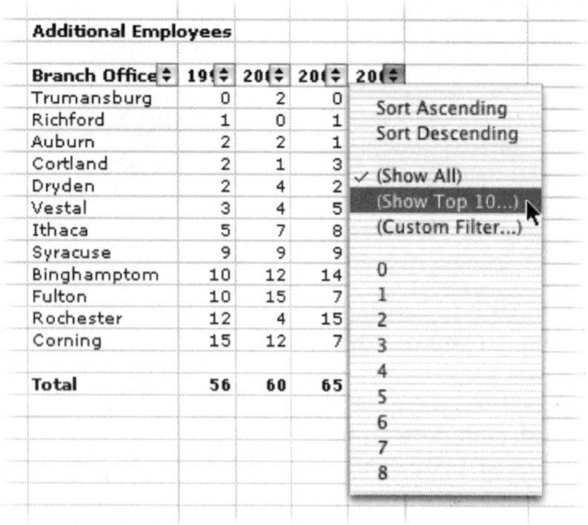

Figure 14-22:
You can quickly and easily sort the rows of selected data by choosing Data→Filter→AutoFilter, then choosing from the pop-up menus that appear. For example, this command shows only the highest ten values within this column; all other rows of the table are temporarily hidden.

- **Filter.** When you choose AutoFilter from this submenu, you get pop-up menus at the top of each column in your selection (Figure 14-22); you can use them to hide or show certain rows or columns, exactly like the filters found in list objects (see page 464). AutoFilter pop-up menus can be applied to only one selection at a time in a worksheet. Also on the Filter submenu, Show All displays items that you hid using the AutoFilter pop-up menus, and Advanced Filter lets you build your own filter. (Consult the online help if you want to build an advanced filter.)

- **Subtotals.** This command automatically puts subtotal formulas in a column (or columns). The columns must have headings that label them (Figure 14-23 illustrates an example).

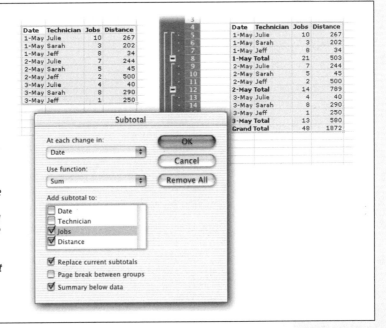

Figure 14-23:
Top left: Select a set of data that could stand some subtotals.

Bottom: When you choose Data→Subtotals, the Subtotal dialog box appears. In this box, you can choose the column that determines where subtotals go (in this case, at each change in the date), which function is used, and in which columns the subtotal appears.

Top right: When you click OK, the subtotals appear in your data, grouped appropriately according to the column you selected in the Subtotal dialog box. (Excel uses its outlining notation, as described on page 559, making it easy to collapse the result to show subtotals only.)

Validating Data

To ensure that the right kind of data is entered in a cell or cells, use a built-in Excel feature called Data Validation. This feature makes sure that dates, for example, don't end up in cells meant for currency.

To set up data validation for a cell or cells, select them and then choose Data→Validation, which brings up the Data Validation dialog box. This box has three tabs: Settings, Input Message, and Error Alert.

In the Settings tab, you can choose which data types are allowed to be entered (such as whole numbers, decimals, or lists). In the Input Message tab, you can enter a message that will pop up when you (or whoever uses this spreadsheet) select the cell in question. The Error Alert tab, meanwhile, lets you specify which error message Excel should display when someone enters the wrong kind of data.

To use this feature, select the relevant columns, including their headings, and then choose Data→Subtotals. In the Subtotal dialog box that pops up, you can tell Excel which function to use (your choices include Sum, Count, StdDev, and Average, among others). If you've selected more than one column, you can add the selected function to whichever column or columns you choose.

- **Text to Columns.** Suppose you've pasted a phrase into a single cell, and now you'd like to split each word into a separate column. Or maybe a cell contains several cells' worth of text, each separated by a nonstandard delimiter (such as a semicolon) that you'd like to split in a similar fashion. Text to Columns is the solution, as shown in Figure 14-24.

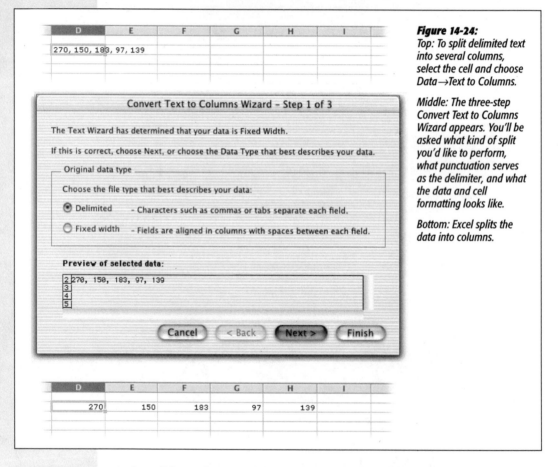

Figure 14-24:
Top: To split delimited text into several columns, select the cell and choose Data→Text to Columns.

Middle: The three-step Convert Text to Columns Wizard appears. You'll be asked what kind of split you'd like to perform, what punctuation serves as the delimiter, and what the data and cell formatting looks like.

Bottom: Excel splits the data into columns.

- **Consolidate.** The Consolidate command joins data from several different worksheets or workbooks into the same area, turning it into a kind of summary. In older versions of Excel, this command was important; in Excel X, Microsoft recommends that you not use it and instead simply type the references and operators that you wish to use directly in the consolidation area. For example, if you track revenues for each region on four different worksheets, you can consolidate that data onto a fifth worksheet. Figure 14-25 shows the procedure. (To learn more, read the "Consolidate data" entry in Excel's online help.)

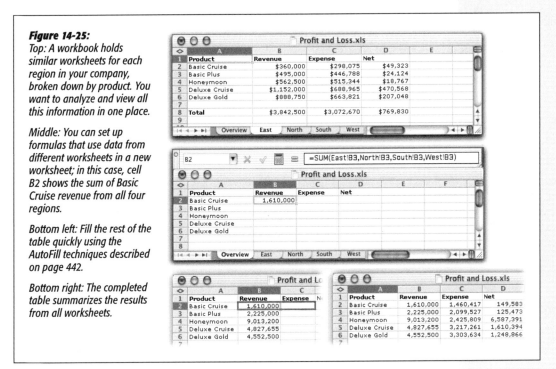

Figure 14-25:
Top: A workbook holds similar worksheets for each region in your company, broken down by product. You want to analyze and view all this information in one place.

Middle: You can set up formulas that use data from different worksheets in a new worksheet; in this case, cell B2 shows the sum of Basic Cruise revenue from all four regions.

Bottom left: Fill the rest of the table quickly using the AutoFill techniques described on page 442.

Bottom right: The completed table summarizes the results from all worksheets.

Data form

A spreadsheet is certainly a compact and tidy way to view information. But for the novice, it's not exactly self-explanatory. If you plan to turn some data-entry tasks over to an assistant who's not completely at home with the row-and-column scheme, you might consider setting up a *data form* for him—a little dialog box that displays a single spreadsheet row as individual blanks that must be filled in (see Figure 14-26). Data forms also offer a great way to search for data or delete it one row (that is, one record) at a time.

To set up a data form, start with a series of columns with column headers at the top—a list does nicely. These headers serve as categories for the data form. Then, with the cursor in the list, choose Data→Form, which brings up the data form window for that list (Figure 14-26).

When the form appears, the text boxes show the first row of data in the list. You can scroll through the rows (or records) using the scroll bar. On the right, eight buttons let you perform the following functions: add a new record (or row) of data at the bottom, delete the currently selected row, click Criteria to enter search criteria in the text boxes next to the field names, and then search for that information using Find Prev and Find Next. Finally, the Close button closes the window.

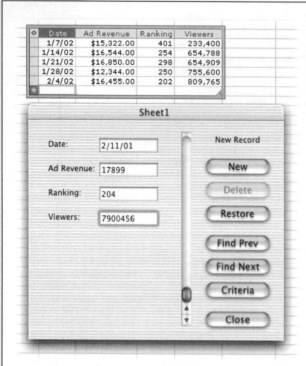

Figure 14-26:
The fields in a data form correspond to the columns in the spreadsheet. Data forms work like miniature databases. With them, you can quickly add and remove whole rows of data in a list, as well as search through a list for all matches.

Viewing Your Data

Excel worksheets can grow very quickly. Fortunately, Excel has some great tools to help you look at just the data you want.

Custom views

Excel can memorize everything about a workbook's window: its size and position, any splits or frozen panes, which sheets are active and which cells are selected, and even your printer settings—in a *custom view*. Custom views are snapshots of your view options at the time that the view is saved. Using custom views, you can quickly switch from your certain-columns-hidden view to your everything-exposed view, or from your split-window view to your full-window view.

To create a custom view, choose View→Custom Views, which brings up the Custom Views dialog box. To make Excel memorize your current window arrangement, click Add (and type a name for the current setup); switch between custom views by clicking a view's name in the list and then clicking Show.

Reports

Reports combine sheets, views, and scenarios into a convenient printable format. They're great when you have a sprawling spreadsheet from which you want to print only a few key cells. For example, if you want to create a report with just the capital expenditures sheet of a huge yearly budget, the Report Manger can do the trick.

Note: The Report Manager is yet another feature that's available only if you take the trouble to install it using the Value Pack installer described on page 681.

To create a report, choose View→Report Manager. In the Report Manager, you can create, edit, print, and delete reports by clicking the buttons on the right.

For example, to create a new report, click Add; in the Add Report dialog box, name the new report, then create a report section—choose a sheet, an optional view, an optional scenario, and click Add. Note that you can create multiple sections, too. When you've created all your sections, click OK, which returns you to the Report Manager window. You should see your newly minted report in the Reports list. Print it by selecting it and then clicking Print.

Outlining

In Excel, *outlines* help to summarize many rows of data, hiding or showing levels of detail in lists so that only the summaries are visible (see Figure 14-27). Because they let you switch between overview and detail views in a single step, outlines are useful

Figure 14-27:
Top: An outlined spreadsheet fully expanded.

Bottom: The same spreadsheet that's been partially collapsed. Clicking a + or – button opens or closes detail areas.

	A	B	C	D	E
1	Date	Show	Ad Revenue	Ranking	Viewers
2	35854	Iron Chef	$103,500.00	273	23563
3	35854	Dexter's Lab	$55,200.00	321	18245
4	35854	Alias	$61,400.00	239	31388
5	35854	Oz	$175,000.00	104	14555
6	35854	Kids in the H	$29,750.00	378	12344
7	1-Mar Totals		$424,850.00	1315	100095
8	35855	Iron Chef	$113,850.00	457	24296
9	35855	Dexter's Lab	$60,720.00	280	18978
10	35855	Alias	$67,540.00	318	32121
11	35855	Oz	$192,500.00	98	15288
12	35855	Kids in the H	$32,725.00	250	13077
13	2-Mar Totals		$467,335.00	1403	103760
14	35856	Iron Chef	$108,600.00	455	46526
15	35856	Dexter's Lab	$55,470.00	255	35890
16	35856	Alias	$62,290.00	319	62176
17	35856	Oz	$187,250.00	295	28510
18	35856	Kids in the H	$27,475.00	101	24088
19	3-Mar Totals		$441,085.00		
20	Grand Totals		$1,333,270.00	2718	203855
21					

	A	B	C	D	E
1	Date	Show	Ad Revenue	Ranking	Viewers
7	1-Mar Totals		$424,850.00	1315	100095
8	2-Mar	Iron Chef	$113,850.00	457	24296
9	2-Mar	Dexter's Lab	$60,720.00	280	18978
10	2-Mar	Alias	$67,540.00	318	32121
11	2-Mar	Oz	$192,500.00	98	15288
12	2-Mar	Kids in the H	$32,725.00	250	13077
13	2-Mar Totals		$467,335.00	1403	103760
19	3-Mar Totals		$441,085.00		
20	Grand Totals		$1,333,270.00	2718	203855
21					

for worksheets that teem with subtotals and details. (If you're unfamiliar with the concept of outlining software, consult page 211, which describes the very similar feature in Microsoft Word.)

You can create an outline in one of two ways: automatically or manually. The automatic method works only if your worksheet is properly formatted, as follows:

- Summary *columns* must be to the right or left of the data they summarize. In Figure 14-28 at top, the D column is a summary column, located to the right of the data it summarizes.

- Summary *rows* must be immediately above or below the cells that they summarize. For example, in Figure 14-28 at bottom, each subtotal is directly below the cells that it adds together.

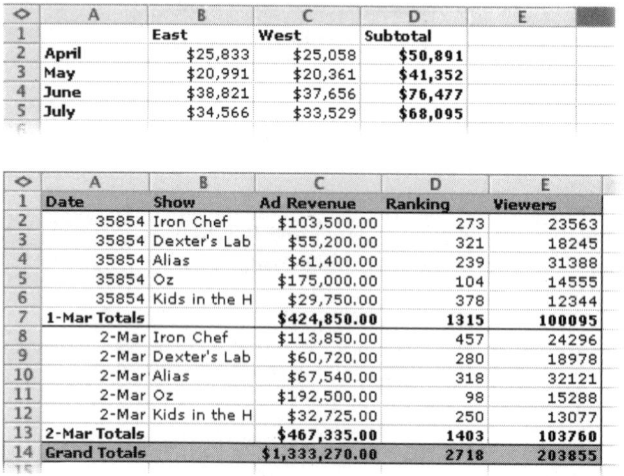

◇	A	B	C	D	E
1		East	West	Subtotal	
2	April	$25,833	$25,058	**$50,891**	
3	May	$20,991	$20,361	**$41,352**	
4	June	$38,821	$37,656	**$76,477**	
5	July	$34,566	$33,529	**$68,095**	

◇	A	B	C	D	E
1	Date	Show	Ad Revenue	Ranking	Viewers
2	35854	Iron Chef	$103,500.00	273	23563
3	35854	Dexter's Lab	$55,200.00	321	18245
4	35854	Alias	$61,400.00	239	31388
5	35854	Oz	$175,000.00	104	14555
6	35854	Kids in the H	$29,750.00	378	12344
7	**1-Mar Totals**		**$424,850.00**	**1315**	**100095**
8	2-Mar	Iron Chef	$113,850.00	457	24296
9	2-Mar	Dexter's Lab	$60,720.00	280	18978
10	2-Mar	Alias	$67,540.00	318	32121
11	2-Mar	Oz	$192,500.00	98	15288
12	2-Mar	Kids in the H	$32,725.00	250	13077
13	**2-Mar Totals**		**$467,335.00**	**1403**	**103760**
14	**Grand Totals**		**$1,333,270.00**	**2718**	**203855**

Figure 14-28:
Top: Because the column of subtotals (column D) is to the right of the data to which it refers, this spreadsheet can be automatically outlined.

Bottom: Each subtotal is beneath the cells that it summarizes, making this spreadsheet, too, a fine candidate for automatic outlining.

If your spreadsheet meets these conditions, creating an outline is as easy as selecting Data→Group and Outline→Auto Outline.

If your data isn't so neatly organized, you'll have to create an outline manually. Select the rows or columns of data that you want to group together into one level of the outline; choose Data→Group and Outline→Group. A bracket line appears outside the row numbers or column letters, connecting that group. Keep selecting rows or columns and grouping them until you've manually created your outline.

Outlines can have eight levels of detail, making it easy to go from general to specific very quickly. Thick brackets connect the summary row or column to the set of cells that it summarizes; a + or – button appears at the end of the line by the summary row or column.

To expand or collapse a single "branch" of the outline, click a + or – button; if you see several nested brackets, click the outer + or – buttons to collapse greater chunks of the outline. Also, the tiny, numbered buttons at the upper left hide and show outline levels and correspond to Level 1, Level 2, and so on, much like the Show Heading buttons on the Outlining toolbar in Word (see page 211).

Tip: Although outlines were originally designed to hide or reveal detail, you can use them to hide *any* rows or columns that you like.

POWER USERS' CLINIC

Proofing Tools

A spelling error can ruin the credibility of an otherwise brilliant spreadsheet, especially when you've gone through the trouble of getting it to look just right. Running a spell check on your spreadsheet before you show it to others can prevent just such an embarrassing mishap. Fortunately, Excel is part of a larger office suite—one that includes spelling tools.

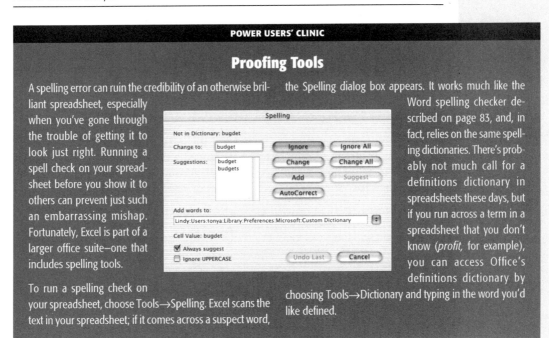

To run a spelling check on your spreadsheet, choose Tools→Spelling. Excel scans the text in your spreadsheet; if it comes across a suspect word,

the Spelling dialog box appears. It works much like the Word spelling checker described on page 83, and, in fact, relies on the same spelling dictionaries. There's probably not much call for a definitions dictionary in spreadsheets these days, but if you run across a term in a spreadsheet that you don't know (*profit,* for example), you can access Office's definitions dictionary by choosing Tools→Dictionary and typing in the word you'd like defined.

Figure 14-29:
To flag a file for follow-up, click the Flag for Follow Up button in the Standard toolbar (top), which brings up the Flag for Follow Up dialog box (bottom). In this box, you can set a time and date to be reminded that you need to attend to your worksheet. (Press Tab if you have trouble moving the insertion point around in the dialog box.) Once the date is set, click OK and save the document. Excel creates a task in Entourage; the reminder will pop up at the specified time, provided an Office X program is running at the time.

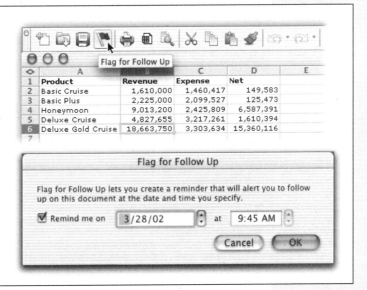

Flag for Follow-Up

Sometimes, when you're presenting the contents of a workbook to someone else—or when you're up battling a bout of insomnia by going through your old Excel workbooks—you come across something in a spreadsheet that needs updating, research, explanation, or some other kind of follow-up. Excel's *flag for follow-up* feature lets you attach a reminder to a file, which you can program to appear (as a reminder box on your screen) at a specified time. See Figure 14-29 for details, or page 397 for more on Office X reminders.

Adding a Comment

Here's another way to get your own attention (or somebody else's): Add a *comment* to a cell—a great way to annotate a spreadsheet. A note might say, for example, "This estimate seems way too high—call me," or "If you hadn't noticed, the dot-com era is over, pal." See Figure 14-30 for details.

To edit a comment that already exists, select the cell and then choose Insert→Edit Comment. To *delete* a comment, select the cell with the comment and choose Edit→Clear→Comments. You can also reveal all comments on a worksheet at once by choosing View→Comments.

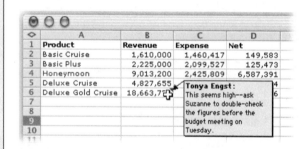

Figure 14-30:
To add a note to a cell, click the cell and then choose Insert→Comment. A nice yellow "sticky note" opens with your user name on the top (as it appears in the Excel→Preferences→General tab). Type your comment in the window. When you click elsewhere, the note disappears, leaving only a small triangle in the upper-right corner of the cell. To make the comment reappear, let the cursor hover over the triangle.

POWER USERS' CLINIC

Add-Ins

Hungry for even more customization? Excel can satisfy even that appetite with add-ins—little plug-in programs that add new capabilities to Excel. Several come with Excel, and a few others are available for download on the Internet.

To use an add-in, you must first put it into the Microsoft Office X→Office→Add-Ins folder on your hard drive. Once it's there, launch Excel and choose

Tools→Add-Ins. You get the Add-Ins dialog box, in which you can enable the add-ins of your choice by turning on the checkboxes next to their names. Click OK to load your add-ins.

A useful add-in for power users is the Analysis ToolPak, which, when turned on, adds a series of engineering, financial, and statistical options to Excel's function lists.

Tip: Like the Stickies program on every Mac, Excel comment boxes lack scroll bars. If you have a lot to say, keep typing past the bottom boundary of the box; Excel expands the note automatically. You can press the up and down arrow keys to walk your insertion point through the text, in the absence of scroll bars.

(Alternatively, drag one of the white handles to make the box bigger.)

Macros: Making Excel Work for You

A *macro* is a recorded series of actions that Excel can play back automatically, at high speed and with perfect accuracy. Macros are useful for automating tedious processes, such as formatting or data entry tasks.

For example, if you're constantly getting malformed expense reports because someone in Sales insists on changing the formatting in mileage cells to Currency instead of Number, you can write a macro that selects the mileage column and reformats it as Number in the blink of an eye.

But that's just the beginning. People who develop high-level macro-writing skill can use it as a full-on programming language. Their macros can throw dialog boxes onto the screen to ask users for information, plug the provided responses into appropriate cells in a spreadsheet, massage it with formulas, and format it for beautiful printing. Such a macro, in other words, can ask for five stock symbols and their closing prices over a week, and then produce a neatly formatted percentage-of-change table for you.

You can record your own macros or run macros you find embedded in a worksheet that came from somebody else.

Recording a Macro

To record a macro, choose Tools→Macro→Record New Macro. The Record Macro box appears (Figure 14-31), giving you the chance to name your new macro (and provide a description).

At this point, you can also specify where you want to store the macro. Using the "Store macro in:" pop-up menu, you can choose to store it:

- **In the currently open workbook.** It will ride along with the data that was used when you created it, but you won't be able to use the macro without opening the workbook that contains it.

- **In a brand-new workbook created to store the macro.** This option is useful when you don't want to sully the workbook that you're working on with a macro, but still want to use a macro with it.

- **In your personal macro workbook.** The Personal Macro Workbook is a special workbook that stays with the copy of Excel where the macro is created. Think of it as a library where you can store all kinds of macros for use in any workbook. It's the perfect place for macros that you'll be attaching to menu items or buttons (see page 630 for details).

When you click OK, Excel puts up the macro toolbar (complete with a Stop button) and begins to watch and memorize your every move; each click, drag, and menu command becomes a part of the macro. Excel macros are surprisingly versatile: Besides just data entry and formatting, they can drag data around, resize and move chart elements, and execute menu commands that involve dialog boxes.

Like anything that sounds too good to be true, though, there are some limitations. Macros don't understand what the data actually means; if you alter the landscape of a spreadsheet by moving some of its data and formulas around (without modifying the macro to notice the new locations), the macro assumes that everything is in its old place; when it runs, it'll move the wrong things around.

Tip: When you record a macro, you can use the Relative Reference button on the macro toolbar to ensure that the macro refers to relative cell coordinates, which helps alleviate the problem of altering the wrong data with a macro. To solve the problem completely, you must keep your worksheets largely untouched after you've recorded a macro.

Using Macros in Menus and Toolbars

You don't have to use the Macro dialog box to trigger a macro you've recorded; you can assign it to an Excel toolbar or even a menu, putting its power only a click away.

To assign a macro to a toolbar button, choose Tools→ Customize→Commands tab. In the categories list, select Macros; drag a Custom Button to the toolbar where you want the macro button to appear, as shown here. Click OK, then click the new custom button. This brings up the Assign Macro dialog box, in which you choose the macro to link to the button. Once you've done so, click OK. Now, every time you click the toolbar button, the macro attached to it runs.

You can turn a macro into a menu command, too. Choose Tools→Customize→Commands tab. Select Macros in the Categories list, and then drag the Custom Menu Item in

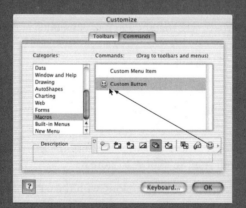

the Commands list to the menu where you want it to appear. (See page 630 for more on customizing menus.) Once it's in the menu, double-click the menu item to open the Command Properties dialog box; now you can change its name to something recognizable. Click OK, then OK again to dismiss the Customize box.

Now click your new menu command, which brings up the Assign Macro dialog box. Select the macro that you want to assign to the menu command; click OK. From now on, when you choose the new menu command from the menu, Excel will run the macro you assigned.

Note: These macros *must* be saved in your Personal Macro Workbook. Otherwise, you'll need to open the workbook that contains the macro every time you want to use the button or menu command.

Once you've done everything that you want the macro to do, click the Stop button on the toolbar. You've just created a macro.

Playing a Macro

To play a macro that you've recorded (or that someone has embedded in the currently open workbook), choose Tools→Macro→Macros, which brings up the Macro dialog box. In it, double-click the name of the macro you want to play (or click it once and click Run).

Tip: If you've specified a key combination for your macro, just press the key combination to run it, bypassing the visit to the Macro box.

Excel now plays back the macro, doing everything that you specified when you recorded it—but at very high speed and with computerish precision.

Figure 14-31:
Top: The Record Macro dialog box offers a chance to choose a keyboard combination (called a Shortcut key in Excel) that will trigger the macro during your everyday spreadsheet work.

Bottom: In the Macro dialog box, click Run to trigger the highlighted macro, whether it takes over the world—or just merges a few cells and adds a border around the outside.

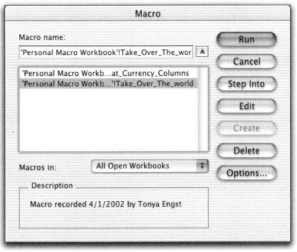

Sharing Macros

To share a macro with someone else, save your macro in a workbook when you create it, and then hand the workbook off to your macro tradee. When that person opens the workbook, your macro is available in the Macro dialog box.

WORKAROUND WORKSHOP

The Trouble with Macros

Although they seem simple on the surface, macros represent a messy, controversial subject (for Excel, PowerPoint, and Word veterans), thanks to the fact that they're an ideal carrier of *viruses*. It's perfectly possible for some maladjusted social deviant to write a destructive little program that, say, erases your entire spreadsheet.

Fortunately, most macro viruses are written so that they work only on Windows PCs. Furthermore, the Office X programs themselves help guard against macro viruses. When you open a document containing an embedded macro, for example, you see the warning shown here, which offers to disable any macros attached to the document (thus rendering them harmless). If you're still worried about macro viruses, you can buy antivirus software (and keep it up-to-date); modern antivirus programs can scan for macro viruses in Office documents.

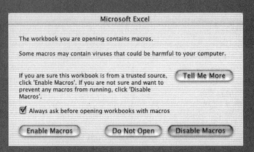

Macros are also a messy, controversial subject because behind the scenes, they're written in a programming language called Visual Basic for Applications. If you aspire to writing or editing macros by hand, then take a peek at the VBA code by choosing Tools→ Macro→Macros, clicking a macro name, and then clicking the Step Into button. This catapults you into Microsoft's VBA editor, where the macro's *source code* is visible.

If you're convinced that perhaps you don't want to become a programmer after all, click any visible portion of your workbook to get rid of the VBA editor. On the other hand, if you're interested in editing your macro by changing the code (or perhaps learning how to code these things by hand), this source code is an excellent place to begin your studies. A book or Web site on VBA programming is another good idea.

Part Four: PowerPoint

4

Basic PowerPoint

W hen you have a point to get across—to the boss, the board of directors, or your spouse—PowerPoint is your program. PowerPoint lets you combine graphics, text, sounds, and movies on a series of slides (or what amounts to a series of drawing documents), which link together to form a slide show. You use that slide show to get your *point* across in a *powerful* way. (So much for our theory on the origins of the name PowerPoint.)

The Big Picture

PowerPoint makes it easy to create and organize your presentation's outline, slides, and speaking notes. In PowerPoint's three-pane Normal view (Figure 15-1), you can see these three major elements together and work with them simultaneously.

To construct a slide show, you generally start by writing an outline (in the Outline pane). Here, you can type in the titles for your slides and then drag them around into a logical order. You then do most of the nitty-gritty design work in the Slide pane, in which you mix text, graphics, and backgrounds to create individual slide designs. Finally, the Notes pane lets you type speaker's notes and attach them to individual slides, so that you have facts at your fingertips while giving a presentation.

Step 1: Specify a Design

Before you can get more than a single screen into the program, you must answer an important question: What will your slides look like?

The slides in your show may display different kinds of information—one may show some text statistics, another may display a diagram, a third may contain a chart, and so on. Even so, however, you'll probably want all of these slides to have a consistent design, no matter what's on them: the same fonts, background graphics, color scheme, and so on.

That's why, as soon as you launch PowerPoint, the first thing you see is the Project Gallery, which should look familiar if you've used Word X or Excel X. In PowerPoint's case, the Project Gallery offers several templates that can get you started building your slide show without having to waste a lot of time on the design elements—or even composing the text on the slides.

Tip: If you, PowerPoint master, don't need the Project Gallery intruding into your personal space at every program launch, turn off the "Show Project Gallery at startup" checkbox at the bottom of the window. Or, you can toggle the checkbox in PowerPoint→Preferences→View panel.

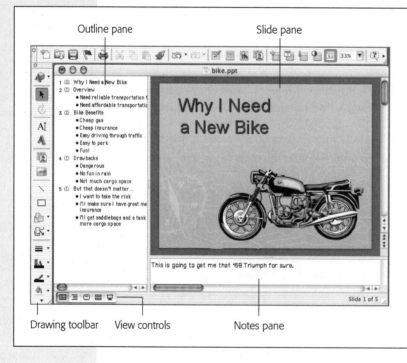

Outline pane   Slide pane

Figure 15-1:
You can see how the different parts of your presentation go together in Normal view. This three-paned window includes an area for the slide show's outline, a smaller area for notes, and an area in which you actually build the slide. *Finally, PowerPoint's view controls sit in the lower-left corner of the main window.*

Drawing toolbar   View controls   Notes pane

When project deadlines are looming and there are a million things that need to be done (including creating a presentation), you'll welcome these timesaving features.

Canned, Professionally Designed Templates

In the Project Gallery, open the Presentations category by clicking the flippy triangle to its left (see Figure 15-2). Then click Designs. In the middle of the Project Gallery window, you now see a huge selection of predesigned slide show templates—

either a list of their names or tiny thumbnail images of representative slides (depending on whether the View pop-up menu at the bottom of the window says List or Catalog).

In the List view, click one of the design templates (such as Azure, Blue Diagonal, or Bold Stripes); on the right side of the window, you see a miniature version of the slide design. While several of the templates in the gallery are, shall we say, inspirationally challenged, some may be worth considering.

If any of these templates looks like it will work for your purposes, double-click it. The New Slide dialog box appears, as described on page 574.

Tip: The design template that will work best depends not only on your taste and the purpose of your presentation, but also on how it will be presented. All of the included designs look terrific when projected from the Mac itself (using a portable projector, for example). If you plan to *print* the various slides, on the other hand, the designs with solid colors in the background might not be so appropriate. Not only will they take forever to print (and a lot of ink or toner), but the blended backgrounds on some of these designs may not look as smooth as they do on the screen.

Complete Slide Shows, Including Prewritten Text

You don't have to spend very much time in the corporate world to begin to feel like every meeting is the same. Based on that convenient fact of life, Microsoft has taken the liberty of providing several templates for complete slide shows. These templates include both a design theme (complete with backgrounds, font choices, and standing graphics and an outline befitting the situation).

For example, if you choose the Communicating Bad News template, you get a seven-slide outline to help you through the process of telling your colleagues about rocky times ahead, complete with a positive spin (and a placeholder for morale-building information bits). Such *content templates,* in other words, provide a canned but thoughtful structure for your presentation.

To survey a list of these ready-made shows, click Presentations in the Category list (of the Project Gallery window) and then click Content. You see a long list of ready-to-use slide shows, such as Marketing Plan, Motivating A Team, Project Overview, and so on (see Figure 15-2).

If you find a promising suggestion, double-click its icon. After a moment, you arrive in the three-pane Normal view (Figure 15-1), with the outline and design of your slide show already in place. You're ready to go about replacing the dummy text of this outline with phrases specific to your pitch, as described on page 575.

Custom-built Slide Shows Based on Your Input

If starting out your presentation building with a completely formatted, ready-to-go slide show feels too much like cheating, you may prefer to take advantage of the very similar AutoContent Wizard. This feature draws upon the same set of canned slide-show designs as the Content list described in the previous paragraphs, but gives you the opportunity to tailor the starter slides up front, rather than after PowerPoint has created them.

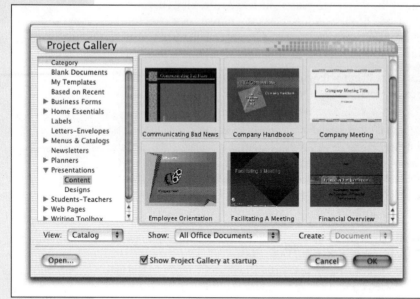

Figure 15-2:
PowerPoint provides a large collection of templates for your presentation needs, including a template for breaking bad news, from "Your stock options are worthless" to "Honey, I wrecked the car today." To choose a template, select it and click OK, or just double-click the one you want. (If the View pop-up menu at the bottom of the window says List, click the name of a slide show to see a preview of it.)

In the Project Gallery, click Blank Documents in the Category list. Then double-click AutoContent Wizard in the list to its right. The wizard proceeds to take you through the following steps:

1. **Choose a presentation type.**

   The first screen of the AutoContent Wizard asks you what kind of presentation you're planning. Start by using the Category pop-up menu to tell PowerPoint the overall nature of the presentation you're planning (General, Corporate, Projects, or whatever). You'll see a list of design templates appropriate for the category you've chosen; click each to see a preview of that slide design at the bottom of the window. Click Next to continue.

2. **Specify the presentation medium.**

   The wizard screen asks you to choose how you're going to deliver your slide show—on a computer screen, as black-and-white overheads, as color overheads, or as 35 mm slides. Your choice affects both the measurements of the slides and the color scheme: darker colors for computer screens and 35mm slides, lighter colors for color overheads, and, of course, black and white for black-and-white overheads. Click Next.

Tip: You can adjust the dimensions of your slide show later by choosing File→Page Setup (when reusing the show for a different projection method, for example). However, as the graphics and text boxes on each slide may shift in the process, it's best to pick the appropriate size for your slides at this early phase.

3. **Give your show a name.**

   On the final wizard screen, you're asked to enter the presentation's title, descriptive information, and any "footer" text that you want to appear at the bottom of each slide (such as your name or your department name).

When you finally click Finish, you wind up with a slide show document containing several ready-to-customize slides. A quick examination will show that they're filled with bogus information, such as dummy numbers in the charts and irrelevant data plotted in the graphs—but the point is that the designs and sequence are already in place. Now's your chance to change the actual text and numbers to suit your purpose; after all, you probably don't want to start off a motivational presentation with a slide that says, "Title goes here."

Starting from Scratch

If you're the kind of PowerPoint pro that Microsoft executives collectively dream about, then you might be inclined to design your slide show from scratch, beginning with a blank, white screen. To get there from the Project Gallery, click the Blank Documents category and then double-click PowerPoint Presentation. Or, if you're already in PowerPoint, choose File→New Presentation (⌘-N).

Either way, you're now facing the New Slide dialog box, from which you can choose a layout for your first slide (see page 574). To make your slides look less boring, you can use PowerPoint's various text and drawing tools to build each slide from scratch

---

POWER USERS' CLINIC

Adding Your Own Templates

In many corporations, PowerPoint slide shows are an everyday occurrence. In such situations, you may even be asked to use a PowerPoint template, approved and designed by your company, as the basis for any slide shows you give. (Remind your superiors that such templates from the Windows version of PowerPoint work just fine on your Mac.)

It's easy to make one of these templates show up in your Project Gallery, ready for easy access each time you begin to create a slide show. Just drag the template file into Microsoft Office X→Templates→My Templates folder. It'll show up in the Project Gallery under the My Templates category. In fact, you can transform any PowerPoint file into a template by dragging it into this folder.

When you open it, you'll get a blank *copy* of that file (called "Presentation1," for example), even if it wasn't a PowerPoint template per se. PowerPoint is smart enough to figure: "If it's in the Templates folder, I'm probably supposed to treat it as a template."

(see Figure 15-3). Although designing slides this way involves a lot more work than simply choosing a template, you'll be rewarded with a presentation that doesn't *look* like it came out of a can.

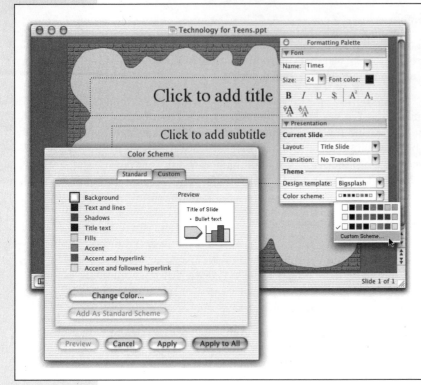

Figure 15-3:
Top: The Theme portion of the Formatting Palette lets you select various canned design templates and color schemes. Choosing a color scheme is as easy as picking one from the list. (Selecting a new color scheme changes the colors of all of the elements on a slide.) If you want to create your own color collection, choose Custom Scheme from the "Color scheme" pop-up menu on the Formatting Palette.

Bottom: In the resulting Color Scheme dialog box, you can choose new colors for the slide's background, text, shadows, fills, accents, and links.

The New Slide Dialog Box

When you create a new presentation, whether by using the Project Gallery or by choosing File→New Presentation, you come face-to-face with the New Slide dialog box (Figure 15-4). This box offers 24 slide designs in a scrolling list, each with a place for some text, a picture, a table, a chart, or a media file—or some combination of these elements. Each has been predesigned with centered text, neatly framed graphics, and so on. When you choose a layout and click OK, PowerPoint creates a new slide with those elements.

Which slide form you choose for each slide depends on what you want to do with that slide, as shown in Figure 15-4.

Tip: You can always change a slide from one of these canned layouts to another by choosing Format→Slide Layout. The equivalent of the New Slide dialog box reappears so that you can choose a different layout for the current slide.

Step 2: Writing the Outline

Step 1:
Specify a Design

The built-in PowerPoint starter slide shows save you a few minutes of design effort, but sooner or later you'll actually have to write the *words* that will appear on your slides. Outlining your presentation helps you organize your thoughts and write those all-important words.

One great way to go about this is to use PowerPoint's Outline view, which looks much like Normal view except that the Outline pane is wider. You switch into Outline view by clicking the Outline View button near the bottom left of the main window.

Tip: You can use the secret of Outline view anytime the sluggishness of PowerPoint's Normal view makes you feel like you're jogging through quicksand. It's not sold in stores, not listed in the View menu; you get to it by clicking the *second* tiny icon at the lower-left corner of the main window.

The Slide pane and Notes pane shrink a bit, but at least your typing won't be shackled to a slug.

The basics of typing an outline are simple: Each slide icon at the left of the Outline pane represents an individual slide. Whatever you type adjacent to the slide icon becomes the corresponding slide's title (see Figure 15-5).

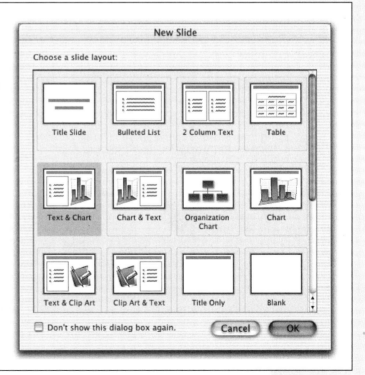

Figure 15-4:
When you add a new slide to your presentation, you'll be presented with the New Slide dialog box, from which you can choose one of 24 different layouts. These layouts make it easy to add various elements to your slides by providing placeholders for bullet lists, charts, artwork, tables, and even movies.

To generate more outline text, you can:

- Press Return after typing a title to start another title. Each title corresponds to a slide.

- Press Tab to *demote* a title into a bullet point under the previous title. If you continue pressing Tab, you can continue the demotion, down to five levels below the title. (Demote is outlining jargon for "make less important," or "move down one level in the outline.")

- Press Shift-Tab to *promote* a bullet point into a more important bullet point or a title. (Promote, as you might guess, means to "make more important," or "move up one level in the outline.")

- Press Return after typing a bullet point to start another bullet point.

- Press Control-M after typing a bullet point to start a title for a new slide.

If you create more than an occasional PowerPoint show, you'll make your life much easier if you master a few of these key combinations:

Keystroke	What it does
Tab	Demotes a heading
Shift-Tab	Promotes a heading
Return	Creates a new heading at the same level

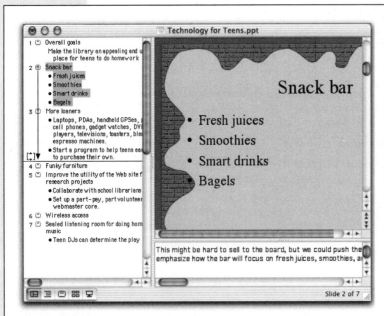

Figure 15-5:
You can drag topics or bullet points into a different order as you build your outline, just by dragging a tiny slide or bullet icon. A horizontal line indicates where PowerPoint thinks you want to place the item when you release the mouse. As you work on your outline in the left-hand Outline pane, you get to see the matching slide in the Slide pane.

Shift-Option-right arrow	Demotes a heading
Shift-Option-left arrow	Promotes a heading
Shift-Option-+	Expands (shows) the points below the current heading (use the + on the numeric keypad)
Shift-Option-–	Collapses (hides) the points below the current heading (use the + on the numeric keypad)
Shift-Option-down arrow	Moves a heading down by one line in the outline
Shift-Option-up arrow	Moves a heading up by one line in the outline
Option-arrow (any direction)	Moves the cursor one word or line in that direction

If all these keyboard shortcuts make you itch, you can promote, demote, and rear-range by simply dragging slide icons or bullet points left, right, up, and down. Also, if pushing buttons is your thing, you can use the Outlining toolbar. (Choose View→Toolbars→Outlining to make it appear.)

For reasons of both for space clarity, keep your main topics to a minimum, and keep your supporting points short and sweet. Also, don't pile too many of these subtopics on any given slide.

As you type your slide show's outline, you can watch the slide being built in the Slide pane—handy feedback to avoid typing too much text for a bullet. There's a draw-back, however—you may have to type relatively slowly to avoid outracing Power-Point, which may take a moment per letter to build the slide as you type.

Using a Word Outline

The PowerPoint outliner isn't the only outliner in Office X. If, having cuddled up with Chapter 6 for several evenings, you're already proficient with the outliner in Word X, you may prefer to write up your slide show in Word. Fortunately, you can easily import such an outline into PowerPoint.

POWER USERS' CLINIC

Typing Directly into Your Slides

Not everybody uses the Outline pane to hash out the shape of a presentation. Some people prefer to type their text directly onto the slides themselves.

If you fall into that category, begin the slide show by choosing only a design template, not a content template as de-scribed at the beginning of this chapter. Then, each time you want to add a slide to your show, choose Insert→New Slide (Control-M) or click the New Slide button in the Stan-dard toolbar.

The New Slide window appears (Figure 15-4). Double-click the slide type you want. After PowerPoint returns you to the main window, you can fill in the details by clicking the various text or graphics placeholders and then typing or importing text to fill those placeholders.

You can make more room in the Slide pane by dragging the bar that separates the Outline pane from the Slide and Notes panes.

To do so, launch PowerPoint and choose File→Open to bring up the Open dialog box. Select All Outlines in the Show pop-up menu, and then select the Word document that you want to import.

After you click Open, the Office Assistant asks you if you want to open the outline in Word or in PowerPoint; choose PowerPoint. PowerPoint now converts your outline into the basis for a slide show; each top-level heading becomes the title of a new slide, and subheadings become bullet points on each slide.

Tip: You can perform this trick from inside Word, too. With the outline open in Word X, choose File→Send To→Microsoft PowerPoint. PowerPoint opens (if it's not already open) and converts the outline into a presentation automatically, saving you several steps.

Step 3: Building the Show

It's much better to show blank white slides containing an effective message than fancy graphics that don't say anything. That's why it's an excellent idea to begin your presentation planning with the Outline pane.

Once the outline's in good shape, it's time to start thinking about the cosmetics; how your slides look. PowerPoint's tools make it easy to adapt your design (or Microsoft's design) for all the slides simultaneously.

Caution: Choose File→Page Setup and set the Size options *before* you design your slides. A radical change to these options later in the game may result in cutoff graphics or unintended distortions, as though your slides were being projected through a fun-house mirror.

Using Masters

A *master item* is a background element that appears on every slide—a logo or a background, for example. When you add, delete, move, or replace a master item, you see the change reflected in all of your slides that use that master item. For example, if you want to change the background color of all of your slides, just change the background on their *slide master;* PowerPoint updates all the slides instantly.

In fact, PowerPoint offers four different categories of master items: slides, titles, handouts, and notes. Here's how they work.

Slide master

The *slide master*—or, as most people would call it, the master slide—is a special slide whose background, font size and style, bullet style, and footer (whatever appears at the bottom of every slide) determine the look of these elements on every slide it controls.

Editing the slide master

To look at and change the slide master, choose View→Master→Slide Master. Now you're face-to-face with the slide master itself (see Figure 15-6), which comes with these master items:

- **Title Area.** This usually contains some dummy text, a placeholder for the real text that will appear in your slides. The title area is surrounded by a dashed line.

- **Object Area.** The settings you make in this area determine how the body of your slides—text, charts, pictures, and media clips—will look and where they will sit.

- **Date Area, Footer Area, and Number Area.** These boxes at the bottom of the slide master show where the date and time, slide number, and miscellaneous footer text will appear on each slide. (These same boxes appear in the preview in File→Page Setup→Header/Footer→Slide tab.)

Note: In View→Master→Slide Master mode, the placeholder text (such as "Click to edit Master title style") is irrelevant. Don't bother editing it; doing so has no effect on your actual slides.

By changing the font size, style, color, and placement of these items, you can change where PowerPoint puts those elements on your slides. For example, if you want all of your slides' titles to be in 24-point Gill Sans Ultra Bold, just click once inside the placeholder text to select the box; then use the Formatting Palette to change the font to 24-point Gill Sans Ultra Bold. Now, any existing slides that have titles (and any *new* slides you make) will display the title in 24-point Gill Sans Ultra Bold.

Figure 15-6:
The slide master generates certain elements that will be reflected in every slide in the presentation—except for title slides, which have their own title master. Slide Master view also has a small toolbar of its own with two buttons: Slide Miniature (produces a miniature image of an actual slide in the presentation, which lets you see how your changes to the master slide affect it) and Close (takes you back to whatever slide you were viewing).

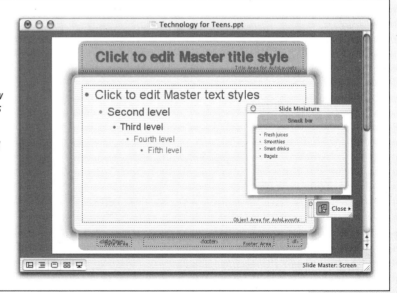

Adding new elements to a slide master

The title, bulleted text items, and various footers revealed on your slide master can appear on every slide; all you have to do is fill them in. But if you need *additional* text to appear on each slide (such as your department or project name), you can create additional default text blocks on your slide master.

To do so, use the Text Box button on the Drawing toolbar, which usually floats at the left edge of your screen, as shown in Figure 15-9. (If it's not there, choose View→Toolbars→Drawing.) If you can't find the Text Box button, point to each button in turn without clicking and read the yellow tooltip that appears (the tooltip reveals the button's name). Click the slide master where you want the new text box to appear, type some dummy placeholder text, and then use the Formatting Palette to set its font, color, and style.

You should also feel free to draw or paste graphics onto the slide master—your corporate logo or a background graphic, for example. Anything you place here will appear on every slide that's based on this master.

Title slide master

The *title slide master* is a special kind of slide master. It controls the layout of only one kind of slide: the title slide, usually the first one your audience sees. To view and edit the title master, choose View→Master→Title Master.

Once you understand that this master design applies only to title slides, you can use this slide master exactly like the slide masters described earlier, since elements that you put on the title slide master show up on all title slides. (When you insert a new slide via Insert→Slide, you'll find the Title Slide option at the upper left of the New Slide dialog box. You can also switch any slide to title slide status: while viewing it in the Slide pane, choose Format→Slide Layout, and then double-click Title Slide at the upper left of the Slide Layout dialog box.)

Handout master

You can read more about *handouts* on page 620. For now, it's enough to know that a PowerPoint handout is a special page design that lets you place several slides on a single sheet for printing and distributing to your audience.

Set up the design of your handouts by choosing View→Master→Handout Master, and then adding or editing the elements you want.

Notes master

In PowerPoint terminology, a note is another form of handout—one that features a miniature slide at the top half of the page, and typed commentary at the bottom (see page 620). Once again, you can specify the basic design of your notes printouts by choosing View→Master→Notes Master, and then editing the design you find here (such as altering the font or adding graphics); once again, those changes appear on every notes page in the presentation.

View Controls

To get the most out of PowerPoint, you should become familiar with the program's View controls, which are in the lower-left corner of the PowerPoint window (see Figure 15-1). These five buttons let you switch between PowerPoint's five view modes:

- **Normal view** is the standard three-pane view, as illustrated in Figure 15-1.

- **Outline view** expands the Outline pane so that it dominates the main window, shrinking the Slide pane and Notes pane to make room. You may prefer this view when you're working up the contents of your talk and still fiddling with the wording. As noted earlier, when you're typing up your outline, the typing itself goes much faster in this view than in Normal view.

- **Slide view** shows only the current slide. You'll probably prefer this view when you're putting the finishing touches (such as the charts and graphics) on your slides, after the outlining process is complete.

Tip: In any multipane view, you can drag the thin striped boundaries between the panes to make individual panes larger or smaller. (A tiny row of dots in the center of these lines denotes a draggable boundary—but you don't have to put your cursor on the dots themselves.)

• **Slide Sorter view** (Figure 15-7) displays thumbnail images of all of the slides that you've created, so that you can rearrange them by dragging. Drag either a single slide or several at once; Shift-click them to select more than one, or ⌘-click the first and last in a range. A vertical "your slide will go here" line appears when you drag selected slides.

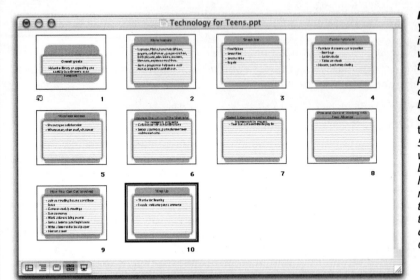

Figure 15-7:
You can delete slides in the Slide Sorter view by selecting them and then pressing Delete (or choosing Edit→ Delete Slide). You can also work with transitions (page 597) in Slide Sorter view; a small icon below a slide, shown here on slide 1, represents a transition. Click the transition icon to see a miniature preview of your transition.

You can use this view as a handy navigational aid; double-clicking a slide in Slide Sorter view opens the slide in your previous view.

• **Slide Show.** If you click this button, PowerPoint actually begins the slide show; see page 602 for more detail.

Navigation

No matter which view you're using, moving among the slides in your show is easy. For example:

• **Normal view or Outline view.** The outline is always on the left of the slide; all it takes to move from slide to slide is a click on the corresponding outline heading. If, for example, you want to go to the fourth slide in the presentation, just click the fourth element. PowerPoint displays that slide on the right side of the window.

• **Slide Sorter view.** In the Slide Sorter view, you can move from slide to slide by clicking the slide, or by using the arrow keys to move the selection rectangle around. If you double-click a slide, PowerPoint switches to the previous view with that slide selected.

- **Slide view.** The Slide view shows a single slide, filling the window. To move to the next slide in the show, you can click the scroll down arrow, or click the Next Slide button in the lower-right corner of the window, or press the Page down key. To move to the slide *before* the current slide, click the scroll up arrow, or click the Previous Slide button (also in the lower-right portion of the window), or press the Page up key.

- **Slide Show.** When you're in Slide Show view, each individual slide takes up the entire screen or window—no menus, no scroll bars, no controls. There are lots of key combinations that help you move around while in Slide Show view (see page 602). For now, you can use the right or down arrow key to move to the *next* slide in a slide show, or the left or up arrow key to move to the *previous* slide. Press the Esc key to return to the previous view.

Manipulating Your Slides

As you construct the show, new ideas will inevitably pop into your head; topics you originally expected to fill only three bullet points on a single slide may expand to require several slides—or vice versa. Fortunately, it's no problem to adjust the slide sequence as you go.

Inserting new slides

Inserting a new slide into the lineup once you've created a few is easy. Just click anyplace in the outline topic or the slide *before* the spot where you want the new slide to appear, then choose Insert→New Slide (Control-M). The New Slide dialog box appears, as described on page 574.

Tip: In Outline view, creating a new slide is even easier. Just click after an existing heading and press Return; the new heading represents a new slide (unless it's indented, of course).

Inserting old slides

You can also recycle slides from other presentation files simply by choosing Insert→Slides from File. The Choose a File dialog box appears; locate and single-click the PowerPoint file whose slides you want to import.

At the bottom of the dialog box, choose "Import all slides" or (if you want to hand-pick the slides worth importing) "Select slides to insert." Then click Open.

If you chose "Select slides to insert," you now see a dialog box offering miniatures of the slides. If you want to import slides with their existing design intact, as opposed to letting them inherit the new presentation's master slide design, turn on "Keep design of original slides." Shift-click the slides you want, click Insert, and then—after PowerPoint inserts the slides behind the dialog box—click Close.

Deleting a slide

Easy one: Click the slide and then press Delete, or choose Edit→Delete Slide.

Moving slides around

The easiest way to rearrange your slide sequence is in the Outline pane (by dragging the tiny slide icons up and down) or in Slide Sorter view (by dragging thumbnails around). In either case, the Cut, Copy, and Paste commands work.

Tip: The trick in Slide Sorter view is, before pasting, to select the slide just *before* the spot where you want the pasted slides to appear.

How to Build a Slide

The outliner is an excellent tool for building the overall flow of your slide show. But sooner or later, you'll probably want to visit the actual slide pictures themselves—to add charts or other graphics, to edit your concluding slide when new data becomes available five minutes before a meeting, and so on.

Using Backgrounds

Creating an individual slide is a bit like painting on a canvas: You first paint the background and work your way to the foreground, layer by layer.

For example, PowerPoint lets you set a background color, gradient, pattern, or graphic for your slide. You can also create a backdrop by adding shapes and importing graphics.

Changing backgrounds

Every slide begins life with a backdrop, courtesy of its slide master. If you'd like to override or enhance that backdrop on a particular slide, however, choose Format→ Slide Background, which brings up the Background dialog box (Figure 15-8). In this box, you see a sample slide with the current color scheme. At the bottom, a pop-

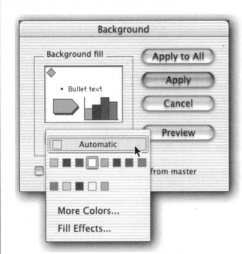

Figure 15-8:
The Background dialog box shows how your background fill color looks when applied to a slide with the current color scheme. (If you feel confident overriding Microsoft's professional color groups, choose More Colors from the pop-up menu; the standard Apple color picker dialog box appears, offering access to any color under the sun via several different Color Pickers, as described on page 651.)

up menu lets you choose, from a swatch of eight coordinated colors, a new background color.

Note: The technique described here *overrides* the background fill color specified by the slide master, just for a single slide. To change the background for *all* of the slides, choose View→Master→Slide Master, and then edit the background of that master slide. Doing so changes the backgrounds of all corresponding slides—except for those that you've changed yourself.

If you want something more than a solid background color, choose Fill Effects from the pop-up menu, which brings up the Fill Effects dialog box. This box lets you choose one of four effects by clicking one of the four tabs along the top: Gradient (a smoothly shifting color blend), Texture (a photograph of some natural material, such as wood grain, marble, or burlap), Pattern (simple, two-color patterns, such as stripes and dots), or Picture (a graphics file from your hard drive). See Chapter 18 for much more on these special tabs.

Tip: Be careful with this feature. Photos, textures, and gradients can make your text very difficult to read. (On the other hand, depending on the news you have to share with your colleagues, that may be exactly what you were hoping.)

Working with Text

There are two ways to add text to your slides; both are quite straightforward. First, if your slide master includes text placeholders, as shown in Figure 15-6, you can click the individual placeholder text items (which typically read something like "Click to Add Text"), and then type in your own words to replace the dummy text. Because these placeholders are linked to the slide master, they reflect its font characteristics.

WORKAROUND WORKSHOP

Shutting Off Two Annoying PowerPoint Features

If, as you add text to a box, you notice that the words and paragraphs are shrinking, don't be alarmed. PowerPoint is just trying to make your text fit into the placeholder text box. PowerPoint makes the text spill over onto another line only if shrinking the font size and line spacing fails.

If you find this feature annoying, never fear. You can turn it off easily enough: Just choose PowerPoint→ Preferences, and, in the dialog box, click the Edit tab. On the Edit panel, turn off the option called "Auto-fit text to text placeholder," and then click OK.

Another favor PowerPoint tries to do you: When you select more than one word and end your selection halfway through a word, PowerPoint selects the rest of that word for you. (This feature may sound familiar; the same thing happens in Word.)

This behavior can be frustrating when all you want to do is get rid of an errant suffix. To turn *this* feature off, choose PowerPoint→Preferences→Edit tab and turn off "When selecting, automatically select entire word." Now you can select as much or as little of a word as you like.

The other method is to add new text boxes (with no corresponding placeholders on the master) to a particular slide. Simply click the Text Box button on the Drawing toolbar (Figure 15-9), and then click the slide where you want to add text. PowerPoint adds a text box to the slide in which you can type any text you like.

Editing and formatting text

Adjusting the type characteristics of any kind of text box is easy. First, click the Select Objects tool (see Figure 15-9), and then click the text that you want to adjust. You've just activated the text box; now you can select part or all of the text to change its font, size, or style, using the Formatting Palette or the Format menu.

Note: In general, editing text on a slide changes it in the outline, and vice versa; the outline and text on a slide are just different representations of the same text. The one exception: When you add a text box to a slide by using the Text Box tool, your outline doesn't know anything about this new text, and doesn't display the new text.

Select Objects tool   An added text box   Reshaping handles

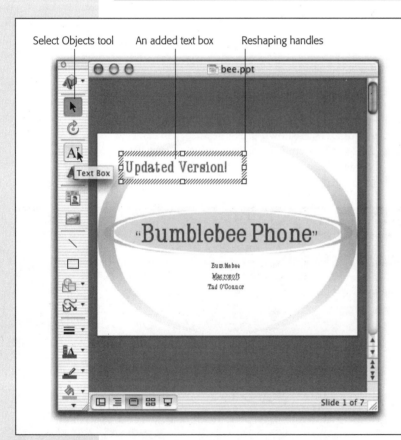

Figure 15-9:
The Select Objects tool (an arrow tool by any other name) lets you select text, pictures, and other items on a slide. The tooltip identifies the Text Box tool, which was used to create the new text box shown here. To move the text box, position the cursor over its border so that the cursor becomes a tiny hand, then drag; to reshape it, drag one of the white handles. (Press Shift while dragging a corner handle to keep the proportions steady as you resize.)

Formatting bullets

Since bullet-point lists play such a big role in business presentations, learning how to format the bullets is a key skill.

To change the bullet style, put the cursor in the text in which you want to make the change; open the Bullets and Numbering section of the Formatting Palette; and then choose a bullet style from the Style menu you find there.

Other characters as bullets

You don't even have to be content with the mundane dot (•) as your bullet symbol. You can choose any character from a variety of fonts by choosing Character in the menu (see Figure 15-10).

Figure 15-10:
Top: The Bullets and Numbering section of the Formatting Palette lets you choose the style, color, and size of your bullets.

Bottom: The Bullet dialog box contains a pop-up list of dingbat fonts (fonts whose characters are symbols). Browse these fonts to find just the right bullet for the point you're making. Click the character that you want to use and then click OK.

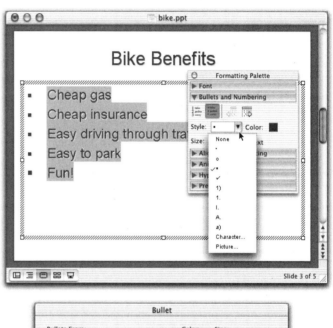

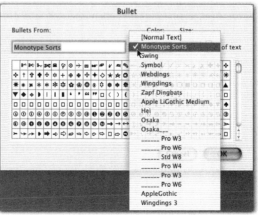

Graphics as bullets

You can even use a little graphic as the bullet, such as a JPEG file that shows a pointing hand, a checkmark, or your boss's head.

To specify a graphics file on your hard drive that you want to use as a bullet, proceed like this:

1. **Click the slide just to the right of the bullet that you want to modify.**

    The insertion point flashes next to the bullet point.

2. **On the Formatting Palette, in the Bullets and Numbering section, open the Style pop-up menu and choose Picture.**

    The Choose a Picture dialog box appears.

3. **Navigate to and double-click the graphic you want to use as a bullet.**

    You return to your slide, where the image automatically replaces the bullet at the same size of the text. Again using the Formatting Palette's Bullets and Numbering section, you can adjust the bullet size by entering a new percentage in the "Size % of text" box. Use the Color pop-up menu to give the bullet a custom color.

Adding Graphics, Charts, and Tables

Text and backgrounds aren't the only things that you can put onto a slide. You can also place graphics, movies, tables, charts, and other objects in your presentations. For example, you may want to insert a video clip of your company president explaining why this year's sales numbers aren't *quite* what they should be. Or, if you want to include a picture of your product when giving a marketing presentation, you can import it into your slide. Here's how to go about using these specialized objects.

Graphics

PowerPoint gives you lots of options for bringing graphics into your slides via the Insert menu—from Office's Clip Art collection, from a file on your hard drive, by inserting a Word table, by using an AutoShape, an Office Organization Chart, or WordArt, or by capturing an image directly from a scanner or digital camera. Use the Insert→Picture command (or the buttons on the Standard toolbar) to insert these special graphics, which Chapter 18 describes in detail.

Microsoft Word tables

If you've mastered (or even toyed with) the flexible table-making tools in Microsoft Word, here's an instant return on your investment: PowerPoint stands ready to teleport you into Microsoft Word, wait while you design a table for your slide, and then slurp the result into the PowerPoint slide. It works like this:

1. **Choose Insert→Picture→Microsoft Word Table.**

    The Insert Table dialog box appears.

2. **Type the number of rows and columns you want, then click OK.**

Strangely, enough, you're no longer in PowerPoint; you've been deposited in Microsoft Word, in a window called Document in *Sales Pitch* (or whatever your PowerPoint file is called). Now you can use all of the Word table tools described on page 165.

3. **Design your table. When you're finished, close the Word document.**

You return to PowerPoint. Your Word document vanishes as though it never even existed, but the table itself materializes on whatever PowerPoint slide you were editing. Want to work on the table some more? No problem—just double-click the table on the PowerPoint slide to return to Word.

PowerPoint tables

If you don't have the patience to flip into Microsoft Word every time you want to slap a table onto a slide, you may prefer to use PowerPoint's own table-making tools. They're not as flexible as those in Word, but more than adequate for most modern slide shows.

When you choose Insert→Table, a small window lets you specify how many columns and rows you want in your table; when you click OK, PowerPoint inserts the table into your slide. Or, for even less fuss, use the Insert Table pop-up button on the Standard toolbar, shown in Figure 15-11.

Once the table appears, you can adjust its size by dragging the resize handles at each corner, and you can move it or rearrange its interior by dragging the table's borders.

Tip: You can also *draw* a table directly on your slide by calling up the Table toolbar (View→Toolbars→Tables and Borders) and then using the Draw Table tool. It works just like its Word counterpart, detailed on page 165.

Inserting a table also brings up the Table toolbar. It contains just enough tools to let you make changes like these to your PowerPoint table:

- **Change border lines.** To change a border's style, width, or color, make your selections using the Border Style, Border Width, and Border Color controls in the upper part of the toolbar, and then click the borders you want to change using the Draw Table tool.

- **Change text alignment.** To change how text is aligned in a cell, select the cell (or cells); then click the Text Alignment buttons in the toolbar, which let you align text at the top, center, or bottom of the cell. (You can also use the text-alignment buttons in the Formatting Palette to do this job, as well as to modify the left-right alignment.)

- **Merge or split cells.** By erasing the line between two cells using the Eraser tool, you can tear down the barrier between them, creating one long cell. (Another method: Select the cells that you want to merge by Shift-clicking them, and then click the Merge Cells button.)

On the other hand, you can also split a cell in two. Click the Draw Table tool and then drag to "draw in" the new border (Figure 15-11). Alternatively, select the cell you want to split and then click the Split Cell button, which vertically divides the cell.

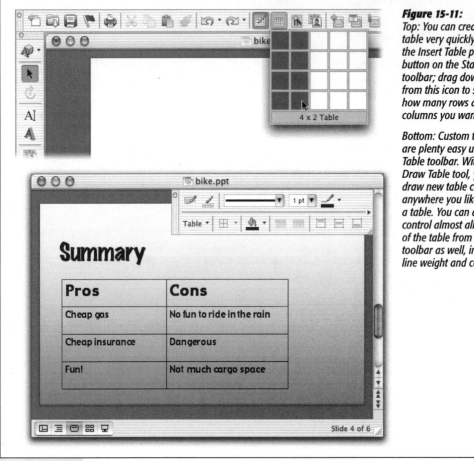

Figure 15-11:
Top: You can create a table very quickly using the Insert Table pop-up button on the Standard toolbar; drag downward from this icon to specify how many rows and columns you want.

Bottom: Custom tables are plenty easy using the Table toolbar. With the Draw Table tool, you can draw new table cells anywhere you like within a table. You can also control almost all aspects of the table from this toolbar as well, including line weight and color.

- **Add or remove columns and rows.** The menu commands in the Table pop-up button (see Figure 15-12) let you insert columns and rows as well as delete them. They also let you merge and split cells, set how borders look, and specify how cells are filled.

Movies and sounds

These days, showing your colleagues a bunch of motionless pictures isn't very flashy (if indeed flashiness is what you're after). Via the Insert menu, PowerPoint can import movies and sounds in six different formats—from the Clip Gallery, from files, and from CD audio tracks; you can also record your own sounds directly into PowerPoint.

- **Movie from Gallery.** Microsoft's Clip Gallery has lots of animated GIF files (short cartoons) that illustrate typical business situations, such as a stock ticker and a checklist. To insert a motion clip from the Gallery onto one of your slides, choose Insert→Movies and Sounds→Movie from Gallery. Use these animated GIFs sparingly; they can quickly turn an otherwise fine presentation into something tacky.

  When, during a slide show, you arrive at a slide containing a movie from the Gallery, it plays automatically, looping over and over until you move on to the next slide.

Tip: From within the dialog box that appears when you choose Insert→Movies and Sounds→Movie from Gallery, you can visit Microsoft's clip art Web site to search for more animated GIFs. Just click the Online button, which automatically takes you to Design Gallery Live.

Figure 15-12:
In addition to its toolbar buttons, the Table toolbar has a menu of commands that let you insert and remove columns and rows as well as split and join cells. You can also select a row, a column, or an entire table using this menu.

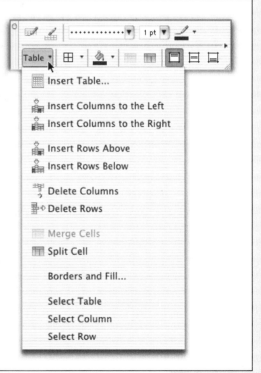

• **Movie from File.** The Insert→Movies and Sounds→Movie from File command lets you select a movie of your own to import into your presentation. It brings up an Open File dialog box, in which you can choose a QuickTime-compatible movie.

When you insert a movie, Excel asks if you want it to play automatically when the slide comes up during the slide show. If you click No, the movie won't play until you click it.

In either case, embedding a movie brings up the Movie toolbar, whose buttons let you insert a movie, play a movie, show its controller scroll bar, make the movie loop over and over, specify the movie's poster frame (a frame of the movie which serves as its icon), and bring up the Format Picture dialog box.

Tip: Be careful when you embed movies in your PowerPoint presentation. These movies are *not* saved inside your PowerPoint presentation. Instead, the presentation maintains a *link* to the movie on your hard drive. If you copy your presentation to, say, your laptop, but forget to copy the movie file as well, you'll be in for a rude surprise when the conference-room lights dim. The slide will appear showing the "poster frame" icon of the movie, but nothing will happen when you click it.

Avoid this problem by saving your multimedia PowerPoint presentation as a *package*—a single folder that contains the PowerPoint file and every linked file it needs, ready for backing up, burning to CD, copying to your laptop, and so on. Choose File→Save As, and then, in the Format pop-up menu, choose PowerPoint Package.

Figure 15-13:
The small filmstrip icon in the lower-left corner of an embedded movie (left) is actually a switch that, when clicked, reveals a simple movie controller (right).

- **Sound from Gallery.** The Insert→Movies and Sounds→Sound from Gallery command opens the Clip Gallery and lets you browse for the appropriate sound clip, much as though you're browsing for motion graphics in the Gallery. Turn on the Preview checkbox to display a small Preview window; then you can play a sound in the Clip Gallery by clicking the triangle in the Preview window. These embedded sound files show up as small speaker icons in your presentation; click to play.

Because these sound clips don't take up much space, PowerPoint generally embeds them directly in the PowerPoint file. This time, you generally *don't* have to worry about bloating your presentation or losing the link to the sound file when you move the presentation to a different disk. (If you choose PowerPoint→Preferences→General, you'll see that you can specify the sound-file threshold for automatic embedding. For example, PowerPoint makes sounds smaller than 101 K part of your presentation's file, but it leaves larger ones on the hard drive, like the movies described in the previous tip.)

You *do* have to worry about the cheese factor when embedding sound files, however. It doesn't take many to ruin an otherwise fine presentation.

Note: If your version of Office doesn't have many (or any) sounds or motion clips in the Gallery, use the Value Pack installer to install the Clip Art and Sound Effects options (see page 681).

- **Sound from File.** Choosing Insert→Movies and Sounds→Sound from File brings up an Open File dialog box, which lets you choose your own audio file to import—including MP3 files. Once again, PowerPoint asks if you want the sound to play automatically when its slide appears during your slide show. If you click No, you'll have to click the sound icon (a small speaker) to make it play.

You can drag this icon anywhere on the slide.

Note: Planting a large sound file on a slide is like planting a movie there: you're actually installing a *link* to the sound file on your hard drive, not the file itself. This feature keeps the size of your presentation much smaller, but it also means that you have to remember to move the sound file when you move the presentation to another machine. Otherwise, you'll find yourself with a soundless presentation.

Once again, the best way to be sure your sounds travel with you is to save your show as a PowerPoint package (see the tip on page 592). To do so, choose File→Save As. Name your show; then pop up the Format menu and choose PowerPoint Package.

- **Play CD Audio Track.** Although the recording industry may not particularly appreciate it, you can also grab a track from a music CD to serve as a soundtrack for your slide show. When you select Insert→Movies and Sounds→Play CD Audio Track, PowerPoint displays the Play Options dialog box (Figure 15-14), where you can set the start and end points for your sound. When this slide appears during the actual presentation, the song will begin to play automatically (or when you click it, at your option).

Note: The music won't play unless the actual audio CD is already inserted in your Mac at the time of your presentation.

- **Record Sound.** The Insert→Movies and Sounds→Record Sound command lets you record your own sounds that are then inserted into the presentation.

  To record a sound, first visit the Speech panel of your Mac's System Preferences program. Click the Listening tab and make sure that your Mac's microphone is selected, attached, and working. Quit System Preferences.

  Now, in PowerPoint, choose Insert→Movies and Sounds→Record Sound. PowerPoint presents a Record Sound dialog box. Click Record, speak or sing or squawk into your Mac's microphone, and then click Stop. You can play back the sound by clicking Play to make sure it's just what you want. If so, click Save.

  You'll find a little speaker icon on your PowerPoint slide. Click it during a presentation to hear your recording. (Unlike imported sounds and movies, these sounds are part of the PowerPoint file rather than links to separate files on your hard drive. Be aware that sound files can greatly inflate the size of your PowerPoint document.)

Figure 15-14:
In Play Options, you can choose which CD tracks are included and what portion of the tracks are played; perhaps you only want fifteen seconds of the Rolling Stones' "Satisfaction." You can also turn on "Loop until stopped," which causes the sound to repeat until you click or move to a new slide.

Charts

If your presentation is just crying out for a chart—and what presentation isn't?—just choose Insert→Chart to launch Microsoft Graph. This little application (a part of Office) lets you quickly create a graph, using a stripped-down, Excel-like spreadsheet window. When you choose Graph→Quit & Return to [Your PowerPoint file's name], PowerPoint *embeds* your chart into the current slide. (Embedding puts the output of one program into a document belonging to another. In this case, Graph's output is appearing in a PowerPoint document.)

Once the chart appears in your slide, you can double-click to edit it, launching Microsoft Graph again in the process. (That's key to an embedded object: you can edit it again in its parent program.) For more on Microsoft Graph, see page 668.

How to
Build a Slide

Tip: The true graphing genius in Office lies not in Microsoft Graph, but in Excel. If you want a full-fledged chart, or you've already created one in an Excel workbook, just copy and paste it from the workbook or use the Insert→Object command, described next.

Other objects

The Insert→Object command is the first step to embedding several other kinds of visuals onto a PowerPoint slide. The objects can come from such other Office programs as Equation Editor, Excel, Microsoft Graph, Organization Chart, or Word. (Equation Editor, Graph, and Chart are described in Chapter 18.)

Note: If you were hoping to add equations to your slide, but don't see Equation Editor listed as an object type, you'll have to first install the software from the Value Pack; check page 681 for details.

As shown in Figure 15-15, the resulting dialog box lets you either choose an existing document to install onto your slide, or create a new one. If you plan to insert an existing file into your slide, *first* choose the object type and *then* click "Create from file." The instant you turn on "Create from file," the standard Mac OS X Open File dialog box appears so that you can select the document you want.

What happens next depends on what you do in the Import Object box:

- **"Create new" with "Display as icon" turned on.** An appropriate icon now appears on the slide. You can click the icon to open the corresponding program and create a new document. Choose File→Close & Return to [Your PowerPoint file's name] when you finish your work.

- **"Create new" with "Display as icon" turned off.** The appropriate program opens so that you can create your new object. Choose File→Close & Return to [Your PowerPoint file's name] when you finish. Your new object appears on the slide.

- **"Create from file" with "Display as icon" turned on.** PowerPoint takes you back to your slide, where an icon for your embedded object appears. Double-click the icon should you ever want to edit or display the object.

- **"Create from file" with "Display as icon" turned off.** The chart, equation, or document appears on the slide. (For Word or Excel files, you see only the first page or worksheet.) Double-click to edit or view the object in its parent program.

You may reasonably scratch your head at the prospect of placing an entire Word or Excel document onto a slide, especially if the document is larger than the slide itself.

After scratching for a few moments, though, you'll probably realize that Microsoft has provided a dandy way to link supporting documents and reference materials to your PowerPoint presentation. When, during your pitch, some muckraking co-worker objects, "But that's not the marketing plan we talked about last month," you can click the Word document's icon that you've placed on the slide in anticipation of just such a ruckus—and open the actual Word file, in Word, for all to see.

> **Note:** Unfortunately, the "Display as icon" and, indeed, this whole object-embedding business, relies on a message technology called Object Linking and Embedding, abbreviated OLE and often pronounced "o-LAY." As noted in the more complete discussion on page 659, Object Linking and Embedding has a reputation for behaving oddly, although it's not nearly so dangerous as it was in Mac OS 9. It works best when linking to very small documents on computers that have lots of memory.

Hyperlink

The Insert→Hyperlink turns the selected text or graphic into a clickable link, capable of opening another PowerPoint file, any Macintosh file or program, or a specified Web page on the Internet. You'll find a complete description of this feature on page 293.

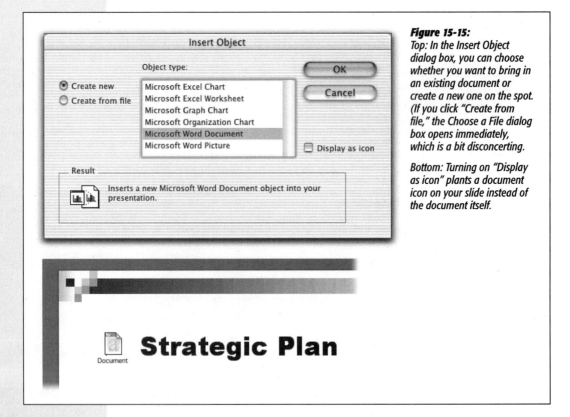

Figure 15-15:
Top: In the Insert Object dialog box, you can choose whether you want to bring in an existing document or create a new one on the spot. (If you click "Create from file," the Choose a File dialog box opens immediately, which is a bit disconcerting.)

Bottom: Turning on "Display as icon" plants a document icon on your slide instead of the document itself.

Advanced PowerPoint

B uilding individual slides in PowerPoint can be lots of fun, if that's your idea of a good time. But the real muscle of the program lies in its ability to pull those images togeth

er into a running slide show. Although good taste sometimes suffers as a result, you can dress up your slide presentations with flashy cinematics, music, sound effects, and voice narration. You can then rehearse your PowerPoint shows to work out the split-second timing. You can even turn your masterpieces into printouts or a Web site for the benefit of those who missed the presentation, or save your slide shows as QuickTime movies, then edit them again later (back in PowerPoint).

This chapter shows you how to harness these potent PowerPoint features.

Making a Slide Show

Chapter 15 discusses building slides and finding your way around PowerPoint. Now it's time to dig in and look at the big picture—how to bring those images together into a complete slide show with all the trimmings.

Transitions

PowerPoint gives you broad artistic license in the way you switch from one slide to the next. By varying the *transitions*—the between-slide special effects—you can create a sense of movement or put some zip into otherwise lackluster material such as tables, flowcharts, and scenes from your Cancun honeymoon. PowerPoint transitions range from simple *cuts* (with one slide quickly replacing another) to fancier effects such as *dissolves* (where one slide melts into the next) and checkerboard *wipes* (in which slides transmogrify with a moving checkerboard effect). Even with all this variety, though, it's a good idea to rely on simple transitions and use the pyrotechnics sparingly.

How transitions work

Transitions, as the term implies, appear in the spaces between slides in a show. To add a transition in PowerPoint, you first need to specify the location by selecting the slide that *begins* the switcheroo. If, for example, you want to insert a transition between the fourth and fifth slides in a show, select slide four in one of the following ways:

- In Normal view, click in the outline heading.

- In Slide view, summon the slide.

- In Slide Sorter view, click the slide thumbnail.

After selecting a slide, you can add a transition in any of several ways:

- On the Formatting Palette, scroll down the Transition pop-up menu and pick the transition you want to use.

- Choose Slide Show→Slide Transition; or in Slide Sorter view, Control-click a slide and choose Slide Transition from the contextual menu.

  The Slide Transition dialog box appears, offering a pop-up menu with a list of transitions. Scroll down the list and make your choice, then click Apply.

- In Slide Sorter view, use the Slide Sorter toolbar that appears automatically; it offers a Transitions pop-up menu.

Kinds of transitions

Although you'll probably end up using simple cuts and other tried-and-true favorites over the course of your slide show career, PowerPoint dangles before you a mouth-wateringly long list of special effects. They fall into two general categories: PowerPoint transitions (those that come with the program) and *QuickTime* transitions, which are part of Apple's QuickTime movie software. The method used for retrieving them is slightly different, but in practice, PowerPoint and QuickTime transitions work the same way.

UP TO SPEED

Avoiding the Cheese Factor

PowerPoint makes it easy to load up your presentations with funky transitions, sounds, and other cheesy gimmicks. But with power comes responsibility. While you may be tempted to show off all the program's entertaining features in a single presentation, bear in mind that old design adage: Less is more. It's usually best to keep your transitions and sounds simple and your designs basic. That way, you won't distract the audience from the important part of the presentation—your message—with a bunch of dazzling gewgaws.

Tip: If the provided transitions don't adequately express the inner you, try downloading and installing the shareware Effects Packs from Buena Software at www.buena.com. You can try them at no charge; if you wind up making them part of your everyday transition diet, the cost is $30 each, $50 for the Effects Pack Bundle 2 Pack, or $70 for the Effects Pack Bundle 3 Pack.

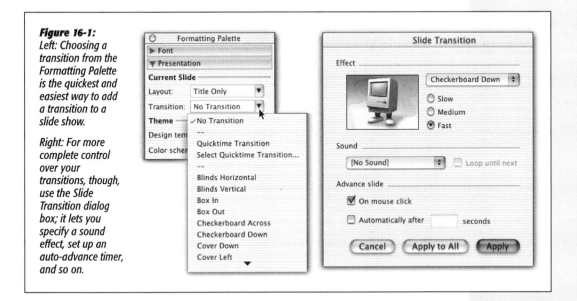

Figure 16-1:
Left: Choosing a transition from the Formatting Palette is the quickest and easiest way to add a transition to a slide show.

Right: For more complete control over your transitions, though, use the Slide Transition dialog box; it lets you specify a sound effect, set up an auto-advance timer, and so on.

PowerPoint gives you a total of 40 transitions, grouped into twelve basic types (described here by their visual effects):

- **Blinds.** The first slide closes like a set of blinds, either horizontally or vertically. As that image moves out, the next one emerges in its place.

- **Box.** The incoming slide wipes over the previous image with an expanding or contracting box, opening from either the center or the edges.

- **Checkerboard.** The first image breaks up into a pattern of adjacent squares, which turns into the next image as it sweeps across or down the screen.

- **Cover.** The new slide scoots in from off-screen to cover the previous image with a framed, three-dimensional effect. The eight variations in this group match the directions from which the incoming slide can enter: top, bottom, left, right, and the four corners.

- **Cut.** The next slide in the show simply pops in place of the previous one. No frills, no fireworks. This is the most basic, and therefore the most useful, of all the transition types; it's also the "transition" you get if you don't specify *any* transition.

- **Dissolve.** One slide fizzles out and morphs into another in an impressionistic, "pixellated" fashion. Think of Captain Kirk beaming up and you've got the idea.

- **Fade Through Black.** Here, the first slide fades out to black, then the next one materializes in its place. This transition is similar to Dissolve, but without the granulated, melting-in-acid effect.

- **Random Bars.** Irregular horizontal or vertical slats appear across the image, quickly disintegrating and giving way to the next slide.

- **Split.** The first image splits into doors that open either horizontally or vertically to reveal the next slide. Or, doors showing the second image close in over the first image.

- **Strips.** As seen in countless old movies, the incoming image wipes across the screen diagonally from one corner to the opposite corner.

- **Uncover.** The existing slide moves off screen to expose the next image lying behind it. Shrewd readers will recognize this as the reverse of Cover.

- **Wipe.** In an effect that's similar to Cover but with more of a squeegee effect, the incoming slide moves vertically or horizontally into view as it wipes away the previous slide.

QuickTime transitions

Apple's QuickTime software offers even more variety—eleven basic transitions, each of which can be modified to your liking. To add a QuickTime effect to your presentation, go to the Formatting Palette and choose Select QuickTime Transition from the Transition pop-up menu. (You can also get there by choosing Slide Show→Slide Transition; from the Transition pop-up menu, choose Select QuickTime Transition.) This brings up the Select Effect dialog box shown in Figure 16-2. Here you can choose a QuickTime transition by clicking in the left panel, and then adjust its settings in the panel on the right.

Caution: Not all transitions look good, or even work at all, when you export your presentation as a QuickTime movie (see page 614). If you'd like to avoid unpleasant surprises, stick to QuickTime transitions or the PowerPoint transitions that are on Microsoft's "we think they'll work" list. These likely-to-work transitions are: all Covers and Cuts, all Splits and Uncovers, and Fade Through Black.

If you use any other PowerPoint transition, save your presentation as a movie early on and test it. That way, you'll nip goofy transition problems in the bud.

Customizing your transitions

Once you've chosen a transition effect, you can tinker with its settings to add variety or to make them conform to your presentation's overall style. Customizing transitions is also a good way to set your slide show apart from the efforts of less-creative PowerPoint users. (Just allow yourself enough time before the big pitch to refine your transitions.)

Using the Slide Transition dialog box (Slide Show→Slide Transition), you can control just about every aspect of how transitions behave. Here's a look at some of the things you can manipulate in this box (see Figure 16-1):

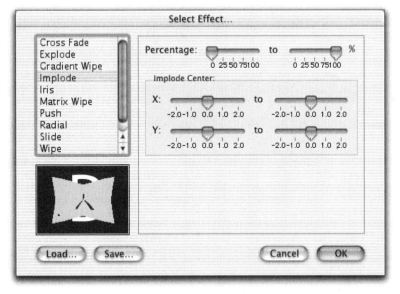

Figure 16-2:
QuickTime transitions are versatile little effects that can be tweaked and molded to create many more variations. (These, by the way, are the same transitions that QuickTime uses with video in other programs.)

- **Effect.** You can use this section to preview transition effects by choosing a new transition or selecting a new speed. PowerPoint responds by playing your new effect in the thumbnail of Max, the Office Assistant cartoon character (if you haven't turned the little bugger off, that is). This is an extremely useful feature, because most transition types have several, sometimes subtle, variations, and the names of some transitions give few clues to their function. Also, some of the more intricate effects, like Cover and Checkerboard, look more impressive at slower speeds.

- **Sound.** In the gratuitous-bells-and-whistles department, nothing beats the Sound section. Using this pop-up menu, you can add a sound effect to your transition: applause, breaking glass, a car driving by, or anything else you find in your Microsoft Office X→Office→Sounds folder. (Or choose Other Sound to use a sound located elsewhere. PowerPoint recognizes sounds in many common file formats; search for "sound" in the online help to see the full list.)

Tip: You can add new sounds to the pop-up menu by dropping your own WAV (.wav) sound files into the Microsoft Office X→Office→Sounds folder.

The occasional explosion or whoosh can bring comic relief, help you underscore a point, or draw special attention to an image. But for the sanity of those viewing your slide show, go easy on the noise. Don't apply sound to every transition, or the next sound you hear will be the silence of an empty auditorium.

Tip: Don't use these sound effects for background music. For that purpose, insert a sound object in a given slide using the Insert command, as described on page 593; or use a CD as a sound track, detailed on page 616.

- **Advance slide.** Here's where you tell PowerPoint the method you want to use for advancing to the next image in your slide show. You have two basic choices: advance when you click the mouse, or advance automatically after a number of seconds that you specify (the preferred choice of trade-show booth personnel worldwide). You can also turn on both options, thereby instructing the program to change slides after a number of seconds *unless* you click the mouse first.

Putting On the Show

Now that you know how to build individual slides and insert transitions, it's time to start getting ready for making the presentation itself.

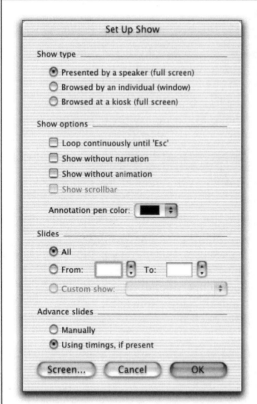

Figure 16-3:
The Set Up Show dialog box also lets you choose which slides to use and how you want them to be advanced: manually, with a mouse click; or automatically, using preset timings. You can also choose an annotation pen color for the onscreen writing tool that allows you to scrawl arrows, circles, cartoons, or quaint Latin expressions on your slides to underscore a point (or keep yourself entertained while the audience is napping).

Setting up

Before you slick your hair and strut out on stage, the first preparatory step is to choose Slide Show→Set Up Show. In the dialog box that appears (see Figure 16-3), you can choose the *type* of presentation you want it to be—a typical full-screen slide show, a small show for an individual reader to browse, or a self-running kiosk-style show that keeps playing until you (or the police) shut it off.

Rehearsing your presentation

As P-Day (Presentation Day) draws near, you can use PowerPoint's *rehearsal mode* to run through the slide show and work out the timing. It can be very helpful to know how long it takes to show each slide, especially if you have a tight presentation schedule. This handy feature even allows you to factor in sufficient time for the laughter to subside after your well-rehearsed "off the cuff" jokes.

To begin the rehearsal, choose Slide Show→Rehearse Timings. The screen fills with the first slide, and PowerPoint shifts into presentation mode. A timer appears in the lower-right corner of the slide, ticking off the number of seconds the slide is spending on the screen. Each time you advance to a new slide, the timer resets itself to zero and begins the count anew for *that* slide.

When you've gone through the whole show, PowerPoint asks if you want it to record those timings for use later in an automated show. If you answer yes, PowerPoint logs the timings automatically in the "Advance slide" portion of the Slide Transition dialog box (Figure 16-1). The program then asks if you want it to note those timings in Slide Sorter view, as shown in Figure 16-4. You may as well do this; it's pretty handy to see those time allotments, even if you decide to ignore them and advance the slides manually.

Figure 16-4:
After you've done your timing run, PowerPoint marks the slide duration beneath each slide in Slide Sorter view. It's important to note that the duration of transitions is not factored into the timing of each slide. So if you've chosen some of the slower, fancier transitions, be sure to take their length into account when calculating the timing of your show.

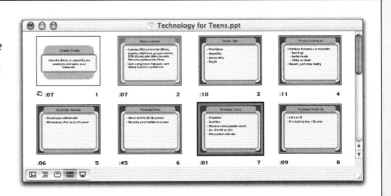

Choosing a navigation scheme

If you choose PowerPoint→Preferences→View tab, you'll find some useful preference settings that affect the appearance of the show you're about to give. In the Slide Show area, for example, you'll find a pop-up menu with choices including:

- **Pop-up menu button.** Turning on this option means that when you twitch the mouse during your slide show, PowerPoint will make a subtle toolbar appear in the lower-left corner. Clicking it gives you the same pop-up menu of useful controls (Next, Previous, End Show, and so on) that you'd usually get only by Control-clicking the screen.

- **Slide Navigator.** If you choose this option, then you'll see a peculiar, detached scroll bar floating near the bottom of each slide (Figure 16-5 shows the bar). You can use it to navigate your slide show: click the left- and right-pointing triangle buttons to advance or retreat through your slides, or use the scroll bar to jump around in the show. As you scroll, PowerPoint pops up slide miniatures on the Slide Navigator bar, making it easy to stop scrolling at the correct slide.

The Preferences→View tab also offers an "End with black slide" checkbox, which is well worth turning on. That way, when you reach the end of your slide show, you won't awkwardly drop back into the disorganized world of icons and menus that will shatter the illusion of tidiness you've so carefully projected.

Presenting on screen

Your formal wear is clean and pressed. Now the moment has come—it's time to run your show. Once you have it loaded and ready to go, PowerPoint gives you three ways to put your show up on the screen.

Any one of the following options starts the slide show:

- Click the Slide Show view button in the lower-left corner of the main window. (It looks like an old-time home movie screen—the rightmost button.)

- Choose Slide Show→View Show.

- Choose View→Slide Show.

At this point, the program fills the screen with your first slide (or, in some cases, with the slide that was previously selected). Unless you've chosen to use preset timings, the first slide stays on the screen until you manually switch to the next slide (by clicking the mouse or pressing the Space bar, for example).

PowerPoint gives you several ways to move around: A simple mouse click or a press of the Space bar moves you to the next slide, as does pressing the down arrow or right arrow key. (One exception: If you've set up an animation on a slide, these advance keys trigger the animation instead of summoning the next slide. More on animations later.)

After you've reached the end of the show, PowerPoint returns you to its previous view.

Note: If you rehearsed your slide show and chose to save your timings, the show will play automatically to the end, displaying each slide for the predetermined number of seconds.

While your slide show is running, you can Control-click anywhere on the screen to bring up a contextual menu that offers such self-explanatory navigation options as Next, Previous, and End Show. It also gives you some less obvious options that are worth pointing out:

- **Meeting Minder** opens a floating window in which you can enter minutes of your meeting or list action items to be taken up after the meeting.

  Later, you can export these notes to Word for printing, distribution, and follow-up. To do so, choose Tools→Meeting Minder and click the Export to Word button.

- **Pointer Options,** as you might imagine, let you pick the kind of onscreen cursor you want to use—Automatic, Hidden, Arrow, or Pen. (Automatic gives Power-Point the authority to choose a pointer for you; Hidden makes the pointer go away; Arrow is the standard Mac arrow-shaped pointer; and Pen turns the pointer into a writing tool; see Figure 16-5.)

- Finally, the **Screen** submenu's commands let you pause a running slide show that's otherwise on autopilot, put up a black screen during a discussion, or erase any graffiti that you made with the aforementioned pen tool.

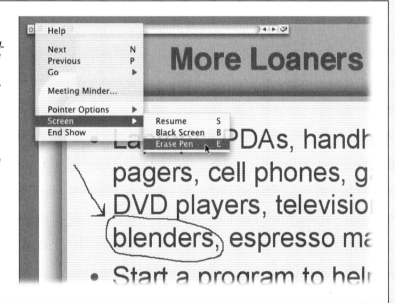

Figure 16-5:
To view the contextual menu in a slide show, either Control-click a slide or, if you've turned on the Slide Navigator bar (top left) in the PowerPoint→Preferences→View tab, click the Slide Show Controls button on the bar. The resulting menu (shown here) gives you a lot of power; for example, you can choose Pen from the Pointer Options submenu and then scribble circles, arrows, underlines, and other real-time doodles on your slides during the presentation. (You can later erase your additions by choosing Screen→Erase Pen from the contextual menu.)

Controlling the show

Here's the rundown on helpful keystrokes you can use while the slide show is running:

What to do	How to do it
Next slide (or start an animation)	Mouse click, Space bar, Return, N, Enter, right arrow, down arrow, Page down
Previous slide or animation	left arrow, up arrow, Page up, P, Delete
End a slide show	⌘-period, hyphen, Esc
Jump to a certain slide number	a number key and then Return
Jump to the first slide/last slide	Home, End
To/from a black screen	B, period
To/from a white screen	W, comma

Putting Controls on Slides

If you don't feel like memorizing keystrokes, you can embed a host of useful command buttons (for advancing slides, jumping to the end of the show, and so on) right on the slide when you're preparing the show. You can place buttons on individual slides or many slides at once:

- If you want to add a button to just one slide, switch into Normal view or Slide view, and bring up the slide in question.

- If you want to add a button to the same location in a group of slides—or all of them—place it on the slide master. Start by choosing View→Master→Slide Master. (See page 579 for a refresher on working with the slide master.)

Note: Don't try this shortcut if you'll be saving your presentation as a QuickTime movie. For QuickTime movies, you must put the buttons on each slide individually.

Once the slide where you want to stick your button is showing, make sure the Drawing toolbar is also showing. (Choose View→Toolbars→Drawing if it's not.) On the Drawing toolbar, use the AutoShapes pop-up button to choose from the Action Buttons submenu (see Figure 16-6).

UP TO SPEED

Using a Projector

The screen on Apple's PowerBook G4 may be big, but it's still not big enough for a conference room full of your colleagues. Many PowerPoint slide shows, therefore, are destined to be displayed by big, TV-style monitors or by special projectors that throw those slides onto a large screen.

Every current PowerBook, iBook, Power Mac, and iMac model has a *video out* connector on the back or side panel, which lets you connect the computer to a projector that can take either VGA or S-video input. (Older iBooks and

iMacs lack this jack. Some laptop models require a small adapter cable.)

Connect your Mac's video out port to the projector's video in port. Then you can use the Displays panel of System Preferences if you need to turn *mirroring* on or off. (Mirroring is when two screens show exactly the same thing.) You'll find the Mirror Displays checkbox on the Arrange tab.

Once you've got your Mac's video desktop showing up on the projector, you can run your slide show on the big screen.

On the Action Buttons palette are twelve buttons. The four in the middle of the palette help you jump around during the show: Previous Slide, Next Slide, First Slide, and Last Slide.

To put an Action Button on your slide, click the button you want. (Alternatively, choose a button name from the Slide Show→Action Buttons submenu.) Then drag diagonally on the slide as though using one of PowerPoint's drawing tools. Power-Point draws the button for you, then opens up the Action Settings dialog box shown in Figure 16-6.

In this box, you can specify exactly what your newly created button will do. The proposed settings are fine for most purposes, so you can generally just click OK. It's worth noting, however, that you can use these controls to make your button do much fancier tricks, as described in Figure 16-6.

(By default, your action will be triggered when you *click* the corresponding button. But if you click the Mouse Over tab in the Action Settings dialog box, you can also specify that something happens instead when you just point to it.)

Later, when the slide show is running, press the A key to make the arrow cursor appear, then click your newly created button to trigger the associated event.

Caution: Planning to save your show as a QuickTime movie? Watch out for action settings that don't work out well with movies! For example, Microsoft recommends that you avoid all mouse overs; hyperlinks to last slide viewed, end of show, custom show, other PowerPoint presentation, other file, and email address; run program and run macro; object action; play sound; and highlight click.

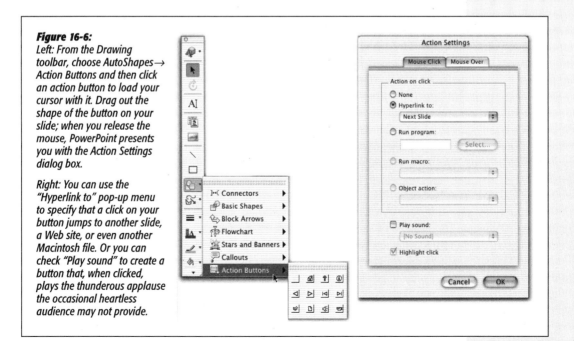

Figure 16-6:
Left: From the Drawing toolbar, choose AutoShapes→ Action Buttons and then click an action button to load your cursor with it. Drag out the shape of the button on your slide; when you release the mouse, PowerPoint presents you with the Action Settings dialog box.

Right: You can use the "Hyperlink to" pop-up menu to specify that a click on your button jumps to another slide, a Web site, or even another Macintosh file. Or you can check "Play sound" to create a button that, when clicked, plays the thunderous applause the occasional heartless audience may not provide.

You can put any of eight other Action Buttons on your slides. Some come with pre-set icons and some have preset Action Settings that match their individual functions. **Custom** lets you customize your own action button (by running a macro or launching a program); **Home** zips back to the first slide in the show; **Help** lets you create a link to a help slide that you've designed; **Information creates** a link to an information slide that you've added; **Last Slide Viewed** takes you back to the last slide you saw (which, if you've been jumping around, isn't necessarily the slide before this one in sequence); **Document** launches a Macintosh file or program that you specify; **Sound** triggers a sound; and **Movie** starts rolling a movie that you've set up beforehand.

If you want to change the appearance of an Action Button—or any other AutoShape—double-click on the button to bring up the Format AutoShape dialog box.

Tip: You don't have to use one of the predrawn shapes on the Action Buttons palette as your visible button; PowerPoint can turn *any* graphic object into a button. Just Control-click it and choose Action Settings from the contextual menu, then proceed as described in the preceding paragraphs.

Recycling Your Presentations

PowerPoint lets you create multiple custom shows in a single document. This feature comes in handy if, for example, you want to have both long and abbreviated versions of the same show, or if you want to tailor some material you've used before to a different audience. It's also great for creating shows that *branch*. Anyone who's using your document in a one-on-one situation can follow different branches by clicking hyperlinked buttons. You could even get fancy and give each branch a different slide master.

But let's take the first case. Suppose you're going to address two different groups on the topic of deer. You have lots of great slides on the topic. But there's a good chance the group from the Bambi Fan Club wouldn't sit through the show you've got planned for Hunters Anonymous. You could solve this moral dilemma by creating a *customized show* for each group, each of whose slides are a subset of the complete deer presentation.

To build such a custom show, choose Slide Shows→Custom Shows. The resulting dialog box gives you four choices: New, Edit, Remove, and Copy.

When you click New, a dialog box pops up that lets you choose the slides you want to include in the custom show (Figure 16-7). You can also reorder the slides in your custom show and give your custom show a name.

Then, when it's time to give the actual presentation, choose Slide Shows→Custom Shows to bring up a window that lists the custom shows you've built. Click the one you want to present and then click Show; your custom show now begins.

Hiding slides

There may be times when you want to hide a slide from view without actually deleting it. The slide needs more work, for example, or it's not appropriate for a certain audience. There are a couple of ways to go about preventing a slide from showing up in slide shows. First, you can select the slide you want to hide and then select Slide Show→Hide Slide. You can also use the Slide Sorter view to hide slides by selecting the slides you want to hide and then clicking the Hide Slide button in the Slide Sorter toolbar. (If that toolbar isn't visible, choose View→Toolbars→Slide Sorter.) PowerPoint simply skips over hidden slides when you run the slide show.

To bring a hidden slide back into view, Control-click it in Slide Sorter view and select Hide Slide to turn off the checkmark.

Figure 16-7:
Using the Define Custom Show dialog box, you can choose a subset of slides from the currently open slide show and reorder those slides any way you want to create a customized presentation.

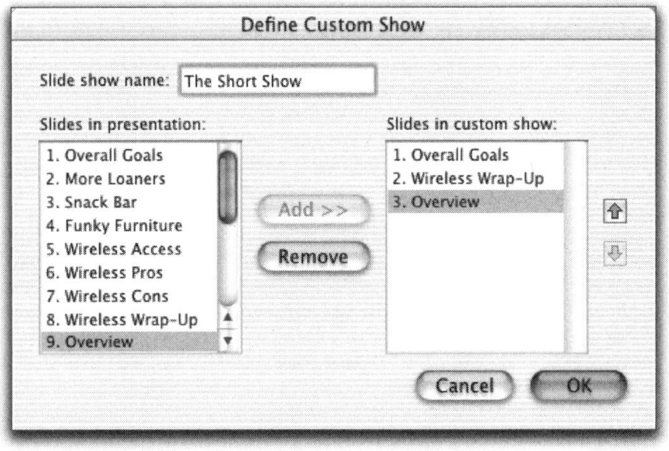

Multimedia Effects

PowerPoint puts at your disposal a Spielbergian selection of special effects. In addition to the transitions you insert between slides, the program lets you animate particular elements in an image. It also enables you to add a soundtrack or voice narration to your slide show—features that are especially useful if you want to save the presentation as a stand-alone movie.

Adding Animations

One of the simplest ways to jazz up a PowerPoint presentation is to animate an element in a slide—be it text, an image, or even a movie. Animated objects whisk into view when triggered by an advance key, then dart away the next time you press the same key. You can control the animated object's path of motion and also choose whether its action is accompanied by a sound effect.

As always, these effects do nothing to make up for lack of a meaningful message in your presentation, and seem primarily designed for making glitzy demos of Power-Point at trade shows; use them sparingly and with good taste.

Tip: You've been warned: Animations may not show up when you export your PowerPoint presentation as a QuickTime movie (as described on page 614), especially if you've also created transitions between slides.

Standard animations

To animate an object using one of PowerPoint's ready-made special effects, first select the object you want to animate—click inside a block of text or click an image, for example.

Note: Not all standard animations work with all kinds of objects. Laser Text and Typewriter, for instance, affect only text, not graphics. If a particular effect isn't applicable to the object you've selected, that option is grayed out on the Animations menu.

Then choose an animation style from the Slide Show→Animations submenu, which offers fourteen different animations (plus an Off option to remove an animation). A few examples:

- **Fly In.** The selected object shoots in from the left with a *swish* sound and comes to rest at its rightful spot in the layout.

- **Fly Out.** The selected object pops off the slide and exits to the right with the same *swish.*

- **Fly In/Out.** The selected object flies onto the slide from the left and lands in its proper position, then, with another press of the advance key, rockets off to the right. An audible *swish* accompanies both motions.

FREQUENTLY ASKED QUESTION

Bullet by Bullet

I've seen these really tall, smart, good-looking people do presentations where their bullet lists don't show up all at once. Instead, each point whooshes onto the screen on command. Can I do that too?

It's easy to animate the arrival of your bullets. Choose Slide Show→Animations→Custom, click the Effects tab, and then select the text object (the one that contains your bullets) in the box to the left. From the "Entry effect" pop-up menu, choose an animation style (such as Fly In From Left, by far the most popular choice among tall, smart, good-

looking people).

If you click OK, your bullet points will now fly in one at a time, each time you click the mouse (or press an advance key). If you click the Order and Timing tab, you can specify instead that they appear a certain number of seconds apart. And, if you click the Options tab, you can choose the bullet level that you want to group together—something that will make sense only if you've actually created bulleted lists *within* bulleted lists.

- **Drive-In/Out.** The selected object enters the slide from the right and, with the sound of a car motor and screeching tires, skids into its resting place. Another press of the advance key sends the object off the slide to the left with the same infernal racket.

- **Flash Once.** No sound here. The selected object simply flashes once in a silent, subliminal kind of way.

- **Dissolve.** The selected object gradually materializes before your eyes, a few pixels at a time.

- **Appear.** In this, the simplest of all PowerPoint's animations, the selected item just pops into its predetermined spot on the slide.

Tip: To preview an animation, choose Slide Show→Animation Preview. A little window pops up, showing you just how the animation looks when it kicks in (although in this preview, you don't have to click the mouse or press a key to trigger each phase of the animation).

Custom animations

If none of the preset animations suits your fancy, you can fiddle with them to create an effect you like better. The Custom Animation dialog box is the shop where you soup up animations and control multiple animations on the same slide. To open this window, choose Slide Show→Animations→Custom, or click the Customize button in the Animation section of the Formatting Palette.

In the Custom Animation dialog box (Figure 16-8), you can exercise control over almost every aspect of an animated object, such as how it enters or exits a slide and what sounds it makes. This is also where you let PowerPoint know which animations to trigger if you have *more* than one per slide.

The left side of the Custom Animation dialog box shows a list of all the text boxes, graphics, and other objects on the slide. To animate one of these objects or adjust the animation style you've already applied, click the one you want to work with. Below that list is a Preview pane with Stop and Play buttons; use these, if you wish, to show how your adjustments have affected the slide.

The Custom Animation window has three tabbed sections: Effects, Order and Timing, and Options. Here's an overview of their functions:

- **Effects.** Using the five pop-up menus in this section, you can choose what animated effect PowerPoint uses to whisk an object on or off the slide, and whether an effect happens with or without sound; you can choose from among the program's sixteen preset sounds or select an "Other Sound" from your hard drive. You can choose from the "After animation" pop-up menu to add a color effect to an animated object after it has made its grand entrance on the screen. For instance, after a new bullet point has flown onto the screen in brilliant orange to get the audience's eye, you might decide that it should settle down into a more demure color to match the other bullet points that have already arrived.

- **Order and Timing.** When you have more than one animated object on a slide, use this tab to specify their arrival order. The Animation order box lists all animations scheduled for the slide. After clicking a white area of the box to deselect them, you can change their order by selecting an animation's name and then clicking the up or down arrow buttons. Come here also to tell PowerPoint how you want the animations to be triggered—either with a click of the mouse, or automatically after a given number of seconds.

- **Options.** This tab lets you set options for any other programs or media that you've selected to use as part of your presentation. For example, if you're planning to show a QuickTime movie clip, here's where you instruct PowerPoint whether to pause or continue the slide show while the movie is playing, and also whether to show the movie just once or to loop it continuously until you tell it to stop. If you have text selected for animation, use this tab to choose whether it enters the slide all at once, one word at a time, or one *letter* at a time.

Once you've customized your animations, click OK to close the window.

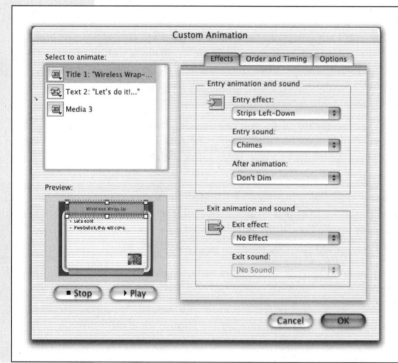

Figure 16-8:
The Custom Animation dialog box is animation headquarters, your personal Dreamworks studio. Its pop-up menus give you access to tons of animation effects—far more than the paltry fourteen

Narration

If you're worried about laryngitis on the day of your presentation, if you're creating a self-running kiosk show, or if you have an unnatural fear of public *squeaking*, you might want to record voice narration for your slide show ahead of time. That way, you can sit back and relax while your confident, disembodied voice plays along with the show.

To add recorded narration to your presentation, you need a Mac with a microphone, of course. (PowerBooks and iMacs have built-in mikes; USB microphones are available for Power Macs, Cubes, and iBooks; and older Power Macs came with a small plastic microphone and corresponding jack.) You might want to visit the Speech panel of System Preferences (click the Listening tab) to make sure that you've selected the correct microphone for input. Quit all other sound-recording programs, if any are running. Then:

1. **Choose Slide Show→Record Narration to bring up the Record Narration dialog box.**

    This box shows the current recording settings, including your maximum recording time based on your free hard-drive space. Since sound files can be huge, the "Link narrations" checkbox lets you save your narration files to any location you like, such as an external hard drive with plenty of free space, rather than embedding them in the presentation file. Click Set to choose where PowerPoint saves linked narrations. When you finish recording, that location will contain one AIFF sound file for each slide in your presentation.

Note: If you link your narrations, moving your presentation to another machine will break the links. (As always, the PowerPoint Package format avoids this problem, as discussed on page 592.)

---

2. **Click Record.**

    PowerPoint starts running through your presentation. As you advance through the slides, PowerPoint makes a separate, linked AIFF sound file for each slide. Or, if you didn't link the recording, PowerPoint attaches the audio you recorded as a sound object on each slide.

    There's no easy way to re-record just one flubbed slide; for most purposes, it's simplest to start over with a new "take." To start over, end the slide show using whatever method you normally use (press Esc for instance). Then, choose Slide Show→Record Narration and begin again. (And if you're *really* having trouble, you can always record individual sound files for each slide, then attach them as described on page 593.)

Note: These voice clips override any other sound effects in the slide show, so if you're using a recorded narration, embedded sound effects (including transition sounds) don't play.

---

3. **Record whatever you want to say for each slide; advance the slides as you normally would (by clicking the mouse, for example).**

    When you reach the end of the slide show, PowerPoint asks if you want to save the timings (to record the amount of time you spent on each slide) along with your narration. If you click No, PowerPoint saves only the narration. If you click Yes, PowerPoint saves the timings along with the narration, overwriting any existing timings.

If you choose not to include the timings, each sound will play when you manually advance to a given slide. In that way, you can let the narration play and then have some discussion with each slide, moving on only when you're ready.

Warning: Voice recordings can eat up a lot of disk space, so be sure you have enough room on your hard drive to hold the sound. If not, consider saving your voice files to an external hard drive or some other industrial-strength storage area.

Once you're done recording your narration, you've got a self-contained slide show, suitable for parties or board meetings.

Saving Presentations as QuickTime Movies

PowerPoint X's predecessor, PowerPoint 2001, introduced a great new feature: the ability to save presentations as QuickTime movies. This is a nifty idea for two reasons: Anyone with QuickTime installed—Mac users, Windows users, whoever—can play these movies even if they don't have PowerPoint. That's a great way for your associates and underlings to give the same kinds of pitches you give without having to spring for a copy of Office. Also, a presentation movie thus converted can be opened and edited in PowerPoint as if it were a PowerPoint file.

Note: PowerPoint Viewer 98 is a utility for playing PowerPoint presentations on Macs that don't have PowerPoint. You can download it from Microsoft's Web site (in PowerPoint, choose Help→Visit the Mactopia Web Site, or point your browser at *www.mactopia.com*).

Viewer 98 still plays many PowerPoint X presentations, but it doesn't handle exit animations, graphic bullets, QuickTime Transitions, or animated GIFs. In general, the Save as Movie option described on these pages is far more flexible and compatible with far more computers.

Before you proceed, remember that not every bell and whistle of a PowerPoint slide show survives the conversion into a QuickTime movie. As noted here and there throughout this chapter, things like action buttons on master slides, certain PowerPoint transitions, and certain actions (mouse overs, certain kinds of links, play sound, and so on) won't work at all.

To turn an open PowerPoint presentation into a QuickTime movie, choose File→Make Movie. This brings up a Save dialog box, which you can use to name your movie file and choose a folder location for it.

As you save your movie, PowerPoint gives you a chance to fine-tune some of its settings. To begin, turn on the Adjust Settings radio button. Now click Save. PowerPoint responds by opening the Movie Options dialog box shown in Figure 16-9.

The most important settings worth examining here are Movie Dimensions (see Figure 16-9) and the Optimization pop-up menu. The latter lets you specify which you value more: compact file size, smooth playback of animations, or picture quality. Depending on the complexity of your file and the screen size you've specified, these virtues may be mutually exclusive; if you want the highest quality animations, for example, the file won't be very small on your hard drive, and the quality of animated photos may suffer.

Tip: After you've saved your slide show as a QuickTime movie, you may notice your PowerPoint transitions acting a little flaky. Microsoft has identified the following transitions as being definite problems: Blinds, Box, Checkerboard, Dissolve, Random Bars, Strips, and Wipe. As a general rule, use QuickTime transitions if you plan to convert your show into a movie.

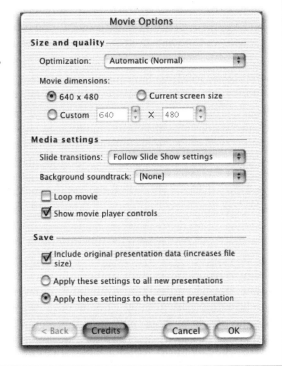

Figure 16-9:
This dialog box lets you specify the size of the QuickTime movie; 640 x 480 won't fill most of today's 15-inch or larger screens. Using the "Background soundtrack" pop-up menu, you can choose an MP3 file or another file to play during the whole slide show—a handy option in self-running, kiosk situations. Notice the radio buttons in the Save area that let you select whether PowerPoint should use your new settings for just this presentation or use them for future presentations as well.

This dialog box also lets you import a sound file to use as a soundtrack. Chosen tastefully, music or some other nondistracting sound (rainfall or ocean waves, perhaps) can make your movie a more well-rounded presentation. Tread carefully, though, to avoid crossing that fine line between "nondistracting" and "sleep-inducing." These background sound files can be in any number of formats, including AIFF, QuickTime audio, WAV, and MP3.

To add a background soundtrack, choose Select Soundtrack in the Background soundtrack pop-up menu. PowerPoint asks you to locate the sound file that you want to use, which it then attaches to your presentation when you click OK. Power-Point will mix the soundtrack sound with any embedded sounds, including voice narration.

Finally, the Movie Options window lets you decide whether PowerPoint adds the *presentation data* to the movie file. If you choose this option, you or your colleagues will be able to reopen the movie file *right back into PowerPoint* for further editing—a truly impressive stunt. However, you'll make the resulting movie file much bigger on the disk.

Saving Presentations for the Web

PowerPoint lets you create presentation files that are formatted, coded, and ready to be posted on the Internet. With just a few mouse clicks, you can save your slide show as a Web page, complete with some nifty JavaScript programming that gives viewers a high level of control over how they watch your show.

Before you move your presentation onto the Web, you'll first want to see how it looks after the conversion. To preview your presentation as a Web page, choose File→Web Page Preview. PowerPoint generates all the necessary graphics, HTML, and JavaScript coding, then transfers the whole enchilada into your browser. You can then use your browser to click your way through the presentation, which actually looks very much as it would if you were viewing it in PowerPoint's Normal (three-pane) view.

To save your presentation as a Web page (or rather, a set of them), choose File→Save as Web Page. PowerPoint asks where you'd like to save your show. Clicking Web Options opens a dialog box that lets you tell the program such things as what colors to use, where to place navigation buttons, and how to encode images. Once you're satisfied with the options you've chosen, click OK. To actually save the presentation, click Save. PowerPoint automatically renders your presentation as HTML files com-

---

TROUBLESHOOTING MOMENT

Funky Fonts

When viewing a presentation that's been converted into a Web page, you may notice that the fonts don't fit quite right—a by-product of the fact that the HTML language of Web pages isn't terrifically brilliant about managing fonts. Although PowerPoint does its best to compensate, sometimes type rendered in HTML is just too large for the allotted space, so chunks of text bump down to the next line.

You can do a couple of things to combat this fat-font problem. Keep your font sizes a shade smaller than you ordinarily would, and try not to squeeze too much copy on a single line. And whenever possible, avoid tables with multiple lines of text; these babies are just *waiting* to bunch together and run over.

plete with embedded JavaScript and accompanying Web-ready graphics files. You wind up with a home page and a folder full of HTML files, graphics files, and sound files. You can upload these files to your Web server as you would any other Web page files (see page 304).

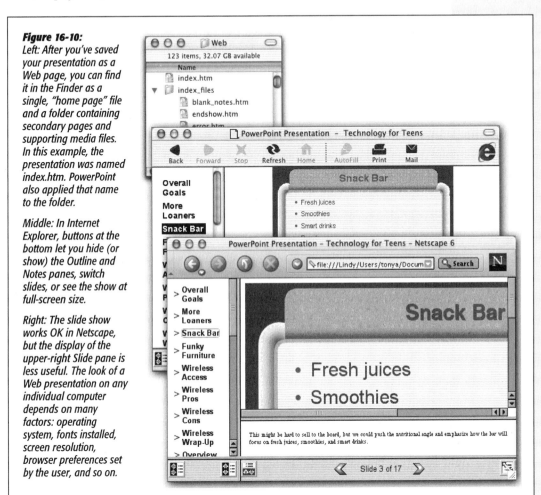

Figure 16-10:
Left: After you've saved your presentation as a Web page, you can find it in the Finder as a single, "home page" file and a folder containing secondary pages and supporting media files. In this example, the presentation was named index.htm. PowerPoint also applied that name to the folder.

Middle: In Internet Explorer, buttons at the bottom let you hide (or show) the Outline and Notes panes, switch slides, or see the show at full-screen size.

Right: The slide show works OK in Netscape, but the display of the upper-right Slide pane is less useful. The look of a Web presentation on any individual computer depends on many factors: operating system, fonts installed, screen resolution, browser preferences set by the user, and so on.

Saving Slides as Graphics

Among its many other gifts, PowerPoint allows you to save individual slides—text and all—as graphics files. This can be a handy little feature whenever you want to make sharp-looking, high-resolution images of your presentation to pass along to your friends (or your agent).

To save a PowerPoint slide as a graphics file, first open the slide you want to convert, then follow these few steps:

1. **Choose File→Save As.**

   A dialog box appears, offering several options.

2. **From the Format pop-up menu, select a graphics file format.**

   JPEG is a great choice for photos; PICT is good, too, but it's a Macintosh-only format. Use GIF or PNG (see page 288) for smaller files, especially if you intend to use the resulting still images on a Web page and if your audience will be using relatively recent versions of the popular Web browsers.

3. **Click Options.**

   At the bottom of the resulting Preferences window, you can choose whether you want PowerPoint to save *all* the slides in the show as graphics or just this one. In addition, you can set up the file resolution and dimensions. (The dimensions is an important setting; you don't want your monitor to chop off part of the slides.) Finally, you can specify whether to compress the file (smaller files, worse quality).

Tip: You don't need to set up these options time after time; you can set up your preferred settings only once, on the PowerPoint→Preferences→Save tab. There you'll find the identical graphics-saving options, which affect the proposed values for all your subsequent graphics-saving exploits.

---

4. **Change the settings as desired, click OK, then name the still image and click Save.**

   If you opted to save all of the slides, PowerPoint automatically creates a *folder* bearing your file's name. Inside the folder are the individual graphics files, with names like Slide1.jpg, Slide2.jpg, and so on.

Printing Your Presentation

Although PowerPoint is primarily meant to throw images onto a monitor or projector, you can also print out your presentations on good old-fashioned paper—which is especially useful, of course, for printing handouts, overheads, and notes. Whatever the format, all printing is done through the same basic procedure: Open the presentation you want to print, make a few adjustments in the Page Setup dialog box and the Print dialog box, then fire away.

Page Setup

Before printing your presentation, you should pop open the hood and take a peek at the Page Setup dialog box (see Figure 16-11). After all, this important window is the engine that controls the size of your slides, whether they're for onscreen viewing or printing. Be sure to make any size adjustments early in the game; if you fiddle with the knobs in Page Setup *after* the slide has been made, it'll stretch to fit, possibly giving the image a warped or distorted look, or knocking certain graphics off the edges altogether.

You can use the settings in this dialog box to morph your slide show into something appropriate for another format—taking it from an overhead projector to a Web banner, for instance. Also, if you want to send your presentation out to be printed, you can adjust the presentation's resolution by clicking the Options button in the Save dialog box.

To open the Page Setup dialog box, choose File→Page Setup. Doing so brings you face to face with Microsoft's version of the Page Setup box, which presents you with a pop-up menu offering preset slide sizes: On-screen show, US Letter, US Ledger, A3, A4, B4, B5, 35mm slides, Overhead, and Web banner (Figure 16-11, top). If you have a custom slide size in mind, you can set its width and height here as well.

Figure 16-11:
Top: The basic options in the Page Setup dialog box let you size your slides and set a separate orientation (portrait or landscape) for slides and other documents–notes, handouts, and outlines–that you want to print.

Bottom: If you choose Microsoft PowerPoint in the Print dialog box, you gain access to several important options, including the various printout types shown in the Print What pop-up menu. Further, you can shrink your document to fit the available paper; print in color, grayscale, or pure black and white; print any hidden slides; or put a snappy little frame around each slide printout or thumbnail on a handout. Finally, the Preview button can save you a lot of time; click it to generate a Preview document.

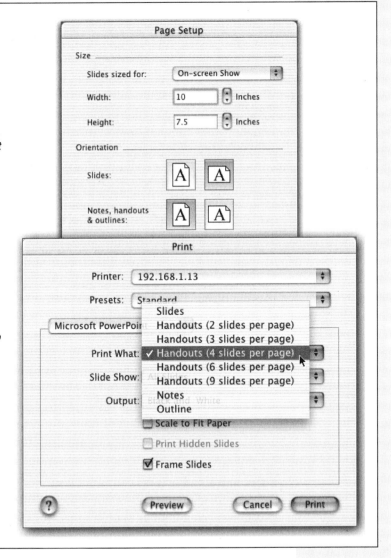

Click Header/Footer to make text (such as a slide number, page number, or date) appear on the top or bottom of every slide, or every note and handout. On each tab in the Header and Footer dialog box, click the checkboxes and watch the Preview at the lower right to see where the different text elements appear. Once you've turned on a checkbox, select the box's related options and enter text as appropriate.

For example, working in the Slide tab, you can insert a slide number at the lower right corner of each printed slide (or slide thumbnail on a handout) by turning on "Slide number" and then entering a starting slide number. Turn on "Don't show on title slide" at the bottom of the dialog box if you'd like that number hidden on *title* slides. (A title slide is usually the first slide in your presentation, but title slides can theoretically appear anywhere in the show.)

Printing Your Slides

When you're ready to commit your presentation to paper, choose File→Print (⌘-P) to bring up the Print dialog box. Here's where you tell PowerPoint exactly what you want to print—slides, handouts, notes, or an outline.

In the Print dialog box, from the Copies & Pages pop-up menu, choose Microsoft PowerPoint to reveal special, PowerPoint-related print settings (see Figure 16-11, bottom). Here, you can select which chunks of your presentation you want to print (slides, handouts, notes, or the outline). From this spot you can also choose to print a custom show, if you created one earlier. When you're ready, click Preview to check your choices one last time, or click Print to send your document to the printer.

Notes and Handouts

It didn't take the world long to dispel the myth of the paperless office, and that's evident every time your audience asks you for a hard copy of your presentation. Sure, you can steer some audiences to the Web version of your presentation that you've cleverly posted to the Web in advance (be sure to point this out to your boss as a cost-saving measure you've adopted). But when that approach fails, PowerPoint can print out your notes and handouts or convert them to PDF files for electronic distribution.

Every PowerPoint slide can have *notes* attached to it: written tidbits to help you get through your presentation, or to clarify points for your audience. As you build your presentation, the Notes pane in PowerPoint's Normal view provides a place to type notes for each slide as it's active. (These notes appear on Web pages if you leave "Include slide notes" checked in the Appearance tab of the Web Options dialog box when saving your presentation as a Web page.)

Handouts are printouts of your slides, usually featuring multiple slides per sheet of paper. They let your audience take your entire show away with them on paper, to spare them from having to take notes during the meeting. Handouts don't include notes; you'll have to print those out separately.

Note: Both notes and handouts have master pages, which work the same as slide masters; see page 579 for details.

To print your notes and handouts, choose File→Print (⌘-P) and then select Microsoft PowerPoint from the Copies & Pages pop-up menu. This brings up the settings specific to PowerPoint. In the Print What pop-up menu, you can choose to print notes or handouts in layouts that contain two, three, four, six, or nine slide miniatures per sheet. Here again, if you click Preview, you'll be shown an onscreen preview of the printout-in-waiting, which you can save as an Acrobat (PDF) file by choosing File→Save As PDF.

Tip: You can choose the Layout item in the Copies & Pages pop-up menu to print one, two, four, six, nine, or sixteen slides per page. With Layout chosen, use the "Pages per Sheet" pop-up menu; your printer will substitute one slide per page. (You won't see your custom layout in Preview, but it will print.)

Part Five:
Microsoft Office as a Whole

5

Customizing Office

Microsoft desperately wants the approval of Mac fans; its programmers seem willing to do almost anything to make Office X a hit. For example, its software design seems to subscribe to the theory, "If you don't like something, change it yourself."

Very few elements of the way you work with Office are set in stone. Word, Excel, and PowerPoint each let you redesign the toolbars and even rework the menus. In Word and (for the first time) Excel, you can also choose different keyboard equivalents for commands. (Only Entourage is off-the-rack software. You can't work it over in the same ways.)

Even if you're a novice, customization is worth exploring. There will almost certainly come a day when you wish you could choose an easier keystroke for some function than the one Microsoft chose. With this chapter as your guide, you can.

Customizing Your Toolbars

One way to customize your toolbars is to drag them around the screen and change their shapes to fit your whims (and your monitor shape). To move a toolbar, just drag it, using its skinny title bar (next to the close button) as a handle.

You'll soon discover that toolbars are "magnetic." That is, they like to snap against the sides of the monitor, other toolbars, the Formatting Palette, or to the Office Assistant's window—just about anything except an actual document window.

Tip: This snappiness is designed to help you keep your screen tidy, but if you want to stifle your toolbars' social tendencies, press Shift as you drag them.

You can also reshape your toolbar by resizing it as if it were a window: just drag the diagonally striped area in the lower-right corner, as shown in Figure 17-1.

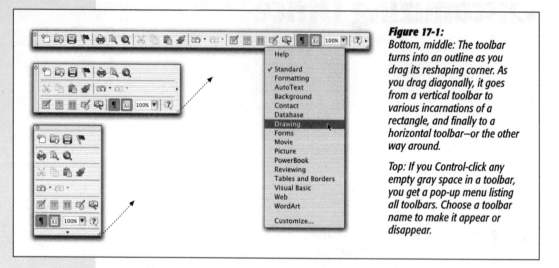

Figure 17-1:
Bottom, middle: The toolbar turns into an outline as you drag its reshaping corner. As you drag diagonally, it goes from a vertical toolbar to various incarnations of a rectangle, and finally to a horizontal toolbar—or the other way around.

Top: If you Control-click any empty gray space in a toolbar, you get a pop-up menu listing all toolbars. Choose a toolbar name to make it appear or disappear.

Showing Other Toolbars

Excel, PowerPoint, and Word each come with a toolbar or two that pop up when the program opens, but that's just the beginning. In fact, Word has 24 toolbars, PowerPoint has 17, and Excel has 23, each dedicated to a certain purpose (such as graphics work, Web design, or reviewing comments). Some toolbars appear automatically when you use a related command or open a corresponding editing area. Others you can summon or dismiss as you need them.

You can go about opening and closing toolbars in any of three ways:

- Control-click the More Buttons toolbar icon (usually at the far right or bottom edge of an open toolbar or palette), or Control-click an empty area on any open toolbar or palette. As shown in Figure 17-1, you get a pop-up menu of what Microsoft considers to be the most useful toolbars. Choose the name of the one you'd like to open or close.

- Choose from the View→Toolbars submenu. Here again, you see over a dozen of the most important toolbars.

- Choose Tools→Customize, and then click the Toolbars tab. Now you see a list of *all* of the toolbars, even the obscure ones. Click a checkbox to make the corresponding toolbar appear or disappear instantly. (Because you don't even have to close the dialog box between experiments, this is the fastest way to have a quick look at all the available toolbars.) Click OK to close the dialog box.

Creating Custom Toolbars

The likelihood of Microsoft *perfectly* predicting which buttons you'd like on which toolbars is about the same as finding the shoes you want, in your size, in the right color, at the first shoe store you visit. Fortunately, it's very easy to delete or add buttons on Excel, PowerPoint, or Word toolbars. In fact, you can, and should, create entirely new toolbars that contain nothing but your own favorite buttons. If you use Word's styles, as described on page 141, for example, it's a no-brainer to create a palette of your favorite styles, so that you can apply them with single click.

To move a button or delete it from a toolbar

To move a button, open the Customize dialog box by choosing Tools→Customize and then just drag the button to a new spot on the toolbar—or even to another toolbar. (You can ignore the Customize dialog box itself for the moment. Although it seems counterintuitive, the Customize dialog box needs to be open for this dragging to work). The button assumes its new place, and the other buttons rearrange themselves to make room.

To get rid of a button, Control-click the button you wish to remove, and then choose Hide Command from the contextual menu that appears. If you already have the Customize dialog box open, you can delete a button by dragging it off the toolbar to the desktop or anywhere else in the document window. (Either way, you can get the button back later if you like; read on.)

To add a button or design a new toolbar from scratch

Every now and then, you'll wish you had a one-shot button that triggers some useful command—for inserting the current date into your document, for example.

To add a button to an existing toolbar, choose Tools→Customize, and then click the Commands tab. A list of command categories appears, grouped by menu, along with the actual commands in each category. It's a staggeringly long list that includes almost every command in the program.

You'll notice that the names of Office's commands in the All Commands list are a tad user-hostile. No spaces are allowed, and the name of the command often runs together with the menu that contains it (such as ToolsSpelling). You'll also notice that each of your Office programs offers *hundreds* of commands that don't appear in the regular menus. Furthermore, the names of some commands don't quite correspond to their menu bar equivalents. For example, the command for Insert→Comment is InsertAnnotation in the All Commands list.

Tip: Trying to move around quickly in the All Commands category? You can type a letter (or letters) to move to the part of the list beginning with that letter. For instance, type *v* to scroll to commands for viewing or *ins* to jump to commands for inserting.

You can drag *any* of the commands in the Customize dialog box onto a toolbar, as shown in Figure 17-2. Some of them even take the form of pop-up menus, such as Font Color, which then become part of your toolbar. In fact, if you drag the com-

mand at the bottom of the Categories list called New Menu onto a toolbar, it turns
into a pop-up menu that you can fill with any commands you like. You might decide
to set up several custom pop-up menus filled with small lists of related styles—one
just for headings, for example. The more logical the arrangement, the quicker the
access. You can rename your homemade pop-up menu as described in the Tip below.

Weirder yet, look at the top of your screen—there's a *duplicate menu bar* there, floating
on its own toolbar! Click one of these phony menus to open it. Now you can drag
any menu command *right off the menu* onto your new toolbar, where it will be available for quicker access. Once buttons are on the toolbar, you can drag them around,
or even drag them off the toolbar to get rid of them, as long as you don't close the
Customize dialog box.

Tip: If you double-click a toolbar button or pop-up menu while the Customize dialog box is open, you
summon the Command Properties dialog box. Here's where you get to specify how you want the command to look in the toolbar: as a little icon, as a plain English word, or both (see the box on the facing
page). You can also add a separator line before the button (above it or to its left) by turning on "Begin a
group."

You can even perform this kind of button editing when the Customize window *isn't* open—in the middle of
your everyday work. The trick is to Control-click the button and choose Properties from the contextual
menu.

Designing a completely new toolbar works much the same way. Choose
Tools→Customize, select the Toolbars tab, and then click the New button. You'll be
asked to name your new toolbar, which then appears as an empty square floating

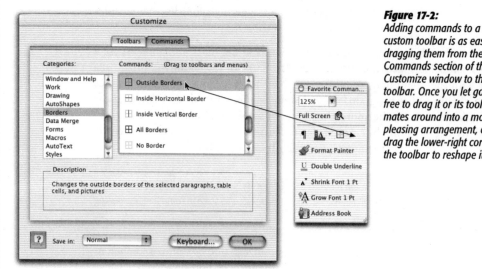

Figure 17-2:
*Adding commands to a
custom toolbar is as easy as
dragging them from the
Commands section of the
Customize window to the
toolbar. Once you let go, feel
free to drag it or its toolbar-
mates around into a more
pleasing arrangement, or
drag the lower-right corner of
the toolbar to reshape it.*

oddly above the Customize dialog box—a toolbar just waiting for you to provide commands. Now click the Commands tab and begin populating your new toolbar with commands and buttons, just as described earlier. Click OK when you're finished.

Attaching Custom Toolbars to Documents

In general, a toolbar you've created or edited is stored in the Normal template (see page 202), so that it will be available for use in any new documents you create. But after spending 20 minutes handcrafting the world's most brilliant toolbar, the last thing you want is to confine it forever to your own Mac.

Fortunately, you can pass on your brilliance to other people just by attaching the custom toolbar to an Excel workbook or a Word document (PowerPoint lacks this feature).

- **In Excel.** Choose Tools→Customize, then click the Toolbars tab. Click a toolbar's name in the pane on the left side of the Customize window, and then click Attach.

  The Attach Toolbars window appears. It works exactly like the Organizer, described and illustrated on page 207. Use it to select the destination document and copy the toolbar into it.

- **In Word.** Choose Tools→Templates and Add-Ins. Click the Organizer button. Use the Organizer described on page 207 to copy any toolbar into any document *or* template.

OBSESSIVE USERS' CLINIC

Drawing Your Own Buttons

Not all commands that you drag onto your toolbars come with associated picture buttons. Most of the time, all you get is a *text* button. If you'd prefer an icon, though, you can add one.

The trick is to Control-click the new button and choose the Properties command. You get the Command Properties dialog box, shown here, where you see a little blank button icon in the upper left corner. Click the pop-up menu attached to find 42 alternative button icons vying for your affection. If one of Microsoft's ready-made buttons will do, choose it from this pop-up menu.

If you don't care for any of Microsoft's microscopic masterpieces, you can design your own button in some other program (Photoshop or AppleWorks, let's say). Copy it, switch to the Office program you're editing, and then paste the graphic onto a button by choosing Paste Button Image from the menu. Microsoft recommends a 20 x 20 pixel image for maximum good looks. (If your menu doesn't have a Paste Button Image command, install Service Release 1, as described on page 12.)

To restore the button's original icon (or lack of icon), choose Reset Button Image at the bottom of the menu.

Note: When you open a Word document in which someone has embedded a homemade toolbar, a dialog box offers a word of caution. It lets you know that the toolbar could conceivably contain a macro virus (see page 566).

Redesigning Your Menus

Not only can you build your own toolbars in Excel, PowerPoint, and Word, you can also twist and shape the *menus* of these programs to suit your schemes. You can add and remove menu items from the various menus, and you can even move the menus themselves so that they appear in different places on the menu bar.

More than one Excel owner, for example, has found happiness by stripping out over half of the default commands that he found he never used. Conversely, you're missing out in Word if you don't *add* commands to the menus that you usually have to trigger by burrowing through nested dialog boxes.

As noted earlier, choosing Tools→Customize doesn't just open the Customize dialog box. It also opens a strange-looking *duplicate* menu bar just beneath the real one. If you click a menu name on this Menu Bar "toolbar," the menu opens, revealing all of the commands in that menu.

Adding a command

To add a command to a menu, choose Tools→Customize, and click the Commands tab. Find the command that you want to add (by clicking the appropriate category on the left side first, for example). Then drag the command out of the Commands list and straight onto the *name* of the desired menu (on the *duplicate* menu bar), as shown in figure 17-3.

Note: Excel has *two* menu bars—a Worksheet Menu Bar and a Chart Menu Bar. They're listed individually in the Customize dialog box's Toolbars tab. That's because Excel's Data menu changes into a Chart menu when a chart is selected. These menu bars are independent, so if you make changes to the Insert menu item on the Chart Menu Bar toolbar, those changes *won't* be reflected in the Insert menu item on the Worksheet Menu Bar.

As you drag your command over the duplicate menu, the menu opens automatically. As you drag down the menu, a line shows you where the new command will appear when you release the mouse.

Tip: You can even rename your newly installed menu command: Open the duplicate menu bar, then double-click your command to open the Command Properties dialog box. Type the new name and press Return.

Removing a menu command

Suppose that you never use the Dictionary command in Excel's Tools menu; the only word *you* need to know is "Profit."

Getting rid of a menu command—whether you put it on the menu or not—is easy. Choose Tools→Customize to summon the strange duplicate menu bar shown in Figure 17-3. Now click the menu title (in the duplicate menu bar) that contains the offending command. Finally, drag the command itself off the menu.

Tip: In Word only, there's a faster way to remove a menu command, one that doesn't even involve the Customize dialog box: Just press Option-⌘-hyphen (on the main keyboard, not the number pad). The cursor is now "loaded," as reflected by its status as a big, bold – sign. Now just *choose* the menu command you want to nuke, using the regular menus. When you release the mouse, the command is gone, and your cursor returns to normal.

Figure 17-3:
Once you've chosen Tools→ Customize, you get the duplicate, editable menu bar. By dragging menus and commands as shown here, you show Office how you want to modify your real menu bar. Here, a Meeting Minder command is being added to the Slide Show menu in PowerPoint.

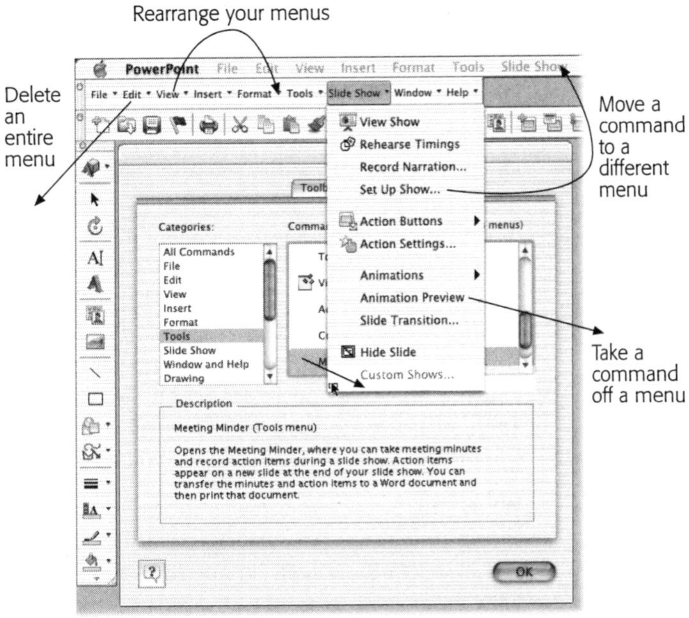

Removing commands from menus doesn't delete them from the program, of course. To restore a command you've removed from a menu, reinstall it as described in the previous section.

Adding a menu

You can do more than just add commands to existing menus. You can also create completely *new* menus, name them whatever you please, and fill them with any commands you like, in any order you like. This feature opens up staggering possibilities of customization: You can create a stripped-down "just the commands you really need" menu for an absolute novice, for example, or build a menu of your macros.

To do so, choose Tools→Customize; click the Commands tab; scroll to the bottom of the Categories list; and click New Menu. Drag the New Menu command from the Commands list (right side of the window) to the Menu Bar toolbar. Put it anywhere you want—between the File and Edit menus, for example, or to the right of the Help menu.

With the new menu still selected, Control-click your new menu and choose Properties from the contextual menu (or click the Modify Selection button in the Customize dialog box). Type a name for your new menu into the Name field. Finally, press Return. (Control-clicking also offers the Begin Group command, which inserts a separator line into your menu-under-construction.)

Your new menu is installed. Now you can add to it any commands you want, using the same technique described in "Adding a command," on page 630.

Removing a menu

You don't have to stare at Microsoft's complex menus if you rarely use one of them. If you never use tables in Word, for example, by all means get rid of the Table menu.

Doing so couldn't be easier. Choose Tools→Customize to make the phantom double menu bar appear. Point to the name of the menu you no longer need and drag it directly downward and off the menu bar. Once it's gone, the other menus close up to fill its space. (Never fear: You can always bring it back, as described below.)

Moving whole menus, or specific commands

Even the order of menus on the menu bar isn't sacrosanct in Office X. If it occurs to you that perhaps the Fonts menu should come before the Edit menu, choose Tools→Customize. Now you can start dragging around the menu titles themselves (on the duplicate menu bar) until you've reached an arrangement that you like.

While you're at it, you can also drag individual commands from menu to menu. As shown in Figure 17-3, start by choosing Tools→Customize. Then bring the menu command to the screen by opening its current menu in the duplicate menu bar. Now drag the command to the *name* of a new menu, which opens automatically; without releasing the mouse, drag downward until the command is positioned where you want it. Finally, release the mouse button.

Resetting everything back to normal

When you delete a command, it's not gone from Office. You've merely removed it from its menu or toolbar, and it's easy enough to put it back—a handy fact to remember when you've made a mess of your menus through overzealous exploration.

Open the Customize window (by choosing Tools→Customize). Click the Toolbars tab. In the list at left, click Menu Bar, and then click Reset. You've just restored your menus and commands to their original, factory-fresh condition.

Tip: You can use this technique to reset any of the factory toolbars, too. On the Tools→Customize→Toolbars tab, just turn on the checkbox next to the toolbar you want to restore, and then click Reset.

Reassigning Key Combinations

A staggering number of Office commands can be triggered by pressing an equally staggering number of keyboard shortcuts. The only problem arises when you discover that Microsoft has chosen something bizarre (like Option-⌘-R for Thesaurus) instead of something more natural (like ⌘-T).

The good news is that you can reassign key combinations for any menu command— in Word and Excel, anyway. You can't fiddle with the keyboard commands in PowerPoint or Entourage. (But hey, in Office 2001 you couldn't change key commands in Excel either, so at least Microsoft is making *some* progress.)

To begin, choose Tools→Customize. In the Customize dialog box, click the Keyboard button.

Now the Customize Keyboard window appears (see Figure 17-4). It works much like the toolbar-editing dialog box described earlier in this chapter. At left, click a command category; at right, click the name of the command you want to reassign. (After clicking or tabbing into one of these lists, you can jump to a particular category or command by typing the first couple letters of its name.)

Figure 17-4:
Here, the Spelling and Grammar command (which Word calls ToolsProofing) is being given another keyboard shortcut— Option-⌘-S. Word warns that Option-⌘-S is already in use by another command ("DocSplit," which splits the document window into two panes); if you don't care, just click Assign.

After highlighting the command for which you'd like to change or add a key combi-nation, click in the box beneath the "Press new shortcut key" field. Now press the keys you'd like to use as the new key combo, using any combination of the Shift, ⌘, Option, and Control keys along with a letter, Fkey, or number key.

If that keystroke already "belongs" to another command in the Office X program you're using, the Customize dialog box shows you which command has it (Figure 17-4). To reassign that keystroke to the new command anyway, click the Assign but-ton. To keep the current setting, press Delete, and then try another keystroke.

Obviously, you can't have two commands linked to a single keystroke. However, you *can* create more than one keyboard shortcut for a single command. For instance, in Word X, both ⌘-B and Shift-⌘-B are assigned to Bold.

Tip: If you find yourself frequently triggering some command *accidentally,* you may want to *remove* its assigned keystroke. To do so, click the command name in the list, highlight the keystroke in the "Current keys" list, and then click the Remove button. Click OK to save the changes.

If you don't like the key combinations that you've edited, you can always reset them by clicking the Reset All button in the lower-right portion of the dialog box.

Faster Keyboard Reassignment in Word

Word offers a shortcut for assigning a keyboard shortcut to a menu: Press Option-⌘ and the + sign on your nu-meric keypad (at the right side of your keyboard). The mouse pointer changes into a large ⌘ symbol.

Now click the toolbar button, or choose the menu com-mand, for which you want to set up a keystroke. A special keyboard-reassignment box appears, looking something like the one in Figure 17-4. Just press the keystroke you want as described above. You've just saved yourself sev-eral steps.

The Graphics Programs of Office X

Office comes with Word for text, Excel for numbers, PowerPoint for slides, and Entourage for email and scheduling. From reading the box, you might conclude that Office is therefore missing one of the cornerstone Macintosh programs: graphics software.

In fact, however, Office comes with a minor army of graphics programs. Microsoft Graph, Equation Editor, Clip Gallery, AutoShapes, WordArt, and other tools are built right in and shared among Word, Excel, and PowerPoint. (They're not available in Entourage.)

Because they take advantage of the Mac OS X Quartz drawing technology, these programs produce better results than ever in Office X. The benefits include smoother (*antialiased*) lines and new transparency effects.

Inserting a Graphic

You can drag, paste, or insert a picture into a Word, Excel, or PowerPoint document. To insert a graphic, choose Insert→Picture (or click the Insert Picture button on the Drawing toolbar) and then choose one of the following from the submenu:

- **Clip Art** opens the Office Clip Gallery, as described below.

- **From File** opens a dialog box where you can choose any graphics file on your Mac.

- **Horizontal Line** (Word only) is a quick way to put a horizontal line between paragraphs without opening the Borders and Shading dialog box. These lines are actually GIF files. They're more decorative than standard lines and borders, and ideal for use on Web sites (see Chapter 7).

- **AutoShapes** are an expanded, elaborate version of the familiar circles and squares that you create with drawing tools. For instance, AutoShapes include arrows, cubes, banners, and talking balloons (see page 540).

- **Organization Chart** opens Microsoft Organization Chart, a specialized mini-program that creates corporate charts showing how executives, managers, and assistants relate to one another (see page 663).

- **WordArt** allows you to change the look of text in a number of wacky, attention-getting ways. After typing the text, you can stretch, color, and distort it, using Office's drawing tools (page 540).

- **From Scanner or Camera** lets you import directly from one of these devices connected to your Mac—sometimes. Its success depends on your model of digital camera or scanner.

- **Chart** (Word only) creates a chart from any Excel file on your Mac. (Of course, you can use Excel charts in PowerPoint, too. But in PowerPoint, the command is right on the Insert menu, not on the Picture submenu. See Chapter 13 for details on charts.)

- **Microsoft Word Table** (PowerPoint only) opens a dialog box to start building a spreadsheet-like table (see page 589).

UP TO SPEED

Pictures and Drawings

There are two distinct kinds of graphics in the computer world, which, in Office, are known as *pictures* and *drawings*.

Pictures include *bitmap files, raster graphics, painting files,* JPEG or GIF images, photographs, anything scanned or captured with a digital camera, anything grabbed from a Web page, and Office clip art. What all pictures have in common is that (a) they're composed of individual, tiny colored dots, and (b) you can't create them using the tools built into Office. You can make pictures larger or smaller, but if you stretch something larger than original size, it may look blotchy.

Drawings include AutoShapes, Word Art, and any graphics you create using Office's own drawing tools. Drawings, also known as *vector* or object-oriented graphics, are stored by the Mac as mathematical equations that describe their size, shape, and other characteristics. That's a fancy way of saying that you can resize, rotate, squish, or squeeze drawings as much as you like without ever worrying that they'll print jagged or blotchy.

Keeping these distinctions in mind may help you understand why your Office programs function like they do when you work with graphics.

The Clip Gallery

Clip art refers to a canned collection of professionally drawn, cartoonlike illustrations designed for use in a wide variety of documents. Designing a Christmas card? You can count on finding a Santa head or snowflake in any self-respecting clip-art collection. Need a sketch of an airplane taking off for a newsletter article about business travel? Off you go to the clip art collection.

Fortunately, Office comes with about 200 pieces of ready-to-use art (more if you install the additional clips from the Value Pack, as described on page 681) in a collection called the Clip Gallery. To review them, choose Insert→Picture→Clip Art. The Clip Gallery opens, as shown in Figure 18-1. (Clicking the Insert Clip Art button near the middle of the Drawing toolbar opens it, too.)

Tip: In true Mac OS X fashion, the Clip Gallery has its own Dock icon, but don't get too excited: Even if you make it a permanent Dock installation (by Control-clicking its Dock icon and choosing Keep in Dock from the contextual menu), you won't be able to *open* the Gallery from the Dock. Its Dock icon serves primarily as a quick way to pull its window forward if it gets buried.

Figure 18-1:
Click a category in the list at the left to see thumbnails of the available clips, one of which is Search Results (after you've done a keyword search, as shown here). Click a thumbnail and then click Insert (or just double-click the thumbnail) to place the full-size version in your document. (Turn on the Preview box to see the full-size image in a separate window.) You then have to click Close to ditch the dialog box.

Categories

The Categories button in the Clip Gallery window opens a dialog box where you can delete categories from, or add categories to, the Clip Gallery. Neither process deletes or adds any actual pictures;—they stay where they always were—in the Microsoft Office X→Clipart→Core folder. You're just deleting or adding category names into which the pictures can reside.

Online

If you click the Online button, Office asks your permission to launch your Web browser and connect to the Microsoft Design Gallery Live Web site, which offers thousands of additional clip art files in a searchable database. You can download them individually or in groups by turning on their boxes.

Best of all, when you click the "download clips" link in Design Gallery Live, Word automatically imports the new clips into the Clip Gallery and opens the gallery to display them. New clips arrive in the category called Favorites, as well as into other existing categories based upon their keywords. To move them around, see "Properties," below.

Adding Your Own Clips

You're not limited to clip art from Microsoft. Not only can you transfer your own images into any Word document with the Insert→From File command, but you can also make them part of the Clip Gallery. This gives you the opportunity to use the Clip Gallery's search function and organizing features and see thumbnails of your own clip art, too. (iPhoto it ain't, but this feature can be handy.)

To do so, choose Insert→Picture→Clip Art to open the Clip Gallery; click Import. Use the Open window in the Import dialog box to navigate on your Mac to the graphics files that you want to bring into the Clip Gallery. (Make sure the Show menu shows "Clip Gallery Images"; the kinds of images you can import are JPEG, TIFF, PICT, GIF, PNG, or Photoshop files, as well as clip art from Microsoft.)

Use the radio buttons at the bottom of the dialog box to indicate whether you'd like Word to store a copy of the clip (leaving the original in place), move the original from its current location into the Clip Gallery, or just place an alias of the original file in the Clip Gallery. Since it's possible to delete clips from the Clip Gallery (see below), this alias method is the most prudent. It also saves on disk space.

Click to select the image (Shift-click to select multiple images); click Import. The Properties dialog box opens, offering you a chance to rename the image and assign categories to it.

Deleting Clips

If you want a clip out of your life forever, click it in the Clip Gallery and choose Edit→Clear. Word asks for confirmation before nuking it.

Properties

Every image in the Clip Gallery is associated with a list of *properties* that identify and define it. Some, like file size, you can't change (at least not from within the Clip Gallery). Other properties, such as Description, Category, and Keyword, you can change, and thereby control how the Clip Gallery is organized. These bits of descriptive text are the "handles" you'll need later to *find* particular clips among the seething graphic masses you've accumulated.

To work with a clip's properties, click it in the Clip Gallery and click Properties. The Properties dialog box appears, as shown in Figure 18-2.

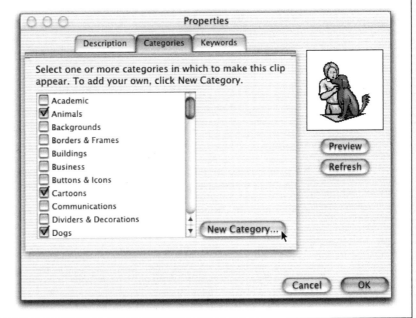

Figure 18-2:
Be sure to check out all three tabs—Description, Categories, and Keyword—when setting a clip's properties. All three will help you find the clip later.

- **Description.** The description you enter here becomes the *name* that the Clip Gallery uses for the image. The file information on the rest of this tab shows the real file's name and where it's located on your Mac.

- **Categories.** Turn on the boxes for *all* the categories where you may expect to look for this clip later; there's no limit to how many you can choose. You can even add new categories to the Clip Gallery by clicking New Category.

- **Keywords.** Each clip has its own unique list of descriptive *keywords*; again, there's no limit. These words pull up the clip when you search for them. Thus, if you're adding a clip of a dolphin swimming, you may want to give it keywords such as *fish, ocean, wildlife, mammals, animals, marine life, water,* and *Flipper.*

The Properties dialog box is also the place to "delete" a clip from a certain category. When you turn off a checkbox on the Categories tab, the clip will no longer appear on that category's panel.

Search

When you enter a word in the Search box at the top of the Clip Gallery and click Search, Word finds all the clips that match (or are related to) that keyword. For instance, if you type in *automobile*, Word pulls up all the clips that have "automobile" as keywords. Cooler yet, it also finds clips with "car" or "vehicle" as keywords—it relies on the Office X Thesaurus to figure out which possible keywords mean the same thing as what you typed!

Working with Clip Art

After placing a piece of clip art into your document, you can click it to produce eight tiny square handles at its perimeter. By dragging these handles, you can resize the illustration in a variety of ways:

- **Drag** a handle to resize the figure in that dimension—drag the top one to make it taller, a side one to make it wider, and so on.

- **Shift-dragging** a corner handle keeps an object in its original proportions as you resize it.

- **Option-dragging** any handle resizes the object from the center outward in the direction you're dragging. (This method does not maintain proportion.)

- **Shift-Option-dragging** a corner handle resizes an object from the center outward *and* maintains its proportions.

- **⌘-dragging** any handle overrides the *drawing grid* (see page 648).

You can also move a graphic around the screen by dragging it freely.

AutoShapes and WordArt

There are two kinds of drawings in Word: those you make yourself using Word's drawing tools (see page 644), and those Word makes for you, through features such as AutoShapes and WordArt.

AutoShapes

An AutoShape is a ready-made drawing object. As with the simple circle, square, and triangle of times past, you simply drag to size and place them in your document. However, you now have many more choices. The AutoShapes in Office X include a smiley face, callout balloons, flowchart boxes, and all manner of star shapes.

To use an AutoShape in your document, click the AutoShapes button on the Drawing toolbar. (If it's not already open, choose View→Toolbars→Drawing. Or, if you can't get enough of that genie effect, click the Drawing button on the Standard toolbar.)

As shown in Figure 18-3, each AutoShape menu provides a palette of choices. Click one, then release the mouse; now drag in your document to place the AutoShape— you can always resize or move it later.

Note: In Word, adding an AutoShape flips you automatically into Page Layout mode; that's because Word treats such shapes as objects rooted to a certain spot on the *printed page,* not embedded into the text. In fact, if you return to Normal view, the AutoShape *doesn't appear at all.* Many a Word fan has grown alarmed, thinking that the carefully modified shape has disappeared forever.

You *can* convert the new AutoShape so that it interacts with your text, however; see page 164.

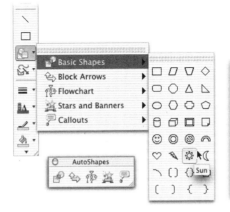
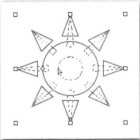

Figure 18-3:
Left: The drawing tools on the Drawing toolbar give you (top to bottom): lines, rectangles, AutoShapes, and other assorted lines. You can keep a mini palette (bottom) of them open by dragging the palette off the Drawing toolbar.

Right: Called the "adjustment handle," the yellow diamond lets you play with the AutoShape's shape without actually resizing it.

Like other drawing objects, AutoShapes can be grouped (see page 646) and combined with other drawing objects, such as lines. For example, you can combine the Flowchart AutoShapes with arrows to create a flowchart.

POWER USERS' CLINIC

Make Your AutoShapes Talk

You can add text to any enclosed AutoShape. When you do, the text becomes part of the shape and moves along with it, as shown here—a great way to use AutoShapes as callouts and flowcharts.

To begin, Control-click the AutoShape and choose Add Text from the contextual menu. The AutoShape changes to look eerily like a text box, with

an insertion point waiting for you to start typing.

There's just one little hitch worth mentioning: When you rotate an AutoShape, the text direction doesn't change. To rotate the text, select it and choose Format→Text Direction, or use the Orientation tool on the Alignment and Spacing section of the Formatting Palette.

Tip: As you drag to create an AutoShape, press Shift to keep the shape in equal length-to-height proportion. For instance, select the rectangle shape and Shift-drag to create a square, or select the oval and Shift-drag to create a perfect circle. As noted earlier, you can also press Shift when dragging to resize such an object without distorting its original proportions.

If you change your mind, there's a quick way to swap one AutoShape for another without deleting one and creating a new one. Just click the AutoShape with which you're dissatisfied, click and hold the Draw button at the top of the Drawing toolbar, click Change AutoShape from the pop-up menu, and choose a new one from one of the palettes.

POWER USERS' CLINIC

More of the Same

Say you've got your AutoShape just the way you want it, and you want to use the same banner—outlined in blue and filled in with yellow—at the top of every page. You don't have to change the line and fill color each time you create the banner. Just Control-click the first one and choose Set AutoShape Defaults from the contextual menu.

Now every time you create another banner in this document, it will appear with the same line and fill colors (and shadows and 3-D effects, for that matter). To change the default settings, just change one of the AutoShapes and choose Set AutoShape Defaults again.

WordArt

Like an AutoShape, a piece of WordArt is a type of ready-made drawing object; in this case, it's used for special text effects—3-D, wavy, slanting, colored, and various other permutations—that would be just right on a movie poster (but should be used sparingly in other situations). Figure 18-4 illustrates some examples.

To create some WordArt, choose Insert→Picture→WordArt. (Alternatively, you can click the Insert WordArt button on the Drawing toolbar, which looks like a three-dimensional A). Then proceed as shown in Figure 18-4.

When you click a piece of WordArt, the WordArt toolbar appears (Figure 18-4, lower right). Most of its tools take you to dialog boxes for formatting WordArt. Clicking Edit Text takes you back to the Edit WordArt dialog box; double-clicking the WordArt itself does the same thing. There are also buttons for the WordArt Gallery and the Format→WordArt dialog box.

The bottom row contains tools—spacing and alignment, for example—that format the actual text of your WordArt. The most powerful button here is the second one, Vertical Text, which takes the WordArt and strings it downwards, so that one letter appears below the other. Clicking the first one, Same Letter Heights, stretches the nonascending and descending letters of the selected WordArt so that all letters line up, top and bottom.

Note: As with AutoShapes, adding WordArt to a Word document flips you into Page Layout mode. Again, if you return to Normal view, the WordArt may seem to vanish. See page 160 for instructions on making text wrap around the graphic, if that's what you want.

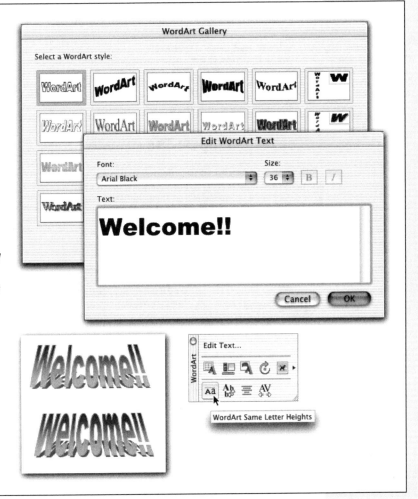

Figure 18-4:
Top left: In the WordArt Gallery, choose a text design that strikes your fancy, and then click OK.

Top right: Now the Edit WordArt Text dialog box opens. Choose a typeface, then type in your spectacular text banner message here; click OK when you're finished.

Lower left: Your new WordArt instantly appears in your document, shown here before and after applying Same Letter Heights.

Lower right: The WordArt toolbar. If you can't find the WordArt toolbar, it's probably not open. Click a WordArt object or choose View→Toolbars→WordArt.

Although most of the features of WordArt are the same as for other drawing objects, some features are unique:

- **Free rotate.** When you click the Free Rotate button on the WordArt toolbar and drag the round green handles, you rotate either the word itself or its shadow (if any).

• **Changing color.** To change the color of WordArt, don't use the Font Color tools in the Formatting Palette; they don't work. Instead, use the Fill Color control on the Formatting Palette (page 109) to change the color of the letters.

In most cases, WordArt letters also have a line around them; you can use any of Word's line formatting tools (such as the one on the Formatting Palette) to change the letter border's color and even its thickness.

• **Changing shape.** While you can alter the shape of a WordArt by dragging its sizing handles, there's also a way to change its shape altogether: Click the WordArt Shape on the WordArt toolbar (see Figure 18-4) and select one of the overall patterns from the palette. When you let go of the mouse, the selected WordArt changes shape automatically.

Lines and Shapes: The Drawing Toolbar

Even with the immense variety of AutoShapes and WordArt, some days you just need to unleash your creative spirit. With Office's drawing tools, you can draw free-form lines and shapes and combine them with arrows and AutoShapes to build your own masterpieces.

Figure 18-5:
When a toolbar menu has a strip of dotted lines at the top, you can drag it off the toolbar (left) to create a floating palette (right). The Lines palette contains tools for straight lines, arrows, double arrows, curved lines, free-form shapes, and scribbled lines.

To get started, summon the Drawing toolbar by choosing View→Toolbars→Drawing. Click the Line, Rectangle, or Lines toolbar icon, as shown in Figure 18-5. Choose a line type from the Line Style pop-up menu; then drag in your document to place the line, rectangle, or shape you've selected from the Lines pop-up button. (As with AutoShapes and WordArt, lines lie *on top of* text in Word—and are invisible in Normal view—unless you wrap them around the text, as described on page 160.)

If you've opted for the Lines tool, you'll find that each of the options in its pop-up button menu works a bit differently:

• **Line.** Drag for the position and length of the straight line you want; the cursor turns into a tiny cross. To resize the newly drawn line, drag the handles on each side, or reposition it by dragging the line itself (at which time the cursor turns into a hand).

- **Arrow and double arrow** work just like lines. When you draw a single arrow, the point appears where you *stop* dragging; a double arrow automatically springs points on both sides.

- **Curve.** Unlike lines, you draw curves by clicking, not dragging. Click to create a starting point; as you move the mouse, the curve follows. When you click a second time, the line gently curves from the first point to the second. Continue in this same manner. (The curve tool works best for wiggles and waves rather than closed shapes.) When you're done, double-click to finish off the curve. To enclose the shape, click as close as you can to your starting point.

- The **Freeform** tool is a two-in-one special. When you drag with it, the cursor turns into a pencil and works like a pencil—you can draw lines with any bend and direction without the limitations of the Curve tool. The instant you let go of the mouse button, the cursor turns into a cross and becomes a line tool. Clicking the mouse again now draws a straight line, just as with the Line tool. Hold down the mouse button again to go back to freehand drawing. (Nobody ever promised that Office would be a simple program.)

- The **Scribble** tool is like Freeform without the straight-line feature. You drag it to draw a freehand line; the line ends when you let go of the mouse button.

Tip: Clicking one of the Drawing toolbar icons loads your cursor with just *one* line or shape. After you've dragged in your document window, Office automatically switches you to the Select Objects tool (arrow cursor). If you plan to make several lines or shapes in a row, you'll quickly tire of reselecting your desired tool after each shape.

The workaround: *Double-click* a toolbar icon. Now your selected tool remains in force, no matter how many times you drag in your document, until you select a different one yourself.

Editing Drawing objects

To change the color and thickness of lines and the shapes you've drawn, use the Line formatting tools on the Formatting Palette or Drawing toolbar. Here are some of the other options on the Drawing toolbar or, if you Control-click the object, the contextual menu:

- **Edit Points.** Don't worry if your line or drawn object doesn't come out perfect on the first try. Just do the best you can, and then select the shape and choose Edit Points from the Draw pop-up menu at the top of the Drawing toolbar (or from the contextual menu). You can then drag the little black dots to resize and re-shape the line. This trick is especially useful for the Curve, Freeform, and Scribble tools.

- **Open Curve.** This unusual command (available on the contextual menu only) "disconnects" the point where you closed a Curve, Freeform, or Scribble object. Now you can use the edit points to reshape the object. Should you ever want to close the gap again, Control-click the shape again and choose Close Curve.

• **Nudge.** Although you can always move a picture or drawing object by dragging with the mouse, your hand movements on the mouse may not be precise enough. Fortunately, Office offers finer control.

To give your object a more controlled nudge, click the flippy triangle at the end of the drawing toolbar and choose Nudge→Up, Down, Left, or Right. If you've got Snap to Grid turned on (see page 648), you'll nudge the object one gridline at a time.

If Snap to Grid is turned off, each nudge moves the object only one pixel at a time. Of course, it's far less effort to simply tap the arrow keys, which also moves a selected object one pixel at a time.

Grouping the Parts

Every now and then, you may want to combine various drawing objects—arrows with flowchart boxes, callouts with AutoShapes, text boxes with lines—and keep them together. With Office's *grouping* features, you can combine drawing parts and then move, resize, and even format them as a unit.

To group objects, first select the ones you want to combine. Here's how: Using the Select Objects (arrow) tool on the Drawing toolbar, click one of the objects and then Shift-click the others one by one. The objects can be overlapping or completely separate. (To remove one of them from the group, click it again.) Then, from the pop-up menu at the top of the Drawing toolbar, click Draw→Group.

From now on, when you move or resize the drawing, or use any of the formatting tools described in the next section, its elements respond as a unit.

If you do wish to work on just one element of the grouped object, click it and select Draw→Ungroup on the Drawing toolbar. The individual objects appear with their own handles, so that you can go to town with your adjustments.

To regroup objects when your tweaks are complete, just click Draw→Regroup. You don't have to reselect all the pieces first; Word regroups the objects that you most recently ungrouped. If you have more than one set of objects ungrouped, click any *one* object in the set that you want to regroup.

Stacking Objects

In Word or Excel, you may use graphic objects only occasionally; in PowerPoint, graphics may be your primary weapon. Either way, sometimes you may wind up with several graphics on the screen at once. Using the Office *stacking* commands, you can control which graphic is *in front* of, or "covers up," another by shuffling your various graphics as though they're on separate sheets of clear plastic. Once you understand the commands, you can create intricate layers of text and objects.

First, ungroup the objects you're working with. Then use the commands described below to arrange the layers.

Tip: In Word, there's another layer to contend with: the one that contains your text. Word offers elaborate control over how graphics interact with the text—for example, how the text wraps around graphics on the page. When you're stacking objects, you can even have one object behind the text, and another object (or grouped object) directly in front of it, so that the text flows over the background object but wraps around the front one. Just select each object and choose its text wrapping style separately (see page 160).

- **Stacking with text (Word only).** To layer drawing objects and text (whether it's a text box or text on the page), select the *object*. Then, from the Draw pop-up button on the Drawing toolbar, choose Arrange→Behind Text or In Front of Text. You can also choose Format→Object→Layout tab and then "Behind text" or "In front of text," or use the Wrapping panel of the Formatting Palette.

  Note that the text-layering commands operate independently from the Bring to Front/Send to Back and Bring Forward/Send Backward commands described next.

Tip: It's possible to move and format a drawing object while it's layered behind text—the only trick is selecting it. To switch from the text selection tool (which looks like an I-bar) to the drawing selection tool (which looks like an arrow cursor), click the arrow icon on the Drawing toolbar. Now click to select the object.

- **Bring to Front/Send to Back.** This pair of commands comes in handy when you're layering more than two objects. On the Drawing toolbar, choose Draw→Arrange→Bring to Front or Send to Back to send the selected object *all the way* to the bottom or *all the way* to the top of your stack.

- **Bring Forward/Send Backward.** When you choose Draw→Arrange→Bring Forward or Send Backward on the Drawing toolbar, Word moves the selected object forward or back *one layer*. For instance, if you have three stacked objects and send the top one backward, it becomes the meat in the middle of the sandwich.

Tip: To make a quick copy of a drawing object, just Option-drag it. When you let go of the mouse button, an exact duplicate of the object appears.

Aligning Drawing Objects

When you have multiple drawing objects on a page, you may want them to be equally spaced apart or evenly aligned by their top edges. Instead of working out the measurements and aligning them yourself, use Word's built-in alignment features.

To do so, select the objects that you need to line up or arrange (Shift-click each one). Then choose one of the following options from the Align or Distribute menu of the Draw pop-up button (on the Drawing toolbar). Use the tiny icons on this menu as a visual clue to their functions.

- **Align Left, Center, or Right.** These commands bring the selected objects into perfect vertical alignment by their left or right edges, or centerlines.

- **Align Top, Middle, or Bottom.** These commands bring the selected objects into perfect *horizontal* alignment by their top or bottom edges, or centerlines.

- **Distribute Horizontally or Vertically.** Use these commands to spread your drawing objects across the page or from top to bottom—with an equal amount of space between each one.

You can also use the above commands on a single object, to place it at either side or in the center of a page.

Tip (Word and PowerPoint only): If you choose Draw→Arrange or Distribute→Relative to Page (or Slide) before using any of the alignment commands, Office includes the page itself as one of the alignment objects. Choosing Align Top, for example, moves the objects so that their top edges are flush with the top of the page.

The Drawing grid

Even without using the alignment commands, you may have noticed that it's fairly easy to pull objects into alignment with one another just by dragging. That's because each Word page has an invisible alignment grid that objects "snap to," as if pulled into line by a magnetic force.

To see the grid, choose Draw→Grid on the Drawing toolbar. Turn on "Display gridlines on screen" in the Drawing Grid dialog box, specify a gridline separation in the "Horizontal every" box (and the "Vertical every" box too, if you like), and then click OK. Now you can see the grid's faint gray lines superimposed on your document.

Note: In Excel, the gridlines are the cell boundaries themselves. You can either snap to these gridlines or "To Shape" (see "Snap objects to other objects," below).

Now that you know what the grid looks like, here's how to use it:

- To turn the grid off so that you can drag objects around with no spatial restriction whatsoever, turn off the "Snap objects to grid" box.

Tip: When the grid is turned off, ⌘-drag an object when you *do* want it to snap to the grid. Conversely, when the grid is turned on, ⌘-dragging a graphic moves it exactly where you put it, *without* snapping to the grid.

- You can use the "Snap objects to other objects" box with or without snapping to the grid. When this box is turned on, a dragged object snaps into alignment with the edges of the closest nearby object. If the grid is on, the nearest object overrides the grid.

- Change the default grid spacing (an eighth of an inch) by changing the measurements in the "Grid settings" boxes.

- The "Grid origin" settings control where the grid begins, measuring from the upper-left corner of the page. For instance, you can start the grid 1" from the upper-left corner by setting both the horizontal and vertical origins to 1".

- Turn on "Use margins" to limit the grid to the area within the margins, using the margins as the guide. This option ignores the page edges and, at least in terms of alignment, makes the area within the margins a world unto itself. This option is recommended if the margins are not exactly centered on the page, but you want everything *within* the margins to be centered within the margin area.

Click OK to apply the grid changes to your document.

Rotating Drawing objects

You can rotate drawing objects in either of two ways: freely with the mouse, or in precise 90-degree increments.

- To Free Rotate, click the object, and then click the rotation tool (a curved-around arrow) on the Drawing toolbar. The handles on the object become green dots. Drag any dot to rotate the object on its own axis. The object jumps into its new orientation when you let go of the mouse button. (*Option*-drag to rotate the object on its end instead.)

- To rotate in 90-degree increments, click the object, and then choose Draw→Rotate or Flip→Rotate Left or Rotate Right on the Drawing toolbar. Repeat the process to continue rotating the object a quarter turn at a time.

WORKAROUND WORKSHOP

Drawing with Clip Art

Many of the tools for formatting drawing objects don't work on *pictures* (see page 636 for a definition). But in Excel and PowerPoint, you can turn one special kind of picture—Microsoft clip art—*into* a drawing object. Then you can use the drawing tools on it, such as rotate, flip, and stacking.

To do so, Control-click the picture. Choose Edit Picture or Grouping→ Ungroup from the contextual menu. Either way, a message box asks if you'd like to convert the picture into a drawing. Click Yes.

Suddenly, your clip art image has turned into a mass of drawing objects. All their tiny white handles are now visible at once, which can be disconcerting, as shown here. Click a component object to see its four

handles, which you can then drag independently to adjust the graphic itself. You can also apply the usual drawing commands to it—alignment, layering, rotating, flipping, fill, edit points, and so on.

Word doesn't exactly allow you to turn the picture into a drawing, but there is a way to use the Drawing tools on it. Control-click the picture; from the contextual menu, choose Edit Picture. Word opens the picture in a new window, where you can move the picture's component pieces independently, turn on the edit points, and use any other Drawing tools you wish. When you're finished redesigning the picture, click Close Picture on the tiny toolbar to return to your document.

- To flip a selected drawing object, choose Draw→Rotate or Flip→Flip Horizontal or Flip Vertical on the Drawing toolbar. Flip Horizontal reverses the object from side to side; Flip Vertical turns it head-over-heels.

Formatting Pictures and Drawings

Once you've placed a graphic into a document, you can touch it up in a number of ways, from fixing a scanned photo to fattening up an arrow you've drawn.

Microsoft offers these image tools in triplicate, just to make sure you can't miss them.

- **The Formatting Palette.** When you click a picture or drawing, whichever sections you're used to seeing there (Font, Borders and Shading, and so on) are replaced by an arsenal of graphics controls (Fill, Line, Size, and so on).

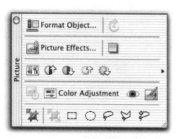

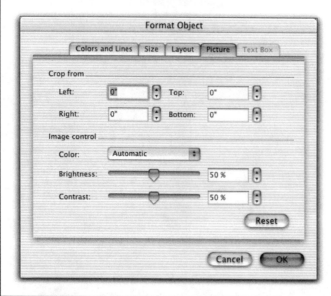

Figure 18-6:
Top: The Picture toolbar is a quicker route to many of the settings that are unique to pictures.

Bottom: The Format Picture dialog box offers the same controls, and more.

- **The Drawing or Picture toolbar.** This toolbar appears on your screen whenever you click a graphic of the corresponding type. The formatting controls available to you are different for each kind of graphic (*drawing* or *picture; see* page 636).

Note: The Picture toolbar doesn't appear when the Formatting Palette is open. Just this once, Microsoft is saving you a scrap of redundancy.

- **The Format dialog box.** When you *double-click* a drawing or picture in Word or Excel, this massive, multitab dialog box appears (see Figure 18-6). Its various panes let you specify every conceivable aspect of the selected graphic.

The following discussion focuses on the Format dialog box, since it's the most complete. Most of the choices described in this section also appear, however, in the Formatting Palette and the appropriate toolbar.

Colors and Lines Tab

On this tab of the Format dialog box, you can specify a color, picture, or pattern that will fill in the interior of your picture or drawing.

Note: The Colors and Lines tab is designed to fill in the background of *drawing objects* and *Office clip art.* It generally has no effect on other kinds of pictures.

Fill Color: Standard palette

Office comes with a standard palette of 40 colors (see Figure 18-7). Click a swatch to open the palette, and then click the color you want.

Figure 18-7:
The HSV color picker (shown here) is easy to use even if you don't learn all the theory behind it. Just move the bottom slider to about 50% to see all available hues. Click on an appealing color in the circle, and then move the slider to adjust the brightness.

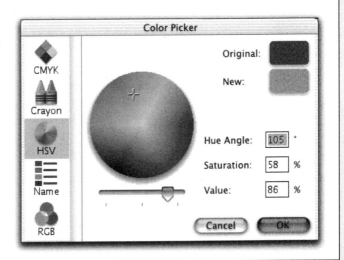

Fill Color: More Colors

If none of the 40 meets with your artistic standards, Word offers six ways to mix your own electronic paints. To open the Mac's Color Picker dialog box, choose More Colors from the Fill Color pop-up menu.

Apple has provided six different ways to mix the elusive shade you're seeking. Icons at the left side of the Color Picker dialog box represent them. Here are the various color pickers you can try:

- The **CMYK** (Cyan, Magenta, Yellow, Black) picker has a slider for each of these four color elements (which correspond to the four ink colors used in the printing business).

- The **Crayon Picker** is the easiest one to use, as easy as picking a crayon out of a box. (The names are lots of fun, too.)

- The **HSV** (Hue, Saturation, Value) picker is a circle controlling three elements of color. The *hues* (pure colors) are located around the edge of the circle—0 degrees for red, 60 for yellow, and so on. As you venture toward the middle of the circle, the *saturation* (amount of hue) decreases, going down to zero in the middle. The *Value*, controlled by the slider at the bottom of the pane, is the amount of black mixed with the hue: zero for all black and 100 for no black. You can describe any color by specifying particular percentages of Hue Angle, Saturation, and Value. (Most of the time, no one will quiz you on these numbers.)

- The **Name** picker is a single slider that lets you choose from the spectrum of colors that can be described in HTML code. (These, as Web designers are well aware, are hexadecimal numbers like FF9900.) As you move the arrow along the spectrum, the picker displays the HTML code for the color you're choosing (and limits you to colors that reproduce consistently in Web browsers). If you save your document as a Web page, these hexadecimal numbers will transfer into your source code, instructing browsers which color to display. (The actual color varies depending upon the browser and monitor on which the page is viewed.)

- The **RGB** (Red, Green, Blue) picker is similar to the CMYK picker, but is more intuitive. Most people are more familiar with mixing red, blue, and green to make different colors than they are with mixing cyan, magenta, and yellow. (So how do you make yellow with an RGB color picker? By mixing red and green, of course.)

Note: In Office X, Microsoft has removed the old HLS color picker. Of course, you can achieve the same effects with the HSV picker.

Fill Color: Fill Effects

If you choose Fill Effects from the Fill Color pop-up menu, you get the secret dialog box shown in Figure 18-8. It offers four tabs of its own, each offering a dramatic way to fill in the background of the selected drawing object.

- For example, the **Gradient** tab lets you apply smoothly shifting colors within the interior of the drawing object—for rainbowlike, shimmery effects. Use the top controls to specify the colors you want to shift from and to; use the bottom controls to indicate the direction of shifting. And because you're in the new world of Office X, you can apply transparency to the gradient colors by using the sliders at the lower right.

- The **Texture** tab is your personal Home Depot for marble, granite, burlap, and other building materials. When you need to dress up, say, a title or heading by "mounting it" on a stately, plaque-like rectangle, these squares are just the ticket. (Click Other Texture to choose a graphics file on your Mac that you'd like to use instead as a tiled, repeating background pattern.)

- The **Pattern** tab offers a variety of two-color patterns. Using the pop-up menus at the bottom of the dialog box, you can specify which is the dark color and which is the light one.

- Finally, when you click the **Picture** tab, you'll find no pictures to choose from— at first. Click Select Picture to choose any picture file on your Mac, including but not limited to Office clip art. Click Insert to bring the picture into the Picture tab, where you can see what it will look like. Click OK to use the picture as a fill for your Drawing object.

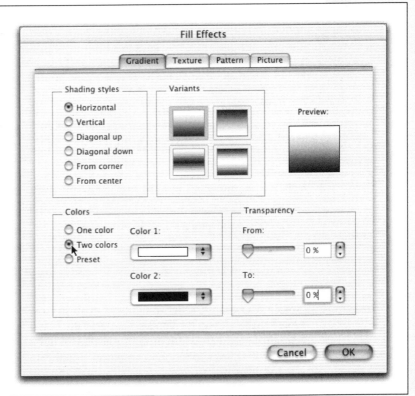

Figure 18-8:
Clicking the Colors radio buttons on the Gradient tab lets you use any of Word's color picking tools to choose the colors to apply to the gradient effects. The Preset choice gives you a list of preinstalled custom color combinations with poetic names such as Late Sunset and Fog. The Transparency sliders add transparency to either end of the gradient effect.

Transparency

This slider, found on the Colors and Lines tab and the Formatting Palette, changes whatever color you've chosen into a transparent version. The text or objects layered above or below it remain visible through the color, courtesy of Mac OS X's Quartz graphics technology.

Line pop-up menus (Drawing objects only)

In the Line section of the Colors and Lines tab, you can choose colors, dash and dot patterns, styles (single, double, and so on), weight or thickness, and transparency. All of it applies to the lines that constitute the selected drawing. (*Weight* is measured to the nearest .25 point.)

As you'll soon discover, this option is dimmed for picture objects like clip art and digital photos.

Tip: On the Line Color palette (found on the Drawing toolbar and Formatting Palette), there's an extra choice: Patterned Lines. Just as for fills, you can choose from a palette of patterns, with or without colors, to apply to the selected line. Try them on lines 4 points or more in thickness.

Pick Line Color/Pick Fill Color

Choosing this eyedropper tool on the line or fill color *palettes* (not the Format dialog box) lets you click to pick a color anywhere on your Mac's screen. It can be in any open window, such as a Web page in your browser. When you click a color with the eyedropper, the line or fill takes on that color to match. That color is then added to the bottom of all Office color palettes for your future use.

Arrows (Drawing objects only)

If you've drawn a simple line (as opposed to an enclosed shape), you can add an arrowhead to one or both ends, using the Arrow controls here.

Size Tab

While you can always resize a picture right in your document by dragging its handles, the Size tab offers other invaluable features. For example:

- **Height, Width.** These boxes let you specify precise measurements for the height and width of your drawing object, in hundredths of an inch.

- **Rotation.** This option lets you rotate a drawing object (not a picture) to any angle.

- **Scale.** These controls let you enlarge or shrink a selected graphic by a specified percentage. (If you turn on **Lock aspect ratio** before adjusting size, the drawing's original height-to-width proportions remain the same. The **Relative to original picture size** box applies only to pictures, not drawings; it lets you use the boxes in the Scale section to change the picture's size by a percentage of the original size. Thus, by changing the percentage to 200, you can double a picture's size without calculating the exact measurements.)

Tip: Making bitmapped images (like digital photos) *larger* than they originally appear is a recipe for blotchiness. And if you intend to print such graphics, be aware that their standard screen resolution, 72 dots per inch, is not fine enough to produce high-quality prints. For that purpose, use digital images of 150 dots per inch or higher.

- **Reset.** Word remembers the original size and aspect ratio (proportion of height to width). Click this button to restore the picture to its original size and shape, no matter how much you've played with it. (This option isn't applicable to drawings.)

Layout Tab (Word Only)

This tab of the Format dialog box lets you choose a text-wrapping option for a graphic placed in your text; see page 160 for details.

Advanced Layout (Word only)

You can lay out a Word page in a flash—by dragging. However, there may be times when you need to be more precise, as, for example, when you want a certain graphic to appear exactly 1.23 inches from the top of the page. For those times, use the Advanced Layout options.

To open the Advanced Layout dialog box, highlight a graphic in the document; double-click it; click the Layout tab; then click the Advanced button. There are two tabs within this inner dialog box: Text Wrapping and Picture Position.

Text Wrapping

These advanced text-wrapping-around-graphics options are described on page 160.

Picture Position

Use these controls to specify exactly where the picture lies relative to the page, and whether or not the graphic should stay attached to its text. (In other words, if you delete some text on an earlier page, should the graphic slide upward?)

Note: Most of the controls here apply only to drawings, not pictures. The exception is shown in Figure 18-9.

- **Horizontal.** These settings control the horizontal relationship between a drawing object and other parts of the page. Clicking a radio button activates the two menus where you choose options for the horizontal setting.

    For example, the **Alignment** controls let you choose left, right, or centered alignment on the page, and most importantly, what to align the object *with*—page, column, character (text), or margin. For instance, choosing "Left relative to Margin" aligns the left edge of your graphic with the left margin, meaning the image will stick to the left margin even when you adjust the margins.

Book Layout is instrumental when you're using a two-facing-pages format. You can align the object with the inner (gutter) margin or outer margin, or the inner or outer page edge.

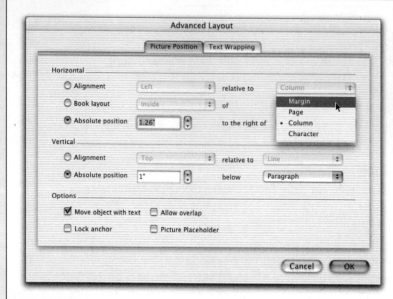

Figure 18-9:
The Picture Placeholder option is available only for pictures, not drawings. Checking this box is a way to swap the selected picture with another. When you click the picture after closing the Format dialog box, the Choose a Picture dialog box opens, so that you can import any picture file on your Mac. Until you actually choose a new picture (or uncheck the Picture Placeholder box), that dialog box will open every time you click the picture.

Absolute Position always measures the distance in inches from the right of a page landmark, such as Column, Margin, Page, or Character (text). Note that you can use the Column setting even if there's only one column on the page.

- **Vertical.** You have two options for vertical alignment. **Alignment** lets you line up your drawing object with a margin, page, or line (of text)—but this time, the alignment is from top to bottom. For instance, "Bottom relative to Page" tacks the bottom of your object to the bottom of the page.

  You can also choose an **absolute position**, in inches, below a Paragraph, Margin, Page, or Line (of text), always measured from the *top*.

- **Move object with text.** Turn on this box to keep the object with the surrounding text, even if you cut and paste it or edit around it.

- **Lock anchor.** Turning on this box keeps the surrounding paragraph attached to the drawing or picture, even if you move the object to a different place.

- **Allow overlap.** This command lets two objects overlap, as long as they have the same text wrapping style. The text will wrap (or not wrap) around both of them together.

- **Picture Placeholder.** Exclusively for pictures, this option lets you swap one image for another (Figure 18-9).

Picture Tab (Picture Objects Only)

The tools on the **Picture** tab, as shown in Figure 18-6, provide a great deal of control over how your image looks. For example:

- Use the **Crop from** boxes to specify, in hundredths of an inch, how much you'd like to trim off each side of a picture. (There's a crop tool on the Picture toolbar, of course, but it doesn't permit this kind of numerical accuracy.)

- The **Color** menu lets you turn your color graphic into grayscale, black and white, or watermark. (The watermark setting produces an extremely faint image, light enough that you can still read text that flows over it. Of course, you can do the same thing using the Transparency slider on the Colors and Lines tab).

  These choices affect only the image itself, not the fill. You adjust the fill on the Colors and Lines tab as described above.

- **Brightness and Contrast** are mainly useful for touching up photographs, but they do affect clip art and other images. Increase brightness and contrast for a crisper look; decrease them for a softer effect.

If you change your mind about anything you've done to a picture, remember you can undo your changes one by one by choosing the Edit→Undo command. Or, to start all over again, click the **Reset** button here; this will restore your picture to its original, pristine condition.

Position Tab (PowerPoint Only)

The Format dialog box offers this tab only in PowerPoint. Its simple controls let you specify exactly where your graphic appears on the slide, relative to the center or corner of the slide.

Protection and Properties Tabs (Excel Only)

You can lock a graphic independently of the other spreadsheet elements, preventing anyone who doesn't have the password from deleting or modifying it. That's the purpose of the Protection tab's sole checkbox. (As noted in the dialog box, however, you must still lock the spreadsheet itself as a next step; see page 524.)

The Properties tab controls how your graphic should respond when you move or resize the spreadsheet cells on which it lies. That is, it determines whether or not the graphic *should* move or resize in kind. It also offers a "Print object" checkbox that, if turned off, renders your object invisible in printouts.

The Picture Toolbar

The Format Picture dialog box described in the previous pages may be overrun with features, but when it comes to touching up pictures (scans, JPEG images, Office clip art, and so on), it's only the beginning. The Picture toolbar, which appears automatically when you click a picture, offers many more ways to dress up your images. (You can also summon it by choosing View→Toolbar→Picture. And by the way, this command is not available if the Formatting Palette is open, because the same tools automatically appear there if you select a picture.)

Move the cursor over the buttons on the toolbar to see their pop-up labels, as identified here:

- **Picture Effects** applies Photoshop-like filters to a photograph, allowing you to radically change its look with a single click. You can make it look as if it were drawn in charcoal, for example, or made of stained glass. Click the Picture Effects button to see the full gallery of choices.

- The **Shadow** button puts a shadow behind any type of picture, making it look as though it's floating just above the surface of your document. Click Shadow Settings to open a toolbar where you can choose a different color for the shadow, and nudge it closer to or further away from the picture.

- When you click the **Set Transparent Color** button, the cursor turns into an arrow pointer. When you click that pointer on a solid color in your picture, everything of that color turns transparent. When your picture is a photograph, this is the way to eliminate its background and wrap text tight against the foreground image. It works best if the photograph's background is a solid color. (This tool is not available on clip art pictures.)

- The **Color Adjustment** tool works for both photographs and clip art. Clicking it opens a dialog box where you can increase or decrease the *saturation* (making the image colors appear more intense or washed out), or adjust the amount of red, blue, or green in the image. You can do this just for effect, or to correct a photograph that has a distorted tint from improper lighting.

  It's OK if you've never done this before; just click one of the radio buttons and watch what happens in the preview windows. Now you can see exactly how the image has changed. Click Reset Settings to return to the original, or Apply to make the change permanent. If you click Color Adjustment again, your altered image becomes the new "normal," so that you can adjust the color further. (To return to the true original color, use Edit→Undo as many times as necessary.)

- **Fix Red Eye** and **Remove Scratch** are, of course, special tools for correcting photographs once you've inserted them in a Word document.

- The **Marquee** tools along the bottom of the Picture toolbar are for selecting parts of photographs and other bitmap images. Click on one of the tools and drag it over the image to select the desired area. (To cancel a marquee selection, double-click anywhere in the document.) Now you can click the **Cutout** button to remove that area, or use the Cut, Copy, and Paste commands to place that part of the picture somewhere else.

- The **Magic Lasso** tool (at the lower right) is the most exciting. It lets you click repeatedly around an irregularly shaped item in your picture (a person, for example); the shimmering selection marquee hugs the outline of the item. To close the marquee and complete the selection, double-click back at the starting point.

Once you've highlighted a portion of the picture in this way, you can cut out the selection, removing your ex from the picture forever, for example. You can also apply certain effects to that portion of the picture inside or outside the lasso, applying a dry brush effect to the background while leaving the people inside the lasso clear.

Object Linking and Embedding (OLE)

Linked and *embedded* objects are both chunks of data, like drawings or spreadsheets, nestled within a document in one Office program but actually created by another.

You edit them in whatever program created them, but behind the scenes, there's a big difference in where their data is stored. A *linked* object's data is stored in a separate file (what Microsoft calls the *source* file). An *embedded* object, on the other hand, is an integral part of the file in which it appears. All its data is stored right there in the document. That's why an embedded object bloats the file size of the document that contains it. However, embedding an object means that you'll never have to endure that sickening jolt when you realize you're missing an important speech that you copied to your laptop (as you might if you had only used linking).

The whole process is called Object Linking and Embedding, or OLE for short. You can't get very far on a Microsoft newsgroup or discussion board without seeing that acronym. At user group meetings, the preferred pronunciation is olé.

UP TO SPEED

Helper Programs: Chart, Equation Editor, and Graph

Office comes with several helper programs, each of which is dedicated to one specific task: organization charts, equations, and graphs.

You're not meant to open these programs by double-clicking them, as you would a normal Mac program. In fact, Equation Editor doesn't even *have* a Save command, and Microsoft Graph can't be launched by a double-click. Instead, you open one of these helper programs from within another Office application. For example, if you're working in Word or PowerPoint, and you want to embed a graph (but you don't want to go through the hassle of opening Excel to do the job), simply choose Insert→Object.

Office presents you with a list of the possible object types that Word can insert. Double-click the one you want, such

as Microsoft Graph. Now Microsoft Graph opens, and Office puts a placeholder graphic in your Word document (it shows where the graph will appear when you quit Graph).

Once your graph is finished, close Microsoft Graph; the graph that you created appears automatically at the point that you chose—no copy and paste necessary. (In fact, the chart or equation appears there even if you close the helper program's window without saving changes! Choosing Edit→Undo is the quickest way to delete the aborted image from your document.)

If you've already created an equation, graph, or chart using one of these applications, you can edit it by double-clicking the object. The appropriate helper program opens automatically.

Creating Linked Objects

To add a linked object to your Office document, you first must create that object in a program that offers OLE features. On the Mac, that includes Word, Excel, and PowerPoint X. For example, you can use linking to incorporate a drawing, spreadsheet, or chart into a Word document; weirdly enough, even another Word document can be incorporated into a Word document.

When you've created the source document, save the file, open the destination Word document, and choose Insert→Object. Click From File to open the Insert as Object dialog box (Figure 18-10), where you can navigate to the source document. (If you can't seem to find where you saved the file, click Find File to launch Word's search function.)

When you've located the source document, select it, turn on Link to File, and click Insert. The entire contents of the source file appear in the destination document inside a resizable border. You can format this object using Word's picture formatting tools—but to edit the *content* of the linked object, you must open the actual source file.

Editing Linked Objects

To edit a linked object, simply double-click it. (If you have many linked objects in one document, choose Edit→Links, and then click the link you want to edit in the list box. Links can be identified by the name of the source file.)

If it isn't already running, the source program launches, and the source document opens. Now you can edit the story, rotate the drawing, or revise the numbers in the spreadsheet. When you close the source document, the linked object is automatically updated.

It's easy to see the limitation of linked objects: Without the source file and the destination file on the same Mac, you can't edit the linked object. If you copy a document containing a linked object to a Zip disk, email it, or transfer it to your iBook, you'll be able to see, but not edit, the linked object. The bottom line: If you must edit it on the road, be sure to copy the source file onto the same disk or laptop.

Repairing a broken link

If Office can't find the source file for a linked object, perhaps because you've moved or renamed it, there's a way to remind Office of its location. Choose Edit→Links and select the link in question; click Change Source. An open file box appears where you can choose the source file; this is what tells Office to reconnect it to that link. Navigate to the file and double-click it.

You can use the same technique to change a linked object to a new source file altogether—such as a different illustration or a new fiscal year's ledger. Bear in mind that the new source file must be in the same program as the original one.

Tip: This is also the technique to use if you want to create a link to only a certain part of a source file—for example, a range of cells in an Excel spreadsheet or an excerpt of a Word document that you've marked with a bookmark (see page 233 for details on bookmarks). Type the name of the range or bookmark in the Range/Bookmark box.

Figure 18-10:
Checking the "Display as Icon" box in the Insert as Object dialog box creates an icon (left) that links to the source document. Both linked and embedded objects can be displayed as icons.

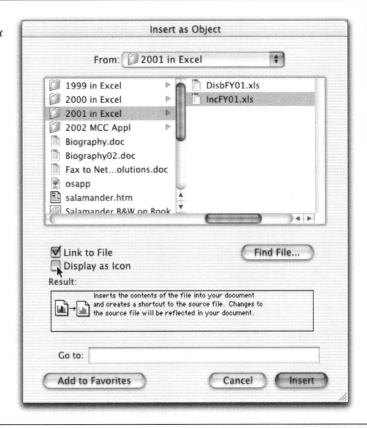

Overriding Automatic Updating

Office automatically updates linked objects every time you edit the source document. If, however, you want the linked object to remain unchanged (permanently or temporarily), there are a number of ways to go about it. Begin by choosing Edit→Links to open the Links dialog box.

- **Break Link.** This button uncouples the connection between source document and object. (Because this choice is irrevocable, Office asks if you're sure.) From now on, editing the source document does nothing at all to the destination document. You can't even repair the link, since the object no longer *is* a link. It becomes a picture, however, and still can be formatted as such (see page 657).

Tip: If you act quickly, you can reinstate a broken link by choosing Edit→Undo Links or pressing ⌘-Z.

- **Locked.** This box prevents changes to the source document from affecting the destination object. You can still double-click the link to open the source document, but any editing you perform there won't have any effect until you turn off the Locked box again *and* click the Update Now button in the Links dialog box.

- **Manual Updating.** Automatic is Office's default way of updating linked documents. When you choose the Manual radio button at the bottom of the Links dialog box, Word updates the linked object only when you click Update Now.

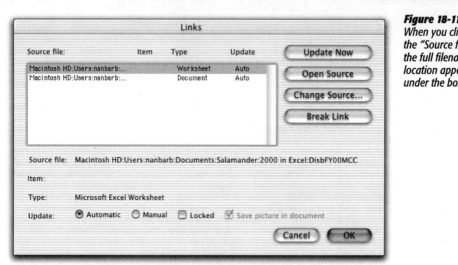

Figure 18-11:
When you click a link in the "Source file" box, the full filename and location appear just under the box.

Creating Embedded Objects

Creating an embedded object from an existing file is the same as creating a linked object, except you do *not* turn on Link to File.

To bring in an external file using this technique, choose Insert→Object. In the dialog box, proceed like this:

- **If the file you want to embed already exists:** Click From File. Navigate to and open the source document to embed a copy of it in your Office document.

- **To create a new file (for embedding) on the spot:** In the list box, double-click the kind of object you want to create: Chart, Worksheet, Picture, or whatever. A new window opens, complete with menus and toolbars, where you can begin creating the object. When you're done, close the window; the object appears in your document.

Tip: When creating an embedded picture, you can use any of Word's drawing tools, as described earlier in this chapter. However, when you close the window, the result is a *picture,* not a drawing. To edit it with picture tools, you must double-click to open its window, as described below. This is a great way to use both drawing tools and picture tools (picture effects, brightness, and so on) on the same object.

If, on the other hand, you simply want to insert a drawing object in a Word, Excel, or PowerPoint document, just open the Drawing toolbar (see page 650) and draw away!

Editing Embedded Objects

Like a linked object, an embedded object has a frame around it. You can format it using Office's picture tools (see page 657).

To edit it, though, you must double-click it. (Or click it and choose Edit→Object→Edit. The Edit menu changes to specify the type of object you've selected—Document Object, Worksheet Object, and so on.) The object opens in a separate document window, where you can edit it using the appropriate menus and toolbars.

You can edit an embedded object in any compatible program on your Mac. Just click the object and then choose Edit→Object→Convert. Choose a program in the list that appears, and then click OK. (Most of the time, the Microsoft Office programs will be the only ones available.)

Organization Chart

MS Organization Chart is dedicated to creating that unique artifact of corporate culture: the organization chart. These charts detail the hierarchy inside a company, noting, with a series of boxes and lines, who reports to whom. Each employee is represented by a rectangle containing a name, title, and notes.

This rather unpolished, sometimes cranky program is in the Microsoft Office X→Office folder. The only way to launch it, though, is by choosing Insert→Object from within Word, Excel, or PowerPoint, and then selecting it from the list in the Object dialog box.

Creating a Chart

When first inserting an organization chart, you get a sparse window containing a toolbar and an area for creating your chart (see Figure 18-12).

You start out with a chart showing positions for a manager and three subordinate co-workers. Use the toolbar button to add employee boxes to your chart, which expands to accommodate new boxes. Here's how:

- **Select.** This arrow-shaped tool lets you select boxes or lines in your organization chart. It also allows you to select text inside a chart item, before copying, cutting, dragging, or formatting it.

- **Enter Text.** This tool lets you type text snippets directly on your organization chart without putting them in an "employee box."

- **Zoom.** This tool toggles between larger and smaller images of your chart. (With the Zoom tool selected, click the chart itself.)

- **Subordinate.** Click this button, then an existing employee box, to create a box below the box you just clicked, creating a subordinate employee.

Tip: Clicking the Subordinate button (or one of the other box-name buttons) more than once before clicking a box in the diagram creates multiple boxes simultaneously. For example, click the Subordinate button four times and then click a box in your diagram to give that box four underlings.

- **Left Co-worker, Right Co-worker.** These tools add a box for a co-worker to the left or right, respectively, of the box you click.

- **Manager.** This tool creates a box above the box you click in, which indicates a manager for that employee.

Tip: ⌘-click this icon to insert a box between a manager box and its subordinate. (Highlight the subordinate box first.)

- **Assistant.** This tool creates a box *below and to the side* of an employee box, indicating an assistant to that employee.

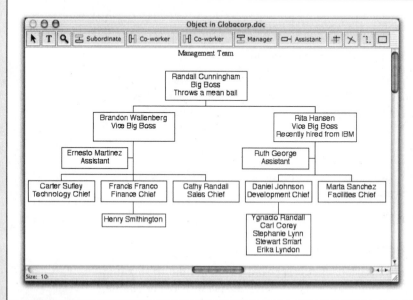

Figure 18-12:
To move someone's box (because of a promotion or reassignment), use the Select (arrow) tool to drag it. Most of the time, you'll want to drag a box so that it's squarely superimposed on another box. Move the cursor to the bottom edge of the target box to make the box you're moving an underling, or to the left edge to make it an equal, and so on. To delete an box, click it and then press Delete. What a feeling of power!

Changing employee information

Each employee box that you create contains two lines of text: *Type Name Here* and *Type Title Here.* To edit this info, click the Select (arrow) tool, click a box, and type the employee's name. Hit the Tab or Return key to highlight the placeholder for the employee's title, and then type right over it. You can also type in two lines' worth of comments below each employee's name and title. (If you click outside the box, the <Comment> placeholders disappear.)

When your company reshuffles, you can drag the boxes around to reflect the new corporate structure. When it's had a good night's sleep, Chart changes your cursor into a box or an arrow as you drag one box on top of another, to indicate where it will go when you release the mouse button (Figure 18-12). The most effective technique is to drag the box in an L shape: directly onto another box, and then downward (to make the dragged box subordinate) or left or right (to make it an equal).

Tip: Press Shift-Tab to move backward through the lines in an employee's box.

More tips:

- ⌘-drag a box onto its new co-worker or manager to move a box *without* moving its subordinates.

- Shift-drag a box up or down to move its group up or down.

- Drag the topmost box downward to move the whole chart on the page.

Using different chart styles

The Styles menu (see Figure 18-13) lets you set one of a number of styles for the boxes in your chart. Select all or part of the chart, and then choose from the menu to apply a style.

- **Compact Tree** is the standard view where subordinates are arrayed directly below their managers. Its cousin, **Spread Tree,** is a fanned-out version of the same thing, where boxes are below *and to either side* of the boxes above, so that no box is directly below any other.

- **Stacked Groups With Boxes/Stacked Groups No Boxes** turn the chart into a kind of outline form, with each layer of employees indented to the right of their supervisors.

- **Boxed Groups** is an unusual, telescopic view, in which groups of employees appear *inside* their supervisors' boxes.

- **Assistant** turns the selected box into the assistant of the manager above it.

- **Co-Manager** is for those hellish business situations where an employee has more than one manager. In this case, you can apply a *co-manager* style to an employee box, making that employee the co-manager of her co-workers.

Tip: Along the way, use the Text, Boxes, Lines, and Chart menus to specify the fonts, colors, line styles, and colors used by your chart.

Closing the window returns you to your Office document, where the graph is now in place.

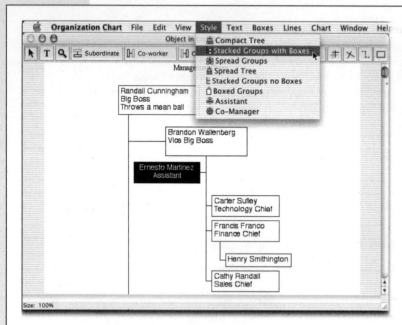

Figure 18-13:
These styles govern how boxes are positioned and linked together. To apply a style, select a box, or several boxes (by Shift-clicking them), and then choose a style from the menu. The Stacked Groups with Boxes style is shown here.

Equation Editor

For the scientifically minded, Microsoft offers the Equation Editor program, which lets you create equations worthy of any Ph.D. student at CalTech.

To open this valuable program in Word, Excel, or PowerPoint, choose Insert→Object and double-click Microsoft Equation Editor. A window in which to type your equation opens, along with a double-row toolbar across the top that's filled with equation element templates—fractions, radicals, integrals, summation, and set theory templates. Each offers a variety of symbols that you can incorporate into equations as complicated as you'll ever need.

Note: Equation Editor isn't part of the regular installation. You have to install it using the Value Pack installer, as described on page 681.

To create an equation, simply type it into the main window. When you run across a symbol that you can't enter via the keyboard (the standard Apple keyboard lacks an integral key, for example), click the toolbar template button that contains the symbol you want to enter, and then select the symbol itself from the palette that pops up. If the symbol normally contains a few different places for other elements (such as a summation symbol), the symbol that you insert has placeholders for the elements surrounding the symbol.

Figure 18-14:
Pythagoras would be proud— or at least satisfied. With its double-row of symbol buttons, Equation Editor lets you insert just about any mathematical and logical symbol available.

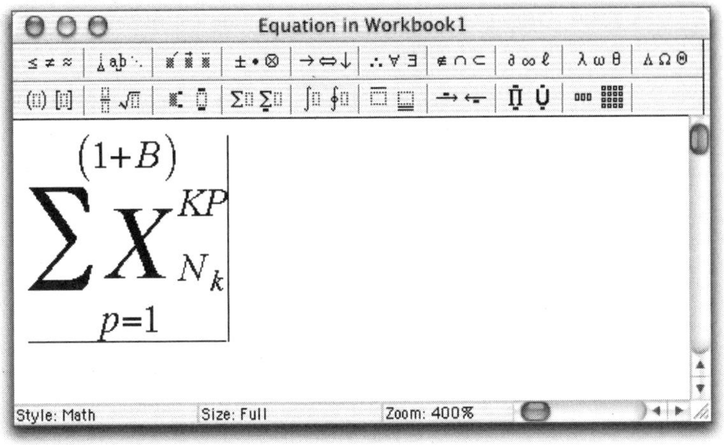

As you work, you can:

- **Change views.** Equation Editor lets you magnify or reduce your view of the equation you're building; use the View menu to change zoom level.

- **Change spacing and alignment.** When creating an equation, it's important to control spacing—especially when creating a matrix. The Format menu lets you align your equation, as well as control how elements are spaced within an equation.

- **Choose a style.** Equation Editor lets you choose one of seven typographical styles for the equations that you write—Math, Text, Function, Variable, Greek, Matrix-Vector, and Other (which lets you define your own style). To create your own style, choose Style→Define; this command lets you set all kinds of characteristics for the elements of your equations (such as how text, variables, and symbols appear).

- **Change sizes.** To quickly swap between normal and superscript sizes, use the Size menu, which presents six options—as well as the option of defining your own text size.

Equation Editor has no Save command. When you're finished designing the equation, close the Equation Editor; the equation lands in the Word, Excel, or PowerPoint document from which you began this exercise.

Microsoft Graph

Microsoft Graph is a stripped-down version of Excel's charting functions. You're likely to use it most often in Word or PowerPoint; after all, there's little point to using it in Excel, whose charting functions are much more highly evolved.

From within a Word or PowerPoint document, choose Insert→Object. The Microsoft Graph window appears, carrying unmistakable echoes of Excel. It consists of four main elements:

- **Cells.** Just as in an Excel spreadsheet, Graph draws the information for its charts from its own set of cells. However, you can't type formulas into them, this time; you must type the numbers themselves into each cell.

- **Graph preview.** This window shows you what your graph in progress looks like as you work.

- **Standard toolbar.** Its commands let you manipulate items in your chart and in Graph's spreadsheet.

- **Formatting toolbar.** The Formatting toolbar contains formatting commands similar to those in Excel's Formatting Palette, such as text alignment, style commands, and cell formatting commands.

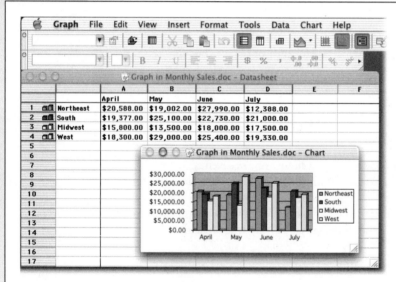

Figure 18-15:
The best time to use Microsoft Graph rather than Excel is when you want to whip up a quick graph without bothering with Excel. If, on the other hand, the data you want to graph is already in an Excel worksheet, go ahead and create the chart in Excel.

Entering Data

To get started in Microsoft Graph, plug numbers into the cells. Navigating through Graph's cells is similar to moving through an Excel sheet (press Tab to move right one cell, Shift-Tab to move left; Return to move down one cell, Shift-Return to go up). You can also click the cell you want to edit.

As in Excel, cells are labeled with letters and numbers; unlike Excel, Graph's spreadsheet has an extra row at the far left and an extra column at the top. You're supposed to type row and column headers into these special dedicated areas. Graph will then use these cells in the chart for its axes and for the legend.

As you work, you can make these kinds of changes to your chart:

- **Change the chart type.** Microsoft Graph can produce every chart type that Excel can, but it starts out with a vertical bar graph. To change this chart type, choose one of the eighteen options found in the Chart Type pop-up button in the Standard toolbar. (If you can't figure out which icon it is, point to the toolbar icons without clicking and read the resulting tooltips). (See Chapter 13 for a discussion of which chart type to use with which kinds of data.)

  To use a chart type that isn't present in the Chart Type palette, choose Chart→Chart Type to open the Chart Type window. This window is nearly identical to the Chart Type window in Excel and features the same range of chart types.

- **Swap axes.** If Graph is showing the data on the wrong axes, click the By Row or By Column button in the Standard toolbar—either will swap the chart's horizontal and vertical dimensions.

- **Change element colors.** To change colors in a chart, simply click the element that you want to change (such as a bar or its background) and then select a new color from the Fill Color pop-up button (the "pouring paint can" icon) in the Standard toolbar.

- **Move or resize something.** You can move the chart's legend by dragging it. Most other graph elements are fixed in place, but you can resize something (such as the legend or the chart's plot area) by clicking it and then dragging one of the resize handles that appear at its corners. If you have a 3-D item in a chart, you can also drag its corners to rotate it, just as you can in an Excel chart containing a 3-D element.

Tip: If you *really* want to fine-tune control over a 3-D object, choose Chart→3-D View, which produces a control window in which you can control the exact rotation of a 3-D object.

- **Change the fonts.** You're not stuck using Geneva in your tables. To change the font, select the item in question (label, axis, whatever) and then choose Format→Font to bring up the Format window, where you can tweak the font size, style, color, underline, and so on. Click OK to save the changes.

- **Add a data table.** If you want to include a *data table* (which displays the cells used to make the chart), click the Data Table button in the Standard toolbar. It plops the data table below the chart.

Advanced chart options

Choosing Chart→Chart Options brings up the Chart Options dialog box, where you can control your chart's title, axes, gridlines, legend, data labels, and data table. It's essentially the same as Excel's Chart Options window, which is detailed on page 503.

Tip: To import an Excel worksheet (or a tab- or comma-delimited text file) into Graph, choose Edit→Import File.

Windows Media Player

On the Macintosh, the standard movie- and sound-playing software is QuickTime Player. On Windows, it's Windows Media Player.

Thanks to a bizarre intersection of Microsoft corporate strategies, there's now a program called Windows Media Player (WMP) for Macintosh (Figure 18-16). You have to install WMP from the Value Pack (see page 681), or, if you can't bear to dig out that CD again, you can download it from *www.microsoft.com/mac/downloads.aspx*.

WMP combines some of the features of iTunes and QuickTime Player. Unlike iTunes, however, WMP for the Mac can't play MP3 files or burn music CDs—in fact, it can't even *play* CDs.

Still, WMP is the only game in town if you want to experience streaming audio and video that are available only in Windows formats (.asf, .asx, .wm, .wmp, and so on). A Fall 2003 version called Windows Media Player 9 for Mac OS X brings even more formats to the Mac, including WMP 9—Microsoft's latest and greatest video and audio format. More online WMP files than ever, including certain movie trailers, will be playing in a browser near you—including both Safari and Internet Explorer.

WORKAROUND WORKSHOP

Installing WMP: Not for Wimps

Like many newly Carbonized programs, Windows Media Player needed some time to learn how to play nice with Mac OS X. For the best chance at success, make sure you've installed the most recent versions of both Mac OS X and the player. (If your WMP opens in Classic instead of Mac OS X, then you definitely need to download a newer version.)

If you don't have the latest and greatest, you may encounter errors while trying to run the WMP installer. The following workaround usually succeeds at sorting things out:

Locate the WMP installer on your Mac, but don't launch it

yet. Instead, launch Internet Explorer in OS X (version 5.1.4 or later is preferable). Only then should you double-click the WMP installer. When installation is completed, close the installer, and then quit Internet Explorer. Finally, relaunch Internet Explorer. This procedure forces Explorer to find its new plug-ins in your Mac's Library→Internet Plug-Ins→Windows Media Plugin folder.

If you've installed WMP successfully, but can't get any streaming media to play, then try the same trick. Launch Explorer, launch Windows Media Player, and then quit and relaunch Explorer.

After installation, you can find Windows Media Player in its own folder in the Applications folder. To get started, double-click its icon, which looks like a little blue-and-yellow Play button.

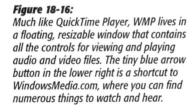

Figure 18-16:
Much like QuickTime Player, WMP lives in a floating, resizable window that contains all the controls for viewing and playing audio and video files. The tiny blue arrow button in the lower right is a shortcut to WindowsMedia.com, where you can find numerous things to watch and hear.

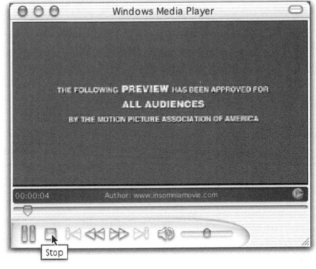

Operating the Player

If you've used QuickTime Player, the Windows Media Player will look familiar. As shown in Figure 18-16, it's a blank screen with a bank of VCR-like controls. You can bring audio or video clips or streams onto the screen by using the Open command, by choosing from the Favorites menu, or by clicking links on Web sites. Click the Hide Video Area button to collapse the window to a narrow bar—perfect for when you're just listening to an audio channel in the background.

At the bottom are volume, play/pause, stop, rewind, and fast-forward buttons. You'll also find a *Seek bar*—a scanning control. Drag it to move forward or backward through an audio or video clip. If you need to take a phone call while watching a news story you've downloaded, just replay the part you missed.

Finally, the little blue arrow button at the lower right opens the Windows Media Guide, the same Web site you get by choosing Favorites→WindowsMedia.com.

Skins

A *skin* is a visual overlay, a "look" that you can change—and an idea made insanely popular among MP3-playing programs for Windows. In WMP for Mac, you can choose among them by choosing View→the Select Skin submenu. The Default skin looks like Mac OS X. Modern approximates what WMP looks like in Windows XP. Mini is a smaller version of Modern, and only works for audio files, not video clips.

A tannery's worth of additional skins awaits on the Windows Media Web site and elsewhere on the Internet, but don't get too excited: They don't work in WMP for the Mac.

Playing files on your Mac

The File→Open command doesn't actually open anything. It simply lets you select a media file on your hard drive that you want to play. The file can be any Windows media file you've downloaded from a Web site, received as an email attachment, and so on. (Remember that WMP can't play MP3 files or audio CDs; use iTunes for those tasks.)

Using Streaming Media

Streaming media means music or video files that play on your Mac in real time, as it receives them from Web sites (as opposed to files that you must download or save first)—movie trailers, news reports, music videos, and so on. Some streaming media have a limited play time, such as music videos. (These are also called *progressive downloads,* because WMP keeps a download of the file, which you can replay.) Other streams, notably Internet radio stations, are "live" and broadcast continuously.

To play streaming media, click any link that says, "listen now" or "listen live." Most streaming media on the Web is sent to you in formats known as RealOne Player, QuickTime, or Windows Media Player. Some streams only work in Windows Media, which is probably why you're reading this section.

If you've never tried streaming media before, here's a way to get started:

1. **In Windows Media Player, choose Favorites→WindowsMedia.com.**

   WMP launches your Web browser and opens the WindowsMedia.com home page.

2. **Click one of the movie links or video clip links located in the middle of the page.**

   In a few moments, the clip opens in the Windows Media Player and starts to play. (This may not work if your standard browser isn't Internet Explorer.)

Note: Sometimes streaming media plays in your browser window instead of the Windows Media Player window—an effect called an *embedded player.* The Media Player window just hangs out in the background.

That's OK; you can even close the WMP window, and the embedded player will still work. You still need to have WMP on your Mac in order to use Windows Media embedded players—but it doesn't need to be running.

Listening to Internet radio

In Windows Media Player, Internet radio always begins with clicking a link on a Web site. While you can always search for radio station Web sites using Google or another search engine, WMP offers a timesaving shortcut via the Favorites menu.

1. **In Windows Media Player, choose Favorites→Internet Radio.**

   Your browser opens to the WindowsMedia.com Radio page.

2. **Click one of the links located near the top of the page.**

   Or, if none of the featured programs appeals to you, click one of the categories under Find Radio Stations at the left of the page; a list of Internet radio stations in that category appears to the right. (The MSN Music channels don't work in Windows Media Player for the Mac, so don't bother clicking that category.)

   Click one of those links to go to the station's Web site. Note that some Web sites work better than others: Some offer you a choice of programs or channels, so you have to click more than once to find a link that says "listen"; others require you to sign in before listening.

Tip: If you have a high-speed Internet connection, be sure you've told Windows Media Player about it. Choose Windows Media Player→Preferences→Connection tab. On this panel, choose your specific Internet connection (56 K modem, DSL, or whatever), so that you receive bigger movies and better sound, where available.

WORKAROUND WORKSHOP

Not-So-Streaming Media

Because there are so many streaming media Web sites and so many different people programming them, the day will undoubtedly come when you click a streaming media link and nothing happens. Usually, you have a better chance of playing a file when you've saved it on your Mac than when you rely on a Web site to download it to WMP.

To transfer the file onto your Mac, Control-click the link and, from the contextual menu, choose "Download link to disk." Save the file into your Music folder or somewhere else on your Mac. Now you can play it as described on the facing page.

Part Six:
Appendixes

6

Installation and Troubleshooting

Installing Office

There are two ways to install Microsoft Office X on your Mac:

- Drag the Microsoft Office X folder from the Office CD-ROM onto your hard drive. This method is fast and simple, requires 200 MB of hard drive space, and gives you all four primary programs.

- Run the Office Installer, a more traditional method of installing Mac software. Use this method if you want to control how Office is installed on your Mac and specify which components you want.

Both of these methods are described in the following sections.

UP TO SPEED

Office X Hardware and Software Requirements

To use Microsoft Office X, your computer must have at least:

- A G3 PowerPC chip.

- Mac OS X, version 10.1 or later.

- 200 MB of disk space for drag-and drop installation, or an "easy install," of Office. You get all four Office programs—Entourage, Excel,

PowerPoint, and Word. You can save disk space if you don't install all of these programs.

- A color monitor that can show 800 x 600 pixels or more. (Tell your boss—or your spouse—that 1024 x 768 is recommended.)

- 128 MB of RAM. If you care about speed, more is better, of course.

Regardless of the primary installation method you chose, you can also install a few eccentric, optional Office components by running something called the Value Pack; see page 681.

Caution: Microsoft recommends that you install Office on a hard drive that's been formatted using *Mac OS Extended (HFS +),* the default format for OS X. If your Mac came with OS X preinstalled, chances are excellent that your disk is already formatted in this way.

If, however, your cousin built you a custom Mac on the cheap and you're not sure how OS X made its way onto your hard disk, check your disk's format by running Apple System Profiler, a program in your Applications→Utilities folder. After launching System Profiler, look in the Devices and Volumes tab, find the name of your hard disk, and then click its flippy triangle.

If it turns out that your disk uses the wrong format, but you're not sure how to proceed, be aware that you are treading firmly on power-user territory. See *Mac OS X: The Missing Manual* for more information about disk formatting—or make your cousin solve the problem.

Drag-and-drop Installation

Microsoft's Macintosh Business Unit—the people responsible for building Mac programs at Microsoft—have done a lot of research to find out what Mac people want in their programs. One finding was, surprisingly enough, people don't like complicated installers. So Microsoft came up with the drag-and-drop installation, which set a new world standard for simplicity and speed. (Or, more accurately, it returned to an *old* standard. In the early days, all Mac software was installed this way.)

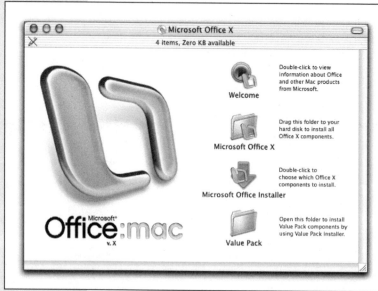

Figure A-1:
The major item of interest in this window is the Microsoft Office X folder. To install Office, drag this folder onto your hard drive. The most logical place to put it is in the Applications folder on your hard disk.

Here's how it works.

1. **Put the Microsoft Office:mac v.X CD into your CD-ROM drive. Double-click the resulting Microsoft Office X CD icon.**

   The Microsoft Office X window opens. Inside you'll see four icons: Welcome, Microsoft Office X, Microsoft Office Installer, and Value Pack (see Figure A-1).

2. **Drag the Microsoft Office X folder into the Applications folder on your hard drive.**

   After the Finder has finished copying about 800 files onto your hard drive (which should only take a few minutes), the first part of your installation is done. You're ready to run your first Office program.

3. **Open the Microsoft Office X folder on your hard drive (not the one on the CD). Double-click one of the Office programs.**

   Word, Excel, and PowerPoint make good choices. (Save Entourage for later, until you're ready to enter the technical specs for your email account, as described on page 310.)

   The first time you launch one of these programs, the Microsoft Office X Setup Assistant pops up. This introductory program's purpose is to collect your CD Key number, process your registration, and copy various files (such as *shared libraries,* which are chunks of computer code that the various Office applications can share to avoid duplication) into special nooks and crannies of your hard disk.

4. **Fill in your name and (if you like) your organization's name, and then the many-digit CD Key that came with Office.**

   You'll likely find this number inside the back cover of the booklet that came with your CD.

5. **Click Next.**

   Office asks you to confirm that you typed the number correctly.

6. **Click Accept if you typed it correctly. Otherwise, click Back and try again.**

   The Assistant shows you a product ID code and asks you to write it down. You'll be asked for it when you call Microsoft's help line. Truth is, though, you don't actually need to remember it; you can always retrieve it by choosing the About command from the Word, Excel, PowerPoint, or Entourage menu.

7. **Click Next.**

   A window pops up asking you to register Office (that is, to provide your name and address so that Microsoft can send you junk mail). It gives you two choices: Register Now and Register Later. (Apparently, Never Register isn't an option.)

8. **Click Register Now or Register Later.**

Register Now closes the window and opens your Web browser to take you to Microsoft's registration Web page. Register Later dismisses the window. In either case, your program opens at last. The text at the upper right of the welcome screen tells you what's still being installed.

Using the Traditional Installer

If you like using a more traditional installation program, Office has you covered. You may want to use this installer if, for example, the drag-and-drop approach gives you more software components than you'd like.

1. **Insert the Microsoft Office:mac v. X CD in your CD-ROM drive, and then double-click the Microsoft Office X CD icon.**

The Microsoft Office X window opens.

2. **Inside the Microsoft Office X window, double-click Microsoft Office Installer.**

When the program launches, you see a standard installation window like the one shown in Figure A-2.

3. **From the pop-up menu in the upper-left corner, choose Easy Install or Custom Install.**

Use the Easy Install if you just want to install Office and don't need—or want—to specify exactly which Office features you want to install. (You'll get exactly the same components you'd have received using the drag-and-drop installation method.) Use a Custom Install if you'd prefer to specify exactly which parts of Office you want to install.

You're immediately offered a list of Office components, as shown in Figure A-2. You can click the little I button for a brief description of each element, but the basics are clear enough: To save disk space and installation time, you can turn off the checkboxes for certain Office software bundles. Look in the lower-left corner to find out where the Office Installer plans to install Office. If you don't like the location, choose a new one.

4. **Click Install.**

The Installing window appears, showing colorful illustrations for each application as the installation proceeds. Meanwhile, the installer tosses the software from the CD to your hard disk. When the installer completes the job, it pops up a message, asking what you want to do next. Click Continue only if, for some reason, you want to install Office onto another hard drive.

5. **Click Quit.**

Take a moment to check your hard disk. You should see a Microsoft Office folder in the location you selected earlier.

6. To complete the installation, double-click one of the Office applications, such as Word or Excel.

   The Microsoft Office X Setup Assistant presents its personalization screen.

7. Fill in the blanks.

   You may find your CD Key inside the back cover of the booklet that came in the box with your CD.

8. Click Next and then advance through the remaining screens of the assistant.

   When you finish, the software displays a welcome screen while it starts up.

Figure A-2:
If you use the Office Installer, you can choose between Easy Install and Custom Install. A Custom Install (bottom) lets you choose exactly which parts of Office you don't want. You have individual control over each of the four major Office programs and over some add-on software such as the Clip Gallery and Microsoft Graph, by clicking the flippy triangle next to Office Tools.

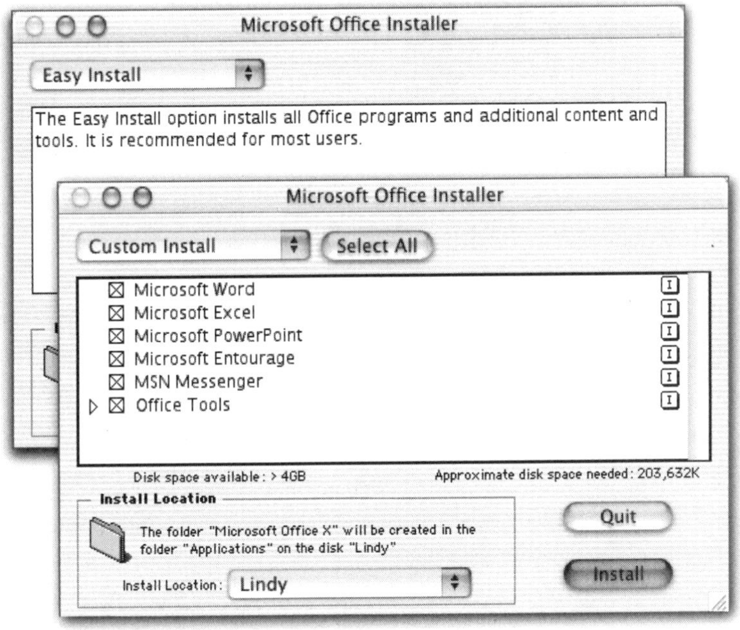

Installing the Value Pack

No matter how you install Office X, you're not getting everything that Office has to offer. And that's why there's the Value Pack Installer. It can install hundreds of megabytes' worth of useful components, including more Assistant characters, more fonts, more clip art, more templates, the Equation Editor, Remove Office (software that can un-install Office), Windows Media Player (see page 670), and so on. Most of these components are described in the appropriate chapters of this book.

To install items from the Value Pack, insert the CD, double-click the Microsoft Office X CD icon that appears on the desktop, double-click the Value Pack icon in the Microsoft Office X window, and then (finally!) double-click Value Pack Installer. Now you can choose the items that you want to install. If you want to go hog wild, click the Select All button, which gives you the whole enchilada—more than 7,000 files. Now *that's* value!

Even More Valuable Downloads

Check out the Mactopia Web site at *www.mactopia.com* to find fixes and utilities for Office. There's no telling what you'll encounter on any given day at this Microsoft site, but you may find important goodies—like *service releases*.

Service releases are a nice way of saying "bug fixes and updates." They contain bug fixes, bits of software that didn't make it onto the CD, enhancements that nobody had even thought of when the CD shipped, and so on. The June 2002 service release, for example, is essential for any Office X user's sanity. (See page 12.)

Self-Repair and Troubleshooting

Once you've installed Office, you're supposed to leave its thousands of software pieces where they lie. If you drag Word out of the Microsoft Office X folder, for example, it won't work; double-clicking it gives you only a stern reprimand—and a suggestion that you put Word's icon *back* where it came from.

Tip: Dragging the icons for the Office programs that you use often to your Dock is an excellent idea; nobody wants to burrow into the Microsoft Office X folder to find the Word icon 23 times a day. Or, if you don't use the Dock, at the very least Option-⌘-drag the programs' icons out of the Microsoft Office X folder and onto your desktop, creating aliases that remain convenient for quick launching.

Unfortunately, the occasional Mac owner still experiments, sometimes throwing out mysterious files bearing Microsoft's name, moving software pieces around, and so on. After hearing from one too many an Office user who couldn't open Excel because of some missing file, Microsoft decided to do something about it. The result was an improvement to Office 98, which is still with us today, called *self-repair*.

Self-repair means that Office keeps a stash of *duplicate copies* of every system-related file that it needs to function properly. If one of those files ever goes missing, Office quietly reinstalls the necessary file. All you experience is a delay as Office copies the proper file to the proper location.

Similarly, as you launch Office applications, your software creates settings and preference files that keep track of how you use and customize the software. For example, if you change the font that Excel uses automatically in new spreadsheets (which you do on the Excel→Preferences→General panel), Excel stores that standard font setting in a file called Excel Settings (10).

Occasionally, a settings file or a bit of software becomes *corrupted*, causing all manner of strange behavior, odd crashes, and chaos. If you're experiencing strange crashes, investigate the possibility that a settings file or a bit of Microsoft software has gone bad.

Check for a bad settings or preference file:

To test for a corrupt file, quit all Office programs, and then drag onto your desktop Microsoft Office Settings (10) and any Preference (or Settings) files that relate to your problem software. When you next start the program, it will create fresh, clean copies. If your problem goes away, move the old, corrupt files from your desktop to the Trash. If the corrupt files contain a lot of customization work, you can try further testing to see which specific file causes the problem, or—if you have backups— try restoring a slightly older version of the file. Here's where you can find these preference and settings files:

- You can find most of them in your user directory in your Home folder→Library→Preferences→Microsoft.

- Word stores custom style settings in a template called Normal, and this template may be the cause of your woe. You can most likely locate Normal in your computer's Applications→Microsoft Office→Templates folder. However, if you do not have write access to this folder, you'll find Normal hanging out in your Home→Library→Preferences→Microsoft folder along with all of the other settings and preference files.

- Entourage stores custom information (and email) for its main user in Home→Documents→Microsoft User Data→Office X Identities→Main Identity. This folder (and all identity folders) are well worth backing up; if a file in Main Identity (or any identity folder) becomes corrupt, you'll have no recourse but to start again if you don't have backups.

Uninstall Office and then install again

With previous versions of the Macintosh OS, it was fairly easy to remove Microsoft shared libraries and such from the System Folder as a quick test to see if they were corrupted. Under Mac OS X, this picky procedure takes the skills and patience of a brain surgeon. You can save yourself a lot of time by simply installing the Remove Office program from the Value Pack (page 681) and then running Remove Office, which takes about five seconds.

Remove Office does a thorough job of removing Microsoft Office–related files from your hard disk. You can reinstall Office and—if your problem was a corrupted Office-related file—the problem should be solved.

> **Warning:** Perhaps it goes without saying, but after running Remove Office, you can't use Office until you install it again. And that will entail re-entering your CD Key number.

Research your problem online

If you want to hunt online for information, you can always try Microsoft's Knowledge Base at *http://support.microsoft.com*. Or, if your geek rating is at least a 6 on a scale of 1 to 10, try *www.microsoft.com/mac/officex/ork/default.asp*. That's the Office Resource Kit, which has lots of information aimed at network administrators and consultants—the people who are *supposed* to fix problems when all else fails.

The Office Help System

Microsoft's electronic help screens may not explain all the burning myster-
ies of life, or even of Office X, but they're often enough to get you out of
a jam. They're also great for showing you different, and often faster, ways
of doing something and for revealing Office features you never knew existed.

In Office X, the Help system has been both improved and pared down. For example,
if you're a Mac user from way back, you may have already noticed something missing from the Help menu: the Show Balloons command. Because help balloons no
longer exist in Mac OS X, they no longer exist in Office X. Tooltips and the Description panels of dialog boxes fill in much of the gap. (Open Preferences and watch
what happens at the bottom of the box when you pass the cursor over the various
options.) Still, you may find you're spending more time than ever visiting the Help
index.

Fortunately, Microsoft has improved the help system's search function. When you
search the help system, Office now searches for *all* words related to your search,
instead of the former, question-based search method. This way you don't have to
worry about what Microsoft calls the topic. Even using your own words, you'll generally find the Help page you want, as long as the word you're searching for is in
there somewhere.

There are two ways to access Office's online help: the main Help index window and
the more interactive, if somewhat goofy, animated Assistant.

The Assistant

When you first launch Office and open a document, a little window pops up alongside your document window, showcasing a little Mac Plus with feet and a repertoire of cutesy mannerisms. This is Max, the Assistant.

Tip: To witness all of Max's moves, Control-click him and choose Animate! from the contextual menu. Max performs a different animation each time.

You can make Max's window smaller by dragging the lower-right corner, and close his window using the button in the textured bar at the left side. And of course, as with any Office toolbar, you can move Max around on the screen by dragging the bar.

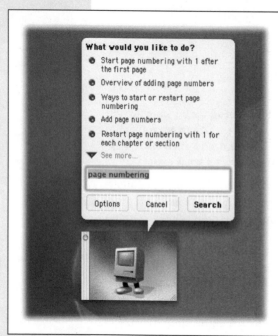

Figure B-1:
Max, the Office Assistant, doing what he's designed to do: showing search results from the Help files. But if it's been awhile since you've typed anything, he'll start turning himself into Rubik's Cube configurations out of sheer boredom, and finally keel over with a clunk.

To the surprise of many, Max was not, in fact, designed purely to annoy you. His primary function is to provide access to Office's help screens, like this:

1. Click the Max window, or choose Help→Search Office Help, click Help on the Standard toolbar, or press the Help key.

   Max's speech balloon opens, asking, "What would you like to do?"

2. Type a question, or a few key words, into the balloon window and click Search (or press Return).

For example, you might type *page margins* or *How do I make a table?* Office searches the Help system and displays a list of topics in Max's speech balloon that more or less match your query.

3. **Click the blue button beside a promising-looking topic.**

A Microsoft Office Help window opens to the selected topic. (See "The Help Index" on page 689 for more detail on navigating this window.)

To look at a different topic, click Max again to bring back the search balloon and list of topics; when you click another blue button, the next topic appears in the Help window. The Help window has Forward and Back buttons to navigate among the help screens you've seen thus far.

Tip: You can work in your document with the Help window open. If you don't need it anymore, click its Close button to dismiss it.

More Assistant Characters

Why do so many Mac fans react negatively to the Help character? Is it the notion of an onscreen peeping Tom who's observing your actions? Or is it Max himself?

If it's the Mac Plus itself that bugs you, then choose a different Assistant from the set of thirteen at your disposal. ITo access them, you must first install them from the Value Pack on the Office X CD, as described on page 681.

Once you've installed the entire gamut of Assistants, you can switch among them by Control-clicking the Assistant and Choose Assistant from the contextual menu. The Office Assistant dialog box opens to the Gallery tab. Click the Back and Next buttons to view all of the Assistants available and listen to a sample sound snippet of each. (Hint: The Office Logo is the least obtrusive Assistant.) Click OK when you find an Assistant that you can live with.

The Office Assistant dialog box closes and the new Assistant takes Max's place.

Assistant Options

Sometimes, as you're working along, the Assistant chimes and displays a light bulb icon. Clicking the light bulb displays a tip about the Office feature that you appear to be stumbling with. Other times, the Assistant offers to launch a Help topic, such as when you start to draw a table, open a wizard, or start to format a letter.

You can always ignore the tip, or click Cancel if you don't want to use the Letter Wizard, but it's possible to prevent the Assistant from even suggesting such a thing. The place to control the Assistant's behavior is the Office Assistant dialog box (Figure B-2). To open it, click Options in the Assistant's speech balloon. You can always open this dialog box by control-clicking the Assistant and choosing Options from the contextual menu.

Some of the options are self-explanatory; here are a few that may not be:

- **Respond to Help key.** If you uncheck this box, pressing Help will open the Office Help system window (see "The Help Index" on the next page) instead of opening the Assistant's balloon.

- **Help with wizards.** When you use a wizard in Office (as when opening a template, for example), the Assistant can offer additional tips as you work. Clearing this box turns this feature off.

- **Move when in the way.** This option makes the Assistant's window hop around so as not to block open dialog boxes. It also shrinks it to a smaller size if you haven't used the Assistant for five minutes.

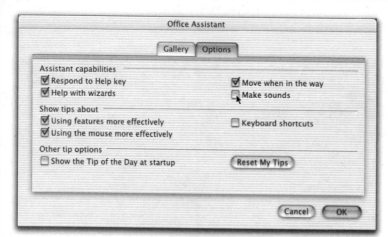

Figure B-2:
If you're trying to sleep and you hear your Mac making clanking noises from the next room, it may just be the Office Assistant up to his usual tricks. In this dialog box, consider turning off "Make sounds."

- **Show tips about.** The three checkboxes on this panel control what kinds of tips the Assistant offers while you're working.

- **Show the Tip of the Day at startup.** Office can show a different learning-this-program tip each time you launch any Office program. Usually, they contain useful information ("To repeat most commands and actions, press Command-Y"). Occasionally, Microsoft's programmers throw in attempts at humor ("You can hurt yourself if you run with scissors").

   Clicking "Reset My Tips" reshuffles startup tips you've already seen into the pile. Office warns you that you may see repeat tips when you click this button.

Click OK to position your new settings, or click Cancel to exit the Office Assistant dialog box without changing any settings.

Turning the Assistant Off

Just clicking the Assistant window's Close box makes Max wave goodbye and vanish, but he may still reappear now and then. If you'd rather not include him in your Office experience *ever*, use the Office X command that has a certain population of Mac fans cheering: Help→Turn Assistant Off.

For help turning the Assistant off, choose Help→Office Help Contents, click Help on the Standard toolbar, or press the Help key. All of these methods open the Help Contents window (see below). Tips are still available when the Assistant is turned off; a light bulb appears next to the Help button on the Standard toolbar when Office is offering a tip.

Tip: Sometimes, when you turn on the Assistant from the Help menu after working without Max's (or Bosgrove's) help for a while, the Assistant window appears completely white and empty when it opens. Even the close button doesn't work. As with many Office X annoyances, this one goes away if you install Service Release 1, as described on page 12 .

The Help Index

The Office Assistant has its charms, but help screens are the real meat of Microsoft's help. These screens—which are supposed to take the place of a hard-copy manual in Office X—appear when you use one of these methods:

- Do a search using the Office Assistant, as described on page 686.

- Choose Help→Office Help Contents.

- Turn the Assistant off (as described above), and click the Help button on the Standard toolbar or press the Help key.

The Help window opens, as shown in Figure B-3. The three buttons at the top of this window offer three approaches to finding information in the Help system:

- The **Contents** button displays the master list of topics in the left pane of the Help screen. Click one of these topics (you don't need to click the flippy triangle) for a list of subtopics, as shown in Figure B-3. Each subtopic is a hyperlink that opens the topic's help screen in the right pane.

- Clicking the **A-Z Index** button changes the contents of the left pane to a list of hyperlinks, one for each letter of the alphabet. Clicking a letter shows a list of topics that begin with that letter. Click a topic name to see a list of subtopics, which are once again links to pertinent help screens. This method may be the quickest when you know exactly what you want to look up—margins or tables, for example.

- Clicking **Search** opens a text box and a Search button in the left pane. Type a few key words into the box and click Search—this approach is exactly the same as, and produces the same results as, typing into Max's search window. The topics found by the search are listed below the Search button in the left pane. As always, these topics are links that open the corresponding help screens.

Web-Based Help

Microsoft does a fine job of keeping you updated about what's happening in the world of Office for the Mac. The Microsoft Office for the Mac Web site (called Mactopia.com) contains Frequently Asked Questions pages, instructional articles, updates for download, and, when all else fails, a gateway to Microsoft's technical support department.

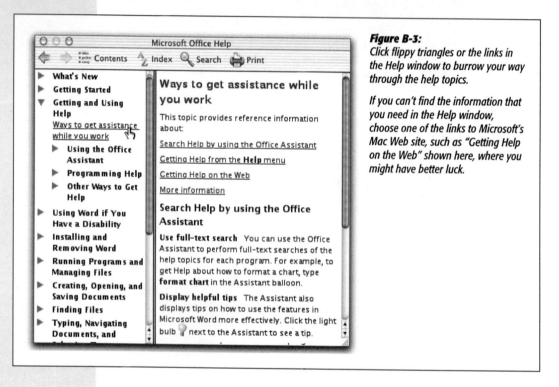

Figure B-3:
Click flippy triangles or the links in the Help window to burrow your way through the help topics.

If you can't find the information that you need in the Help window, choose one of the links to Microsoft's Mac Web site, such as "Getting Help on the Web" shown here, where you might have better luck.

To go directly to Microsoft's Mac Web site, choose Help→Additional Help Resources. Office launches your Web browser and displays an introductory page. It contains a list of hyperlinks to five of the most useful support areas on *www.microsoft.com/ mac:*

- The links under **Late-Breaking News** are a little misleading. They don't contain any new information; they don't even link to the Web where, presumably, the latest news is. They simply open the Read Me files that have been on your Mac, in the Microsoft Office X→Read Me folder.

  Still, if you've never read the Read Me's, they're worth a look, since they explain some of the more obscure quirks of the Office programs.

- **New Components** links to the page where Microsoft posts updates to Office X (and earlier versions of Office, too) along with a host of other free software items, including the latest versions of Internet Explorer, Outlook Express, and even some kids' games. Some of these updates are more useful than others. For instance, everyone with a Hotmail account who uses Entourage will want to download the Hotmail Updater. The Excel Add-in patch, on the other hand, applies only to those who use the French version. This page is also where you download Windows Media Player (page 670) and any updates to it.

- **Support on the Web** offers a direct link to Mactopia's Office X home base. Although much of this page is directed toward selling Office to that handful of holdouts who haven't yet bought the program, links at the left side offer FAQ pages, How-to articles, and news announcements.

  One of the most critical links on this page is **Office Support**, which takes you to a technical-help page. Here you'll learn that you're allowed to call for free Office help on two different issues before Microsoft starts charging $35 for each phone call. There's also a link to Microsoft's **Knowledge Base,** a vast, searchable collection of how-to and informational articles (most of which are about Windows products).

  How-to Articles is a direct link to a collection of step-by-step procedures, illustrated with screen shots, for such Office tasks as business forecasting in Excel, using movies in PowerPoint, organizing Entourage contacts, and publishing a flyer in Word.

  Finally, even if you're not a big newsgroup fan, don't overlook the **Newsgroups** link. By clicking this link, you can access newsgroups for all of the Office programs *in your Web browser,* as if they were plain old Web-based message boards. Without even owning a newsreader, you can post your Office question to a group of fellow users, many of whom have been in your shoes and are happy to share the answer.

- **Getting Started with Microsoft** X isn't a link at all, but a reminder to go read the 169-page "Getting Started" book in the Applications→Microsoft Office X folder. This manual, which opens in Adobe Acrobat, contains step-by-step instructions for various Office tasks and includes much of the same information as the online how-to articles described above.

- Finally, under the **Microsoft Office X Assisted Support** heading, there's a brief explanation of Microsoft's support system, and another gateway to technical-help pages.

Index

OFFICE X FOR MACINTOSH: THE MISSING MANUAL

OFFICE X FOR MACINTOSH: THE MISSING MANUAL

P

OFFICE X FOR MACINTOSH: THE MISSING MANUAL

formatting cell borders and color, 482–486
hiding, 521
manual formatting, 480–486
merging cells, 491–492
moving, 521
naming, 436
printing, 512–518
properties, 531
protecting cells, 485
renaming, 521
scrolling through sheet tabs, 521
selecting cells, 445–446
sharing, 522–524
size of, 436
types of data, 439–441
wrapping text
around graphics, 655–656
in Word, 160–163
in Word Web pages, 288
writing styles, Spelling and Grammar and, 89–90
Writing Toolbox, Project Gallery, 17
WYSIWYG (what-you-*see also*-is-what-you-get)
fonts, 112
styles, 144

X

XML (extensible markup language), exporting
Excel files, 530
XY (scatter) charts, 499

Z

zooming Word documents, 36

Colophon

This book was written in Word X on various Macs around the country and edited using the tracking feature described in Chapter 5.

The screenshots were captured with Ambrosia Software's Snapz Pro X *(www. ambrosiasw.com)*. Adobe Photoshop 7 and Macromedia Freehand *(www.adobe.com)* were called in as required for touching them up.

The book was designed and laid out in Adobe PageMaker 6.5 on a PowerBook G3 and Power Mac G4. The fonts used include Formata (as the sans-serif family) and Minion (as the serif body face). To provide the and ⌘ symbols, a custom font was created using Macromedia Fontographer.

The book was generated as an Adobe Acrobat PDF file for proofreading and indexing, and finally transmitted to the printing plant in the form of PostScript files.

International Distributors

http://international.oreilly.com/distributors.html • international@oreilly.com

UK, EUROPE, MIDDLE EAST, AND AFRICA (EXCEPT FRANCE, GERMANY, AUSTRIA, SWITZERLAND, LUXEMBOURG, AND LIECHTENSTEIN)

INQUIRIES
O'Reilly UK Limited
4 Castle Street
Farnham
Surrey, GU9 7HS
United Kingdom
Telephone: 44-1252-711776
Fax: 44-1252-734211
Email: information@oreilly.co.uk

ORDERS
Wiley Distribution Services Ltd.
1 Oldlands Way
Bognor Regis
West Sussex PO22 9SA
United Kingdom
Telephone: 44-1243-843294
UK Freephone: 0800-243207
Fax: 44-1243-843302 (Europe/EU orders)
or 44-1243-843274 (Middle East/Africa)
Email: cs-books@wiley.co.uk

FRANCE

INQUIRIES & ORDERS
Éditions O'Reilly
18 rue Séguier
75006 Paris, France
Tel: 33-1-40-51-71-89
Fax: 33-1-40-51-72-26
Email: france@oreilly.fr

GERMANY, SWITZERLAND, AUSTRIA, LUXEMBOURG, AND LIECHTENSTEIN

INQUIRIES & ORDERS
O'Reilly Verlag
Balthasarstr. 81
D-50670 Köln, Germany
Telephone: 49-221-973160-91
Fax: 49-221-973160-8
Email: anfragen@oreilly.de (inquiries)
Email: order@oreilly.de (orders)

CANADA

(FRENCH LANGUAGE BOOKS)
Les Éditions Flammarion ltée
375, Avenue Laurier Ouest
Montréal, QC H2V 2K3 Canada
Tel: 1-514-277-8807
Fax: 1-514-278-2085
Email: info@flammarion.qc.ca

HONG KONG

City Discount Subscription Service, Ltd.
Unit A, 6th Floor, Yan's Tower
27 Wong Chuk Hang Road
Aberdeen, Hong Kong
Tel: 852-2580-3539
Fax: 852-2580-6463
Email: citydis@ppn.com.hk

KOREA

Hanbit Media, Inc.
Chungmu Bldg. 210
Yonnam-dong 568-33
Mapo-gu
Seoul, Korea
Tel: 822-325-0397
Fax: 822-325-9697
Email: hant93@chollian.dacom.co.kr

PHILIPPINES

Global Publishing
G/F Benavides Garden
1186 Benavides Street
Manila, Philippines
Tel: 632-254-8949/632-252-2582
Fax: 632-734-5060/632-252-2733
Email: globalp@pacific.net.ph

TAIWAN

O'Reilly Taiwan
1st Floor, No. 21, Lane 295
Section 1, Fu-Shing South Road
Taipei, 106 Taiwan
Tel: 886-2-27099669
Fax: 886-2-27038802
Email: mori@oreilly.com

INDIA

Shroff Publishers & Distributors PVT. LTD.
C-103, MIDC, TTC Pawane
Navi Mumbai 400 701
India
Tel: (91-22) 763 4290, 763 4293
Fax: (91-22) 768 3337
Email: spdorders@shroffpublishers.com

CHINA

O'Reilly Beijing
SIGMA Building, Suite B809
No. 49 Zhichun Road
Haidian District
Beijing, China PR 100080
Tel: 86-10-8809-7475
Fax: 86-10-8809-7463
Email: beijing@oreilly.com

JAPAN

O'Reilly Japan, Inc.
Yotsuya Y's Building
7 Banch 6, Honshio-cho
Shinjuku-ku
Tokyo 160-0003 Japan
Tel: 81-3-3356-5227
Fax: 81-3-3356-5261
Email: japan@oreilly.com

SINGAPORE, INDONESIA, MALAYSIA, AND THAILAND

TransQuest Publishers Pte Ltd
30 Old Toh Tuck Road #05-02
Sembawang Kimtrans Logistics Centre
Singapore 597654
Tel: 65-4623112
Fax: 65-4625761
Email: wendiw@transquest.com.sg

AUSTRALIA

Woodslane Pty., Ltd.
7/5 Vuko Place
Warriewood NSW 2102
Australia
Tel: 61-2-9970-5111
Fax: 61-2-9970-5002
Email: info@woodslane.com.au

NEW ZEALAND

Woodslane New Zealand, Ltd.
21 Cooks Street (P.O. Box 575)
Waganui, New Zealand
Tel: 64-6-347-6543
Fax: 64-6-345-4840
Email: info@woodslane.com.au

ARGENTINA

Distribuidora Cuspide
Suipacha 764
1008 Buenos Aires
Argentina
Phone: 54-11-4322-8868
Fax: 54-11-4322-3456
Email: libros@cuspide.com

ALL OTHER COUNTRIES

O'Reilly & Associates, Inc.
1005 Gravenstein Hwy North
Sebastopol, CA 95472 USA
Tel: 707-827-7000
Fax: 707-829-0104
Email: order@oreilly.com

O'REILLY®

TO ORDER: **800-998-9938** • **order@oreilly.com** • **www.oreilly.com**
ONLINE EDITIONS OF MOST O'REILLY TITLES ARE AVAILABLE BY SUBSCRIPTION AT **safari.oreilly.com**
ALSO AVAILABLE AT MOST RETAIL AND ONLINE BOOKSTORES